THE REVOLT
AGAINST
THE MASSES

THE REVOLT

AGAINST

THE MASSES

And Other Essays on
Politics and Public Policy

BY

AARON WILDAVSKY

BASIC BOOKS, INC., PUBLISHERS

NEW YORK   LONDON

© 1971 by Basic Books, Inc.
Library of Congress Catalog Card Number: 70–147009
SBN 465–06949–5
Manufactured in the United States of America
DESIGNED BY VINCENT TORRE

THINGS I NEVER KNEW:

A PREFACE

Sometimes it pays to be obtuse. Things I never knew have helped me most. In nearly every contact I had with academic folk wisdom my experience ran counter to what I later learned were commonly held views.

I was never told that Brooklyn College was a vulgar, proletarian backwater, staffed by instructors whose obscurity was matched only by their lack of talent. So I encountered a succession of brilliant teachers. In the political science department I "majored" in Samuel Konefsky, a mentor beyond compare. His passion for scholarship shone in everything he did. My interest in social policy and federalism dates from a superb course he gave, far ahead of its time, on "Social Reform Under the American Federal System." Not yet aware that history was out of style and political theory a subject fit only for unscientific dilettantes, I spent a splendid final year with him examining the attempts of the founding fathers to reconcile justice with majority rule.

Kenneth Organski showed me that humor and politics were not only compatible but perhaps inseparable. Good fun and analytical rigor, in his class, went hand in hand. Charles Ascher, whose fund of anecdote and insight was apparently inexhaustible, introduced me to the study of bureaucracy. Anyone who could observe brilliant historians like Hyman Kublin, Arthur Charles Cole, and Jesse Clarkson give meaning to the past should consider himself fortunate. Professor Clarkson's lectures on Russian history to 1900 ranged widely and deeply, and included comparisons with developments in Western Europe and trends in intellectual history. They remain vividly in my mind as incomparably the finest I have ever heard. On my return from the army, wondering how I might get back to my studies in the middle of a semester, Randolph Goodman offered to let me take his course in modern drama, guaranteeing that no matter what happened, I would not flunk. I received my undeserved "C" and with it something of his passionate feeling for the theater. (I omit the name of the teacher whom I clocked in 187 renditions of "A-N-D - SO - TH-EN" in one fateful hour.) Since the idea that political activism was incompatible with scholarship had not yet gained widespread currency, I feasted on both; it would be hard to say from which I learned more. The vital importance of controlling the mimeograph machines is something not ordinarily taught in the formal curriculum.

No doubt someone neglected to inform me that Australia was a nation without modern political scientists, and I went there in 1954 on a Fulbright Grant. Once there I took for granted the existence of a corps of talented scholars, Rufus Davis, Henry Mayer, Robert Parker, and Richard Spann, who are the equal of any men in American political science. Under the dedicated tutelage of Henry Mayer (who showed me 14 Sydney libraries in one day) I wrote a monograph, *Studies in Australian Politics, the 1926 Referendum.* Any year in which one writes a book, attends over 100 Labor party meetings, learns to play the recorder, hitchhikes 6,000 miles, and lives in a hostel for Asian students can't be all bad. And there was more.

One day Rufus Davis came to Sydney and asked if I would teach a course on American politics at the University of Queensland so that he could get on with his work on federalism. Barely conscious of what was involved in teaching, dimly aware that I should have pleaded lack of qualification, I accepted the invitation. The next day I went to my room, took out a sheaf of foolscap, wrote various major headings on the top (Parties, Interest Groups, Presidency, Congress, and so forth), and put down what I knew about each of them. Three hours later I was finished and discovered that my ignorance was appalling. For six weeks I read about American politics day and night and emerged with a series of lecture notes that helped me for years to come. Without a conscious plan I found my days at Queensland filled with seeing students and doing research. The combination of teaching and writing made me happy. To my surprise I had discovered a vocation.

How could I have failed to realize that in 1955 the Yale University political science department was fast becoming a hotbed of vile and amoral behaviorism, not to say an emporium of hyperfactualism and vulgar empiricism? I came to study Soviet politics with Frederick Barghoorn, from whom I learned a vast amount. I stayed to study public administration with James Fesler. He possessed an unerring sense for the critical problem. Whatever insight, clarity of mind, and a sense of proportion could do for his students, he did. I might have missed the whole thing but someone had neglected to inform me that only fuddy-duddies ventured into public administration. (It took a new name, "organization theory," to make the ancient field of bureaucracy respectable once again.) Had anyone told me that case histories were out of fashion and did not constitute true social science, I should never have spent an exciting year with Allan Sindler doing a dissertation on the Dixon-Yates case.

Although I did no formal work with him, conversations with Robert Dahl, with his zest for inquiry, his insistence upon rigorous thought, and his disdain for pseudoscientific claptrap, made a big difference. He set the standards. Though economists who are not devotees of formal mathematical models were then in low repute, the word had not yet gotten around to me, and I was able to sit in on the best seminar I have known. To watch Charles E. Lindblom "break-the-back" of a book, dissolve it into its fundamental propositions, and relate these to basic theories in the social sciences, was a privilege. His scholarly work has had a powerful impact on my own.

Rumor had it that men who taught at small liberal arts colleges never emerged from oblivion. Their presence was manifested in pathetic form at national meetings, with no scholarly accomplishments to their names, and only a few dull stories about the escapades of their favorite students. But I was too busy working to listen. So I spent four splendid years at Oberlin College.

John Lewis, my chairman, exemplified the life of reason that enveloped the members of the government department. There was always mutual respect among us and dedication to teaching and research. Conversations on foreign policy with Robert Tufts and George Lanyi were a constant source of enlightenment. Our students were aspiring scholars. They taught me to increase my reading list so I would seem more serious to them. I had been told, while deciding whether to accept a job offer from Oberlin, that a man could not make an impact on the profession through teaching undergraduates. That was wrong as could be. In my last year our department had seven winners of Woodrow Wilson awards, a larger total than many universities. Over a dozen of the students I worked with in four years at Oberlin have doctorates in political science.

Had I known, of course, that meeting the insistent demands of bright students in an institution devoted to teaching would eat up my time and sap my energies, had I only realized that teaching and research were incompatible, I should not have been so pleased. Oblivious, as usual, I did both to the fullest and enjoyed every minute. I taught the Introduction to American Government (twice a year), Comparative Politics (The United Kingdom, France, Germany, and Sweden), State and Local Government, the Presidency and Public Administration, and a seminar for senior majors on national conventions, budgeting, or whatever I happened to be working on. During those years, from 1958 through 1962, I did most of the work on three books: *Presidential Elections* (with Nelson W. Polsby), *The Politics of the Budgetary Process,* and *Leadership in a Small Town.*

These books were finished in a year in Washington, D.C. at Resources for the Future, a research organization specializing in the analysis of natural resource policies. RFF had asked me to do another case history of a resource policy modeled on my earlier study of the Dixon-Yates case. Failing to realize that young men did not talk back to old organizations, I persuaded them instead to let me pursue my study of budgeting. Under the wise leadership of Vice President Irving Fox, RFF was the very model of what a research organization should be: its officers always had time to assist you when you needed help, and they were always too busy with their own work to burden you with trivialities. Had someone bothered to tell me that political scientists could neither understand nor cope with high-powered mathematically sophisticated economists, I might not have sat in on the weekly seminars there in which men like John Krutilla and Alan Kneese taught me much about economics and, perhaps more importantly, about how economists go about their work. It is one thing to read a finished study, and another to observe a man in the middle of his work, struggling to make it come off.

Oberlin was too good. It was too warm and comfortable and congenial. I should, I thought, not grow old in one place. I must try the other end of the world, a place as different from Oberlin as could be imagined. That was Berkeley.

Berkeley, I was told, was a good place to visit but you would not want to live there. It was full of academic beasts who chewed up young men and spit out the pieces. It was too far from the centers of action and culture on the East Coast. Somehow those arguments never got through to me.

I have often regretted leaving Oberlin, but never once having come to Berkeley. Berkeley suffers from an excess of (dis)affection. We are all, faculty and students, like children who press their noses against shop windows in the Christmas season to see the infinitely desirable and utterly unobtainable luxuries inside. Amidst the incredible beauty of the countryside and the extraordinary intellectual vitality of the institution, the disparity between aspiration and achievement is at its height. I am reminded of a novel by Thomas Wolfe in which the main character—as usual, himself—stands outside the great Harvard library overcome by sadness because there is so much there and he can only get to a small part of it.

To me Berkeley will always be the place I met Peter Odegard and Jacobus tenBroek in the last years of their lives. Even while a mechanical pacer tried vainly to match his life force, Peter soared above us all. His joy in life was matched by his zest for politics. He never let me forget that our duty was not only to contribute to a discipline called political science but to a nation that needed better public policy. All I knew about Jacobus tenBroek at first was that he had an indefinable quality called wisdom; his advice on departmental policy was at once disinterested and compelling; I thought long and hard before challenging his judgment. As I read his published work I became aware that he combined originality in scholarship with profound social concern. His work has done more to improve the life of citizens than any man I have known. I wish that I could hear again his deep laughter or retain the comfort of knowing that if I could convince him on a disputed question I could confidently expect to persuade others, because no one else could raise so powerful a challenge.

One piece of conventional wisdom did turn out to correspond more to reality than I would have liked. When I became chairman of the political science department at Berkeley I was told that the administrative duties involved would make it impossible to undertake any sustained piece of scholarly work. That was true. Hence this collection of papers with which I have whiled away my time in between manning the barricades, comforting secretaries overcome by tear-gas fumes, reconciling differences whose origins are lost in antiquity, and learning why I have always found original sin to be so appropriate a doctrine. During those times I have often recalled the Don Quixote who lived in M. J. Bernardette's great class at Brooklyn College as a person who knew what one man ultimately required from another: not justice but mercy.

CONTENTS

PART III

Political Anthropology

PART IV

Political Analysis

PART V

What Difference Does Reform Make?

THE REVOLT
AGAINST
THE MASSES

INTRODUCTION

Because no man can really stand exposure, writing a personal essay is a vulnerable enterprise. Yet an introduction to a collection of one's papers must be personal; it would be evasive if it did not reflect the man who wrote them. I will try to answer, for my own essays, questions I have often had about scholars who have influenced me. How did they write the papers I liked? Why did they write them? How did they go about the tasks of research and writing? Thus the first section discusses the kinds of essays I write and the second describes how I came to write them. The subject of the third section is craftsmanship, broadly conceived to include both modes of work and organization of time. The fourth section seeks to relate my interest in public policy in a democratic society to my own experience. Presumably this essay will not demonstrate by analogy the wisdom of the adage, attributed to Bismarck, that if one wishes to have respect for politics or sausages one should not see how either is made.

The Kinds of Work I Do

For the past two decades I have been engaged in the study of politics and public policy. Why? Because I like it. That it gives me great pleasure should be evident. Every man needs a craft through which he can express himself to the extent of his abilities, and I have found mine. There is also the fulfillment of obligation. Self-government is one of the noblest and most difficult aims of mankind. A pessimist about human nature, I cannot regard its ultimate prospects as certain. If a man can contribute to the survival and extension of free government in the smallest way, he has done well.

I could have organized these essays around the substantive areas—budgeting, the presidency, political parties, domestic and foreign policy—that have interested me most. I have not done so because I want the book to reflect the ways in which I think about my work. I have, therefore, designed the contents to reveal the kinds of work I do, from the analysis of issues to the impact of ideas on public policy to the advocacy of reform.

In analyzing issues, I first ask what differentiates the issue under examination from other issues? Does the way in which the issue arose or was posed to the participants affect the ways in which they deal with it? When the special qualities of the issue have been isolated, I attempt to account for them. Then I try to explain what happened to this issue through knowledge of its characteristics.

In thinking over the reaction to the sporadic violence that has occurred on campus and in the community in the past several years, I came to feel that the issues involved had been misconstrued. The dichotomy between the idealists who resorted to violence and the materialists who deplored it seemed to me misdirected. I could not reconcile the self-portrait of the radicals either with my own experience or with the effects of their actions in the world. People who really wanted to end the war in Vietnam, for example, would not have done it by systematically alienating the very people they had to convince. I thought that the behavior of the violent could be better explained (and the issues they symbolized discussed) if it were understood that they represented a variety of elitist contempt for the mass of citizens rather than a manifestation of popular revolt against an unrepresentative establishment. The title of the essay—"The Revolt Against the Masses"—expresses my viewpoint succinctly.

The problem in "The Empty-Head Blues" is to account for the exasperating quality of an issue in which the apparent recipients of benefits curse those who are allegedly trying to help them. The "anger plus opportunity" theory takes a step in that direction by showing how attempts to alleviate problems can make people feel worse about them, at least in the short run. The argument of "Race and Research: The Moynihan Report and the Politics of Controversy" is that the close identification of class and race among black people, a phenomenon not encountered in other areas of American politics, helps explain why what seems like proper experimental procedure to social scientists appears like just another example of discrimination to the control group that does not get the new services.

"The Political Feasibility of Income by Right" contains a political cost-benefit-analysis of proposals to help poor people by increasing their income. It turns out that guaranteed income is repugnant to widely and deeply held American values, such as work and equality of opportunity. Guaranteed income is also more expensive and less efficient than alternative policies. Income policies are favored, however, because they promise to bring political support to the American system of government. The key to understanding income maintenance lies in its emergence from an extraordinary issue—the failure of existing welfare programs to gain support from the people they are supposed to help.

As I read about the controversy surrounding the antiballistic missile

(ABM), it became clear that the arguments on both sides were, if not specious, at least insufficiently conclusive to help an intelligent man make up his mind. I was puzzled by the fact that ABM supporters were moving away from the old deterrence theory while opponents of ABM were embracing it. Here, it seemed to me, was a significant reversal of position, and I then set out to study the history of the issue to see why this had happened. The opponents of ABM, it turned out, did not choose the issue so much as it offered itself up to them as an opportunity to enlarge the political opposition to defense expenditures. Having once taken a position, the opponents were stuck with it when the Nixon administration changed its line. They thus found themselves devising arguments about deterrence (destruction of a large part of the Soviet Union was assured; ABM was unnecessary because there was no real threat to American deterrence forces) they would not have contemplated using even a few months before.

"Presidential Succession and Disability" poses unusual difficulties in issue-analysis. How does one act on an important matter when neither history nor theory provides a guide? In the case of Presidential succession, it proved possible to limit the difficulties caused by human error; in regard to the disability problem, however, the cure may prove to be worse than the disease. There is no way to be right every time. The existence of a problem does not necessarily imply a solution. It is wise, lest we suffer unnecessary disappointment, to circumscribe the realm of problems that cannot be solved.

If knowledge is to be accumulated, issues must be placed in categories that carry with them predictions about how similar issues will be handled in the future. A beginning toward a classification of issues is contained in "The Analysis of Issue-Contexts in the Study of Decision-Making." It was written because my initial study of the Dixon-Yates case left me puzzled. Why did the President of the United States repeatedly ignore information which would have helped him immensely? After defining the problem more clearly, I got the idea that the public-versus-private-power controversy had created a polarizing effect that led each side to disregard what the other said. After writing *Dixon-Yates: A Study in Power Politics,* I looked around for another case history that would illustrate the opposite kind of environment for decision-making. *Gotham in the Air Age* by Herbert Kaufman, concerning a case in which it took a long time for the participants to figure out which side they were on or even what the sides were, was just right for my purposes. To clarify my thoughts on issue-analysis further, I intend to teach a course on the subject.

Part II explores how the way men think about social problems influences the kinds of policies they recommend. In the late 1950s and early 1960s I became intrigued with the growing body of literature on defense policy. Perhaps, I thought, the experts were too close to the problem; perhaps they had missed the importance of some of the general ideas guiding their specific analyses.

The "Practical Consequences of the Theoretical Study of Defense Policy" shows that unexamined models of international conflict, whether one believes the problem to be appeasement of aggressors or avoidance of the deadly cycle of misunderstanding among nations, are of critical importance in determining how decision-makers fix their stands on defense matters. The same process is at work in the field of budgeting. Thinking about budgets in terms of narrow economic efficiency has profound implications for the mechanisms of resource allocation and the policy outcomes one will accept. In "The Political Economy of Efficiency" I attempt to show the basic political values that underlie apparently neutral efficiency concerns in cost-benefit analysis, systems analysis, and program budgeting.

When the editors of *Daedalus* asked me to contribute an essay about politics in a volume on natural resource policy, I first considered doing a piece on conflicts involved in determining resource policies. When I read the other essays in the volume, however, most of which had already been completed, I saw in them a fascinating clash between the devotion of economists to efficiency and their love of the unspoiled outdoors. "Aesthetic Power, or the Triumph of the Sensitive Minority Over the Vulgar Mass" illustrates the dilemmas that occur when economists discover that the objective of increasing national income, based on efficiency considerations, will not enable them to realize their aesthetic goals in the area of natural resources. Rather than debase economic analysis, I recommend mobilizing support to deal with political conflicts over resource policies.

In future work—Naomi Caiden and I are engaged in a study of the relationship between planning and budgeting in low-income countries—I hope to explore the power of planning as an idea. The extraordinary problems confronted everywhere in planning are in an important sense encapsulated in the different and multiple meanings of the word itself. Conceiving of planning as an activity engaged in by men called planners leads to quite different policies from those reached when defining planning as a social process that is a product of an entire nation's capacities. To know how men think about planning is to understand much about what they try to do and even more about why they fail.

The essays in Part III, "Political Anthropology," employ an approach one would use in trying to understand a tribe whose customs were strange and whose activities sometimes appeared odd to an outside observer. I attempt to get inside the skin of the people I am writing about, to look at the world through their eyes insofar as that is possible. The assumption behind this approach is that you cannot understand why people behave as they do unless you know how the world looks to them.

" 'What Can I Do?' The Ohio Delegate's View of the Convention" is centered around delegates' reactions to problems that arise when it may be in the interest of the leading candidates to present misleading information and the truth is hard to convey. The essays on the "Goldwater Phenomenon" and "The Meaning of Youth in the Struggle for Control of the Democratic Party" concern differing conceptions of political activity. If one wants to know something about the political styles of party activists at national conventions, he observes their behavior and asks them questions about what they are doing and how they feel about what is happening elsewhere. The ways in which they characterize their favorite candidates, for example, can be used as an indicator of the style of politics they prefer. A similar approach, involving interviewing to look at the world from the viewpoint of actors situated in different places, served well in discovering how a new arrangement, the zero-base budget, worked in the Department of Agriculture. The interviews led us to pose a more analytical question: why did each participant swear the zero-base budget was no good for himself but insist that all the others must have benefited? To understand why a man like Bill Long is so active, it helps to view the opportunities and risks of social action as he does. The main requirement for this kind of research is a great deal of thought about the questions to be asked and a huge amount of energy in pursuing the people to be questioned.

The essays under the heading of "Political Anthropology" go where the evidence leads them; the interviews are designed to generate hypotheses rather than confirm them. The essays in Part IV, "Political Analysis," however, are directly analytical. Each begins with a hypothesis. Each poses a question and seeks evidence to help in answering it. If you wonder whether the President is more successful in foreign than in domestic policy (perhaps there are "Two Presidencies"), you seek a source of data that tells you how Presidents have fared with Congress in both policy areas. If you gather hints that budgetary behavior (summarized in "Budgeting as a Political Process") is exceedingly regular, you try to test these uniformities on the available data—Presidential budget requests for agencies and congressional appropriations—thereby creating "A Theory of the Budgetary Process."

I have rarely been interested in empirical questions for their own sake. In the back of my mind has always been a concern with evaluating the likely consequences of reform proposals suggested by others as well as thinking about changes I might recommend. Thus my work on budgeting includes both an analysis of the consequences of program budgeting ("Rescuing Policy Analysis from PPBS") and my own proposals for reform ("Toward a Radical Incrementalism"). These essays should reflect a strong personal sense of responsibility for public policy.

Thinking about reform imposes a strong discipline on the writer because he must establish the causal connection between the change under discussion and the good or bad consequences likely to ensue. The essay on "Salvation by Staff" not only evaluates suggestions for reform in the Presidential office, but also includes criteria for changes that are designed to help (rather than unintentionally hinder) the Chief Executive.

My admiration for *Don Quixote* stems from Cervantes' recognition of the essential contrariness of human life in which there is often so little connection between our intentions and the consequences of our actions. Many of the papers in this collection revolve around conditions that stimulate a desire to do good and my concern that attempting to do good may have harmful consequences.

It is difficult to place the essay (coauthored with Max Singer) on "A Third-World Averaging Strategy" because it encompasses several kinds of work presented in this collection. It belongs partly with the essays on the influence of ideas, for difficulties in American foreign policy toward developing nations stem in part from faulty conceptions of the international system. Creating an averaging strategy depends on issue-analysis; a critical policy question—whether to deal with all these nations on the same basis or to treat each one individually—lies at the center of our recommendations. Our proposal for uniform treatment of third-world countries also depends on analysis that gives evidence of their low and diminishing importance to the economy and security of the United States. The essay is included in the section on reform because it is fundamentally concerned with advocating changes in American foreign policy. I hope this paper and others like it show that a concern with moral issues—a concern with what is right and wrong in the world—is compatible with a life of scholarship.

My research into leadership at Oberlin was designed not only to discover who made decisions in the past but also to prescribe how capable citizens might gain larger shares in future decisions. One day, while I was reading the Sunday *New York Times,* I came across three separate commandments directing citizens to increase their rate of political participation. One book review contained the prescription that no citizen could retain his self-respect without reading the lengthy list of books the author felt were indispensable for intelligent consideration of his favorite policy. The "News of the Week in Review" recommended that citizens who were not utterly selfish and cared a little for their country participate in organizational activity on behalf of some noble policy. A politician was quoted in a news story as requesting all moral persons to join him in a crusade. It occurred to me that if a man like myself, who devoted himself entirely to the study of public affairs, could not find time for most of these activities, citizens who had different responsibilities would be even more frustrated. Telling people to be active in everything all the time is not useful, so I determined to write "A Strategy for Political Participation" that would contain advice a man might actually use.

Lost in History

The complete genesis of these essays is lost in history. I kept no notes. Even if I had, I would not necessarily have been conscious of the full range of personality and circumstance that combined to produce them.

Enough has remained with me, however, to reconstruct the pattern of design and accident that make up the irregular pulse of scholarly life. Rather than attempt to account for the history of every piece in this collection, I would like to illustrate the checkered origins of several bodies of work from the most conscious intention to the most accidental occurrence.

Budgeting is the field in which my work is best known. Yet I have often wondered how I became involved with a subject that appeared to offer so little promise. Would you take a course called "Financial Administration"? Read a book on the minutiae of budgetary procedure? I certainly would not. It so happened, however, that at Yale the preliminary examinations for the doctorate in the subfield of Public Administration usually had a question on budgeting. It was, therefore, incumbent upon those who wished to prepare for this ordeal to acquaint themselves with the literature, no matter how painful or unrewarding that might be. I did the necessary reading without complaint, but also without enthusiasm, and ended up writing an answer to a question about budgeting. (Hopefully, no one will ever dig it up.) The literature I had read was incredibly dull, lifeless, and irrelevant. Still, I knew that getting money must be a prime object for government agencies and the officials who run them, and I wondered how they went about doing it. But the literature had essentially nothing to say about how men behaved in the process of budgeting.

So far as I can remember, I had no thoughts whatsoever about budgeting in the two years that followed the examinations. Then, for reasons which may always remain obscure, I began to think about the subject. On pure faith, Oberlin College gave me a few hundred dollars to take a student to Washington so that both of us could interview people involved in budgeting. I spent the next few weeks trying to think of a few simple questions that I could ask of budget officers in the hope of getting some interesting response. How do you decide what to ask for? How do you go about getting it? Who is most important to you in getting funds? How often do you talk with them? Judd Kestler and I spent six weeks in Washington interviewing from morning to night. We were not certain whether it was encouraging to discover that no academic investigator had ever spoken to these important people about their work before. At the end, we thought we had something, but we were not quite sure what it was.

Later that summer, I tried to write what eventually became the "Political Implications of Budgetary Reform." But it would not get written. Too ignorant about welfare economics to do the theoretical part, I stopped to gain some additional knowledge, then tried again. Four or five more drafts appeared to no avail. I dropped the writing and decided to try another tack. The following winter, when time permitted, I laid out on the table in my office the notes we had made of our interviews and tried to sort them into meaningful categories. The initial result was a paper called "A Preliminary Guide to the Budgetary Process," which was never published, but which proved to be an invaluable aid to my thinking. I tried three more times to write the paper on "Political Implications" and failed. Months later everything seemed to fall into place and the paper got done.

Two years later, using the "Preliminary Guide" to direct my efforts, I engaged in another bout of interviewing in Washington and finished a draft of *The Politics of the Budgetary Process*. All the essays on budgeting, except for "The Political Implications of Budgetary Reform," were written after the book was published. "Budgeting as a Political Process," which was prepared for the *International Encyclopedia of Social Sciences* to summarize the state of existing knowledge, gives the reader some idea of my findings as well as references to practices in foreign governments.

Although I cannot say exactly how my interest in budgeting developed, I can specify precisely the events which led up to devising, with Otto Davis and Michael Dempster, the equations that are at the heart of "A Theory of the Budgetary Process." Had I not been frustrated by the Bureau of the Budget, that paper and the work which follows from it might never have been done. My intention had been to sit in on a budgetary cycle of two agencies, the Bureau of Land Management in the Department of Interior and the Soil Conservation Service in Agriculture, in order to do a detailed study of how budgeting was actually carried on. The study was to include activities in Congress and the Budget Bureau. I proceeded carefully. I got a letter from the director of the Budget granting me permission to see bureau files and interview their personnel. Top agency officials gave their assent. When it came time to sit in on critical meetings, however, I found that the Bureau of the Budget objected. After strenuous negotiations, in which I was helped by Joe Fisher, the president of Resources for the Future, it appeared I could see everything in the files for previous years, except for the recommendations of the Director's Review, the top decision-making body within the Bureau of the Budget. This was not what I had hoped for, but I accepted it anyway. A few weeks later, in the best bureaucratic fashion, a telephone call informed me that everything in the bureau files concerning the two agencies referred in some way to the recommendations of the Director's Review; therefore I would be unable to see anything. I was furious, but there seemed to be nothing I could do.

Determined to overcome these obstacles, I wondered how it was possible to study budgeting without actually being on the spot to observe behavior as it occurred. I threw myself into another round of interviews. But it seemed to me that I did not learn one new thing. All I heard were the same old stories. Then it dawned on me that I was running away from an important finding: behavior in the budgetary process must be exceedingly uniform if all I got was the same response over and over again. I could try to express in formal language the regularities I had found and test them out on available data. My enthusiasm waned, however, when I discovered that I did not know how to go about the task.

At that critical moment, Otto Davis literally walked in my door. He was introduced to me as an economist interested in political phenomena. I explained to him at some length what I wanted to do. He read the manuscript of my book on *The Politics of the Budgetary Process* and said that he thought it could be done. We formulated the general ideas behind the equations and he set to work. Months later important statistical problems had arisen; if they were not resolved, the theoretical basis for our work would be undermined. Essentially, the problem that goes under the imposing name of "auto-correlation of the residuals" involves the substantive question of whether we were not claiming as findings what we ourselves had put into the equations. Chasing your own tail is not recommended. To our good fortune, Michael Dempster agreed to try to prove a new theorem that would allow us to proceed as we wished. We waited for months until he accomplished the task. His work and the more technical parts of the analysis were reported in a separate publication for specialists.[1] I took on the task of preparing a paper for an audience of political scientists who might conceivably be interested in the general problem but who were not familiar with the terms and notation. "A Theory of the Budgetary Process" is still, admittedly, not easy to read, but I believe that a determined student can master it without prior technical training.

While trying unsuccessfully to study the budgetary process in the Soil Conservation service, I discovered that the Department of Agriculture was in the midst of an interesting experiment with a "zero-base" budget, which involved treating major expenditures as if no previous commitments had been made and they all had to be justified anew. Another Oberlin student, Arthur Hammond, joined me in Washington, and we did the set of interviews on which "Comprehensive Versus Incremental Budgeting in the Department of Agriculture" is based.

When program budgeting came into vogue in the federal government, I was often asked to comment, but felt that I did not have enough to say. After some thought, I decided to take a close look at the fundamental analytical processes on which program budgeting appeared to rest. My experience at Resources for the Future proved invaluable in appraising the literature on cost-benefit analysis. In view of the fact that program budgeting had been exported in a sense from the Defense Department, I also thought it wise to read about the systems analysis practiced there. Then I studied the books on program budgeting written by its leading advocates. Having done the reading, I saw how cost-benefit analysis, systems analysis, and program budgeting could be treated as increasing levels of economic imperialism on political subjects.

In the years since the Bureau of the Budget first refused me its cooperation, I have sent many students to Washington to work on budgetary matters and have made many acquaintances among practitioners. Now it is hard to freeze me out. Whenever I come through Washington (usually about four or five times a year) I make it a point to speak about current developments with several men engaged in budgeting. In recent times that has meant emphasis on program budgeting. When I discovered that the

Budget Director himself did not actually use the program budget to make decisions, I thought the time had come to say another word on the subject. What concerned me most was the cynicism of budget officials, who had been forced to engage in an exercise—program budgeting—which no one knew how to do. This bad experience had the adverse effect of creating antagonism not merely toward program budgeting in particular but toward policy analysis in general. I wanted to explain both why program budgeting did not work, and why this failure should not be cause for rejecting policy analysis. That is why I called the piece "Rescuing Policy Analysis from PPBS."

It is one thing to tell others that their ideas leave something to be desired and quite another to come up with a better one yourself. The American Enterprise Institute's desire to sponsor a paper on budgetary reform from the congressional viewpoint challenged me to do just that. So far as I can tell, my proposal for a "radical incrementalism" has fallen into the void. Someday, I keep telling myself, its evident wisdom will be acknowledged.

I wrote a paper about political style without being aware that was the subject I was working on. Upon arriving at Oberlin, Ohio, I was told that the bankers ran the town. If they were not the ones who controlled everything, then it was the town's merchants. No one even remotely considered that a slightly rumpled and rotund individual named Bill Long, who managed the Co-op book store and had a reputation as a wild-eyed radical, would get anything more than bruises for his efforts to change Oberlin. In four years I observed him use prodigious amounts of skill, knowledge, and energy to lead the community through a major transformation. I thought that other people would be interested in knowing about the impact that a remarkable man could have on public policy and wrote "Bill Long: Portrait of an Activist." I did not then realize that the political style he epitomizes—instrumental, pragmatic, oriented to accomplishment on substantive policies—was not the only possible one.

My acknowledged interest in political styles dates from a failure. Awarded a grant to attend the 1960 Democratic Convention, I developed a research design hypothesizing that after several ballots have failed to select a candidate, the pattern of communication among delegates is crucial in developing support for the eventual nominee.[2] Though I believed that Kennedy would win the nomination, as did everyone else, I decided to try out my research design on the Ohio delegation. Observing these political men and writing about them was a lot of fun, even if chasing them around from morning until night was exhausting. But there was no chance to observe communication on nonexistent second and third ballots. In retrospect, however, I realized that in " 'What Can I Do?' The Ohio Delegate's View of the Convention," I had painted a picture of traditional party men who were groping around to find a winner.

When the 1964 Republican Convention beckoned across the Bay in San

Francisco, I saw it as a chance to study the special qualities of the Gold-water supporter. But as the article on the "Goldwater Phenomenon: Purists, Politicians, and the Two-Party System" relates, efforts to ask them about their views on public policy led to nothing interesting. Thrashing about for some good way to make use of my time, I came up with the idea of asking them how they approached politics, how they felt about winning and losing, and what they considered the proper stance to take in political life. That paid off so well that I arranged for a group of students from Berkeley and Chicago to help me do the same sort of thing at the 1968 Democratic Convention. Taken together, the papers on the Goldwater forces and on the struggle between the McCarthyites and the party regulars reveal a growing emphasis on style in the political activity of elites. I plan to look at the trend again in 1972.

Occasionally one does a paper that takes on a personal meaning out of proportion to its value as a piece of scholarship. The critique of Duverger's *Political Parties* (not included here for lack of space) originated as a graduate course paper, but it has since assumed a larger significance for me. Coming to grips with that work, achieving an understanding of what a general theory of political parties was supposed to do, took months of effort and seventeen drafts. Done for a course brilliantly taught by David Truman, the paper was so schematic and detailed that I could not imagine giving it in class and therefore requested my fellow students to read it in advance and give me their comments. (I thereby discovered a good way of running research seminars. Anyone who has heard students drone on reading complex papers in class knows it to be an awful experience. My students deposit their papers in a convenient place several days in advance, and when the class convenes it discusses material it has been able to consider at some leisure.) Most members of the class at Yale were kind enough to write me a few sentences. Nelson Polsby wrote two bluebooks of tightly packed and detailed criticism; we have been friends ever since. Told that the Duverger paper, a product of so much sweat and toil, should be published, I blithely sent it off. There followed a series of rejections by the major journals of this country. One anonymous critic suggested that I rewrite the piece praising Duverger's book instead of criticizing it. I returned to my teachers and was told that if I thought the article was good, I should keep sending it around and lick my wounds in private. In the years since *The Journal of Politics* finally accepted it,[3] the article has been reprinted numerous times.

In recent years my interest in the substance of public policy has grown. The reason for writing any article is likely to be an intense concern about the problem it covers. While racial conflict was breaking out in the summer of 1966, for example, I encountered numerous people expressing anger, dismay and, most of all, puzzlement at this state of affairs. They could not make sense out of it and neither could I. As a student of public policy I was able to work out these anxieties by turning my attention to the problem. I took seriously the complaint of those who felt that the racial situation was anomalous. Instead of trying to say it was all really too simple, I tried to explain to them (and first of all to myself) why the situation appeared so perverse at the time. That is the origin of "The Empty-Head Blues," a title I took as a parody of the old Bessie Smith song, "The Empty Bed Blues," because so many people kept telling me they were worried about racial violence, but that they did not have a thought about it in their heads. My research involved reading a book about the Moynihan Report that led to ideas incorporated in the review on "Race and Research."

As it became apparent that urban problems were really national problems and that "the urban crisis" was in part a euphemism for racial conflict, I began thinking about policies that would respond to the situation. Inequality of income, it seemed to me, lay behind the concerns that were voiced on all sides. Therefore, I seized upon an invitation to do a paper on the political feasibility of proposals to give poor people income as a right. I had for years been talking and writing (see "The Political Economy of Efficiency") about the desirability of including appraisals of political feasibility as part of the analysis of policy proposals. A good policy analysis could not merely be one that was published in a journal or that languished on the writer's desk, but also had to be one that was adopted and survived in the political environment. A talented graduate student, Bill Cavala, helped with the interviewing and assisted me in unraveling some of the complex questions of political theory involved in giving people money they have not directly earned. The paper illustrates one of the risks of dealing with contemporary problems: life may soon prove us wrong.

I have included "The Theory of Preemptive Revolution" not merely because it was fun to write but because it led to more serious work. I mailed the piece to Max Singer at the Hudson Institute, who responded with one of his own that had a similar, though less fanciful, thrust. Both of us were concerned about the unseemly position of the United States rushing out to "save from communism" every little country in the world. We did not like it when Uncle Sam got kicked around for his pains. Out of that concern we wrote "A Third-World Averaging Strategy."

You never know whether you really have anything to say until you try to write it down. Many ideas seem great until you discover they will not write. Thoughts rush out in a jumble; you have to unscramble them. Nature never comes in straight lines; men have to put them there. Sometimes they fail. A few lines may be in order, therefore, about the papers that never got written.

Sometimes you can't get the requisite information. If the Bureau of the Budget refuses access to its files and lets you interview people only in groups of three or more with the chief glaring at the Indians, that piece is not going to get done. If your research design depends on studying the reaction of convention delegates to information received during the second ballot, it is a little hard to implement when the first ballot ends the whole affair. A few years ago I thought it would be interesting to use organization charts to demolish once and for all the canard that organizations never die. Part of the difficulty was that the federal government has not made the charts on consistent rules so it was hard to tell from one department to another what a change in organizational status meant. The big problem, I confess, lay in finding a sample of defunct agencies to study.

The most interesting cases of papers that will not write are those involving conceptual difficulties. My files contain a half-finished essay called "Reflections on Non-Issues." Robert Dahl's *Who Governs?* and (less often) my *Leadership in a Small Town* had been criticized because their concentration on actual decisions in New Haven and Oberlin appeared to preclude consideration of those "non-decisions" that might have been made but were not. How do you examine the little man who wasn't there? Would it make sense, let us say, to study the British Parliament in terms of those decisions it might conceivably have made but did not? I tried to reformulate the criticism to refer to the difference between accounting for the historical development of existing governmental relationships versus the marginal changes likely at any one point in time. But writing about things rarely contemplated and never done proved as elusive as (perhaps because it was) the subject itself. I never could get hold of it properly.

Even if the thought is in you there is no guarantee it will come out. Between the thought and the deed there is a vast chasm. That gulf can be bridged only by taking seriously the task of organizing work. In addition to having things to say, the ability to write depends on developing appropriate habits, finding the right kind of place, obtaining useful criticism, learning how to arrange material, working out a suitable physical style, combining teaching and research, overcoming temptations to divert energies, and surmounting the obstacles created by administrative demands.

In the Same Place, at the Same Time, and in the Same Way

In getting my work done I cannot overestimate the importance of habit and rhythm. Insofar as possible I try to work in the same place, at the same time, and in the same way. Once the rhythm of work begins to take hold, it carries you through fallow periods; it keeps you going through the inevitable descriptive passages that contain nothing new but are essential for the story you are telling or the point you wish to make. Willa Cather's *The Professor's House* contains the best description I know of the impact of a place of residence on a man's work. When the professor moves to another house, he loses his sense of ease and comfort and knowing where he is for the purpose at hand.

I have never worked at home. There is something appalling to me about gazing at my own entrails. Perhaps this is due to the huge mess I create in the process of writing, so that my desk is piled high with all sorts of debris. I like to leave the scene of the crime to begin anew the next day. (For the same reason, I maintain physical separation between my research and administrative offices.) For the past several years my writing has been done in a loft three blocks from the main campus of the university, where there is a small office measuring 8 by 11 feet. It has a desk, a telephone, two chairs, the material I am working on at the moment, and no adornment of any kind whatsoever. The monks had the right idea.

There is, I am convinced, no one time of day to write that is good for everyone. I am a morning person myself; if I attempt to write in the evening it is a sure sign of desperation rather than choice. The important thing is to work at roughly the same time every day so that body and mind expect to be called on and will respond.

I write when I sit and I think when I walk. I like to write for an hour or two and then (hopefully having gotten somewhere) walk and think over the next steps. There is something about releasing the physical energy kept under control while writing that makes it easier to begin again. It is a mistake to push oneself when the flesh is weak and the spirit unwilling.

Writing is not only a mental but a physical process in which a sense of touch connects thought with word. In my early college days I wrote everything out in longhand first and then typed the final draft. Losing the contact of pen on paper, I thought, would stem the flow of ideas. Faced with the necessity of completing four papers in one week, however, I discovered that I could type the initial drafts. Typing saved a lot of time and there was something about pounding the machine (I have never been able to tolerate electric typewriters because you can't feel what you are doing) that created the necessary physical contact.

When I became department chairman I had to change my work method to conform to circumstances in which writing time might be limited to an hour or two a day. There was time to think and to read; the difficulty lay in putting together enough consecutive hours to write. If I could knock out a first draft, I would occasionally be able to finish something of essay length. Reluctantly and over some period of time I gave up my affair with the typewriter and began dictating.

For the contact with the typewriter I substitute the sensation of sheets of paper appearing whole and clean out of the void. I press heavily with pencil in making revisions, so that I feel a little more like a craftsman. After the sheets of paper get so covered with my scribbles that they are virtually illegible except to devoted secretaries, they are retyped and the process of revision continues. New paragraphs are written; old ones are abandoned; whole sections are moved from one place to another; the would-be essay is typed several times more until either I or the subject is exhausted. To compose passages that prove exceedingly recalcitrant, I reestablish contact with the typewriter. The time has come when I can even dictate into a machine and not feel as if I have forever lost touch with real life.

Before studying with Arthur Charles Cole, a historian who lived and breathed research, I did not know how to organize a large piece of work. Notes were stuck in odd places. It was anyone's guess whether they would ever be retrieved. Professor Cole taught me how to work systematically from notecards. I list the topics to be covered. Then I shuffle the cards around until a coherent presentation of themes emerges. When the material on the cards has been put into place or discarded, it is time to begin writing. I have continued that practice ever since for works of book length or complicated papers like "The Political Economy of Efficiency."

Shorter papers come in various ways. Sometimes they flow on in a straight line from start to finish, like "Rescuing Policy Analysis From PPBS." At other times they are full of stops and starts, like "The Empty-Head Blues." I had so much difficulty organizing that piece I almost gave it up. It was only after I removed what was essentially a book review about the Moynihan Report from the center of the essay that "The Empty-Head Blues" took final shape.

Sometimes I employ a form of free association. I jot down a number of points and write a paragraph or two about each of them without paying attention to their relationship to one another. More points and more isolated paragraphs follow. If I think there is enough to work with, I knit various paragraphs together with analytic threads. Revision follows revision. "The Politics of ABM," "The Two Presidencies," and "The Meaning of Youth in the Struggle for Control of the Democratic Party" were written that way.

Writing is a process of self-discovery which sometimes leads you to say more than you knew was in you or carries you far from original intentions. That is why I have learned not to worry about introductions to books or the first few paragraphs of an essay. There is no sense in trying too hard to get them "right," because you don't know what that will be until you finish. The purpose of a beginning is to get you started; when the work is completed, you can go back to the beginning and tell the reader not what you thought you were going to say but what you ended up saying.

Oftentimes you get stuck in the course of writing. You sit at your desk and nothing happens. Sometimes the only thing to do is to leave it alone. But there are other ways. If you are writing a book, some parts always seem easier than others. It helps to gain confidence by turning to something that does write more easily. When one part of a paper seems utterly impossible, others, which had previously appeared just as difficult, seem easier by comparison. Through a process of sequential reduction, you arrive at a point where only a few critical passages remain and there is the incentive of knowing that when these difficulties are overcome the paper will be completed.

"The Political Economy of Efficiency" occupies a special place in my affection because it is one of the few papers that was written almost effort-lessly. Perhaps the explanation may be found in my working conditions. It was done in three days without interruptions on a light-weight portable typewriter while I was in bed recuperating from an illness.

I get as much help as I can in improving my work. In Oberlin it was obviously not possible in a four-man department to find people who shared my precise interests. After getting general comments from one or two of my colleagues, I would send preliminary drafts of papers to friends all over the country. At Berkeley I will ordinarily get five or six comments before sending a batch of 20 or 30 to various people who might be inter-ested in the subject and be willing to give me comments. This is a common practice that serves to facilitate communication among scholars. One of the hard things about academic life is that one's friends and colleagues get scattered. Circulating papers not only helps improve the quality but ena-bles me to keep in touch with people I like but rarely get to see.

One of the glories of academic life is the ability to go from one subject to another as the spirit moves. I would not give it up for anything. Main-taining this diversity of interests—defense and domestic policies, Ameri-can and foreign governments, local and national politics, political parties, the presidency, budgeting—raises the problem of reading enough to keep up with new knowledge. In view of the huge amount of research done on these subjects, it is not possible to follow developments closely in each of them. I can read everything in English on budgeting because the total out-put is small. On the presidency, I read all the serious analytical work and an occasional historical study; the vast outpouring of literature on the sub-ject is generally of no interest because it rarely attempts to explain any-thing and is usually a rehash of some muddy idea about the alleged characteristics of great men or the supposed alternation between weak and strong Presidents. Every couple of years I take a few days to read the accumulated literature on national conventions. Beyond that, I wait until I research a paper and then read what I can find until diminishing returns set in. As a general practice, I subscribe to major journals in political sci-ence and economics and scan them for material of interest. People send me things they are working on. I get clues about worthwhile reading from book reviews but more often from friends. I try to read something most days.

Reading is indispensable for writing; it can also be the enemy of writ-ing. There is a time to read and a time to say that picking other men's brains must stop. The most convincing argument anyone can give himself for not writing is that he has not read everything there is and is therefore not properly prepared to begin. The excuse is so plausible it is hard to re-sist. Yet there is always something else one might read. The next book may somehow change one's mind; not, however, if the thought is ever to give birth to the word.

Writing is a severe discipline. The writer puts himself on the line. His words stand exposed. He is subject to criticism, if not to ridicule. He is alone with himself for long periods when no one is there to provide support. He cannot depend on the surface push of events to carry him along. In his isolation and precariousness, a setback may seem overwhelming. The temptation to withdraw into the self is sometimes irresistible, for it is easy to invent one excuse after another to stop writing. When a man has been writing for some time, he is also subject to less obvious temptations to stop writing, less obvious because they flow from previous accomplishments.

The creative years are often spent in obscurity. The scholar unknown, spends his time working. Then something he writes takes hold. He is called upon to give lectures at distant places. Each trip he takes seems justified at the time by the interest of the locale, the worthiness of the cause, or the attractiveness of the people. The more he talks, however, the less he has to say. He has been using up his intellectual capital, and if he does not watch out his services will become more and more in demand as his thoughts are less and less worth hearing.

Temptation is a conference. Is it not pleasant to attend a fine meeting with many distinguished people amidst lovely rural surroundings? Often the subject is just slightly different from work already done, so that it appears possible to get by through a little regurgitation. If the subject is far removed from areas of previous competence, it is flattering suddenly to become a universal genius whose opinions are sought on every conceivable matter. But running and writing are not compatible.

My trial came with program budgeting. For a couple of years it was the rage. Local, state, national, and international bureaucracies had to have it. Being one of the few national critics of program budgeting, I was called upon to go everywhere. No one should believe that I resisted this temptation. For six months I was in full flight. I knew I should stop, but it was hard. Finally, I refused outright to discuss program budgeting. The only measure of defense was not to cut down the evil but to eliminate it altogether. The fact that repeated exposure led me to loathe the topic made it a little easier.

There is a Gresham's Law—good little projects drive out better big ones—that results from giving in to an insidious form of temptation. There are invitations to contribute articles to symposia, prepare special reports for governmental bodies, and submit papers for publication in leading reviews. The temptation is insidious because there is nothing wrong with the requests. Each proposal is desirable in and of itself; the subject is interesting; the research required is worthwhile; and the scholarly purpose is eminently justifiable. The trouble is that these good little projects represent diversions from the main line of scholarly inquiry. It is so easy to find one's self committed two years in advance to do one little interesting thing after another, so that the whole is, alas, considerably less than the sum of its parts. One defense is simply to say no to everything. A better way, I have found, is to accept only those projects that fit in with one's longer-range scholarly plans. I will take an assignment that promises to teach me something about issue-analysis but will reject one that represents a slight variation on what I have done before. I recently accepted a request from the Public Land Law Review Commission to write a report on budgeting in the areas of recreation and land management. I am interested in both budgeting and natural resources, but that alone would not have led me to accept the job. The project required several weeks of interviewing, collaboration with students, and a good deal of writing time. I took it on because I was thinking about converting *The Politics of the Budgetary Process* into a comprehensive monograph. One chapter, I thought, should provide a kind of before-and-during (it cannot yet be after) study of program budgeting in a specific area of policy. The commission provided the necessary access to governmental officials and the financial resources to do the job.

The best way to avoid some kinds of temptations is to give in to others. I seek out projects that have multiple uses. My ideal is to undertake research and writing that will serve as a focus of classroom lectures and seminar discussions. "The Political Economy of Efficiency," for example, provided the basis of several discussions in my graduate seminar on budgeting. "The Political Feasibility of Income by Right" was useful for discussion in my undergraduate honors seminar on Oakland's policy problems. When I am in the first-draft stage, I like to give lectures on the subject of the paper because it helps me think.

There is a widespread belief that teaching is opposed to research. The more you do of one, supposedly, the less you do of the other. I disagree. Teaching and research belong together. Teaching is more interesting and more valuable when the instructor has done original work and has known the discipline of writing down his thoughts and having them subjected to criticism by his peers. There is no better guarantee of a teacher's interest in his students than that they should be working together on a subject which is of scholarly interest to him. Teaching is an invaluable aid in writing. It helps clarify thoughts and increases fluency. My experience has been that men who take scholarship seriously enough to want to share it with others make the best teachers; writing is, after all, a form of teaching.

Teaching has been an invaluable aid in my research, just as research has enhanced my teaching. One of my books, *Leadership in a Small Town,* was wholly conceived and developed in an undergraduate course. Upon being told to teach a course on state and local government at Oberlin, I was dismayed because I had scarcely heard of the subject. After reading several texts and various articles in the field I was appalled. The existing literature was dull and uninformative. It dealt largely with the minutiae of muncipal administration and contained numerous cliches like "the superiority of the city manager form of government" without any evidence to back them up. I simply could not subject myself and my students to counting manhole covers all semester. In desperation I recalled that two of my friends at

Yale, Nelson Polsby and Raymond Wolfinger, were working with Professor Robert Dahl on a community power study of who controlled the decision-making process in New Haven, Connecticut. I sent for their material, read widely in the literature, and decided that students might as well get some contact with the world by finding out how things were done in the town of Oberlin. In the next three years successive classes in State and Local Government accumulated (and used for its reading lists) numerous papers on how specific decisions were made. We even did a small survey to determine the extent of citizen interest and activity and to compare ordinary citizens with political activists. By that time I found myself involved with the personalities and drama of political events in Oberlin. It was only when preparing for the fourth year of classes that I read through the student material and realized that with another year's work on my part there would be enough to write a book.

The idea for a paper often comes from a lack of adequate class material. In teaching courses on the presidency at Oberlin and Berkeley, I tired of describing the President's powers and then talking about the few case histories we had showing Presidents in action. There was a need for analytic thrust to differentiate among Presidential activities. Thus, the paper on "The Two Presidencies" originated as a classroom lecture.

If teaching and research may be compatible, there is less reason to be sanguine about the relationship between writing and administration. As chairman of the political science department, with its 50 faculty, 900 undergraduate majors, 300 graduate students, and 14 secretaries, I soon discovered it was impossible to carry on the intense personal contact required by the job and then leave it for a while in order to read, reflect, or write. The pace of events was too swift. So I tried, with modest success, to set aside mornings for scholarly work. I began early and kept at it until the telephone proved too insistent or my colleagues hunted me out in desperation.

On hectic days, it all seemed impossible. Between consulting with my colleagues, coping with a few minor disasters, trying to recruit good men to the faculty, arranging the appropriate coalition for the next department meeting, soothing the outraged and the injured, and trying to invent new educational policies, there was no time for anything else. The worst deprivation, however, was not the actual time spent on departmental matters, but the diversion of mental energies from scholarly channels. Whereas I used to walk and think about the theoretical problems of my research, I found the latest department crisis preempting my attention.

On better days, with quiet mornings spent reading, writing, or talking to students, I felt that the combination of scholarly thought and administrative action had something to be said for it. The two kinds of activities tire out different parts of the mind and body. You can be exhausted in one and still have energy to carry out the other. They gratify different senses and arouse different anxieties. Harmony among them depends on getting sufficient time to give each its due. They do share one common requisite: unflagging energy. In the end there is the consolation of knowing that the worst that can happen to you as an administrator is to be fired so you will have more time for the main work of your life.

Limitations of time have led me to see the virtue of collaboration. If I want to do a monograph on the history of ancient budgeting (because it pleases me, because it is not relevant to anything whatsoever, because it must be done solely for a love of the subject), I can read enough to outline the work to be done. But I cannot spend the long months required to investigate the specialized literature on governmental practices and social life in ancient Greece, Rome, India, China, Japan, and so on. A great pool of underutilized talent at the university is composed of wives of faculty members. One of them, Carolyn Webber, will coauthor a monograph on ancient budgeting with me.

Like writing itself, willingness to collaborate depends on early and successful experience. Nelson Polsby and I wrote a paper on party reform at the Yale Graduate School. Later I encouraged him to prepare for publication a paper he had done formalizing the literature on national conventions. On a snowy Thanksgiving in Oberlin, where Nelson was visiting me, we discovered that we each had done a fair amount of work on Presidential conventions and elections. There was born the idea, reinforced by earlier experience, of collaborating on a book called *Presidential Elections*.

Since I tend to write long and Nelson to write short, I took on the task of blending together the various papers we already had. He shortened and tightened my rough draft and wrote new sections of his own. After doing what we could with the manuscript by mail, we discovered it was not up to the standard we had set. So the next summer we met in Washington daily over a period of weeks. Each afternoon we read over a portion of the manuscript to decide what had to be changed and to agree upon a division of labor. Nelson, being a night person, wrote his contribution in the evening, I prepared mine in the morning, and we met again to continue the process. It was a remarkably satisfying experience.

A Man's Life and His Work Are One

A man's life and his work are one. No man springs full grown into the world, and I am no exception. My interest in democracy stems directly from personal experience.

My parents fled from Bolshevik Russia to democratic America. They delivered no sermons on patriotism, but they left no doubt about their preference. When I once suggested to my father that he might enjoy going back to Russia to see his family, he was indignant. Would any sane man, he asked, voluntarily return to the scene of a hateful life?

Politics was an avid subject of conversation in our house. My mother used to read me stories from the *New York Daily News,* an early experience which taught me how selective perception can make one comfortable with a newspaper whose editorial views are utterly opposed to one's beliefs. My father vigorously argued with his friends over foreign policy questions. There was no debate about the New Deal because we were all Democrats. I was 14 before I met a live Republican. The earliest political chant I remember is: "Roosevelt in the White House, rah rah rah!/Landon in the ashcan, hah hah hah!"

In 1930, when I was born, my father was in the hospital recovering from the loss of a leg due to an industrial accident. He could no longer pursue his trade as a bookbinder. Fortunately he was able to use workman's compensation funds to begin a new life. He bought an apartment house, fixed it up, sold it for a higher price if he could get it, and moved on. As his real estate ventures declined during World War II, the shortage of labor enabled him to go back to work. During that time we rented an apartment in a house we did not own. I learned to live with a situation in which our tenants complained about their landlord, we complained about ours, my father complained about his boss, and the superintendent hired to take care of our building complained about him. I cannot think of a better way to get an objective view of social relations than to be landlord and tenant, employer and employee all at once. The necessity of enabling diverse and conflicting interests to get along were apparent even in the small network of activities surrounding my family.

My first contact with partisan politics came from negotiating over housing matters for my parents with City Hall through the local Democratic club. At 14 I distributed leaflets for Franklin D. Roosevelt on his tour through Brooklyn. But it was Brooklyn College that led to intense personal involvement.

I did not learn about Communists and fellow travelers from books; I learned by observing their behavior in student politics. I was amazed to discover that one of the cliches about them was true: they *were* subject to outside guidance by the Communist party and they *did* all say the same thing. It got so that I could finish their sentences for them. During one hilarious period in 1950, I accidentally discovered a way of getting the *Daily Worker* a couple of hours before it was available near campus. Every few weeks there was bound to be a change in the party line on some question. I would take up the matter with the local types and hear them repeat the old line. Several hours later I would return with the same question and hear a new line. It was amazing what a few hours of reflection would do.

I remember the heated conversation I had with a date on the New Lots IRT subway. She had joined a group dedicated to civil liberties, together with a number of students who belonged to an organization called the Labor Youth League. I told her that although they might be fine people individually, they would not hesitate to sacrifice the purposes of her civil liberties group to the higher dictates of their cause. She vehemently objected to my *a priori* argument, since I did not know personally all the people involved and their character might be different. The next week they used their control of the mimeograph machine to put out leaflets taking positions on which the members of the group as a whole were not consulted. My social life improved.

After shopping around for a congenial political organization, I joined the youth division of the New York State Liberal party because it combined welfare liberalism with opposition to totalitarianism. In campaigning for Harry Truman in 1948 I learned an invaluable lesson about the potential of active minorities. With three people in it, our Young Liberal Club could hardly do anything. When our membership expanded a full 100 percent we were able to keep one member at the mimeograph and five others covering every entrance and exit to Brooklyn College. We had an impact far beyond our numbers.

One of the beliefs prevalent in the student political culture of the time (1948–1950) was that you could not beat the Communists at their own game. If they were determined to take over an organization of innocents, they could not be stopped. But their effort to turn a conference on student participation in educational policy to the ends of Soviet foreign policy provoked me to challenge that belief. I read as much as I could on Communist tactics and political activism in general. A group of us, ranging from the Liberal and Democratic parties to the Socialists and Trotskyites, formed the "Democratic Coalition Committee" in an effort to counter the Communist influence. We came early; we stayed late; we memorized Robert's Rules of Order; we worked day and night, and we prevailed. My grades took a precipitous drop but my knowledge of political activity sharply increased.

While I was taking Professor Jesse Clarkson's course on modern Russian history, I was also attending lectures given by Max Schactman, a learned Trotskyite leader who could tell you what happened every minute during the critical days of the Bolshevik Revolution. Noting certain glaring inconsistencies in their theories, I asked Professor Clarkson how I might decide between the two versions. I would see that he was right, Clarkson said, if I read a multivolume set of documents on the revolution put out by the Hoover Institution. A few days later I posed the same question to Mr. Schactman. You will see that I am right, he said, by reading the documents put out by the Hoover Institution.

In view of this background it is not surprising that I went to Yale Graduate School with the intention of specializing in Soviet politics. But after two years of study I decided against it. I finally realized that my activist temperament was unsuited to studying a political system at long range as if through the wrong end of a telescope. Moreover, the conviction began growing on me that Soviet politics as it was then conceived was too simple. A small, ideologically devoted cadre used force and persuasion to bend a population to its will. If persuasion failed, they just used more force. What was so hard about that? Getting people to consent to live together by reconciling their differences seemed infinitely more complicated and interesting. I realized that I did not want to spend my life in a negative enterprise criticizing a system I did not like. I would much rather explore the potential of democracy. And that is what I have tried to do in my subsequent teaching and writing.

I consider myself a representative of the passionate and committed center. Mostly I push hard for small changes compatible with the little knowledge and limited moral sensibility of mankind. My life and my work embody both a deep-seated pessimism about man's ability to control the evil in him and an abiding faith that it is worth trying to perfect his capacity for self-government.

NOTES

1. Otto Davis, Michael Dempster, and Aaron Wildavsky, "On the Process of Budgeting: An Empirical Study of Congressional Appropriation," in Gordon Tullock, ed., *Papers on Non-Market Decision Making* (Charlottesville: Thomas Jefferson Center for Political Economy, University of Virginia, 1966), pp. 63–132.
2. The research design is the second half of Nelson Polsby and Aaron Wildavsky, "Uncertainty and Decision-Making at the National Conventions," in N. Polsby, R. Dentler, and P. Smith, eds., *Politics and Social Life* (Boston: Houghton Mifflin Company, 1963), pp. 370–389.
3. "A Methodological Critique of Duverger's Political Parties," *Journal of Politics,* 21, no. 2, May 1959, pp. 303–318.

PART I

The Analysis
of Issues

1

THE REVOLT AGAINST
THE MASSES [1]

The revolutionaries of contemporary America do not seek to redistribute privilege from those who have it to those who do not. These radicals wish to arrange a transfer of power from those elites who now exercise it to another elite, namely themselves, who do not. This aspiring elite is of the same race (white), the same class (upper-middle and upper), and the same educational background (the best colleges and universities) as those they wish to displace. The goal of this white, radical, privileged elite is clear: a society purged by them of the values, tastes, preferences and policies desired by the mass of Americans. The white elite is in revolt against the masses.

By the masses I mean all of the working class and the vast preponderance of the middle class. The elite can be located by reduction. It is part (perhaps five to ten percent of the population is involved) of an upper-middle and upper-class revolt against the culture of the masses. Among the culturally discontented, the elite forms part of the New Left political movement. The elite itself—those who have abandoned regular political activity in favor of coercive assaults on social institutions—is the most violent segment of that movement. Members of the elite make up no more than three and probably less than one percent of the population.[2] They are my subject and I shall begin with them. I shall deal with the things they have in common: their differences would be the subject of another essay.

Hostility Toward the Masses

The mass of people in the United States have not undergone much political change in the past decade. They support democratic institutions and accord legitimacy to their government. They are strongly identified with the major political parties, with a majority seeing themselves as Democrats. They have traditional American values. For them, America is still the land of opportunity, and they would like to share in it.

The great political changes in America have occurred within its voluble elites. However small in number, their voices are amplified throughout the land. They lead demonstrations; they proclaim themselves and others to be alienated; they suffer, and impose upon others, a sense of malaise; their negative interpretation of conditions and their growing hostility to the current organization of the American political system creates the sense of crisis that we all experience.

A small but significant segment of the upper middle and upper class has become disaffected. The origins of their anger against existing American society may be found in growing industrialization and affluence. The extraordinary degree to which the common man of the 1930s has enriched himself threatens this elite. Its stunning decline in expected privilege is felt most directly as a loss of amenity. A man has to be much richer than ever before in order to be visibly better off. In the 1930s, for example, a man who could afford a decent-sized boat had the rivers and lakes much to himself. Now he must share them with the hordes of people who crowd existing facilities. It is necessary to travel further and pay more in order to restore the old notions of privilege that rest on distance from the mass. A few months ago I read a news report about the army of people who come to the Southern California desert with dune buggies, motorcycles, and other apparatus, so that it is difficult for anyone to find solitude there. It is the extension of former elitist privileges to the masses on a thousand fronts that threatens the white elite.

When the masses were truly poor, their opinions could largely be ignored. They dressed differently from other people, they stayed in their own neighborhoods, and they kept in their place. The rise of mass affluence has exerted a strong influence on public culture. Media and fashions bend to mass tastes. The life styles of the white elite are being obliterated by the sheer numbers of people who possess the outer appurtenances of culture—just at the moment these radicals had hoped to set public taste. They lose power to the majority of their own economic class which either identifies with the culture of the masses or which is content to make money by catering to this culture. The radical elite hates the establishment not because it exploits the masses but because it does not repress their cultural desires enough.

Members of the radical elite are characterized by enormous hostility to what they perceive as the idiocy of mass taste. They despise everything about the masses—the clothes they wear; the houses they live in; the furniture they buy; the length of their hair; their sexual and sanitary habits; their speech; the way they treat their wives, husbands, and children; the TV programs they watch; the newspapers they read; the politicians they like; their work habits; the way they talk to one another; their neighborhoods—everything that goes into making what is called the American way of life. The elite also hates the masses for the injustices they commit against those less fortunate than themselves. It has sometimes been true that the radicals were so occupied with hating, they had no love to spare for people. Their protestations about love, love, LOVE, LOVE! only amplify the point. They protest too much. One cannot talk to a member of the radical elite without understanding that they will make the masses behave or else.

The radical elite adores the underprivileged because it can do things for them. The downtrodden can be shown *noblesse oblige*. They can be manipulated, in their own interest of course. People who can help themselves must be dealt with as equals not as wards.

An aristocratic bid for power and privilege cannot succeed under the conditions of American life. But it can be dressed in democratic garb. The slogan of the white elite is "participatory democracy." Strangely enough, this doctrine, under which everyone allegedly participates, rules out the mass of working and middle-class Americans. The mass has to work. The mass lacks the flexible occupation that allows the professional and the student to choose their working hours. It is not qualified by temperament and training to continually engage in agitation. It may be manipulated by symbolic oratory but it cannot lead in that process. To the degree that mass representative institutions—political parties, legislatures, elected executives—are denigrated, the mass is without the means for effective active action. In the agitational society of participatory democracy, the elite, not the mass, rules.

The Crisis of the Achievement Culture

The conflict between the radical elite and the conservative mass is rooted in deep subcultural differences in American society. The conflict has emerged with additional force and clarity because the pool from which the elite is drawn—the upper middle class and upper class—has expanded markedly. The accompanying chart, "Conflict of Subcultures," is merely suggestive of some of the many dimensions of life on which mass and elite differ. Books could (and have) been written on any one of them. All I can do here is comment briefly on two of these cultural dimensions.

Achievement depends on meeting standards of accomplishment, while *ascription* depends on who the person is, not on what he does. When a society is specific in the political realm, its political activities are largely specialized in institutions devoted to the purpose, such as parties and legislatures. When a society is governed by diffuse political norms, virtually all institutions are seen as arenas of political conflict. Economic achievement and political specificity have been the prevailing norms (though rarely without challenge) for most of American history. The current attempt to move from achievement back to ascription, and to enforce it by going from specificity to diffuseness in politics, present the basic cultural perspective within which the radical elite may be understood. Their attempt to politicize everything from child care to churches in order to break down prevailing standards of achievement and substitute political ones creates the crisis we all experience.

TABLE 1-1
Conflict of Subcultures

DIMENSION	RADICAL ELITE	MASS
1. Religion	atheistic or mystic	agnostic or formal church
2. Authority	derision	respect
3. Family	permissive	discipline
4. Work ethic	weak	strong
5. Status	ascription	achievement
6. Style	hip	square
7. Drugs	marijuana, yes; others, mixed; alcohol, indifferent	all "no" except alcohol
8. Living arrangements	communal	individual family
9. Equality	result	opportunity
10. Patriotism	low	high
11. Foreign policy	internationalist	nationalist
12. Politics-scope	diffuse; virtually all institutions politicized	specific; limited to institutions devoted to the purpose
13. Politics-salience	high	low
14. Politics-rate of participation	high	low
15. Politics-direction	radical	conservative
16. Form of decision-making	participatory democracy	representative democracy
17. Assessment of American political system	totalitarian	democratic
18. Evaluation of American society	irredeemably bad	has faults but basically good

The major manifestation of the crisis of the achievement culture is the rebellion of some of its members against the standards they have traditionally imposed upon themselves. This rebellion is obvious to us all. But its dimensions are more complex than generally recognized. Specifically, I discern three types of rebels:

The first rebels against the achievement norm itself. He seeks to establish other realms in which he can live. The most conspicuous representatives of this type are the hippies.

The second rebel does not necessarily want to change or abolish the achievement culture but to get around it. The almost-professionals—schoolteachers, social workers and others on the fringes of the educational elite—are the best representatives of this tendency. Throughout the country, with a little embarrassment, they now want to join the trade unions (with their own versions of seniority) to guard against the judgment of outsiders.

The third rebel, the man or woman with exorbitant need for achievement and fear of failure, stands at the center of our analysis. This type of person wants to replace the economic indices of success (so prevalent in American society) with political ones, which are at once less subject to accurate measurement and better suited to men with general education but no special vocation. He is the man on the campus who wants to abolish exams but has a doctorate granted by a committee he has helped establish. He is part of the radical elite that wishes to transform the achievement culture by gaining control over political institutions.

I do not mean to say that the radical elite possesses no characteristics in common with the mass. Like other Americans, the elite is enormously energetic and has a strong sense of craftsmanship that manifests itself in incessant activity (sometimes including the manufacture of weapons, even if an occasional bomb does blow up in their hands). Elite and mass share a pervasive competitiveness—it matters little whether this shows up in the acquisition of money and conspicuous consumption or in the race to see who can dispose of the outer appurtenances of wealth fastest and with the most publicity. Knowledge of differences and similarities between elite and mass enables us to understand an otherwise puzzling phenomenon: the elite is anxious to share wealth in order to enforce economic equality but it will never grant cultural equality to the mass. The radical egalitarianism of the elite is limited to the values it cares least about.

Where Do They Come From?

With the cultural differences between mass and elite in mind, it is worthwhile inquiring how youth is recruited into the radical elite rather than developing and maintaining an identification with the mass of Americans. One hypothesis is that radical students are good sons and daughters. They are simply carrying the values—hostility to government, contempt for mass culture, rejection of authority—that they were taught at home. If they appear more radical than their parents, this may be because they are freer to work out the implications of the beliefs they share with their families. There is always the possibility, however, that we are misled by a few famous family names into believing that transmission of radicalism through the family is the major operative force. It could work just the other way around. An equally plausible hypothesis is that children who enjoy strong relationships with their parents do not engage in (or justify) violence, no matter what brand of politics the family is selling. Children with adequate self-regard do not wish to destroy the essentially benevolent world that is the extension of their happy home life.

In any event there are not enough radical families to make the elite grow. Some young people without supportive family traditions are radicalized and recruited into the elite. The more likely candidates for that distinction are youth from families uncertain and troubled about their views of society. They participate in the capitalist largesse but they either do not believe in the worth of their own contribution or they do not know how to express it. The motion picture called "The Graduate" is a splendid example of this phenomenon. The young man in the story continually whines about life, and his parents do nothing to straighten him out. They are middle class. They work and make money. They send the graduate to college. All they ask in return is a little chance to show him off to their friends and the hope that he will find work. The graduate refuses to cooperate; he will not be pleasant and he will not work. He cannot follow his own ideas because he doesn't have any. His parents might justify their existence, though they do not realize it, by virtue of the productive relationship they have to society. All the graduate can produce, except possibly for illegitimate children, is contempt for his parents. One hopes his lovely girlfriend will not get him, or keep him. His qualities are more appropriate to a spoiled child than a man. His parents have failed him, not because they are necessarily unworthy, but because they do not have (and cannot, therefore, communicate to him) a sense of their own worth. The only person who comes off well is Mrs. Robinson. She is defeated because her only pleasure lies in fleeting sensuality. Nevertheless, she is straight. Her honesty consists of resisting the temptation to blame others for her own failures. Her defeat is, therefore, tempered by integrity. The graduate's victory (he subdues his parents, gets the girl) is tainted by hypocrisy. The self-indulgence of his despair is at variance with his intellectual and moral pretensions. Mrs. Robinson assumes a prone position for her pleasure. The graduate is always lying symbolically on his back and whining, "society did it to me."

The graduate's anger is diffuse, not directed against any specific target outside his family. He is ripe for mobilization. Whether or not he becomes a revolutionary depends on a balance of circumstance and personality that no one understands. But some young men, like him, will fall into that category.

The analysis I have presented is not favorable to the white, radical, privileged elite. There is certainly room for disagreement about the tendencies of the movement they lead in American society, but I believe my interpretation of their characteristics transcends personal bias. As evidence, I refer the reader to "Young Intelligentsia in Revolt," [3] an article written by Richard Flacks, a young sociologist who identifies himself with this movement, who has participated in it, and who has studied it. In an interview study, Flacks found that "Both the [New Left] activists and their parents were hostile to the self-denying, competitive, status-oriented individualism of bourgeois culture. . . ." This is another way of saying that the radical elite decries the cultural values espoused by the vast majority of Americans. Segments of the American intelligentsia, Flacks continues, whose special role is to act as critics of the dominant culture, "have begun to develop a family structure and value system at odds with the traditional capitalist, protestant ethic, middle-class culture." In other words, segments of the intelligentsia are challenging the achievement culture. Flacks concludes that "despite the apparent material security of many in this class [the intelligentsia], its trajectory is toward revolutionary opposition to capitalism." If they could persuade the people they would not have to use force. Thus the radical student movement of the past decade has, in Flacks' words, "transformed itself from a nonideological movement for vague principles of social justice . . . into a movement spearheaded by revolutionaries tending, more and more, to look to classical revolutionary doctrine as a guiding principle and to embody, more and more, classical models of revolutionary action as their own."

Where Flacks and I disagree, of course, is over the moral worth and social purposes of the New Left Revolutionaries. We both believe that, in his words, the movement "ought not survive if it conceives itself to be an elite band of professional revolutionaries, aiming to 'seize power' in the midst of social chaos and breakdown." The difference is that Flacks thinks the elite doesn't want to seize power—and I think they do. Flacks befogs the point by prefacing "revolutionaries" (a good word in his lexicon) with "professional" and "band." Presumably this persuades the reader that the "seizure of power" hypothesis is absurd since most young college idealists don't belong to a "band" and most radicals aren't "professional revolutionaries." But once this point is unraveled, the deceptive character of his formulation is evident: there *are* professional revolutionaries in America; they *are* loosely organized into bands; and the radical elite *does* aim "to 'seize power' in the midst of social chaos and breakdown" which they untiringly attempt to create.

Morality

While by ordinary standards members of the radical elite would be counted powerful, their taste for power grows with their fury at the vulgarization of American life. Since they have a much higher sense of political efficacy than other people—they are, after all, richer, better educated, more fluent—they are in a position to act out their beliefs. They are, they think, better than others. Their values are superior, their behavior more honest, their motives more noble. At times it appears as if they were the first to discover morality. In their hearts, as the Goldwaterites used to say, they know they're right. The power of the revolutionaries, their ability to move others, stems ultimately from their hold on the moral conscience of Americans. If these Americans did not respond to (were not conflicted by) the moral claims of the radicals, this elite could not so easily escape punishment for their misdeeds.

The charge of moral cowardice is the strongest hold the radicals have over other Americans. The radicals look at the state of black people, for instance, and ask why it has lasted so long. To them the answer is the same as it was in Nazi Germany in the 1930s: no one had the courage to stand against it. Their argument has much to commend it: not to condemn evil is to condone it; not to actively oppose evil is to involve oneself in the guilt. It is not the argument itself, however, but the use the radicals make of it that leads to perverse moral consequences.

The radicals are overcome by the American strain of moral absolutism: if something is not all good it is all bad. Reason itself is rejected because it has erred; it has been used to support war and racism. We are all either "good Germans" or active Nazis. If you think that things could be better, but do not wish to tear down your government, then you are a "good German"; that is, you are branded a moral coward. The only thing worse than being a Nazi is to be a collaborator. The ultimate radical value is integrity. They shake with fear at the thought of selling out. No cost is too great to rid themselves of any possible taint. The corollary is that personal absolution from guilt through violence is more important than ending the causes of guilt through social justice. They are justified, they believe, in doing anything to eliminate this danger. Violence smites the evil and cleanses the good. Hence morality becomes a license to destroy.

But surely one must give the revolutionaries credit for moral sensitivity to war and racism. Up to a point. The best of them once made sacrifices in the civil rights movement and opposed the Vietnam war somewhat earlier than others. But they soon tired of mere reformism. To observe members of the radical elite is to see that their modes of action, centering on violence and coercion, increasingly come to dominate their lives. As time passes, people are attracted into the movement less for its stated moral values and more for its activities, participation in and justification of violence.

What can be said of the radical moral position now? Is it moral to help the black tenth of the population by inciting them to attack the white nine-tenths who are certain to destroy them? Moral posturing is not enough to prove moral worth. A discussion of the Vietnam situation will illustrate the subtlety of the moral issues involved. From there I will go on to consider the moral stature of the characteristic arguments they use to justify both their own privileges and the incapacity of the masses to decide what is good for them.

Consider how the radical protestors have gone about convincing people to oppose the Vietnam war. The radicals say, in effect, "Your dress is vulgar, your behavior is immoral, your beliefs are despicable, your words reek of hypocrisy, your way of life is vicious; make a public confession of your sins and support our opposition to the Vietnam war." By their actions, the radical elite communicates the view that the way to end violence in Vietnam is to initiate it at home. They demonstrate their love of peace by making war on their fellow Americans.

If it were not for the hostility that the protestors cause among the mass of citizens, support for the war would be much less than it is. Citizens are torn between their dislike of the war and their anger at the coercive tactics of the demonstrators. The basic facts about public opinion on Vietnam are that the hawks are opposed to continuation of the war without victory and the doves dislike the violent demonstrators. Many hawks and doves, therefore, reluctantly accept gradual withdrawal because it will get America out of the war without granting approval to domestic disorder.

To get the people to end the war, the white elite would have to accept the basic worth of the mass of Americans. The white elite would have to approach their fellow citizens as people with whom they share common beliefs and whose ideas they wish to change on a single policy question. From that basis they could approach with considerable success the "hard-hats" who also do not like the war. Perhaps the radicals' dislike of the American system is so great they sacrifice their opposition to the war to it. Perhaps they find their interests served by a perverse situation in which the nation finds itself mired in a vicious war while the character of the protest movement makes it difficult to organize a normal political response to end it. The radicals should get no moral credit for actions that actually help prolong the war.

Opposition to American involvement is one thing; support for the Viet Cong is another. The revolutionaries identify with the Viet Cong not because these guerrillas fight against repression—once in power they are the epitome of repression—but because the radical elite also hopes to achieve power through insurrectionary violence. The extraordinary popularity of the Al Fatah guerrillas with the elite (extraordinary because of the reactionary social elements and ideology the guerrillas represent) undoubtedly stems from their affinity for violence as a means of drastic social change in nations where the masses are powerful. The instinctive, almost visceral hatred of the radicals for Israel may be traced to the fact that it is the apotheosis of a successful achievement culture. The fact that the Israeli government has vast support from its people is not a stumbling block to the radical elite, once one understands that it is precisely the success of these masses in America they resent.

There is a vast difference between a revolution by the masses and a revolution for them. Why can't the people have their own revolution if they want one? Why must it be imposed on them? The answer can only be that the people are not competent.

The members of the radical elite say that the people do not follow them because the people are being misled. This thesis of "capitalist indoctrination," which was once called "false consciousness," states that the real preferences of people are perverted and subverted by capitalist control of the media of communication and information; that is why the people are manipulated to support war and racism when their real interests are just the contrary. They need the radical elite to show them their true interests.

The thesis of capitalist indoctrination is self-protecting. It cannot be refuted because there are no conceivable future events that invalidate it. Whatever happens can be explained away by saying that they (the capitalists, the establishment, the ruling class, or whoever) wanted it that way. The fact that officials in positions of power often are unhappy with the media is easily explained away as a clever effort to deceive the people. If underground shelters are being suggested by the government, that shows the persuasive power of the capitalists. If the people will have none of the shelter nonsense, that merely shows that the establishment reconsidered and turned to more nefarious schemes to make profits.

What is lost in the swirl of words is the basic inhumanity of the elitist position. The indoctrination thesis is used to deny value to the masses who oppose the elite. The masses are told they are easily fooled; this testifies to their credulity. They are told they do not know what is good for them; this makes them child-like. But, when the people are told they cannot trust their own feelings, when their desires are alleged to be unworthy, when their policy preferences should be disregarded because they are not genuine, these people are being deprived of their humanity. What is left for the masses if they are deprived of judgment, wisdom, feeling, desire and preference?

This moral perversity stems from a personal background that makes aspiring radicals peculiarly insensitive to the feelings of other Americans. They have been isolated from the ordinary forms of violence associated with working class or poverty life. Unfortunately they have also emerged from early adolescence without a coherent framework for organizing political reality if, as eventually happens, they encounter meaner life-styles. Their first, forced meeting with the situations of other less fortunate people, who were not present in the relatively homogeneous suburban home environment, is likely to be in college. Here the basic principles of decency that were given at least lip service in the home are shattered by the undeniably less fortunate situation of others. Their response is outrage and a demand that the situation (whatever it is, poverty, racism, rent-gouging) be immediately rectified. They discover, however, that their outrage changes nothing, that they are powerless to do anything about the situation. This leads to a second type of fury: one where their moral wishes do not automatically translate into reality.

What should happen is that they recognize this is a large country with a lot of people who want different things and that most things take a good deal of time and organization, but are possibly attainable. In fact, however, neither the family nor the school has given them the type of analytical framework necessary to reach this conclusion. Faced with a world that will not meet their standards, and not knowing what to do about it, they are easily won over to radical doctrines counseling complete systemic change-over, doctrines which do make a lot of sense if your major political activity is collecting atrocity stories.

The political perspectives of Americans newly available for radical causes lack two critical dimensions. The first is their lack of a "horizontal perspective." Radicals seem amazingly unaware of the size of this nation, of the vastly different peoples it contains, or of their divergent preferences. They may in some sense be aware of some of this through reading, but only personal contact with different people would (a) reduce the sense of moral outrage at some of the non-upper-middle-class facts of life these people discover, and (b) put in perspective their sense of powerlessness (after all, there are 200,000,000 + Americans, and most of these new radicals have more than 1/200,000,000th of American political power). The second is their lack of a "vertical perspective." They reveal little conception of the time needed to accomplish anything, of the need to dedicate oneself for relatively long periods if one is serious about any political goal, of the way in which political changes *are* secured over time. This, of course, partly ties in with the number of different types of people who need to be persuaded, a task of which the new elite is emotionally unaware and for which it is stylistically unprepared.

Once having become radical, members of the elite might face a moral crisis over their superior position in society. If they are so moral why do they remain privileged? The argument by which members of the elite sustain this position is a thing of beauty which must be experienced in person, together with appropriate gestures, to be fully appreciated. Here is one of many conversations. I have reproduced it as faithfully as memory will allow. "When I was a liberal I used to think that way," the radical begins, with something between an innocent and knowing look. "I used to bleed for the poor and the blacks and the guys who died in the war. Was I guilty! I almost gave up my car. [with great sincerity] But then I became a radical. How do I know? You know, I think the real difference between a liberal and a radical is that the liberal thinks others are exploited and the radical knows that he is also a victim. In fact, I think we are exploited worse because it is so insidious you don't realize what is happening. The damn system guides you into competing for grades just like everyone else. Before you know it you've got a good job that's part of the war machine or you're on a research team doing your little bit to keep the establishment going. Your whole life is run by others and you have no say. When I realized they wanted my soul, man, I knew it was time to resist. Then I wasn't guilty any more. I resisted. And I took every advantage the lousy system had to offer—money from home, food stamps, fellowships, grades for anything. When you feel you are as far down as you can go, inside I mean, you take anything."

This theory of psychic exploitation—the better off you seem on the surface the worse off you are down below—fits in easily with the standard repertoire of left radicals. They begin by dividing the world into the good guys and the bad, the exploiters and the exploited, the capitalists and the workers. When capitalists exploit people of color abroad they are called imperialists. When they do it at home they are called racists. Thus racism and imperialism are simply joined together. Here are the explanations, all two of them, that one needs to explain any world phenomenon he doesn't like. Why is there war? Because capitalists require it to make profits. Why is there racism? Because the economic system requires people to exploit. Why is there imperialism? Because capitalists began to run out of victims at home. An honored place is reserved for intellectuals. Why is the intelligentsia especially victimized? Because the alleged freedom and tolerance of the system is actually a subterfuge to hide their complicity in repressing others. This is not a caricature; this is all there is; the rest is minor embellishment.

Romantic Revolutionary Violence

There is (despite the crudity of thought) a real parallel between the forces determining the growth of a white, privileged, radical elite and the forces Marx thought would provide the impetus to proletarian revolution. In the beginning, Marx proclaimed the doctrine of the increasing misery of the proletariat. After a time, this doctrine proved impossible to maintain. Marx therefore created additional arguments to justify the revolutionary potential of the working class. He claimed that although the proletariat might be materially better off, it was getting worse off in two important respects: (1) the gap between its improved condition and the still better position of the upper classes was increasing; (2) the proletariat's sense of alienation from its work and the social system that supported this capitalist mode of production was growing. A similar argument applies to America, with the critical exception that the target group is not the proletariat, of course, but the radical, privileged elite.

They are the ones who feel threatened by the lessening distance between them and the mass. They are the ones who feel alienated from the conditions of their life that would consign them to only a modest share of power in society. They are the ones who threaten to lead a revolt in the name of all, so that they may gain power for a few.

Their hero, Fidel Castro, exemplifies their creed. Here is a member of the Cuban upper class who turned his full fury on the other members of his class and destroyed them. Here is a bohemian in power. Here is the ultimate ideal of the white elite—voluntaristic violence through which a tiny group imposes its values on the rest of the population. Today Fidel is teaching the Cuban people the virtue of work, whether they like it or not.

In a brilliant article in *Encounter,* Richard Lowenthal has traced the growing preference of radical elites for voluntaristic violence—revolutions as an act of will. If Marx suggested that violence might be necessary to overthrow a recalcitrant capitalist regime, he stressed even more the principles of scientific socialism under which certain objective conditions had to exist before a revolution was possible. One of the attractive features of Marxist thought to an earlier generation was the belief that they understood which way history was going and were hitching a ride. While Lenin developed the active role of the professional revolutionaries who made up the vanguard of the proletariat, he also insisted on analysis of social conditions before undertaking violent action. The role of violence grows in the thought of Mao Tse-tung but he still insists that the men who make the revolution must analyze the conditions of the peasantry and work with them. The stress of the Viet Cong on continual terrorism, as Chalmers Johnson has observed in the June 1968 *Asian Survey,* is not entirely compatible with Mao's thought. Fidel Castro and Che Guevara carried voluntaristic violence to a new height. They insisted that a tiny group, literally a handful, if sufficiently determined and willing to use force, can overturn an entire nation, and their success in Cuba has given some credence to their claim. Among radical movements today, not only in America but around the world, there is a denigration of reason and a glorification of violence. Their common assumption is that acts of terror will undermine existing systems, and it is perfectly all right to figure out what the new regime will be like when the time comes.

Because modern revolutionaries appear to lack a program, observers ask with near hysterical insistence: What do the radicals want? What *do* they want? Yet the repetition of the question reveals more about the anxieties of the asker than the difficulty of obtaining an answer. After all, radical spokesmen tell us what they want. If they are asked what they will do once they get into power, they say they will decide when that glorious day comes. If one looks at their behavior, the answer is all too obvious: they want power. And they want to get it through revolution.

All the energies and thoughts of the radical elite are caught up with justifying revolution and figuring out how to accomplish it. They impatiently shrug shoulders and say that asking what they will do after they are in power is, in and of itself, a counter-revolutionary move. Being required to spell out how they would act under circumstances they cannot predict would stultify action on their part. Efforts at theoretical construction divert their attention from the act of revolution and turn it toward the act of governing. Compelling them to focus on specific future policies, about which they would undoubtedly disagree, would create internal dissension, but they can all agree that the present system is intolerable and must be replaced by violent action. It is apparently hard for some questioners to accept the answers they get because they find it difficult to believe that there are people who really think seriously about doing them in.

It is impossible to speak to members of the radical elite and not sense their hatred of the majority of Americans whom Flacks says they must persuade. Unless most Americans suddenly want to commit suicide, they will not willingly turn over their destinies to those who despise them. How, then, will members of the radical elite accomplish their aims?

The Search for Allies

The elite condemns the mass while trying to lead mass movements. Hence its success at the polls is limited compared to its ability to create a pervasive sense of disruption. Yet it must make alliances if it is to become more than a small sect. But who will give the elite the power it seeks? Who can it use to break down the bastions of society?

The hippy and the radical elite appear to form a strange alliance. The flower children are apolitical, and sensory experience rather than the manipulation of symbols is their game. Yet these differences, while real, hide important similarities. Both the hippy and the radical reject a politics of persuasion, the hippy by withdrawal and the radical by coercion. Moreover, in its apparently apolitical way, the hippy phenomenon represents a politics of outrage. Their bizarre dress and habits are not culturally neutral; they are a manifestation of hostility toward prevailing mores. They do not so much try a different style of life (the Mennonites who *live* a different life outrage a few people) so much as they condemn the lives other people live. Hippies drive other citizens out of the neighborhoods they invade. In words and in outward visage, hippies communicate the fact that they find the mass of Americans to be disgusting. It is only a matter of time before this inner malice becomes converted into outer aggression.

The alliance of the radical elite with the hippy movement is by its very nature unreliable. As the street people become more violent and more drugridden, they repel the rest of society. Their volatility, which makes them so useful for street warfare, is a handicap for more stable forms of organization. There is also the danger that members of the elite may get caught up in the drug syndrome with all its debilitating effects. Revolutionaries impose strict rules against hard drugs because people who take them are not dependable. Who, then, will provide the elite with massive force to apply against the system?

As a self-styled revolutionary vanguard, the white elite has sought a proletariat and believes it has found it in the black masses. The combination of moral outrage against injustice, a cultural style different from that of the prevailing middle class, and an available underclass is virtually irresistible. The cultural style of the white elite is angry and committed. It is cool and sophisticated. It swings. Yet not even its style is its own; it is borrowed from black people. It is hard to say whether black culture first attracted them or whether they sought it out for political purposes. But their imitation of black music, dance, and language does serve a political function for them; it leads them to believe they have a natural alliance with blacks.

During the period of the growth of black political consciousness, when it was fashionable to put forward maximal rage, the alliance was a natural one. Black spokesmen vented their spleen at the world around them and the white elite could not have enjoyed it more. Its members wrote articles and made speeches explaining why black rage was just and intensely therapeutic. Although the Vietnam war was never the main cause for black militancy, the resulting diversion of funds from civilian to military purposes provided a handy point of agreement with the white elite. Black spokesmen, however, are not interested merely in attacking the legitimacy of the political system; many of them have particular aims in mind to improve the condition of their people. Accordingly, their coalition with the white elite is precarious.

In recent years Negroes in the United States have been conceived as an undifferentiated black mass led by a minuscule but militant elite. It will help if we break down the elite into component elements so that we can better determine their future alliances. The black elite should at least be divided into two groups: those who are essentially ideological and expressive versus those who are pragmatic and oriented toward remedial action. The ideologues have a natural affinity for the white elite, which affords them deference through cultural imitation and arms them with a simplified Marxist terminology. This expressive black elite serves as symbols of persecution. They die to provide the white elite with martyrs. The less dramatic black elite, however, focuses on policy decisions to benefit deprived black citizens. Accomplishment in specific areas serves as a substitute for ideology. Consequently, they are more nationalistic and less concerned with provocation for its own sake. They are deeply suspicious of whites who want alliances for their own purposes. They are leery of demonstrations and of shootouts with police for vague purposes. These pragmatic militants will stay with the system (while criticizing it) so long as there are incentives for making gains.

The rise of concern over the quality of the environment as a major public issue, for instance, is likely to split nationalist black militants from the white elite. In this issue the elite's dominant concerns with power and amenity come together. They wish to force government to spend billions of public money to satisfy their aesthetic preferences. So long as the rhetoric concentrates on "the rape of the environment" and desire to purify the air, conflict remains muted. But as soon as the realization dawns that this issue takes attention from the plight of black people, that billions spent on pollution cannot be spent on social programs, that you have to be well off to be inordinately concerned with these issues, the anger of black militants against the white elite will rise. The concern of white radicals with over-population just makes the blacks more furious.

It did not take long for people concerned with pollution to understand that the major cause of environmental deterioration is other people. There are too many of them. The waste products of their consumption pollute the beaches with foam from detergents, the cities with gas fumes, the rivers with aluminum beer cans. Like hordes of locusts, they overwhelm our na-tional parks. The natural response of the white, radical, privileged elite is to call for a limitation on population and a reduction of consumption by the masses. Thus one finds, in one of the marvelous ironies of our age, radical sympathizers who support integration, black self-determination, and zoning ordinances that limit occupancy to one house an acre. Imagine telling black people that the trouble with the country is over-consumption!

Radicals notice that Nixon and Reagan have seized upon the environ-mental issue as a means of deflecting protest into more lawful channels. This is not a case of rape, however, but of seduction. The alleged victims were all too willing; they only needed someone to make the connection be-tween their loss of amenity and the deterioration of the environment. The ecology issue, moreover, has the same beauty for students as their protest against current educational practice; they can feel they are condemning the establishment while gaining greater privileges for themselves.

That the radical elite seeks power in the universities comes as no sur-prise when one realizes that the campus is the place where the upper-mid-dle and upper classes congregate. Although the elite is small, its potential for recruitment is greatest where the pool from which it takes its members is largest and least diluted. The fact that universities are not organized for self-defense and are therefore weak compared to other social institutions adds the possibility of power to that of recruitment.

Coercion on campus is directed at taking power away from the faculty so that radicals can use the university as a base to attack the community. The demands of radical students for educational reform come down to nothing—no exams, no grades, no requirements. In this way, they reduce the pressure on themselves for academic performance and allow more time for political activity. They are so alienated, it seems, they can't bear to leave.

Student radicals, ready to use mass coercion and/or violence to gain power on the campus, do not number more than a few percent of the total student population. Our concern, therefore, is not only with the student radicals but also with a significant stratum anywhere from ten to thiry per-cent of the student body, who lend their support in times of crisis. The radicals could be contained if it were not for their ability (on occasion) to mobilize the larger body of "liberal" supporters. What's in it for them?

The radicals curse out the University establishment and their student followers can get some vicarious pleasure from that. That pleasure would, however, be short-lived were it not for the followers' approval of the educational policy (or rather, the lack of it) propounded by the radicals. They proclaim instant educational freedom—no requirements of any kind whatsoever: no requirements of admission, no required courses, and no requirements for graduation. Everything is to be done in a personal way. Classes are to be smaller, the student plans his own program and he is judged personally by those who have gotten to know him best and with whom he has chosen to work. He is treated as a friend, a person to whom special consideration is due because of close personal attachment, a person whom it would be wrong to treat like any other. What attracts the liberal student stratum, in a word, is radical support of a movement from achievement back to ascription. The radicals promise to reverse the development of industrial society so as to make accomplishment depend more on the personal characteristics of the student than on any ostensibly objective measure of his accomplishment.

When students complain about depersonalization, they mean that there are so many others like them that it is difficult to treat them as unique individuals. They are complaining, in essence, about mass education. The incredible increase in college students from about 5% of the eligible population in 1900 to 40% today has necessarily meant a decline in the status of the student. He is not distinguished merely by virtue of entering college, but must compete for distinction among many others like him. The very fact that he is part of a mass educational system means that he is dispensable. If he does not survive, others will be there to take his place. The talk of being cogs in the wheel, of being reduced to a mere cipher, of being a waste product of society, has its basis in the common understanding that mass education has made each individual less essential than he was before.

Dissemination of the idea that man has to be creative at a time when so many have been exposed to higher education gives rise to expectations that cannot be met. New creations can only become the property of the few; if all are "original," none are. There is an immense contradiction here between the pressures on the educated to find new forms of expression, and the common perception of originality as something rare and unusual. The result is widespread anger at a system that denies special status to its aspiring elites. Rather than compete with so many others for former aristocratic privilege, the liberal students join in when the radicals act on their fantasies of dethroning the masters who enslave them.[4]

In accounting for the ability of student radicals to mobilize a mass following, the influence of music and dance should not be discounted. In the forties and fifties the children of the white elite sang folk songs to themselves; other kids sang popular songs. Rock conquered all in the sixties. Love of this music and the dance that went with it spread to all sectors of the population. Radicals, who otherwise had no entree into mass culture, were able to use this musical scene to gain access to many young people whose styles had previously made them foreign to one another.

The pervasive character of student disruptions might suggest that this stratum could supply the mass base required by the radical elite. Perhaps. But there are problems. When students move out of the universities they are subject to social pressures that make it difficult to maintain a radical posture. The incessant support of similarly minded people is lacking. The endless time required for agitation is taken up by work and family. The need to make accommodations with coworkers and neighbors makes absolutist, let alone violent, positions rather difficult. That is why the radical elite is now developing an "enclave strategy." They wish to drive citizens out of favored communities (mostly university towns) in order to become the dominant group. Then they can guard their membership against contaminating outside influences as well as maintain a sanctuary for attacking a hostile world.

Even while he is at the university the liberal student is not perfectly malleable for radical purposes. He may want his courses to serve his private needs and is therefore willing to ally himself with radicals to end all conceivable educational restrictions. But the student interested in personal goals does not take kindly to the radicals' use of classrooms for their purposes. The basic conflict between therapy and agitation has not yet come to the fore but it surely will.

Reason is in full flight. God is not dead; He is merely in hiding behind the endless numbers of Taro cards, zodiacs, and swamis. A substantial minority of students seek not divine aid but divination in making their choices—when they do not simply farm them out to the latest pretender who claims to be in touch with the spiritual vibrations of the universe. If reason is racism for the more politically minded (to cite a once popular slogan), it does not meet the needs of the therapists. They want the classroom to serve as their spiritual center and angrily reject it because it cannot. In a column from the May 29, 1970 edition of the *Daily Californian,* a student named Sandy Kress spoke of "The University as Church": In fact, it is since the demise of the Church that we have been able, I think, to discover the institution that can and should spiritually lead the community. And that is the University . . . only here can we achieve our social and even religious salvation."

The student liberals, on whom the radicals depend for mass support, are meliorists at heart. Their work, as radicals know, results in reform of the existing system that improves its chances for survival. Ultimately, therefore, it is the liberals who are the enemy of the radicals and against whom their wrath will ultimately prove most severe.

Liberal students still have interests to defend. Liberals may be mobilized around issues like Vietnam that make the government look bad and that hurt them personally through military service. But radical economic policies would destroy the income advantages that these middle-class liberals have and hurt the families on which they depend for support. Black racism, when fueled by white elitist hostility to the masses, frightens the liberals. They begin to sense that they may soon become the Establishment that stands in the way of the white elite. Given a choice, liberals will choose stylish politicians like Robert Kennedy who combine ameliorative politics within the system and a congenial personal life style. The allegiance of liberals to the radical cause is a sometimes thing.

Radicals always face the danger that liberals will become "overmobilized" and take over the movement. The Cambodian crisis is a good case in point. So long as Vietnam demonstrations were on the decline, radicals could occupy prominent places. But as soon as large numbers of students became activated, they insisted on dealing with the issue at hand and would not allow the purveyors of violence to turn it into a general attack on the university and society—that is, ultimately on themselves.

There is no need to spend much time on a possible alliance between workers and the white elite. The proletariat does not look favorably on the attack being made on its fundamental values by the elite. If the workers had their way, there would be no elite left to contemplate making revolution. From time to time radical groups make forays into the laboring ranks by trying to forge coalitions on strike issues. These efforts, despite occasional brief success, have proven abortive. It is hard to win them over when you really want to do them in.

Just as leaders sometimes find themselves chasing their followers, the radical elite is always in danger of being co-opted by those it seeks to mobilize. The elite commitment to the black cause, for instance, may have reached a point where its members find it difficult to oppose anything black militants wish to do. When manifestations of stylistic contempt for the masses prove unproductive, or "trashing" becomes a way of life,[5] to take other examples, the elite may have trouble switching off its hippie followers, or even the habits of its own members. Between random, ritualized violence and ordinary garden-variety reform, the elite is too easily corrupted.

Although its political prospects are bleak in the real world, the white elite can still seek metaphorical allies. They have been working hard to persuade themselves that *they* are the people. Yet the very slogan of the white elite, "Power to the People," betrays them. If they were the people, they would have the power. The fact is that it is not the ruling elites they are against, but the mass of people who is their enemy.

The Sense of Impending Disaster

The great strength of the radical elite lies in its ability to convey its sense of doom to others in society. If all is hopeless, why struggle against them?

The elite and its supporters in the communications media, the professions, and the social sciences overidentify with change. They point out the

various inequities that exist in our society and they urge those who presumably suffer most, especially black people, to act against these conditions. They seek to create a climate of opinion for rapid change. The elite
lacks sympathy with the mass of Americans (especially striving, former
lower-class ethnics) whose resistance to rapid change is put down to ignorance, special privilege or outright bigotry.

The vast mass of white citizens underidentifies with change. They see
change as taking place at their expense. It is their jobs which are sought
for blacks, their schools which are invaded by other people, and their children who are bussed to strange locations. They have trouble earning
enough to live up to the standards they have set for themselves. They work
hard and their lives are difficult in numerous ways. They wonder whether
their newly-found gains will be taken away or whether inflation will erode
their incomes. They are upset by the threat to their values of work, stability, family and achievement that is posed by elite agitation. If there were
such a person as an objective observer, he would find that in the last
twenty years their real income has increased, their housing has improved,
and they have access to more diverse educational and cultural opportunities. On the negative side, he would find a deterioration in the situation in
regard to crime and drugs. All in all, he might note considerable social
change, a fair amount of which might ordinarily be labeled as progress.

By and large, things are getting better. But the elite would define progress as much too little, while the mass would consider change much too
rapid. The result is a phenomenon to which we are all witness: many
things get better but everyone feels worse.

Public officials are in the grip of a similar dilemma. The incredible rise
in expectations generated by the elite has made it exceedingly difficult for
governments to get credit for anything they do. The demands are both
vague (somehow a sense of malaise is gripping the country for which only
revolutionary change is appropriate) and overwhelming (equality of
achievement between black and white, revamping of the environment, vast
reduction of inequality of income, and on and on). Government is called
upon to intervene everywhere and is criticized for its growing bureaucracy.
Coercion is used to vastly increase welfare payments, and the resulting
high cost is used to discredit the program. Blacks are urged to simultaneously integrate with whites and control their own communities. Inflation
should be curbed while vast expenditures are made for every conceivable
purpose. The black have-nots are plunged into conflict with the white
have-littles, and the inevitable consequences are used to suggest that the
country is in bad shape. Heightened conflict is urged and created, and its
presence then becomes further evidence of the deterioration of social relations. Anything less than miraculous changes in long-standing social conditions is portrayed as evidence of failure. Public officials are constantly
urged to be responsive to the people as the tiniest of minorities carries slogans saying *they* are the people.[6] In this context the impulse of public offi-

cials to escape the arduous task of making public policy may become irresistible. If there is no way to win, they can at least stop from losing, when losing is defined as anything they might conceivably do.

Revolution?

Ways of life are in contention; that is why our image of America as a single nation, indivisible, is shaken. Sometimes those who are most dissatisfied with the way things are see more sharply than those who are happy with the existing order. The critics look for faults; they find them with a welcoming eye. When the prosperous fifties left America smug, the critics of its achievement culture unerringly went South to expose its deepest contradictions. They came back home to make the South the image of campus and nation; it confirmed what they knew. As time passed their protest became routinized; touch the right nerve and reflex action set in. It was another triumph of technique over purpose. The original moral impulse gave way to perpetual motion. The new recruits literally became "the movement" and made it into their own image—march, shout, sit, run, throw, leap, crash. Violence is the opiate of the radicals; they get high on action. There was no quiet place to restore vision. To move toward the mass was to sell out. All that remained was to run even faster, by outbidding others for more violent rhetoric. It was only time before the deed approached the word. For the mass had hidden all the distinction there was in its vast, formless self. There was apparently no way to be something except by attacking the evil beast at its source. Mass America would listen, indeed it would applaud, or it would howl.

Can the radical elite cause a revolution? The prognosis is poor but not hopeless. Can they get the kind of revolution they promise? That is less likely. They may simply open the floodgate of power to the onrushing forces of the right. But their personal goals will be filled. By the time revolutionary upheaval is a genuine possibility their lust for power will make it easy for them to (a) switch sides; or (b) fight their guerrilla war exactly as their daydreams tell them it should be fought. Hiding at night in the hills; swooping down to burn a hayfield during the day. Then back to the hills where the women are cooking soup, to celebrate and sing revolutionary songs.

What can be done to prevent elitist revolution? Deny them a mass following. Phase out the war in Vietnam and continue to improve the position of blacks, Chicanos and the poor in general. Resist provocations to radicalize the temporary followers of the radical elite by repressing them. Refuse to countenance violence by steady and specific measures against those who employ it. Show that violence does not pay but that peaceful politics does. Rewards must not go to those who merely agitate but must be obtained only by capturing public office through participation in electoral politics.

Do not panic. The greatest weapon the radical elite possesses is its ability to convince others that society is falling apart. Fire-bombings, window breakings, and shooting at police, however deadly or upsetting they may be, are mere pin pricks. They cannot, by themselves, move the levers of power. Only inappropriate responses by those in power can do that. Neither capitulation to violence nor indiscriminate repression will help. So long as most Americans do not abandon their posts, the radical elite can only kill or annoy; it cannot rule.

Perhaps the worst thing the radical elite has done is to make their reactions the standard measure of public policy. If they do not scream and if they cannot organize mass protest, then by implication the policy being pursued is all right. The invasion of Laos, which promises the merest hope of temporary gains and risks further erosion of political legitimacy in America, is defended by saying that the radicals are no longer able to mount demonstrations against it. What is bad for them is not necessarily good for us. The impotence of the radicals is not necessarily a source of virility for other Americans. American life, in Croly's famous phrase, still haunts us with its unrealised promise. Our task, as always, is to make our lives conform to that promise.

NOTES

1. I am grateful to Bill Cavala, Andrew Janos, Byron Shafer and Phil Siegelman for valuable insights. Naturally, no two people agree entirely on this subject, and we are no exception.

2. The Michigan Survey Research Center estimates that white people who take the strongest position against the war *and* approve the tactics of the demonstrators make up about 3 percent of those who voted in 1968.

3. Richard Flacks, "Young Intelligentsia in Revolt," *Trans-action* (June 1970), pp. 47–55.

4. The fantasies of white liberal students are not far from the fear of black people that genocide will be visited upon them. The fact is that no one really wishes to commit genocide on black people and no one really believes that it is about to happen. Why, then, is the fear so oft repeated? The answer is not that blacks expect white extremists to murder them. These blacks are concerned in a more fundamental way with conditions of modern industrial society. They fear that their low skill makes them dispensable in the most frightening way; they could disappear from the earth and society would go on much as before. That is why they are so insistent upon carving out a place for themselves in the new society. That is why they want a politics of distribution, rather than a politics of production. To be men, they must be part of society so that their lives are part of the lives of others. All must live, they say, or none.

5. A gentleman named Moe, who runs a bookstore on Telegraph Avenue in Berkeley, posted:

A FEW THOUGHTS ABOUT THE JULY 4TH TRASHINGS

From peaceful demonstrations to demonstrations punctuated by police violence to police-violent cop-baiting demonstrations with a side-order of trashing, to pure trashing, I trace a definite political decline.

Does petty and not-so-petty trashing have anything to do with revolution? I thought revolutionists picked the widest possible turf and made massive, illegal (but not necessarily violent) thrusts against the system. But trashing small businesses to defend a playground . . . somehow lacks revolutionary stature.

Isn't trashing more a kind of pseudo-revolutionary game for speed freaks—frisbees by day and rocks by night? . . .

6. A graduate student in the Political Science Department at Berkeley, Byron Shafer, sent me the following illustration: "The incident which sums up the whole radical thing for me was one I had the pleasure of witnessing when I was in Ann Arbor last fall. The radicals were trying to shut the University down over the issue of a discount book store. That night there were S.D.S. speakers haranguing the crowd about the need for the shut-down; they were on a large plaza, which filled up quickly. Down in front were a lot of their supporters, white radicals, but all around the rear were a large number of faculty members on their way home, citizens passing by, and students getting out of late class. One speaker finally brought it to a head, and asked for a vote. "All those who think we should strike." There was a loud "Yes, right on, etc." from down front. "All those who think no." There was a deafening "No" from the rear and the edges, clearly the overwhelming voice of the crowd. To which the S.D.Ser on the rostrum replied, "Why don't all you folks in the back go home, and let the people decide this."

2

THE EMPTY-HEAD BLUES:
BLACK REBELLION AND
WHITE REACTION

Liberals have been moaning those empty-head blues. They feel bad. They
know the sky is about to fall in. But they can't think of anything to do.
Having been too sanguine and too self-righteous about their part in the
civil rights movement, they are too easily prey to despair when their contribution is rejected by those they presumed to help. Torn between a nagging guilt and a secret desire to turn on their black tormentors, white liberals have become spectators watching with frozen horror as their
integrationist ideals and favorite public programs disintegrate amidst violent black rebellion. How did this maddening situation come about? What
can be done about it?

How to Enrage Whites without Helping Blacks

A recipe for violence: promise a lot; deliver a little. Lead people to believe they will be much better off, but let there be no dramatic improvement. Try a variety of small programs, each interesting but marginal in
impact and severely underfinanced. Avoid any attempted solution remotely
comparable in size to the dimensions of the problem you are trying to
solve. Have middle-class civil servants hire upper-class student radicals to
use lower-class Negroes as a battering ram against the existing local political systems; then complain that people are going around disrupting things
and chastise local politicians for not cooperating with those out to do them

From *The Public Interest*, no. 11 (Spring 1968), pp. 3–16. Reprinted by permission. Copyright © 1968 by National Affairs, Inc.

in. Get some poor people involved in local decision-making, only to discover that there is not enough at stake to be worth bothering about. Feel guilty about what has happened to black people; tell them you are surprised they have not revolted before; express shock and dismay when they follow your advice. Go in for a little force, just enough to anger, not enough to discourage. Feel guilty again; say you are surprised that worse has not happened. Alternate with a little suppression. Mix well, apply a match, and run. . . .

The dilemma of liberal politicians is exquisite. Now they play only "minus-sum" games in which every player leaves the contest worse off than when he entered. The first rule is to get yourself hooked on purely symbolic issues. This guarantees that if you fail to get your policy adopted you are revealed as impotent and useless to the deprived. If you win your policy objective, you are even worse off because it is soon clear that nothing has changed. A typical game played under this rule is called "Civilian Police Review Board." The objective is to force a racist response from the voters who are fearful of their safety on subways and in the streets. The game begins with a publicity campaign focusing on fascist police, various atrocities, and other lurid events. The police and their friends counter with an equally illuminating defense: nothing is wrong that a little get-tough campaign would not cure. The game ends with a ballot in which white voters are asked to choose between their friendly neighborhood policeman and the specter of black violence. The usual result is that the whites vote for the police and defeat the review board. If a review board is created, however, it soon becomes apparent that a few judgments against policemen have no effect on the critical problem of securing adequate protection for Negroes. But the game is a perfect loser: everyone's feelings are exacerbated and the conflict continues at a new height of hostility.

There are many similar games. In Milwaukee, for example, wave after wave of Negro demonstrators cry out for a fair housing ordinance. The certain result is that whites are made furious. The sad thing is that, if the punitive marches succeed in their immediate goal, only a handful of Negroes at most will be helped. Or consider the drive to achieve school integration by bussing children to different parts of the city. If such integration is accompanied by huge efforts to create equality of educational achievement among black and white, all praise is due. But if black children continue to read poorly, race hatred may well increase. Black radicals will then be certain to condemn the liberal integrationists who have again left them and their children holding an empty bag.

The liberal politician is damned if he does and damned if he doesn't. He breaks his back to get two historic civil rights acts passed only to find himself accused of coming in too little and too late. The rat control bill is a perfect example of the classic bind. When Congress originally failed to pass the bill, it was made into a bitter example of inhumanity. Yet it can safely be said that had the bill sailed through Congress it would also have joined the list of those liberal measures that are not good enough to do the job. Too little and too late. How much all this is like Groucho Marx's famous crack that any country club willing to have him as a member wasn't exclusive enough for him to join.

We have learned some hard lessons. Every time we try to deal with problems of race we end up with symbolic gestures that infuriate everyone and please no one. Why? The American dilemma is a compound of racism suffused with class differences. Since America appears to be richer in economic resources than in brotherly love, it would be natural to tackle economic problems first. Few of us expect a quick solution to the lesser problems posed by large class differences among white people. None is surprised that upper-class whites do not integrate with their lower-class racial cohorts. Yet we persist in following policies that attack racism before economic equality has begun to be established. The result is that neither poverty nor racism is diminished.

Disheartened by the magnitude of the change required in racial behavior, unwilling to recognize the full extent of the resources required to improve economic conditions, we are tempted to try a lot of small programs that create an illusion of activity, ferment, and change. But nothing much happens. Confusion is rampant because it looks to some (mostly white) like so much is being done, and to others (mostly black) that nothing is happening. Hence the rival accusations of black ingratitude and white indifference. It is apparent that we should abandon symbolic policies that anger whites and do not help blacks and should concentrate instead on programs that will materially increase the well-being of poor people in the United States. Programs should be large rather than small, and provide tangible benefits to many citizens, not symbolic rewards for a few.

Income and Education

The most compelling need is for a fast and vast job program designed to virtually end unemployment among Negroes. The best alternative would be a superheated economy in which jobs searched for people and employers served their own interests by training any available man. Inflation would be a problem, but one of much lesser magnitude than present dilemmas. The next best alternative would be large government subsidies to finance decent jobs with futures, again leaving training to employers and motivation to indigenous groups and the near-universal desire for legitimate gain. Nothing else is possible until we end high rates of unemployment.

But any program designed to improve the longer-range prospects of the disadvantaged would also have to involve a fundamental change in elementary education. There are many things we do not know about improving education. But we do know that the child who reads well can do most anything, and the child who cannot is lost. If you are 14 and cannot read, you know there is no future for you in ordinary American life. Following the principle of "bottleneck" planning (that is, concentrating every effort on the most critical resources), one might abolish all subjects in the curriculum except reading and a little mathematics. Every six months there would be examinations in reading, and teachers whose classes fell behind would be held to account. Principals would be promoted on the basis of the accomplishment of their students in reading. Although family conditions may overwhelm all other factors in ability to learn, as the Coleman report suggests, this is a conclusion to which we should be driven only after making the absolute maximum effort to get every child to read.

Would these employment, income, and education policies stop black rebellions? [1] That is bound to be the question. Alas, it is a mean-spirited question because it deflects attention from human needs. But it will raise itself insistently, so we had better attend to it, especially if (as I believe) rebellions are bound to increase for a time. Let us assess the adequacy of these remedies by evaluating them in the context of theories of racial rebellion.

Reward and Blackmail Theories

We are everywhere confronted with exceedingly primitive notions of the causes of racial disturbances. According to one popular model, rebellions are caused by giving rewards to the people who engage in these activities. The reward theory posits ever-increasing violence in response to the hope of getting ever-increasing rewards. This vulgarized version of learning theory (Christians call it sinning to abound in grace) suggests that outbursts will continue so long as Negroes are rewarded by governmental policies designed to improve their conditions. Would it be true, then, that the less that is done for Negroes, the less the probability of racial rebellion? What will we do when at all future moments we will be looking back at past rebellions, passing through present rebellions, and anticipating future rebellions?

Another currently held model suggests that white people help black people only because black people rebel. Blackmail is an appropriate designation for this theory. Rebellions by blacks cause whites to provide rewards; these rewards presumably lead to a reduction in hostility. But, on this theory, a decrease in hostility inevitably leads to a lesser willingness by whites to give rewards to blacks. Hence there will be more riots.

Obviously, if one begins by assuming a connection between riots and rewards, one can only conclude that riots cause rewards or rewards cause riots. Disaster is predicted if help is given and doom if it is not. Perhaps a slightly more complex analysis would be helpful.

The Theory of Relative Deprivation

America is a country to which people who were worse off have come to be better off. And so it has proved to be for most of us. But not for Negroes. Not in slavery and not afterward. The southern system of slavery so effectively cut off Negroes from former home, family, and culture that comparisons with the past which sustained so many others against the initial adversity of life in America became meaningless. Being better off than in slavery hardly recommends itself to anyone as a criterion of judgment. For better or worse, black men have been born anew in America. Negroes can only compare their positions to their recent past or to others in America. They have evidently chosen to be Americans if they can. That is our common hope. But it can also be our despair because it is so difficult to satisfy people whose standard of comparison is the richest segment of the richest nation on earth.

Imagine that our fondest dreams were realized: we had secured virtually full employment and higher income for Negroes as well as other Americans. There would certainly be an improvement in the Negro condition. But there would also be an increase in "relative deprivation." The higher starting point for other Americans would guarantee that result. The arithmetic is as follows:

Assume that Negroes make $4,000 a year and that other Americans they compare themselves with make $10,000 a year. If whites increased their income 5 percent a year, Negroes would have to gain an incredible 15 percent a year in order to gain equality of income in ten years. If we take the more reasonable assumption about the best that could happen—a 10 percent increase per year for Negroes and a 5 percent for others—the absolute difference in income would actually continue to increase for the first decade! So, if rebellions are caused in part by relative deprivation— by resentment at inequality—there will be more rebellions.

Now take education. The most optimistic assumption about education would be that the gap between whites and blacks would narrow dramatically in 10 or 20 years and not sooner. While the quality of education might improve significantly and quickly if we are very lucky, the benefits would take time to manifest themselves. Moreover, higher educational achievement, while desirable in itself, would likely lead to still higher aspirations. Ergo: things will get worse before they get better.

Job, income, and education policies may be necessary to stop rebellions in the future, but they will not suffice to halt them now. Before accepting this melancholy conclusion as the final sentence on our racial crimes, let us see if a closer look at black rebellion will not suggest to us additional remedies.

The Anger-Plus-Opportunity Theory

The most straightforward explanation of riotous behavior is that the violence is a combination of anger and opportunity. That whites have long despised Negroes is no secret. That Negroes suffer numerous indignities on account of their color is all too evident. When extraordinary levels of unemployment (running as high as 30 percent for black youth) are added to these daily causes of resentment, it is no wonder that many Negroes feel enraged. But it is one thing to feel mad and angry and another to feel safe enough to act out those feelings. The relative lack of black violence in the South may be partly attributed to the well-founded fear by Negroes that severe retribution will be visited upon them. Just as soon as Negro strength increased sufficiently in northern cities and whites became troubled about brutal retaliation, it became safer for Negroes to act on violent feelings. The faint stirrings of white conscience may have had the paradoxical effect of legitimizing black violence without simultaneously leading to actions that dramatically alleviated oppressive conditions.[2]

To the degree that this overly simple theory is correct, it also helps explain the essential perversity of the racial situation. The theory implies that one way of mitigating violence would be to reduce the pattern of injustice that gives rise to feelings of rage. So far, so good. But recognition of the problem and mobilizing political support to begin to act require widespread dissemination of information on just how bad things were and continue to be. The message to Negroes is that they have been and are being treated badly. There cannot help but be the suggestion that Negroes are justified in taking strong actions to improve their position. There are bound to be white people whose guilt disarms them when faced with destructive acts. Thus the laudatory efforts to reduce the desire of Negroes to act violently actually increases their opportunities for using force without the corresponding expectation of severe punishment. The two sides of the desire-plus-opportunities theory of racial violence are not in balance; attempts to reduce the desire have the exasperating effect of increasing opportunity.

Black violence has reduced support for measures designed to help Negroes. Yet the polar opposite tactic—nonviolent pressure—is impossible to maintain. The emphasis of the civil rights movement on nonviolence was unnatural. It reassured whites and helped get bills on voting rights passed in Congress. But it left no place for self-defense. Where was all that black rage to go? Instead of a normal stress on self-defense, therefore, many Negro activists have shifted from turning the other cheek to abusing the man. One extreme has simply been substituted for another.

In such a situation it is easy for black men to succumb to a politics of outrage in which violent rhetoric provides a substitute for remedial action.

Caught between rage and impotence, held responsible by no mass following of their own, Negro spokesmen compete in ragging the white man. Negroes can't help enjoying the fun, but we should be as clear as they are
that the whole act is directed toward "Whitey." If whom a man loves can
be determined by whom he can't resist talking to, then Whitey has captured all the affection these people have. No doubt this perverse form of
Uncle Tomism will eventually be exposed by Negroes who want leaders to
pay attention to them. In the meantime, we risk the consequences of a
rhetoric of violence that angers whites without aiding blacks.

I conclude that all of us in America will need an acute sense of humor
to survive the next decade. There will be rebellion if we do the best we
know how. There will be even more violence if we do not. Almost harder
to bear will be the incredible provocations—mixtures of arrogance, slander,
paranoia, and duplicity. There are spectacular fantasies among black people about the deaths of Kennedy and Malcolm X right next to saccharine
remarks about law and order from whites who have long practiced violence against Negroes. The one truth which white liberals are supposed to
avow is that they do not know, have never known, and will never know
anything about black people. Yet one would suppose that if two groups
have contact, each would have an equal chance of failing to know the
other. The old truth may have been that blacks were invisible men for
whites. The new truth is that whites are invisible because they all look
alike.

The language of "black power" should not, however, be dismissed without serious consideration. The fact that it means so many different things
to different men does not prevent our observing that the slogan strikes a
responsive chord among black men. At a minimum, black power signifies
a widespread concern for a political dimension that has been conspicuously missing from previous theories of racial conflict.

The Identity and Legitimacy Theory

It will add to our understanding if we decide which features of the black
rebellions we want to explain. The extensive looting, for example, does not
appear especially deserving of explanation. There is looting all over the
world when riots occur. That is why martial law is so often declared in the
wake of natural disasters. When the police appear uncertain or absent, the
urge to loot is apparently more than most of us can resist. Nor do we need
to spend an excessive amount of time on the snipers. Virtually every society has small groups with an urge to disrupt its activities. The interesting
question is why the mass of citizens in the ghettos did not react against the
snipers and the incendiaries who put the torch to their neighborhoods.

The beginning of wisdom about black rebellion is that we are dealing with a problem in social control, with feelings widespread in an entire community, and not with just a few wild men. An entire community has become disaffected. That is not to say Negroes share common views on public policy. Indeed, they can hardly agree on anything. But they will not turn in one of their own to the white man. They will not defend what they have against the violence of their own people, not necessarily because they have nothing to lose, but because they do not have enough of the one thing that they would otherwise risk losing—participation in a common American life.

The great question raised by black rebellion is: who will call himself an American? That has been the modal drama of life in America. Loyalist and patriot, patrician and plebeian, slave and free man, southern man and northern man, employer and workers, ethnic and Wasp, all have shattered the quiet of our vast continent with their wars. Today's rebellion is part of this struggle to forge a worthy American identity for black men. Black rebellion presents a crisis of legitimacy—a questioning of "white" authority. Hence the incessant demands for new power relationships. The immediate problems posed by black rebellion are, therefore, political, and require a political response.

Political Solutions

The most obvious political need is for mechanisms to reduce the blatant conflicts between Negroes and police with the police being the most visible and oppressive manifestation of governmental authority. Increasing the number of Negro policemen (and firemen) might help by blurring the purely racial nature of the encounters. The measures necessary to accomplish this end—allowing entry to people with minor police records, changing various requirements for health and examinations—are within our grasp. There are also various proposals for altering the role of policemen by putting them more in the role of helpers, and by sensitizing them to the problems of life among the severely deprived. It is difficult to quarrel with such humane measures. Yet they do not quite go to the heart of the matter. For policemen do have certain evident law-enforcement functions that may be blurred but not hidden. The rest of us manage to get along with police, not through mutual good will, but by avoiding contact with them unless we make a specific request for help. Not love but distance is the answer. A substantial increase in employment and rise in income will reduce the opportunity and need for crime. (Even the dope addict with a higher income is likely to be able to make arrangements that will keep him clear of the police.) Relationships with police could also be markedly improved by following Jacobus tenBroek's proposal to abolish the law of the poor. One reason that we have "two nations" in America is that there is literally a separate law for poor people. The difficulty is not merely that poor people receive less justice, but also that laws about sexual conduct, home finance, drug addiction, and dozens of other matters apply severely to them but laxly to other Americans. Hiring more Negro policemen will not be successful unless the frequency of unhappy contacts between them and the citizenry is sharply reduced.

Even were all this accomplished, however, it would not meet the profound Negro demand for autonomy, for control of some portion of their lives, for the self-esteem that comes from being powerful. If we cast aside the cynicism that tells us no man is truly master of his fate, we can recognize insistent political demands that may be accommodated or crushed but cannot be ignored. For present purposes we can dispense with a lot of research and simply assume that the best way to feel in control is to exercise control. Can this be done at all? Can it be done without generating the violence that will bring about the retribution that ends our hopes?

The usual American response to difficult political problems has been to disperse and fragment them into smaller conflicts that take place in different localities and times. Problems of church and state and education have been handled in just this way. Applying this procedure to racial problems in the past, however, has meant victory for racism or at least the status quo. Deprived of opportunities to exert influence at state and local levels because of official racism or lack of effective political resources, Negroes had no alternative except to look to the national government. This choice of a favored site for conflict was always opportunistic. Calhoun's doctrine of the concurrent majority meant control for regional racists. States' rights and local autonomy were doctrines for keeping the Negro and the poor in their places. Now the old men are justified who say that if you live long enough everything comes full circle. Black nationalists, having little hope of a large voice in national and state politics, are talking about local autonomy. They demand a voice and a veto over policies affecting neighborhoods in which black people are in the majority. Bringing government closer to the people is a slogan that is no longer the exclusive property of conservatives. The pursuit of group interest by blacks thus creates opportunities for unusual political coalitions.

The Heller proposals for bloc grants to states, much of which would be distributed to cities, provide a strong basis for agreement. Local government would be strengthened. Negroes would find it more worthwhile to make demands on city governments. Cities would have the resources to grant some of these demands. The formation of neighborhood corporations or governments would be the next step. Run by elected councils within specified geographical boundaries, the corporations would provide a forum for airing grievances and working out common demands. In order to avoid complete focus on demands, and to provide experience in self-government, the neighborhood corporations would also negotiate with the city government to take over certain limited functions. Education has long been considered a neighborhood function and there are already moves toward further decentralization. If health and housing inspections are serious sources of grievances, cities may be willing to let neighborhood corporations hire and guide local people to do the job. Part of the energies within the neighborhood would thus be devoted to resolving disagreements among the local people about how they should run their own affairs.

We should be clear about what we are doing. The neighborhood corporation involves a return to earlier patterns of local rule that were regarded as offensive to principles of good government. The movement from the spoils system to neutral competence through civil service will, for a time, be reversed. What were previously despised as the worst attributes of boss rule and ethnic depravity—favoritism, trading of jobs for favors, winking at abuses when perpetrated by one's own kind, tolerance of local mores regarded by some as corrupt—will be reinstituted. Political practices worked out to accommodate the needs of lower-class immigrants, arrangements abandoned when they conflicted with rising professionalism and economic status, may understandably be preferred by underprivileged black people. The uneven development of all our people makes it difficult to pursue national practices. And Negroes, too, will have to reconcile themselves to the fact that programs which permit greater autonomy for urban Negroes may leave rural Negroes at the mercy of hostile state and local governments.

Today the black ghettos resemble nothing so much as newly emerging nations faced with extraordinary demands and few resources. There is the same ambivalence toward "foreign" aid: you must have it and yet you hate the giver because of your dependence on him. Highly educated and skilled people (black as well as white) are deeply resented because of the well-founded fear that they will "take over." The greater the disparity between aims and accomplishments, the greater the demagoguery and destructive fantasy life. Yet underneath the pounding rhetoric there are men and women who are learning the skills of leadership. They must be given a chance to learn—that is, to make mistakes. They must have an opportunity to generate growth in human resources in their own communities. Otherwise, they will lack the pride and security to reenter American life on conditions of mutual interest, respect, and allegiance.

We need to be reminded, however, that without a drastic decrease in unemployment no other programs will be meaningful. It will prove extraordinarily difficult to abolish the law of the poor because so many people will be dependent on governmental assistance that the tax burden will generate additional demands for obnoxious restrictions. When so many men cannot make a living now, educational improvement will seem hopelessly long-range. Community action programs suffer the most because of the utter futility of finding local measures to create vast employment. Expectations are raised that no local or state political system can meet. Ordinary politics are discredited. Each generation of community leaders is rejected as soon as it becomes part of an "Establishment" that cannot deliver.

Income, education, and power are mutually supportive. They are the bastions of legitimacy in our political system. Better education will enable Negroes to receive higher income and to gain the communications skills necessary to carry on political activity. The exercise of governmental power will strengthen the sense of mastery that makes the long road of education seem worthwhile. Political power also creates jobs. Good jobs at decent pay provide additional resources for education and political activity.

Political Support

What about the political feasibility of the economic and political programs advocated here? Will the President and Congress agree to spend the $5 or $10 billion a year that a job program will cost? Will mayors and city councils agree to share limited powers with neighborhood corporations? Will a policy of suppression appear more attractive as well as less expensive? There is an old story that goes, "Harry, how's your wife?" "Compared to what?" he replies. The political desirability of these programs depends in part on how they compare with what we have been doing. Take the sad plight of our mayors.

Mayors in the United States are in an incredible position. The only things they can do, such as providing better recreation facilities, improving housing inspection, and the like are strictly marginal improvements. They lack the money and the power to do more. Yet they are held responsible for every evil. Rebellions appear to occur at random, afflicting both cities whose mayors try hard to do the right thing and those whose mayors are indifferent or hostile. What incentives will mayors have to do what good they can do? Since they cannot possibly do enough, the do-nothing mayor appears no worse off than the better mayors. (A major possibility is that mayors will learn to concentrate on the one area in which they might do well and reap credit from some segments of the population—suppression of rebellions.) Therefore, working with neighborhood corporations, invigorated by fresh infusions of federal funds, should prove attractive to mayors who despair of their present situation.

Politicians in the Democratic party are frantically pursuing ways of handling racial problems that will not end in disaster for everyone concerned. Buffeted between the hostility of blue-collar workers to civil rights legislation and the inability to satisfy radical Negroes no matter what, the politicians fear their party will be split on racial grounds. They foresee waves of repression and a permanent estrangement between black and white in America. But consider what a new orientation would have to offer to Democratic party politicians. They would not try to bid for the support of racial radicals, white or black. The Democrats would turn down both mass suppression and mass violence, avoiding especially symbolic issues that embitter whites and do not help blacks. The politicians would primarily espouse policies promising immediate and substantial improvement of the economic condition of poor people. Decent jobs at good pay come first. Next, there should be the most powerful education program that can be devised to enable the presently disadvantaged to participate as equals in the market place and the political arena. These policies should be presented at face value as measures for making good the promise of American life. These policies are consonant with the traditions of the Democratic party, and they need not divide the races. The poor need help. We are a rich nation. We can and should give that help.

No doubt a party promoting these income policies might lose an election or two. But when it did get into power it would have goals worth achieving. The difficulty with existing policies is that even when properly pursued they do not help enough people immediately in direct ways. The usual mode of alleviating difficult problems by incremental attack along diverse fronts does not work because there is no solid base on which to rest these efforts. We will never know what long-run contributions antipoverty programs can make if we continue to insist that secondary programs substitute for primary ones, that supporting programs be adopted in place of the basic efforts they are intended to assist.

Democratic divisions over these issues also provide extraordinary opportunities for Republicans to recover from decades of declining support. The danger is that an anti-Negro stance will appear to offer hope of detaching white voters from the Democratic party. The resistance of these voters to conservative economic policies would be submerged under a tide of racial anger. There is another stance, however, that would be productive at the polls and fit comfortably with Republican principles. A massive employment program could be expected to win over some Negroes and poor whites while not alienating existing Republican support. Such a program would hold out greater long-run hope of alleviating rebellious conditions than would suppression. Republicans would presumably not support federal subsidies for radical community action. But a program that stressed local autonomy through neighborhood governments should prove attractive to conservatives. Indeed, Republicans are much less weighed down than are Democrats with commitments to existing welfare and education policies that Negroes find so disagreeable.

A Response to Rebellion

There will be rebellions; that much we can take for granted. The question is not whether these things will happen but how Americans will choose to react. It is easy to win tactical victories—disperse mobs brutally—and lose strategic battles. In the midst of consummate gall and endless effrontery, there is considerable danger of committing strategic suicide. What we do should depend on what we want. The prevailing confusion makes it advisable to take the risk of restating the obvious.

Just as Lincoln put preservation of the Union above all else in his times, so should we put construction of a multiracial nation as our major objective. Our goal is that we all consider ourselves Americans who pay allegiance to the same political symbols and participate as citizens in the same national life. In pursuit of this goal, we must reaffirm our dedication to integration of the races for all who wish it. Wholly white or black communities can be one mode of participation in a common life. But integration is the preferred way of life for those who believe that there must be a single nation in America. A surface integration, however, must not be pursued at the expense of equality of achievement among black and white, for then integration will become a barrier to the creation of a joint American identity.

If we do not wish white and black men to live as citizens in the same country, we will have no difficulty in finding policies appropriate to that end. We can continue what we are doing. Better still, we can let violence feed on violence. The early riots have largely been aimless affairs in which destruction has been visited by Negroes on their own neighborhoods. Mass repressions visited indiscriminately upon black people can give them new reasons for race hatred and further violence. White people can be turned into proto-blacks—people who fear destruction because of their color. The difference between the races is that whites possess more abundant means of committing mayhem.

Americans who wish to hold open the possibility of emerging as a single people should not engage in mass repression. The surest way for black bigots to get a following is for white racists to create it. We want to open and not to foreclose the possibilities of being American together. There will be riots, and they will have to be put down. But our aim should be to separate the actively violent from the rest of the black community. Force should be limited, specific, and controlled.

Capitulation to lawless behavior would be bad. The hunger for humiliation shown by the New Left can only succeed in demeaning everyone. The black man's dignity cannot be won by the white man's degradation; the bread of humiliation will feed few people. The most destructive elements will simply be encouraged to raise the level of abuse. White anger will rise. Acting out the ritual frenzy of hatred will close all doors.

Our program should be neither suppression nor capitulation, but affirmation of common possibilities in a civil society. Without promising what no man can deliver—an end to the rebellions that are the consequences of our past failures—we can try to do what we now see to be right and just: a massive employment program, a concerted effort to improve educational achievement, and then support for a process of self-generating growth in the urban ghettos.

NOTES

1. One has to be careful not to commit semantic aggression. The word "riot" is too aimless to apply to a phenomenon that is national in scope and that is clearly directed at expressing rage against the conditions of life of black people. To use "revolt," however, would suggest far more leadership, organization, and concerted action than appears to have been the case. So we are left with "rebellion," an appropriate word to designate violence by people who wish to express their hostility toward prevailing conditions but who are not yet organized to attack the larger society.

2. Support for this hypothesis comes from a study of antiwhite violence in Africa, which shows that there was little bloodshed in countries that engaged either in consistent repression or gave independence to the black majority; violence did occur when whites vacillated.

3

RACE AND RESEARCH:
THE MOYNIHAN REPORT AND
THE POLITICS OF
CONTROVERSY

Written in the winter of 1965 by Daniel Patrick Moynihan, then Assistant Secretary of Labor, the Moynihan Report on "The Negro Family: The Case for National Action" was a cry of alarm. The new civil rights acts, laudable as they were, were bound to prove disappointing. They would not substantially change the economic and social position of Negroes for a long time. For even if the legal barriers to equal opportunity were broken by this legislation, many if not most black people would still not be able to take advantage of the new possibilities. They lacked the skills to get the jobs that were available to their better educated brothers. The catastrophic levels of unemployment in most black areas were not likely to instill in people hope for the future that would encourage them to acquire the necessary skills. The Negro family was breaking up under the combined impact of low wages, high joblessness, and a welfare system that did not exactly encourage men to stay home. The legacy of racial oppression was being paid out.

Disaster! Disaster! Disaster! That was Moynihan's message. Expectations were rising and few concrete payoffs were in sight. As Nathan Glazer had observed in an important article in *Commentary,* the demands of some black activists had significantly changed from equality of opportunity to equality of result. This profound change posed several dilemmas. The American commitment toward equality, such as it was, manifestly did not include the vast compensatory mechanisms necessary to secure equality

From *The Activist,* no. 22 (Fall 1968), pp. 20–22. Reprinted by permission.

as a fact. Treating Negroes better than whites—discrimination in reverse
—appeared difficult to sell to politicians and voters alike. How, then,
could political support be obtained for the billions of dollars needed to
create jobs and income? Moynihan apparently reasoned that the policy-
makers could be convinced of the need for these policies by appealing to a
value widely held in America—family stability.

The Moynihan Report was thus a politically directed document designed
to alert high Administration officials to coming dangers and to prepare
them for the evident policy recommendations to follow. In keeping with
his pragmatic action orientation, Moynihan decided not to include a list of
policy recommendations in his report but rather to use the vehicle of a
Presidential speech at Howard University to alert the nation and Congress
to the gravity of the racial problem. That speech was surely the best a
President has ever given on racial problems.

A brilliant policy analysis alerts the Executive Office to imminent danger, the President publicly recognizes the problem, and then . . . nothing.
Rage and fury grow but not at inaction, not at the growing dimensions of
the problem—but rather at Moynihan himself and his report. (Or, rather,
since hardly anyone bothered to get the real thing, at butchered versions in
the press.) How dare Moynihan cast aspersions on the Negro family (he
didn't), which has so superbly adapted to the difficult conditions of ghetto
life? How dare Moynihan (he didn't) say that what Negro families needed
was more social work rather than more income and more respect? A report on the Negro family clearly should not be written at all, certainly not
by a white man, but if it had to be done it should be totally concerned
with the crimes of white men.

The President waited for a lead from civil rights groups. He would respond to their call for action. But all they could agree on was hostility to
the Moynihan Report. So they worked out their disagreements in the traditional fashion—they asked for everything anybody wanted. This barrage
of demands paralyzed the Executive Office. It was a classic case of too
much and not enough. The dozens of demands bogged the mind and paralyzed the will. No single demand emerged as the rallying cry for massive
action. The White House liberals became confused just a little earlier than
other liberals. The equality of opportunity to which they had dedicated
themselves was no longer good enough. Integration, which had been the ultimate goal of their small stock of idealism, was seriously questioned. Neither seemed likely to end dominance by the white man. But if this was the
goal, what role was there for a white government? Confusion reigned supreme.

This unhappy story is told by Lee Rainwater and William L. Yancey in
The Moynihan Report and the Politics of Controversy.[1] They describe how
the report came to be written, analyze its contents, describe the reactions
to it, and discuss the uses of social science research in political disputes. In
addition, the book includes the full Moynihan Report and the more signifi-

cant critiques. The book is splendid in almost every way. While speaking their piece whenever they see fit, the authors are remarkably objective. Their one lapse from grace inevitably concerns President Johnson; the commandment to be fair evidently stops short of the White House. Yancey and Rainwater are for all the right things like human dignity and truth and scholarly commitment, and they exude the admirable faith that these values will not prove incompatible. Their work beautifully exemplifies their creed. Since Rainwater and Yancey are primarily concerned with the use of social science in making governmental policy, let us examine more closely some of the basic problems of research into Negro life that they discuss.

Why is it that so many Negroes are unemployed? Is it because there are no jobs for them or because they do not want to work? If poor education disqualifies Negroes, why don't they do better at school? Is discrimination the basic cause or are there elements of Negro culture that are hostile to formal education? Why are crime and illegitimacy rates so high among Negroes? Is it that society has failed them or that they do not choose to take advantage of what society has to offer?

One part of the answer is all too clear. When people have been disadvantaged for a long time, they (like the ghettoized Jews who refined self-hatred into a high art) may become carriers of their own victimization. As Rainwater and Yancey say,

. . . behind these stereotypes there are people whose adaptations to slum life have resulted in ways of behaving that *are* destructive of their possibilities for taking advantage of any new opportunities that might come their way. There are women who have many illegitimate children and even more that have one or two. There are children who find it difficult to learn in school because their life at home does not provide them with the kinds of experiences that maximize their chances of doing well at school, and there are families who throw garbage out of the window, thereby getting themselves in trouble with their neighbors and others. Just because these things are true, it is not necessary to conclude that segregation and discrimination are not the terrible villains we thought they were. To the contrary, segregation and discrimination *are* the terrible villains we thought they were precisely because they have these kinds of effects as well as other effects on the people who must live in a segregated world.[2]

Yet this insight does not begin to provide precise answers to the big question: to what degree do existing patterns of Negro behavior contribute to their own difficulties? Who or what is responsible for the present conditions of Negroes in America? To even pose this question today is to sense its fierce impact and to know that it is a political declaration as much as an academic query.

The usual approach of social scientists is to isolate race by comparing the behavior of Negroes and Caucasians with various factors such as education and income held constant. Thus, a researcher tries to determine whether differences previously attributable to race will disappear or be markedly reduced when comparing whites and blacks at the same income level. Yet nothing conclusive seems to be established. The difficulty, of course, is partly political. These statistics are potential political weapons. Anything said to demonstrate that Negroes are not well off may be turned around and used to condemn them. Any set of numbers that appears to show that Negroes are better off may be used to suggest that they need no help. I believe the difficulty in achieving understanding goes much deeper than the usual polemical distortions. There is a fundamental defect in this mode of analysis itself, a defect that is directly related to the magnitude of the policy problems with which we are faced. The defect is this: when a single variable explains a great deal about a particular problem, it is absolutely necessary to control for the effects of that variable if the impact of any other factors is to be discovered. Now, unemployment among younger Negroes may have been running at a rate of 30 percent or more for over a decade. Many employed Negroes, moreover, do not make enough to support a family at minimal levels. Here is an extraordinary situation in which a good one-third to one-half of young Negro men are either unemployed or working below a family wage in any single year. If other causes of discontent are to be discovered, employment will have to be statistically controlled. Is there any way of doing this so that the results make sense? I believe the answer is "no."

The control for income, in my opinion, is not useful for comparing groups or communities under present conditions. The disorientation and dismay caused by high unemployment among so large a proportion of the black population is likely to affect the whole group and not just the people directly involved. The existence of this probability must have a powerful effect even on those who are not poor or unemployed. A man's race vitally affects his chances in life; if this were not true, there would be no race problem and we know damn well there is one.

The situation may be so bad in critical cases that no control group exists. The Moynihan Report, for instance, generated a lot of controversy over the desirability of the matriarchal family. As matters stand now, however, the only available choice beyond having mothers head families is no families at all. It would be most instructive to observe how matriarchal families among Negroes with high income ($15,000 a year) compare with whites, but the relevant Negro group does not exist. In the presence of such overwhelming factors as high unemployment, low income, and poor education, it is not possible to get precise and meaningful answers to questions about the impact of family structure, sexual mores, work habits, and the rest.

Even if the problem of statistical controls is solved, political difficulties still block the establishment of proper experimental controls. We can tell whether, say, a new education program directed at the entire Negro population of a city is effective by comparing its results with clearly stated objectives. No controls are then necessary. But since this hypothetical new program costs a great deal, and we do not know in advance whether it will work, the obvious thing is to set up pilot projects. These pilot projects are experiments and require experimental controls. Most children and schools must go on in the old ways to serve as bases of comparison. But as soon as a few schools are selected and controls set up, there is immediate prejudgment of the effectiveness of the experimental programs. "Why can't our children have special curricula, smaller classes, the new methods?" Before the experiment can be tried, it becomes a subject for political pressures, collective bargaining, and mass demonstrations. The result is that at the end it is impossible to tell whether schools with the new programs are better or worse than schools without them.

The conclusion is inescapable: experimental programs that do not encompass entire cities are probably doomed because the application of essential controls—meaning that most children will not be helped immediately—is interpreted as just another example of discrimination at the control sites in the black areas. The moral of this story for public policy must also be understood. Action must precede exact knowledge. Racial problems must be approached through big programs that cover large areas. No one can say that large-scale programs will prove effective. What can be said is that there is no hope of learning or accomplishing anything from miniature experiments. The size of the laboratory must begin to approach the enormity of the problem.

NOTES

1. Lee Rainwater and William L. Yancey, *The Moynihan Report and the Politics of Controversy* (Cambridge: M.I.T. Press, 1968).
2. *Ibid.*, p. 232.

4

THE POLITICAL FEASIBILITY
OF INCOME BY RIGHT

WITH *Bill Cavala*

Our task is to determine the political feasibility of those public policies which would give poor people income as a right. Such a task involves little more than outlining the steps (or, in our case, the major step) through which any policy must necessarily pass, while providing an assessment of the chances of passage. This type of analysis provides information about the nature and strengths of obstacles that stand in the way of a new proposal. It offers counsel to the proponents of a policy, providing them with a set of its predicted strengths and weaknesses to emphasize or modify. The utility of this approach is, of course, founded on several assumptions, the most basic of which is the belief that the political process will continue to function much the same as it has in the past.

If this perspective is accepted, then our task becomes all too simple. Income policies are not politically feasible because few people want them. Why? Policies that provide people with unearned income run counter to widely held and deeply felt American values such as achievement, work, and equality of opportunity. The large tax increase or drastic reallocation of public funds required to guarantee income has few supporters. Labor unions fear that a guaranteed income would render them superfluous. Militant black leaders take the same position for a similar reason. Income policies are not serious subjects for discussion in Congress. Those who do care about them are trying to find ways to put them on the agenda of those issues safe to discuss.

These assertions will be elaborated and defended in various ways. Since congressional enactment is necessary in order for income proposals to be adopted, the first part of the essay will deal with opinion in the Congress. The second section is devoted to a closer look at those aspects of income

From *Public Policy* 18 (Spring 1970), pp. 321–354. Reprinted by permission.

by right—effectiveness, dignity, bureaucracy, equality, incentives, taxes—
that create special political problems. Through a brief analysis of selected
aspects of the recent political history of public assistance and poverty programs in the third section, we appraise the argument that there are important political advantages in giving everyone income by right instead of directing public funds exclusively to the "deserving" poor.

As we mentioned earlier, an analysis of political feasibility is based on
traditional assumptions, one of which presumes that the usual bargaining,
logrolling, and coalition building will take place in the future much as it
has in the past. Yet these assumptions ignore the role which domestic crisis has come to play in our political system. People argue that any reasonable prediction would foresee a situation in which domestic crises might
become so severe that people would abandon long-held beliefs and adopt
any policy promising help. The problem, as we see it, is that most arguments for income maintenance which rest on the premise (or hope) of crisis also assume that these dramatic events would provide no more than lib-
eration from the allegedly stifling process of partisan mutual adjustment.
Their vision is that of the "100 days" in which the bickering that had
impeded new ideas was swept aside by the overwhelming need for "action." Much of the faith in crisis seems rooted in the nostalgia for the
unity of purpose which would give our leaders the freedom to experiment,
to act quickly and creatively in meeting our problems. It has become almost an article of faith among liberal intellectuals that the "Crisis of the
Old Order" will be followed by the "Coming of the New Deal."

Although this essay is not the place for an extended and serious discussion of that premise, it does seem necessary to make clear our belief that
in many ways the analogy of the 1930s is dangerously misleading. The
kinds of crises we face are not, after all, those of universal economic hard-
ship or of a crucial external threat. Rather, they are crises which divide
Americans and set them against one another. The rhetoric of priorities,
furthermore, serves to tie issues of foreign policy to problems of domestic
initiative. Cleavages which formerly served to unite some men on some issues and divide them on others now tend to unite and divide the same men
on a much wider range of questions. The problems of race and the disadvantaged, terribly divisive in themselves, become even more so when
linked with the current attack on the responsiveness of our traditional political processes. Many young people, cynically or idealistically, see no
progress; their protests take the form of increasing hostility to political institutions. A much larger segment of the electorate responds to the violence, not the criticism, and it demands (however inarticulately) a defense
of the institutions through an attack on the critics.

The crisis of legitimacy we would be likely to face is not likely to be a
liberating one which gives freedom of action to our leaders. Pragmatic experimentation works best in a situation where the goals are agreed upon
and only the means are debatable. But when it is the authority of the re-

gime, the legitimacy of our institutions and our traditional forms of politics that are called into question, the margin for error must be greatly reduced. A President facing this type of crisis could not incur an experimental mistake without adding to the magnitude of the problem: modern times of crisis provide opportunities for great failures as well as great successes.

In view of the high cost of failure, proponents of income maintenance have an obligation to take a hard look at the argument that it will both improve the lot of the poor *and* increase support for existing political institutions. For while advertising income maintenance as the panacea for violence may well make it a more "feasible" policy, if the advertisement proves false the ultimate price of that feasibility may be paid in the coin of more expectations crushed, more hostility, and less opportunity for future success. We discuss the relationship between guaranteed income and violence, and ask whether bloc grants to states and cities might be more efficacious in lessening the resort to force. In the last section, we return to our original assumptions about political continuity and make our predictions of the actual course of policy-making. We then compare these predictions with the recent Nixon proposals on welfare to see how much a study of political feasibility aids in prediction. For those unfamiliar with the nature of the proposals being discussed, the general principles and some of the specific plans are described in the Appendix.

Lack of Support in Congress [1]

If the strongest arguments for income plans are the arguments against our present system of public assistance, an initial optimism is justified. There is high awareness of the failures of the present system among members of the 91st Congress. Almost every member has a personal atrocity story dealing with the failure of the poverty program and welfare system in his state or district. All were aware of the disincentives now built into our public assistance programs. With only a single exception, they agreed that the present approaches to the problems of poverty are not working now and would probably not work in the future. Fertile soil, it would appear, for the income-maintenance arguments. But rejection of present welfare policies has not yet been transformed into acceptance of income by right.

Most of the members of Congress we interviewed [2] did not understand what was meant by any of the terms commonly used to describe income by right. After a short explication by the interviewer, however, they did not lack for opinions. Congressmen typically would say, "No, absolutely not, you just can't give people money, you have to leave them some sense of self-respect." Others would speak of "something for nothing" or the "work ethic" to explain why they or their constituents were opposed. As soon as the idea became clear, they immediately made a connection with socialism, planning, and other disagreeable things. "Whatever the plan," one Congressman noted, "if it can be labeled guaranteed income with any kind of correctness, then it would be defeated."

Although we thought the Congressmen would be concerned about work incentives, we did not realize how persistent and deeply felt these feelings would be. A respected and hard-driving Congressman insisted that poverty gives people its own incentive to overcome adversity. "I myself," he said, "would have been a lush if people had paid me not to work." [3] It was not enough to remind the legislators about the disincentives in the present welfare system, for they knew and objected already; their answer, however, was to suggest that the welfare system be made more unpleasant. When we pointed out the resultant human degradation, they would acknowledge it but then claim that a guaranteed income would only worsen the problem: giving away money undermines the pride, responsibility, and motivation of the recipient. These representatives would seriously argue that they were protecting the poor from their own weaknesses by refusing to give them money. They said this, apparently, not out of malice but out of a conviction that men are weak and will take the easy path—to their own ruin. Three of the most powerful and respected members of the House noted that if they in their poor youth had been given a guaranteed income they would be "bums" today.

As in society at large, Congressmen who grew up in hard times do not have much sympathy for income policies. They believe that people have to work for their own salvation. "If you cut your own wood," the philosophy of the conservative legislators went, "it warms you twice." That might be true of adults, we said for the sake of argument, but what about women and kids? The typical answer was consistent with the philosophy of earning one's way: "It's a fine object lesson for kids, having free money in the family. They're not going to learn responsibility *that* way."

High on the list of congressional objections to income proposals (though never mentioned before the moral difficulties) was the necessity for a large increase in income taxes. Everyone had the same arguments: we are facing a taxpayers' revolt; people are unhappy with the present system's cost; redistribution would hurt middle-class incentives; the money isn't available, and so on. The last theme was naturally prevalent among members of the House Appropriations Committee. One of them explained, "We really just don't have enough money to fill our needs, let alone our wants," and he gave the example of a family sitting around after dinner, planning what they'd do if they had the money. They'd build boats, sail around the world, things of this sort. "But," he said, "you eventually have to get up and wash the dishes and leave those plans among the after-dinner smoke."

A return to reality meant that a huge tax increase was required. "To get that kind of money," we were told, "you have to have an increase in taxes, and to get the kind of plan you want through Congress, it would have to be Presidential initiative. Something that big simply couldn't come from the Congress. There is no Congressman big enough. The leadership itself won't move without a Presidential initiative." No one we interviewed was willing to say that he would ask his constituents to support a substantial tax increase at the present time.

Even the most liberal proponents of the plans agreed that the money for income maintenance just would not be there (given other needs and demands) unless defense spending could be cut. Whether true or not, this is the conviction of the Congress; it means that the fight for authorization, and especially for appropriations, will be perceived as an adjunct of the fight against military spending. Alternatives (raising taxes, cutting spending in other areas) are not considered viable by many members. The argument that income plans could be financed out of revenue gained by growth in GNP is not taken seriously: conservatives want to have the money before they spend it; liberals feel that most of this money is already earmarked for increased defense expenditures.

The Congressmen we interviewed did not believe that their middle- and working-class constituents and their union leaders would support income maintenance. Raising the minimum wage is a major goal of labor unions, and that would be weakened by any income plan. Even if some labor union leaders could be persuaded to support income maintenance, the rank and file probably would not, on grounds of equity. Most unions and their members will have to change their views on income maintenance before it is a feasible policy, and most Congressmen will not take this gamble. "In my state," one reported, "it would be political suicide. My supporters are primarily working-class people; they oppose the notion of something for nothing. They tell me they bust their butts over their jobs, and they're not about to have somebody living off the fruits of their energies." Another expressed similar sentiments and ended, "In short, I am extremely pessimistic on almost every ground you can imagine, and I myself am not anywhere near convinced that such a program is morally defensible, let alone politically feasible." Rather than asking why most Congressmen oppose income maintenance, it might be more instructive to ask why a few actually support it.

Support for income maintenance came from Congressmen perceived by their more hesitant colleagues as "safe-seat liberals," that is, from members of the Democratic Study Group (DSG) in the House and from a handful of crusaders in the Senate. Characteristically, they knew only that income maintenance was a liberal ussue and that they were liberals; ergo, their support was automatic. When queried as to what would be required for passage of such a plan, all cited a need for more liberals and fewer conservatives in Congress (about 205 more by our count).

Among the members of the Democratic Study Group we interviewed, there was little concern with the moral or even the knotty technical issues involved in income maintenance. They would merely repeat what became a familiar litany: the more Democrats the more progressives, the more progressives the more support for progressive issues, the more progressive issues the better the chance of a guaranteed income. There was not even much talk about income proposals among DSG members because "everyone knows where each other stands." [4] When asked about the chances of passing an income maintenance proposal, however, they all give the same answer: "None, zero, absolutely no chance."

The strategy adopted by these liberals was to introduce vast comprehensive bills covering everything from guaranteed income to higher education for all to total employment and so on. They do not mean to push these measures, however, but merely to introduce them. If they were really serious, several members told us, important blocs of voters they need for reelection would be mad at them. In addition, party leaders and their fellow Congressmen would be angry at them for exposing the party to danger without any hope of accomplishment. A *pro forma* introduction of a comprehensive bill, however, had certain virtues summed up by a Senator: "It at least presents the issue to the other Senators and gets them thinking about it. It tends to be true that when an idea is written up in bill form it takes on some kind of legitimacy.[5] Also, people looking for a liberal record will probably stand up for it, which gives them a stake in defending it in the future when they run for re-election." Yet even Congressmen with the most liberal constituencies would observe that income maintenance was not popular with the voters in their districts nor with various groups such as labor unions that had provided support for them in the past. Hence their support was "nominal and not really very serious."

Our preinterview guess had been that liberals would favor income plans, that conservatives would oppose them, and that a large body of Congressmen in the middle would have no opinion one way or the other. We wanted to determine whether this group could be reached by a combination of better information and a proposal modified to take their most serious objections into account. What we found, however, was that this "middle group" was virtually nonexistent. The moderates were either opposed on moral grounds or frightened by the political consequences of the issue. In order for them to consider supporting income maintenance, they felt that three things would be needed: (1) modifications to take care of their concern about incentives, equity, and cost; (2) sufficient support in their own constituencies to make the risk worth taking; (3) strong public support from the President. "I'd hate to stand for that issue in 1970," a legislator insists. "I could do it if it were a matter of supporting a Presidential program, but it's tough to stand alone—they'd crucify me." New York liberals might go around introducing "silly" bills but not the man in the middle. "Those boys," a Congressman said, referring to liberals from safe districts, "they don't have to worry about a thing back home in talking to voters, but for people like me—and there are quite a few of us here in the

Congress—it's just too big an issue to stand up on alone. If the President was for it, then we could stand up with him."

Many members of Congress felt that income by right would be a survival issue. It would be highly visible in a campaign and would result in the defeat of Congressmen from shaky districts. The issue would combine higher taxes, increasing numbers of allegedly lazy bums on welfare rolls, and riots and rising crime rates as part of undesirable tendencies in American life. In order to make the income plans sound reasonable, moderate Congressmen would need to supply information of a complex sort to the voter. All felt that conservative opponents could effectively simplify the issue and provide objections which would immediately be understood and favorably received by the voter. Between those Congressmen who shared the views of their constituents that guaranteed income was "a payoff for laziness" and others who considered the political risks too high, the question of political feasibility was uniformly regarded as hopeless for the present. "Right now, it's not even an issue which could be viably discussed."

So they don't like income maintenance, they don't like the present system, and they don't have the money available to do better. Would they do anything about welfare policy? Responses to this question did not vary from liberal to conservative: "An honest day's dollar for an honest day's work." All favor increased job opportunity but they were vague as to what that meant, as to who could work at what level of wages and so on. Some of the Southern members talked in sentimental terms about the value and discipline of the old WPA and CCC camps, which is how they perceive the notion of the government as the employer of last resort. Despite the lack of clarity, job programs were as strongly preferred by members of Congress as they are in the general population.

Virtually all Congressmen agreed that "hunger is a problem" and were sympathetic to Senator McGovern's efforts to eliminate hunger. To them this meant that people should be given food for survival. Poverty meant real hunger, not inability to have what others had. The basic idea, as several Congressmen put it, was that "no one should starve—but to be at a better-off level than starvation one should put some element of oneself into one's work." These Congressmen ". . . don't mind giving away food, but it shouldn't be steak. People should not be satisfied with living on a food stamp program. I'm sure the Agriculture Department could come up with some nutritious food that isn't too tasty so that you'd want to get off it as soon as possible, but that as long as you had to be on it then it would keep you alive." So far as these Congressmen are concerned, all carrot and no stick is not going to work.

Specific Political Difficulties

EFFECTIVENESS

Effectiveness might be judged simply by considering how much of the so-called poverty gap is filled by each of the proposed plans; the most effective would eliminate the greatest number of people from the ranks of the poor. Unfortunately, however, other considerations affect this rather pristine variable. For one thing, we must consider the probability that any income-maintenance program will be adopted (if at all) only at the expense of, rather than in addition to, the present system of public assistance. We must remember that politically it is not the mere desire to eliminate poverty that makes possible the discussion of a guaranteed income proposal; equally if not more important is today's widespread dissatisfaction with the welfare system. Any plan which does not promise substantial reductions in the cost of welfare and the size of its bureaucracy stands little chance of success.

What we must ask, then, is whether the plans under consideration would serve as adequate substitutes for our present system. That is, will some (many?) poor people be worse off after the trade-off than before? Will we simply be shifting the burden of poverty from one group to another? In making this evaluation, critics [6] of the income proposals have noted that only the social dividend proposals (Schwartz and Theobald) would fulfill the criterion of leaving no one worse off than before. The fractional plans (Friedman, Lampman, Tobin) would not reduce the cost of public assistance (by any amount that would be politically visible) without making the poor of several states economically worse off than before.

What this means is that none of the politically feasible proposals (for example, the fractional plans, feasible because they cost less) meets the criterion of economic effectiveness. At the same time, neither of the economically effective plans (with full guarantees) appears to be politically feasible. Tough choices will have to be made. Would it be worthwhile to seek the adoption of proposals which in the short run place the poor in a relatively worse position than before but establish the principle of income by right? Conceivably, once the battle over income maintenance as a principle has been won, the level of the guarantee could be raised later when funds were made available.

In making this decision, it is of course important to know who would suffer. The OASDHI (social security) trust fund totals over $20 billion, held in the form of government securities. (Interesting legal and moral questions arise concerning any proposed disposition of the trust fund, to which employers, employees, and the self-employed have contributed for a particular purpose.) It is not social security that would be cut, however, but the most visible of the present welfare programs: Aid to Families with Dependent Children (AFDC).

While cutting AFDC would not provide much in the way of economic savings (only $2 billion in 1967), it is almost the only assistance program which is politically feasible to slash. It is also the program which has come in for the most criticism. Yet none of the politically feasible lower-cost income plans would serve as an adequate substitute for AFDC. The short-run disadvantages accrued by the adoption of a predictably emasculated income plan would, therefore, fall primarily on the one million mothers and the 3.6 million children who are the primary beneficiaries under our present system.[7] The moral problems raised by these facts are quite obvious. There are those, however, who believe that this (hopefully) temporary loss in income would be compensated for by a gain in dignity under income proposals. We believe that this hope is illusory.

DIGNITY AND BUREAUCRACY

One of the great selling points of income maintenance is its purported superiority over the present welfare system. Conservatives are expected to support it because they believe it provides the opportunity of dismantling the great welfare bureaucracy. Poor people are expected to support it because it substitutes the dignity of "income by right" for the degradation of welfare investigations and the "means test." We must now ask whether the proposals that are feasible do in fact provide more dignity and less bureaucracy than the welfare system.

The answer appears to be a flat "no." For one thing, even if new programs were instituted with a level of appropriations that would make feasible a cutback of present welfare, a bureaucracy would still be required. None of the plans, with the exception of Friedman's proposal, could be administered directly through the existing apparatus of the IRS. All the plans would involve the elimination of state and county welfare machinery; hence a new or expanded national bureaucracy would be necessary. The result would be more centralization, not decentralization. Given the difficulty of forms, the literacy levels of the recipients, and necessity of quarterly payments and estimations of income, the need for bureaucratic assistance is not likely to diminish appreciably. If we assume that the elimination of categories and their concomitant stigma will make more people eligible for aid and more eligible people willing to apply for it, bureaucracy may well increase.

Let us also ponder the problem of coordination of bureaucracies. Will county social workers be administering the federal program? Will the complexities of the new forms require as much of their time as the old investigations? Will not the increased numbers of recipients also increase the need for casework and counseling? Will we then need more social workers, paid by the local government to administer a federal program?

If administrative costs increase or remain the same after adoption of income maintenance, the main argument with political appeal to congressional conservatives is lost. Support from these men would be improbable at best: prior to authorization it must be demonstrated in a clear and convincing way that the size of the bureaucracy will decrease both in cost and in numbers. Unfortunately, the only situation in which such a demonstration could be made is likely to be one in which the present system of aid is eliminated in favor of an income maintenance with low levels of support. This, of course, has the undesirable consequence of making large numbers of poor people economically worse off than they are now.

From the perspective of the poor, some of the arguments which stress the human advantages of income by right over the present system do make sense. Much of the harassment (such as midnight raids) associated with enforcement of degrading rules would be eliminated. There would be no need to spy around for "the man in the house." But these problems could also be eliminated through a simple modification of the present system. The real argument for income maintenance as a source of dignity is stronger: it purports not simply to decrease the indignities of welfare, but promises also to remove the stigma associated with poverty. We seriously question whether income maintenance would achieve this crucial goal.[8] In America the stigma of poverty, after all, lies less in the fact of being poor than in the implication that one is lacking in those abilities which are rewarded. The idea of an income floor is a step toward modifying this implication. It suggests that the poor are not completely responsible for their fate, that they may have lacked a real (as against formal) opportunity to participate in our race for gain. But it is a far different thing to say that the losers in that race will not starve than it is to say that the race itself is not a worthy one.

Income by right would remove the stigma of being poor only to the extent that it succeeded in removing the opposite status from being rich, that is, only to the extent that it signaled acceptance of the principle of equal result rather than equal opportunity. The recognition that equality of result is involved quite naturally leads conservatives to oppose income maintenance in principle. But where, in principle, income by right would lead to a demand for income leveling that truly would remove the stigma (as well as the fact) of poverty, the proposals we are dealing with do not. They do not (at least initially) propose an equalization of the distribution of income in the United States. They do not, as a consequence, eliminate the stigma of being a loser in the competitive race which is American life. What they offer is, in effect, a consolation prize. The amount of dignity which such a prize would salvage is problematical at best.[9]

But if income-maintenance plans are unable to eliminate the stigma of being poor per se, at least they can spare the poor from the indignity and embarrassment of having their condition publicly proclaimed. There are moral advantages to a silent check received in the privacy of one's own home with no strings attached as to how you spend it and no need to justify to someone how you got it. That is the real strength of the income-maintenance proposals: it is private and impersonal, not public, personal, and degrading.

The power of this argument, however, is based on the contrast between the theory of the proposals and the present practices of the welfare system. We have argued that in practice the new proposals would have many of the disabilities of the old. In short, while the benefits of the plans would be invisible and private to the community, the means of obtaining those benefits would be visible and public. (Note that if the stigma of poverty were really removed by such plans the need for privacy would not be there.) The degradation of being publicly identified as poor would remain for numbers of recipients. If the most onerous features of the present system were eliminated, it might be difficult indeed to determine whether categorical assistance or guaranteed income served the value of dignity the best.

EQUITY

The political strength of the present system of categorical aid lies in its strict coverage: no non-needy are supposed to be given support. The abhorrence that some people feel at giving "something for nothing" may be mitigated by their acceptance of aid to the needy. Unfortunately, several of the new plans for guaranteed income are unable to maintain this political credit. Attempts to fill the "poverty gap" completely while at the same time moving toward the idea of income by right tend to produce loose coverage as a necessary byproduct.

An income plan with loose coverage would pay money to substantial numbers of middle- and low-income wage earners as well as to the defined "poor," unless an offsetting tax of high rate is placed against income earned in addition to the subsidy. While there is still widespread sentiment against any form of government aid to the poor, federal policies over the past 30 years have accustomed people to the concept.[10] Income plans with loose coverage, however, do not involve simply redistributing income from the non-poor to the poor; they demand a redistribution from the "wealthy" non-poor to the less wealthy non-poor. Plans which include such leakages could not be defended as aid to the needy. Rather, defenders of such plans would have to justify them in terms of arguments for equality of income.

Thus the first liability which "loose" proposals tend to accrue is a conflict with some of the widely shared values of Americans. While the concept of equality is an important value to mobilize in support of any proposal, it is the notion of equal opportunity rather than equality of result which is basic to the American tradition.[11] Equality may be used to justify removing some of the handicaps which make the opportunity to compete meaningless, but equality of result would negate the idea of competition itself and render equality of opportunity meaningless. Opponents of income plans, we suggest, would be in a much better position to use the persuasive value of the tradition of equality. In more concrete terms, we must ask whether families of about median income can be expected to sit back while poorer families are raised by government subsidy to income levels as high as their own.

The main difficulty with any plan that involves loose coverage, however, lies in the fact that it tends to pyramid liabilities. Where ordinarily the opposition of upper-income groups who are concerned with their economic interests can be countervailed to some extent by an appeal to their moral values, in this case the two would reinforce rather than conflict with one another. It is not wise to allow those groups who would oppose income proposals on strict economic grounds the additional weapon of ideological purity. From this perspective, then, the political recommendation would have to be against opting for one of the proposals with loose coverage. The vital point is the necessity of separating the concept of income maintenance for the *poor* (which could be rationalized in terms of equal opportunity arguments) from the idea of income redistribution per se (which could not be so justified).

These criticisms are, of course, directed primarily at the social dividend proposals of Theobald and Schwartz who set their minimum income level at a high enough point that either a prohibitively high offset rate must be adopted or the break-even point must be raised so as to insure that most of the net payments will go to the non-poor. The high guarantee and/or the high break-even point make substantial leakages to the non-poor a given.[12] These plans also raise the specter of reducing the incentive to work.

INCENTIVES

The problem of incentives involves deeply felt moral values as well as important economic considerations. In form the problem is simple to state: if we are to avoid payments to the non-poor, then as the earned income of the poor rises the amount of the subsidy should decline. The question is: at what rate should the subsidy decline? Or, put differently, what portion of his nontransfer income will the poor person be allowed to retain? As this "offset rate" (the tax imposed on earned income) rises, economic theory tells us that the incentive to work will drop. Under our present welfare system (AFDC-UP and OASDI up to age 72), the offset rate is 100 percent or more.[13] A built-in disincentive to working, this problem has been the source of much of the political criticism of our public assistance programs.

In fact, the high offset rate associated with our present welfare system has served the proponents of income-maintenance proposals as one of their strong arguments. The fact that all of the proposed income plans feature less than 100 percent offset rates on earned income is taken as a major plus factor. Usually this is spoken of as a "bonus," or incentive factor, accompanied by an argument contrasting it favorably with our present "disincentives." [14]

But, at least in theory, any offset of earned income will tend to act as a disincentive. While this is recognized as a disability of our present welfare system, the categorical nature of that assistance has helped to make it at least politically palatable. Among the critics of income assistance there is a widespread conviction that poor people can and should be separated into classes of those who either *can* or *will* work and those who "can't" or "won't." The present system of aid is intended to reach only those who cannot work for some reason or another; thus disincentives are not really a problem. However, income-by-right proposals make no such distinctions between "deserving" and "nondeserving" poor. With every poor person eligible for payment, with no category to eliminate those who could work, the incentive problem will appear much more relevant to critics of the proposals than is now the case.

There are two dilemmas: the economic problem, involving questions of whether productivity will be affected, and the problem of equity. As succinctly stated by a person interviewed in the Gallup Poll, "I don't want my tax money going to someone who is sitting around with his feet up in the air." The answer to both of these objections, of course, could be found if we had empirical evidence which demonstrated that subsidies would not materially impair the incentive to work among recipients. Unfortunately, what evidence we do have on this problem is scanty and contradictory. G. F. Break found little evidence of disincentives among upper- and upper-middle income earners who face a high tax rate.[15] But the political value of this study is dubious; most critics of income maintenance would argue that individuals in this bracket are qualitatively different from those less fortunate: they are committed to the "work ethic"; the poor are not. The problem of generalizability is common to most of the studies on incentives: can they be applied to the situation of those directly affected by the income plans? [16] That is why the Trenton experiment has been undertaken. By actually giving income supplements to people in need one can try to determine what this does to their incentives. Even when results are in, however, we fear that they cannot possibly be conclusive. If the results are mixed, no one will know what to make of them. If they appear to show that incentive is not lost but actually grows, opponents of income maintenance will talk about how the people selected are not quite representative or about an alleged "Hawthorne effect." If the experiment shows a decline in incentive, proponents will argue away the results but they will have a harder time. A positive finding will by no means end the dispute.

These considerations are important because any new income proposal must be sold on the basis that (1) it is more congenial to the work ethic than our present welfare system; (2) it would be less permanent than that system; and (3) it would eventually cost less. The public and their representatives must be convinced that those poor people who are able, when presented with the new opportunities that income maintenance would give them, would seek work and income levels high enough to remove them from the reach of the subsidy. This question does not involve in any substantial number those presently on the welfare rolls: the Kerner Report estimates that only about 60,000 of the 7.5 million now receiving assistance would be aided by new job opportunities; the others are either children, mothers with children, the aged, the blind, or the otherwise handicapped.[17] The real problem concerns the working poor, those who are now employed but receiving low wages: will they find it advantageous to continue to work when the remuneration for their services is cut by some set percentage? We do not know.

The problem of incentives is complicated by the need to maintain some type of offset if only to keep costs down and strict coverage up. With no offset, the high cost of the plan (when combined with present tax rates) would make for high marginal rates on taxable income for upper-middle and upper-income families.[18] And high taxes mean near-fatal political risks.

TAXES

This threat of increases in federal taxation is, quite naturally, a great obstacle to any income proposal. The problem is political feasibility. While the present federal tax rate, even with the surcharge, is lower than the pre-1964 rate, state and local taxes have increased. Since, with few exceptions, municipal taxes are collected in lump sums rather than by means of a withholding system, their political visibility has risen considerably to property owners, who must bear the full burden of property taxation. Any new tax burden would fall primarily on this middle and upper-middle income group. Over two-thirds of them oppose guaranteed income.[19] Yet they are politically articulate and well organized, thus able to resist the imposition of new taxes or to take political retribution upon the imposers.

Even if new money is made available, there will be competing demands for the funds. Most cities have no money, poor revenue sources, and are faced with problems beyond welfare assistance. These city problems—education, sanitation, housing, police and fire protection—are only connected indirectly and in the long run with the problem of poverty. While some of them may be mitigated after decades of increased income for the poor, none will disappear with the adoption of the income proposals, for none of the proposals provides any base from which the city could obtain new revenue in the near future. Income plans will thus be in direct competition with the proposal of bloc grants to the cities.

The adoption of an income proposal which would allow for the virtual elimination of present assistance programs might mean that more state money could be funneled into the cities—but not necessarily. For one thing, safeguards would have to be erected to insure that state administrations would not simply use their savings for tax relief. For another, only the social dividend proposals would allow for much reduction of public assistance. Yet we have seen that they result in loose coverage. They cost so much—$30 to $50 billion a year—that there would be no way to argue that they represented a net saving to the taxpayer. The savings for the states amount to approximately $3 billion a year; considerably less than they could expect to gain in the long run from most of the bloc grant proposals. Finally, while the income proposals have the desirable quality of dealing with rural as well as urban poverty, this also involves dealing, to a certain extent, with rural problems at the expense of the politically more visible cities.[20]

These bleak facts rule out, we think, any possibility of enacting one of the large proposals in the next few years. Any proposal that is adopted would have to be substantially compatible with the two politically more important priorities: the demands of the cities and lower taxes. Analyzed in terms of cost,[21] the only viable proposals would be Friedman's ($10 billion), Lampman's ($8–11 billion), and Tobin's ($10–14 billion). Even with these lower-cost plans, however, most of these political difficulties would remain and new ones would be added because of their lesser effectiveness in reducing poverty.

Why Welfare Policies Have No Support

In view of the overwhelming opposition to income by right, it may appear surprising that it has a band of enthusiastic supporters. When one understands that existing welfare policies have become a huge political liability, surprise may give way to a search for the critical political functions that its proponents expect income policies to perform.

Modern social welfare policy must be virtually unique among major policies in that it has no supporters one can discern. Those who pay and those who receive, administrators and social workers, conservatives and liberals, economists and political scientists, Congressmen and ordinary citizens—all join in a chorus saying the policies are no good. In asking what differentiates welfare policy from other policies, therefore, we must turn to another question, namely, why does this collection of major policies have virtually no support?

There is no difficulty in finding things wrong with the welfare system. Consider the man-in-the-house rule. In order to prevent payments to women with dependent children who were actually being supported by able-bodied men living in the home, a rule was promulgated stating payments could not be made under these circumstances. The results were to encourage men to leave the home and thus deprive the child of any stable male companionship. Then there was the confiscatory tax on earnings. If

all or most of a person's earnings are subtracted from his welfare payments, it reduces his incentive to work. One also thinks of degrading personal questions, miserly allowances, residence requirements, and the like.
When a policy shows weaknesses, however, as all do, the usual course of
action is to modify them in accord with experience. Residency requirements may be abolished. A national standard for welfare may be established. Recipients may be allowed to keep all or a substantial part of additional income up to a specified amount. While these ameliorative devices
are being pursued, no one appears to have much hope for them. The reason is not that they are unimportant; rather, we think that the welfare system itself—the direct provision of funds and services to carefully deline-
ated groups in the population under a series of rules—has become an
enormous political albatross. What is almost worse, the major difficulties
appear to stem from the recipients and their supporters, thus giving the
whole scene a strange and galling quality.

In the 1930s, from whence we can date the modern era of social legislation, it was easy to understand the political facts of life in the field of
welfare. How neat and tidy it all was. The people who got welfare and the
liberals who supported them wanted more money. Conservatives and the
people who contributed the taxes that supported welfare payments wanted
to pay less money. In those nostalgic days you could tell the political play-
ers without a scorecard.

The taxpayer revulsion against welfare is easy to understand. Costs of
welfare programs have been expanding at a great rate, and this sharp increase has come at a time when other costs of local and regional government are going up. At the same time, the cost of aid to dependent children
has risen. Thus it is understandable that some taxpayers do not like to pay
as much as they do. When welfare problems are further given extensive
publicity through the efforts of recipients to improve their lot, the matter
is forcibly brought to the attention of those who pay. It may be that the existing system of social welfare was tenable so long, and only so long, as
taxpayers were not made acutely aware of the real situation in regard to
cost.

The puzzling part of the equation now, however, is not those who pay,
but those who receive. Why have those who ostensibly benefit from welfare
turned against it? Being on welfare has hardly ever been considered pleasant. Despite its numerous indignities, however, recipients have gone
along with it because they could not find any alternative. Nor were they
usually organized to present their claims in an effective way in the political arena. These conditions changed, however, as the war on poverty became mixed with racial hostility. Poor people were being encouraged to
act. The initial idea was that if the poor were organized to put pressure on
the welfare bureaucracy it would become more responsive to their needs.
In those urban areas where a large proportion of the welfare poor were
black, and the administrators were white, the usual disagreeable aspects of

welfare became objects of racial enmity. The flames of conflict were fanned by white middle-class radicals who saw in the organized militancy of the poor an opportunity to strike at the system they disliked.

When black people see that for generations they are on welfare, it is not surprising that they identify their subordinate position with the welfare system. They would much rather control their own economic life so they would not be at the mercy of others. Viewed in this light, the rejection of existing welfare policy is understandable. The fact that many people must continue to live under welfare, however, has led militants to take forceful action to improve conditions while the system lasts. These activities— rejection of the system and militant action to increase benefits and improve conditions—have given the field of welfare policy its perplexing and exasperating qualities.

It would not be too much to say that the social work profession has been traumatized by the growth of black militancy. Their willingness to perform the tasks associated with welfare depends on their belief that the program is good and that they know how to help others. The militants have called both assumptions into question. They claim that the social workers are hostile to poor people and that their experience does not fit them to interpret these people's needs. For our purposes, it hardly matters that some social workers identify with the blacks and others with the Establishment or that still others simply depart. The result is the same: opposition to continuation of the present welfare program.

The position of the radicals has been delightful. They get credit for improving welfare conditions and for opposing the system. That is, they have learned the ultimate political trick of combining the advantages of power with the benefits of opposition. It is not surprising, however, that other people should not be pleased with this happy combination. If the welfare system is being used to radicalize the poor, if the people who receive the money are far from grateful for it, there is no political benefit in continuing the program.

Let us summarize the conclusions apparent to most people involved with welfare policy.

1. Costs go up.
2. Satisfaction goes down.
3. Militancy increases.
4. Support decreases.

Poverty is no longer a popular issue. Every Congressman knows of the failure of the present system and of the war on poverty. This has led to disenchantment with traditional approaches, but not necessarily to a desire to substitute something in its place. A perceptive observer in the executive branch told us of his fear that ". . . problems of poverty will become illegitimate in the eyes of Congressmen. They associate poverty programs with conflict, with anti-political results. They simply will be tired of hearing about it."

Federal revenue sharing is becoming more popular not only because states and cities obviously need more money but because these units rather than the federal government can be blamed for the inevitable failures. "If you give them the money," a legislator observed, "and let them go at it and try to do what they can, that's going to take some of the blame off the Congress when the programs fail."

Where income maintenance has congressional appeal outside the coterie of committed liberals, it is seen as a means of escape from the adverse political consequences of poverty programs. The idea is to take the blame from the political system and place it back on the individual. "If some guy doesn't make it and you're giving him money, you can't blame the administration of the welfare thing, you can't say that it degrades him. At that point the burden is really on him."

Most liberals apparently see in guaranteed income a way of being good to the poor; they do not really look upon income policies as political devices. But there is an important segment of what was once the liberal community that has become desperately concerned with maintaining the stability of democratic institutions. While they are also disenchanted with categorical programs and direct services, their overriding interest now is political: how to increase and maintain support for the democratic process as they understand it. They would like a system that costs less and is appreciated more. If that cannot be had, as is readily apparent, they will take a system that costs more but for which the nation gets political credit.

These beleaguered liberals see in income supplements an answer to their political prayers. Here at one stroke is a means for buying off the poor and eliminating the need for middle men, whether they be white social work bureaucrats or black neighborhood militants. These sophisticated liberals understand the many difficulties that beset income supplements. But the political dilemma posed by existing welfare programs seems so acute, the dangers to democratic government seem so great, that income strategies appear to be a lesser evil.

Guaranteed Income and Political Rewards

Evaluation of any proposal must include some notion of the political rewards to be gained upon its implementation. Such an evaluation is more complex than it might appear at first glance. It is not enough simply to note that income-maintenance plans provide one of the answers to the problem of poverty in America. It is not enough, for one reason, because of the limited consensus in America over whether poverty is a legitimate public as against private or individual problem. Poverty, that is, cannot be reached within the rhetoric and solutions of the equal opportunity formula. As one Congressman put it, "We really lack a national purpose which has as one of its goals the elimination of poverty." In fact, as we have noted, many Congressmen felt the elimination of poverty via income maintenance would also involve the elimination of those values that have been considered central (individual initiative, liberty). We mention this only to emphasize that the vocabulary of justice is not wholly the reserve of the proponents of income-maintenance plans.

Income-maintenance plans unfortunately provide no assurance of producing political credit for their supporters. It is no longer accepted as a given that the poor will be, in some (hopefully electoral) way, "grateful." It is no longer accepted, for one reason, because of the political failure of the poverty program over the past three years; to many Congressmen, that program appears to have increased disaffection rather than gratitude.[22] While it may, indeed, be true that this disaffection is the result of a new hope that produces rising expectations and subsequent frustrations, this thought remains a hollow consolation to the Congressman who has found himself a target for every failure and ignored for every success. Proponents of income maintenance will have to supply convincing arguments that their proposals would produce more tangible political benefits than have past programs.

Those political arguments, in effect, would have to address the problem which increasingly is being used by political men as a standard by which to judge the desirability of proposed public policy in this area: the problem of violence. We should understand, then, that one of the first questions directed to income proposals by our political leaders will be, simply, "Will they bring peace to our cities?" This is a question with several dimensions. It could be interpreted without generosity as a query about the size of the sop needed to keep the masses docile and manipulable. A more generous interpretation would recognize in this question a growing concern with the fate of the Republic, a belief that the new modes of action may well endanger the institutions and values of democracy itself. This second interpretation is important because it asks of income maintenance not simply, "Will it preserve order?" (more money for more police might do that at less cost); it asks whether such plans will help us in our task of evolving a good public order.

The question about peace in our cities involves, then, two important issues. The first and obvious problem is peace itself; the second and more important problem concerns the style and substance of politics in the America to come. Analysis of either aspect of the problem is obviously risky, for whatever tack we take it will be based on premises which are necessarily controversial. Since, however, we believe this problem to be crucial to the assessment of any policy's *desirability* as well as feasibility in these troubled days, we will not pretend to an optimism which we do not feel. If what follows appears to be overly pessimistic or cynical, it may be attributed to our conviction that the problems of democracy involve much more than problems of economics.

The economic argument addressed to the current problem of racial hostility assumes that the root cause lies in the fact that there are many poor people who need to get above the poverty line: the large income-maintenance proposals should lead to a reduction of hostility. Yet there is also a theory that identifies a major cause in the disaffection of elites—the people who are already above the poverty line but who are better able to make their grievances felt. Should this be true, then income maintenance would not necessarily lead to more satisfaction. If the critical problem is to satisfy the demands of those who want greater *control* of political and economic life rather than those who just want more income, merely helping the poorest people will not decrease the present disaffection. These two theories could, of course, be interconnected. One could argue that if the poor were made better off through direct grants of income from the federal government, they would no longer be willing to provide a mass base of tacit support for militant actions. This theory would argue that elite dissatisfaction might continue, but it would be considerably less successful. Should the theory of relative deprivation be operative, however, an income strategy would only slightly ameliorate the situation. Indeed, a belief in relative deprivation would argue that making a large number of people slightly better off might create a resource base for more widespread and more intense forms of protest. There is evidence to suggest that the two groups that engage least in riot activity are (1) the best educated and economically advantaged and (2) the least educated and poorest.[23] Those who are prone to riot behavior appear to be the people who have some income and some education but not enough to achieve substantial rewards. Raising the income of the poorest under this theory, therefore, might make larger numbers of people available for militant action.

Many black militants are presently against and will continue to oppose income policies. A rational explanation is that there would be no need for them to act as brokers for black people if income supplements were available directly from the government. The entire routine by which attention is focused on poverty programs, community action, confrontation, and mobilization would be rendered superfluous. They may reasonably perceive such proposals as the modern equivalent of the civil service reforms that undermined the urban machines of earlier ethnic peoples. Another reason for opposition is that income supplements would still be a form of dependency. While the income would be guaranteed under law, it would still come from white legislators rather than emanating from some black control over the economy.

The term "black militant" encompasses a wide range of people in common parlance. There are those who are interested in furthering riot behavior and perhaps in engaging in guerrilla warfare: enemies of the system, they profit by the failure of its defenders. There are many others who would join the defenders of a reformed system, men who are interested in black control of their communities and in a much larger piece of the economic and political action. These programmatic militants would undoubtedly prefer not to have riots and violence. But since they can do little about it in any event, they are prone to make use of the circumstances to further their own aims. One political objection to income strategies is that they blur the distinction between the two types of militants. Income proposals would unite them because they are a way of bypassing indigenous leadership. Alternatives such as bloc grants might divide them by creating incentives for programmatic leadership and rewards for those who participate in existing structures. But as we shall see, even this alternative has potential crippling disabilities.

In fact, the honest response to the query about bringing peace to our cities—basing that response on the crucial assumption that income maintenance will for a long time preempt the field of social policy—is that these proposals will probably not bring peace. Certainly it is true that the alleviation of poverty and the conditions which poverty breeds stands as a high priority among the various leadership groups of the black community. But they also have other goals of a public and visible nature. They want power and status vis-à-vis whites. To the extent that the acceptance of income-maintenance demands that these other goals be neglected, to that extent the political response to income maintenance will be less favorable than that hoped for by even the liberal members of the Congress.

We mentioned earlier the problem of political competition between income-maintenance plans and the urban-bloc grant proposals. While perhaps doing less in a substantive sense for the urban poor, bloc grants may provide opportunity and action of a kind more visible to ghetto residents. Conceivably they would provide the cities with the economic means to be responsive to the public needs of the ghettos (which income maintenance would not). This responsiveness in turn might strengthen the hand of the moderate leaders of the black community who, by working through more traditional political channels, could return to their people with visible gains.

There is, then, some reason to believe that bloc grants might produce tangible political rewards. They would provide the cities with part of the resources to deal with their problems. They are attractive to the conservative and states' rights coalition in Congress. They are compatible with the desires of the organized black community for power, decentralization, and community control. They place high rewards on the use of traditional political channels, perhaps lessening the need for confrontation politics. Thus they give promise of being a means by which the level of urban disaffection could be brought down. Income maintenance, however, can promise few of these things; periodic and public victories by black leaders on visible issues (schools, housing) would probably produce greater benefits than monthly subsidies. To the extent that the two types of plans are mutually exclusive (for reasons of cost) we might expect that income maintenance will be, by many, rated second best.

Having made this case, we shall now argue why, in practice, we would be less than optimistic about the implementation of this proposal. The idea that bloc grants would be a perpetual source of new money, available each year to placate dissident groups, is not likely to be borne out by experience. State governments, as we have noted, are likely to take a large cut out of the bloc grants before they reach the cities. Then many cities without the worst social problems will get a share because there is no reasonable way to exclude them and they can use the money. Funds will also go to conservative cities that will use them for traditional expenditures rather than income redistribution or social goals. What happens next is a struggle for funds within the cities. Where these struggles are resolved within two or three years, bloc grants from the federal perspective will turn into specific expenditures for special purposes in the cities. There will be agreement on a "base"—the purpose and amount of expenditure that is accepted as part of the usual pattern to be continued in the future. Interests will congregate around "their" expenditure and defend it against attack; city officials will defend it because the political costs of change will be too high, especially after the weariness introduced by the hard-fought conflicts of the past few years. In those cases where the struggle over the new money is prolonged or too severe, city officials may seek to reduce their own discretion as a means of reducing the pressure on them. If they do not control the funds there would be nothing to be gained in badgering them. Hence they will ask that the previously free bloc grant be turned into a restricted, specific expenditure. The much-wanted freedom produced will likely turn out to be a one-time thing.

It might be argued that income policies would get around the problem of violence by withdrawing the incentive. Although militants would initially object to income proposals, they would find it hard to continue protests against policies that give cash to their poor constituents. Assuming that income policies are so large that they preempt the field of welfare, it might be argued that there would be no point in protest because there was nothing to be had. Areas of controversy like housing would not be fruitful grounds for militancy because individuals would have to buy the best they could with their increased income. If there are no prizes, this argument continues, there can be no contest. Militant action, then, would have to be confined to attempts to raise the level of income payments, and that would be a national question where power would go to those who are best able to mobilize votes in national elections. It is this "no incentive" theory of militant protest that provides one of the basic political justifications for income strategies as a means of maintaining political stability. We note only that by moving the scope of conflict from the city to the nation, the collective power of the urban poor is correspondingly reduced. To the extent that the struggle in contemporary America involves questions of power and status as well as of income, such a move might easily increase both political alienation and the violence that appears to accompany it.

In fact, it is entirely possible that neither guaranteed income nor bloc grants nor any other policy proposals will have substantial effect on the level of protest. The violence may simply have little to do with ameliorating social conditions for mass or elite. In a paper on "Black Rebellion and White Reaction," [24] Wildavsky refers to the "anger-plus-opportunity" theory of racial rebellion. Anger at white racism and the resulting deprivation continues to grow as black people become ever more aware of what has happened to them. The "opportunity" side of the theory suggests that violence is also a function of ability to get away with it. There are many peoples in the world who are furious and who do not manifest their hostility in violent behavior because their societies suppress rather than reward violence. Even if we give all possible advantages to bloc grants or income proposals, for example, they might, under some circumstances, lead to greater violence in the cities. No doubt cities would have something to give and militants would be kept busy trying to get it. But if they discover that the most violent get the largest rewards, bloc grants will serve as an incentive for raising the level of violence.

To say this is not, of course, to say that social problems do not have high priority or that poverty and racism are not ultimately causes of unrest. But it may be that acting out anger in violent ways is a problem that must be dealt with on its own terms as well as by attack on social causes. Mere suppression of violence, while necessary, is not enough. It would still be necessary to show that peaceful political activity was a rational policy because it succeeded where violence did not. How this end could be achieved, what reforms would be necessary, is beyond the scope of this essay. The only moral which we wish to attach to this risky story, a story so easily subject to misinterpretation, is that everyone who believes that his favorite social policy will bring racial peace and respect for democratic institutions may be grievously disappointed. We do not feel, however, that adopting this conclusion necessitates abandoning social policies. Rather we prefer to follow the worthy old political adage, "When in doubt, do right." We must return to asking which alternative social program promises to do the most to improve the welfare of the people.

The Future

Income by right is not politically feasible in the near future. The President will not support it and Congress would not pass it if he did. The populace is hugely opposed. The Gallup Poll reports that less than 50 percent of the people with incomes under $3,000 are in favor.[25] We do not believe that the next Democratic candidate for President could win an election in which guaranteed income was the major issue or, if he did, that the Democratic party would gain a sufficiently large majority in Congress to accomplish the purpose.

Before our conclusions are accepted, the limitations of our study should be taken into account. We have interviewed some 50 legislators. Their small number we think less an impediment than the fact that they have been asked to react to a subject they have not thought much about. Had we been able to chart trends in opinion over time on a well-known issue, our findings would deserve greater credence. As it is, opinion may change drastically in response to new events or better and different information. Next year things may be much different. Perhaps. But we do not think so.

We have presented detailed political analyses of income maintenance that suggested additional reasons for its lack of popularity, and we have argued that other alternatives, such as bloc grants, would prove more politically attractive. Here we wish to make a theoretical point about opinion on guaranteed income that can only be borne out or disproved by future events. We believe that the latent structure of opinion is hostile to income by right. The greater the amount of the information (regardless of its quality and direction), the more attention is focused on it, the more hostile public opinion will be. The reason is that income maintenance runs counter to basic American values—equality, work, achievement. As soon as income proposals become better known, people who were not concerned will realize they are opposed. For most people, knowledge will extend to the blatant aspects of the proposals—income by right without work—and not to apparent subtleties, such as superiority to public assistance. The concern with dignity will, we predict, be viewed as reward for laziness and worse by most people.

Foreign trade stands as an illustration of an issue on which the latent structure of opinion is negative.[26] By and large, proponents of free trade have high incomes and higher education and opponents have less income and a lower level of education. An education campaign in behalf of free trade, therefore, has the paradoxical effect of increasing public opposition by activating opponents who might otherwise have been quiescent. Since workers and other low-income people outnumber the proponents of free trade, anything that contributes to mobilization of the general public increases the proportion of the populace opposed to that policy. Even if guaranteed income were eventually to gain majority support by those below the poverty line, they are vastly outnumbered by stable working-class and middle-class people who will be activated into opposition.

If the people or the Congress is asked to vote income maintenance up or down, they will say "no." But a straight vote on the principle of guaranteed income is not the only way the issue can be posed. Indeed, we believe that essentially the same purposes could be accomplished indirectly by discrete policy decisions that avoid a losing battle over the central principle until circumstances render it far more palatable.

Let us suppose that President Nixon were to conduct the same kind of interviews with Congressmen as we did and to base his program on what he found. He would first introduce a program to end or mitigate hunger because there is widespread and intense sentiment to that effect. Later on, he would support bloc grants to states and cities because that also has much support. As more funds become available, he would move toward a large employment program for which there is favorable sentiment everywhere.

If we look at the political pressure on the President emanating from Republican governors, we can expect him to propose a national welfare minimum payment. The pressures will mount in light of the Supreme Court decision abolishing residence requirements for welfare recipients. While it appears that the essential nature of categorical aid programs will be maintained, the more obnoxious requirements will be whittled away. The man-in-the-house rule and the effective tax against earning additional income are out or on their way out. Moves are under way to eliminate means tests.

In a second round of policy proposals the "deserving poor" will receive attention. The poor who are employed but who do not receive sufficient wages to maintain their families will be helped through a subsidy to employers. Social security payments will continue their rapid rise. The aged, blind, and disabled will receive something equivalent to a negative income tax.

By the time these individual policy decisions have been made, the only groups left out will be the "undeserving poor"—couples with no children, single men and women, and the relatively small body of men who are unemployed fathers.

Intensive employment programs will be aimed at the men. By that time, however, the cost of the old and new welfare programs will have risen substantially. It will then not seem like such a great leap to blanket in the remaining "undeserving poor." The advantages of having a single, uniform national program will outweigh the incremental cost. The moral objections will remain, but so much ground will have been given away that they will not appear insuperable. Until the very last step all this may be done without raising guaranteed income as an explicit national issue on which careers are broken and elections are lost.

We predicted that the administration would act in the area of poverty in the following steps: [27]

1. Increased effort to end hunger through food stamps
2. A program of revenue sharing with states and cities through bloc grants
3. The construction of a federal employment program
4. A program of national minimum welfare payments, including less obnoxious AFDC requirements and a less burdensome offset to earned income

5. A program designed to provide benefits for the working poor
6. Increases in Social Security benefits
7. Increases in OAA and Aid to the Disabled and Blind
8. Extension of coverage to include those poor presently outside the system of categorical aid.

Our prediction was that these steps would take place little by little, over a relatively extended period of time. We made this prediction on the basis of an assumption that the President would not wish the authorization of new programs without some assurance of substantial funding. This premise proved to be incorrect. The President evidently decided to seek approval of the delivery system prior to the availability of funds. Thus the initial level of funding for his bloc grant proposal amounts to only $500 million. As a consequence, while the President acted as we predicted (at least, our first six predictions), he did so sooner and in a more comprehensive way than we felt he would.

In the best of all worlds, where the nation possesses virtually unlimited resources, income maintenance and bloc grants would exist side by side at high levels of funding. There would be programs to alleviate mass suffering and elite dissatisfaction. No doubt there will for a long time be a little bit of both, but not enough of either. The critical questions of redistribution of income and of political power will remain in flux. Those who wish to defend the Republic, an imperfect set of institutions and practices, will have to do so with an imperfect set of policies and programs.

Appendix

Following Tobin and Pechman, we understand the series of proposals categorized under the concept of guaranteed income to embody at least the following four characteristics: (1) assistance is to be made available on the basis of need alone; (2) need and entitlement to public assistance would be objectively and uniformly measured throughout the nation in terms of the size and composition of the family unit, its income, and its other economic resources; (3) assistance should be paid in cash, not kind, and should be given for free disposition by the recipient, not earmarked for particular uses; (4) any tax placed on income earned in addition to that provided by the supplement should be less than 100 percent.[28] Proposals designed along these lines are of two main types: those known as negative income taxes, and those categorized as social dividend plans. The negative income tax scheme would require that every family with an income above a certain level pay a positive tax, while everyone below this level is given money. The social dividend plans simply call for each family unit to receive a guaranteed minimum income paid to it by the government.

Usually, such plans also require each family to pay a tax on its earned income above a certain level.

As Green and Lampman [29] have noted, both the social dividend and negative rates taxation plans employ the same three basic variables: (1) an income guarantee; (2) a tax rate applied against a tax base; (3) a break-even point, where tax owed equals the allowance received. Any two of these variables would determine the third. Thus a determination of the guarantee and the tax rate would produce a given break-even point; or a prior determination of the tax rate and desired break-even point would point out the level of guarantee necessary, and so on. Both types of plans are basically the same, involving the transfer of money from richer to poorer through taxation. Such plans differ from our present public transfer programs in several important respects. First, they focus on the goal of closing the "poverty gap," of eliminating poverty as defined by some income level (which, in turn, may be defined in absolute dollar terms or in terms of some prescribed standard-of-living level). Second, they emphasize income criteria, usually related to family size, to determine eligibility for payments. This is, of course, in contrast to our present system which provides payments to those in need only if they fall into a "deserving" category; that is, if they are poor for a "good" reason (age, work history, dependent children, physical disability, etc.). Finally, the two systems differ markedly in the degree to which taxes are used as a means for transferring income. This difference is, of course, related to the differences in philosophy which underlie the two types of programs. The various transfer by taxation plans are based on the philosophy that as a matter of right everyone has (should have) access to some of the benefits of modern society's affluence. Those persons or families that fail to obtain such access through the private sphere (as determined by their income level) should be compensated by the public sphere. While the present system allows the government to draw a line between those able and expected to work and those that are not, the guaranteed income schemes do not draw such lines: all those defined as poor should, ideally, be eligible for payments regardless of the reason.

SPECIFIC PLANS

While a number of varying proposals have been put forward, the following five schemes are the ones most often mentioned in the literature on the subject. These plans may be described in terms of the three variables mentioned above: income guaranteed, the rate at which extra income is taxed, and the break-even point or point at which taxes paid and allowances received are equal. An estimation of the cost of each plan is included. All but the two most costly (those of Schwartz and Theobald) would require the maintenance of existing public assistance in substantial amounts if many people are not to be made economically worse off than they are now.

Friedman Proposal [30] sets the guaranteed minimum income equal to 50 percent of the unused personal exemptions of a family minus its minimum standard deduction ($3,000 for a family of four). Thus the amount received would be calculated by taking a family's total income, subtracting it from the exemptions minus minimum standard deduction, and paying the family 50 percent of the result. For example, if income is equal to $2,000 (family of four) and the exemptions minus minimum standard deduction total is equal to $3,000, then $3,000 minus $2,000 equals $1,000, 50 percent of which is then paid to the family ($500). The total income after the transfer would then be $2,500. If the family earned $3,000, it would receive no payment and pay no taxes (break-even point). If its income were over $3,000, it would pay a tax. *Cost: about $10 billion.*

Theobald Proposal [31] sets the guaranteed minimum income equal to $1,000 for each adult, $600 for each child (total of $3,200 for a family of four). Theobald sets his offset rate at 90 percent; thus the family could keep only 10 ¢ of every dollar it earned up to the break-even point. That point in this plan would be $3,556. *Cost: about $30 billion.*

Schwartz Proposal [32] sets the guaranteed minimum income equal to $4,000 for a family of four. Would place no offsetting tax on other income. Families would pay taxes on their allowances as part of their total income. *Cost: about $23 billion.*

McGovern Proposal (*Child Entitlement Plan*) [33] pays $10 a month to every dependent child ($240 a year for family with two children). The payments would be subject to the regular income tax as part of the total income of the family but no special tax on allowance would be levied and the deductions for children would be maintained. *Cost: about $8 billion.*

Lampman Proposal [34] includes a number of proposals which specify different rates of federal subsidy to be added to earnings as reported under the income tax. The subsidy scales are regressive: as earnings increase, the rate of subsidy declines. (See Table 3–1.) *Cost: about $8 billion.*

Tobin Proposal [35] is similar to Lampman, but with some variations. The government would pay each taxpayer below the $6,000 break-even point $400 a year for himself and each member of his family, commencing at zero income (the $6,000 is based on a family of 5). This allowance would then be reduced by 33⅓ cents for every dollar the family earns above $6,000 (⅓ offset). Thus, at an income of $1,200 per person per year for five people, the allowance would be zero. Above that amount, the family would pay taxes at the rate of 33⅓ percent of each additional dollar. Then, at some higher point, the regular tax schedule would apply. *Cost: $12–$15 billion.*

Tobin's plan, like the others, is open to variation. Thus, if the allowance per person is reduced and/or the offset rate on extra earned income is increased, the total cost of the plan goes down. It is also true that as employ-

TABLE 3–1

Lampman Proposal

Allowance Plan: Four-Person Family with Break-even Point of $3,000 a Year

EARNED INCOME	AMOUNT BY WHICH INCOME IS BELOW BREAK-EVEN POINT	RATE OF SUBSIDY	AMOUNT OF SUBSIDY	TOTAL INCOME, INCLUDING SUBSIDY
None	$3,000	50%	$1,500	$1,500
$ 500	2,500	45%	1,125	1,625
1,000	2,000	38%	750	1,750
1,500	1,500	33%	500	2,000
2,000	1,000	25%	250	2,250
2,500	500	25%	125	2,625
2,800	200	25%	50	2,850
3,000	0	0%	0	3,000

SOURCE: C. Green and R. J. Lampman, "Schemes for Transferring Income to the Poor," *Industrial Relations* 6 (February 1967).

ment and wages rise, so will total income. As total income rises (for previously poor families), the need and amount of the subsidy drops and the cost of the plan drops accordingly.

Nixon Plan would leave the provision for federal assistance to the aged, blind, and disabled unchanged, except that a uniform floor of $65 per month for all such recipients would be established. The proposal would abolish the present system of AFDC, substituting the following plan in its place. The proposal would pay a minimum income of $1,600 to each family of four. Additional earned income would be taxed at a 50 percent rate, but the first $720 of income would not serve to reduce the initial subsidy. At this rate the break-even point for a family of four would be $3,920. (See Table 3–2.) The plan is categorical in that it would not apply to the

TABLE 3–2

Nixon Plan

EARNINGS	SUPPLEMENT	TOTAL
$ 0	$1,600	$1,600
720	1,600	2,320
1,000	1,460	2,460
2,000	960	2,960
3,000	460	3,460
3,920	0	3,920

single adult who is not handicapped or aged, or for the married couple without children. It would allow payments to families headed by unemployed males. The plan is work-related in that recipients must accept training opportunities and "suitable work" when offered. Only the mentally and physically incapable, and the mothers of *preschool* children are exempted from this requirement. If a recipient declines a job or training opportunity designated as "suitable," he would lose his portion of the benefit. The remaining funds (for mother and/or children) would be made available through a local welfare agency. *Cost: an estimated $2.5 billion over the present program.*

NOTES

1. To a large extent our argument in this essay ignores the problems associated with the political aspects of bureaucratic behavior. There may be, for example, bureaucrats whose careers are or could be tied to income maintenance, men or groups whose aid could be critical in the construction of a winning coalition. Our primary explanation for this failure on our part is simple lack of time. A second reason, and perhaps a more justifiable one, is that in the case of income maintenance the issue is much more likely to become an important public question than is usually the case in welfare-related matters. As interest groups and constituents become more concerned with an issue, the influence of bureaucracies on congressional decisions decreases. Income by right is not an issue that will slide by unnoticed.

2. We undertook approximately 50 interviews lasting from 15 minutes to over two hours. House interviews were clustered around three major committees: Appropriations, Ways and Means, and Education and Labor. Our Senate interviews, while containing several representatives of the corresponding relevant committees, were much more broadly scattered. We attempted, both in the case of relevant committee members and of others, to cover a broad spectrum of views which we assumed would be distributed according to a number of measures (for example, party, ideological position within party, type of district, region of country). Although the consistency of responses is persuasive to us, no claims of "representativeness" can be made. The interviews themselves were unstructured and open-ended. So few of the Congressmen interviewed knew anything of the various proposals by any name (negative income tax, income supplements, income maintenance, etc.) that a short description was usually necessary. This tended to be followed by the eventual realization on the part of the interviewee that some sort of "guaranteed income" was involved.

3. There was no end of anecdotes on this subject. One Congressman told of being on a football team. One day he was replaced on the varsity by another player. "All week long I worked my ass off," he reported, but still he was kept with the scrubs. On the day of the big game he was named to start, and then played the best game of his life. Summing up, this Congressman said that "the point lay in incentive." "You take that away and people won't play as hard. They lose the satisfaction of winning while the country loses the benefit of their contribution." Another Congressman made a homely observation to the effect that if you take 50 gallons of pure, clean water and one gallon of bad water and mix them up, you get 51 gallons of bad water. "In the same way," he said, "the guaranteed income, with its destructive quality in terms of incentives, would infect the entire country. Some people would want that because that would leave us in a position where we'd have to move toward socialism and the elimination of freedom." As a final example among many choice statements, a Congressman told the story of a man stranded in the desert, with not a tree in sight. A bear approached. What do you do? "Why, up that tree!" he exclaimed. But there was no tree, we reminded him. "There damn well had to be a tree," he said. His moral was that if the pressure is there, people will find a way to alleviate it.

4. See A. Wildavsky, "The Analysis of Issue-Contexts in the Study of Decision-Making," *Journal of Politics* 24 (1962): 717–732, for a discussion of the structure of similar polarizing issues.

5. See Nelson W. Polsby, "Policy Analysis and Congress," in "The Analysis and Evaluation of Public Expenditures," *Joint Economic Committee,* U.S. Congress, 3:493, for an analytical discussion of this process.

6. J. C. Vadakin, "A Critique of the Guaranteed Annual Income," *The Public Interest* (Spring 1964); G. H. Hildebrand, "Second Thoughts on the Negative Income Tax," *Industrial Relations* (February 1967).

7. Figures taken from *Report of the National Advisory Commission on Civil Disorders,* Chapter 17, part III.

8. It should be clear that we are speaking here of the indignity of being poor per se in a nation where many consider poverty a sign of failure. These arguments do not touch upon the indignities visited upon the poor because their lack of resources closes off so many alternatives to them. Any money from any means helps to alleviate petty victimization by landlords, markets, etc. The syndrome of relative deprivation usually associated with arguments about poverty must refer more to the psychological problems than to the physical facts of being poor.

9. The analogy is suggested by John Schaar, "Some Ways of Thinking about Equality," *Journal of Politics* 26 (1964).

10. E. Mueller, "Public Attitudes Toward Fiscal Programs," *Quarterly Journal of Economics* (May 1965), 215.

11. Schaar, *op. cit.* Few Congressmen interviewed felt that equality in the distribution of goods was required by any moral consideration. Their primary fear was that income maintenance, ostensibly designed to end poverty, would end up as a proposal for total equality of income, indistinguishable from "socialistic" planning.

12. Hildebrand, *op. cit.*

13. In several states, an earned income of $1 not only disqualified potential payment recipients but also made them ineligible for health care and other nonincome benefits.

14. E.g., R. Theobald's proposal for a 10 percent "premium" (90 percent offset) in his *Free Men and Free Markets* (New York: C. N. Potter, 1963).

15. G. F. Break, "Income Taxes and Incentives to Work: An Empirical Study," *American Economic Review* (September 1957).

16. Cf. the controversy between L. E. Gallaway, "Negative Income Taxes and the Elimination of Poverty," *National Tax Journal* (September 1966) and M. Taussig, "Negative Income Taxes and the Elimination of Poverty: Comment," *National Tax Journal* (September 1967).

17. *Report of the National Advisory Commission on Civil Disorders,* Chapter 17, Part III, p. 457.

18. C. Green and R. J. Lampman, "Schemes for Transferring Income to the Poor," *Industrial Relations* 6 (February 1967).

19. Gallup Poll, June 16, 1969. Sixty-four percent of those with an annual family income of $7,000–10,000 oppose such plans; 68 percent of those in the $10,000-and-over category are in opposition.

20. The objection might be overcome if it could be demonstrated that these proposals would dampen rural migration to urban areas. National welfare standards would have a similar effect.

21. Estimates taken from Vadakin, *op. cit.*

22. This, of course, does not apply to all aspects of the poverty program. Some parts (for example, Head Start, Upward Bound) have produced political benefits at little political cost. The same thing cannot be said about those elements "sold" to the Congress as means for alleviating urban tensions (for example, community action).

23. See Everett F. Cataldo, Richard M. Johnson, Lyman A. Kellstedt, "Social Strain and Urban Violence," in Louis H. Masotti and Don R. Bowen, eds., *Riots and Rebellion: Civil Violence in the Urban Community* (Beverly Hills: Sage Publications, 1968), pp. 285–298; and Jeffrey M. Paige, "Collective Violence and the Culture of Subordination" (Ph.D. dissertation, University of Michigan, 1968).

24. A. Wildavsky, "The Empty-Head Blues: Black Rebellion and White Reaction," *The Public Interest,* no. 11 (Spring 1968), pp. 3–16, Chapter 1 of this volume.

25. Forty-eight percent favor; 45 percent oppose; 7 percent no opinion.

26. See Raymond Bauer, Ithiel Pool, Lewis Anthony Dexter, "Public Attitudes on Foreign Trade," in Raymond Bauer et al., eds., *American Business and Public Policy* (New York: Atherton Press, 1964), pp. 80–104.

27. This essay was circulated in draft form prior to President Nixon's recent message containing his welfare reform package, so as to provide an opportunity to compare our predictions with his actions.

28. Tobin, Pechman, and Mieszkowski, "Is a Negative Income Tax Practical?" *The Yale Law Journal* 77 (November 1967).

29. Green and Lampman, *op. cit.*

30. Milton Friedman, *Capitalism and Freedom* (Chicago: University of Chicago Press, 1962).

31. Theobald, *op. cit.*

32. Edward E. Schwartz, "An End to the Means Test," in R. Theobald, ed., *The Guaranteed Income: Next Step in Economic Evolution?* (Garden City, N.Y.: Doubleday, 1966).

33. Senate Bill No. 562, 91st Congress, 1st Session, January 22 (legislative day, January 10), 1969.

34. Green and Lampman, *op. cit.*

35. This is one of a number of variations offered by James Tobin. Cf. his "Improving the Economic Status of the Negro," *Daedalus* (Fall 1965); "Is a Negative Income Tax Practical?" *op. cit.*

5

THE POLITICS OF ABM

I

Issues have lives of their own. Men cannot often choose the ground on which to fight major issues; they must take what the world offers up. There is always the danger, then, that the issue will control the men, rather than the men the issue. The recent controversy over the Safeguard antiballistic missile is a classic case in point. Thus the advocates of ABM—people who in the past were likely to be great believers in the prevailing American doctrine of nuclear deterrence—have taken the lead in challenging that doctrine, while opponents of ABM—people more or less of the left and previously skeptical of the same doctrine—have become ever more firmly wedded to it. Thus, too, some of those who are against ABM are willing to entertain a launch-on-warning policy (that is, a policy which would have the U.S. fire all its missiles to avoid having them destroyed in a suspected enemy attack) for the 1970s, while those who favor the ABM are bitterly opposed to such a policy. And thus, finally, some elements of the opposition to ABM have talked themselves into believing that the 1972 Presidential campaign should be run on the basis of opposition to the power of the military in the United States. One thing, however, is clear: it all began when an always precarious nuclear balance between the United States and the Soviet Union was apparently threatened by new weapons.

American strategy for deterrence is primitive. The United States seeks to have a sufficient number and diversity of nuclear weapons to guarantee that, in the event of a surprise attack by the Soviet Union, it would be able to strike back with enough force to destroy the aggressor. Since the Soviet Union also has sufficient capability to retaliate after an attack, each country is believed to be deterred from launching a surprise attack against the other by the threat of mutual destruction. It is this precarious equilibrium that Robert McNamara has called "assured destruction." No one can know

Reprinted from *Commentary*, November 1969, pp. 55–63, by permission. Copyright © 1969 by the American Jewish Committee.

for sure, of course, how much prospective damage to people and objects would actually deter a would-be aggressor. Estimating the number of casualties required is essentially a mystical enterprise, and the magic number has shifted over time. Since the Soviet Union absorbed 20 million casualties in World War II, that figure is usually considered to be the lowest tolerable point. The highest can run well over 100 million. If a successfully deterrent second strike is put at or below, say, 30 million casualties, then almost all U.S. Minuteman missiles are unnecessary because Polaris and other weapons can do the job. If, on the other hand, the number of "hostages" is set at close to 100 million, then missiles are needed, and protecting them—which is what ABM purports to do—becomes much more significant.

The ability to destroy an opponent after he has launched a first strike depends not only on the yield and accuracy of one's nuclear weapons, but on the number of different ways in which they can be delivered. If there is only one major weapons system, such as the Minuteman, there is always the chance that it will malfunction or be wiped out. American deterrence has, therefore, depended on having at least three ways of getting back at an enemy—the Minutemen in hardened silos on American soil; bombers at "soft" airfields; and Polaris submarines, with their missiles hidden in the depths of the world's oceans. Redundancy has become an essential part of nuclear defense. Yet no one can say how many separate deterrent forces are required to make certain that not all could be overwhelmed at the same time.

American deterrent forces were built to be effective under the conditions of the 1960s. In the process of raising billions of dollars to build them, the weapons were oversold to Congress and the public as relatively permanent answers to nuclear defense. The more sophisticated people involved always realized (and sometimes said in public) that no system of defense could be good for all time or even necessarily for more than a decade. But it is fair to say that these words of caution were lost. What has happened in the last few years is that the effectiveness of two of our three major deterrent systems has been called into serious question.

Of the three, manned bombers have always been the most uncertain because they can be easily destroyed unless there is time for them to take to the air. In November 1967, Secretary of Defense Robert McNamara reported that the Soviet Union was developing a Fractional Orbital Bombardment System that could deliver nuclear weapons from missiles flying in low orbit around the earth. While the accuracy of such a system is poor as compared with intercontinental ballistic missiles, FOB's are more than good enough to wipe out airplanes on the ground. Their low trajectory makes it difficult to detect them with regular long-range radars; and even with newer, over-the-horizon radars, warning time is sharply reduced. In addition, manned bombers are exceedingly vulnerable to missiles launched from submarines.

In December 1967 the Department of Defense reported the development of the Multiple Independently Targetable Re-entry Vehicle (MIRV), a system in which a single vehicle carries multiple warheads that can be maneuvered to separate targets on independent courses. President Johnson's budget message in 1969 called for expenditures to provide multiple warheads for the land-based Minuteman Three and the submarine-launched Poseidon. At the same time, Secretary of Defense Clark Clifford noted the rapid growth of the Soviet Union's force of intercontinental ballistic missiles, which he warned might equal those of the United States by 1970 and would probably have larger payloads. Were the Soviet Union to continue its present rate of deployment, and were the Soviet SS-9 missile to continue to be developed as a MIRV, there might be grounds for questioning the ability of the Minuteman to strike back.

Hence the great ABM debate. Proponents of ABM argued that by the mid-1970s the Soviet Union could have a sufficient number of MIRV's (with accuracies that the United States is capable of achieving today) to destroy about 950 of the 1,000 Minutemen. Opponents argued that the Soviet Union would be able to destroy only a much smaller number and that a sufficient proportion of Minutemen would be left to wreak unacceptable damage. The debate is hard going for even the most informed observers, and one wishes the protagonists would confront each other directly so that the differences in their assumptions and modes of analysis could be exposed.[1]

My purpose, however, is not to make a case for or against the ABM, or even to give a complete account of the multitude of considerations raised by each side. The books and congressional hearings on which this essay is based contain enough of that to satisfy anyone.[2] Now that the Senate has decided by one vote to approve initial deployment of the ABM, rehashing the debate would in any case be anticlimactic and no more informative than it was at the time. We can learn something, I believe, by asking not who was right but why the participants adopted the positions they did. There is more, in other words, to be gained from an examination of why ABM was an issue at all than by evaluating the relative merits of the positions, although some such evaluation is necessary by way of background. Let us begin, therefore, by considering important arguments that do not matter—important because they appeared endlessly in the debate, but that did not matter because they were inherently inconclusive.

II

Everyone agrees that ABM is an exceedingly complex technological system. Even if it does not quite live up to Senator Edward Kennedy's advertisement of it as "the single most complex undertaking man has yet set for himself in his time on earth," the system will not be easy to build and make effective. It requires radars to look over the horizon, track incoming weapons, filter out decoys, and pass information on to other computers which are connected to the Spartan and Sprint missiles and to various command-and-control arrangements, which must guide the outgoing missiles rapidly to the target so that the incoming missiles are destroyed high enough in the atmosphere to prevent serious damage. The Spartan, whose present range is 300–500 miles, would get first crack, and the Sprint, whose range is around 25 miles, would take over as missiles got nearer their targets. In initial deployment, these Spartans and Sprints would be placed around two Minuteman complexes.

Because of its complexity, endless disputes have raged about whether the ABM can do its job or indeed whether it will ever work at all. The major argument of opponents is that defensive systems, like the ABM, are likely to fail because adequate testing is difficult if not impossible. ". . . The history of initial failures of far simpler systems suggests that the probability of catastrophic failure of a defensive ABM is quite high," says physicist Leonard Rodberg. "It is much higher, in fact, than for offensive systems, which are less intricate and more susceptible to adequate testing." The advocates of ABM respond by saying that "no strategic weapons system can be tested realistically in a nuclear war environment whether the system is defensive or offensive." If we are to be around to observe the results, they contend, analysis of nuclear war must proceed without testing in the real environment. But even if it is not desirable to test a system under realistic conditions, proponents of ABM believe it is still possible to take precautions. "If I am concerned at my summer home about being attacked by a mountain lion," Dr. Frederick Seitz said in defense of ABM, "I can go through a great deal of significant preparatory work. I can test cartridges in the basement. I can fire blanks in a gun, and be pretty sure that the system will work, if a mountain lion appears. I don't need to acquire a mountain lion, and have him attack me as an initial test."

In the time-honored tradition of finding counterexamples, Professor Abram Chayes arrived at a different conclusion. "If I were buying a gun to defend my house against burglars, and half the gun experts I talked to told me it wouldn't shoot, and I knew I couldn't try it out until the burglars got there, I think I would start looking around for some other way to protect my house." By now, the nature of the discussion should be clear to everyone. If you believe in the desirability of the ABM for other reasons, then you believe it will, must, and can be made to work. If you decide for other reasons that the ABM is undesirable, then you attempt to show that it cannot and will not work.

How does a decision-maker without technical expertise make a decision when those who should know are so divided? Since he cannot go into the technical problem, he may decide by placing confidence in the advice of men whom he trusts most, perhaps because their policy preferences are generally similar to his own. Argument by authority is not helpful in public, however, because there are so many eminent men on both sides. So the disputants search for historical experience that will appear relevant and accessible to laymen. What does history teach? The proponents of ABM say history teaches that the preponderance of scientists said the H-bomb could not be developed and they were wrong. They point to the outstanding success with complex missions involving interacting technologies, such as Polaris and Apollo. They observe that in the past scientists have been surprised at how rapidly systems considered impossible came into being. Dr. Seitz mentions television, radar, jet aircraft, intercontinental ballistic missiles, and so on. The other side has no difficulty in finding its examples of failures from the Maginot Line, all-weather interceptors, the Distance Early Warning line, Skybolt, and more. What history has to teach us, apparently, is that complex systems often do not work but that sometimes they do and, in addition, that it is very difficult to tell in advance which of these two categories a weapons system belongs in.

One way to resolve the question is to agree with Abram Chayes that ". . . there is an inherent advantage for the side that deploys last. If the offense can see the characteristics of the ABM system ranged against it, it can adopt the tactics best able to overcome that particular system." If your opponent attacks you, of course, before you are ready to respond to a new system, then you are in trouble. There is no system, Albert Wohlstetter remarks, about which it cannot be said, ". . . you can always get something better if you wait." But the argument can be turned around: instead of waiting, perhaps the best way to get information about whether a system will work is to try it. Opponents of ABM would not regard this response as satisfactory.

Throughout the debate on the ABM there has been a swirl of contention about the relative costs of offense and defense. The point has been made, for instance, that the Soviet Union could always build more offensive missiles to negate the defensive value of the ABM. But the point is irrelevant; if enough money is spent, any offense can overcome a defense, and any defense an offense. The question remains how much each will cost, and— even more critical—what is the presumed advantage of offense over defense per dollar spent. The Chayes-Wiesner group contend that "the offense problem is simpler than that of defense, because ICBMs are pretargeted, and they do not have to be aimed within a few moments of launch on the basis of recently acquired target data. Moreover, the timing of the launch is not critical with offensive weapons, unlike the ABM, which must be able to respond on call against a target approaching at seventy-two hundred miles per hour."

Similar considerations, however, can be adduced to support the alleged advantages of a defensive system. In an effort to even out the debate, Albert Wohlstetter has stated that "an increment in defense offsets a larger increment in offense because the defense of missiles doesn't require defending all missiles and one can choose which silos to defend. . . . More-over the defense can choose that at the last minute. The defense has the last move in this sort of a system, whereas the offense cannot know which one is going to be chosen and therefore must attack all." Freeman Dyson takes the position that defensive forces eventually will triumph because they are situated much closer to the scene of action and can adapt more quickly than offensive forces, which must make their moves thousands of miles away and attempt to exert control over incredibly long distances. Here again, as in the dispute over the technical operability of the ABM, we have a clash of rival intuitions that has its interest as such, but is of no real help to anyone trying to make up his mind on an important issue.

In a similar category belongs the dispute over the efficacy of penetration aids, such as decoys and metal chaff, that are designed to confuse radar and thus render an ABM system useless. People who are against ABM claim that it would be relatively easy for the Chinese, not to mention the Rus-sians, to develop simple and cheap penetration aids that would negate high-altitude defense. Supporters of ABM point out that the United States has spent several billion dollars on penetration aids, and experience has shown that they are difficult to devise and deploy. They conclude that the Chinese will have great trouble along these lines, but that countermeasures against Russian efforts are feasible and desirable. To this their opponents reply that one never can tell but what the clever Chinese will make some-thing that American designers have not thought of.

A more interesting charge against the ABM is that its deployment would result in shifting the power to make life-and-death decisions from the Pres-ident to low-level technicians, or even from persons to machines. By the time the President got warning of incoming missiles there might be any-where from 5 to 25 minutes in which to make a decision. If there is to be any certainty of response, some people believe that the actual decision will have to be made by the men in charge of operating Safeguard or by the computers on which they rely. "The point is not," Bill Moyers writes,

that under these or any other circumstances the President relinquishes the ac-tual command decisions—he does not—but that the option when it reaches him is almost no option at all. If the system is to have any chance of intercept-ing actual enemy missiles, it is difficult to see how the President can avoid sur-rendering his decision-making authority to the computers and the junior mili-tary officers who stand over them. The command decision becomes little more than a hurried human reflex, devoid of political and moral consideration, to confirm what the machines say is inevitable.

This statement appears plausible until one considers what the situation would be if there were no ABM. What would a President of the United States do if word reached him that a number of intercontinental ballistic missiles were approaching the United States? Advocates insist that ABM would better enable the United States to ride out an attack with some assurance that there would be enough left with which to respond. There would then be no need to make a precipitate decision that might turn out to begin nuclear war by mistake. "Deciding to launch our ICBM might be the most important decision that will ever have been made," Albert Wohlstetter told the Senate Armed Services Committee. "That is the decision for World War III. I do not want to decide that on radar data. I can think of ways such data might be spurious." The choice, then, is between two kinds of errors: the error that results in sending up an ABM that will explode at high altitude over or near our own country; and the error that will send nuclear missiles winging their way to destroy a large part of the Soviet population, touching off a wave of retaliation, if the Soviets had not intended (or had not launched) an attack in the first place.

Another reason given for rejecting ABM is that it would make a future arms-control agreement more difficult. ABM would add another item to be negotiated, thus increasing the complexity of an already tortuous series of negotiations. As the Russians already have an ABM, however, it is hard to see how this matter can be left out of the negotiations. And in any case, one might think that opponents of the ABM, having insisted that it is too complex to work, should have no reason to believe that the Soviet Union would feel compelled to take countermeasures against it. But ABM opponents say that the Russians will have to *believe* that the system might work and therefore will take precautions against it by increasing the size of their missile force, thus further inhibiting the prospects of an arms-control agreement.

It should come as no surprise that advocates of ABM believe on the other hand that the system will make a positive contribution toward arms control. One of the important barriers to any arms-control agreement is the number of parties who refuse to join. By improving the possibilities for effective defense against lesser powers, ABM, according to its supporters, will enhance the chances for concluding arms-control agreements without the participation of those lesser powers—the more so since the possession of ABM systems by the two superpowers would enable them to relax a little about minor violations.

My own conclusion is that deploying the Safeguard ABM would complicate the arms-control negotiations in some ways and make them easier in others, and that it is not easy to draw the balance. The kind of decision required may be illustrated by analogy to problems concerned with the nuclear test-ban treaty. The unrelenting march of technology always makes it possible for someone to claim that new developments will invalidate the safeguards that exist and hence the value of the agreement, and the fact that there are already dangers that presently cannot be guarded against reduces the prospect of agreement still further. Yet a reasonable man might risk a bet on future American technology. Rather than permitting underground testing, for instance, simply because there were no existing ways of indirect detection (and the Soviets would not allow on-site inspection), I would have preferred taking the risk that, given sufficient motivation, the United States could develop the necessary technology. In the ABM case, a belief that the system is essential would quickly resolve the technological doubts in its favor. Thus the question is not merely one of technology, unless there are strong scientific reasons for believing that the development is impossible *in principle;* rather, the question is one of assessing the technological probabilities and deciding the direction in which we wish to take our risks.

People on both sides of the debate have succumbed to the "funny numbers" syndrome. These are arguments that are constructed in such a way that neither the ABM nor any other system could ever be rejected or, alternatively, approved on the basis of them. Professor Edward Teller, for instance, observes that "the first year of the 'Safeguard' deployment will cost only one half as much as we spend on defense in one week." Since almost all systems have low initial costs, it is hard to think of one that would have been ruled out by this approach; besides, if defense expenditures were drastically reduced, the amount allocated to Safeguard would turn out to be a larger proportion of the whole. Phyllis Schlafly, coauthor of three books on nuclear strategy, *The Grave Diggers, Strike from Space,* and *The Betrayers,* brings to our attention the fact that the Safeguard ABM "will cost only $8 per person per year. Isn't your life worth $8 per year?" she asks with admirable restraint.

On the opposite side of the argument, we encounter talk of the lives that could be saved and the human spirits that could be nurtured if the money to be spent on ABM were devoted to other purposes. The lists that have been drawn up include the "10 million Americans [who] go to bed hungry each night; 26 million [who] live in abject poverty; . . . polluted streams and air, housing, education, transportation. . . ." Of course, anyone who loves the outdoors and wishes to spend money to keep nature in an unspoiled condition must also feel ashamed that his programs will divert funds from widows and orphans.

Finally, John Kenneth Galbraith has found an infallible way of winning the debate over ABM—he simply categorizes everyone who might conceivably be on the other side as a member of the "Military-Industrial Complex." He includes not only military officers, civilians in the Pentagon, defense contractors, members of the Armed Services Committees, but also ". . . the university scientists and those in such defense-oriented organizations as RAND, the Institute for Defense Analyses, and the Hudson Institute who think professionally about weapons and weapons systems and the strategy of their use." Just to make sure he has cast the net wide enough, Galbraith also includes social scientists who "responded eagerly to invitations to spend the summer at RAND. They devoted their winters to seminars on the strategy of defense and deterrence. The only question was whether a man could get a high enough security clearance."

Unfortunately for Galbraith's point, if it were not for the fact that research institutes and universities have spread knowledge of defense policy around the country, it would have been difficult to have a debate on the ABM at all. Indeed, the ABM issue is the only one involving strategic forces in the past decade that was not brought to public attention by disputes within the military services, but rather by "defense intellectuals," and the most impressive arguments on *both* sides have been advanced by these same intellectuals. Galbraith, however, has covered his tracks: all one has to do in order to win an exit visa from the Military-Industrial Complex is to denounce the ABM.

There are, of course, many different phenomena that go under the name of the Military-Industrial Complex. There is reason to be concerned about the large number of ex-Pentagon employees who work for defense contractors, and the difficulties inherent in close and intelligent congressional supervision of military programs are deserving of scrutiny and debate. More serious still in my opinion, though never mentioned, is the fascination of the general public with hardware and technological solutions to complex human problems. The rush on all sides to exclaim that the Apollo moonshot proves that the United States can solve any problem on which it sets its mind is but a recent reminder. But these and other problems cannot be solved by using MIC as a mindless slogan with which to castigate one's enemies. If the people who use it really believed in its full implications, there would in fact be no need for them to debate the merits of individual projects. They could just oppose anything and everything supported by the military on *a priori* grounds.

III

The ABM has several potential uses . . . and abuses. It can be used as a defensive weapon to protect the Minuteman deterrent. It can protect against a small attack from China or any other power in possession of only a few deliverable nuclear weapons. And it may be emplaced around cities in an attempt to reduce civilian casualties in the event of nuclear war. The variety of uses to which an ABM might be put has occasioned dispute within the defense community and has resulted in different emphases being placed upon different purposes at different times. Unable to decide whether an ABM designed simply to protect cities was justified, former Secretary of Defense Robert McNamara came out for a defensive system, allegedly to protect against Chinese attack. The Nixon administration at first adopted a city-defense objective, called Sentinel, and then turned to the present Safeguard whose objective is to protect part of the Minuteman deterrent force. Yet any one of these uses can be converted into any other.

The second stage of Safeguard, for example, will have some modest city-defense capability since it must cover a substantial area of the United States in order to perform its primary mission.

The shifts and turns in the history of the ABM have interacted with the pre-existing anxieties of its opponents to produce an atmosphere of maximum distrust. The anomalies introduced by the change of objectives I have just described, together with the impossibility of adequately distinguishing one from another, have served to infuriate opponents of the ABM. What were they to think when the administration, which initially proposed the ABM to protect against an improbable Chinese attack, then offered to give it up if the Russians gave up theirs? The suspicion soon grew that the idea was to have the ABM no matter what the reason; rationales were seen as pure window-dressing. Thus, a long-time supporter of the defense program like Senator Stuart Symington could speak of "this new and pretty tricky sudden shift from the cities to the missile sites."

The way in which the ABM issue arose gave its detractors a special political opportunity. After the Sentinel ABM was proposed, and immediate efforts were undertaken to select sites for deployment of the Sprint and Spartan missiles near major cities, there was a political uproar reminiscent of the debate over civil defense in President Kennedy's time. In those days the left was outraged at increasing militarism and the ludicrous idea that a defense was possible against nuclear weapons. The right was briefly interested, but eventually decided that the whole thing was cowardly and that offense rather than defense should be emphasized. Despite the conviction expressed at the time that industrial firms, which stood to make billions from having us all burrow underground, would therefore secure a decision to proceed, virtually no support materialized for civil defense and it died.

The Sentinel ABM apparently generated just such a negative reaction among the people it was supposedly designed to protect. Hence it began to appear that there would be wider political opposition to the Sentinel than would normally be the case in matters of military policy and that ABM, therefore, might become an issue on which to take a stand against militarism. Just as many people began to get committed to turning the proposed ABM into a major political issue, however, the Nixon administration changed its line; the program was renamed Safeguard and was directed toward defense of the Minuteman deterrent force. By removing the ABM sites from the cities, where they caused alarm and could be criticized as an attempt to protect the populace prior to an attack on the Soviet Union, the administration reduced the opportunity to make a good political issue out of ABM. By that time, however, the opponents were both angry and committed and began to pick up every rock they could find to throw at the proposal.

The most apparent rationale for opposing the Safeguard ABM is lack of trust in the military. It is perhaps not surprising that an organization like Women Strike for Peace should commit itself "to defeat the ABM and to attempt to turn the country away from the tide of militarism before it is too late." But when the Governor of North Dakota says, ". . . our nation is swept along by contrived hysteria to keep the pipeline of the defense industries full," the defense establishment is obviously in trouble. Evidently, the lesson learned from the Vietnam war has been that the judgment of the military (even when supported by the President) should be questioned everywhere. One should always be as skeptical of the claims of government as of declarations of love, promises of eternal peace, assurances of investment profits, or any other relationship where ego, self-interest, and uncertainty are involved.

But one cannot challenge everything at once. Learning where and when to trust will be difficult. From World War II the U.S. learned to arm itself in order to secure peace. It was wise, Americans thought, to intervene before little wars became big ones and little dictators thought of world conquest. The Vietnam experience apparently teaches us that if a nation has arms it may use them and small wars may become large if big countries are involved. The trouble is that the United States seems capable of learning only one lesson at a time—"look before you leap" (Vietnam) supplants "he who hesitates is lost" (Munich)—when what needs to be asked is under which conditions these proverbial lessons apply.

Since there is little trust, anger at alleged deception is always near the surface. While many opponents of the ABM like to think of themselves as apostles of change, they argue that nothing has happened in the last few years to alter the requirements for nuclear defense. Senator Edward M. Kennedy, for example, writes in his introduction to ABM: *An Evaluation of the Decision to Deploy an Antiballistic Missile System:* "Our nuclear forces are so large, and so sophisticated, that they would deter an enemy from attacking us while we sought an arms limitation agreement with the Soviets over some predetermined period, just as they have deterred our enemies over all the years of the nuclear age." The same line is taken by Theodore Sorensen, who asserts: "Having assured the West Europeans for some years that, even after suffering a first strike, we possessed a second-strike capacity of weapons systems in the ground, underwater, or in the air sufficient to destroy any attacker several times over, we will have a difficult task convincing them now that an ABM system is needed to make this deterrent effective." After a decade in which billions have been spent on nuclear weapons, it galls the critics of ABM to hear others claim that the expenditures were not good for an indefinite future. It seems more likely to them that as the war in Vietnam is—one hopes—being phased out, new excuses are being found to replenish military expenditure.

The climate of opinion in the United States, however, is still such that arguments have to be phrased in terms of advocacy of national defense. No one can win broad support by saying he wants to leave the nation defenseless. So the opponents of ABM must worry about our nuclear deterrent and they must have alternatives to ABM in case the deterrent should be threatened. In order to avoid what they consider the overriding present evil—a useless ABM that will divert billions from domestic uses and strengthen the military politically—they are easily led into excessive reliance on a strategy of assured destruction. Under this doctrine the superpowers would maintain large arsenals of intercontinental ballistic missiles and make no persuasive efforts to defend their own populations; thus, each nation's people becomes hostage for its own good behavior. The attraction of assured destruction as a strategy is that it would appear to result in a nuclear standoff while ruling out all sorts of fanciful and expensive ways of making believe that the nation might render itself safe in the face of nuclear weapons.

The adherents of assured destruction (under which the total vulnerability of the U.S. and the Soviet Union to attack by each other is the guarantor of peace) see every move to increase defensive facilities as a trick to unleash an offensive holocaust. What unimaginable things might an American government not do, they ask, if civil defense or an ABM gave it the idea that it could escape total destruction in a nuclear war? Then the vast urge for destruction in a people prone to violence might spill out and engulf the world. The image of America as a modern dinosaur, with an incredible technical arsenal and a pea-sized brain, comes to the fore. For this image the adherents of assured destruction would substitute that of a man asking his friends, half in terror and half in exaltation, to hold him back lest he commit an act of murder, so great is his deep-seated potential for violence; such is the emotive level of those who believe that for America the only guarantee of national morality lies in being defenseless. This profound lack of trust in a whole people long antedates Vietnam and suggests that any effort at defense would meet with fierce opposition.

But, an advocate of ABM might ask, how would a policy of assured destruction work in practice? Imagine that a nuclear missile is coming. What can the United States do? The proponents of assured destruction say that the United States is capable of a devastating attack on the Soviet Union no matter what happens. Yet that would not stop the missile, and the President is not to be envied who might have to explain why, though he knew missiles were coming, strategic doctrine required that he have no means of intercepting them.

This and other challenges to the doctrine of assured destruction have been put forward by many of the authors represented in *Why ABM?*, a volume published by the Hudson Institute. These men regard mutual suicide as an unsatisfactory basis for national defense; they advocate a different theory of deterrence, calling for substantial ballistic-missile defense by the superpowers together with phased reductions in offensive missiles, which are defined as missiles that can reach the other country. Such a policy could vastly reduce the incentives for third powers to get nuclear weapons and to engage in nuclear blackmail. It would also reduce damage in case of accident or a breakdown of deterrence. It would not, probably, reduce the chances of nuclear war below the present posture of mutual annihilation but it would not markedly increase them either. Should some temporary breakdown in deterrence occur, it would be possible to limit damage and have somebody around to learn the lesson and push for more complete disarmament.

It should be pointed out that responsible opponents of ABM never say that they do not care about protecting the deterrent. On the contrary, they care very much. "I think," Abram Chayes says, "if the Soviet threat should materialize along the lines projected by Secretary Laird, which I believe to be unlikely, and if the strategic arms-control talks fail, we then will have to consider very urgently the goal of protecting our deterrent." Nevertheless, these opponents would still wish to have an alternative to ABM should the Soviets appear in the late 1970s to be able to destroy a very large proportion of Minutemen. According to Herbert York, if we think that two years are available before the period of maximum danger, more Minutemen can be deployed. If four years is a more feasible time period, the number of Polaris submarines could also be increased.

The difficulty with these alternatives is that they would vastly increase the amount of American destructive power and hence might exacerbate Soviet fears of a possible surprise attack. Should the danger period be numbered in terms of weeks, it is possible to go on airborne alert, but this posture would be prohibitively expensive over a longer period of time. These alternatives to ABM, therefore, are either limited, unfeasible, or would tend to increase markedly the destructive power of nuclear weapons and the anxiety of the major powers.

Those who believe that the United States should defend its Minutemen with ABM state that their policy is designed to avoid the worst strategic alternative—launching missiles before they have a chance to be destroyed. Professor Richard Rosecrance insists that:

We *should* defend Minuteman because we ourselves could respond in escalatory and undesirable ways if we fail to reinsure Minuteman's invulnerability to attack. Imagine a situation in which the BMEWS radars give indication of an incoming attack on our land-based forces. And surely Minuteman is what the SS-9's would shoot at. One can imagine enormous pressure upon an American President to launch Minuteman before the incoming warheads land on target. He might or might not yield to that pressure. But he would know that if he did not launch Minuteman within approximately 20 minutes and the radar warning was accurate, he could expect a very large proportion, between 90–99 per cent, of the force to be destroyed in their silos. Under these circumstances it would not be surprising if he authorized launch of Minuteman. Such a decision would certainly result in saving Minuteman, but if the radar indications were erroneous, the measures taken by the President to protect our force could have catastrophic consequences for our own society.

However incredible the idea of a launch-on-warning posture may appear, it too has seriously been mentioned as an alternative to ABM. Jerome Wiesner, for example, writes:

However, if one is truly worried about a full-scale SS-9 attack, it is possible to launch the Minuteman and Titan missiles after unequivocal warning of a large attack is received but before the attacking missiles have hit. The missile warning could be associated with other knowledge, such as information about attacks on bomber bases, Polaris submarines, etc., to provide confirmation that an attack is really under way.

The most feasible immediate alternative to ABM would be the superhardening of existing Minuteman sites. The trouble here is that we do not know the precise effectiveness of hardening much beyond present levels, and in any case as missiles became more and more accurate, whatever effectiveness hardening might have would be rapidly diminished. What the advocates of ABM dislike about hardening—it cannot be easily expanded or adapted—is exactly what the opponents like about it. It is a limited response to a limited threat.

Who could have foretold that eminent spokesmen for peace would seriously contemplate a launch-on-warning policy, or would pledge themselves to rush into huge provocations in the 1970s if a Soviet threat materializes, or would glory in the vulnerability of the populace as a guarantor of restraint? Indeed we have a case here of men being controlled by an issue.

IV

We come now to perhaps the most interesting question of all: why did the ABM debate turn into one of *the* major domestic issues of the decade? The principal reason, in my opinion, is that the debate lent itself to manipulation by people whose primary political interests lay elsewhere— specifically, in bringing the Vietnam war to an end and in opposing on general grounds high defense expenditures. These people had perceived, no doubt correctly, that a major conflict over funds to support the war, or a direct assault on the military men involved, would be politically ineffective. (Despite the evident unpopularity of our engagement in Vietnam, there appears to be no good way of making a political issue out of funds denied to American men under fire.) What the ABM debate offered, quite simply, was a temporary tactical opportunity to test whether opposition to military influence in American life was a sufficiently powerful issue on which to base a successful Presidential campaign.

John Kenneth Galbraith's volume, *How to Control the Military,* is quite explicit on this point. "The goal, all must remember," Galbraith insists, "is to get all military power under firm political control. This means electing a President on this issue next time. This, above all," he repeats, lest we forget so soon, "must be the issue in the next election." If it were up to him, there would be "an organization alert to the military power" in virtually every congressional district that would exact specific promises from candidates "to resist military programs."

Now, the idea of a campaign based on opposition to the military is open to criticism on several counts. A theorist of public opinion, for example, without recourse to actual evidence, might predict that an issue like ABM would not be understood by most voters. The minority of the population who felt they knew something about the matter, moreover, would probably be taken from the better educated portion of the electorate that is traditionally Republican and conservative, and hence would most likely be in favor of military programs in general. All the polls would bear this prediction out. In addition, while there is probably general agreement that defense expenditures are too high, this is not equivalent to support for a holy war against the military profession. To his personal credit, Galbraith says that his "is not an anti-military crusade. Generals and admirals, and soldiers, sailors, and airmen are not the object of attack. The purpose is to return the military establishment to its traditional position in the American political system."

Yet however laudable the distinction, it is certain to be lost. The attack is bound to become vague and vulgar, and the response equally if not more so. Does Galbraith have a candidate to lead the unpatriotic party? Will this candidate wish to spend his time explaining why he reviles the sacrifices of American men in arms? We love our servicemen, he will say, it is just that we hate all the things they do. This line might go over big in some circles but not, I think, in any part of the electorate not already convinced. The strategy would be a disaster at the polls, especially since there is unlikely now to be a Kennedy whose personal popularity might have been so great as to give the appearance that the antimilitary thesis was accepted by a majority of voters. No one really knows what elections mean in terms of specific issues, but they can be made to mean things that voters have hardly contemplated. If an election is ostensibly lost on the issue of military influence, would that mean that generals and admirals had public license to pursue any policy they saw fit?

The most certain result of an antimilitary election strategy would be to lay the groundwork for the further politicization of the American military. Whatever else one might say about military officials in the United States, they have not organized to thwart direct and explicit civilian commands because of their alienation from a hateful system of government. But if they should become pilloried in public as the scapegoats for an entire nation's tragedy, military men would, in effect, be given moral sanction to enter politics en masse to defend themselves against attack. That would be an exceedingly high price to pay for a losing campaign issue.

Presidential campaigns aside, however, we should also consider the probable reaction of military men to the actual positions taken by ABM opponents—dedication to a policy of assured destruction, rejection of defensive systems, and vociferous attacks on the defense establishment. In the face of such concerted antagonism, the strategy of the military and its right-wing allies will undoubtedly be to wait, as they have many times before, for an immediate danger to appear and then to press for an all-out response. If they cannot get part of what they want in advance of a crisis, they will use the crisis to get all they can.

In the United States it only takes one man to make an issue—the President. It is difficult to have a major issue without his participation. Yet instead of running away from conflict over ABM, the President started it. Why did he help make an issue that was bound to stir up antagonism toward the military? One reason is that the Nixon administration did not expect that ABM would become the major issue it turned out to be. If MIRV and this year's Vietnam budget had not caused widespread criticism, there was no reason to expect that ABM would. The administration failed to realize that many Americans who might trust the President to deal with foreign affairs would withdraw that trust in regard to ABM because ballistic missile defense would be seen by them as a domestic matter. It is all right, apparently, to build missiles that threaten havoc abroad (and therefore at home) but not to emplace defensive missiles near cities that will remind people of the potentialities for disaster.

The decision to proceed with deployment of the Safeguard ABM was a political mistake for the nation. Nixon should have realized that his foreign policy will remain mortgaged to the Vietnam war as long as that conflict continues, and that he cannot subject the nation to controversy without opening the floodgates of recrimination. A year's delay in deployment now might have adverse effects on the nation's nuclear deterrent in the mid-1970s, but everything has a price, and the cost of Vietnam has to be paid out until the mortgage is lifted by substantial troop withdrawals.

The ABM debate has followed Gresham's law: bad arguments drive out good ones. There is still time, however, to talk about critical issues, like halting deployment of MIRV in an arms-control agreement and sharply reducing expenditures of the general purpose forces. Most important of all, the nation's current strategic doctrine—assured destruction—should be given the closest scrutiny.

If the United States continues to rely on a doctrine of assured destruction, the prospect of losing that assurance in time of crisis will be immensely threatening. After all, ABM might not work, and it is possible that hardening of the missile sites will not work either; neither can be tested under actual circumstances. What we do know how to do, all too well, is build more Poseidon and Minuteman missiles with multiple warheads, and if we feel our lives threatened we may be pressed into doing all the things we know how to do as quickly (and as expensively) as possible. In the 1980s we might then come to look back upon the period from 1965 to 1975 as one in which modestly hopeful efforts were undertaken to deal with urgent domestic problems before they were swamped entirely by an overwhelming concern with national survival.

Should the ABM debate lead to a consideration of these issues, and to a complete reassessment of American deterrence policy, it may finally be seen to have been to the good. So far, however, the debate has resulted not in public enlightenment but in a heightened disposition on the part of Americans to blame one another for real and imagined errors in public policy. If the debate leads to continued indiscriminate attacks on the military, coupled with an unquestioning belief in the policy of assured destruction, it will manage what no event except for Vietnam has done—it will combine foreign and domestic disaster.

NOTES

1. Fortunately, the Subcommittee on National Security and International Operations of the Senate Government Operations Committee has published the fascinating debate between Albert Wohlstetter on the pro side and George Rathjens and others on the anti side. This exchange, called "Defense Analysis: Two Examples" (91st Congress, 1st session, 1969) is the best brief example of defense analysis I know.

2. Hearings before the Committee on Armed Services, United States Senate, 91st Congress, 1st session in S. 1192, S. 2407, and S. 2546, Parts 1 and 2; Abram Chayes and Jerome B. Wiesner, eds., *ABM, An Evaluation of the Decision to Deploy an Antiballistic Missile System* (New York: Harper & Row, 1969); John Kenneth Galbraith, *How to Control the Military* (New York: Doubleday, 1959); Johan J. Holst and William Schneider, Jr., eds., *Why ABM? Policy Issues in the Missile Defense Controversy* (New York: Pergamon Press, 1969).

6

PRESIDENTIAL SUCCESSION AND DISABILITY: POLICY ANALYSIS FOR UNIQUE CASES

The new constitutional amendment on Presidential succession and disability raises in extreme form the problem of recommending policy for unique cases. These special policies have the following outstanding characteristics:

1. The proposed solutions must work every time.
2. There is little historical experience upon which to base generalizations about future probabilities.
3. Behavioral science does not contain relevant propositions that could facilitate reasonable prediction of the outcomes of different sets of events under varying conditions.
4. The usual way around this kind of difficulty—the application of rules of thumb, like the incremental method, that depend on repeated adjustments of feedback—is not applicable because (a) it is so difficult to get the relevant experience, and (b) there is not enough time. The "error" of "trial and error" must not happen.

These problem characteristics mean that the one certainty is that uniquely favorable solutions cannot be obtained. The existing state of human knowledge means that the problems are insoluble. But there are reasons to believe that no action at all may be worse than any of several alternatives, however unsatisfactory they appear. So how do we proceed? It is possible to clarify the most relevant criteria and to apply them, with some generalizations from political science, to different alternatives. This form of analy-

From Aaron Wildavsky, ed., *The Presidency* (Boston: Little, Brown and Co., 1969), pp. 777–795. Reprinted by permission.

sis allows us to reject the worst; we can then choose among better although imperfect alternatives.

Application of the relevant criteria to Presidential succession will show that the new constitutional amendment represents a reasonable "satisficing" alternative that neither wholly meets nor completely violates the crucial criteria. In the case of Presidential disability, however, the constitutional provisions are a parody of what must be avoided: a prolonged struggle over who has the right to be President. The problem simply cannot be solved in advance. We must rely on the presumed virtues of our political elites to work out solutions for problems as they arise.

In our analyses it will be necessary to consider the relationship of Presidents to their important publics within the United States; for the choice of a successor or a person to act as President during periods of disability depends on the probable reactions of the major publics that, in their mutual interaction, make up the larger patterns we call the presidency. In determining whether a successor might come from a particular institution, moreover, we are required to appraise that institution from a Presidential perspective. Although existing knowledge is not adequate, we must attempt to specify the causal connections between different successors and their likely behavior in the Presidential office. Consideration of reform thus compels us to summarize a substantial part of our knowledge about the presidency.

Great problems of public policy exert an independent force upon the societies that encounter them. Once a problem is recognized, public energies may be mobilized to find solutions and scholarly talents may be directed toward historical inquiries in order to determine how the problem emerged. Yet a great problem of public policy may itself be a source of energy; once its characteristics are determined many new problems arise and numerous old ones become more urgent. Such is the case with the problem of Presidential succession and disability. This perennial problem of the American political structure would hardly concern us now with so deep a sense of urgency if it were not for the specter of nuclear war. Just as the 1964 Presidential elections brought out profound anxieties about which candidate would have his finger on the nuclear button, so have we been led to fear that there might be no one around to wiggle the Presidential finger at mankind after a nuclear attack.

The tragic death of President Kennedy, and recognition of the possibility that Vice President Johnson might have been shot at the same time, has made us aware of the dangers that might face us if we failed to make adequate provision for Presidential succession. That is why we have added the Twenty-fifth Amendment to the Constitution. Two basic questions must still be answered: Who should be next in line if the Vice President is unavailable? How far should the line of succession be lengthened to guard against the possibility of an atomic attack killing all those on call?

In trying to answer these questions, we may ask what history has to tell us. There has never been a need to go beyond the Vice President to fill the presidency, although one or the other office has been vacant for approximately 40 percent of the time since the beginning of the Republic. The first succession act was passed in 1792 when the Senate was dominated by supporters of Alexander Hamilton and the House by friends of Secretary of State Thomas Jefferson. The Senate passed a bill putting the President pro tempore of that body next in line, but the House amended it by placing the Secretary of State first in line. A compromise was finally reached by putting the Speaker of the House second in line behind the President pro tempore of the Senate who, if a vacancy occurred during the first two years and seven months of a Presidential term, would serve until a special Presidential election was held. On November 25, 1885, Vice President Thomas Henricks died, ten days before the first session of the next Congress. A major impetus to change the line of succession was provided by the fact that Cleveland was a Democrat, while the new President pro tempore was a Republican. The Act of 1886 placed succession among Cabinet positions in the following order: the Secretary of State, the Secretary of the Treasury, the Secretary of War, the Attorney General, the Postmaster General, the Secretary of the Navy, and the Secretary of the Interior. After Vice President Truman became President in 1945 there were those who thought that his Secretary of State, Edward R. Stettinius, was not of presidential caliber, and that House Speaker Sam Rayburn would be better. President Truman, who appeared to accept the argument that the Act of 1886 was "undemocratic," waited until the Republicans gained a majority in the House of Representatives and proposed that the succession act be changed to put the Speaker—then Republican Joseph W. Martin—first in line and the President pro tempore of the Senate next.

The Presidential Succession Act passed in 1947 provides a line of succession first through Congress—the Speaker and the President pro tempore—and then through the Cabinet in the order of the 1886 Act with the addition of the Secretaries of Agriculture, Commerce, and Labor. In case a Speaker or President pro tempore was not constitutionally qualified to be President by reason of age or foreign birth, the next qualified person in line would assume the office until a Speaker or President pro tempore who was qualified was elected. The act also said that these officials must resign their existing positions when they act as President. This is essentially the succession plan we have today. Because of the circumstances following Kennedy's death and Johnson's succession—a Speaker in his seventies and a President pro tempore in his eighties—questions have inevitably been raised about the suitability of a plan that would permit them to assume the burdens of the presidency.

What history has to teach us, it appears, is that succession acts have been influenced by somebody's dislike of the idea of a particular person or person of a particular party being next in line to succeed to the Presidency. An examination of the problem that avoids considerations of personality or immediate partisan advantage would seem to be in order. Let us begin by developing a set of criteria with which to evaluate the many complicated proposals for dealing with Presidential succession. Then we can apply these criteria to the major proposals that have been advanced, with special attention to the victorious alternative embodied in the Twenty-fifth Amendment.

Any method for determining Presidential succession must be established with absolute certainty. There must never be any doubt about precisely which person—whether occupying a particular position or chosen in a specified way—is next in line to assume the presidency. Nor must there be any doubt about the new President's term of office or his right to exercise presidential powers. Untold mischief would result if there were two or more claimants for the office or if there was no one with an undisputed right to occupy it. Who, then, could speak for the United States in foreign affairs or rally the nation to meet domestic emergencies? Worse still would be the internal upheaval resulting from the bitter disputes of rival claimants and their supporters. To argue about what the President should do is a normal part of politics in a democracy; to argue over which person should be doing what a President has the right to do is an invitation to civil war.

In addition to being certain, Presidential succession should be immediate. Only a few minutes or at most a few hours should elapse between the demise of one President and the accession of another, as was fortunately the case when Johnson succeeded Kennedy. In an atomic era made immensely dangerous by the existence of weapons of huge destructiveness, we simply cannot afford to be without a President. In many ways we would be better off with any one responsible person rather than no one in the Presidential office, even if this person was inferior to others who might have been chosen.

One reason for insisting that any plan for succession be certain and immediate is that these features help the new President gain acceptance as the legitimate occupant of the White House. When a political system is called "legitimate" the vast majority of people—especially those active in politics—believe that it is the right system of government. Severe policy conflicts are then less likely to overturn the regime. When the legitimacy of a political system is threatened, as was the case in Weimar Germany and Fourth Republic France, even minor political controversies are dangerous because they raise the question not only of "how much shall each interest receive" but also of "whether this form of government shall survive."

If the person who succeeds to the presidency is to be considered legitimate, the plan for determining who he will be should be as stable as possible so that it can gather force from longevity and tradition. Stability is a desirable standard because it gives the greatest assurance that the plan will be known by the largest number of citizens. Taught in the schools and disseminated by the media of information upon suitable occasions, the plan can become part of the political lore that every American is expected to know as part of his basic education. Changing the plan every few years could only result in confusion and lack of widespread understanding of the procedures then in operation. It would then be much easier for someone to challenge the existing plan and to suggest that since the procedures had been changed so often there was nothing sacrosanct in abiding by them. The advantage of stability need not imply that the present arrangement be kept, although it does mean that we should try to keep any new plan for as long as possible.

The gravest danger to stability comes from the efforts of those who would tailor a succession act to fit the particular individual they would like to help or hinder in case the need should arise. While it is not feasible to designate a particular individual by name for succession, it is possible to block a current officeholder, in case he is not thought suitable, or to place another current officeholder who is well-liked next in the line of succession. Following such practices would lead to continual changes in the succession act as those who occupied various institutional positions fell in and out of favor. Since no one can guarantee that all of us will always approve of the person designated as the immediate successor, wisdom would appear to require that we make the best, long-range arrangement that we can. The futile hope that we can always get the man we would most prefer has to be weighed against creating instability.

The third criterion for determining Presidential succession is continuity. Whoever succeeds to the presidency should serve until the next regularly scheduled election. A man who is in office for only a short period of time, and who must soon give way to another person, can hardly be expected to act with confidence, vigor, and dispatch. At best, he could undertake holding actions because he could not commit the executive branch to any policy that lasted beyond a few months. Weakness, indecision, futility, even challenges of the right of a temporary occupant to act like a President would be the most likely consequences of failing to allow a successor to serve until the end of the established Presidential term. It follows, therefore, that any proposal that permits the presidency to be occupied by alternating individuals is to be rejected.

If we are to meet the criteria discussed thus far, the procedures embodied in a succession plan also must be as simple as possible. Simplicity is urged as a criterion because it helps insure certainty, immediacy, and legitimacy. The more complex the plan, the more time is likely to be involved, the more doubt is likely to arise about who is next in line, and the more opportunities are created for something to go wrong. If people are puzzled over what procedures are to be followed, the way is left open for demagogues to claim that the result is not legitimate. If the occupant of the presidency is not determined beforehand, delay and intrigue may be added to confusion. Hence, we should eliminate any proposals concerning succession that involve more than a few simple steps or that involve lengthy deliberations or consultations.

The transfer of power to a new President should be as tranquil as possible. The political life of the country should not be upset by shocks or disruptions in this delicate period, for the death of a President is inevitably traumatic. The nation mourns the loss of the man whose office signifies its unity, virility, and hope. More than we realize, a President provides important guidelines from which we take our bearings in a complicated world. By knowing about him and his customary modes of operation, the world is made somewhat more predictable. Regardless of whether we support his specific policies, his loss creates a void. There is no need, therefore, to add to the disquiet by public contests or controversies, by campaigns or contests that may unleash pent-up emotions.

However admirable a proposal for handling succession might otherwise be, it cannot be acceptable unless it is also consistent with the proper management of presidential disability. Let us suppose that there is no Vice President and the person who is President becomes disabled. A new occupant of the presidency who could serve for the rest of the term or only a few weeks or months until the President recovers is needed. If the person next in line has a very important job, he might be reluctant to resign his position to take over the presidency for a limited period, knowing that he might be unable to regain his former post. Such reluctance, though understandable, would be most dangerous. The successor might be tempted to delay assuming the presidency until well after the full extent of the disability was evident, thus creating a gap in the effective exercise of presidential responsibility. Or the successor might be tempted to hedge about resigning his previous position, thereby creating dangerous uncertainty about his status and hence his legitimacy and longevity in office. Whoever is next in line, therefore, must be placed so that he can either resume his former position without difficulty or have no profound regrets about risking losing it.

Any person who succeeds to the presidency should belong to the same political party as the former President. The party system is an essential element of democratic government in the United States and succession proposals should try to strengthen rather than weaken our parties.

That the person who succeeds to the presidency should be a good man, capable of exercising the highest office in the land, is an evident but elusive criterion. It is difficult to say precisely what combination of characteristics is most desirable in a President. Certain qualities—tenacity, firmness, courage—are so personal that it is impossible to tell whether any man will have them when he needs them. Moreover, assessments of attributes like intelligence, knowledge, and skill are clearly related to one's own political preferences. Would a liberal prefer a highly intelligent but extremely conservative man to a moderately intelligent but extremely liberal person? The President's actions depend upon his values and preferences as well as his personal capacities. We can, of course, do our best to appraise the appropriateness of successors who would be drawn from various institutions such as Congress, the Cabinet, or the Supreme Court. We can say, perhaps, that a successor should have some experience in American politics so that he will have been socialized in acceptable modes of political conduct. It would also be desirable for a potential successor to know something about current developments of special Presidential responsibility, especially in foreign affairs.

Proposals for handling Presidential succession are designed to see that we always have a President who functions with the full powers of the office. There would seem to be little point in adopting proposals at the cost of weakening the presidency or of diluting the quality of the Vice President, who is most likely to take over if something happens to the President. Any plan that would add appreciably to the President's burdens, which are already great, or that would depreciate the worth of the vice presidency, should be turned down. It is difficult, of course, to find any proposal that is costless.

Our ideal Presidential succession, then, would be certain, immediate, and widely regarded as legitimate. The succession plan would be simple and stable. It would lead to the choice of good men from the former President's party, who would maintain continuity in office. The President would be able to exercise the full powers of his office, his successor would be ready to take over if a disability occurred, and the strength of the presidency would remain unimpaired.

Proposals for dealing with Presidential succession proceed in one of two directions. They either specify that the holders of certain institutional positions, such as Cabinet positions, should succeed to the presidency, or they describe a procedure, such as a special election, through which a successor would be chosen. Let us consider the arguments for and against the occupants of institutional positions providing a line of succession and then consider various other procedures suggested for finding a successor.

One proposal, following the Act of 1886, suggests that the Secretary of State, followed by other Cabinet members, should assume the presidency after the Vice President if a vacancy occurs. This plan, supposedly, would keep the presidency moving in the same general direction, especially in the vital field of foreign affairs, because the Secretary of State is assumed to share the President's preferences and usually belongs to the President's political party as well. Moreover, Secretaries of State have often been men of considerable stature who are likely to be qualified for the presidency anyway because of their knowledge and breadth of vision. And the secretary has the additional advantage of being instantaneously ready to assume the presidency.

Perhaps the most serious objection to the Secretary of State is that he is not an elected official and thus might suffer from a lack of legitimacy. In a time of crisis some people might challenge his right to occupy the presidency. Nor is it necessarily the case that the Secretary of State will be a man of stature. The growing importance of foreign policy will lead some Presidents to wish to act as their own policy-maker. They may be wary, therefore, of appointing an individual with an independent national standing or following who might challenge them or make it costly to fire them. Such considerations may have played a part in John F. Kennedy's decision to appoint the little-known and deferential Dean Rusk over the well-known and assertive Adlai Stevenson, who could count on his own support in the Democratic party. It is not even certain that a Secretary of State would follow the foreign policy of the President he succeeded. Certainly Eisenhower and Dulles differed in their approaches.

The network of associations that envelops Cabinet members, centered around the major interests they serve, gives them a narrower view and pulls them apart from a President who must juggle and balance many concerns at once. Although the proposition that Cabinet members are the President's "natural enemies" may be exaggerated, there is no reason to expect them to agree fully on matters of departmental policy, let alone the broad range of foreign and domestic issues.

In order to avoid some of the difficulties associated with the choice of the Secretary of State and still keep succession within the executive branch, it has been proposed that national conventions nominate, and the voting citizenry elect, two vice presidents. In case two vacancies occurred in the Presidential office, the second Vice President would take over. This scheme has the advantage of placing succession in the hands of an elected national official of the same political party who would be kept continuously informed of important developments, who could take over immediately, and whose legitimacy could not be questioned. The major question here is whether this scheme might not create additional difficulties that would be greater than its presumed benefits.

There is, first of all, the problem of getting an outstanding person to accept a position as second Vice President. This official would not have the few formal duties of the first Vice President and he would know that in the course of American history a second Vice President has not been required to assume the presidency. And should a first Vice President look forward to the chance of running for the presidency at some future time, he would know that he had a probable rival right next to him, thus further reducing the incentive for talented and ambitious men to take the job. Debasing the value of the vice presidency in order to meet the more remote contingency that two successors might be required hardly seems advisable.

The introduction of a second Vice President would also lead to what might be called the "politics of polygamy." In polygamous societies, the relationship between the first and second wives is not always noted for light and harmony. Since the President has the discretion to determine what Vice Presidents will or will not do beyond the usual tedium of presiding over the Senate, Vice Presidents such as Richard Nixon and Lyndon Johnson have had to fight to get important assignments. The potentiality of conflict, favoritism, and intrigue would be multiplied with two Vice Presidents looking for work, perhaps by encroaching on the Secretary of State or other highly placed officials. We know that Vice President John Nance Garner was not averse to suggesting means of overturning the "Administration" program to congressional opponents of Franklin Roosevelt's policies. How much greater, then, would be the temptation of mischief with one or even two disgruntled Vice Presidents looking for an outlet for their talents and energies.

Presumably, one Vice President would continue to preside over the Senate and to take on such additional duties as the President saw fit to allot to him. The other Vice President would be assigned as a general presidential assistant. No doubt there is plenty of work around the White House and the President would have no difficulty in finding jobs for any willing hand. But unlike such other high staff assistants as the Director of the Budget and the Chairman of the Council of Economic Advisers, Vice Presidents cannot be fired. Even if the President had originally desired a particular person as second Vice President, the chief executive might change his mind after a year or two and wish to get rid of him. If this Vice President was charged in the Constitution or by statute with specific responsibilities, the President would be in the anomalous position of disagreeing with a high official he could not remove. Moreover, it might be costly to "dump" this Vice President at the next national convention.

It has been customary in recent years for Presidential candidates to choose their running mates. One would imagine that this custom might carry over to the choice of a second Vice President. Yet it is conceivable that party leaders, who are prepared to concede the choice of the first Vice President, might find a rationale for a greater voice in the selection of any additional Vice Presidents. While Lyndon Johnson was able to remove Robert Kennedy from consideration for the Democratic vice presidential nomination in 1964, for example, he might have found it more difficult to justify refusing him a consolation prize if there had been more positions to distribute. Johnson—or any President—would thus be faced with the prospect of offending an important party faction or working with a man whom he patently did not want and who possessed sufficient independent strength to make himself troublesome over the next four years.

The problems created by having two Vice Presidents may be avoided by giving the President the right to choose a new Vice President in case there is a vacancy in that office through the death or disability of either the original President or Vice President. There is much to commend this proposal. The successor would certainly be acceptable to the President, would belong to his political party, would be likely to continue his policies, and would be immediately available. There is something inherently plausible in leaving the choice of a successor to the man who has been elected by the voters and whose replacement should perhaps be like him in essential respects. We trust the President with matters of life and death, so the argument goes, why not trust him to pick his possible successor. Indeed, the operation of the national nominating conventions pretty much assures a President the right to choose his first successor—the man he selects as his running mate.

Yet allowing whoever is President to choose his successor is not without its difficulties. Such personal action, without the participation of a customary legitimizing body such as the national convention, might be regarded as an unwarranted exercise of personal power. Even under the Succession Act of 1886 a President would be choosing a Cabinet member—subject to senatorial confirmation—who might incidentally be his successor, rather than a second Vice President whose major function would be precisely to be available in case he was needed to become the next President.

It is not clear whether having the right to name a successor would help or harm a President. He might be helped if a vacancy occurred at a time when he wished to establish the new successor as his heir apparent in a future Presidential nomination and election. Other people in his party, however, might not approve. Furthermore, a President might be harmed if he wished to retain freedom of maneuver in his choice for his next running mate or for a candidate for his party's nomination in a future election. The very fact that he designated a new Vice President during his term of office might make it difficult for him to disavow that person in the future. President Lyndon Johnson, for example, apparently decided to hold off naming his choice for the vice presidential nomination in 1964 in order to determine which man might be best in the light of future events such as the identity of the Republican candidates. He would have had trouble doing this if he had been forced to name a successor immediately. Presumably a President who succeeded another because of his death or disability would have to name his successor within two weeks or 30 days after assuming office. Yet it is difficult to believe that any President would wish to undertake this difficult assignment when he was desperately trying to guide himself and the nation through a trying period of transition. Further delay, however, would violate the criterion of immediacy.

The attack on the legitimacy of the plan providing for Presidential choice may be mitigated by a somewhat different plan, which calls for acceptance or rejection of the new President's nomination of his Vice President by Congress. While this might solve the problem of legitimacy, this proposal would not meet the wishes of those who feel that the choice of a successor as well as the successor himself should be confined to the executive branch. They would argue that Congressmen have different, narrower constituencies than the President, that the President and Congressmen have different perspectives, that Congress may be controlled by the opposite party, and that the separation of powers would be violated by giving Congress an important part to play. The President could hardly afford to have a nominee rejected; it would severely damage his prestige. A narrow approval might inflict severe wounds and might question the legitimacy of his choice. Hence the President would have to conduct the widest consultations in order to make certain that his candidate was approved by a substantial if not overwhelming majority. In this case the power to reject, to use the traditional formula for senatorial confirmation, might become the power to select. Consequently, the President might be forced to accept someone he really did not want or pay the price of a long and bitter conflict.

A strong case in favor of having Congress act as the legitimizing authority can also be made. If individual Representatives have rather narrow constituencies, Congress as a collective body spans the nation. Moreover, the increasing urbanization of the United States gives Senators more representative constituencies than in the past. A majority of Congressmen, however, might belong to a different political party than the former President and his new successor. This means that bipartisan compromise would be reflected in the choice of a new Vice President so as to assure reasonable cooperation between the legislative and executive branches of government. The separation of powers, as Richard Neustadt has told us, is a form of shared power. Nothing is accomplished by treating the different branches as if they lived in separate worlds when the daily activities of government require their mutual cooperation. While the President might not wish to take the trouble to find an immediate successor and present him to Congress, the chief executive's responsibilities to the nation far outweigh any temporary inconvenience he might suffer in doing so. A man who cannot deal with small political troubles, it might be argued, does not belong in the White House.

Still another variant of the above plan calls for having Congress choose among three to five candidates selected by the President soon after a vacancy arises. But if the President indicated a first preference, even informally, the purpose of the plan would be thwarted, and the President would be faced with the prospect of having his choice publicly rejected. Indeed, there could be no guarantee that Congress would accept any of the President's suggestions or that it would be able to arrive at a decision at all, at least not without extensive hearings and lengthy debates. Aside from the mischief and dissension in Congress that this plan might create, it hardly comports with our ideas of an immediate, simple, and tranquil succession.

In a message to Congress supporting what was to become the existing Succession Act, President Truman declared, "The Speaker of the House of Representatives, who is elected in his own district, is also elected to be the presiding officer of the House by a vote of all the Representatives of all the people of the country. As a result, I believe that the Speaker is the official in the Federal Government whose selection, next to that of the President and Vice President, can be most accurately said to stem from the people themselves." The legitimacy of the Speaker becoming President could not be questioned. More than that, a Speaker is bound to be a product *par excellence* of American political life. Having come up through the ranks over a period of many years, he knows what kinds of behavior are and are not acceptable. He is most unlikely to be an extremist or a person who would threaten our liberties. Conciliation, respect for others, ability to bring men of diverse points of view together for common purposes are his stocks in trade. A Speaker is likely to have a wide-ranging acquaintance-ship with other governmental officials and a broad knowledge of the major issues of the day, especially in regard to domestic affairs.

The objections to the Speaker assuming the presidency are numerous. It is said that the Speaker is of lower caliber than other officials such as the Secretary of State, that he is likely to be too old, that he could not be suf-ficiently well informed, that he has a congressional rather than Presidential orientation, and that he might belong to a different party than the late President or Vice President. Far more evidence than has thus far been supplied, however, would be required to demonstrate that the late Sam Ray-burn would necessarily have been a worse President than any of the Sec-retaries of State who served during his long tenure as Speaker, or that Sec-retary Rusk would make a more vigorous, determined, and forceful Presi-dent than Speaker McCormack. If a Speaker or potential Speaker does not manifest the toughness, administrative ability, intelligence, and force to run a large and unwieldy body such as the House of Representatives, he is not likely to last, as the deposition of two recent Republican leaders sug-gests. The political skills and the breadth of knowledge a Speaker develops provide excellent training for the presidency. Age or seniority is not the prime factor in determining who becomes or survives as Speaker. The man is chosen in a contest between different factions in his party for his ability to lead and serve the membership. In this sense the Speaker becomes expe-rienced in a prime task of the presidency—leading, serving, and resolving conflicts among a broad and rather heterogeneous collection of interests. True, Speakers are usually somewhat older than Secretaries of State, though this is by no means an invariant rule. Yet an infirm man could hardly carry on as Speaker, so great are the demands on his energy. The long service in government he would have acquired by the time he became Speaker may be considered an asset in terms of experience as well as a lia-bility in terms of age. But, in the era of De Gaulle and Adenauer, disqual-ification on grounds of age seems out of place.

It may be that Speakers are more oriented toward a congressional view and to domestic politics, than a Secretary of State. But excessively par-ochial concerns can hardly dominate a Speaker's thoughts and actions when he must accommodate to some degree a large party in the House as well as the President of the United States. Harry S. Truman, the one re-cent President who came to the White House almost immediately after long congressional experience, although not from the speakership, had one of the best records in foreign affairs of any President in our time. A

Speaker is extraordinarily busy and might not have as much time for intensive study as other officials. But it would be foolish to suggest, as have some writers, that the Speaker necessarily would be blatantly uninformed or that the formal separation of powers would provide a serious obstacle to sending information to a person from a rival branch of government. Indeed, it could be argued that a Speaker, with whom the President must cooperate and who has many sanctions at his disposal, is in a much better position to demand information than the much less powerful Vice President is today. Could it be that Secretaries of State are thought to be generally more distinguished than Speakers because their jobs require them to issue lofty pronouncements, while Speakers, like Presidents, are immersed in the muck and mire of partisan politics and domestic strife?

A most serious obstacle in the path of the Speaker is that he might belong to a different political party than the President and might change the party in the White House, contrary to the expressed wishes of the voters. No doubt a Speaker, realizing this and sensitive to his position, would be loathe to alter radically the personnel or the policy direction of the previous President until the voters had made known their approval in an election. He might choose a type of national coalition government in which members of both parties would be represented in the Cabinet. It is also true that the partisan attachments of some Secretaries of State have been ambiguous. In fact, the present Secretary [Dean Rusk] has no base of support in the Democratic party. Nevertheless, a change of party in the presidency should be avoided if possible. The question is whether other plans, which lack this defect, do not contain others of equal or greater importance.

Another obstacle facing the Speaker is that he might be reluctant to resign his eminent position if a case of presidential disability occurred and it appeared that the President might resume his office in a short time. It is difficult to see how proper provision could be made enabling him to resume his seat in Congress once having resigned it, and if this could be managed he might be influenced by the prospect that he will need the support of his colleagues to regain the speakership at a later date. The criterion of compatibility with succession proposals is violated by putting the Speaker next in line unless he is given the vice presidency when a vacancy occurs in that office through the death of a President or Vice President.

There are a host of proposals that leave the decision of a specific successor up to Congress. One calls for the selection of a new Vice President by a majority vote of a joint session of Congress. A second would have the House of Representatives choose the successor, and a third would have the House choose from among a number of individuals nominated by the Senate. A different stipulation is that members of one or both houses should confine their selection to a member of the President's party in Congress. All of these plans share a common defect: they usually propose that part or all of Congress meet soon after a vacancy has occurred. Yet it might be too late if both the President and Vice President are unavailable. To be sure, such plans may provide for an interim President, but instead of violating the criterion of immediacy, they run counter to the criterion of continuity. What could an interim President do while Congress was in the midst of debates on the identity of the successor? If the congressional debates revealed a lack of consensus, the new President would be handicapped from the start, assuming that terrible events had not occurred in the meantime. Should the election be confined to the House, the authority of the Speaker might be undermined by the choice of another person. Confining the choice to members of the President's party is contrary to all congressional precedent. It might be regarded as lacking the legitimacy of full congressional approval, and it would in no way guarantee that the successor would be a follower, rather than an opponent, of the late President. These proposals combine the disadvantages of locating the choice in Congress without the advantages of having an official like the Speaker immediately available for the presidency.

It is apparent that none of the succession proposals give certain promise of meeting all of the relevant criteria. There are five, however, that merit discussion in an imperfect world because they violate the smallest number of criteria. If one is willing to accept the prospect that in the future, Vice Presidents may be of low quality and that they may create continued difficulty for Presidents, the nomination and election of two Vice Presidents may be acceptable. Selection by the President himself may be advocated if one believes that the problem of legitimacy will not be serious, that the President will not have to compromise himself inordinately, that an immediate decision will not prove too taxing for him, and that the nation can afford to wait during the time it takes for him to make up his mind. Nomination by the President and confirmation by both houses of Congress may be appropriate so long as it is thought that the prestige of the President and his possible successor will not be badly damaged, and that the possible lengthy delays in this procedure will not materialize or are not likely to be dangerous if they do. If one believes that succession need not be kept in the executive branch, or that a change of party in the White House ought to be permitted, or that the Speaker would not hesitate about assuming the Presidential office in the event of a disability, then succession by the Speaker may be desirable.

Although we have argued that the Secretary of State would not necessarily turn out to be a better man than the Speaker or a Presidential nominee, there is little reason to assume that he would probably be worse. The Secretary of State would be likely to meet all our criteria except "legitimacy." Yet how would we know that this would be the case? Perhaps we should cease relying on intuition. We could survey voters and political activists on how they would regard succession by the Secretary of State as opposed to a variety of other possibilities. It might turn out that voters and activists would be willing to accept anyone who is chosen in a manner con-

sistent with the appropriate constitutional provisions and statutes. Yet it
might also be the case that certain officials would be widely regarded as
more or less legitimate than others.[1]

We can cut into the criteria in another way by dividing the various proposals into two categories: those that promise to solve the direct problem
of Presidential succession but that may have undesirable side effects, and
those that minimize side effects but that may be less than adequate in dealing with succession. If one chose to put the greatest weight on handling the
succession itself, then the alternative of two Vice Presidents would emerge
as by far the best choice. If one takes the position that other values should
not be sacrificed just to deal with a succession problem that has never yet
materialized, then allowing the President to choose his own successor
would clearly be superior.

Placing the analysis in this light suggests why the Bayh amendment—
named after its chief sponsor, the Democratic Senator from Indiana—
received such widespread support and easily became the Twenty-fifth
Amendment. It provides that vice-presidential vacancies shall be filled
through nomination by the President, subject to a majority vote in both the
Senate and the House. This is a "satisficing" proposal. It sacrifices some
immediacy and creates some instant problems for the President in order to
secure legitimacy and to minimize his problems with the Vice President in
the future. Not every criterion is perfectly satisfied, but neither is any one
criterion blatantly violated. No other proposal is evidently better and many
are clearly worse. Avoiding the worst is not the same as getting the best,
but it has something to be said for it in the context of great uncertainty.

The possibility of an atomic attack that could kill all Cabinet members,
many Congressmen, and a good part of any institution designated to
choose a successor, leads us to consider the desirability of lengthening the
line of succession in addition to the question of "who shall be next in
line." There are those who say that such an eventuality would be so horri-
ble that they do not wish to think about it. It would be morally impermissible for governmental officials to take this view, however. Their task is to
help the living by taking whatever steps they can to promote continuity in
government. The most obvious move is to reduce the probability that all
top governmental officials will be incapacitated at one time. The President
and Vice President can travel separately whenever possible, and there is
certainly no reason why the Secretaries of State and Defense and other
Cabinet members should be in an airplane at the same time, as happened
when President Kennedy was assassinated. Although the likelihood is not
great, however, no one can guarantee that an atomic attack, taking place at
a time such as the delivery of the State of the Union message, might not
create a vacancy in the presidency with no living successor.

We might meet this problem in part by designating additional members
of Congress and men in high executive posts to stand in the line of succession. Further protection might be obtained by including the governors of

the 50 states. A permanent order of precedence among governors might be fixed by adopting a wholly arbitrary procedure—taking the states in alphabetical order or in order of their admission to the Union.

To raise the question how a successor to the presidency should be found may imply that some solution is at hand. It is tempting to define problems as things to which there are solutions. Yet there may be problems for which there are no solutions. Let us examine a problem in a related area —presidential disability—for which there appears to be no apparent solution.

Proposals concerned with Presidential disability are designed to deal with four kinds of events:

1. The President is so badly incapacitated that he cannot communicate with the Vice President.
2. The President knows he is disabled and tells the Vice President to take over.
3. The President recovers his health and takes back his office.
4. The President really cannot carry out his responsibilities but insists on retaining his office.

History has taught us that Vice Presidents have been reluctant to take great responsibility when a President was out of commission because they feared being accused of usurping power. And at least one President failed to ask a Vice President to take over because the chief executive and his friends feared that it would be difficult for him to get his job back. For a long time, however, the matter did not seem urgent and the obvious remedy was not adopted because Congressmen could not agree on any single proposal for handling the entire problem. Different factions coalesced around different plans and it was always possible to show that each plan had some glaring defect. Since Congress would not act, President Eisenhower, aware of public concern over his illnesses, entered into an informal agreement with Vice President Nixon that effectively took care of the first three circumstances outlined above. It was agreed that if the Vice President took over, he succeeded only to the powers and duties but not to the office itself. Therefore, the President, realizing he was disabled, could call upon his Vice President to take over. Or the Vice President, after consulting the Cabinet, could take over if the President was unable to make the announcement. In both cases, the President could take back his job as soon as he felt able to do so simply by announcing that his disability was over. Presidents Kennedy and Johnson have since adopted similar agreements with their potential successors. The fourth instance, however, in which key officials disagree about the President's ability to act as President, remains troublesome.

The possibility that a President might wish to regain office before he is ready must be taken seriously. He might be mentally deranged or he might fear that the acting President was entrenching himself unduly and thus be motivated to take back the office prematurely. Who is to umpire disagreements between the President and Vice President over when the President is ready to go back to work? The Bayh amendment states that this choice would be made by a combination of the Vice President and a majority of the Cabinet whose decision not to let the President back would have to be ratified by a two-thirds majority of both houses of Congress.

On the positive side, the Bayh amendment safeguards the President. By the time the Vice President and a majority of the Cabinet decide that the President is unable to resume his office, and two-thirds of both houses agree, there is very little possibility of a successful plot to deprive the President of his office without due cause. Moreover, the association of the executive and legislative branches of government in this proposal would appear to assure the legitimacy of the action, which would be of the utmost importance when such an unusual act—keeping a duly elected President out of office—was taking place. If one suggests that the scales are being weighted in favor of a President's resuming his office, a proper answer is that he should be denied this right only in the most extraordinary circumstances. Yet there are aspects of this proposal that leave us uneasy.

One could argue that the evils that a dispute over whether the President had a right to his office would bring about would be so great that prevention rather than cure must be our hope. An extended trial procedure in Congress would keep the nation in a state of peril; it would also limit the possibility of emergency action, which is perhaps the greatest good to be obtained by formally dealing with the problem of Presidential disability. If an obviously disabled President seeks to hold on to his office while unable to exercise its duties, Congress might be given the power of impeachment to deal with such sins against the Republic. If impeachment is too severe a remedy, especially since a President could no longer hope to resume office, a President who had, in effect, been declared guilty of hiding his disability could serve no useful purpose either for himself or for his country. A disagreement between the President and Vice President would inevitably be serious but the suggested arrangement, far from aggravating the difficulty, merely recognizes it and at least offers a way out.

Another criticism of involving Congress in the matter is that it might alter the traditional distribution of power—whatever that is supposed to be—between the executive and legislative branches. A hostile two-thirds majority of Congress might then get rid of a President without following the rather arduous impeachment procedures prescribed in the Constitution. Since the Vice President and a majority of the Cabinet would have to initiate the procedure before Congress could act, however, it is improbable that all these people would be able to agree on a course adverse to the President. Indeed, a more cogent objection to the plan may be that it requires such widespread agreement as to make it unlikely that any President could be prevented from exercising his office if he was sufficiently determined. Can we, then, devise any plan that would include sufficient safeguards to be acceptable to a President and that would, at the same time, prevent a determined but disabled President from regaining his office?

It is difficult to see how any solution can be found for the problem of a President who is prepared to ruin his country in order to retain his office. So long as the President remains adamant, his Cabinet and Vice President are unlikely to insist that he give up his powers and duties. Anyone who resisted a President's will in such circumstances would find it rather awkward to continue serving him. Congress would find it difficult to act in the midst of these uncertainties; it would have to institute a lengthy investigation, followed by prolonged and perhaps bitter debate, before it arrived at a decision. If Congress was closely divided near the two-thirds mark, as is possible, the resulting uproar, delay, and chaos would be precisely what we wish to avoid. It may be, therefore, that there is no effective remedy in our system for a President who cannot be trusted to protect the nation when its very existence might be threatened,[2] or that such remedies would have to be worked out on the spot.

By this time the fundamental dilemma has become apparent. The structure of problems like presidential succession and presidential disability is much different than that encountered in making most policy recommendations. Ordinarily, we would expect to accumulate experience and adjust our practices accordingly. If our theory was inadequate or required calculations we could not make, we could try various incremental moves and let these small acts generate consequences that we could study while taking further action. If our policy proved to be successful most of the time we would probably be satisfied. But in the case of Presidential succession, the stakes are so high that we require a mechanism that will work every time, especially the first time. We might not recover from an experience that tells us that whatever policy we adopt has proven disastrous. No science that I am aware of can claim total predictability for chains of circumstances that, if not unique, are at least highly irregular.

To end on this note would, however, be too pessimistic. It is true that we cannot have great confidence that the best alternatives will work out exactly as we would like. But we have, perhaps, not used all the resources of political theory at our command. Let us now add an aspect of American political behavior that we have neglected. I refer to the existence of a subculture of political activists whose members manifest a high degree of commitment to democratic processes and an overwhelming determination that free government should continue. Whatever the unforeseen specific events, therefore, we could expect, with a high degree of certainty, that Presidents, Congressmen, Cabinet members, and other members of national political elites would do everything in their power to prevent catastrophe. Whatever their other differences might be, these men are likely to put preservation of the system before other preferences. If the concept of the "public interest" has any meaning at all, members of the nation's highest political elites would work together to protect their nation against the evils stemming from the absence of a President, disagreement over who is President, or questions surrounding the legitimacy of the man who is President.

NOTES

1. In June 1945, a cross-section of citizens was asked to choose among the Secretary of State, the Speaker, and a special meeting of the electoral college. Forty-seven percent chose the Secretary of State, 20 percent the Speaker, and 18 percent the electoral college, with 15 percent venturing no opinion. Hadley Centril, ed., *Public Opinion 1935-1946* (Princeton: Princeton University Press, 1951), p. 590.

2. Citizens of the United States do not really know whether their political system contains sufficient safeguards against a President who tries to establish a dictatorship for the excellent reason that no President has ever tried to become a dictator. Indirectly, of course, we can argue in principle that the political system does contain effective safeguards. We can show that political leaders go through a socialization process in which men who do not accept basic democratic procedures are screened out. There is plenty of evidence to suggest that political activists manifest a high degree of commitment to democratic norms. Presidents do not wish to become dictators because they and their leading associates, including military officers, have internalized the desirability of such rules as free elections. As in so many other cases, we have "solved" this problem by never having had to face it at all. Its very appearance in serious form might be a sign of extreme degeneration of the political system for which no remedy might be appropriate.

7

THE ANALYSIS OF ISSUE-CONTEXTS IN THE STUDY OF DECISION-MAKING

In the evolving study of decision-making [1] attention has been paid to the personal and social characteristics of the participants, the institutional settings in which they work, the small groups which they form, the pressures to which they are subjected, the flow of information and advice which they receive, their perceptions of reality, the alignment of interests supporting and opposing certain alternatives, and the logic and psychology of situations involving choice. From Mary Parker Follett's "Law of the Situation" to Harold Stein's introduction to the case book, *Public Administration and Policy Development,* much emphasis has also been placed on the situational context of issues. But the very richness of the factual context has apparently inhibited efforts to abstract elements which would facilitate comparisons among the case histories by classifying issue-contexts along various dimensions and examining their consequences for decision-making. The thesis of this essay is that the study of decision-making would gain by making explicit and systematic an analytic category—the contexts of the issues—specifying the situations in which issues occur and their impact on the decision-makers.

The subject matter of the issue—the tariff, public versus private power, conservation—obviously helps determine the interests and the particular decision-makers who are concerned with the problem. It is not immediately apparent, however, that the context in which the issue occurs not only helps determine the decision-maker's perception of the facts and values but also the way in which he seeks out, receives, and evaluates this information. Different issue-contexts invoke different decision-making pat-

From *Journal of Politics* 24 (1962), pp. 717-732. Reprinted by permission.

terns which affect the manner in which the decision-maker goes about trying to solve his problem, and thus influence the final result. Of course, the analysis of issue-contexts is merely one tool which must be used in conjunction with many others to explain what has happened.

We begin with a statement of how differences in issue-contexts affect the behavior of decision-makers. This is followed by a demonstration of how the analysis of issue-contexts may be used to help account for behavior in two major cases—Dixon-Yates and Gotham in the Air Age. Then we present conclusions bearing on the analysis of issue-contexts for explanatory purposes and for assisting administrators.

I

Organizations would find life quite unbearable if they treated each stimulus requiring action as something new. Every decision would then require an agreed definition of the situation, a frame of reference for interpreting events, a specification of the mixture of values involved, a thorough search for policy alternatives, prediction of the likely consequences of these alternatives, and much more. In order to avoid the enormous effort and intellectual capacities required to accomplish these tasks, organizations ordinarily cut their decision costs and their burden of calculation by developing set patterns of responses to frequently encountered stimuli. As the members of the organization learn to interpret the world in fixed ways, they tend to perceive events to fit in with their existing frames of reference. To the extent that members share common simplifications about the world, they reinforce one another in the strength of their convictions. They may block out stimuli which do not fit in with their preconceived notions. They may define the situation in accordance with their stereotypes and drastically restrict consideration of alternatives and consequences. A stimulus may be treated as belonging to a well-known type because of some partially perceived surface characteristics, thus invoking the standard responses, when it actually contains novel features requiring rather different kinds of actions. These difficulties may be countered by trying to build-in sensitivity to the perception of novel problems, and by justifying the complex and costly procedures necessary to deal with them. But severe diseconomies occur and the pressures toward subsuming new stimuli under old rubrics become irresistible. Thus the rival needs for routine and for flexibility exist in a permanent tension.

When a particular stimulus evokes an agreed upon set of responses, knowledge of this context of decision helps the observer to account for the behavior. If the observer can discover the organization's repertoire of responses, its mode of classifying stimuli, and its rules of application, he can explain most of its decisions. The context of decision may be such, however, that the responses which the organization has learned are inappropriate. This may be correctly perceived by the organization which then engages in a much more complex mode of adapting its behavior. Instances also occur in which stereotyping takes place so that the organization encounters difficulty because a routine response to what is perceived as a routine stimulus turns out to be ill-adapted to the actual circumstances. By sensitizing himself to the context of decision, to the relationship between the stimuli impinging on the organization and its decision-making apparatus, the observer can hope to provide at least partial explanations for the unusual cases.

The context of the issue affects the manner in which it is handled and hence the decision that is made. An issue which seems new to the decision-makers will be handled differently than one which appears quite familiar. The search for information, for example, is likely to be much more extensive in the former instance than the latter. An issue which occurs in a context where the mixture of values involved is clear (a result, possibly, of previous experience or strong convictions) would be treated differently than one in which the participants were less certain of what was involved. The likelihood of getting a quick decision, for instance, would be less when the decision-makers were in doubt as to the appropriate values or their desirable mixture. In many issue-contexts the members of the organizations have hardened attitudes and prepared responses ready to be activated by the appropriate stimuli. The chances are, therefore, that the responsible officials will be less likely to assimilate new information than they would if they disagreed among themselves or if their positions were more fluid. Perhaps a series of questions will illustrate the impact of the issue-context.

II

What associations does a particular stimulus call forth in the mind of the decision-maker? Does it present a problem which he is able to relate automatically to past experience and information? Or does he have to investigate the matter with some thoroughness to discover what it is all about? Different procedures in regard to the collecting and reporting of information would be followed, depending upon the answers to these questions.

Is the issue-context one on which the decision-maker's position is immediately apparent to him or does he have to calculate what is at stake, what values are involved? Again, the answer would determine, in part at least, the procedure followed in handling the problem and its ultimate disposition. In the *Wilderness Sanctuary* case, the cues provided by the President's knowledge of the conservation issue and his certainty in regard to his own position permitted him to act after just a few minutes of conversation with an aide.[2]

Does the decision-maker know what the positions of other participants are likely to be or does he have to put out feelers, await developments, bargain, or use some other method of obtaining this essential information? One would proceed differently with knowledge of the disposition of forces than without it.

Certain well-known issues such as the tariff carry their own contexts with them to a certain extent. Their past history is such, the number of conflicts so large, that the participants tend to develop attitudes and predispositions which are activated as economizing devices whenever that subject matter impinges on their consciousness. By studying the history of the issue, the context into which it is likely to be put by a variety of participants may be ascertained.

Some issue-contexts exercise a severe dichotomizing effect in which opinion is polarized into two opposing groups. In others, by no means all of the participants have chosen sides. And there are still other issue-contexts in which the participants are fragmented or diffused into numerous groups taking a variety of positions. The probability, for instance, that an official's advisers will be receptive to opposing views or report the extent of disagreement or perceive the consequences of their actions will vary from issue-context to issue-context depending on the degree to which opinion is severely polarized or highly diffused.

Different issue-contexts, then, evoke varying decision-making patterns. The way in which the decision-maker relates himself to the problem before him, the procedure he goes through in solving it, the nature of his relationship to others in his organization, and the manner in which he relates himself to those outside his organization, depend partly on the type of issue-context.

III

It is desirable to demonstrate how analysis of the issue-context might help to solve a specific and troubling analytic problem. Let us take one aspect of the Dixon-Yates case for illustrative purposes. The solution of the problem, rather than its details will provide the focus of attention, since this is not the place to present a detailed case history. No attempt will be made to suggest more than the barest outline of the facts.[3]

The Dixon-Yates case, as the reader may recall, revolved about an administration-sponsored contract between two private utilities (headed by Edgar Dixon and Eugene Yates) and the Atomic Energy Commission whose purpose was to supply power needed by the Tennessee Valley Authority.

One aspect of the heated controversy over this project involved the role of Adolphe H. Wenzell, a Vice-President of the First Boston Corporation, a firm specializing in the marketing of utility securities, who also served as a consultant for the Bureau of the Budget in the early stages of negotiations with the private utilities. Later on, it developed that First Boston became a financial agent for Dixon-Yates and helped to raise over $100 million to finance the construction of a power plant under the contract with AEC. The opponents of the contract leveled serious charges of conflict of interest in regard to Wenzell's activities, and the Supreme Court later ruled that the Dixon-Yates contract was unenforceable due to conflict of interest involving Wenzell.

Although the possibility of a conflict of interest situation was repeatedly made known to high officials in the Budget Bureau, nothing was done to avoid the danger. The Eisenhower Administration reacted first by trying to withhold knowledge of Wenzell's participation, second by denying that he had anything to do with Dixon-Yates, and then by saying that what he did was of no importance. Long after the opposition had unearthed evidence of Wenzell's activities in connection with the Dixon-Yates project, administration officials, including the President, continued to make embarrassing misstatements concerning his role—misstatements which could be checked by any observer. This was noticed by contemporary observers, including *New York Times* columnist Arthur Krock who wrote that the Administration's guilt ". . . seems to consist of a series of indefensible blunders, including an effort to cover up errors which . . . it should have been obvious would be exposed at the capital. And, as Napoleon cynically remarked, a blunder is worse than a crime." [4]

The analytic problem is to account for the administration's response to public allegations of conflict of interest concerning Wenzell. Why were certain facts, obvious to outside observers, apparently disregarded by an administration which must be presumed not to have desired to injure its own cause and reputation? Several simple explanations offer themselves but scarcely withstand examination.

One is that the administration engaged in "an effort to cover up." This might account for the various attempts to disguise or slight Wenzell's participation in the project. There is, however, a fatal defect in this explanation. It does not account for the administration's failure to give an accurate statement of Wenzell's activities after the facts had come out. And the administration could only harm itself by failure to admit what everyone knew or could easily find out.

Another possible explanation is that the business background of administration officials affected their behavior. The business community does not look upon situations of dual interests with the same disfavor as does government and for that reason may not readily identify them as such. This might explain why some in the administration were not immediately aware of the dangers inherent in Wenzell's position, but it hardly suffices to explain why nothing was done after the seriousness of the situation repeatedly was brought to their attention.

The only way in which a rational pattern of behavior can be posited is to assume a failure in perception. If administration officials did not perceive the "facts" which others perceived, then their actions in regard to the conflict of interest problem may not have been dysfunctional in view of the world as they saw it.

In his book *Social Psychology,* T. M. Newcomb wrote:

> . . . Perception involves a good deal of *omitting . . . supplementing . . .* and *structuring* whatever is available to be perceived. . . . Any object, event, or situation is necessarily sized up in *relation to something,* and this 'something' constitutes the frame of reference. . . . The frame of reference in which a person perceives something determines his motivated response to it.[5]

What, then, constituted for all administration officials a common frame of reference of sufficient strength to account for their different perception of Wenzell's situation and the dangers inherent in their handling of it?

The first clue was that every single participant whom I interviewed emphasized that Dixon-Yates was part of the public-versus-private-power issue. To a man, these approximately 100 individuals insisted that Dixon-Yates could not be understood without knowledge of the larger issue and that knowledge of the power issue would enable one to understand behavior otherwise inexplicable. A second clue was provided by the readiness of the interviews to identify individuals as being on one side or the other and to express hostility toward those with whom they disagreed. Indeed, the most common term they used to describe the other side was "those bastards." These clues suggested the need for an investigation of the history of the public-versus-private-power issue.

Although no history of this important controversy has been written (a sign of the neglect of issue-contexts), fugitive materials were revealing. The public-versus-private-power issue has been one of the most persistent and dramatic controversies of twentieth-century American politics. It has been fought òut hundreds of times at the city, state, county, and national levels of our politics in the past 60 years. A 50-year-old private or public-power executive, or a political figure who has become identified with one or another position, may well be able to look back to 25 years of personal involvement in this controversy. The long years of dispute had served to polarize opinion so that virtually everyone in public life who dealt with this issue was identified with private or with public power. The power issue had introduced a dichotomizing element into public life which profoundly affected the administration's reaction to the Wenzell episode.

With this in mind, it became possible to construct a series of propositions stating that the public-versus-private-power issue carries with it certain important consequences influencing the behavior of those who make decisions:

1. A large percentage of the participants in the controversy are divided into two well-defined camps with opposing views. Active individuals who are impartial, uncommitted, or who dissent from the two major views are rare.

2. Professional bureaucracies have developed, with full time staff who make a career out of fighting this issue.

3. Since the opposing groups have long since been formed, their active members are acutely aware of who is on the opposing team. If there is doubt about which side a participant is on, intelligence is rapidly passed out placing him in one of the two categories.

4. Personal contacts are largely restricted to individuals on one's own side.

5. Having good reason to believe they have "heard it all before," the disputants are disinclined to listen to arguments on the other side.

6. The participants on each side have long since developed a fairly complete set of attitudes on this issue which have crystallized through years of dispute.

7. They have in reserve a number of prepared responses ready to be activated in the direction indicated by their set of attitudes whenever the occasion demands.

8. Views on this issue are held with considerable passion, leading to a strong tendency to oversimplify, to regard events and personalities in terms of black and white. Opponents are regarded as inherently suspect of all kinds of devious actions while supporters are considered to be above suspicion.[6]

9. While the participants may have a direct economic stake in the controversy, in time they come to feel that more is involved than money and property. Victory and defeat are seen in terms of overriding general principles which must not be sacrificed.

These propositions must be evaluated against a background of some of the most elementary things we know about the pressures working on top government officials. They are normally so busy that even fairly important matters must be considered in an exceedingly short time. The official acts partly, if not largely, on the basis of his past capital of accumulated information, attitudes, and prepared responses. And it is precisely in regard to the great and long-standing issues (like public versus private power) that his set of attitudes and prepared responses is likely to be best developed and to provide him with a much needed framework within which snap appraisals and judgments may apparently be made most safely.

In the helter-skelter of the day's activities the cost of accepting and evaluating new information may be so great that it is automatically rejected or classified as part of the previously familiar pattern. The official thus slips into a pattern of selective listening and selective limitation of the probable consequences of contemplated actions. This makes it easier for him to function without being deluged with more work than he can handle.

Given the long history and the polarizing effect of the issue under consideration, it is not surprising that all the President's advisers shared the same views—highly favorable to the private power companies and hostile to public power as represented by TVA. In this "hothouse" atmosphere with its mutual reinforcement of similar opinions on the power issue, the disinclination to see anything wrong in Wenzell's dual role does not appear quite so extraordinary. Where others saw a potentially explosive situation, the President's advisers saw a dastardly plot to discredit its private power policy—a tactic so vile as to deserve no notice from wise and honest men except to say that of course none of it, whatever it was, could possibly be true.

If the opposition wickedly contended that Wenzell's activities involved a conflict of interest, the administration was likely to interpret: conflict of interest suggests dishonesty; we are honest; the allegation was false; there was no truth in it or those who made it; Wenzell's role must have been entirely proper. If the opposition said that Wenzell was important, this came across as another public power slander whose very utterance would lead a knowing man to realize that Wenzell must have had nothing to do with it, because this was just the kind of dirty trick the opposition would be likely to play. It was the suspect and contaminated source of the accusations against which the administration reacted, and not the surface noise itself (undoubtedly a cover for selfish interests).[7]

When repeated questions arose as to Wenzell's role and the public clamor about it climbed to fever pitch, the administration's disinclination to pursue the matter was so great that the President was put in the position of making untenable statements whose accuracy could have been checked by a phone call. The President's advisers and purveyors of information, busy men all, were set to react to a preconceived picture of events provided by the power issue; reinforced in this view by contact with one another and men of similar views, they acted to meet the dangers of the world as they saw it—a world of events which differed radically from those perceived by other observers.

IV

Illustrating the diffused issue-context is Herbert Kaufman's, "Gotham in the Air Age," [8] from which we take an account of how New York Mayor William O'Dwyer dealt with the task of completing the construction of Idlewild Airport. The analytic problem is to account for the Mayor's prolonged indecision.

At the end of Mayor LaGuardia's term in 1945, it appeared that Idlewild would soon be completed. Construction was well-advanced, contracts with the airlines had been signed, and it was expected that operating revenues would be adequate to discharge the huge debt which the city would incur. It soon became evident, however, that these revenues would not be sufficient, and that the city could not afford to spend as much as $130 million of its legal debt limit in view of the pent-up demand for services which had been denied during the war. Robert Moses, a man in whom Mayor O'Dwyer placed great trust, favored setting up a separate airport authority to raise the necessary funds, thus relieving immediate pressure on the debt limit. This meant that the existing administrative structure, the Department of Marine and Aviation, would not be used. LaGuardia protested vigorously but the newly-elected O'Dwyer paid no heed.

The mayor immediately asked the State Government to pass legislation establishing a City Airport Authority. He supported Moses again by rejecting a suggestion by the nonpartisan Citizens' Union that the project be turned over to the Port of New York Authority. Despite opposition from LaGuardia and the airlines (who feared that the Airport Authority could not raise the money), the mayor persisted and the bill establishing the Authority was passed with a number of modifications. O'Dwyer lost no time in appointing Harry F. Guggenheim as Chairman and General James Doolittle and Laurence Rockefeller as members.

We can see that the Mayor knew what he wanted, accepted the advice of Robert Moses, refused to consider other alternatives, and was prepared to act vigorously. Then developments occurred which shattered these certainties and discomforted O'Dwyer.

Wearing one of his many hats as City Construction Coordinator, Robert Moses was apparently determined to control the Airport Authority. To make his point clear, Moses had its funds cut, its authority circumscribed, and its operations planned by himself. His objectives were achieved in a way: Doolittle had a rather hypothetical resignation suddenly accepted and Guggenheim resigned as Chairman, a bare three months after his appointment. But, Kaufman writes, "In gaining control, Moses had in effect discredited the Authority . . ." (p. 175) and it ceased to be an obviously good way to meet the City's objectives. The mayor was shocked by Guggenheim's resignation and no longer put such great reliance on Moses' advice. Having begun his administration in January convinced that "Moses had the right answer, [O'Dwyer] showed signs in August of wondering whether there were any right answers at all" (p. 183).

In the following months, Kaufman reports, the mayor was troubled, "And he left no doubt that he intended to investigate conscientiously every possible alternative. . . . There was a disturbed interlude of indecision" during which the administration found itself "deluged in a flood of competing ideas and interpretations that did not make a final choice any easier" (p. 183).

Deprived of firm moorings, Mayor O'Dwyer decided to open up the field. He let it be known that he would consider the previously rejected technique of city construction and operation; he instructed an engineer to submit a plan for a smaller airport facility; and he invited the Port Authority to make a study preparatory to submitting a plan for taking over all of the city's airports. A group of consultants shattered any fleeting idea that Idlewild might be abandoned by making a high estimate of future traffic and declaring that the field had to be put into operation as soon as possible. The Citizens' Budget Commission, a well-known research organization, recommended that the city build the airport and lease it to a terminal company, made up largely of airlines, at a rental equal to the charge on the city's debt. The Regional Plan Association advocated the development of a series of regional airports to be operated by a new tri-state agency. The Port Authority presented a $191 million program for three municipal airports but local officials were unhappy over many provisions which seemed quite onerous. A committee of architects, hired by the city for the purpose, submitted a reduced plan costing around $70 million. Meanwhile, the Airport Authority was still functioning and presented its own proposal with an estimated cost of $80 million. Thus the Mayor was caught between proposals for the city to build and operate, to build and lease, to turn everything over to a bi-state (Port) authority, or a tri-state authority. The price-tag varied from $70 to $191 million. In the midst of all this confusion and uncertainty, Mayor O'Dwyer turned the whole thing over to a five-man committee of city officials.

Under a heading entitled, "Perplexity At City Hall," Kaufman recounts how attacks were made on the Airport Authority's ability to raise funds. Then the Port Authority made a somewhat better offer. The mayor declared that if the city operated the airports, he would establish a separate Department of Aviation. The Regional Plan Association said it would support the Port Authority. At an open hearing before the Board of Estimate, it appeared that the Airport Authority probably could not raise the necessary funds while the Port Authority could. Comptroller Lazarus Joseph argued in favor of city operation, lest New York give away the valuable resources it had invested. The proposal for a terminal company was abandoned by its sponsors, who contented themselves with criticizing others. Out of the blue, O'Dwyer came up with the notion that the airlines might finance and build their own hangars if New York City constructed and maintained the other basic facilities at the airport. But the airlines later decided they could not do the job.

Amidst reports of a revised and much more attractive offer from the Port Authority, the mayor called a meeting of his five-man committee to study the proposal. He said that his mind was still open. "The discussion apparently produced still more confusion," Kaufman notes, and a three-man committee was named "to coordinate the thinking and recommendations" of the five-man committee (p. 189).

The three-man committee reported in a few days that it was strongly opposed to operation by either the Airport Authority or the Port Authority and in favor of city operation for the time being. But the Board of Estimate did not agree; Mayor O'Dwyer appointed a two-man committee to seek agreement with the Port Authority on the terms to which the three-man committee had objected. The negotiations were successful and the decision to let the Port Authority take over was made some eighteen months after Mayor O'Dwyer had first wrestled with it. His choice had been made easier because all of the alternatives except for operation by the city and the Port Authority had been withdrawn or discredited during the passage of time, and the imperatives for reducing the burden on the debt limit still existed. When the Port Authority proved willing to give the city a better deal, O'Dwyer made the decision in its favor.

"Gotham in the Air Age," is especially valuable for our purposes because it was the radical shift in the context of the issue which created difficulties for the mayor and led him to continually postpone a decision. The problem was not the complexity of the airport issue; it was no more or less complex when the mayor was ready to move ahead rapidly with the Airport Authority than when he had difficulty in making up his mind. Nor was the problem initially one of inability to calculate the stakes involved; the values remained essentially what they had always been throughout the case. More accurately, these considerations did not appear to be problems to the mayor when he operated under a polarized issue-context.[9] He accepted the need for altering the arrangement for Idlewild and put complete trust in Moses and the Airport Authority solution which he had devised. Calculation of the complex values involved, extensive consideration of competing alternatives, a search for the disposition of forces, all this was rendered unnecessary when his effective advisory apparatus was solid and trusted. When Moses acted in such a way as to bring his own alternative into disrepute, however, the Mayor began to lose confidence in him and the issue-context suddenly became diffused.

The results from the change in issue-context accord well with our schema. The mayor's position was no longer immediately apparent to him, so he began the painstaking process of calculating what was at stake. Thus Kaufman concluded that the mayor moved from one value to another, "endeavoring to do the right thing without perhaps ever fully having in mind what he meant by the right thing. . . ." (p. 193). Instead of confining himself to a consideration of one or two policy alternatives, the mayor began a search to dredge up every one he could find. This took time and further complicated his decision problems because of the difficulty of determining the likely consequences of each alternative. A period of great uncertainty ensued partly because the mayor lacked a frame of reference to give meaning to the "facts" which poured in from all sides. His indecision might have lasted indefinitely had there not been inescapable time pressure accompanied by events which removed many of the alternatives from consideration.

V

Simply suggesting that issues differ is trivial, but identifying elements in the contexts of issues which lead to different decision processes is important, particularly if this enables researchers to derive useful propositions and administrators to anticipate difficulties in their mechanisms for decision. Within the limitations that one always encounters in a new field of inquiry, enough has been said here to indicate how the analysis of issue-contexts could be used to develop propositions about decision-making.[10] One could explain why the memoranda prepared for the President on a polarizing issue would be advocates' briefs designed to secure his approval for action favorable to one side, without presentation of opposing views with anything like full force. One could also explain why everyone high in the President's office would be likely to share the same opinion. It would follow from the analysis of this kind of issue-context that these advisers would be likely to restrict face-to-face contacts to those who agreed with them. This in turn would reinforce existing opinion, and lead to a high degree of stereotyping about the opposition and to other predictable consequences.

Considering a diffused issue-context, let us suppose that a technological development occurred in the weapons field—a development so revolutionary as to cast doubt upon past approaches to national defense. It is doubtful whether the usual pattern in the President's office would be followed in approaching the new problem. The search for information and advice would range far outside the usual channels. All kinds of advice would flow in, much of it contradictory. Face-to-face contacts between the President's advisers and outside persons would be extensive. Although different individuals and agencies would in time become identified with different views and tendencies, so would the President's advisers be divided. The memoranda for the President would present a variety of conflicting views, or, possibly, would be delayed because of the conflicting views. The danger of disregarding relevant information and prematurely discounting political costs would be decreased by this diffused issue-context but the danger of bogging down and failing to come to any clear-cut decision would be increased.[11] "Gotham in the Air Age" illustrates a similar process.

VI

The administrator need not be a passive instrument who knows that different kinds of issue-contexts affect the process of decision in different ways but who is unable to do anything about it. Actions may be taken to mitigate expected difficulties. When dealing with a polarizing issue-context which unites his organization against others, the administrator may insist upon full reporting of information; he may seek outside information and advice to offset the undesirable consequences of monolithic internal opinion. When faced with a diffused issue-context which leaves his organization uncertain and divided, the administrator may place limits on the acquisition of information and the time available for decision; he may push for action to avoid perpetual indecisiveness.

Administrative effectiveness in this regard depends on our ability to accumulate experience by specifying the major ways in which issue-contexts differ in their tendency to invoke various processes of decision. A clearer and more complete specification of the differences among issue-contexts which affect the way they are handled will pay dividends to both the theorist and the practitioner. The possibility of using issue-contexts to make comparisons among the mass of case histories already accumulated is especially inviting.

NOTES

1. The term "decision-making" is as broad or broader than political science itself. We delude ourselves if we think that the adoption of this increasingly popular nomenclature has in any way delimited our traditional field of inquiry. "Decision-making"—referring to a choice among alternatives—is used here partly for convenience and partly to denote a convergence of interest in the social sciences on situations in which choices are made.

2. *Inter-University Case Program,* Series Number 13.

3. The factual material is taken from A. Wildavsky, *Dixon-Yates: A Study in Power Politics* (New Haven: Yale University Press, 1962). This manuscript contains complete documentation of all the factual statements made here. See also Sherman Adams, *Firsthand Report* (New York: Harper & Row, 1961), pp. 314–315; *United States* v. *Mississippi Valley Generating Company,* 364 U.S. 520; and the writer's "TVA and Power Politics," *American Political Science Review* 55 (1961): 576–590.

4. *New York Times,* November 29, 1955, p. 28.

5. T. M. Newcomb, *Social Psychology* (New York: Holt, Rinehart and Winston, 1950), pp. 90–95, 212, 221.

6. The disposition to disregard unfavorable aspects of one's own position is solidified by a common phenomenon: the activization of an issue results in an increase of hostility between the conflicting groups and an increase of solidarity within them. See B. R. Berelson, P. F. Lazarsfeld, and W. N. McPhee, *Voting, A Study of Opinion Formation in a Presidential Campaign* (Chicago: University of Chicago Press, 1954).

7. It might be said that this argument cuts both ways. Since each side expects the other to use foul means and is, therefore, on guard against the other, it would be just as logical to argue that the administration would do everything in its power to make certain it was above suspicion on such matters as corruption and conflict of interest. If this were true, then "political naïveté" might provide an acceptable explanation of the administration's early actions. But it hardly suffices to explain why the administration continued to act in a set pattern. The thesis propounded here is that the very factors which heightened the administration's suspicion and enmity toward its public-power opponents also blinded it to information which was perceived to come from the enemy and serve his evil purposes.

8. Harold Stein, ed., *Public Administration and Policy Development* (New York: Harcourt, Brace, 1952), pp. 143–197.

9. The propositions in the following paragraphs are essentially the reverse of those given for the polarized issue-context in the Dixon-Yates case above.

10. Some might not think it necessary to add that in American national government, where influence is highly fragmented, different decision areas (scopes) are likely to involve different decision-makers. Yet since the notion of the "power elite" dies hard and there still exists a disposition to seek out general influentials without regard to the decision area, there may be no harm in underscoring the obvious. In the absence of a single power center able to arrive at a position on most issues of importance and to get its way against opposition, national policy is made largely by a series of ad-hoc coalitions which vary with each issue area. The affected interests mobilize support from agencies and bureaus, congressional committees and individual Congressmen, the political parties, other interests, the Executive Office, and elsewhere. Much of this work is done on an informal basis which makes it difficult to describe, but those involved in a particular area get to know what has to be done and are able to chart a path through this complex maze. Some work in American politics has been done in describing the politics of agriculture, labor, veterans' affairs and so on, so that researchers need not start from scratch in charting the usual pattern of relationships. However, far more systematic effort is called for in covering all the major decision areas and mapping out the interests that are involved, their channels of communication, and the relationships among them. Increased stress on issue-contexts should help achieve this result.

11. The degree of confidence to be accorded to these predictions would depend, to be sure, on gathering a decent sample of issue-contexts. But there need be no barrier to this if the importance of the analysis of issue-contexts is recognized. It will be found, of course, that other factors alter the picture, thus necessitating reformulation of the original proposition to take the relevant circumstances into account. Far from being a cause for despair, this step should provide interesting opportunities for analysis. At the very least, the analyst will have been made aware that a deviant case exists and requires investigation.

The construction of a fully developed typology of issue-contexts which would indicate the observed consequences for decision in the different categories would be most desirable. This task, however, must await the sensitization of researchers to the usefulness of the analysis of issue-contexts and their attempt to apply it to a wide variety of decision areas.

PART II

The Practical Consequences of Theory

8

PRACTICAL CONSEQUENCES
OF THE THEORETICAL STUDY
OF DEFENSE POLICY

This is a venture in the sociology of knowledge. The ways in which national defense policy is studied, rather than its content, is the subject of this essay-review. Its concern is more with the structure of arguments than with their substance. My thesis is that the nature of the problem—preventing or recuperating from nuclear war—helps generate consequences which go far beyond the original subject matter.

The Study of Defense Policy as a Problem in Theory

No one has had experience with nuclear war. Indeed, the major purpose of devising defense policy is to avoid such a war. Defense policy may be described, therefore, as dealing with future states we do not know and manifestly do not wish to discover. Many possibilities must be considered to avoid them. If a person believed that there was a one in ten probability of suffering a slight scratch during the day, he would ordinarily be justified in taking only modest precautions. But if he believed that there was a one to a hundred probability of being killed, he might wish to take far more extensive precautions, despite the relatively low chance he was taking. The improbability of the alternative must be weighed against the magnitude of the danger. The enormous threat posed to the entire society by the specter of nuclear war strongly suggests that all sorts of improbable situations must be taken into account. The study of defense policy, accordingly requires expertise in the improbable, if not the farfetched.

From *Public Administration Review* 25 (March 1965), pp. 90–102. Reprinted by permission.

How could a nuclear war be prevented? How might it start? How might it be terminated if it did start? Could damage be limited and, if so, how could this be done? If experience provided answers to the questions, we would probably not be in a position to make use of them except in the problematical attempt to construct a new civilization. We can, however, imagine how a war might start, what it might be like, and how it (or we) might end. We need to create artificial worlds, based on various assumptions, and try to work out the consequences. Models of conflict (or conflict-avoidance if a euphemism is preferred) must take the place of the experience we do not wish to have.

In the imaginative and disciplined creation of the artificial worlds used for analysis, the participants have to be specified and given motives and degrees of rationality or irrationality. In the beginning, actions and reactions are given and decision-rules for generating new alternatives are specified. The trains of consequences generated under different conditions may be worked out and intellectual experiments made which vary key factors in order to observe the changes which take place. "Confirmation" of a kind may be sought through historical analogy, rules for determining internal consistency, or by testing central propositions in other environments. When experience means disaster, the world of theory is the only one appropriate for the study of nuclear war.

The point is not that specific defense policies can be built directly out of abstract models. That would defeat both the purpose of the models and of the policies. Theories mean simplification and abstraction from reality; if we could at once comprehend the world in all its complexity we would need no theories. Circumstances alter cases and policies require adjustment to particular situations. In this sense, there is no substitute for good judgment. Because there is also no substitute for theories in defense policy, however, the theories provide the basis from which adjustments are made to fit specific circumstances. The real question is not whether defense policy shall be based on some proposition which is necessarily a simplification but, rather which simplification shall inform the policy.

The Anti-Intellectual Approach

The study of defense policy is at once fascinating and terrible. The problems provide a challenge for the most ingenious mind, highlighted by the realization that human destinies are implicated in the analysis. Work can hardly be done without a professional attitude. The proverbial jokes of psychiatrists and the grizzly humor of surgeons help maintain the detachment these professionals need if they are to work in the midst of tragedy. The defense intellectual's emotional resources would soon be depleted if he expended a huge amount of effort on every aspect of his macabre subject matter. It would hardly be productive to spend all day saying "my God" or "isn't it terrible." Yet the contrast between the flow of ink in the model worlds of the analysts and the flow of blood inevitable in nuclear war is bound to be provoking. If sufficient outrage is generated at this disparity, the result may be a sophisticated form of anti-intellectualism. The motives of the defense intellectuals may be challenged rather than their ideas. Only the rationale of deterrence may appear to be questioned, when actually the objection is to discussing the subject at all.

In an essay entitled "Critique of Strategic Thinking," Anatol Rapoport first says:

. . . that there is an inherent tendency in strategic thinking to simplify the analysis of a situation in order to make a decision problem more tractable. Decision problems can be cast into several models, which can be arranged in an ascending order of complexity. The more complex the model, the more problematic becomes the estimation of data required to solve the associated decision problem. Accordingly, pressure is constantly operating on the strategist to simplify the situation, either by casting it into a simpler model or by skirting around the estimation problem. The concomitant danger is in the omission of possibly the most essential features of the problem.[1]

Rapoport, it appears, would settle for models which represent the essential features of the problem as he sees them. His comments are reasonable and he is part of the tradition he is criticizing. As the emotional intensity of his writing rises, however, Rapoport abandons this approach:

The strategist's idea of making a conflict more realistic is simply to make strategic considerations more complex. We have accordingly accumulated a vast collection of Rube Goldbergian contraptions, whose paramount attractiveness to virtuoso strategists is 'ingenuity.' In spite of our hopeless entanglements in this monstrous maze, most of us are quick to accuse those who would reformulate the issues and problems in human terms of muddleheadedness and naïveté. We have translated the game of strategy (where men may engage in ruthlessness and cunning to their heart's content *because* it is only a game) into a plan of genocidal orgies, and we call the resulting nightmare 'realism.'[2]

Just as certain Senators blanched at the thought that *Strategic Surrender* should be a topic of research, let alone a public book, Rapoport simply does not want nuclear war discussed at all.

Kenneth Boulding, on the other hand has not given up on the mind. In *Conflict and Defense* he writes:

There is no way to Eden, to innocence or to ignorance; having eaten of the fruit of the tree of knowledge, it is Zion or nothing. . . .
We do have the gift of understanding, even of the systems that we create ourselves. It is not too much to hope, therefore, that man can learn to fly the great engine of change that he has made and that it may carry us not to destruction but to that great goal for which the world was made.[3]

He is utopian, perhaps, but stands firmly in the intellectual tradition. At one point, however, Boulding commits a regrettable lapse. Referring to a famous RAND Report on civil defense he says that:

The Rand Corporation is financed mainly by the United States Air Force, so that its studies must be accepted with the same kind of reserve that, shall we say, we might greet a study of the Reformation by Jesuits based on unpublished and secret documents in the Vatican; there is the same combination of honesty in the value system and bias in the commitment.[4]

There is no reason why Boulding has to agree with the RAND Report or the elaborations of these ideas by Herman Kahn in *On Thermonuclear War*. He is free to do what Dentler and Cutright have done [5]—try to refute, with the best intellectual tools in his possession, the idea that our society could be reconstituted after a nuclear attack. But to condemn potentially important propositions on the grounds that their source is suspect is to make learning impossible. The *ad hominem* road to peace looks easy but I doubt if it will lead very far.[6]

For some time the personal attacks on Herman Kahn created such a heavy smoke screen that it was difficult to see through it all and find any discussion of his ideas. The emotional force behind *On Thermonuclear War* comes from Kahn's strident insistence that we must think about the war itself. His thesis is that what happens after the war does matter. The moral duty of government officials is not to slit their throats but to save as many people as they can. Part of one's judgment depends on how one reacts to the possible results of civil defense. "After all, we saved 50 million people." Or "150 million people died and all is lost." Another part of this judgment might depend on the estimates of types and distributions of attack. At some levels of megatonage little life would survive, at other levels and locations a great deal. Civil defense preparations might also alter the likelihood of nuclear war or blackmail, and the costs should be compared with benefits from alternative expenditures. Having taken a close look at these and other factors, having found "the courage and the means to look *directly* at Americans under nuclear attack and after an attack," [7] it is perfectly proper for Dentler and Cutright to doubt the efficacy of a civil defense program. To say that the subject should not be discussed at all, however, is to abandon reason itself. A moral posture may guide thought, but is no substitute for it.

Here is a case in point. Several years ago C. P. Snow, speaking for the dual sovereignties of art and science, made an awesome prediction. He announced that at any one time there was a specific probability of a nuclear accident leading to a nuclear war taking place. In a relatively short time, therefore, by multiplying the probabilities, a nuclear war was inevitable unless something drastic was done to alter the world situation. Time is running out on that famous prediction, and we have learned that it is impermissible to multiply the probabilities since the question of whether they are cumulative is what we really want to know. It would take no great effort to announce a new, stunning, and hopeful discovery to the world. There is at any one time a finite probability of peace breaking out. If the probability would be .1, in 15 years there would not only be peace, there would be 150 percent of peace.

Simple moral judgments have a way of eluding one's grasp in the realm of defense policy. Secretary of Defense McNamara proposes a counter-force strategy in which the United States informs the Soviet Union that if a nuclear confrontation begins, the United States will direct its weapons to missile sites rather than to cities. The hope is that the Soviets will see the advantages of protecting their cities by saving our own. A large arsenal of nuclear weapons is required to implement this policy because it is far more difficult to destroy dispersed and protected missile emplacements than cities. Those who prefer a minimum deterrence policy would reject this alternative because they fear that the large number of weapons required might result in an intensification of the missile race. By keeping the number of American missiles and bombers down, they hope to help stabilize relationships among the great nuclear powers. In order to do this, and still deter nuclear attack, however, the smaller number of nuclear weapons must be trained on Soviet cities. Here we confront a paradox. Men like Dentler and Cutright who evidently think of themselves as oriented in a peaceful direction, end up reluctantly supporting a policy which results in holding women and children hostage, while the Defense Department tries to escape this dreadful course.

Students of defense policy are dealers in other peoples' futures. They traffic in the life and death of civilizations. Their knowledge can never be more than a poor match for the difficulty of their subject. The combination of elements which characterizes their profession guarantees eternal dissatisfaction with what they do. They (1) have no immediate experience, (2) must simplify, (3) are concerned with the improbable, (4) never are certain they are right, and (5) may exert a direct or indirect influence over the destiny of mankind. The desire not to be stepped on is more than a Texas tradition. Students of defense policy, by virtue of what they do, can expect to be attacked as demigods; they do "trifle" with the destiny of others. In attacking the entire basis of their enterprise, however, one risks attacking man's ability to control his destiny through the application of whatever limited intelligence he possesses. One could argue that intuition would serve us better. The real question, however, is whether disciplined intuition (meaning theorizing) has something to offer over the untutored kind.

The Spiral Model of Nuclear War

The study of defense policy brings one back to the most fundamental questions of social life. Whether or not some civil defense measures would be desirable, for example, depends in part on our ability to reconstitute civil society at various levels of damage and demoralization. In *On Thermonu-clear War* Herman Kahn has made a significant contribution to this prob-lem, first, by insisting on its importance, and, second, by developing meth-ods for making some kinds of estimates, however imperfect, of damage and recuperation under different conditions. Kahn may well be wrong in some of his specific conclusions, yet Cutright and Dentler use similar tech-niques in disagreeing with him. The authors of *Hostage America* make a notable contribution in drawing upon the many studies of disasters in order to find comparisons with the attack and post-attack phases of nuclear war. They would be less worried about initial panic and more about the possibilities of survival later on than Kahn shows himself to be. To decide among the rival interpretations, we would have to know a great deal more about how social life begins and what keeps people together. We would have to create whole polities in theory if we wished to get some idea about whether free institutions might survive or be capable of reestablishment. Grand theorizing has its faults. But we can expect it to thrive when the al-ternatives literally lack life.

In building model worlds one must make explicit decisions about the re-lationships that prevail. One's attention has to be focused on the forces that move the participants. To talk about defense policy in this context, therefore, is to talk about conflict. The model builder is perforce thrown back on his most elemental conception of what motivates different kinds of men and nations to cooperate and conflict under a variety of conditions. By turning his attention to the study of conflict in a broad sense, more-over, the analyst liberates himself to some extent (and at some cost) from dependence on direct observation of nuclear war. He can simulate war and peace. He can set up experiments among people and attempt the hazardous task of extrapolating to nations. He may gain control of his observations at the expense of relevance to defense policy. But no matter how he proceeds he must take conflict into account. If he does not do this explicitly, as we shall see, his implicit notions of conflict powerfully affect his work.

Robert Dentler and Phillips Cutright, the authors of *Hostage America,* seek "a simple yet powerful dynamic that will help substantially in revers-ing the spiral of nuclear terror that continues unchecked at present." [8] "A dreadfully regular pattern of events plays itself out whenever the process of extreme conflict gets going. . . ." While the origins of the cold war might be of some importance, the two sociologists care most that the great conflict between the United States and the Soviet Union "is in motion, and that this motion is likely to continue in one direction: toward unlimited nuclear war." The dynamics of this conflict, "the patterns common to all conflicts," begin when "the original issues in the controversy become dis-torted. The issues coagulate and change from specific concerns to a *general* dispute. . . . Original differences . . . become magnified. Disagreement grows into hatred. . . . The process in general grows because of involun-tary reactions to which participants fall victim." Conflicts not only tend to grow; they also polarize the opponents so that they take "either-or" positions and develop powerful, one-sided loyalties. "Strong action against an opponent, indeed, depends on polarization extreme enough to allow misperception of the other side. An opponent becomes an enemy when he can be viewed as totally bad." [9] The intense emotional involvement generated by the conflict leads men to *"want to act to resolve the conflict:* not to delay, negotiate, or search for solution. . . ." Caught up in the conflict, men are prevented from "taking the role of the opponent," from looking at the problem the way he does, and from generally seeking alternative ways of dealing with the situation. "Stale slogans that worked in past conflicts may be hauled out and substituted for new solutions." The frame of reference becomes oversimplified. "Issues are not considered on their merits but only through the distorting lens of commitment to one's own side of the conflict." Views become so rigid that anything the opponent does is seen as evil, while one's own side is basically good. At the very end, the noise of a futile attempt to establish a balance of terror drowns out the signals of the approaching ultimate conflict. [10]

The dangers resulting from the final culmination of the spiral process might be mitigated in one of two ways: the causes of the mutual misunderstanding might be dealt with or the fateful consequences of being caught up in the spiral might be reduced. Dentler and Cutright decide to take the cold war for granted. Their "goal is therefore to stabilize the most critical sector of the cold war frontier: to control the odds against thermonuclear catastrophe. To achieve this end, the United States and its allies should call for a multilateral pact to ban the production, testing and use of nuclear weapons and delivery systems." [11] Deterrence would not be abandoned; it would be scaled down. Each side would possess a small number of well-protected nuclear missiles such that no side could hope to destroy the other's ability to retaliate by a surprise attack. "Under this condition, an aggressor attempting a first strike would know with certainty that a reprisal on his own country's centers of population would prove fatal for national survival." [12] The United States and the Soviet Union would thus have only two options: they could do nothing or they could launch a mutually destructive nuclear war. If the scheme worked, the probability of a nuclear war occurring would be reduced at the expense of guaranteeing that if any kind of exchange occurred both sides would destroy each other. The kind of multiple options and gradations of violence for which Secretary of Defense Robert McNamara has been striving would be out of the question.

Dentler and Cutright capture very well the spirit of the spiral model of events leading to nuclear war. The key words are "in motion" "involuntary," and "misperception." Somehow it is all a dreadful mistake. This is how a nuclear war comes about when no one wants it. Men and nations get caught up in a cycle of events in which their responses become involuntary and extreme as they misperceive the situation. Each side expects the other to do the worst and, by its very precautions, justifies for the other its initial predictions. The conflict escalates as each party responds to the presumed provocations of the other until the spiral of events gets completely out of hand.

Although he uses fictional names (Andersland and Jedesland) the entire thrust of Anatol Rapoport's argument in *Fights, Games, and Debates* suggests that he finds a similar interpretation of the balance of terror quite convincing:

> . . . Suppose both have their missile-launchers zeroed in on each other's cities. The 'necessity' to launch the first attack now seems imperative. There is, however, perhaps a speck of sanity left in those who control the final irrevocable act. Yet, as they become aware of the 'necessity,' they cannot but become convinced that *the other is probably coming to the same conclusion.* The perceived 'necessity' is thus self-confirming. The more certain it seems, the more inescapable it becomes at an accelerating rate, ultimately ending in a mad rush on *both* sides to the launching platforms. Two scorpions in a bottle, to use Robert J. Oppenheimer's gloomy comparison.[13]

Infuriating, is it not? Perhaps some investigation into the psychology of perception—since all of this seems to be based on some crazy error— might reveal the source of the difficulties.

The adherents of the spiral model pay a good deal of attention to perception. Rapoport presents the following propositions:

> 1. Perception is a selective process, where not only stimuli are selected but also the way these stimuli are linked to form perceptive wholes.
> 2. There is resistance to change in the perceptive pattern. . . . Controversial issues tend to be polarized not only because commitments have been made but also because certain perceptions are actively excluded from consciousness if they do not fit the chosen world image.[14]

Since the basic difficulty involves the mental states of the participants, it is not surprising that Rapoport advocates a form of permissive psychotherapy. According to Rapoport, in the first step, the "novel experience of being heard and understood without being judged opens up for the patient potentialities of mobilizing his inner resources for reorganizing his image." When the opponent knows that he has been heard and understood he will be more inclined to listen to and to understand another point of view.[15] The second step calls for *"Delineating the region of validity of the opponent's stand."* [16] No matter how preposterous an assertion is, Rapoport informs us, one can always find some context in which it is valid, thereby further reassuring the opponent that he has been heard. Finally, an attempt is made to get the opponent to make *"the assumption of similarity,"* that is to see one's own side of the story. But this is hard. Rapoport says that "No rules can be stated for carrying it out, because an explicit following of rules is self-defeating; it makes the invitation appear as a strategy and calls for a counter-strategy." [17] The difficulty of carrying out the last step seems to be borne out by the fact that Rapoport and others have published attempts to see the world through Soviet eyes but that to the best of my knowledge no similar attempts by Soviet citizens have appeared in the public media.

Both Rapoport and Boulding devote considerable attention to "Richardson process" models, named after a British mathematician who developed a mathematical theory of war. The essence of Richardson processes consists in the mutual interdependence of the moves by participants in a conflict situation. An act by one participant changes the environment of the other, produces a reaction by the other, which in turn compels the first participant to adjust his move and so on. The excellent fit between this kind of process and the spiral model can be seen in Rapoport's revealing quotation from Richardson: "The equations are merely a description of what people would do if they did not stop to think."

In various places throughout his book on *Conflict and Defense* Kenneth Boulding compares business cycles to wars.

Thus, in the business cycle, we have a process of deflation, increasing unemployment, decreasing investment and output, and so on—the familiar vicious spiral. . . . Similarly, in international relations, within the general system of diplomacy, we can have a worsening process in which relations seem to go from bad to worse and in which arms races develop, feelings are exacerbated, and fears increase. This frequently leads to a crisis in the form of a war.[18]

While the bulk of his book, like Rapoport's, is given over to a theoretical discussion of various types of conflict, Boulding also contributes a variant to the spiral model. Having observed earlier that frequently "the character of an organization is determined by the nature of its enemies," [19] Boulding asserts:

The myth of the modern national state is that its armed forces are its servants, to protect it from having to submit to the will of other states or to enable it to impose its will upon others. What, in fact, seems to be the case is that the armed forces of the world form a social system of their own. . . . This paradoxical situation arises because what an armed force is organized for is to fight another armed force; hence the existence of national armed forces is completely self-justifying: each armed force justifies the existence of its potential enemy and has practically no other justification for its existence. . . .

One wonders, therefore, whether the path to national security does not lie through detaching and weakening the organizational and hierarchical bonds that bind the armed forces to the civilian state and through a corresponding strengthening of the bonds that connect the various armed forces of the world with one another. It may be more important to exchange generals with . . . potential enemies, than to exchange professors and concert artists. . . . Once we realize that the object of a disarmament conference is not necessarily to agree to disarm but to build an organization that unites the various national armed forces, the road to disarmament, which has seemed so hopeless, may be opened up. Once the armed forces of the world are united into a single organization, their functions obviously will cease, and, like the ideal Marxian state, they will wither away or, perhaps, one should say, fade.[20]

Could it be that one reason the spiral model of nuclear war is so attractive is that it permits the analyst to assume that basic conflicts do not exist among nations—at least between the United States and the Soviet Union? Dentler and Cutright see the nuclear weapons themselves as carrying the curse; Rapoport finds the danger in misperception; and Boulding discovers a symbiotic relationship in which armies are not dangerous manifestations of conflicts among nations but, rather, feed on one another.[21] Tragedy replaces evil in the world drama and then turns into a comedy of errors. The final scene of *Hamlet* is played over again but a new postscript is added: the dead hero's father appears, just returned from a business trip, and discovers that everybody has died because of some trivial misunderstanding concerning his whereabouts.

A basic fault of the spiral model is that the central phenomenon on which it depends—selective perception—is simply a statement of the human condition. We cannot see or know or comprehend everything. So we try to simplify and conquer. We develop partial pictures of the world and interpret events within our existing frame of reference. To say this, however, is not to say very much. Here we stand because of the human limits on cognition and, to paraphrase Luther, we can do no other.

In order to apply the spiral model to any specific situation we would need a set of criteria or decision rules, with appropriate weights, to tell us whether the structure of events corresponds to the structure of this model. The usual injunctions to consider everything or to reformulate one's frame of reference every morning are not helpful. While it is possible to perceive friendship as hostility, it is also possible to do the reverse. Prophecies may not only be self-fulfilling, they may also be self-destroying. I have in mind, of course, the appeasement model. In this model acts of friendship are viewed as signs of weakness by a hostile power. Its desire for aggrandizement is fed by delusions, which it fosters, that it wishes to find peaceful solutions to outstanding differences. As this power grows stronger, whetting its appetite on foolish concessions by nations which misperceive its intent, its aggressions multiply until it finally resorts to war. The prophecies of its deluded opponents are self-destroying in the sense that their false views of its friendship lead to their demise. Yet the proponents of the spiral model do not suggest how it is to be differentiated from the appeasement model or any other model.

Suppose we consider how Churchill and Chamberlain would fit into the mechanisms of the spiral model. Clearly, Churchill would have to emerge as the villain. He considered Nazi Germany as an enemy determined to take over his country and others if it could. His view solidified early and he refused to change it. Seemingly friendly acts by Hitler were interpreted to coincide with Churchill's fixed frame of reference. At no time was Churchill willing to look at the world through Nazi eyes; he felt that he knew the enemy all too well for that. Chamberlain, on the other hand, was determined to find whatever goodness existed in the situation. He not only put himself in the place of the Nazis, seeing that they did have some just grievances, but he was careful to accord Hitler the full measure of respect and equality. The great question, it would appear, is not whether one has considered everything, but whether one's necessarily limited view of the world is more nearly correct than alternative partial views.

In order to interpret a nation's actions one would have to know something (or make an assumption) about its interests, intentions, and goals. It is quite conceivable that a "hostile" act may be designed to promote greater friendliness. General DeGaulle's activities may be interpreted in this way. Failing to get approval for his proposal that the United States, Great Britain and France form a sort of directorate of equals to determine allied strategy, he has since taken slaps at American policy all over the world. No doubt the General has succeeded in reminding America of France's independence, and he may succeed in getting a greater voice in decisions affecting his country. Thus DeGaulle may rebuff moderate offers of friendship not because he is hostile but because he wants still more. Reversing the situation, friendly actions may incur hostility if they are interpreted as an act of weakness. In the case of new nations, some acts designed to be friendly may be rejected as bribes, or they may lead these nations to make outrageous demands which cannot be met. Henry Kissinger once wrote an article in which he observed that some neutral countries in the United Nations wished most of all to remain equidistant between the positions of the great powers. Consequently, American actions to accede to the assumed preferences of these nations and take a more moderate position only resulted in pushing them further toward the Soviet position. One might sigh for a real world in which love begat love but that is often not the kind of place the world has been.

It is not even necessarily true that correcting distorted perceptions nations have of each other would improve the chances for peace. It is just possible that if United States leaders had known the full measure of the unremitting hostility which Stalin and his advisers may have felt toward their country, they would have initiated a war. Surely, correct perception of Hitler's ambitions might have led to armed clashes in the 1930s. There may be unsuspected advantages in the inevitable degree of uncertainty which surrounds the purposes of men and nations.

The one historical case which the spiral model appears to fit (in regard to rigid mobilization plans) is pre-World War I. The appeasement model refers, of course, to pre-World War II. The debate over defense policy in the United States may be interpreted as posing this question: does the cold war resemble pre-World War I (spiral model) or pre-World War II (appeasement model)? There is no reason, to be sure, why many other models might not provide a better fit for our times. In deciding among the spiral and appeasement models, however, estimation of Soviet goals, intentions, behavior is crucial. The difficulty is that the participants in the debate do not usually formulate their positions precisely so that they agree in advance on what Soviet initiatives and responses mean for the validity of their models. If Soviet reductions in armed forces are deemed hostile what shall we say about increases? If the Cuban missile crisis does not show hostile Soviet intent, what would, short of war? It is to the credit of William Gamson that he has taken a first step in the direction of clarifying the situation.[22]

A Theory of Deterrence

Conflict is accepted as an inevitable part of relations among nations by writers like Kahn, Schelling, and Snyder. Following in the tradition of theorists from Aristotle to Spinoza and Madison, they ask how conflict can be made to serve good purposes, how the predictable hostility among men can be so channeled and diverted as to serve creative instead of destructive purposes. Like their distinguished predecessors, they may theorize for the ages, but they are compelled to prescribe for the moment. Painfully aware that the knowledge they need falls far short of the knowledge they have, they seek to provide the best guidance they can for the momentous policy decisions that will not wait for fully developed theories.

As the policy orientation of the defense analysts increases, their devotion to theory decreases. While their dependence on theory may ultimately be great, they have to show greater concern with fitting general ideas to specific problems. They revel in paradox and hard choices. They delight in finding unsuspected relationships. They stretch their minds to follow the ramifications of policies as far as fertile imaginations can carry them. Consequently, we find lists of factors to be taken into account, types of relationships to be considered, rather than statements of invariant conditions and consequences. The context is enormously enriched, somewhat at the expense of rigor and a sense of completeness. There are endless discussions of what may be expected if one nation does "A" and the second responds with "B" and the first counters with "C" and the second with "D" and on and on. A kind of introspective navel-gazing, a learned and astute intuition of possibilities, follows policies where formal analyses leave off. The result is, I believe, that there is no full-fledged theory of deterrence. What we have instead is an accretion of insights—dazzling, instructive, full of breathtaking leaps and whirls—yet incomplete and limited.

The kind of hard problem which students of defense policy like Schelling, Snyder, and Kahn have in mind involves the relationship between guarding against surprise attack and avoiding an accidental firing of atomic weapons.[23] If one had only to guard against surprise attack, it would be easy enough to set the retaliatory forces so that they would go off at the slightest indication of approaching missiles or bombers; if the "enemy" turned out to be a flock of geese that would just be unfortunate. If the only defense problem were to prevent an atomic accident, it would be easy enough to put so many locks on the weapons that it would take a long time to open them. The real problems arise when one must balance ability to respond immediately to a surprise attack against the desire to avoid accidents. The lesson to be learned is an important one: surprise attack and preventing atomic accidents must be considered together. The underlying logic of this argument, however, is neither developed nor connected with other cases except in the acknowledgment that the really tough problems involve conflicts among objectives.

The central theme of Glenn Snyder's rich and informative books is the essential conflict between deterrence—ability to dissuade an enemy from attack by making the risks outweigh the gains—and defense—reducing the damage the United States would suffer if deterrence fails. This paragraph from *Deterrence and Defense* is a good example of this mode of analysis:

A strategic retaliatory air force sufficient only to wreak minimum 'unacceptable' damage on Soviet cities—to destroy, say, 20 cities—after this force had been decimated by a surprise Soviet nuclear attack, would have great value for deterring such a surprise attack and might be an adequate deterrent against that contingency. But if deterrence were to fail and the Soviet attack took place, it would then not be rational to *use* such a minimum force in massive retaliation against Soviet cities, since this would only stimulate the Soviets to inflict further damage upon us and would contribute nothing to our 'winning the war.' If we are interested in defense—i.e., in winning the war and in minimizing the damage to us—as well as in deterrence, we may wish to have it (if technically feasible) a much larger force and probably one of different composition—a force which can strike effectively at the enemy's remaining forces (thus reducing our own costs) and, further, either by actual attacks or the threat of attacks, force the enemy to surrender or at least to give up his territorial gains.[24]

Snyder immediately observes that in the absence of an ability to knock out a very large part of an enemy's missile force (counterforce), any attempt to engage in full-scale retaliation against a Soviet move into Europe would be irrational because of the enormous losses we would suffer. Yet if we have such a counterforce ability this might work against the efficacy of deterrence because the enemy, fearing that we would strike him first, might decide to get in the first blow himself. If deterrence is our major objective, Snyder notes later on, we might wish to build-in an automatic response so that the enemy would know we would hit him with everything we had if he attacked. But if our goal is to limit our losses after an attack, we might do much better to hold back some forces for bargaining purposes "at the risk that deterrence might be weakened by the enemy's discovery of this intention." [25]

The Strategy of Conflict contains a superb essay on "Surprise Attack and Disarmament," with the most astute and complex analyses. In this Thomas Schelling states that a "number of anomalies and paradoxes . . . have to be faced if we are to recognize the virtues and defects of particular schemes and to comprehend the motives behind them." [26] One important conclusion he reaches is that disarmament, especially a large reduction in the number of protected missiles, might not always be a good idea. While it might be desirable to limit the number of missiles, the balance of terror —which appears to be the best we can hope for despite its uncertainties —can be made more stable by increasing the number of missiles each side is permitted to have. Schelling advances two main reasons to back up his conclusion.

First, the larger the number on both sides, the greater is the absolute number of missiles expected to be left over for retaliation in the event that either side should strike first, and therefore the greater is the deterrence to an attempted first strike. Second, the larger the number of missiles on both sides, the greater must be the absolute and proportionate increase in missiles that either side would have to achieve in order to be capable of assuring, with any specified probability, that the other's left-over missiles would be less than some specified number [large enough to deter] after being attacked. Thus the difficulty of one side's cheating, by disguising and concealing extra missiles, or breaking the engagement and racing to achieve a dominant number, is more than proportionately enhanced by any increase in the starting figures on both sides.[27]

Any number of disarmament proposals today are based on Schelling's argument. For if, as Secretary of Defense McNamara claims, the United States and the Soviet Union have such a large number of missiles, so well protected, that each can wreak havoc on the other after an initial attack, then the requirements for inspection are obviously much less than they would be if the addition of a few more missiles would make a crucial difference.

Having shown the illuminating insight and the unexpected connection, having demonstrated beyond any question the complexity of the relationships involved in thinking about defense policy, writers on this subject are prone to leave their readers with long lists of factors to be taken into account. According to Glenn Snyder, for example, there are ten major variables which enter into the determination of American minimum deterrence requirements.

1. The number and type of the enemy's attack vehicles likely to be used in the surprise attack

2. The reliability, accuracy, and 'yield' of the enemy's vehicles

3. The enemy's firing efficiency—i.e., his ability to coordinate firing of his delivery vehicles so as to maximize the effect of the initial surprise salvo

4. The accuracy of the enemy's intelligence concerning the location of our own striking forces

5. The timeliness and reliability of our warning system

6. The efficiency of our air defenses

7. The effectiveness of our passive force defenses—i.e., dispersal, hardening, mobility, concealment, etc.

8. The efficiency of the enemy's air defenses
9. The efficiency of the enemy's civil defenses
10. The enemy's threshold of acceptable damage.[28]

Yet Snyder is aware that the United States Government can only "attempt to guess how these factors are visualized by the Soviet Union," and must remain doubtful about how much prospective damage would be sufficient to deter the Soviets.[29] According to Snyder, the aggressor's calculation of risk is essentially the result of how he values his war objectives, the costs he expects to incur through a variety of possible enemy responses, the probability of these responses occurring, including lack of any response, and the likelihood of winning the war objectives as a function of various enemy responses. Snyder goes on to say, however, that "obviously, we are dealing here with factors which are highly subjective and uncertain, not subject to exact measurement, and not commensurate except in an intuitive way." [30] Where, then, is a theory of deterrence?

After observing that the horror of nuclear war has led to a stress on the impact of military capability on the enemy's mind rather than on his body, Herman Kahn insists that "If one wishes to discuss deterrence precisely, then one should first specify all the alternatives available to the enemy, and then the various threats and promises we can make to influence his choice among these alternatives." [31] Moreover, Kahn distinguishes between deterring an attack on North America, deterring an extreme provocation, and deterring limited moves. As he goes about the seemingly endless task of specifying catalogues of possible interactions between us and our enemy, Kahn is careful to point out the ambiguities and uncertainties. While the top Soviet leader might well wish to dominate the world, for instance, he probably does not want it at even the "low price" of losing Moscow and Leningrad, nor does he want it "enough (we hope) to start a war in cold blood—at least not unless we have been incredibly careless." [32] Is deterrence, then, based on hope as well as fear?

Either there is no theory of deterrence or it is so blatant that it is encapsulated in the very statement of the deterrence situation. One nation will refrain from launching a first strike against a second nation because there is a very low probability of the first nation destroying enough of the second nation's retaliatory power to avoid enormous destruction of life and property. Presumably, the will to live and to enjoy modern industrial life is being tested here. It is not necessary to postulate a great deal of rationality to believe in this notion of deterrence. All that is required is sufficient rationality so that no government will commit (1) suicide and/or (2) homicide on its population and resources. If both sides are highly vulnerable, stable deterrence would appear to have been achieved. Yet it is by no means clear, as Schelling, Kahn, and Snyder observe many times, whether what is incredible for one side will be equally incredible for the other. Nor can we be certain how nations will respond to all sorts of provocations which might lead to escalation originally intended by no one. While one might have confidence even in subjective probabilities which appear reasonable and which are hedged about by making the most pessimistic assumptions and allowing the largest margin for error, this confidence is rapidly dissipated at the end of an involved change of interactions. The motivation assumed for deterrence is at once so compelling and simple-minded that one tends to vacillate between belief that it could not (because it must not?) fail, or that it is bound to (because it must?) fail.

A signal failure in the study of deterrence is the nearly universal tendency to deal with nations as if the most crucial decisions were made by single individuals instead of groups of leaders operating under the constraints of a particular political system. The best theory may be useless if it is not so conceived as to be able to enter into the decision-making processes of the governments involved. Since Bernard Cohen has made a splendid statement of the case I would make here,[33] I shall content myself with the statement that an organization theory of deterrence might make a great deal of sense. We need to know not so much about individual rationality as about organization rationality in particular types of political systems. Internal bargaining over policy is no less an important subject than bargaining among nations. Administrative theory should, therefore, play a central part in theories of deterrence.[34]

Despite the lack of a whole theory—deterrence is based on a catalogue of propositions like beads on a string—defense policy is evidently based on deterrence. What has been done, in my opinion, is to give deterrence a limited, technical, and highly operational meaning which is immensely useful in providing detailed criteria for defense policy but which also avoids posing some of the most difficult problems. "Our strike-back capability," Snyder writes, "should be strong enough so that in all reasonably conceivable political crises, and in all degrees of limited conflict, striking first at the United States will not appear to be the best of all the available Soviet alternatives." [35] And Schelling declares that the balance of terror, meaning deterrence, "is stable only when neither [side] in striking first, can destroy the other's ability to strike back." [36] By using these definitions and by adopting the most pessimistic assumptions and taking into account America's great wealth, defense planners can build a high degree of invulnerability into the system. While to be invulnerable is not necessarily to deter, an operational definition of invulnerability has taken the place of a theory of deterrence.

The authors of the books discussed here respond to the lack of a satisfactory theory of deterrence in their own way. Boulding and Rapoport vacillate between trying to build a theoretical structure for the study of conflict and wishing to abandon deterrence (and conflict) as too fragile a reed for the safety of mankind. Schelling takes central components of deterrence—promises, threats, commitments—and subjects them to rigorous statement and some empirical testing. Snyder brings together what is known about deterrence so that the argument as a whole can be appraised and some methods found to make choices among alternative policies. Kahn is understandably concerned about what might happen if deterrence fails. Dentler and Cutright choose the form of deterrence which appears to them to be least threatening for human survival. In so far as they seek to build or base their analyses on models of conflict, all the authors are dedicated to the same goals using variants of the same methods. All of them would agree in large measure with Kenneth Boulding when he writes that the prevention of nuclear war requires rapid learning.

The difficulty is that we cannot learn from the actual payoff system, for mistakes can be fatal. The payoffs from which we have to learn can exist only in the imagination; hence the problem may very well be one of quickening the imagination. . . . In this process the development of a convincing body of theory is of the first importance. The body can learn only from experience; the mind can learn from the imagination. We learn by imagining theoretical models and projecting consequences from them. An experience that is fatal offers no opportunity for learning.[37]

Some Practical Consequences

In the absence of direct experience with nuclear war, compelled to depend on imagination, yet desiring rigor, where could we turn for help? Who specializes in the controlled use of imagination? The answer would appear to be: social scientists gifted in abstract thought and physical scientists willing to deal with problems involving people. Economists, for example, appear to have been especially successful in the field of defense policy. No doubt the kind of training they receive is responsible for their special aptitude. They learn how to manipulate symbols. They are taught to take a variety of assumptions, relate them to each other, and work out the myriad consequences in a formal and rigorous manner. Logical and (sometimes) quantitative techniques are part of reducing complex phenomena to symbolic form and working out the implications with some precision. Neither the reader nor the practitioners need to be told that their conclusions are no better than their assumptions. Whatever the reasons, defense policy has become the special province of a breed of men interested in abstract theory and capable of utilizing a wide variety of techniques for gathering the building blocks with which to compose their model worlds.

As late as the 1930s the number of people outside the military establishment who were professionally engaged in the study of defense policy could be numbered on the fingers. Today there are hundreds of such men. The evident importance of defense policy in an era of nuclear weaponry would undoubtedly have led to some increased emphasis on the subject. But the military might well have dominated the field had traditional criteria—experience and position—been sufficient to acquire entry. Instead, the military have had to recognize the importance of abstract thought. They have begun to train their own defense intellectuals in universities, war colleges, and research corporations. Now it is possible for a military officer to make a reputation enhancing his opportunities for promotion by writing technical papers which are well received by civilian defense intellectuals. The United States may be on its way to getting the best educated military leadership in all its history and possibly in most of world history as well. All the preaching about the need to improve military education has not had anything like the effect of competition by civilian intellectuals who established primacy in the abstract arts of vicariously creating worlds which the military are forbidden to experience.

Striking evidence for this point of view comes from a recent letter by Secretary of the Navy Paul H. Nitze concerning the selection of top naval officers. Writing to the President of the 1965 Flag Selection Board on May 18, 1964, Nitze declared:

> After giving careful consideration to qualification for sea command and required specializations, I believe the selection board should place great stress on seeking evidence, in the past performance of prospective flag officers, of the qualities of flexibility of mind, analytical thought processes, creativity and imagination which will best qualify them to compete with the increasingly professional and intellectual civilian leadership within an increasingly integrated Defense Department.[38]

Freely translated, Nitze's remarks suggest that it is well and good to have admirals who can run ships. No one wants to see carriers run aground. But there is a tough bunch of civilian intellectuals in the Defense Department whose standards must be met if the Navy is to continue to run its own affairs. Unless an Admiral can exercise what Nitze later calls "unique intellectual leadership," unless he is prepared to "rely less on the lessons of past experience and more on his basic qualities of intellect and thoughtfulness," [39] his future and the Navy's future may be bleak.

The rise of the defense intellectuals has given the President of the United States enhanced ability to control defense policy. No longer is he dependent for advice on the military. He can choose among defense intellectuals from the research corporations and the academies for alternative sources of advice. He can install these men in his own office. He can play them off against each other or use them to extend spheres of coordination. Presidents can now generate more alternatives, from a wider range of sources than ever before. (Part of the summer of 1914 crisis might have been avoided had there been informed civilian criticism of rigid military plans.) In an analogous situation, the Secretary of Defense has been able to enhance his control of departmental policy because of his ability to bring in men who could compete with professional soldiers.

Without a body of doctrine, however, without at least some common vocabulary and concepts, Presidents and Secretaries of Defense might be too bewildered by the complexity of nuclear situations to act at all. But knowledge of doctrine about deterrence has been widely diffused; it can be picked up by any intelligent person who will read books or listen to enough hours of conversation. As a result, civilians can feel that they understand what is going on in defense policy.

Consider the Cuban missile crisis. The actions of the American Government can be read, in part, as a gloss on Thomas Schelling's *The Strategy of Conflict.* Although top decision-makers may not have read Schelling, his major ideas were certainly "in the air." An important part of American strategy at the outset required following a Schellingesque rule: get in the first unambiguous ultimatum! In this way the burden of initiating disastrous conflict, or of acts which may escalate into such conflict, is thrown upon one's opponents. Public statements were made and troops called up in order to give firm evidence of American commitment, while care was taken to permit the Soviet to decommit. Certain military communications were made public in order to convince Soviet leaders that America was firm but not inordinately hostile. All this is strikingly reminiscent of Schelling's work on the patterns of actions and communications by which commitments are established and broken down. In Schelling's work one also finds experiments in which people are given maps and told that if they pick the same point to meet as another person they will be rewarded. Quite often, one feature of the map or picture turns out to be so prominent in the minds of the subjects that they agree to meet there without any communication. From his insights and from experiments like these, Schelling propounds notions about the importance of maintaining certain evident distinctions as part of implicit agreements between contestants which help reduce conflict. Great care was taken, along these lines, to avoid killing Soviet troops in order to maintain the useful convention of no direct armed attacks.

Perhaps the most extraordinary feature of Presidential action during the Cuban missile crisis was the degree to which the Commander-in-Chief of the Armed Forces insisted on controlling even the smallest moves. From the positioning of ships to the methods of boarding, to the precise words and actions to be taken by individual soldiers and sailors, the President and his civilian advisers were in control. Aside from the benefits conferred by modern means of communication, the President could not have done this without the support of defense intellectuals and the fund of doctrine which they were able to draw upon and share with him.

The prevention of nuclear war is the great problem of our time. We can afford to deal with other problems only so long as we keep this one from blowing up on us. Thus it would not be surprising if the modes of analysis and the intellectual style which have proved useful in the area of national defense would be accorded the highest form of flattery—imitation. Governor Brown of California calls on talent from the aero-space industries to apply systems analysis to difficult state problems. Department heads consider the advisability of surrounding themselves with a group of "whiz kids." The Corps of Engineers moves toward more systematic analysis of water problems. More and more men who can create artificial worlds will be called on to solve the problems of the "real world." I have no doubt that there will be a great deal of abuse and inappropriate use of these tools. But I am even more certain that we have just begun to feel the impact of the study of defense policy on the values and practices of public administration.

Students of public policy usually attempt to account for how decisions are made to deliver prescriptions about how they ought to be made. In both cases policy is treated as the dependent variable which has to be explained. Enough has been said, however, to suggest that the ways in which the dominant problems of the time are handled may set the style for dealing with other areas of policy. The attempt of the Soviet Union to place missiles in Cuba, for instance, is not unlike Khrushchev's virgin lands policy or the practice of "storming" to achieve production goals; Soviet decision-makers characteristically attempt to deal with deep-seated problems of industrialization by furious, last-minute campaigns involving some "gimmick." The myriad ramifications of the study of defense policy give eloquent testimony to the power of thought. The characteristic mode through which major policies are attacked thus becomes an independent variable which may be given explanatory power in accounting for ways of problem solving. The analysis of intellectual fashions deserves greater emphasis than it has yet received.

NOTES

1. Anatol Rapoport, "Critique of Strategic Thinking," in Roger Fisher, ed., *International Conflict and Behavioral Science: The Craigville Papers* (New York: Basic Books, 1964), p. 112.

2. *Ibid.*, p. 234.

3. Kenneth E. Boulding, *Conflict and Defense: A General Theory* (New York: Harper & Row, 1963), pp. 342–343.

4. *Ibid.*, p. 332.

5. Robert A. Dentler and Phillips Cutright, *Hostage America: Human Aspects of a Nuclear Attack and a Program of Prevention*, assisted by Robert Van Dam and Peter W. Morrison (Boston: Beacon Press, 1963).

6. Rapoport's latest book substantiates this conclusion. The proportion of diatribe to analysis (the d/a ratio) has become very high. See Anatol Rapoport, *Strategy and Conscience* (New York: Harper & Row, 1964).

7. Herman Kahn, *On Thermonuclear War* (Princeton: Princeton University Press, 1961), p. ix.

8. Dentler and Cutright, *op. cit.*, p. xii.

9. *Ibid.*, p. 79.

10. *Ibid.*, pp. 80–81.

11. *Ibid.*, p. 81.

12. *Ibid.*, p. 82.

13. Anatol Rapoport, *Fights, Games, and Debates* (Ann Arbor: University of Michigan Press, 1960), p. 173.

14. *Ibid.*, pp. 254, 258.

15. *Ibid.,* p. 286.
16. *Ibid.,* p. 287.
17. *Ibid.*
18. Boulding, *op. cit.,* p. 250.
19. *Ibid.,* p. 150.
20. *Ibid.,* pp. 339–340.
21. Roughly similar views are held by Morton Deutsch, E. James Lieberman, Urie Bronfenbrenner, Lester Grinspoon, and Arthur I. Waskow in their essays in Fisher, *op. cit.*
22. William A. Gamson, "Evaluating Beliefs about International Conflicts," in Fisher, *op. cit.,* pp. 27–40. Gamson shows that different beliefs about Soviet behavior, a strong indication of the difficulties involved in reaching unambiguous conclusions.
23. Thomas C. Schelling, *The Strategy of Conflict* (Cambridge: Harvard University Press, 1963); Glenn H. Snyder, *Deterrence and Defense: Toward a Theory of National Security* (Princeton: Princeton University Press, 1961).
24. Snyder, *op. cit.,* pp. 5–6.
25. *Ibid.,* p. 67, fn. 11.
26. Schelling, *op. cit.,* p. 233.
27. *Ibid.,* p. 236.
28. Snyder, *op. cit.,* p. 55.
29. *Ibid.,* pp. 55–57.
30. *Ibid.,* pp. 12–13.
31. Kahn, *op. cit.,* p. 126.
32. *Ibid.,* p. 134.
33. Bernard C. Cohen, "Military Policy and the Art of the Possible: A Review," *Journal of Conflict Resolution* 6 (June 1962): 154–159.
34. Boulding does talk about organizations, and Kahn sees the necessity for studying committee systems and improving the structure of defense organizations. Grinspoon and Fisher also consider organizations and decision-making structures in essays in Fisher, *op. cit.*
35. Snyder, *op. cit.,* p. 60.
36. Schelling, *op. cit.,* p. 232.
37. Kenneth Boulding, "Toward a Theory of Peace," in Fisher, *op. cit.,* pp. 85–86.
38. Senate Committee on Government Operations, Subcommittee on National Security Staffing and Operations, *Administration of National Security, Hearings,* 88th Congress, 2nd session, 1964, p. 589.
39. *Ibid.,* pp. 589–590.

9

POLITICAL IMPLICATIONS OF
BUDGETARY REFORM

A large part of the literature on budgeting in the United States is concerned with reform. The goals of the proposed reforms are couched in similar language—economy, efficiency, improvement, or just better budgeting. The President, the Congress and its committees, administrative agencies, even the interested citizenry are all to gain by some change in the way the budget is formulated, presented, or evaluated. There is little or no realization among the reformers, however, that any effective change in budgetary relationships must necessarily alter the outcomes of the budgetary process. Otherwise, why bother? Far from being a neutral matter of "better budgeting," proposed reforms inevitably contain important implications for the political system, that is for the "who gets what" of governmental decisions. What are some of the major political implications of budgetary reform and where should we look to increase our knowledge about how the budget is made? We begin with the noblest vision of reform: the development of a normative theory of budgeting that would provide the basis for allocating funds among competing activities.

A Normative Theory of Budgeting?

In 1940, in what is still the best discussion of the subject, V. O. Key lamented "The Lack of a Budgetary Theory." He called for a theory which would help answer the basic question of budgeting on the expenditure side:

From *Public Administration Review* 21 (Autumn 1961), pp. 183–190. Reprinted by permission.

"On what basis shall it be decided to allocate X dollars to Activity A instead of Activity B?" [1] Although several attempts have been made to meet this challenge,[2] not one has come close to succeeding. No progress has been made for the excellent reason that the task, as posed, is impossible to fulfill.[3] The search for an unrealizable goal indicates serious weaknesses in prevailing conceptions of the budget.

If a normative theory of budgeting is to be more than an academic exercise, it must actually guide the making of governmental decisions. The items of expenditures which are passed by Congress, enacted into law, and spent must in large measure conform to the theory if it is to have any practical effect. This is tantamount to prescribing that virtually all the activities of government be carried on according to the theory. For whatever the government does must be paid for from public funds; it is difficult to think of any policy which can be carried out without money.

The budget is the life-blood of the government, the financial reflection of what the government does or intends to do. A theory which contains criteria for determining what ought to be in the budget is nothing less than a theory stating what the government ought to do. If we substitute the words "what the government ought to do" for the words "ought to be in the budget," it becomes clear that a normative theory of budgeting would be a comprehensive and specific political theory detailing what the government's activities ought to be at a particular time. A normative theory of budgeting, therefore, is utopian in the fullest sense of that word; its accomplishment and acceptance would mean the end of conflict over the government's role in society.

By suppressing dissent, totalitarian regimes enforce their normative theory of budgeting on others. Presumably, we reject this solution to the problem of conflict in society and insist on democratic procedures. How then arrive at a theory of budgeting which is something more than one man's preferences?

The crucial aspect of budgeting is whose preferences are to prevail in disputes about which activities are to be carried on and to what degree, in the light of limited resources. The problem is not only "how shall budgetary benefits be maximized?" as if it made no difference who received them, but also "who shall receive budgetary benefits and how much?" One may purport to solve the problem of budgeting by proposing a normative theory (or a welfare function or a hierarchy of values) which specifies a method for maximizing returns for budgetary expenditures. In the absence of ability to impose a set of preferred policies on others, however, this solution breaks down. It amounts to no more than saying that if you can persuade others to agree with you, then you will have achieved agreement. Or it begs the question of what kind of policies will be fed into the scheme by assuming that these are agreed upon. Yet we hardly need argue that a state of universal agreement has not yet arisen.

Another way of avoiding the problem of budgeting is to treat society as a single organism with a consistent set of desires and a life of its own, much as a single consumer might be assumed to have a stable demand and indifference schedule. Instead of revenue being raised and the budget being spent by and for many individuals who may have their own preferences and feelings, as is surely the case, these processes are treated, in effect, as if a single individual were the only one concerned. This approach avoids the central problems of social conflict, of somehow aggregating different preferences so that a decision may emerge. How can we compare the worth of expenditures for irrigation to certain farmers with the worth of widening a highway to motorists and the desirability of aiding old people to pay medical bills as against the degree of safety provided by an expanded defense program?

The process we have developed for dealing with interpersonal comparisons in government is not economic but political. Conflicts are resolved (under agreed upon rules) by translating different preferences through the political system into units called votes or into types of authority like a veto power. There need not be (and there is not) full agreement on goals or the preferential weights to be accorded to different goals. Congressmen directly threaten, compromise, and trade favors in regard to policies in which values are implicitly weighted, and then agree to register the results according to the rules for tallying votes.

The burden of calculation is enormously reduced for three primary reasons: first, only the small number of alternatives which are politically feasible at any one time are considered; second, these policies in a democracy typically differ only in small increments from previous policies on which there is a store of relevant information; and, third, each participant may ordinarily assume that he need consider only his preferences and those of his powerful opponents since the American political system works to assure that every significant interest has representation at some key point. Since only a relatively few interest groups contend on any given issue and no single item is considered in conjunction with all others (because budgets are made in bits and pieces), a huge and confusing array of interests are not activated all at once.

In the American context, a typical result is that bargaining takes place among many dispersed centers of influence and that favors are swapped as in the case of logrolling public works appropriations. Since there is no one group of men who can necessarily impose their preferences upon others within the American political system, special coalitions are formed to support or oppose specific policies. Support is sought in this system of fragmented power at numerous centers of influence—Congressional committees, the congressional leadership, the President, the Budget Bureau, interdepartmental committees, departments, bureaus, private groups, and so on. Nowhere does a single authority have power to determine what is going to be in the budget.

The Politics in Budget Reform

The seeming irrationalities [4] of a political system which does not provide for even formal consideration of the budget as a whole (except by the President who cannot control the final result) has led to many attacks and proposals for reform. The tradition of reform in America is a noble one, not easily to be denied. But in this case it is doomed to failure because it is aimed at the wrong target. If the present budgetary process is rightly or wrongly deemed unsatisfactory, then one must alter in some respect the political system of which the budget is but an expression. It makes no sense to speak as if one could make drastic changes in budgeting without also altering the distribution of influence. But this task is inevitably so formidable (though the reformers are not directly conscious of it) that most adversaries prefer to speak of changing the budgetary process, as if by some subtle alchemy the irrefractible political element could be transformed into a more malleable substance.

The reader who objects to being taken thus far only to be told the obvious truth that the budget is inextricably linked to the political system would have a just complaint if the implications of this remark were truly recognized in the literature on budgeting. But this is not so. One implication is that by far the most significant way of influencing the budget is to introduce basic political changes (or to wait for secular changes like the growing industrialization of the South). Provide the President with more powers enabling him to control the votes of his party in Congress; enable a small group of Congressmen to command a majority of votes on all occasions so that they can push their program through. Then you will have exerted a profound influence on the content of the budget.

A second implication is that no significant change can be made in the budgetary process without affecting the political process. There would be no point in tinkering with the budgetary machinery if, at the end, the pattern of budgetary decisions was precisely the same as before. On the contrary, reform has little justification unless it results in different kinds of decisions and, when and if this has been accomplished, the play of political forces has necessarily been altered. Enabling some political forces to gain at the expense of others requires the explicit introduction and defense of value premises which are ordinarily missing from proposals for budgetary reform.

Since the budget represents conflicts over whose preferences shall prevail, the third implication is that one cannot speak of "better budgeting" without considering who benefits and who loses or demonstrating that no one loses. Just as the supposedly objective criterion of "efficiency" has been shown to have normative implications,[5] so a "better budget" may well be a cloak for hidden policy preferences. To propose that the President be given an item veto, for example, means an attempt to increase the influence of the particular interests which gain superior access to the Chief Executive rather than, say, to the Congress. Only if one eliminates the element of conflict over expenditures, can it be assumed that a reform which enables an official to do a better job from his point of view is simply "good" without considering the policy implications for others.

Arthur Smithies may stand as a typical proponent of a typical reform. Identifying rationality with a comprehensive overview of the budget by a single person or group, Smithies despairs of the fragmented approach taken by Congress and proposes a remedy. He suggests that a Joint (congressional) Budget Policy committee be formed and empowered to consider all proposals for revenue and expenditure in a single package and that their decisions be made binding by a concurrent resolution. And he presents his reform as a moderate proposal to improve the rationality of the budget process.[6] If the proposed Joint Committee were unable to secure the passage of its recommendations, as would surely be the case, it would have gone to enormous trouble without accomplishing anything but a public revelation of futility. The impotence of the Joint Committee on the Legislative Budget,[7] the breakdown of the single Congressional attempt to develop a comprehensive legislative budget,[8] and the failure of Congressional attempts to control the Council of Economic Advisers [9] and the Budget Bureau,[10] all stem from the same cause. There is no cohesive group in Congress capable of using these devices to affect decision making by imposing its preferences on a majority of Congressmen. Smithies' budgetary reform presupposes a completely different political system from the one which exists in the United States. To be sure, there is a name for a committee which imposes its will on the legislature and tolerates no rival committees—it is called a Cabinet on the British model. In the guise of a procedural change in the preparation of the budget by Congress, Smithies is actually proposing a revolutionary move which would mean the virtual introduction of the British Parliamentary system if it were successful.

Smithies suggests that his proposals would be helpful to the President.[11] But the membership of the Joint Committee would be made up largely of conservatives from safe districts who are not dependent on the President, who come from a different constituency than he does, but with whom he must deal in order to get any money for his programs. Should the Joint Committee ever be able to command a two-thirds vote of the Congress, it could virtually ignore the President in matters of domestic policy and run the executive branch so that it is accountable only to them.

I do not mean to disparage in any way the important problem of efficiency, of finding ways to maximize budgetary benefits given a specified distribution of shares. In principle, there seems to be no reason why policy machinery could not be so arranged as to alter the ratio of inputs to outputs without changing the distribution of shares. One can imagine situations in which everyone benefits or where the losses suffered in one respect are made up by greater gains elsewhere. There may be cases where such losses as do exist are not felt by the participants and they may be happy to make changes which increase their felt benefits. The inevitable lack of full information and the disinclination of participants to utilize their political resources to the fullest extent undoubtedly leave broad areas of inertia and inattention open for change. Thus, the "slack" in the system may leave considerable room for ingenuity and innovation in such areas as benefit-cost analysis and the comparability and interrelatedness of public works without running into outstanding political difficulties or involving large changes in the system. Most practical budgeting may take place in a twilight zone between politics and efficiency. Without presenting a final opinion on this matter, it does seem to me that the problem of distributing shares has either been neglected entirely or has been confused with the problem of efficiency to the detriment of both concerns.

The Goals of Knowledge and Reform

Concentration on developing at least the rudiments of a descriptive theory is not meant to discourage concern with normative theory and reform. On the contrary, it is worthwhile studying budgeting from both standpoints. Surely, it is not asking too much to suggest that a lot of reform be preceded by a little knowledge. The point is that until we develop more adequate descriptive theory about budgeting, until we know something about the "existential situation" in which the participants find themselves under our political system, proposals for major reform must be based on woefully inadequate understanding. A proposal which alters established relationships, which does not permit an agency to show certain programs in the most favorable light, which does not tell influential Congressmen what they want to know, which changes prevailing expectations about the behavior of key participants, or which leads to different calculations of an agency's fair share, would have many consequences no one is even able to guess at today. Of course, small, incremental changes proceeding in a pragmatic fashion of trial and error could proceed as before without benefit of theory; but this is not the kind of change with which the literature on budgeting is generally concerned.

Perhaps the "study of budgeting" is just another expression for the "study of politics"; yet one cannot study everything at once, and the vantage point offered by concentration on budgetary decisions offers a useful and much neglected perspective from which to analyze the making of policy. The opportunities for comparison are ample, the outcomes are specific and quantifiable, and a dynamic quality is assured by virtue of the comparative ease with which one can study the development of budgetary items over a period of years.

NOTES

NOTE: This research was begun on a Ford Foundation Grant for Research in Public Affairs awarded through Oberlin College which made it possible for the author and a student, Judd Kessler, to interview some fifty officials involved in budgeting in Washington, D.C. Further work is continuing under a grant from Resources for the Future. I would like to thank these organizations for their support. I am also grateful to V. O. Key, Jr., Charles Lindblom, Nelson Polsby, and Allan Schick, for their useful criticisms. I would welcome comments from students and practitioners interested in studying the budgetary process.

1. V. O. Key, Jr., "The Lack of a Budgetary Theory," *American Political Science Review* 34 (December 1940): 1137–1144.

2. Verne B. Lewis, "Toward a Theory of Budgeting," *Public Administration Review* 12 (Winter 1952): 42–54; "Symposium on Budgetary Theory," *Public Administration Review* 10 (Spring 1954): 28–31; Arthur Smithies, *The Budgetary Process in the United States* (New York: McGraw-Hill, 1955).

3. Key, in fact, shies away from the implications of his question and indicates keen awareness of the political problems involved. But the question has been posed by subsequent authors largely in the terms in which he framed it.

4. See Charles E. Lindblom, "The Science of 'Muddling' Through," *Public Administration Review* 17 (Spring 1959): 78–88 for a description and criticism of the comprehensive method. See also his "Decision-Making in Taxation and Expenditure" in National Bureau of Economic Research, *Public Finances: Needs, Sources, and Utilization* (Princeton: Princeton University Press, 1961), pp. 295–327, and his "Policy Analysis," *American Economic Review* 48 (June 1958): 298–312.

5. Dwight Waldo, *The Administrative State* (New York: Ronald Press, 1948); Herbert A. Simon, "The Criterion of Efficiency," in *Administrative Behavior,* 2nd ed. (New York: Macmillan, 1957), pp. 172–197.

6. Smithies, *op. cit.,* pp. 192–193ff.

7. Avery Leiserson, "Coordination of the Federal Budgetary and Appropriations Procedures Under the Legislative Reorganization Act of 1946," *National Tax Journal* 1 (June 1948): 118–126.

8. Robert Ash Wallace, "Congressional Control of the Budget," *Midwest Journal of Political Science* 3 (May 1959) 160–162; Dalmas H. Nelson, "The Omnibus Appropriations Act of 1950," *Journal of Politics* 15 (May 1953) 274–288; Representative John Phillips, "The Hadacol of the Budget Makers," *National Tax Journal* 4 (September 1951): 255–268.

9. Roy Blough, "The Role of the Economist in Federal Policy-Making," *University of Illinois Bulletin* 51 (November 1953); Lester Seligman, "Presidential Leadership: The Inner Circle and Institutionalization," *Journal of Politics* 18 (August 1956) 410–426; Edwin G. Nourse, *Economics in the Public Service: Administrative Aspects of the Employment Act* (New York: Harcourt Brace, 1953); Ronald C. Hood, "Reorganizing the Council of Economic Advisors," *Political Science Quarterly* 69 (September 1954): 413–437.

10. Fritz Morstein Marx, "The Bureau of the Budget: Its Evolution and Present Role II," *American Political Science Review* 39 (October 1945) 363–398; Richard Neustadt, "The Presidency and Legislation: The Growth of Central Clearance," *Ibid.,* 48 (September 1954) 631–671; Seligman, *op. cit.*

11. Smithies, *op. cit,* pp. 188–225.

10

THE POLITICAL ECONOMY OF
EFFICIENCY: COST-BENEFIT
ANALYSIS, SYSTEMS ANALYSIS,
AND PROGRAM BUDGETING

What contribution can political scientists make to the study of the content of public policy? As the profession has been increasingly concerned with the processes through which policy is made, various political scientists have become worried about the apparent neglect of the substance of the major policy choices made by governments. It is particularly appropriate for political scientists to inquire about the impact on political life of different ways of arriving at and justifying public policies. In recent years economists have developed a number of important approaches to aid in the determination of public policy. The apparent success of cost-benefit analysis, systems analysis, and program budgeting in facilitating rational choice has led some high government officials and political scientists to champion their widespread adoption. Yet questions remain: Are these modes of analysis effective in making economic choices, and if so, are they equally helpful in making political decisions? In this essay I propose to describe cost-benefit analysis, systems analysis, and program budgeting, analyze the strengths and weaknesses of each method for particular purposes, and estimate the utility of each approach for governmental officials and political scientists.

From *Public Administration Review* 26 (December 1966), pp. 7–14. Reprinted by permission.

Efficiency

There was a day when the meaning of economic efficiency was reasonably clear. An objective met up with a technician. Efficiency consisted in meeting the objective at the lowest cost or in obtaining the maximum amount of the objective for a specified amount of resources. Let us call this "pure efficiency." The desirability of trying to achieve certain objectives may depend on the cost of achieving them. In this case the analyst (he has graduated from being a mere technician) alters the objective to suit available resources. Let us call this "mixed efficiency." Both pure and mixed efficiency are limited in the sense that they take for granted the existing structure of the political system and work within its boundaries. Yet the economizer, he who values efficiency most highly, may discover that the most efficient means for accomplishing his ends cannot be secured without altering the machinery for making decisions. He not only alters means and ends (resources and objectives) simultaneously, but makes them dependent on changes in political relationships. While he claims no special interest in or expertise concerning the decision-apparatus outside of the marketplace, the economizer pursues efficiency to the heart of the political system. Let us call this "total efficiency." In this vocabulary, then, concepts of efficiency may be pure or mixed, limited, or total.

A major purpose of this paper is to take the newest and recently most popular modes of achieving efficiency—cost-benefit analysis, systems analysis, and program budgeting—and show how much more is involved than mere economizing. I shall try to show that *even at the most modest level of cost-benefit analysis, it becomes difficult to maintain pure notions of efficiency. At a higher level, systems analysis is based on a mixed notion of efficiency. And program budgeting at the highest levels leaves pure efficiency far behind its overreaching grasp into the structure of the political system. Program budgeting, it turns out, is a form of systems analysis, that is, political systems analysis.*

These modes of analysis are neither good for nothing nor good for everything, and one cannot speak of them as wholly good or bad. It is much more useful to try to specify some conditions under which they would or would not be helpful for various purposes. While such a list could not be exhaustive at this stage, or permanent at any stage (because of advances in the art), it provides a basis for thinking about what these techniques can and cannot do. Another major purpose of this paper, therefore, is to describe cost-benefit and systems analysis and program budgeting as techniques for decision-making. I shall place particular stress upon what seems to me the most characteristic feature of all three modes of analysis: the aids to calculation designed to get around the vast areas of uncertainty where quantitative analysis leaves off and judgment begins.

Cost-Benefit Analysis

. . . One can view cost-benefit analysis as anything from an infallible means of reaching the new Utopia to a waste of resources in attempting to measure the unmeasureable.[1]

The purpose of cost-benefit analysis is to secure an efficient allocation of resources produced by the governmental system in its interaction with the private economy. The nature of efficiency depends on the objectives set up for government. In the field of water resources, where most of the work on cost-benefit analysis has been done, the governmental objective is usually postulated to be an increase in national income. In a crude sense, this means that the costs to whoever may incur them should be less than the benefits to whoever may receive them. The time streams of consumption gained and forgone by a project are its benefits and costs.

The aim of cost-benefit analysis is to maximize "the present value of all benefits less that of all costs, subject to specified restraints." [2] A long view is taken in that costs are estimated not only for the immediate future, but also for the life of the project. A wide view is taken in that indirect consequences for others—variously called externalities, side effects, spillovers, and repercussion effects—are considered. Ideally, all costs and benefits are evaluated. The usual procedure is to estimate the installation costs of the project and spread them over time, thus making them into something like annual costs. To these costs are added an estimate of annual operating costs. The next step involves estimating the average value of the output by considering the likely number of units produced each year and their probable value in the marketplace of the future. Intangible, "secondary," benefits may then be considered. These time streams of costs and benefits are discounted so as to obtain the present value of costs and benefits. Projects whose benefits are greater than their costs may then be approved, or the cost-benefit ratios may, with allowance for relative size, be used to rank projects in order of desirability.

Underlying Economic and Political Assumptions

A straightforward description of cost-benefit analysis cannot do justice to the powerful assumptions that underlie it or to the many conditions limiting its usefulness. The assumptions involve value judgments that are not always recognized and, when recognized, are not easily handled in practice. The limiting conditions arise partly out of the assumptions and partly out of severe computational difficulties in estimating costs and especially benefits. Here I can only indicate some major problems.

Cost-benefit analysis is based on superiority in the marketplace,[3] under competitive conditions and full employment, as the measure of value in society. Any imperfection in the market works against the validity of the results. Unless the same degree of monopoly were found throughout the economy, for example, a governmental body that enjoys monopolistic control of prices or outputs would not necessarily make the same investment decisions it would under free competition. A similar difficulty occurs where the size of a project is large in comparison with the economy, as in some developing nations. The project itself then affects the constellation of relative prices and production against which its efficiency is measured. The assumption based on the classical full-employment model is also important because it gives prices special significance. Where manpower is not being utilized, projects may be justified in part as putting this unused resource to work.

The economic model on which cost-benefit analysis depends for its validity is based on a political theory. The idea is that in a free society the economy is to serve the individual's consistent preferences revealed and rationally pursued in the marketplace. Governments are not supposed to dictate preferences or make decisions. The Grand Inquisitor is out.

This individualist theory assumes as valid the current distribution of income. Preferences are valued in the marketplace where votes are based on disposable income. Governmental action to achieve efficiency, therefore, inevitably carries with it consequences for the distribution of income. Projects of different size and location and composition will transfer income in different amounts to different people. While economists might estimate the redistributive consequences of various projects, they cannot, on efficiency grounds, specify one or another as preferable. How is this serious problem to be handled?

Benefit-cost analysis is a way of trying to promote economic welfare. But whose welfare? No one knows how to deal with interpersonal comparisons of utility. It cannot be assumed that the desirability of rent supplements versus a highway or dam can be measured on a single utility scale. There is no scientific way to compare losses and gains among different people or to say that the marginal loss of a dollar to one man is somehow equal to the gain of a dollar by another. The question of whose utility function is to prevail (the analyst's or that of the people involved, the upstream gainers' or the downstream losers', the direct beneficiaries' or the taxpayers', that of the entire nation or a particular region, and so on) is of prime importance in making public policy.

The literature on welfare economics is notably unable to specify an objective welfare function.[4] Ideally, actions would benefit everyone and harm no one. As an approximation, the welfare economist views as optimal an action that leaves some people better off and none worse off. If this criterion were applied in political life, it would result in a situation like that of the Polish Diet, in which anyone who was damaged could veto legislation. To provide a way out of this impasse, Hicks and Kaldor proposed approval of decisions if the total gain in welfare were such that the winners could compensate the losers. But formal machinery for compensation does not ordinarily exist, and most modern economists are highly critical of the major political mechanism for attempting to compensate: logrolling in Congress on public-works projects.[5] It is a very imperfect mechanism for assuring that losers in one instance become winners in another.

Another way of dealing with income distribution is to accept a criterion laid down by a political body and maximize present benefits less costs subject to this constraint. Or the cost-benefit analyst can present a series of alternatives differing according to the individuals who pay and prices charged. The analyst must compute not only the new inputs and outputs, but also the costs and benefits for each group with which the public authorities are especially concerned. No wonder this is not often done! Prest and Turvey are uncertain whether such a procedure is actually helpful in practice.[6]

Income redistribution in its most extreme form would result in a complete leveling or equality of incomes. Clearly, this is not what is meant. A more practical meaning might be the redistribution of income to the point where specific groups achieve a certain minimum. It is also possible that the operational meaning of income redistribution may simply be the transfer of some income from some haves to some have-nots. Even in the last and most minimal sense of the term it is by no means clear that projects that are inefficient by the usual economic criteria serve to redistribute income in the desired direction. It is possible that some inefficient projects may transfer income from poorer to richer people. Before the claim that certain projects are justified by the effect of distributing income in a specified way can be accepted, an analysis to show that this is what actually happens must be at hand.

Since the distribution of income is at stake, it is not surprising that beneficiaries tend to dominate investment decisions in the political arena and steadfastly refuse to pay for what they receive from government tax revenues. They uniformly resist user charges based on benefits received. Fox and Herfindahl estimate that of a total initial investment of $3 billion for the Corps of Engineers in 1962, taxpayers in general would pay close to two-thirds of the costs.[7] Here, greater use of the facilities by a larger number of beneficiaries getting something for nothing inflates the estimated benefits that justify the project in the first place. There may be a political rationale for these decisions, but it has not been developed.

In addition to redistributing income, public-works projects have a multitude of objectives and consequences. Projects may generate economic growth, alleviate poverty among some people, provide aesthetic enjoyment and opportunities for recreation, improve public health, reduce the risks of natural disaster, alter travel patterns, affect church attendance, change educational opportunities, and more. No single welfare criterion can encompass these diverse objectives. How many of them should be considered? Which are susceptible of quantification? The further one pursues this analysis, the more impassable the thicket.

Limitations in the Utility of Cost-Benefit Analysis

One possible conclusion is that at present certain types of cost-benefit analysis are not meaningful. In reviewing the literature on the calculus of costs and benefits in research and development, for example, Prest and Turvey comment on "the uncertainty and unreliability of cost estimates . . . and . . . the extraordinarily complex nature of the benefits. . . ." [8]

Another conclusion is that one should be cautious in distinguishing the degree to which projects are amenable to cost-benefit analysis.

. . . When there are many diverse types of benefits from a project and/or many different beneficiaries it is difficult to list them all and to avoid double counting. This is one reason why it is so much easier to apply cost-benefit analysis to a limited purpose development, say, than it is to the research and development aspects of some multi-purpose discovery, such as a new type of plastic material. . . . It is no good expecting those fields in which benefits are widely diffused, and in which there are manifest divergences between accounting and economic costs or benefits, to be as cultivable as others. Nor is it realistic to expect that comparisons between projects in entirely different branches of economic activity are likely to be as meaningful or fruitful as those between projects in the same branch. The technique is more useful in the public-utility area than in the social-services area of government. [9]

If the analysis is to be useful at all, calculations must be simplified. [10] The multiple ramifications of interesting activities can be taken into account only at the cost of introducing fantastic complexities. Prest and Turvey remark of one such attempt, "This system . . . requires knowledge of all the demand and supply equations in the economy, so is scarcely capable of application by road engineers." [11] They suggest omitting consideration where (1) side effects are judged not terribly large or where (2) concern for these effects belongs to another governmental jurisdiction. [12]

If certain costs or benefits are deemed important but cannot be quantified, it is always possible to guess. The increasing use of recreation and aesthetic facilities to justify public-works projects in the United States is disapproved by most economists because there can be a vast but hidden inflation of these benefits. For example, to attribute the same value to a recreation day on a reservoir located in a desert miles from any substitute source of water as to a day on an artificial lake in the heart of natural lake country is patently wrong. Economists would prefer to see recreation facilities listed in an appendix so that they can be taken into account in some sense, or alternatively, that the project be presented with and without the recreation facilities, so that a judgment can be made as to whether the additional services are worth the cost.[13]

Economists distinguish between risk, where the precise outcome cannot be predicted but a probability distribution can be specified, and uncertainty, where one does not even know the parameters of the outcomes. The cost-benefit analyst must learn to live with uncertainty, for he can never know whether all relevant objectives have been included and what changes may occur in policy and in technology.

It is easy enough to cut the life of the project below its expected economic life. The interest rate can be raised. Assumptions can be made that costs will be higher and benefits lower than expected. All these methods, essentially conservative, are also highly arbitrary. They can be made somewhat more systematic, however, by sensitivity analysis, in which length of life, for instance, is varied over a series of runs so that its impact on the project can be appraised.

Lessening uncertainty by hiking the interest or discount rate leads to greater difficulties, for the dominance of "higher" criteria over economic analysis is apparent in the frustrating problem of choosing the correct interest rate at which to discount the time streams of costs and benefits essential to the enterprise. Only an interest rate can establish the relationship between values at different periods of time. Yet people differ in preferences for the present versus the intermediate or long-run value. Moreover, the interest rate should also measure the opportunity cost of private capital that could be used to produce wealth elsewhere in the economy if it had not been used up in the form of tax income spent on the project under consideration. Is the appropriate rate the very low cost the government charges, the cost of a government corporation like TVA which must pay a somewhat higher rate, the going rate of interest for private firms, or an even higher rate to hedge against an uncertain future? As Otto Eckstein has observed, ". . . the choice of interest rates must remain a value judgment." [14]

If the efficiency of a project is insensitive to interest costs, then these costs can vary widely without mattering much. But Fox and Herfindahl discovered that if projects of the Corps of Engineers raised their interest (or discount) rate from 2⅝ to 4, 6, or 8 percent, then 9, 64, and 80 percent of the projects, respectively, would have had a benefit-cost ratio of less than unity.[15] This single value choice among many has such large consequences that it alone may be decisive.

The Mixed Results of Cost-Benefit Analysis

Although cost-benefit analysis presumably results in efficiency by adding the most to national income, it is shot through with political and social-value choices and surrounded by uncertainties and difficulties of computation. Whether the many noneconomic assumptions and consequences actually result in basically changing the nature of a project remains moot. Clearly, we have come a long way from pure efficiency, to verge upon mixed efficiency.

Economic analysts usually agree that all relevant factors (especially nonmarket factors) cannot be squeezed into a single formula. They therefore suggest that the policy-maker, in being given the market costs and benefits of alternatives, is in effect presented with the market value he is placing on nonmarket factors. The contribution of the analyst is only one input of the decision, but the analyst may find this limited conception of his role unacceptable to others. Policy-makers may not want this kind of input; they may want *the* answer, or at least an answer they can defend on the basis of the analyst's legitimized expertise.

The dependence of cost-benefit analysis on a prior political framework does not mean that it is a useless or trivial exercise. Decisions must be made. If quantifiable economic costs and benefits are not everything, neither would a decision-maker wish to ignore them entirely. The great advantage of cost-benefit analysis, when pursued with integrity, is that some implicit judgments are made explicit and subject to analysis. Yet, for many, the omission of explicit consideration of political factors is a serious deficiency.

The experience of the Soil Conservation Service in lowering certain political costs may prove illuminating. For many years the service struggled along with eleven major watershed projects involving big dams, great headaches, and little progress. Because the watersheds were confined to a single region, it was exceedingly difficult to generate support in Congress, particularly at appropriations time. The upstream-downstream controversies generated by these projects resulted in less than universal local approval. The scs found itself in the direct line of fire for determining priorities in use of insufficient funds.

Compare this situation with the breakthrough that occurred when scs developed the small watershed program. Since each facility is relatively inexpensive, many of them can be placed throughout the country, markedly increasing political support. Agreement on the local level is facilitated because much less land is flooded and side payments are easier to arrange. A judicious use of cost-benefit analysis, together with ingenious relationships with state governors, places the choice of priorities with the states and yet maintains a reasonable level of consistency by virtue of adherence to national criteria. Errors are easier to correct because the burden of calculation has been drastically reduced and experience may be more easily accumulated with a larger number of small projects.

Consider the situation in which an agency finds it desirable to achieve a geographical spread of projects in order to establish a wider base of support. Assume (with good reason) that cost-benefit criteria will not permit projects to be established in some states because the value of the land or water is too low. One can say that this is just too bad and observe the agency seeking ways around the restriction by playing up benefits, playing down costs, or attacking the whole benefit-cost concept as inapplicable. Another approach would be to recognize that federalism—meaning, realistically, the distribution of indulgences to state units—represents a political value worth promoting to some extent and that gaining nationwide support is important. From this perspective, a compromise solution would be to except one or two projects in each state or region from meeting the full requirement of the formula, though the projects with the highest benefit-cost ratio would have to be chosen. In return for sacrificing full adherence to the formula in a few instances, one would get enhanced support for it in many others.

Everyone knows, of course, that cost-benefit analysis is not the messiah come to save water-resources projects from contamination by the rival forces of ignorance and political corruption. Whenever agencies and their associated interests discover that they cannot do what they want, they may twist prevailing criteria out of shape: two projects may be joined so that both qualify when one, standing alone, would not. Costs and benefits may be manipulated, or the categories may be so extended that almost any project qualifies. On the other hand, cost-benefit analysis has some "good" political uses that might be stressed more than they have been. The technique gives the responsible official a good reason for turning down projects, with a public-interest explanation the Congressman can use with his constituents and the interest-group leader with his members.

This is not to say that cost-benefit analysis has little utility. Assuming that the method will continue to be improved, and that one accepts the market as the measure of economic value, it can certainly tell decision-makers something about what they will be giving up if they follow alternative policies. The use of two analyses, one based on regional and the other on national factors, might result in an appraisal of the economic costs of federalism.

The burden of calculation may be reduced by following cost-benefit analysis for many projects and introducing other values only for a few. To expect, however, that the method itself (which distributes indulgences to some and deprivations to others) will not be subject to manipulation in the political process is to say that we shall be governed by formulas and not by men.

Because the cost-benefit formula does not always jibe with political realities—that is, it omits political costs and benefits—we can expect it to be twisted out of shape from time to time. Yet cost-benefit analysis may still be important in getting rid of the worst projects. Avoiding the worst when one can't get the best is no small accomplishment.

Systems Analysis

The good systems analyst is a *chochem,* a Yiddish word meaning "wise man," with overtones of "wise guy." His forte is creativity. Although he sometimes relates means to ends and fits ends to match means, he ordinarily eschews such pat processes, preferring instead to relate elements imaginatively into new systems that create their own means and ends. He plays new objectives continuously against cost elements until a creative synthesis has been achieved. He looks down upon those who say that they take objectives as given, knowing full well that the apparent solidity of the objective will dissipate during analysis and that, in any case, most people do not know what they want because they do not know what they can get.

Since no one knows how to teach creativity, daring, and nerve, it is not surprising that no one can define what systems analysis is or how it should be practiced. E. S. Quade, who compiled the RAND Corporation lectures on systems analysis, says it "is still largely a form of art" in which it is not possible to lay down "fixed rules which need only be followed with exactness." [16] He examined systems studies to determine ideas and principles common to the good ones, but discovered that "no universally accepted set of ideas existed. It was even difficult to decide which studies should be called good." [17]

Systems analysis is derived from operations research, which came into use during World War II when some scientists discovered that they could use simple quantitative analysis to get the most out of existing military equipment. A reasonably clear objective was given, and ways to cut the cost of achieving it could be developed, using essentially statistical models. Operations research today is largely identified with specific techniques: linear programming, Monte Carlo (randomizing) methods, gaming and game theory. While there is no hard and fast division between operations research and systems analysis, a rough separation may perhaps be made. The less that is known about objectives, the more they conflict, the larger the number of elements to be considered, the more uncertain the environment, the more likely it is that the work will be called a systems analysis. In systems analysis there is more judgment and intuition and less reliance on quantitative methods than in operations research.

Systems analysis builds models that abstract from reality but represent the crucial relationships. The systems analyst first decides what questions are relevant to his inquiry, selects certain quantifiable factors, cuts down the list of factors to be dealt with by aggregation and by eliminating the (hopefully) less important ones, and then gives them quantitative relationships with one another within the system he has chosen for analysis. But crucial variables may not be quantifiable. If they can be reduced to numbers, there may be no mathematical function that can express the desired relationship. More important, there may be no single criterion for judging results among conflicting objectives. Most important, the original objectives, if any, may not make sense.

It cannot be emphasized too strongly that a (if not the) distinguishing characteristic of systems analysis is that the objectives either are not known or are subject to change. Systems analysis, Quade tells us, "is associated with that class of problems where the difficulties lie in deciding what ought to be done—not simply how to do it—and honors go to people who . . . find out what the problem is." [18] Charles Hitch, former comptroller of the Defense Department, insists that:

. . . learning about objectives is one of the chief objects of this kind of analysis. We must learn to look at objectives as critically and as professionally as we look at our models and our other inputs. We may, of course, begin with tentative objectives, but we must expect to modify or replace them as we learn about the systems we are studying—and related systems. The feedback on objectives may in some cases be the most important results of our study. We have never undertaken a major system study at RAND in which we are able to define satisfactory objectives at the beginning of the study. [19]

Systems analysts recognize many good reasons for their difficulties in defining problems or objectives. Quade reaches the core: "Objectives are not, in fact, agreed upon. The choice, while ostensibly between alternatives, is really between objectives or ends and non-analytic methods must be used for a final reconciliation of views." [20] It may be comforting to believe that objectives come to the analyst from on high and can be taken as given, but this easy assumption is all wrong. "For all sorts of good reasons that are not about to change," says Hitch, "official statements of national objectives (or company objectives) tend to be nonexistent or so vague and literary as to be non-operational." [21] Objectives are not only likely to be "thin and rarefied," according to Wohlstetter, "but the relevant authorities are likely to conflict. Among others there will be national differences within an alliance and within the nation, interagency, interservice, and intraservice differences. . . ." [22]

Moreover, even shared objectives often conflict with one another. Deterrence of atomic attack might be best served by letting an enemy know that we would respond with an all-out, indiscriminate attack on his population. Defense of our population against death and destruction might not be well served by this strategy,[23] as the Secretary of Defense recognized when he recommended a city-avoidance strategy that might give an enemy some incentive to spare our cities as well. Not only are objectives large in number and in conflict with one another, but they are likely to engender serious repercussion effects. Many objectives, like morale and the stability of alliances, are resistant to quantification. What is worth doing depends on whether it can be done at all, how well, and at what cost. Hence, objectives really cannot be taken as given; they must be made up by the analyst. "In fact," Wohlstetter declares, "we are always in the process of choosing and modifying both means and ends." [24]

Future systems analysts are explicitly warned not to let clients determine objectives. A suggestive analogy is drawn with the doctor who would not ignore a patient's "description of the symptoms, but . . . cannot allow the patient's self-diagnosis to override his own professional judgment." [25] Quade argues that since systems analysis has often resulted in changing the original objectives of the policy-maker, it would be "self-defeating to accept without inquiry" his "view of what the problem is." [26]

I have stressed the point that the systems analyst is advised to insist on his own formulation of the problem because it shows so clearly that we are dealing with a mixed concept of efficiency. Objectives are being changed. It may still be the case that if you build a better mousetrap the world will beat a path to your door. But it is apparently advisable for the wary sponsor to make sure he has not got a cheaper way to catch mountain lions in his basement.

Adjusting objectives to resources in the present or near future is difficult enough without considering future states of affairs which hold tremendous uncertainty. Constants become variables; little can be taken for granted. The rate of technological progress, an opponent's estimate of your reaction to his latest series of moves based on his reaction to yours, whether or not atomic war will occur, what it will be like, whether we shall have warning, whether the system we are working on will cost anything close to current estimates and whether it will be ready within five years of the due date—on most of these matters there are no objective probabilities to be calculated.

An effective way of dealing with uncertainty must be a major goal of systems analysis. Systems analysis is characterized by the aids to calculation it uses, not to conquer uncertainty, but to circumvent and mitigate some of its pervasive effects. Before a seemingly important factor may be omitted, for example, a sensitivity analysis may be run to determine whether its variation significantly affects the outcome. If there is no good basis for calculating the value of the factor, arbitrary values may be assigned to test for extreme possibilities. Contingency analysis is used to determine how the relative ranking of alternatives holds up under major changes in the environment, say, a new alliance between France and Russia, or alternations in the criteria for judging the alternatives, such as a requirement that a system work well against attacks from space as well as from earth. Contingency analysis places a premium on versatility, as the analyst seeks a system that will hold up well under various eventualities even though it might be quite as good for any single contingency as an alternative system. Adversary procedures may be used to combat uncertainty. Bending over backward to provide advantages for low-ranking systems and handicaps for high-ranking systems is called a fortiori analysis. Changing crucial assumptions in order to make the leading alternatives even, so that one can judge whether the assumptions are overly optimistic or pessimistic, is called break-even analysis.[27] Since all these methods add greatly to the burden of calculation, they must be used with some discretion.

A variety of insurance schemes may also be used to deal with uncertainty. In appraising what an opponent can do, for instance, one can assume the worst, the best, and sheer inertia. In regard to the development of weapons, insurance requires not one flexible weapon, but a variety of alternatives pursued with vigor. As development goes on, uncertainty is reduced. Consequently, basic strategic choice involves determining how worthwhile it is to pay for the additional information by developing rival weapons systems to the next stage. The greater the uncertainty of the world, the greater the desirability of having the widest selection of alternative weapons to choose from to meet unexpected threats and opportunities. Alchian and Kessel are so wedded to the principle of diversified investment that they "strongly recommend this theorem as a basic part of systems analysis." [28]

As a form of calculation, systems analysis represents a merger of quantitative methods and rules of thumb. First, the analyst attempts to solve the problem before he knows a great deal about it. Then he continuously alters his initial solution to get closer to what he intuitively feels ought to be wanted. Means and ends are continuously played off against one another. New objectives are defined, new assumptions made, new models constructed, until a creative amalgam appears which hopefully defines a second-best solution, one that is better than others even if not optimal in any sense. In the famous study of the location of military bases conducted by Albert Wohlstetter and his associates at the RAND Corporation, widely acknowledged as a classic example of systems analysis, Wohlstetter writes:

The base study . . . proceeded by a method of successive approximations. It compared forces for their efficiency in carrying a payload between the bases and targets without opposition either by enemy interceptors or enemy bombers. Then, it introduced obstacles successively: first, enemy defense; then enemy bombardment of our bombers and other elements needed to retaliate. In essence, then, the alternative systems were tested for their first-strike capability and then they were compared for their second-strike capacity. And the programmed system performed in a drastically different way, depending on the order in which the opposing side struck. In the course of analyzing countermeasures and counter-counter-measures, the enemy bombardment turned out to be a dominant problem. This was true even for a very much improved overseas operating base system. The refueling base system was very much less sensitive to strike order. It is only the fact that strike order made such a difference among systems contemplated that gave the first-strike, second-strike distinction an interest. And it was not known in advance of the analysis that few of the programmed bombers would have survived to encounter the problem of penetrating enemy defenses which had previously been taken as the main obstacle. The analysis, then, not only was affected by the objectives considered, it affected them.[29]

The advantage of a good systems study is that when the analysis is run through in theory on paper, certain disadvantages of learning from experience may be avoided.

If the complexity of the problems encountered proved difficult in cost-benefit analysis, the burdens of calculation are ordinarily much greater in systems analysis. Many aspects of a problem simply must be put aside. Only a few variables can be considered simultaneously. "Otherwise," Roland McKean tells us, "the models would become impossibly cumbersome, and . . . the number of calculations to consider would mount in the thousands." [30] Formulas that include everything may appear more satisfactory, but those that cannot be reduced "to a single expression are likely to convey no meaning at all. . . ." [31] Summing up their experience, Hitch and McKean assert that:

> . . . analyses must be piecemeal, since it is impossible for a single analysis to cover all problems of choice simultaneously in a large organization. Thus comparisons of alternative courses of action always pertain to a part of the government's (or corporation's) problem. Other parts of the over-all problem are temporarily put aside, possible decisions about some matters being ignored, specific decisions about others being taken for granted. The resulting analyses are intended to provide assistance in finding optimal, or at least good, solutions to subproblems: in the jargon of systems and operations research, they are suboptimizations.[32]

Although admitting that much bad work is carried on and that inordinate love of numbers and machines often gets in the way of creative work,[33] practitioners of systems analysis believe in their art. "All of them point out how the use of analysis can provide some of the knowledge needed, how it may sometimes serve as a substitute for experience, and, most importantly, how it can work to sharpen intuition." [34] Systems analysis can increase explicitness about the assumptions made and about exclusions from the analysis. The claim is that systems analysis can be perfected; sheer intuition or unaided judgment can never be perfect.

Yet there is also wide agreement that systems analysts "do philosophy," [35] that they are advocates of particular policy alternatives. What Schelling calls "the pure role of expert advisor" is not available for the analyst, who "must usually formulate the questions themselves for his clients." [36] Beyond that, Wohlstetter argues that systems analysts can perform the function of integrating diverse values. New systems can sometimes be found that meet diverse objectives.[37] The politician who gains his objectives by inventing policies that also satisfy others, or the leader of a coalition who searches out areas of maximum agreement, performs a kind of informal systems analysis.

All these men, however, work within the existing political structure. While cost-benefit analysis may contain within it implicit changes in existing governmental policies, it poses no direct challenge to the general decision-making machinery of the political system. Program budgeting is a form of systems analysis that attempts to break out of these confines.

Program Budgeting

It is always important, and perhaps especially so in economics, to avoid being swept off one's feet by the fashions of the moment.[38] So this new system will identify our national goals with precision . . .[39]

On August 25, 1965, President Johnson announced that he was asking the heads of all federal agencies to introduce "a very new and revolutionary system" of program budgeting. Staffs of experts set up in each agency would define goals using "modern methods of program analysis." Then the "most effective and the least costly" way to accomplish these goals would be found.[40]

Program budgeting has no standard definition. The general idea is that budgetary decisions should be made by focusing on output categories like governmental goals, objectives, end products, or programs, instead of inputs like personnel, equipment, and maintenance. As in cost-benefit analysis, to which it owes a great deal, program budgeting lays stress on estimating the total financial cost of accomplishing objectives. What is variously called cost-effectiveness or cost-utility analysis is employed in order to select "alternative approaches to the achievement of a benefit already determined to be worth achieving." [41]

Not everyone would go along with the most far-reaching implications of program budgeting, but the RAND Corporation version, presumably exported from the Defense Department, definitely does include "institutional reorganization to bring relevant administrative functions under the jurisdiction of the authority making the final program decisions." In any event, there would be "information reporting systems and shifts in the power structure to the extent necessary to secure compliance with program decisions by the agencies responsible for their execution." [42] Sometimes it appears that comprehensiveness—simultaneous and complete examination of all programs and all alternatives to programs every year—is being advocated. Actually, comprehensiveness has been dropped (though not without regret) because "it may be too costly in time, effort, uncertainty, and confusion." [43] There exists considerable ambivalence as to whether decisions are implicit in the program categories or merely provide information to improve the judgment of governmental officials.

Programs are not made in heaven. There is nothing out there that is just waiting to be found. Programs are not natural to the world; they must be imposed on it by men. No one can give instructions for making up programs. There are as many ways to conceive of programs as there are of organizing activity,[44] as the comments of the following writers eloquently testify:

It is by no means obvious . . . whether a good program structure should be based on components of specific end objectives (e.g. the accomplishment of certain land reclamation targets), on the principle of cost separation (identifying as a program any activity the costs of which can be readily-segregated), on the separation of means and ends (Is education a means or an end in a situation such as skill-retraining courses for workers displaced by automation?), or on some artificially designed pattern that draws from all these and other classification criteria.[45]

Just what categories constitute the most useful programs and program elements is far from obvious. . . . If one puts all educational activities into a broad package of educational programs, he cannot simultaneously include school lunch programs or physical education activities in a Health Program, or include defense educational activities (such as the military academies) in the Defense Program. . . . In short, precisely how to achieve a rational and useful structure for a program budget is not yet evident.[46]

In much current discussion it seems to be taken for granted that transportation is a natural program category. But that conclusion is by no means obvious.[47]

A first question one might ask is whether, given their nature, health activities merit a separate, independent status in a program budget. The question arises because these activities often are constituents of, or inputs into, other activities whose purpose or goal orientation is the dominating one. Outlays by the Department of Defense for hospital care, for example, though they assist in maintaining the health of one segment of the population, are undertaken on behalf of national defense, and the latter is their justification.[48]

The difficulties with the program concept are illustrated in the space program. A first glance suggests that space projects are ideally suited for program budgeting because they appear as physical systems designed to accomplish various missions. Actually, there is a remarkable degree of interdependence between different missions and objectives—pride, scientific research, space exploration, military uses, etc.—so that it is impossible to apportion costs on a proper basis. Consider the problem of a rocket developed for one mission and useful for others. To apportion costs to each new mission is purely arbitrary. To allocate the cost to the first mission and regard the rocket as a free good for all subsequent missions is ludicrous. The only remotely reasonable alternative—making a separate program out of the rocket itself—does violence to the concept of programs as end products. The difficulty is compounded because the facilities that have multiple uses, like boosters and tracking networks, tend to be very expensive compared to the items that are specific to a particular mission.[49] Simple concepts of programs evaporate upon inspection.

Political realities lie behind the failure to devise principles for defining programs. As Melvin Anshen puts it, "The central issue is, of course, nothing less than the definition of the ultimate objectives of the Federal government as they are realized through operational decisions." The arrangement of the programs inevitably affects the specific actions taken to implement them. "Set in this framework," Anshen continues, "the designation of a schedule of programs may be described as building a bridge between a matter of political philosophy (what is government for?) and . . . assigning scarce resources among alternative governmental objectives." [50]

Because program budgeting is a form of systems analysis (and uses a form of cost-benefit analysis), the conditions that hinder or facilitate its use have largely been covered in the previous sections. The simpler the problem, the fewer the interdependencies, the greater the ability to measure the consequences of alternatives on a common scale, the more costs and benefits that are valued in the marketplace, the better the chances of making effective use of programs. Let us take transportation to illustrate some of the conditions in a specific case.

Investments in transportation are highly interdependent with one another (planes versus cars versus trains versus barges, etc.) and with decisions regarding the regional location of industry and the movements of population. In view of the powerful effects of transportation investment on regional employment, income, and competition with other modes of transport, it becomes necessary to take these factors into account. The partial equilibrium model of efficiency in the narrow sense becomes inappropriate and a general equilibrium model of the economy must be used. The combination of aggregative models at the economy-wide level and interregion and interindustry models that this approach requires is staggering. It is precisely the limited and partial character of cost-effectiveness analyses, taking so much for granted and eliminating many variables, that make them easy to work with for empirical purposes. Furthermore, designing a large-scale transportation system involves so close a mixture of political and economic considerations that it is not possible to disentangle them. The Interstate Highway Program, for example, involved complex bargaining among federal, state, and local governments and reconciliation of many conflicting interests. The development of certain "backward" regions; improvement in the flow of defense supplies; redistribution of income, creating countervailing power against certain monopolies; not to mention the political needs of public officials—all these were involved. While cost-utility exercises might help with small segments of the problem, J. R. Meyer concludes that, "Given the complexity of the political and economic decisions involved, and the emphasis on designing a geographically consistent system, it probably would be difficult to improve on the congressional process as a means of developing such a program in an orderly and systematic way." [51]

On one condition for effective use—reorganization of the federal government to centralize authority for wide-ranging programs—proponents of program budgeting are markedly ambivalent. The problem is that responsibility for programs is now scattered throughout the whole federal establishment and decentralized to state and local authorities as well. In the field of health, for example, expenditures are distributed among at least 12 agencies and six departments outside of Health, Education, and Welfare. A far greater number of organizations are concerned with American activities abroad, with natural resources, and with education. The multiple jurisdictions and overlapping responsibilities do violence to the concept of comprehensive and consistent programs. It "causes one to doubt," Marvin Frankel writes, "whether there can exist in the administrative echelons the kind of overall perspective that would seem indispensable if federal health resources are to be rationally allocated." [52] To G. A. Steiner it is evident that "the present 'chest of drawers' type of organization cannot for long be compatible with program budgeting." [53] W. Z. Hirsch declares that "if we are to have effective program budgeting of natural resources activities, we shall have to provide for new institutional arrangements." [54] Yet the inevitable resistance to wholesale reorganization would be so great that, if it were deemed essential, it might well doom the enterprise. Hence the hope is expressed that translation grids or crossover networks could be used to convert program budget decisions back into the usual budget categories in the usual agencies. That is what is done in defense, but that department has the advantage of having most of the activities it is concerned with under the secretary's jurisdiction. Some program analysts believe that this solution will not do.

Recognizing that a conversion scheme is technically feasible, Anshen is aware that there are "deeply frustrating" issues to be resolved. "The heart of the problem is the fact that the program budget in operation should not be a mere statistical game. Great strategic importance will attach to both the definition of program structure and content and the establishment of specific program objectives (including magnitude, timing, and cost)." [55] The implications of program budgeting, however, go far beyond specific policies.

It will be useful to distinguish between policy politics (which policy will be adopted?), partisan politics (which political party will win office?), and system politics (how will decision structures be set up?). Program budgeting is manifestly concerned with policy politics, and not much with partisan politics, although it could have important consequences for issues that divide the nation's parties. *My contention is that the thrust of program budgeting makes it an integral part of system politics.*

As presently conceived, program budgeting contains an extreme centralizing bias. Power is to be centralized in the presidency (through the Budget Bureau) at the national level, in superdepartments rather than in bureaus within the executive branch, and in the federal government as a whole instead of state or local governments. Note how W. Z. Hirsch assumes the desirability of national dominance when he writes: "These methods of analysis can guide Federal officials in the responsibility of bringing local education decisions into closer harmony with national objectives." [56] G. A. Steiner observes that comprehensiveness may be affected by unrestricted federal grants in aid to the states because "such a plan would remove a substantial part of Federal expenditures from a program budgeting system of the Federal government." [57] Should there be reluctance on the part of state and local officials to employ the new tools, Anshen states "that the Federal government may employ familiar incentives to accelerate this progress." [58] Summing it up, Hirsch says that "It appears doubtful that a natural resources program budget would have much impact without a good deal of centralization." [59]

Within the great federal organizations designed to encompass the widest ramifications of basic objectives, there would have to be strong executives. Only the top executive, cutting across the subunits of the organization, could put the program budget together, as is done in the Department of Defense. A more useful tool for increasing the executive's power to control decisions vis-à-vis his subordinates would be hard to find. [60]

Would large-scale program budgeting benefit the Chief Executive? President Johnson's support of program budgeting could stem in part from his desire to appear frugal, and could also be directed at increasing his control of the executive branch by centralizing decisions in the Bureau of the Budget. In the case of foreign affairs, it is not at all clear whether it would be preferable to emphasize country teams, with the budget made by the State Department to encompass activities of the other federal agencies abroad, or to let commerce, agriculture, defense, and other agencies include their foreign activities in their own budgets. Program budgeting will unleash great struggles of this kind in Washington. An especially interesting possibility is that the Bureau of the Budget might prefer to let the various agencies compete, with the bureau coordinating (that is, controlling) these activities through a comprehensive foreign-affairs program devised only at the Presidential level.

Yet it is not entirely clear that Presidents would welcome all the implications of program budgeting. It is well and good to talk about long-range planning; it is another thing to tie a President's hands by committing him in advance for five years of expenditures. Looking ahead is fine, but not if it means that a President cannot negate the most extensive planning efforts on grounds that seem sufficient to him. [61] He may wish to trade some program budgeting for some political support.

In any event, that all decisions ought to be made by the most central person in the most centralized body capable of grabbing hold of them is difficult to justify on scientific grounds. We see what has happened. First pure efficiency was converted to mixed efficiency. Then limited efficiency became unlimited. Yet the qualifications of efficiency experts for political systems analysis are not evident. [62]

We would be in a much stronger position to predict the consequences of program budgeting if we knew (a) how far toward a genuine program budget the Defense Department has gone and (b) whether the program budget has fulfilled its promise. To the best of my knowledge, not a single study of this important experiment was undertaken (or at least published) before the decision was made to spread it around the land. On the surface, only two of the nine program categories used in the Defense Department appear to be genuine programs in the sense of pointing to end purposes or objectives. Although strategic retaliation and continental defense appear to be distinct programs, it is difficult to separate them conceptually; my guess is that they are, in fact, considered together. The third category—general-purpose forces—is presumably designed to deal with (hopefully) limited war anywhere in the world. According to Arthur Smithies, "The threat is not clearly defined and neither are the requirements for meeting it. Clearly this program is of a very different character from the other two and does not lend itself as readily to analysis in terms either of its components or of its specific contribution to defense objectives." [63]

What about the program called airlift and sealift? These activities support the general-purpose forces. Research and development are carried on presumably to serve other defense objectives, and the same is true for the reserve forces.

No doubt the elements that make up the programs comprise the real action focus of the budget, but these may look less elegant when spread into thousands of elements than they do in nine neat rows. When one hears that hundreds of program elements are up for decision at one time,[64] he is entitled to some skepticism about how much genuine analysis can go into all of them. Part of the argument for program budgeting was that by thinking ahead and working all year round it would be possible to consider changes as they came up and avoid the usual last-minute funk. Both Hitch [65] and Novick [66] (the RAND Corporation expert on defense budgeting) report, however, that this has not worked out. The services hesitate to submit changes piecemeal, and the secretary wants to see what he is getting into before he acts. The vaunted five-year plans are still in force, but their efficacy in determining yearly decisions remains to be established.

One good operational test would be whether the department's systems analysts actually use the figures from the five-year plans in their work or whether they go to the services for the real stuff. Another test would be whether or not the later years of the five-year projections turn out to have any future significance, or whether the battle is really over the next year that is to be scooped out as part of the budget. From a distance, it appears that the services have to work much harder to justify what they are doing. Since the secretary's office must approve changes in defense programs, and he can insist on documentation, he is in a strong position to improve thinking at the lower levels. The intensity of conflict within the Defense Department may not have changed, but it may be that the disputants are or will in the future be likely to shout at a much more sophisticated level.

How much this was due to McNamara himself, to his insistence on quantitative estimates, or to the analytic advantages of a program budget cannot be determined now. It is clear that a program budget, of which the secretary alone is master, has helped impose his will on the Defense Department.

It should also be said that there are many notable differences between decision-making in defense and domestic policy that would render suspect the transmission of procedures from one realm to the other. The greater organizational unity of defense, the immensely large amounts of money at stake, the extraordinarily greater risks involved, the inability to share more than minimal values with opponents, the vastly different array of interests and perceptions of the proper roles of the participants—these are but a few of the factors involved.

The Armed Services and Appropriations Committees in the defense area, for example, are normally most reluctant to substitute their judgment on defense for that of the President and the Secretary of the Department. They do not conceive it to be their role to make day-to-day defense policy, and they are apparently unwilling to take on the burden of decision. They therefore accept a budget presentation based on cavernous program categories even though these are so arranged that it is impossible to make a decision on the basis of them. If they were to ask for and to receive the discussion of alternative actions contained in the much smaller program elements on which the secretary bases his decisions, they would be in a position to take the Department of Defense away from him.

There is no reason whatsoever to believe that a similar restraint would be shown by committees that deal with domestic policies. It is at least possible that the peculiar planning, programming, and budgeting system adopted in defense could not be repeated elsewhere in the federal establishment.

Political Rationality

Political rationality is the fundamental kind of reason, because it deals with the preservation and improvement of decision structures, and decision structures are the source of all decisions. Unless a decision structure exists, no reasoning and no decisions are possible. . . . There can be no conflict between political rationality and . . . technical, legal, social, or economic rationality, because the solution of political problems makes possible an attack on any other problem, while a serious political deficiency can prevent or undo all other problem solving. . . . Non-political decisions are reached by considering a problem in its own terms, and by evaluating proposals according to how well they solve the problem. The best available proposal should be accepted regardless of who makes it or who opposes it, and a faulty proposal should be rejected or improved no matter who makes it. Compromise is always irrational; the rational procedure is to determine which proposal is the best, and to accept it. In a po-

204 The Practical Consequences of Theory

litical decision, on the other hand, action never is based on the merits of a proposal but always on who makes it and who opposes it. Action should be designed to avoid complete identification with any proposal and any point of
view, no matter how good or how popular it might be. The best available proposal should never be accepted just because it is best; it should be deferred, objected to, discussed, until major opposition disappears. Compromise is between
a good and a bad proposal.[67]

We are witnessing the beginning of significant advances in the art and
science of economizing. Having given up the norm of comprehensiveness,
economizers are able to join quantitative analysis with aids to calculation
of the kind described by Lindblom in his strategy of disjointed incrementalism.[68]

Various devices are employed to simplify calculations. Important values
are omitted entirely; others are left to different authorities to whose care
they have been entrusted. Here sensitivity analysis represents an advance
because it provides an empirical basis to justify neglect of some values.
Means and ends are hopelessly intertwined.

The real choice is between rival policies that encapsulate somewhat different mixes of means and ends. Analysis proceeds incrementally by successive limited approximations. It is serial and remedial as successive attacks are made on problems. Rather than waiting upon experience in the
real world, the analyst tries various moves in his model and runs them
through to see if they work. When all else fails, the analyst may try an in-
tegrative solution reconciling a variety of values to some degree, though
meeting none of them completely. He is always ready to settle for the second or third best, provided only that it is better than the going policy.
Constrained by diverse limiting assumptions, weakened by deficiencies in
technique, rarely able to provide unambiguous measures, the systems,
cost-benefit, and program analyst is nonetheless getting better at calculating in the realm of efficiency. Alas, he is an imperialist at heart.

In the literature discussed above there appears several times the proposition that "the program budget is a neutral tool. It has no politics." [69] In
truth, the program budget is suffused with policy politics, makes up a
small part of President Johnson's partisan politics, and tends toward system politics. How could men account for so foolish a statement? It must be
that they who make it identify program budgeting with something good
and beautiful, and politics with something else, bad and ugly. McKean and
Anshen speak of politics in terms of "pressures and expedient adjustments," "haphazard acts . . . unresponsive to a planned analysis of the
needs of efficient decision design." From the political structure they expect
only "resistance and opposition, corresponding to the familiar human disposition to protect established seats of power and procedures made honorable by the mere facts of existence and custom." [70] In other places we hear
of "vested interests," "wasteful duplication," "special interest groups," and
the "Parkinson syndrome." [71]

Not so long ago less sophisticated advocates of reform ignored the political realm. Now they denigrate it. And, since there must be a structure for decision, it is smuggled in as a mere adjunct of achieving efficiency. Who is to blame if the economic tail wags the political dog? It seems unfair to blame the evangelical economizer for spreading the gospel of efficiency. If economic efficiency turns out to be the one true religion, maybe it is because its prophets could so easily conquer.

It is hard to find men who take up the cause of political rationality, who plead the case for political man, and who are primarily concerned with the laws that enable the political machinery to keep working. One is driven to a philosopher like Paul Diesing to find the case for the political:

> . . . the political problem is always basic and prior to the others. . . . This means that any suggested course of action must be evaluated first by its effects on the political structure. A course of action which corrects economic or social deficiencies but increases political difficulties must be rejected, while an action which contributes to political improvement is desirable even if it is not entirely sound from an economic or social standpoint.[72]

There is hardly a political scientist who would claim half as much. The desire to invent decision structures to facilitate the achievement of economic efficiency does not suggest a full appreciation of their proper role by students of politics.

A major task of the political system is to specify goals or objectives. It is impermissible to treat goals as if they were known in advance. "Goals" may well be the product of interaction among key participants rather than some *deus ex machina* or (to use Bentley's term) some "spook" that posits values in advance of our knowledge of them. Certainly, the operational objectives of the Corps of Engineers in the water resources field could hardly be described in terms of developing rivers and harbors.

Once the political process becomes a focus of attention, it is evident that the principal participants may not be clear about their goals. What we call goals or objectives may, in large part, be operationally determined by the policies we can agree upon. The mixtures of values found in complex policies may have to be taken in packages, so that policies may determine goals at least as much as general objectives determine policies. In a political situation, then, the need for support assumes central importance. Not simply the economic, but the *political* costs and benefits turn out to be crucial.

A first attempt to specify what is meant by political costs may bring closer an understanding of the range of requirements for political rationality.[73] Exchange costs are incurred by a political leader when he needs the support of other people to get a policy adopted. He has to pay for this assistance by using up resources in the form of favors (patronage, logrolling) or coercive moves (threats or acts to veto or remove from office). By supporting a policy and influencing others to do the same, a politician antagonizes some people and may suffer their retaliation. If these hostility costs mount, they may turn into reelection costs—actions that decrease his chances (or those of his friends) of being elected or reelected to office. Election costs, in turn, may become policy costs through inability to command the necessary formal powers to accomplish the desired policy objectives.

In the manner of Neustadt, we may also talk about reputation costs, i.e., not only loss of popularity with segments of the electorate, but also loss of esteem and effectiveness with other participants in the political system and loss of ability to secure policies other than the one immediately under consideration. Those who continually urge a President to go all out—that is, use all his resources on a wide range of issues—rarely stop to consider that the price of success in one area of policy may be defeat in another. If he loses popularity with the electorate, as President Truman did, Congress may destroy almost the whole of his domestic program. If he cracks down on the steel industry, as President Kennedy did, he may find himself constrained to lean over backward in the future to avoid unremitting hostility from the business community.

A major consequence of incurring exchange and hostility costs may be undesirable power-redistribution effects. The process of getting a policy adopted or implemented may increase the power of various individuals, organizations, and social groups, which later will be used against the political leader. The power of some participants may be weakened so that the political leader is unable to enjoy their protection.

The legitimacy of the political system may be threatened by costs that involve the weakening of customary political restraints. Politicians who try to suppress opposition, or who practice election frauds, may find similar tactics being used against them. The choice of a highly controversial policy may raise the costs of civic discord. Although the people involved may not hate the political leader, the fact that they hate each other may lead to consequences contrary to his desires.

The literature of economics usually treats organizations and institutions as if they were costless entities. The standard procedure is to consider rival alternatives (in consideration of price policy or other criteria), calculate the differences in cost and achievement among them, and show that one is more or less efficient than another. This typical way of thinking is sometimes misspecified. If the costs of pursuing a policy are strictly economic and can be calculated directly in the marketplace, then the procedure should work well. But if the costs include getting one or another organization to change its policies or procedures, then these costs must also be taken into account.[74] Perhaps there are legal, psychological, or other impediments that make it either impossible or difficult for the required changes to be made. Or the changes may require great effort and result in incurring a variety of other costs. In considering a range of alternatives, one is measuring not only efficiency, but also the costs of change.

Studies based on efficiency criteria are much needed and increasingly useful. My quarrel is not with them at all, as such. I have been concerned that a single value, however important, could triumph over other values without explicit consideration being given these others. I would feel much better if political rationality were being pursued with the same vigor and capability as is economic efficiency. In that case I would have fewer qualms about extending efficiency studies into the decision-making apparatus.

My purpose has not been to accuse economizers of doing what comes naturally. Rather, I have sought to emphasize that economic rationality, however laudable in its own sphere, ought not to swallow up political rationality—but will do so if political rationality continues to lack trained and adept defenders.

NOTES

NOTE: I am more than ordinarily indebted to the people who have improved this essay through their comments. Win Crowther, John Harsanyi, John Krutilla, Arthur Maas, Arnold Meltsner, Nelson Polsby, William Riker, and Dwight Waldo saved me from errors and contributed insights of their own. The responsibility for what is said is entirely mine.

1. A. R. Prest and R. Turvey, "Cost-Benefit Analysis: A Survey," *Economic Journal,* 75 (December 1965): 683–685. I am much indebted to this valuable and discerning survey. I have also relied upon Otto Eckstein, "A Survey of the Theory of Public Expenditure Criteria," in National Bureau of Economic Research, *Public Finances: Needs, Sources, and Utilization* (New York: Princeton University Press, 1961), pp. 439–504; Irving K. Fox and Orris C. Herfindahl, "Attainment of Efficiency in Satisfying Demands for Water Resources," *American Economic Review* (May 1964): 198–206; Charles J. Hitch, *On the Choice of Objectives in Systems Studies* (Santa Monica, Calif.: RAND Corp., 1960); John V. Krutilla, "Is Public Intervention in Water Resources Development Conducive to Economic Efficiency?" *Natural Resources Journal* (January 1966), pp. 60–75; John V. Krutilla and Otto Eckstein, *Multiple Purpose River Development* (Baltimore: Johns Hopkins Press, 1958); and Roland N. McKean, *Efficiency in Government through Systems Analysis with Emphasis on Water Resources Development* (New York: John Wiley, 1958).

2. Prest and Turvey, *op. cit.,* p. 686.

3. In many important areas of policy such as national defense it is not possible to value the product directly in the marketplace. Since benefits cannot be valued in the same way as costs, it is necessary to resort to a somewhat different type of analysis. Instead of cost-benefit analysis, therefore, the work is usually called cost-effectiveness or cost-utility analysis.

4. A. Bergson, "A Reformulation of Certain Aspects of Welfare Economics," *Quarterly Journal of Economics* (February 1938); N. Kaldor, "Welfare Propositions and Interpersonal Comparisons of Utility," *Economic Journal* (1939): 549–552; J. R. Hicks, "The Valuation of Social Income," *Economica* (1940): 105–124; I. M. D. Little, *A Critique of Welfare Economics* (New York: Oxford University Press, 1950); W. J. Baumol, *Welfare Economics and the Theory of the State* (Cambridge: Harvard University Press, 1952); T. Scitovsky, "A Note on Welfare Propositions in Economics," *Review of Economic Studies* (1942); 98–110: J. E. Meade, *The Theory of International Economic Policy,* vol. 2: *Trade and Welfare* (New York: Oxford University Press, 1954).

5. For a different view, see James M. Buchanan and Gordon Tullock, *The Calculus of Consent: Logical Foundations of Constitutional Democracy* (Ann Arbor: University of Michigan Press, 1962).

6. Prest and Turvey, *op. cit.,* p. 702. For a contrary view, see Arthur Maas, "Benefit-Cost Analysis: Its Relevance to Public Investment Decisions," *Quarterly Journal of Economics* 80 (May 1966): 208–226.

7. Fox and Herfindahl, *op. cit.,* p. 200.

8. Prest and Turvey, *op. cit.,* p. 727.

9. *Ibid.*, pp. 729, 731.

10. David Braybrooke and Charles Lindblom, *A Strategy of Decision* (New York: Free Press, 1963).

11. Prest and Turvey, *op. cit.*, p. 714.

12. *Ibid.*, p. 705.

13. See Jack L. Knetch, "Economics of Including Recreation as a Purpose of Water Resource Projects," *Journal of Farm Economics* (December 1964): 1155. No one living in Berkeley, where a "view" contributes to the cost of housing, could believe that aesthetic values are forever going to remain beyond the ingenuity of the quantifier. There are also costs and benefits, such as the saving and losing of human life, which can be quantified but can be valued in the marketplace only in a most peculiar (or ghoulish) sense. See Burton Weisbrod, *The Economics of Public Health: Measuring the Economic Impact of Diseases* (Philadelphia: University of Pennsylvania Press, 1961), for a creative attempt to place a market value on human life. Few of us would want to make decisions about public health by use of this criterion—not, at least, if we were the old person whose future social-value contribution is less than his cost to the authorities.

14. Eckstein, *op. cit.*, p. 460.

15. Fox and Herfindahl, *op. cit.*, p. 202.

16. E. S. Quade, ed., *Analysis for Military Decisions* (Chicago: Rand McNally, 1964), p. 153.

17. *Ibid.*, p. 149.

18. *Ibid.*, p. 7.

19. Hitch, *op. cit.*, p. 19.

20. Quade, *op. cit.*, p. 176.

21. Hitch, *op. cit.*, pp. 4–5.

22. Albert Wohlstetter, "Analysis and Design of Conflict Systems," in Quade, *op. cit.*, p. 121.

23. See Glenn H. Snyder, *Deterrence and Defense* (Princeton, N.J.: Princeton University Press, 1961).

24. Wohlstetter, in Quade, *op. cit.*, p. 122.

25. Quade, *op. cit.*, p. 157. Quade attempts to soften the blow by saying that businessmen and military officers know more about their business than anyone else. But the import of the analogy is clear enough.

26. *Ibid.*, pp. 156–157.

27. Herman Kahn and Irwin Mann believe that *"More than any single thing,* the skilled use of a fortiori and break-even analyses separates the professionals from the amateurs" (*Techniques of Systems Analysis* [Santa Monica, Calif.: RAND Corp., 1957]). They think that convincing others that you have a good solution is as important as coming up with one.

28. Armen A. Alchian and Reuben A. Kessel, *A Proper Role of Systems Analysis* (Santa Monica, Calif.: RAND Corp., 1954), p. 9.

29. Wohlstetter, *op. cit.*, pp. 125–126.

30. McKean, "Criteria," in Quade, *op. cit.*, p. 83.

31. Quade, *op. cit.*, p. 310.

32. Charles J. Hitch and Roland N. McKean, *The Economics of Defense in the Nuclear Age* (Cambridge: Harvard University Press, 1961), p. 161.

33. See Hitch on "Mechanitis—putting . . . machines to work as a substitute for hard thinking" ("Economics and Operations Research: A Symposium. II," *Review of Economics and Statistics* [August 1958]: 209).

34. Quade, *op cit.*, 12.

35. *Ibid.*, p. 5.

36. T. C. Schelling, "Economics and Operations Research: A Symposium. V. Comment," *Review of Economics and Statistics* (August 1958): 222.

37. Wohlstetter, *op. cit.*, p. 122.

38. Prest and Turvey, *op. cit.*, p. 684.

39. President Lyndon Johnson, quoted in David Novick, ed., *Program Budgeting* (Cambridge: Harvard University Press, 1965), p. vi.

40. *Ibid.*, pp. v–vi.

41. Alan Dean, quoted in *ibid.*, p. 311.

42. Roland N. McKean and Melvin Anshen in *ibid.*, pp. 286–287. The authors say that this aspect of program budgeting is part of the general view adopted in the book as a whole.

43. Arthur Smithies in *ibid.*, p. 45.

44. A look at the classic work by Luther Gulick and Lyndall Urwick, *Papers on the Science of Administration* (New York: Columbia University Press, 1937), reveals considerable similarity between their suggested bases of organization and ways of conceptualizing programs.

45. Anshen in Novick, *op. cit.* pp. 19–20.
46. G. A. Steiner in *ibid.*, p. 356.
47. Smithies in *ibid.*, p. 41.
48. Marvin Frankel in *ibid.*, pp. 219–220. I have forborne citing the author who promises exciting discussion of the objectives of American education and ends up with fascinating program categories like primary, secondary, and tertiary education.
49. See the excellent chapter by M. A. Margolis and S. M. Barro in *ibid.*, pp. 120–145.
50. In *ibid.*, p. 18.
51. In *ibid.*, p. 170. This paragraph is based on my interpretation of Meyer's work.
52. In *ibid.*, p. 237.
53. In *ibid.*, p. 348.
54. In *ibid.*, p. 280.
55. In *ibid.*, pp. 358–359.
56. In *ibid.*, p. 206.
57. In *ibid.*, p. 347.
58. In *ibid.*, p. 365.
59. In *ibid.*, p. 280.
60. See my comments to this effect in *The Politics of the Budgetary Process* (Boston: Little, Brown, 1964), p. 140. For discussion of some political consequences of program budgeting, see *ibid.*, pp. 135–142.
61. See William H. Brown and Charles E. Gilbert, *Planning Municipal Investment: A Case Study of Philadelphia* (Philadelphia: University of Pennsylvania Press, 1961), for an excellent discussion of the desire of elected officials to remain free to shift their commitments.
62. It may be said that I have failed to distinguish sufficiently between planning, programming, and budgeting. Planning is an orientation that looks ahead by extending costs and benefits or units of effectiveness a number of years into the future. Programming is a general procedure of systems analysis employing cost-effectiveness studies. In this view program budgeting is a mere mechanical translation of the results of high-level systems studies into convenient storage in the budgetary format. No doubt systems studies could be done without converting the results into the form of a program budget. This approach may have a lot to recommend it, and it appears that it is the one that is generally followed by the Department of Defense in its presentations to Congress. But if the systems studies guide decisions as to the allocation of resources, and the studies are maintained according to particular program categories and are further legitimatized by being given status in the budget, it seems most unlikely that programming will be separated from budgeting. One is never sure whether too much or too little is being claimed for program budgeting. If all that program budgeting amounts to is a simple translation of previous systems studies into some convenient form of accounting, it hardly seems that this phenomenon is worth so much fuss. If the program categories in the budget system are meaningful, then they must be much more than a mere translation of previously reached decisions. In this case, I think that it is not my task to enlighten the proponents of program budgeting, but rather that it is their task to make themselves clear to others.
63. In Novick, *op. cit.*, p. 37.
64. See U.S. House Appropriations Committee, Subcommittee on Department of Defense Appropriations for Fiscal 1965, 88th Congress, 2nd session, Vol. 4, p. 133. McNamara asserted that some 652 "subject issues" had been submitted to him for the fiscal 1965 budget.
65. Hitch, *Decision Making for Defense* (Berkeley: University of California Press, 1965).
66. Novick, *op. cit.*, p. 100.
67. Paul Diesing, *Reason in Society* (Urbana: University of Illinois Press, 1962), pp. 198, 203–204, 231–232.
68. Braybrooke and Lindblom, *op. cit.* See also Lindblom, *The Intelligence of Democracy* (New York: Free Press, 1965).
69. Anshen in Novick, *op. cit.*, p. 370.
70. In *ibid.*, p. 289.
71. *Ibid.*, p. 359.
72. Diesing, *op. cit.*, p. 228.
73. I am indebted to John Harsanyi for suggestions about political rationality.
74. In the field of defense policy, political factors are taken into account to the extent that the studies concentrate on the design of feasible alternatives. In the choice of overseas basing, for example, the question of feasibility in relation to treaties and friendly or unfriendly relationships with other countries is considered. Thus it seems permissible to take into account political considerations originating outside the country, where differences of opinions and preferences among nations are to some extent accepted as legitimate, but apparently not differences internal to the American policy.

11

AESTHETIC POWER OR
THE TRIUMPH OF THE SENSITIVE
MINORITY OVER THE VULGAR MASS:
A POLITICAL ANALYSIS OF
THE NEW ECONOMICS

How does the "old economics" of natural resources differ from the "new economics"? The old economics was mostly economics. The new economics is mostly politics. The agonizing question confronting the new economics has troubled political theorists from the time of the Hebrew prophets to this very day: How shall society be organized so that the preferences of the morally or aesthetically sensitive minority will triumph? Where majorities are rarely mobilized, the question may be rephrased to ask how our *good* minority may prevail over their *bad* minority. If only a superior few truly love the remote and virgin wilderness, for instance, how may this opportunity for solitary communion with nature be preserved against hostile masses or rival elites? The new economics of natural resources appears to be designed to answer this question indirectly without quite raising it to a conscious level.

The terms new economists use to describe the deterioration of the natural environment are sufficiently expressive to convey the feeling behind them. The landscape has been assaulted and degraded, if not raped; genocide has been practiced against certain animal species; the air threatens to become a poisonous gas; the odor of dead fish testifies to the pollution of our water; human marauders invade and despoil isolated areas. The tone is strident; the mood, a mixture of rage and disgust. The metaphors belong

From *Daedalus*, Fall 1967, pp. 1115–1128. Reprinted by permission.

more to the battlefield than the market place. It is not surprising, then, that Athelstan Spilhaus urges us to take risks in enhancing the environment comparable to those we would take in war; nor that Nathaniel Wollman suggests a political structure with administrative environmental boards possessing "the power and authority that is now accorded the military establishment . . . because the penalty of inexpert decisions may be just as disastrous for the human race as the effect of military weapons." Unfortunately, the old economics does not provide the necessary weapons for what many evidently see as the war for environmental quality.

In the beginning, the rationale for the Conservation Movement was one of preserving basic resources that were becoming increasingly scarce. Wood, coal, and iron were essentially fixed in given lumps; use was a kind of desecration. As demand increased and supply decreased in an industrial society, these resources would become more and more valuable. The larger the part played by natural resources in the economy and the higher their price in comparison with other goods, the easier it was to make an economic case for protecting them. To the extent that the votes of a misguided or ignorant people would not protect these precious resources through the political arena, the symbolic casting of ballots in the more rational economic market place would restrict use by raising prices. If politics were involved at all, it would be not for economic reasons, but merely to undo the evil restrictions upon the free market that special interests had worked out with conniving politicians.

Even when economic theorists arrived at a justification for governmental intervention to overcome certain imperfections in the market place, the political arena proved vexing. When a large dam would impose costs on those who did benefit from it, for example, it was deemed appropriate for the government to intervene to rectify the situation. But, as it turned out, the politicians marched to music of their own and were only remotely interested in following the lead of economic science. The interest rate, that old puritan arbiter between present consumption and future desires, was kept artificially low so that many projects were justified on economic grounds without valid reason. Cost-benefit analysis, designed to increase national income by assuring that the benefits to whoever received them would exceed the costs to whoever paid them, was twisted out of shape in notorious fashion. Things were arranged so that general taxpayers received less and the direct beneficiaries far more than their economically justifiable shares. A project with a low benefit-cost ratio might be joined with another having a much higher ratio so that the "new" combined project could qualify. So-called intangibles like recreation values were credited with increasingly large shares of the benefits, thus representing a "finagle" factor that could be enlarged almost at will to provide justification. A decentralized party system and a highly fragmented national political system with strong regional interests proved resistant to making decisions on economic grounds. Comments about narrow local interests, selfish minorities, and violations of the public interest filled the economic literature. While politics was proving so disappointing, the former economic rationale for protecting resources suffered severe blows.

The market mechanism, together with man's remarkable technical ingenuity, drastically changed the supply-and-demand relationships for many natural resources. New sources of supply were continuously discovered, and new products substituted for old. Industrial and farm production grew exceedingly large and immensely more efficient. Consequently, the prices of resources commodities continually decreased in comparison with those of other goods and services. The contribution of natural resources to Gross National Product showed a corresponding, proportionate drop. The decline in the price of resource commodities made it more difficult to justify special treatment on the grounds of economic efficiency. The contribution that these resources made to production was too small, and it is getting smaller. This change in the economic importance of resources lies behind the plaintive cry that it is not possible to justify on economic grounds most large programs designed to improve the quality of the natural environment.

Reevaluations of the abundance of natural resources illustrate another aspect of their new position. We now know that we have more forest resources than we had thought and that new growth may exceed demand. Although water may be in short supply in some areas, technological advance and the shift of existing supplies to more productive uses should provide amounts more than adequate for the future. Despite the hue and cry about the advancing tentacles of the monster called urbanization, only 2 or 3 percent of the nation's land is or will be devoted to urban uses in the next few decades. The immediate conclusion is all too evident. Resource problems will, by and large, not be critical for economic purposes. A technological advance here or a local adjustment there will take care of the worst difficulties. From a strictly economic viewpoint, nothing much need be done.

The terrible difficulty for economists is that problems of environmental quality do not look so bad as they ought. If present modes of economic justification are used, there is no way of preserving the basic values these men hold as users of the natural environment. To have personal values done in by professional values is no fun at all. Hence, a "new economics" has emerged to get around the old. If the old economics will not let you have what you know is right, it follows that a new economics is evidently needed. The term *new economics of natural resources* is used to designate an emerging trend, discernible in this volume, and permits economists to avoid direct confrontation with political problems by bringing in aesthetic factors to make economic analysis come out "right."

Since the new economists of today are the old economists of yesterday, a certain ambivalence about their enterprise might be expected. It is tempting to retain an economic vocabulary for essentially noneconomic processes. The deep woods with clear lakes, white-water streams, and rare animal species may be called unique and irreplaceable, like the White House or the Liberty Bell or a man's children or his sweetheart. One could say that no price is too high for these treasures except that the concept "price" is really inapplicable. These treasures are not to be bought and sold at all. They are literally "priceless"—that is, outside any market. The usual system for determining what is allowable in the market place is political or in some sense deeply traditional or social, but in no case may it be called economic. The old economist considers it ridiculous for a society to spend $20 billion to rid itself entirely of water pollution when marginal benefits of spending the largest fraction of that sum elsewhere would be much higher. The new economist says "why not" and invents rationales. After all, at current rates of economic growth, $20 billion a year represents only a few months delay in reaching a GNP that much higher. This marginalist fallacy, a variant of the old argument that for want of a nail a war was lost, suffers from a fatal defect. We can all think of huge expenditures to accomplish highly cherished ends that could be justified if only people would wait a little while longer to become richer. All the wilderness areas and fine old buildings might be preserved for even less, and many experimental cities might be built. The wealth is here. Presumably, all that is required is the will. We undoubtedly can have some of the things some of us want, but not all the things all of us want. Otherwise, there would be no problem of scarcity, no need for allocation. This is not a new economics but a "non-economics."

The old economists cried out against the use of "finagle factors" that might in some sense be important, but that could not be measured in the market place. In preference to having such factors expanded or contracted at will, they preferred that these be brought to the attention of decision-makers who could take them into account. To do otherwise would be to compromise fatally the economic part of the analysis. The new economists are tempted to abandon this position. Maintaining the wilds may be justified, without being able to specify size or cost or conditions, on the grounds that people like to leave a legacy to their children. Outdoor recreation may be alleged to have great psychic benefits, though demonstrating its dimensions or comparing it with television or people-watching on crowded streets is another matter. Yet alternative expenditures may also serve some values people hold, and the economic problem is to justify one expenditure rather than another on something more than personal grounds. Surely economics is not to become a parody of a parody, the social-science version of Saul Bellow's *Henderson the Rain King* who plunges throughout time and continents shouting ever more loudly, "I want, I want."

No one will argue that the values of economic man in the market place are the only ones that count. Who is so vulgar and insensitive as to claim that only what is objectively demonstrable is important? Will progress be made, however, by undermining the rationale for economic analysis or by concealing intransigent political problems under an economic guise? The new economics poses for itself essentially political problems. Which decisions shall be made through the market and which not? What decision structures will best assure environmental quality? How can aesthetic feelings be translated into public policy? What happens if strong aesthetic impulses are shared by only a small minority? Consideration of the problems surrounding public preferences will help throw the many political dilemmas into sharper focus.

Let us assume, for the moment, that all problems of directly measuring public preferences in regard to the quality of the environment were solved through opinion surveys or other devices. Would our problems of allocating resources then be solved? In one sense, they would be solved all too well. The problem of the interpersonal comparison of utilities, the relative preferences among different people for shares in things like housing, transportation, space exploration, or ballet, must be solved before environmental quality may be given its place. If the results of the survey are accepted, then all allocation problems in society have been solved. Such a state of affairs is usually called utopia.

Suppose, however, that some people prefer a different mix of goods than was provided in the grand allocation mechanism. Perhaps they are among the relatively small groups that intensely desire long canoe trips through completely wild areas and have been outvoted (or "outpreferenced") by others who want skin diving near where they live or who prefer large indemnities to black people to repay them for decades of service in slavery. These minorities would certainly challenge the existing state of preferences. They might argue, as democratic theorists have through the ages, that strict majority rule should not prevail. Minorities like themselves should be given some proportionate share of good things (though it is doubtful whether they would agree that every minority, including ones opposed to their desires, should get similar consideration regardless of what they wanted). The wilderness minority might say that people should not get what they want, but what they ought to have, according to the principles of the sensitive few. Perhaps many people decide in ignorance and ought to be educated before their preferences are counted or weighed equally with those of the more knowledgeable. Things might be different if people were encouraged through subsidies to experience elementary contact with nature, which would in turn alter their previous preferences. What turns out to be crucial is not merely knowledge of preferences but a set of rules for putting them together so that policy decisions emerge. Yet we have not even mentioned the knotty problems of accounting for intensity of preferences. Should the intense minority triumph over the apathetic majority? Should we satisfy the widespread norm of equality by treating all citizens equally or only equals equally? Extraordinary difficulties arise when public preferences must be translated into public policy.

Should their sensitivities be sufficiently outraged, the wilderness minority might question the procedures through which public preferences for governmental expenditures are determined. The use of opinion polls to derive a rank order of public preferences is suspect in many ways. The process of seeking preferences may create preferences where none existed before. People may feel they have to respond to a questionnaire without ever having thought of the matter before or having any real preference. Many citizens may discover that they have preferences only after an act to which they can respond has taken place. It is difficult to get people of low education to understand the wording of questions and the complex choices involved. Highly educated people will also have trouble sorting out their feelings if they are required to make a series of comparisons leading to a ranking of some 15 or 20 major areas of public policy. If the ranking is performed by a survey analyst, the rules for determining the hierarchy of preferences may be challenged as inadequate or controversial. Political leaders like the President are known to influence the determination of public preferences from time to time. What a President may get from a survey, therefore, is an echo of his own voice. Since opinion is mutable, the opposition can say that if they will just work harder, public preferences will come closer to their values in the future. Although the temptation is understandably great, the hard problems of making interpersonal comparisons of utility cannot be avoided by fobbing off the task on other people through an opinion survey.

For the old economics, the political system unfortunately did not produce decisions that met the strict criteria of economic rationality. It was desirable economically, for example, to take into account as many measurable consequences for others as possible. The larger the area covered, the greater is the number of externalities that can be internalized within the analysis. If economic criteria were to be followed, bargaining, horse-trading, log-rolling, or other practices that might introduce inconsistencies had to be kept to a minimum. Thus, a unitary government with highly centralized parties and powerful hierarchical leadership would appear to be preferable to a federal system with extremely decentralized parties and fragmented leadership continuously engaged in bargaining to accommodate the most diverse range of interests. But the desirability and feasibility of abolishing the federal system, the separation of powers, and decentralized parties are not usually considered because such matters go beyond economic analysis.

The new economics need not face the same problems. It is concerned, after all, with getting away from rigid economic analysis and the strict application of efficiency criteria. Its practitioners are committed to values favoring the enhancement of environmental quality. The new economists are advocates as well as scholars. For them, policy outcomes cannot simply be the result of a set of analytic procedures. They want some results and not others. They want to develop the best arguments they can for securing the results they favor. In cases of doubt and indeterminacy, the new economists want the values they favor included rather than excluded. But they are inhibited by a nostalgia for the credibility accorded to the old economists they once were. Caught between the desire to insure certain outcomes and the pull of their economist's conscience, they risk being neither economists nor effective advocates.

The new economics is in danger of misconstruing its mission. Its goals are laudatory (that is, I share them), but they cannot be achieved by self-deception. Little is to be gained and much lost by compromising the old economics. It should be perfected according to its own lights, so that at least part of the spectrum of values will be properly illuminated. What is first required is an accurate statement of the political problems involved in realizing environmental values.

There is no evidence to suggest widespread and intense support for drastically improving the quality of the environment. Most people are probably indifferent. Some care a little, but are unwilling to sacrifice much. Only a relatively small minority cares deeply enough to make significant sacrifices. The best available evidence comes from a survey of attitudes toward government programs conducted in 1961 by Eva Mueller through the Michigan Survey Research Center.[1] The survey is especially valuable because people were asked whether they would give up income in the form of higher taxes in order to pay for expenditures they believed desirable. Of 14 types of public policy mentioned, the item called "Parks, recreation facilities" provides a fair test of public support for improving the environment. No doubt more people care about parks than about the remote backwoods, but 10 percent of the people interviewed have no opinion on these resource programs, and 48 percent think that existing governmental expenditure is about right. Thus, 58 percent of the population is essentially indifferent to a change in public policy. It is true that a larger minority favors more rather than less expenditure (27 to 15 percent), but the favorable minority declines by almost 400 percent (27 to 7 percent) when asked if they would pay higher taxes to support this resource policy. Larger proportions of the population are willing to pay through higher taxes for help for the old and needy, education, defense, and highways. Indeed, the number of people willing to pay to explore outer space is twice that willing to pay to improve the earthly environment (14 percent as compared to 7 percent).

Public sentiment may have changed since 1961. Perhaps people would now be willing to pay more to deal with water pollution. When a candidate for governor of California suggests selling part of the state's wilderness areas, however, and still receives overwhelming endorsement by the electorate, it is difficult to believe that the wilderness minority is very large. Though small, the wilderness minority is not always impotent. Yet the victories recorded here and there all appear to stem from an intense campaign run by a few dedicated individuals. When this middle- and upper-

TABLE 10-1
Attitudes Toward Government Programs

PROGRAM	MORE	LESS	SAME	NO OPINION	TOTAL	MORE EVEN IF TAXES HAD TO BE RAISED[b]
	%	%	%	%	%	%
˰lp for older people	70	3	23	4	100	34
˰lp for needy people	60	7	28	5	100	26
˰ucation	60	7	25	8	100	41
˰m clearance, city improvement[a]	55	9	24	12	100	e
˰spital and medical ˰care	54	9	28	9	100	25
˰blic works[a]	48	11	31	10	100	e
˰fense, rearmament[b]	47	6	34	13	100	30
˰pport for small business[a]	37	11	31	21	100	e
˰ghway construction	36	10	45	9	100	13
˰employment benefits	29	14	45	12	100	10
˰rks, recreational facilities	27	15	48	10	100	7
˰ace exploration[b]	26	32	28	14	100	14
˰pport for agriculture	20	26	34	20	100	6
˰lp to other countries[b]	7	53	28	12	100	2

˰uestion asked only in June 1961.
˰uestion asked only in November 1961.
˰navailable.
˰RCE: Eva Mueller, "Public Attitudes Toward Fiscal Programs," *The Quarterly Journal of Economics* 77 (May 1963).

class effort fails to materialize, nothing happens, except the loss of another site of scenic splendor.

The provision of subsidies on behalf of the aesthetic minority— subsidies like the British Broadcasting Company's Third Programme —might suggest that a unitary and centralized political system would be more receptive to demands of this nature. But this result depends on the existence of a privileged minority to which great deference is accorded. The cultural conditions for this phenomenon do not exist in the United States, nor, on other grounds, would many of us prefer such a situation. In America, a centralized political system that registered immediate majority demands could well wreak havoc with the policies preferred by the aesthetic minority. Bigger and better highways might always be preferred to clean air, or parks, or refuges for wildlife.

A system like the American one that provides special opportunities for skillful and well-organized minorities would appear well suited to the characteristics of the aesthetic few. How should they go about realizing their preferences? How can they mobilize their forces? What organizational structures and strategies are best suited to translating their preferences into public policy? What kinds of administrative arrangements will help obtain favorable results in the future? Although satisfactory answers are not likely to be immediately forthcoming, these questions are foremost among the right ones to ask.

There is no reason to suppose that the most aesthetically interested members of society are politically disadvantaged. They probably do not suffer from being denied the right to vote or from low educational attainments or poor family backgrounds that would deny them the skills necessary to compete in political life. Like those with special interests in theater or ballet or sailing, the aesthetic minority is likely to be composed of middle- or upper-class people who do not have to struggle for the necessities of life and can afford to be sensitive. Their problems of political mobilization are likely to be quite different from those of the poor and downtrodden. Given a choice between political activity in behalf of their preferences for environmental quality or individual economic action, they may well choose the latter. They can move to the suburbs to get away from air pollution or travel to where the remote wilderness still exists. Things may have to get worse before they find it less costly to spend time in political activity than in raising income to satisfy their aesthetic preferences. Yet they are also capable of reasonably long-run perspectives. The leaders of this minority must first convince people who share their preferences that political action is necessary now if they want their children to be able to enjoy a natural environment of higher quality in the future.

Political elites are far more likely to share the preferences of the aesthetic minority than are the mass of people. While long-term efforts of mass education may be desirable, short-term results depend on the men in power. Since various interests oppose certain specific measures, and alternative objects of expenditures compete for existing resources, ways must be found to enable public officials to support the policies most of them would like to see implemented. The questions of who will pay and how are crucial. In the best of all possible worlds, a new process is discovered that produces a good like wood pulp more cheaply and with far less noxious waste than before. Everyone gains, and no one loses; or those who win in one transaction compensate the losers in another. In most cases, however, the questions of who will pay and how much loom large. Costs can be transferred to large industries or to those who consume their products, to general taxpayers or to specific industries, to citizens or to foreigners, from one region or class of citizens to another. Citizens with low incomes are notorious for their willingness to seek greater public benefits, and their unwillingness to pay more taxes. The wealthy are famous for the ingenuity with which they escape the full burden of the income tax. The acknowledged principles of the public-finance literature—ability to pay and benefits received—are inadequate when there are severe disagreements over the justice and applicability of each principle. The difficulties are compounded when a desired objective, say reduction of air pollution, can be accomplished if and only if an objectionable mode of assigning costs is accepted. If it turns out to be much easier to pass the burden on in the form of hidden consumer taxes than to assess the polluters or desecraters of the wilderness, difficult choices must be made.

In the past, there has been considerable public support for conservation in some western states. Mass support may now be generated in various areas in regard to water and air pollution, but the possibilities of support may be slim for a subtle policy specifying so much reduction of pollution here, a little less there, and none someplace else (the kind of policy favored by the old economics). The price of mass support may be massive programs to wipe out pollution entirely. Again, a difficult choice may have to be made between too little effort to reduce pollution and too much.

Presently we do not have the knowledge that would enable us to choose the kinds of organizational structure that would lead to decisions in favor of improving environmental quality. We can, however, identify critical choices. The number of governmental organizations concerned with natural resources is already large and growing. These agencies traditionally perform specialized functions for a particular clientele and are closely tied to local interests and their congressional advocates. To these divisive forces are then joined narrow organizational loyalties. The legitimization of new functions by society, such as desalinization, pollution abatement, and highway beautification, has been accompanied by the creation of separate organizations to devise and implement programs. For people concerned with rationalizing policy in the resource field, the rapid proliferation of autonomous organizations is alarming. It points to the need for larger units or coordinating structures that will presumably produce decisions which take into account a wider range of values. Leaving aside questions of the feasibility and cost of such a change, it is not clear whether it would further the cause of the aesthetic minority. New and "narrow" agencies supporting environmental quality with ever greater determination might be preferable. Subunits within larger multipurpose agencies dealing with extensive geographical areas might be used to great advantage in the cause of the aesthetic minority. We do not know and are hardly in a position to guess.

Another critical issue involves the choice between setting-up or strengthening a regulatory agency or trying to enact legislation that contains automatic incentives making it advantageous for the affected parties to do the right thing. When outrage over pollution or destruction of forests bursts out, it is tempting to pillory the offenders and to control their future conduct by establishing a regulatory commission of some sort. But the history of regulation has not been an entirely happy one. With the best of motives, the original regulatory passion begins to wane. The people whose interests are most directly affected maintain constant vigilance, while the rest of us turn to other pursuits. The regulatory agency is surrounded by the interests it is supposed to regulate. The inevitable accommodations may leave little regulation intact. Moreover, the existence of friendly regulatory bodies is used as a rationale for avoiding the necessity of other and possibly more stringent measures. We have little evaluated experience in developing incentives in the form of tax measures, bonuses for keeping land or water in certain conditions, support for competitive products, or other devices that might accomplish the task.

If action is to be based on some knowledge, the consequences of varying institutional arrangements for major values must be specified. In different times and places, there has been considerable variety in organizational arrangements and legal patterns. Knowledge of what results ensued under different conditions might give direction to future judgments. New techniques of organizational analysis also provide splendid opportunities for current research. The development of computer simulation models is especially promising. These models view organizations as problem-solving mechanisms that use certain rules for arriving at decisions in a complex environment. These rules can be derived from interviews and observations, and programmed on computers. By recapitulating the processes of decisions on computers, it should be possible to explain how the organization works. One can then experiment with alterations in the assumptions guiding the organization, its specific rules for decisions, and its environment, and determine how these changes affect its policy outputs. Organizational changes can be experimentally produced as a better guide to action than mere guesswork.

There is, in general, an appalling lack of information on the causes and consequences of environmental deterioration. If environmental quality is broadened to include the design of urban living (and hence poverty and race relations), the absence of knowledge is even more startling. The availability of better information might reveal a wider range of choice and thus result in different political decisions. There is overwhelming need for experimentation. We could use more than one experimental city. Thus, there is an important role for the man who does not find it becoming to devote his talent to direct political questions of mobilizing support to preserve the wilderness or the cultures of the city. He may feel that his desires are not more worthy than those of other men. Such a man may be prepared to have his minority preferences overridden. But by working to improve the information base for decision-making, he may hope to make everyone wiser about the scope of their interests and the possibilities of reconciliation with others.

We do not wish to restrict ourselves to the values appropriate to economic man in the market place. (Failure to preserve superb redwoods because the economic worth of the income produced by cutting them down exceeds their presently known aesthetic value would be tragic.) Nor do we wish to become mere schemers who, so long as they can muster the political power necessary to achieve their personal objectives, do not care about other people's feelings. (Failure to alleviate the psychic deprivation suffered by people who will lose their jobs if the redwoods are protected, and whose identity is bound up with the lumber trade rather than selling souvenirs to tourists, would be cruel.) Yet, like Dostoevski's underground man, whose appreciation of the endless depths of every question rendered him unfit for any action, the cost of taking everyone's preferences into account may be paralysis. Worse, it may result in grand opportunities forgone or in irreversible damage to the environment. Weak and frail as we are, beset by doubts and anxieties, undoubtedly partial in our views, we must act. If those who love the wilderness will not save it, who will?

NOTES

NOTE: Having come late to this symposium, I have had the opportunity of profiting from and reacting to the other papers. My obligation to the authors of these papers is gratefully acknowledged. I would like to thank Irving Fox, Jerome Milliman, Vincent Ostrom, Jeffrey Pressman, David Wentworth, and Carol Wildavsky for their valuable comments. All of these people disagree with me in significant ways and are not responsible that I often did not take their excellent advice.

1. Eva Mueller, "Public Attitudes Toward Fiscal Programs," *The Quarterly Journal of Economics* 77 (May 1963): 210–235. For questions, see Table 10-1.

PART III

Political Anthropology

12

"WHAT CAN I DO?"
THE OHIO DELEGATE'S VIEW
OF THE CONVENTION

Although there is a great deal of descriptive literature dealing with the more glamorous aspects of national conventions, there is no account of how delegates view the convention. The purpose of this study is to show how individual delegates react to the convention environment, how they feel about it, and how they interpret what they see and hear. This is not merely a matter of curiosity. For the ways in which delegates adjust to the convention situation and perceive the events that take place within it affect their behavior. Of course, a delegate does not simply respond to an abstraction known as the convention. He acts within a specific set of political pacts created by his state delegation which limits and shapes the kinds of things he does. It made a great deal of difference to the delegates from Ohio that they were pledged to John Kennedy in a primary vote and that they had an active governor with aspirations to state and national influence. It is essential, therefore, that we begin with the preconvention history of the Ohio delegation.

Local Politics and National Conventions

In seeking to understand behavior at national conventions it must never be forgotten that the delegates come from state parties which are going institutions with an internal life of their own. The delegates spend only four

From Paul Tillett, ed., *Inside Politics: The National Conventions* (Dobbs Ferry, N.Y.: Oceana Publications, 1960), pp. 112–130. Reprinted by permission of Oceana Publications and the Eagleton Foundation, Rutgers University.

days every four years at convention sessions but they must live with one another within the state party for over 1,400 days between these occasions. It would certainly be unwise to commit acts at the convention which would damage one's chances at home or lead to bitter internal rivalries which might last for years. This is especially true for those leaders whose fortunes are tied up with the accomplishments of a state party. To interpret the behavior of a state delegation, therefore, one must know a good deal about internal factional politics in that locality. This holds true for candidates as well, for a man with a good intelligence service which informs him of internal differences within a state places himself in an excellent position to manipulate the circumstances to his own advantage.

The structural fact that Ohio has a Presidential primary in which delegates are publicly (though not legally) pledged to a particular candidate vitally affects the strategies of the participants. Primaries are important not merely for the votes they may bring but more so because the results provide an indication of a candidate's popularity with the electorate and provide some answer to the question everyone wants to know—"Can he win the election?" Generally speaking, a candidate would be a fool to enter a primary unless he were reasonably certain he could win. This applies with special force to the candidate who believes himself well ahead in delegate support. All he can gain is a few additional votes, but he can lose his entire existing support by a bad showing in the primary. But a candidate like John Kennedy, who needs to demonstrate powerful support in order to stand a chance, has little to lose by entering a primary. If he wins, he has gained votes and made an essential demonstration of his popularity. If he loses, he is hardly worse off than if he had not entered at all. Thus, Kennedy did not have to threaten to enter the Ohio primary; it was apparent to everyone that he would be strongly impelled to do so.

If the existing state leadership is united and has demonstrated a strong following among the electorate, it may be in a better position to check a candidate whose ambitions are deemed detrimental to the party. The state organization may wish to remain uncommitted in order to increase its bargaining power by making a claim on the winner in return for throwing support to him. The party may fear that the intrusion of several candidates would be a divisive influence leaving it in a shattered condition. Consequently, the state leadership may request candidates to stay out and may threaten to throw the weight of the organization against them if they disobey. But if the state organization is split, as in Ohio, a candidate may gain support of one faction and threaten to combine forces with it to defeat those who oppose him. Loss of the primary may carry far reaching implications for state politics, since it may be interpreted as a loss of state leadership by the defeated faction. The interrelationships between local and national politics were foremost in the thoughts of Ohio's political leadership as the 1960 Presidential nominating campaign approached.

Preview

At the Democratic National Convention, Congressman Wayne Hays was berating State Chairman William Coleman over the fact that Ted Kennedy had been permitted to address the Ohio caucus in behalf of his brother, John Kennedy, while a representative of Lyndon Johnson had been told that no speeches would be permitted. Coleman explained that Ted Kennedy had unexpectedly walked in with Ray T. Miller, leader of the Cuyahoga County (Cleveland) organization, and nothing could be done about it. "That's not so," said Governor Michael DiSalle. "He [Ted Kennedy] walked into the meeting with Miller—but actually when I met with [John] Kennedy Sunday, he suggested sending one of his brothers to talk to the delegation to thank them for supporting him." Later, DiSalle called a press conference to say again that he had personally spoken to candidate John F. Kennedy. Not to be outdone, Miller told reporters that Kennedy had made a special point of greeting members of the Miller faction when they went to his convention headquarters at the Biltmore, and he had shaken hands with each one and called him by name. To understand the "I am closer to Kennedy than you are" duel between DiSalle and Miller, it is necessary to reconstruct the factional situation in Ohio which led to two rival groups fighting a party primary battle over which was best entitled to support John Kennedy at the Democratic Convention.

Ohio Comes Out for Kennedy

In the years following World War II the Ohio Democratic party was hardly the model of a cohesive, centrally directed organization. Although Frank Lausche managed to win a series of elections to the governorship, he depended primarily on personal contacts and popularity with the electorate rather than on the party apparatus. The other centers of power in the party were scattered in the county organizations and even they often could not hold their support against independents in primaries.

When Michael DiSalle finally was elected governor in 1958 he sought to create a unified state party under his leadership. His hope was to make the governor's program the party's program, and to have the views of the state leadership count in patronage and in nomination to party and public office. In these efforts he was opposed, if not thwarted, by the Cuyahoga County organization where the fires of local pride and importance burned fiercely. Conflicts developed as Ray T. Miller, the County Chairman, opposed DiSalle's policies and registered protests to the effect that the rightful claims of populous Cuyahoga County were not being met. Then Presidential aspirant John Kennedy entered the picture.

John Kennedy did himself a lot of good by his gracious acceptance of defeat for the Vice-Presidential nomination in 1956. Out of the impression he left there, and through his own efforts to make himself widely known, came an invitation to address the annual party gathering, the Steer Roast, of the Cuyahoga County Democratic Party. County leaders liked him and decided that he was of Presidential calibre. They also believed that Governor DiSalle was against Kennedy and for Symington. After all, DiSalle had been appointed head of the Office of Price Administration by Truman, and Symington was Truman's candidate. Since DiSalle was believed to want a favorite son delegation pledged to him, Ray Miller and his associates decided that they would invite Kennedy into the primary, back a slate pledged to him, gather support from other sections of the state, and defeat the governor. The only rationale they needed was that Kennedy was obviously the popular choice; if the governor did not choose to heed the voice of the people, so much the worse for him. The Cuyahoga County leaders did not have to add that they could use Kennedy as a club to beat the governor and undercut his efforts to establish a state organization under his control. Their spirit of local separatism was unbounded although they would not have objected to a state organization with its center in Cuyahoga County.

At a private meeting with Cleveland Democrats, Miller urged Kennedy to enter the Ohio primary without even consulting the governor. Others who were present, however, and not so intimately connected with the county organization, urged Kennedy not to upset traditional practice and at least consult DiSalle. So a meeting between the two men was arranged.

DiSalle was in a spot. If he ran against Kennedy and lost to the slate backed by Ray Miller, the governor might no longer be able to play important roles in either state or national politics. Defeat would mean not only getting the cold-shoulder from Kennedy but also would prevent the governor from exercising any control over the state delegation to the convention, thereby gaining favor with some other candidate. This would decrease the probability of a cabinet post. Defeat might also result in a tremendous loss of prestige in state politics; and this might lead to loss of control over most of the state party, denial of renomination as governor (or a governorship shorn of real authority), and inability to secure a shot at a senatorship if and when that became open.

Victory in a primary against Kennedy would have cured all these ills but it appeared unlikely. DiSalle polled county chairmen for their preferences and had a private poll of the electorate taken. The news was all black. Kennedy would swamp DiSalle and Lausche, too, if he decided to try his luck. And there was no way of persuading Kennedy not to enter the primary which he needed so badly and which promised to be successful.

At some point in this process, Governor DiSalle hit upon a plan which offered him the most advantages and had the fewest drawbacks.

DiSalle announced that he would run as a favorite son pledged to Kennedy for as long as he had a reasonable chance of winning. This served the
function of guaranteeing that the governor would be head of the delegation, a position appropriate to one who wished to maintain and strengthen
his position of leadership. At the same time, DiSalle did not really limit
his freedom of action to an unacceptable degree. A Kennedy victory would
establish the governor as a man of influence who had been among the first
to support the successful nominee and President. And if Kennedy could
not win the nomination, DiSalle would still be able to switch his support
to a prospective winner and get a foot in that camp. At the state level, the
governor's action might force the Cuyahoga County people to accept his
choice of delegates at the convention and, by implication, his predominance within the state. If the Miller forces decided to run their own slate,
the struggle would then be between rival state and county bodies both
pledged to the same man, and the weight of the larger organization might
be expected to prevail.

Capture of the Ohio delegation was the first big coup for Kennedy and
helped establish him as a serious contender for the nomination. Yet he did
not have to expend time and energy in an expensive primary battle in
which, at best, he was likely to lose a few of the district contests. Since
Kennedy felt that he had to win on an early ballot, the prospect of defection by the governor on a later one did not seem worth fighting about.
Promise of "love eternal" by Miller and his men was not to be rejected,
but neither was the more temporal but equally satisfactory "love while
Kennedy has life" as a candidate.

Despite agreement on a candidate, the factional struggle went on. Governor DiSalle did not take kindly to the Cuyahoga County request to name
all delegates from its area plus 25 percent of the delegates at large—a
proportion equal to the percentage of Democratic voters from that area.
By this method of assigning delegates the governor would be left as a mere
figurehead after the large counties got their share. In order to differentiate
itself from the governor's slate, the Cuyahoga County party declared that it
wanted the entire delegation pledged not merely to vote for Kennedy on
the first few ballots but also to be at Kennedy's disposal if he wanted to
switch them elsewhere. One of the Cuyahoga leaders stated that if Kennedy wanted to make a deal and get support on early ballots by promising
to throw his weight to another candidate at a later time, the Senator had to
be able to dispose of his voting strength as he wished. But DiSalle would
not buy this argument. Despite efforts by other party leaders to bring the
two sides together, they each entered rival slates of delegates, one pledged
to Kennedy through DiSalle and another pledged to Kennedy through Cuyahoga County leader Albert S. Porter, a Miller supporter.

We cannot here go into the details of this vigorous and sometimes vicious primary campaign. Politicians in the Cleveland area were cross-pressured to serve and support one or another delegation. One consequence was that several were dropped from party posts by the Cuyahoga County organizations. The election resulted in a clear but not overwhelming victory for Governor DiSalle as his slate captured 53 delegates and Porter's only eight. Both sides claimed victory and publicized their intimacy with Kennedy and their assured places in his inner council. Such was the situation when the Ohio delegation arrived at the Democratic Convention.

Adjusting to the Convention Situation

"Conventions are fun; they are attended by fun-loving Americans who enjoy themselves immensely. Anyone can see that this raucous, boisterous occasion is a happy one, for all but a few losers, and even they usually manage a smile." This is the accepted picture of national conventions. It is certainly not a completely false picture because many delegates do enjoy themselves at one time or another. But it fails to do justice to elements which induce anxiety among delegates and influence their behavior in many ways. The outside observer who asks them what they think is happening, how they feel about things, what they're doing, soon notices a troubled current beneath the surface flow of gaiety.

The convention brings the delegates into a strange place in which they must participate, or appear to participate, in making an important decision in a terribly short period of time, under hectic conditions, where most of them never find out precisely what is going on and many are full of misinformation.[1] "Can't find a G—damn thing in this place," is the typical plaint of a delegate who finds it difficult to orient himself quickly, especially in Los Angeles which few delegates have visited before and where distances are great. It is not surprising, therefore, that some delegates develop an initial sense of not being in the right place, just at the time when events are moving so quickly that they need all the security of a familiar place to anchor themselves. "Do you think I ought to be at the Biltmore or some place?" [2]

Public mores invade private conscience and impose tremendous demands on the delegate. He should know what is going on, and if he doesn't, something is wrong with him. But on occasion he considers himself lucky if he can find out where he is supposed to be for formal party functions. "Do you know when we'll caucus?"

True, information is thrown at him from all directions but he hardly knows who or what to believe. One day in the papers a Kennedy victory is inevitable and the next it is doubtful and he is slipping. A Johnson staff man patiently explains why his candidate's victory is certain only to be succeeded by Kennedy and Symington people with different stories. One acquaintance says this and another says that. "If you know what's going on you're a better man than I am," responded a delegate who would feel insulted to give such an answer if he were asked about events in his county. "At home I know," said another delegate, "and here . . ." The comment trailed off with an expressive shrug.

A few delegates found it rewarding to go to convention headquarters to seek out their counterparts from other states, newspaper or television reporters, and candidate staff men. But only the most hardy come through unscathed. The more fortunate ones came back at least with conversation pieces and perhaps a word from a famous television personality who could be counted a celebrity. But for the most part these delegates found themselves crushed by the masses of people, uncertain of whom to speak to (especially before delegates' badges were issued as identification) and subject to rebuff. "I never thought that Ed Murrow was such a sour type," said one delegate who felt that he had been brushed off. "Don't go down to the Biltmore," a second delegate advised, "there's just a lot of people trying to find out what others are going to do."

Some delegates feel that they are important people back home. But at the convention the delegate often feels like "a little fish in a big pond" and worries about his status in his new environment. Why is he not consulted and why are his opinions not accorded customary deference by others? He may have only a few acquaintances among the other delegates and these may be political, not personal friends. Conversation may lag because his political acquaintances have different styles of life and do not share his interests in political issues, in horses, or in the weather. There may be difficulty in locating people to talk to and a feeling of loneliness may develop. "Seems like everybody comes from someplace else."

The governor and his top aides are busy people, appearing and disappearing at odd moments and for mysterious purposes. All the delegate may get is a perfunctory handshake. If a delegate has budding feelings of inferiority—"I'm a small man," "What can I do?," "I don't expect to set any records," "Little men don't change things,"—these may be exacerbated by countless little indications that he is out of the know.[3]

It is in this context that the problem of getting a good seat at the convention or tickets for wives and friends takes on special importance. Many delegates come to regard the dispensation of these favors as indices of their status, that is, of the way others regard them. If a delegate finds himself in the back rows where it is difficult to see and hear, he may well consider this a sign of low esteem and a direct slap at his person. He can hardly believe that he got a bad seat by a random occurrence or that other people were just lucky in getting more tickets than he did. "Looks like my place is at the back . . ." one wistful delegate reported; and did not attend the next day's session because, as he put it, you could not very well enjoy the proceedings from that bad location. A good deal of State Chairman

William Coleman's time was spent trying to smooth over ruffled feelings of this sort. That these efforts were not always successful is indicated by the fact that the harshest arguments I heard concerned the distribution of tickets.

It is not surprising the delegates feel troubled when one considers that from their viewpoint the situation is highly unstructured—most of them have no formal role to play. Hence the nagging question of what a particular delegate is supposed to do may recur persistently without his being able to find a satisfactory answer. And if he does not ask himself that question, he feels that the people back home will casually, but insistently, ask him precisely what he did, what his contribution was at the convention.[4]

The governor and a few party leaders are not subject to the same anxieties as the ordinary delegate; they have special ones of their own, for they have direct, personal interests in the outcome of the convention which less influential men do not share. The governor is but one of a number of men who are seeking the candidate's ear. In a fluid political situation the governor can hardly be certain that he will remain in the candidate's confidence or that other more ardent auditors will not usurp his place. The experience of others in past conventions may warn the governor that promises of future indulgences (usually more tacit than explicit) may be cast aside as the candidate's needs change.[5] DiSalle's incessant chant to the effect that he was Kennedy's counselor has the sound of the lady who protests too much, especially in view of the fact that the governor's public preference for Vice President, Stuart Symington, was not chosen.

Mechanisms for Reducing Anxiety

As the convention provides an environment conducive to anxiety, so it also provides opportunities for adjustment. Anxiety induced by strangeness of place can be mitigated but not erased by familiarizing oneself with the surroundings. There is not enough time for that. Instead, the delegates immediately seek out familiar connections with the past. The cry goes out, "Are there Rotarians to make up a meeting?" and soon a quorum is found and a convivial group goes through the old ritual. Mayors breakfast together, Negro delegates converse and go off to a convention-wide meeting of their fellows, Congressmen meet their associates from the Capitol, union members converse about their special policy interests, and delegates from the large counties seek each other's company. Still, some are left out.

Where lack of reliable knowledge is a source of concern, information costs may be cut by an acceptable stance which requires the bare minimum of awareness. "We're supposed to be for Kennedy so what do I care about all these rumors." Or "I go as the Governor goes. That's all I need to know." It was a visible source of relief for some delegates to turn a question about what was happening into an explanation that they were morally committed to Kennedy. The more apathetic may say that "they won't tell me what's going on." Who are "they"? "The big shots."

There are delegates with special contacts who do possess bits and pieces of information which enable them to feel knowledgeable. Negroes may nod wisely and say yes, the civil rights plank is acceptable to their race; union men shake their heads and say no, Johnson is not acceptable to labor; and a few with a line to the governor or Ray Miller or someone on the Kennedy staff generate confidence about Kennedy's chances, often mentioning what individual states are likely to do (right on Pennsylvania, wrong on California). Where the need to appear informed is great and the delegate or alternate lacks access to reliable information, he may become an inside dopester and trade on rumor and invention. He specializes in secret conclaves between shadowy figures behind-the-scenes, where evidence for or against is not likely to be forthcoming. One such person took me aside and whispered in confidential tones that (and this was off the record) he had secret information from the highest authority that Johnson and Kennedy were going to debate before a closed meeting of the Texas and Massachusetts delegations. He called people in Ohio only to learn that they had heard the story on TV and were preparing to watch the debate. More than one delegate discovered by phone or mail that the people back home seemed to have better information than he did.

Some delegates see themselves as spectators. One says that he is present because "The convention is so interesting. I like to see the way in which things work out." Another feels that "political appeal is like sex appeal; don't know why but it's fascinating." Or he may take a scholarly stance and explain that he is a student of the subject and watches it with a sort of clinical detachment. Here is at once an explanation for what he is doing or not doing, a defense against involvement, since he is "really an observer like you," and a rationale to account for his not being terribly important, since his function is to follow whatever happens rather than work for a particular outcome.

Delegates who regard the convention as a vacation site have a set line for dealing with the problem of their personal involvement. They go to the races or Hollywood or Disneyland and justify it by asserting that what anyone does is of little or no importance. In that case, why not get some fun out of the trip. Of course, they could find out the trivial stuff that everyone else does, but it wouldn't count so why bother? "Take it from a man who knows, sonny, they're all wasting their time. Hey, Joe, put five bucks on. . . ."

Men who are active on behalf of a candidate present a contrasting picture. They know who they are for and what they are going to do to help their candidate. They seek to locate and convince potential waverers. If this fails, they may call on someone who is in a position to influence the waverers. The activists may go around buttonholing delegates and putting in a good word for their man. They are realistic about it for the most part. "Who you are speaks more loudly than what you say. If you're the Governor this speaks loudly; if you are just one delegate like . . . [me] this doesn't mean much but occasionally it helps."

Virtually all activists were for Kennedy but there were a few deviants who had a special claim to fame. They were for some other candidate and they let everybody know it. "I'm going to switch on the second ballot regardless of what the Governor does and I'll tell him so." (When the roll was called at the party caucus asking for preferences on the first ballot, this delegate told everyone that he would switch on the second.) After prophesying in the presence of reporters that Ohio would desert Kennedy on the second or third ballot, another deviant went on to tell of the slick trick he had pulled on a local political opponent and how he had told off a government official.

Active delegates appear to feel more self-assured because they are doing something and they have no trouble in explaining to themselves or their friends the significance of their participation in the convention. But what of the other delegates? Their chief claim to fame is that they are official delegates, important people by virtue of being chosen for this honor. Yet this is not quite enough; they have to do something. Convention speeches do not help the delegate meet his needs. The speeches may add to the reputation of the man doing the talking but they do not enhance the delegate. Everyone at home can listen to the speeches, probably under more comfortable conditions. And this helps to explain why many delegates make no attempt to listen to them. The demonstrations, on the other hand, provide an opportunity for active participation ("Did you see me on TV?") in a colorful event which the delegate can recount at home. The marching and the shouting not only serve to indicate support for a candidate but also may serve the function of reducing anxiety by giving the ordinary delegate a role to play.

Political advantage may be taken of the delegate's need to feel important. The task of a leader like Governor DiSalle is to convince delegates to attach their prestige to that of the state party, to assure them that a more significant role for the state enhances their individual importance. Indeed, the essence of the governor's remarks at party caucuses was that for the first time in many a year Ohio had a great role to play in determining the Presidential candidate, and that this chance must not be impaired by a lack of unity which would make all their efforts worthless. In his appearance at the caucus, Ted Kennedy had a word along this line for everyone. On behalf of his brother, he wished to thank every individual delegate for the invaluable contribution they had made to John's success. John Kennedy was where he was because of Ohio and he would always remember, yes he would always remember, even after his election, that Ohio came in when he needed support the most.

In view of the preceding comments, the function which personal attentions like handshakes by leading candidates and pictures taken with prominent persons perform for delegates should be evident. Richard Nixon's practice of having a separate photograph taken of himself with every delegate, however exhausting and perfunctory this may appear, demonstrates a real appreciation of what this gesture means to many delegates.

The Delegate's Perceptions of the Convention

Most delegates share a few major political goals. They want to choose a man who can win the election, they want to get a claim on him (perhaps through their state party), they want to advance their state party or faction, they want to keep the national party together if they can do so without too great a sacrifice of policy preferences. The information required to meet these goals—what the electorate will do, what the convention will do, what the effects on local candidates will be, what other party groups will accept—is never fully available to anyone,[6] certainly not to the ordinary delegate. A great premium is thereby placed on the manipulation of information, for if a sufficient number of delegates and their leaders believe that a certain candidate is likely to win they may act on their conception of reality and bring about a self-fulfilling prophecy as others, observing their behavior, seek to get on the bandwagon. In a closely contested convention, the candidate who makes the picture of events favorable to his chances the one shared by most of the delegates is likely to win. This is particularly the case in convention decision-making choices which must be made rapidly, under conditions of uncertainty, without an opportunity to test one's notion of reality against the outcome of events in time to change one's course of action. Even in the 1960 Democratic convention, where the nutcracker of opinion formed by all the public media of information insisted that Kennedy was going to win, the delegates evidenced considerable variations in perception. We may profitably pay attention to the process of perception even though, in this case, the convention did not go a sufficient number of ballots for us to observe the full political consequences of shifts in the delegate's perceptions of reality.

Will Jack Win?

The first great question, of course, was whether Kennedy would win the nomination. (In a convention without a strong front-runner the question would be, "who will win?") The range of responses may be graded in order of the degree of certainty. "It was all over after West Virginia. Kennedy had it sewed up before we came." "It's Kennedy before the end of the first ballot." "New Jersey will switch to Kennedy at the end of the first ballot. Meyner isn't strong enough to hold the delegation. Then Jack will win." Most predicted Kennedy would win on the second ballot; a few on the third. A sizable minority believed that if Kennedy did not make it on the first or second ballot at the latest, he was through. These were the delegates who speculated about where the delegation might go if Kennedy did not make it. (Johnson appeared to have the most support, followed by Symington and then Stevenson.) A few had serious doubts about Kennedy's ability to win the nomination because the other candidates would gang up against him, because of his religion or youth, because the old pro Harry Truman did not want him, or for some other definable reason. But most of the doubters just felt that the convention was so unpredictable (at least for them) that you just could not know. "With 4,000 delegates around anything can happen," was a typical comment. The number of delegates certain that John Kennedy would win increased after Ted Kennedy informed them that Pennsylvania would give most of its votes to his brother and this was confirmed later that day. The number of doubters increased after the Stevenson demonstration occurred and after stories about how Kennedy was slipping began to circulate. If perceptions were this far apart when so many signs pointed to Kennedy, one can imagine what the case would be when no one candidate had emerged as the overwhelming favorite.

A Religious War?

Yet most delegates clearly had some idea that Kennedy was going to win and the question of who was expected to win did not occasion as much comment as it might have at other conventions. Often, a delegate would brush right past this question and ask what I thought Kennedy's chances were in the election or add that he wished Kennedy's chances in the election were so good as those for the nomination. This was the way the delegates had of bringing up what was troubling them most—the Catholic issue and its effect upon Kennedy's electoral chances. There was more comment on this than anything else although I never introduced the subject. Religion, for the delegates, was an especially painful topic because the very mention of it violated deeply held norms of what was proper behavior in public life. Religious conflict was un-American, disgraceful, violated the Constitution, against our way of life, and "I shouldn't even be talking about it." Having brought up the subject himself, a Negro delegate flared up saying, "Don't you tell me discussion of religion is not right; segregation isn't right either but it's a fact of life."

Before they arrived at the convention the delegates began to collect personal impressions on which to base an opinion on the impact of the religious factor. "I talked to a trainman . . . he was a Mason and he said that he had spoken to a hundred Masons in the past few days and none of them would vote for Kennedy because in the past the Pope had said some nasty things about the Masons." An automobile trip brought a delegate in touch with members of the Holiness sects. These fundamentalists would not vote for Kennedy, he was sorry to say, but there was one ray of light. A Jehovah's Witness had told him that he would vote for Kennedy since it seemed to be God's will that America have a Catholic President.

The memory of the Al Smith Campaign in 1928—"That was not so pretty"—was strongly imprinted in the minds of many older delegates who feared "a religious war." "The Kennedy people say that Smith was 25 years ago but I don't know," one perplexed delegate said. "People are different now," said a delegate. "I think their children have inherited that disease," another replied. His apprehension was increased when, like other Ohio delegates, he saw anti-Catholic signs and demonstrations at the Biltmore where the theme was that America must not be ruled from Moscow or Rome.

A very few delegates were of the opinion that Kennedy was using the religious issue for his own benefit. One delegate had the sneaking suspicion that the Kennedy people put up these [anti-Catholic] signs to gain sympathy. Another had a Catholic friend in Texas who asserted that the Church had tried to pressure him into supporting Kennedy. Without doubt, the religious issue brought some delegates to a more vigorous defense of Kennedy than might otherwise have been the case, as they demanded, "It's time we practiced what we preach [about religious freedom]." Many questions by the interviewer about the approach used by the Johnson staff men who visited the Ohio delegation revealed that none of them tried the traditional tactic of claiming that Kennedy could not win. Why not? "That," in the words of a Johnson man, "would have been interpreted to mean a reference to the religious issue."

An antidote to scattered attacks on the influence of Kennedy's religion was humor. "I'm more afraid of the Republicans than I am of the Pope," retorted one Protestant delegate. Upon being informed that if Kennedy became President "the Pope would move into the White House and bring his wife and children too," a delegate gleefully reported, "that's how much they know about it." Humor was the weapon of Catholic delegates who declared that the Pope would certainly not enter the White House until Kennedy had cleaned it up.

Who's Making All That Noise?

Of lesser concern but nevertheless of considerable interest to the delegates was the Stevenson demonstration on the second day of the convention. To be sure, those who look upon the convention as a vacation ground had no reaction because they were not there. The small group actively working for Kennedy were totally unimpressed. "It was all in the galleries as far as I could see." "They don't vote in the galleries." "Who is there to impress? The people demonstrating outside the convention hall were all from California." "I saw a fellow who said he was a Texan for Stevenson but he never saw Texas." The whole thing was "bought and paid for" or it was "a lot of hullaballoo" presumably signifying nothing. Any candidate would have gotten the same, an activist asserted, and pointed out that the loser always has to make more noise as evidenced by the Southern shout on the platform vote. There are always a few delegates who claim to know how it was all done. "I stood by [Senator Mike Monroney] while he directed it." Or, the "tickets were given to the Stevenson people the day before yesterday." Delegates who looked on the convention largely as spectators, particularly those who had not been to three or four conventions, were visibly impressed. "Remarkable, never saw anything like it." "It was disturbing —something in it—must have been spontaneous." They felt that Kennedy was definitely weaker now but since they were pledged to him the only speculation concerned what might happen on the second ballot.

Perhaps the most revealing comment came when a woman delegate, at a convention for the first time, revealed that she had applauded loud and long for Stevenson. She admired him and he had led the party for two elections. "But," she said, embarrassed, "I didn't know anyone would think I was actually going to vote for him."

What the Governor Wants

At the first Ohio Caucus on Monday morning, Governor DiSalle sought to head off any possible defections from Kennedy. Beginning with a gesture toward the delegate's sense of self-importance—no commitments would be made on behalf of the delegation until it took action; it would be kept informed—the governor reminded them that they were pledged to Kennedy. Anyone with contrary ideas had an opportunity to file a separate slate. A moral commitment was all that was asked for but there was nothing more important in politics than the man who gives his word and keeps it. There was no way, continued the governor, of getting a man to keep his commitment. All the leadership asked was that the delegate tell them what he was going to do and give his reasons in caucus. Ending with a magnanimous gesture, the governor declared that he could not remember who had voted for whom at the last convention but it was important that the delegation stay together.

There was remarkably widespread agreement among the delegates on the governor's position. He was thought to want a cabinet post in Washington. Why? "Well, we know he does." "DiSalle likes it in Washington." "He has complained about the low salary he gets as Governor." In order to accomplish this purpose, he had to deliver the delegation to Kennedy. And this would also serve to solidify his position as head of the state party.

Defections?

With possibly one or two defections, it was assumed that all of Ohio would go for Kennedy on the first ballot. But after that, there was much less certainty. The range of responses to a question about defection on the second ballot went from none to 20; few felt able to venture a prediction on the third ballot, an eventuality which appeared too remote to contemplate. The hard-core Kennedy supporters would stick with him, most delegates thought, and the governor would sway party officials and state employees. Beyond that, no comment.

Yet, strangely enough, many delegates were convinced they could predict something about how DiSalle would behave if Kennedy dropped out. At all costs, he would try to keep the delegation united under him. If he could not persuade all, as was likely, he would "try to figure out which way the wind was blowing" and move in a direction where the preponderance of delegates would support him because he was, in fact, following them.

The immediate problem was the first ballot and here Representative Wayne Hays of Ohio drew much comment by his well-publicized wavering in the direction of Lyndon Johnson. Reactions varied with the type of delegate. Spectators concentrated on the moral problem as the following conversation reveals: "Are we pledged? Morally. He has none, the way he was talking last night. Hell, this is a free country. He's an exhibitionalist." Said an inside dopester, "He's been promised something," hinting that he knew what but was unwilling to say. The group of delegates who worked in Congress or had some previous experience there, however, were quite explicit in offering an explanation. "Last night I heard that Speaker Rayburn said, 'I'm going to be Speaker for ten years and I have an awfully long memory.'" Another delegate responded, "Sure, Rayburn and Johnson have leverage over Congressmen. Of course, they can't take you off committees once you are on." And a third delegate in that circle added, "But the Speaker can make it tough." And in a manner to give notice that he was speaking only in a semiserious way, the delegate said that "Hays might find it tougher to go overseas on these jaunts and live high on those counterpart funds." The activists were blunt: "He better watch out." Their conclusion, however, was that Hays would talk big but that he would have to honor his commitment to Kennedy on the first ballot in order to avoid stirring up resentment within his home district. Amidst muttering about freedom on the second ballot, Ohio voted solidly for Kennedy on the first and there were no more.

No Strife, No Excitement

Aside from a few strong words about possible defectors, there was little serious dispute in the delegation. With both the DiSalle and Miller slates committed to Kennedy, there was no open disagreement among them except, perhaps, in vying for their candidate's favor.[7] When the Miller faction caucused on the opening day, they decided that since they were outnumbered six to one, they would attend the regular state meetings and create no difficulties. While they were all Kennedy supporters, Miller told his group, they should show courtesy to other candidates and listen to them respectfully.

Courtesy appeared to be the watchword and there was little invidious comparison of the candidates within the delegation. The delegates would say, "We have four good men and there's nothing wrong with any of them." Enthusiasts for Kennedy were by no means as numerous as his supporters and there was not too much stress on his attributes. Mention was made of Kennedy's war record, his courage, and, above all, his will to win. But there was also a defensive attitude with praise negatively stated. "He's smart even if he didn't write that book himself." "Any religion a man has is a good thing." "People don't realize that in the 1920s men had to work before finishing school, began their careers in their thirties. Today they finish in their twenties, and get a lot of experience by the time they're thirty."

Lyndon Johnson's "ability to get men to work together" counted heavily with his partisans, while he was not quite liberal enough for others or at least they thought this sentiment would block his nomination. Most of the Negro delegates, especially those with congressional contacts, were favorably inclined toward Johnson although not actively. "I know him. He's a practical Southerner. He knows that things can't go on the way they are." Symington had some support but excited virtually no interest except as a vice-presidential nominee. There was even less support for Stevenson who was admired in a general sort of way and then disqualified. "He's a good brain but the pro's are against him because he lost twice." "A smart man but he's got the taint of an appeaser on him." One delegate had a special theory about why Stevenson was doomed to defeat. "You gotta be married to succeed today—a lot of women voting—everyone knows about Stevenson's divorce. Knew a single fellow who ran for office and oh the stories they told about him. He lost."

The platform occasioned virtually no comment whatsoever from anyone. Negroes noted with satisfaction that it met their desires and that was all. A question about the platform did serve to embarrass some delegates, and one replied that he did not know but, in any case, the delegation was bound by the unit rule and would follow the governor. Of course, there was no unit rule, but if one could believe that there were, and that the decision belonged to someone else, then one need not feel guilty about an excusable lack of knowledge concerning the platform.

The relative lack of controversy within the delegation, as well as the dullness of the first two days' proceedings, were a source of disappointment to some delegates. After this came up spontaneously a few times, I began asking delegates if they felt this was so and why. The Kennedy activists rejected the question as unimportant, saying that "the convention will be fine with me so long as it comes out all right." Some delegates, however, tried to find a reason for it. "This one's not as lively as the previous conventions I've been to. At previous conventions many states had candidates they were really for. Not now. Many people who will vote for Kennedy are not really for him. It is just that other candidates all have something wrong."

Missionaries

There was one dedicated band of men who manifested unflagging interest in the affairs of the Ohio delegates—the candidates' staff members assigned to the delegation. They haunted the hotel rooms and the lobby, zealous in the service of their man. Taking no chances, the Kennedy staff was there radiating confidence in all directions. "Let's get it over on the first ballot. Why waste time. Let's begin work on the election. Jack's over the top now." Listening to him, a delegate suggested that it "might be better for the party if it [the balloting] went further; no charges of rigging, then." But he made no impression. On Wednesday morning, with more talk of defection than usual, a Kennedy staff man arrived breathless announcing, "I'm worried about a couple of defections."

At the Monday caucus, a wealthy businessman representing Lyndon Johnson listened to Ted Kennedy say that brother Jack was beyond the necessary 760 mark. "The way he talks, it's all over," he muttered. Undaunted, he proceeded to demonstrate to the delegates surrounding his seat why Johnson would be a certain winner in the election. He would win all the southern and border states and then he'd need only 61 more electoral votes. Furthermore, Johnson would win the nomination by switches on the third ballot, since Kennedy would fall short on the first and no one else had enough strength. On Tuesday several delegates reported visits from Johnson men in their hotel rooms. Johnson was, it appeared, the most mature, best qualified, most harmonious candidate, and certain of victory too. Hope still burned bright on Wednesday as the Johnson representatives spread the word that Maryland was wavering (it was bound by primary law). There would be plenty of moves toward Johnson on the second ballot, they assured their listeners, but they did not expect any on the first in view of Ohio's previous commitment to Kennedy.

A representative from Symington's headquarters was in evidence but he followed his candidate's lead by playing his hand in a low key. His pitch was: "Let the people vote. We don't want six or seven politicians to decide." Naturally, Ohio delegates were pledged to Kennedy on the first and he respected that. But on the second there would be defections. In fact, he wanted to give everyone a chance, Johnson and Stevenson too, so that there would be an open convention.

Adlai's man did not show up until early Wednesday morning, tapped me on the shoulder and inquired, "Do you know who's supporting Stevenson here?" Discovering that I was not a delegate and the nearby representative of the city police vice-squad (sent to watch for pick-pockets and prostitutes) could not help him either, he found some delegates. An hour later he was full of confidence and figures: 14 for Stevenson on the second plus 23 more his side had to speak to. "The trouble with Stevenson," one of his small group of Ohio supporters later said, "was that he started too late."

A Final Word

Wednesday afternoon saw the second Ohio caucus addressed by prominent speakers. Lyndon Johnson stated that he came, not to convert but to give the delegates a chance to size up another candidate. He stressed the success of Democratic Congresses, his liberalism, and his mature judgment as "a trustee for you and your children." A delegate in the crowd commented, "effective; but no matter what happens he can't be nominated." Stuart Symington seemed apologetic about talking so much on defense— but it was his committee—and dared anyone to have a better voting record than his. Mike Monroney spoke for Stevenson stressing the gravity of the world situation, the need to find a man of sufficient stature to handle it, and the delights of a Stevenson-Kennedy ticket.

Chairman Coleman popped up to say that he was sorry there were not sufficient tickets to go around and that some alternates were "seated in the peanut gallery." If the alternates would take badges labeled "demonstrators," that might get them on the floor. If that did not work the same stratagem tried the day before would be used—a shuttle system for badges with page boys as messengers.

Governor DiSalle appeared for his final word before the voting. All the candidates had been heard and there was not one who would not make a great leader. For the first time in 40 years Ohio was trying to build a cohesive party. Now, the delegates were being bombarded with telegrams. But they must adopt a correct measure and compare the numbers of telegrams with the number who voted for them in the primary. There was no reason why Ohio should not present a large undivided vote on the first ballot and for the first time in many years become a force in the nation. Kennedy would be the nominee and he would know that we were there first with the most.

Had there been a series of ballots during which several of the favorites dropped out, it is possible that delegates in search of a candidate might have been swayed by the personal appearances and the arguments of the staff men. As it was, in no case did I observe these speeches change a vote or an intended vote looking toward a possible second ballot. Rather, those who were positively in favor of a particular candidate were reinforced in their opinions and those without strong feelings were unmoved. The Kennedy activists were impatient. "Oh, what's the use of more talk. Jack's got the vote."

By and large, the delegates were happy with Kennedy's nomination. They could all live with it. Most of them were for him in preference to others even if they did have some uneasy feelings. Few had any strong feelings against him. There had been some excitement at last—the demonstrations—and there was visible relief that the big decision had been made.

Who'll Be V.P.?

Speculation about the vice presidency was rife. Not that the delegates thought they would have a choice; Kennedy admittedly had the right to choose the man if he wanted to. But it was fun speculating about who Kennedy would pick, a game fraught with no dangers, in which all could participate on an equal basis of ignorance. Virtually everyone thought Symington was the logical man. His record was good on defense, labor, civil rights, and farm legislation. He came from a border state, was Protestant, and he had offended no one. Moreover, he had Governor DiSalle's support. Johnson was counted out, not because of his attacks on Kennedy which everyone accepted as part of the political game, but because the congressional specialists kept insisting that he would be a damn fool to give up the powerful job of Senate majority leader. (I mention only in passing the delegate who thought DiSalle would be the vice-presidential candidate, but "don't know if he'll accept.") The Johnson nomination surprised everyone but no one was in a disposition to argue much, considering it Kennedy's prerogative. Placating the south made some sense, a Negro delegate said. "You got to give something to get something."

Satisfaction

Looking back at their convention experiences, most of the delegates were pleased. Their surroundings seemed more familiar, partly because they knew their way around a little better and partly because they had drifted into some acquaintanceships. Kennedy's active supporters had the satisfaction of seeing their man nominated. Party leaders and officials had the satisfaction of seeing the state delegation emerge unified. A county chairman was delighted. "Ohio is in very good shape, came out for Kennedy first. This means federal patronage and it will help local patronage, too. You know, there are Governors and Governors. Not much patronage under Lausche. People have to decide whether they want a two-party system. Now, at least, we have a state party." Those who had come to watch the workings of politics might have preferred to see one more ballot but they felt they had learned a lot and had observed the fascinating Kennedy apparatus at work. The men with the real, the true inside story would wow the folks back home with an account of what really happened. Everyone enjoyed the demonstrations.

There was noticeably more banter: "Watch out, here comes a trend." "How about lunch? It's about time, I've been living on rumors all week." "How come Kennedy won? You can't stop something with nothing." "Hear about the policeman who found a dead horse on Figueroa Street? He moved it to Flower Street because he couldn't spell Figueroa." On that note, the delegation left its hotels and went back to Ohio.

Conclusion

The Ohio delegation did not come close to running the gamut of convention experiences. The continual splits, indecisions, waverings, pressures and hence the bitterness, recrimination, and even tears of the California delegation were not felt by Ohio. Had the Ohio delegation been unpledged, divided, without effective leadership, we should have been able to observe more closely the impact of events upon the delegates and the significance of their responses for decision-making. Had the convention gone several more ballots, the ways in which the delegates acquire different perceptions could have been clarified as well as the consequences of their views of reality upon the eventual nomination. There is no reason to blink at the facts: one cannot study decision-making at a convention when the decision has been determined before the delegation arrived.

Yet the task of the political scientist is not solely to explain how and why decisions get made. His task is also to identify and analyze other phenomena—like perception and adjustment—which impinge on the process of decision. There can be little question that, in this connection, the varying perceptions of the delegates and their different ways of adjusting to the convention environment are important. In some respects therefore, the fact that few major decisions were made at the convention was an advantage. Undistracted by the added excitement of a closely fought convention, we have had an opportunity to examine underlying factors which (though operative at all conventions) might otherwise have been obscured.

NOTES

1. "Kennedy's sure to win," a delegate insisted, "he's got the support of all the big labor leaders like Hoffa . . ."
2. Most of the observations included here were made in the lobby of the Hotel Figueroa, the temporary home of the Ohio delegation, where I interviewed some 20 to 30 delegates a day for periods of five to 25 minutes during the week of the convention. The quotations all come from delegates unless specifically stated otherwise. They were written down immediately following the interview and were transcribed word-for-word as nearly as memory would permit.
3. There were numerous indications of delegates seeking to compensate for feeling unimportant by building themselves up in the eyes of the listener: "When I go back to take care of my apartment houses"; "It won't be Kennedy who'll help the local ticket; I'll help my boys"; "my son's a brilliant boy and when I wrote the General about him, the General hopped right to it . . ."
4. I am not suggesting that the delegates were free of troubled feelings before they came to the convention; obviously, like everyone else, they brought their strengths and weaknesses with them. Nor are the anxiety-provoking aspects of the convention necessarily unique. No doubt, delegates have gone to places which are strange to them before; they have probably had to make important decisions quickly; they may have been a part of events in which their role was not clear and yet they were expected to do something. It is the coming together of all these phenomena in the most famous of our political events that is significant.
5. Jules Abels, *Out of the Jaws of Victory*, recounts the story of how Charles Halleck of Indiana was promised the vice presidency by a Dewey aide in return for contributing support to his nomination. The support was forthcoming but not the nomination, as Dewey decided that Earl Warren was more desirable.
6. In another paper, "Uncertainty and National Conventions," I have explored the importance of uncertainty about vital information and the significance in this context of varying perceptions of events.
7. The one jarring note came on a move to replace the aging Albert O. Horstman as national committeeman because he had done little with the job in the past four years. Governor DiSalle was quoted in the press as saying that "Horstman worked and contributed heavily when there wasn't any real Democratic party in Ohio. Now he wants another term and I think he should have it." The Cuyahoga County faction reportedly feared that Horstman would resign the position and then be replaced by State Chairman William Coleman, a man they disliked. Delegates informed me that Dan Duffy, a leading figure in the Miller group, had gotten Horstman's word that he would not resign and that ended the matter.

13

THE GOLDWATER PHENOMENON:
PURISTS, POLITICIANS, AND
THE TWO-PARTY SYSTEM

The Goldwater phenomenon is the great mystery of American politics. His nomination as Presidential candidate by the Republican party and his campaign for election have profoundly challenged accepted theories of American politics. Merely to enumerate some of the puzzling questions suggests how badly we need explanations.

How was it possible for a Presidential nomination to go to a staunch conservative whose popularity among the electorate was known to be exceedingly low and who was far from being the preferred choice of most Republican voters? Why, in a competitive two-party system in which leaders normally seek essentially the same votes, did the parties seem to be hurtling further apart instead of coming closer together? Why, indeed, did not the minority party (the Republicans) imitate the majority party (the Democrats) in search of votes as had previously been the case? Why did the Goldwater Republicans not follow the traditional practice of "balancing the ticket" by choosing a more liberal person as their vice-presidential candidate? Why did Goldwater and his followers put such great stress on consistency and yet appear so inconsistent in their pronouncements? Since Goldwater said that the race question should not become an issue in the campaign, why did he refuse to take the steps which would have helped accomplish that end—voting for the Civil Rights Act of 1964, and making some conciliatory statement to Negroes? Why did Goldwater slant his appeal to working-class people and Johnson to middle- and upper-class vot-

From *Review of Politics* 27 (July 1965), pp. 386–413. Reprinted by permission.

ers in an apparent shift from the usual tendencies in electioneering? Since the candidates were further apart on issues than at any time in recent decades, why was there so little discussion of issues and so much talk about personalities in the campaign?

To put the questions in this way suggests that we are surprised; that our expectations concerning the behavior of parties and politicians have been violated. Ordinarily, we expect both major parties to choose popular candidates with a good chance of winning. The death wish is not supposed to be dominant among politicians. Party leaders are expected to conciliate groups of voters in order to get at least part of their vote. Abandoning a large number of citizens to the enemy is not usually done. The vice-presidential nominee is usually chosen, as were Lyndon Johnson and Henry Cabot Lodge in 1960, to broaden (not further to restrict) the appeal of the party. And the major parties often accommodate themselves to the most popular part of the opposition's policies in order to enhance their prospects of victory. Yet none of these things happened—at least on the Republican side—in 1964. Why?

In order to answer these questions, I shall try to define the character of the Goldwater movement and to relate it to the traditional practices of American political life. I shall begin with an explanation of why Goldwater won the nomination, go on to an examination of his special political style, and end by drawing out the implications of this analysis for the future of the two-party system.[1]

Delegates Are Different

The convention delegates of the Democratic and Republican parties are elite groups of political activists. While these party leaders undoubtedly share many of the characteristics of their followers among ordinary voters, they also differ from them in significant ways. The leaders are much more interested in public affairs and active in trying to do something about them. They know more about the public issues and care more about them. They are more highly educated. Some 60 percent of the leaders have held public office at one time or another, and the same proportion occupies a party position, usually at the county level. Their identification with and commitment to their political party are much stronger than that of ordinary citizens and voters.

Knowing and caring more about issues and the sort of connections between them, and intensely committed to a partisan stance, Republican and Democratic leaders hold more consistent views on more issues than do their followers. There are sharp, clear, and wide differences between Democratic and Republican leaders on many important issues, and hence policy preferences. Public housing and urban renewal, medical care for the aged, aid to education, reliance on the United Nations, foreign aid, and participation in military alliances are just a few of the issues on which meaningful differences appear. Their followers, however, are much closer together. They differ only moderately from one another along gentle liberal and conservative lines; they do not reflect the wide divisions among party leaders. Furthermore, leaders are far more likely than followers are, to believe that the major parties should hold sharply different views on issues. While some 50 percent of the leaders favor wide differences between the parties, only 20 percent of the followers share this view. Thus the persistent belief that party voters demand sizable policy differences between the parties and are thwarted by calculating politicians who do not care about issues is wrong. If party leaders neglect or blur differences on issues this results not from following their own preferences, but from subordinating them in deference to the electorate.

Do leaders differ from followers? Republican leaders disagree rather strongly with their followers among the voters on a wide range of issues. Indeed, Republican followers are closer to the Democratic rather than Republican leaders on issue preferences. While there are disagreements between Democratic leaders and followers, these are less pronounced and occur less often. After determining the support ratios for leaders and followers on 24 domestic and foreign policy issues, McClosky concluded:

Consideration of the scores of Republican leaders and followers shows not only that they are widely separated in their outlooks but also that the leaders are uniformly more conservative than their followers. . . . The largest differences occur on those issues which have most sharply separated New Deal-Fair Deal spokesmen from the hard core of the Republican opposition—federal aid to education, redistribution of wealth through taxes on business corporations and the wealthy, public ownership of natural resources, public housing, regulation of business, social security, farm price supports, minimum wages, and trade union regulations.[2]

This gives part of the explanation we are seeking. Delegates at the Republican convention may nominate a conservative who is popular neither with the electorate as a whole nor with their own voters because the leaders of the party are much more conservative than their followers. These are, of course, general tendencies, for there are leaders more liberal and followers more conservative than these groups as a whole. Yet the central tendency for divergence between most leaders and most followers is clear and beyond dispute. If this is the case—and it has probably been true since the New Deal period—why did the Republican party, from the 1930s to 1964, fail to nominate an avowed conservative whose policy preferences would more nearly coincide with the views of most of its leaders? Clearly, most Republican leaders have subordinated their personal preferences for a more conservative candidate in favor of other goals. It is worth exploring, then, the goals of party leaders (at least before 1964) as they have been determined in a competitive, two-party system.

The Goals of Delegates

Delegates to the national conventions may have motives which are personally their own: fame, glory, compensation for personal defects, the desire to manipulate others, the wish to be of service, the love of human drama; the possibilities are endless. Fortunately, it is not necessary to play psychoanalyst to understand their behavior. Delegates are party activists. When they come to the convention they enter into a social system in which their roles and expectations are defined with some clarity. What counts for us is not their individual personalities, but their collective goals as party leaders in a two-party system which limits and guides their behavior.

American national parties are loose federations of independent state parties, representing somewhat different combinations of ethnic, religious, sectional, economic, and other interests. What holds them together (particularly those who do not share the prevailing ideology) is the hope of forming a coalition sufficiently broad and inclusive to win the greatest office in the land—the Presidency. In order to accomplish this goal the parties seek to appeal to as many different people as possible. They must broaden their appeal even if this means neglecting some issues, watering down others, and reconciling divergent interests as best they can. It is not surprising, therefore, that the first goal of the delegates may be to find "The Man Who Can Win," for without hope of victory over the years it would be difficult for the party to stay together. A party which cared more about maintaining its ideological purity than about winning would lose all hope of gaining public office and affecting public policy.

It is possible to describe briefly the major goals of most delegates to national conventions: they want not only to nominate a man who can win the election but also to gain power, to unify the party, to obtain a claim on the nominee, to strengthen their state party organization, and to protect their central core of policy preferences insofar as this is consistent with their other goals. Despite the fact that most Republicans hold conservative opinions and would prefer a candidate who shares them, they have, in the past, given primacy to their other goals in order to have a chance of winning in a competitive, two-party system. Yet if the goal of winning the election predominated, as it had in the past, the Republican party would have been unlikely to nominate Goldwater. The next step, then, is to explain how political circumstances operated to decrease the relevance of this goal and to bring others into prominence.

Special Political Conditions

By far the most important special condition of 1964 was that for the first time in 30 years there was no moderate Republican candidate who was both popular with the voters and willing to contest the nomination actively. Whatever the reasons, Nelson Rockefeller simply did not appeal to voters in Republican primaries. Henry Cabot Lodge would not campaign and go on the ballot in California. Richard Nixon had ruled out an active public role for himself. And Governor Scranton could not or would not overcome his reluctance to seek the nomination until it was too late. It is difficult to stop something with nothing, as Goldwater's opponents learned to their sorrow.

Participation in Presidential primaries is usually the preferred strategy of aspirants who cannot be chosen by compromise at the national conventions. Men like Kennedy and Humphrey in 1960 or Goldwater and Rockefeller in 1964 actively contest many primaries because they have to establish overwhelming support before the conventions meet in order to have a chance. Candidates like Nixon, Lodge, and Scranton, however, may reasonably hope to be the choice of the convention after the front-runners have demonstrated that they cannot win. So they stay out of primaries and wait to pick up the pieces. This strategy proved disastrous in 1964 because Nelson Rockefeller was unexpectedly unable to play the role allotted to him; he failed to defeat Goldwater in the California primary and the contest was over before it was supposed to have started.

Another significant condition involved the almost universal expectation that no Republican candidate had a chance of beating Lyndon Johnson. This belief vastly reduced the persuasiveness of the usual argument that the Republican party should put up a popular candidate who might win. Goldwater's opponents had to content themselves with the much weaker argument that another candidate would lose by less.

A strong case might still have been made that the fortunes of Republicans running for state and congressional offices would be improved, or at least not seriously impaired, by running a more popular candidate for the presidency. But this argument was weak in some respects. Republicans from the South and portions of the West and Southwest contended that Goldwater would run as well as, if not better than, any other Republican. And some Republicans were so intensely committed to a conservative victory at the convention, and so frustrated at their previous inability to win the nomination, that they convinced themselves that a "hidden conservative vote" would emerge to help them at the state level.

There were state leaders who winced at the thought of a disastrous defeat in November. But there were fewer such leaders than there might have been precisely because the Republicans are a minority party. There were only 17 Republican state governors at the Republican Convention. These were the men who might have had sufficient hierarchical control over their delegations to keep them from precipitantly joining the Goldwater bandwagon. In the absence of such central leadership, the tendency of most delegates to favor a highly conservative candidate had greater scope to manifest itself.

One might suppose that when the goal of nominating a winner could not be met, some of the delegates would have put a premium on the goal of party unity. To be sure, there was less urgency in achieving unity because victory in the election was not expected anyhow. But if defeat seemed to be inevitable, delegates who cared about the Republican party as an organization might have hoped at least to salvage unity. Goldwater had the advantage here because he could work to unify the party around him. Since he had the lead, his backers could claim that the great danger to party unity lay in stubborn refusal to accept him.

Again, the belief that the Republican party was bound to lose the election not only reduced the need to nominate a popular candidate, but also opened up the possibility of using the conflict over the nomination as a means of gaining control of the various state parties. The leaders still cared about winning, but their notion of the relevant contest changed. Wherever Goldwater had strong support among Republican activists, opposing party factions could be beaten down in the name of support for him. Had there been a popular candidate to oppose Goldwater, the opposition might have elected to fight the battle around this champion. In the circumstances, however, they were faced in many states with the choice of going down to defeat or nominally accepting Goldwater. Some Republican leaders, as was apparently the case with Charles Percy in Illinois, decided to try to maintain their influence within the party by rolling with the Goldwater tide and thus living to fight another day. This is precisely what Governor DiSalle of Ohio did in 1960 when a hostile faction of the Democratic party threatened to use John F. Kennedy's popularity as a club with which to beat him. By supporting Kennedy, he was able to defeat his opponents within the party.

Although its effects are difficult to determine, a third contemporary condition must also be mentioned. The impact of the civil rights issue had given rise to hopes that, for the first time since the unsuccessful Presidential campaigns of William Jennings Bryan (1896, 1900, 1908), a party might win by carrying a coalition of southern and western states. The attraction of such a coalition was that it made a conservative candidate more plausible by removing the necessity to appeal on the basis of welfare issues to the labor and minority groups in the populous industrial states. These carry so much weight in the electoral college that the Republican party has had to appeal to them in the past through moderate candidates and platforms.

Yet even if Goldwater's supporters could convince themselves that his cause was not utterly hopeless, the very fact that they chose him suggests that winning the election was not uppermost in their minds. Politicians have been accused of many things; up till now no one has accused them of wishing to lose elections. Has the United States, then, given birth to a new kind of political activist for whom other things rank above winning office? Interviews held with Goldwater delegates to the Republican Convention may help to answer this question.

Purists vs. Politicians

"The delegates are for Goldwater because they agree with his philosophy of government. That's what you people will never understand—we're committed to his whole approach." This Goldwater delegate was undoubtedly correct. There was a remarkable fit between Goldwater and a substantial majority (approximately 80 percent) of his followers. What they liked about Goldwater, however, was not merely or even primarily his policy positions but rather his "approach," his style of operation. When we asked Goldwater delegates to tell us what they most liked about their candidate only a few mentioned his position on the issues, and those who did were content with brief references to constitutional principles like states' rights.

By far the most frequent characterizations of Goldwater referred to his consistency, honesty, integrity, and willingness to stick by principles. It was not so much his principles (though these were undoubtedly important) but the belief that he stuck to them that counted most with his supporters. "He can be trusted." "He is straightforward." "He does not compromise." "He doesn't pander to the public; he's against expediency." "He is frank." "He has courage." "He stands up for what he believes." "He won't play footsie with the people." "He votes his convictions when he knows he's right." "He doesn't go along with the crowd." "He meets issues head-on." "Goldwater speaks about things others avoid. Most politicians like to avoid issues." "He keeps promises." "He doesn't change his mind." "He is not confused." As one of Goldwater's supporters perceptively observed, "He's different than most politicians." And so are most of Goldwater's followers "different than most politicians."

It thus becomes possible to divide delegates into "politicians" and "purists" according to their characteristic modes of approaching political life. While not all Goldwater supporters were purists (some 20 percent were politicians), all purists were Goldwater supporters.

In order to derive typologies of politicians and purists, let us observe the "pure" types as they were revealed through interviews at the Republican Convention. This Goldwater purist was a delegate from a rural area in Pennsylvania attending his first convention.

Interviewer: What qualities should a Presidential candidate have?

Delegate: Moral integrity.

I.: Should he be able to win the election?

D.: No; principles are more important. I would rather be one against 20,000 and believe I was right. That's what I admire about Goldwater. He's like that.

I.: Are most politicians like that?

D.: No, unfortunately.

I.: What do you like about Goldwater?

D.: I am in sympathy with many of his philosophies of government, but I like him personally for his moral integrity. I always believed that a candidate should carry out his promises. Scranton didn't do that. But now, for the first time in my life, we have a candidate who acts as he believes. He doesn't change his position when it is expedient.

I.: Do you think that if the party loses badly in November it ought to change its principles?

D.: No. I'm willing to fight for these principles for ten years if we don't win.

I.: For 50 years?

D.: Even 50 years.

I.: Do you think it's better to compromise a little to win than to lose and not compromise?

D.: I had this problem in my district. After we fighters had won [the nomination for] the congressional seat the local [Republican] machine offered to make a deal: they wouldn't oppose our candidate if we didn't oppose theirs. I refused because I didn't see how I could make a deal with the men I'd been opposing two years ago for the things they did. So I lost and I could have won easily. I've thought about it many times, because if I had agreed I could have done some good at least. But I don't believe that I should compromise one inch from what I believe deep down inside.

Here we begin to see the distinguishing characteristics of the purists: their emphasis on internal criteria for decision, on what they believe "deep down inside"; their rejection of compromise; their lack of orientation toward winning; their stress on the style and purity of decision—integrity, consistency, adherence to internal norms.

The professionals look at politics quite differently. Here is a California delegate strongly for Goldwater, with more than 15 years in party work, attending his third Republican convention.

Interviewer: You seem different from many of the Goldwater supporters. How would you characterize your position in comparison with them?

Delegate: Yes, I'm more practical. I realize you have to live together. For example, I'm going up now to a meeting of the California Republican committee and we've got to handle a liberal candidate and an ultra-conservative. I'm going to urge them to accept the liberal because we've got to work together. We [the Republicans] are a minority party in California and we can't afford to squabble amongst ourselves. The art of politics is the art of compromise. If I can get a whole loaf, I'll take it. If not, I'll take half rather than lose it all.

I.: What would Goldwater do about the Cuban situation?

D.: Well, it's there now and we'll just have to live with it.

I.: The Berlin Wall?

D.: He won't tear it down; I know him very well.

I.: Social Security?

D.: We've had it for a long time, it's part of our system. That's something some of these Goldwater people don't realize. They're a new breed and sort of naive on things like this. They think you can suddenly shift the whole range of government to the right. What they don't realize is that you can only bend a little back away from the left.

I.: What if Goldwater loses by a landslide?

D.: Well, I don't think that will happen.

I.: Suppose it does?

D.: Well, then, maybe the people aren't ready for a change. . . . Yes, we'll have to try to change, maybe a little more toward the liberal side.

The belief in compromise and bargaining; the sense that public policy is made in small steps rather than big leaps; the concern with conciliating the opposition and broadening public appeal; and the willingness to bend a little to capture public support are all characteristics of the traditional politician in the United States.

Having sketched some of the essential attributes of purists and politicians, we can proceed to a closer examination of these two types, with special emphasis on the purists.

Winning Elections

"I've talked to some of the California delegates," a citizen who observed the convention informed us, "and I don't understand them at all; they talk like they don't care if we win." In a sense he was wrong, because the delegates desperately wanted Goldwater to win. But our informant was essentially correct in the sense that they cared more about maintaining their purity—"I would rather lose and be right"—than about winning. The essential element of this style was a devotion to principles, especially the principle that they should have, maintain, and cherish their principles.

When asked why they entered politics, Goldwater delegates often answered, "For the same reason as any man: principles." When asked if the party should change some of its policies if Goldwater lost badly, the delegates responded by reiterating their devotion to principles. "God, no. These are American principles; these are what we stand for." "No, we want a clear party which will represent principles to the people." "I'd rather stick by the real principles this country was built on than win. Popularity isn't important; prestige isn't important; it's the principles that matter."

Although the politicians put a high premium on popularity with the electorate, there were things they would not do and ways they would not prefer to win. A Scranton delegate, in politics for many years in Philadelphia, pointed out that in his white, upper-class ward he and his party had benefited from a "white backlash" issue in a local election. "But we don't want that; that divides the country. We don't want whites and blacks to fight: it's not good for the country." A New Jersey delegate with many years of political experience did not really like any of the candidates for the nomination and feared that the party would fare badly at the polls if Goldwater were nominated. Yet he felt that things could happen: "a white backlash building up if the Negroes have a lot of big demonstrations in the cities; or if Vietnam blew up in our faces. But I'd rather lose than have those things happen. I'd rather lose than have race fights or war."

One great difference between the purists and the politicians lay in what they would consider grounds for preferring not to win. The politicians emphasized specific unfortunate consequences for people in the country such as race riots and war. The purists emphasized departures from internal principles held by their party leaders such as consistency, integrity, and standing firm. The politicians were oriented toward what happens to other people, the purists toward their individual consciences.

Emphasizing Differences

An important component of the Goldwater style was the guiding principle that the parties ought to be different. The maintenance of wide and sharp differences between the parties was seen as a fundamental purpose of engaging in politics. As an enthusiastic woman delegate from New Jersey put it "I think everything should be an issue, civil rights should be an issue, Cuba should be an issue. This is the first time a campaign will be on issues; I think it's wonderful. It's just terrible the way personality has been in politics, like Kennedy winning on his hair and teeth and Nixon losing because there was a shadow on his chin . . . it's ridiculous."

Hence when Goldwater supporters were asked whether they should balance the ticket with a liberal vice-presidential candidate, they replied: "We don't want a blurred image, we've been a me-too party for too long. We want to take a clear position." If, in order to provide clear differences between the parties, the Republicans lose, that is all right. For "even if the party loses at least we have presented a clear alternative to the people. At least we'll have a strong party." What is meant by strong? "Cohesive, united on principles." The chorus of Goldwater purists rose to a crescendo when they insisted, in almost identical words, "We don't want to become a me-too party, we don't want to be the same as the Democrats." The possibility arose, therefore, that if they were offered accommodations or compromises on issues they would reject them because they wanted to be different.

The ideal party of the purists is not merely a conservative party; it is also a distinct and separate community of cobelievers who differ with the opposition party all down the line. To this extent their style merges with that of the liberal party reformers, described by James Wilson in *The Amateur Democrat,* who wish to see the parties represent clear and opposed alternatives and gain votes only through appeals on policy difference rather than on such "irrational" criteria as personality, party identification, or ethnic status. But the Goldwater purists went even further in their willingness to cast aside whole groups of voters who did not agree with them. "We won't get Negro votes anyway, so there's no point in trying." "They can vote for the other party for all I care." "We won't change our principles just to get a few votes from Negroes." In the same spirit, Barry Goldwater suggested that people who favored the kind of government the United States has had since 1932 should vote not for him but for his opponents.

For the politicians, the desire to win is intimately connected with the belief that a political party should try to get as much support from as many diverse groups as possible. In describing the qualities a Presidential candidate should have, a professional will say, "He should be diplomatic. He should be able to gather support from a lot of groups underneath him. That's what Eisenhower had, that's what Kennedy had, and that's what Johnson has. You know there's one thing about politics, there's no such thing as second place, you don't get anything for coming in second."

Hence the professionals were concerned with losing a substantial part of the small Negro vote they had received in the past. "You just can't go around throwing away votes. The object of a party is to draw voters together to the party, not to push them away." A delegate from Philadelphia was more specific. He had "nothing personal against Goldwater" but feared that if he were to run "we'll get the hell kicked out of us. We've been out of [state] power for ten or 12 years. Now we're getting some of the Polish vote and the Italians don't treat us too bad. The Jews and the Negroes go about 75 percent against us, but at least we get part of the Negro vote and that helps us hold the line in the state generally."

To their dichotomous view of political parties and their belief that issue preferences were the only moral way to choose between them, the purists added a strong desire to simplify political choice: a party for the growth of government and a party against; a party which believes in standing up to the enemy and one which believes in appeasement; a party which believes in private initiative and one which wishes to stifle it; the party of free enterprise versus the party of socialism.

The desire to dichotomize and simplify found expression in ways of locating political supporters and opponents. Perhaps the most charming example came from a California delegate who expressed the wish to see all liberals in the East and all conservatives in the West. Presumably, if one knew where a man came from, one could immediately discern his political tendency. Many delegates voiced the desire to divide friend from foe by simple criteria and then do joyous battle.

The "Privatization" of Politics

We may sum up the Goldwater style by saying that it represented a virtually complete privatization of politics. The private conscience of the leader rather than his public responsibilities became the focal point of politics. Internal criteria—possession of, devotion to, standing up for private principles—became the standard of political judgment. This is far from Burke's principle that the representative be allowed to use his own judgment about what course of action will bring the greatest benefit to his constituents. Rather, the constituents disappear, and we are left with a political leader determining policy on the basis of compatibility with his private principles.

From this perspective we can better understand why Goldwater voted against the Civil Rights Act of 1964 despite his agreeing with the view that the race issue should not become a matter of political partisanship. Goldwater's conscience dictated that he vote against an act which contained two sections he felt violated the Constitution. Although he knew that the act would pass anyway, he was simply unwilling to sacrifice his private conscience in order to achieve what he agreed was the public good. Goldwater undoubtedly believed that adherence to the Constitution was also part of the public interest. The point is that when faced with competing conceptions of public good, he chose a remote abstraction over a direct and specific human value. Nor would he or his supporters agree to make rather innocuous concessions on the civil rights plank in order to placate Negroes because that would have suggested compromise; and compromise suggests that one has not stuck to one's principles.

Once the platform became identified as a Goldwater platform, presumably derived from careful scrutiny of conscience, it became a matter of principle not to permit any alteration whatsoever, even if this meant alienating other party factions on the extremism issue. The very idea that the Republican party should try to balance its ticket with a less conservative vice-presidential candidate was uniformly regarded as immoral and despicable. Such thoughts reeked of inconsistency, me-tooism, expediency, and other political vices stemming from the lack of conscience in politics.

Conspicuously missing from purist thought was consideration of voters. Party was defined entirely without reference to the people who would have to vote for it. True, the purists believed that there was a "hidden Republican vote," and they fully expected a huge upsurge of support as most Americans discovered that a party embracing their most cherished principles had at last appeared on the scene. But the "real Republican Party," as they were fond of calling it, was far removed from vulgar pandering for votes. It stood on its principles. It did not change to attract votes. Voters were attracted to it when people changed.

One can see the privatization of politics at work when Goldwater delegates expressed their feelings about President Johnson and former President Eisenhower. Extremely hostile feelings were expressed about both men because they were seen as traditional politicians gifted in the arts of compromise. Goldwater's castigation of Johnson as a "faker," for example, was uniformly regarded as accurate and appropriate. "Originally and historically," a delegate told us, "Johnson was a conservative, but he's willing to do things, to change to stay in power. This shows weakness of character."

The purists did not think it appropriate that a Senator on becoming President should act differently. If a public official need consult only his private conscience, of course, there should be little change in his actions in different offices. If Johnson acted differently in the two offices this could only be because "he has no principles. L.B.J. is a consummate politician. He is inconsistent and immoral." Goldwater was different. "He doesn't talk from both sides of his mouth."

If the essence of politics is to be found in the relationship between leaders and their principles, one would ask quite different questions and give much different answers to queries about the positions taken by candidates. When we asked delegates about Goldwater's position on racial matters, the purists would always respond by saying that Goldwater himself was not bigoted. They knew the exact percentage of employees in the Goldwater department store in Phoenix who were non-Caucasians. They pointed with pride to this statistic as evidence of their candidate's favorable disposition toward Negroes. There was no mention of what Goldwater might do as President; there was no understanding that the public role of a Presidential aspirant might be of interest. Negro delegates, to be sure, could not have cared less about Goldwater's personal predilections. They wanted to know what he would do for Negroes in his capacity as President of the United States. That Goldwater shared this perspective became evident during the campaign when he asked if Negroes would not rather have a President who dealt with race relations as a matter of conscience instead of as a political football. Since political action is a major method of redressing Negro grievances, it is not surprising that Goldwater failed to get his conscience accepted as a substitute for favorable Presidential action.

The privatization of politics leads to an *a priori* approach to politics. Problems are met by stating one's first principles and assuming that they must be relevant to whatever is in hand. One gets no sense whatsoever that Goldwater purists approached problems by inquiring how special circumstances might be taken into account in order to achieve desirable results. The pragmatic spirit was completely lacking. Indeed, the purists manifested amazingly little interest in specific issues. In our interviews at the convention, we simply could not get them to talk about anything concrete, unless references to welfare-statism and too-much-government are considered specific replies. The purists did express strong belief in the importance of being interested in issues, but this is not equivalent to being interested in specific issues.

All this makes one wonder whether the Goldwater phenomenon did not represent a retreat from politics through politics. Purists are interested in being interested in politics. They care about people caring about politics. They are far more concerned about the need for substantial differences between the parties than they are about the differences themselves. If only one has principles and stands up for them, their position seems to suggest, the messy world of politics—compromise, bargaining, exceptions, modifications, inconsistencies—will disappear. Political style thus becomes a substitute for politics itself.

Campaign Style

The campaign speeches of Barry Goldwater are a testimonial to the extraordinary importance he assigned to political style. It would be difficult to find another candidate so insistent that people not vote for him if they did not share his views. Rarely has so much attention been given to stylistic reasons for supporting a candidate. This approach is epitomized in a Goldwater speech delivered to a rally at Madison Square Garden and its overwhelming stylistic emphasis is noteworthy.

Goldwater began by saying that although he knew what statements would get him the most votes he was not going to make them.

I can't help wondering sometimes, if you've asked yourselves why my campaign is what it is.

I wonder, my fellow Americans, if you think I don't know what views would be most popular. Do you think I don't know what labor wants to hear, what management . . . what housewives and diplomats and white-collar workers want to hear? Do you honestly think, after all these years in politics, that I don't know the easy ways to get votes? The promises to make? The subjects to talk about—and the ones to avoid? Well, I do!   .

He then proceeded to tell his audience why he did not "take the easy way."

First of all, if I just went around telling people what they want to hear, I'd sound like Lyndon Baines Johnson. And I still think the American people are entitled to a choice.

But more important, if I had to cater to every special interest in the country to get elected, I wouldn't want the job.

Like his followers, Goldwater was a political purist who objected to telling people what they wanted to hear, catering to "special interests," or being like the other party in order to gain popularity.

As a political purist, Goldwater was careful about the kind of people who should and should not support him. The Nazi and Fascist types, the

Communists and left-wing radicals, were clearly beyond the pale. But Goldwater included "The lazy, dole-happy people who want to feed on the fruits of somebody else's labor" and people who believed in promises and those "who are willing to believe that Communism can be 'accommodated.' " Most revealing, for our purposes, was his characterization of the people he believed would vote for him.

People who take the trouble to reread, thoughtfully, the Declaration of Independence and the Constitution of the United States will vote for me. . . .

People who have learned to be suspicious of never-ending promises of "something for nothing"—they will vote for me.

People who have the courage and the intelligence to listen to the truth, and think about it. People whose votes can't be bought. They'll vote for me.

People who are sick to death of politicians coming out in favor of happiness and declaring war on misery. People who are fed up with so-called leaders of government promising to legislate worry out of existence. People who will listen for a little while to such transparent, vote-grabbing demagoguery and say —"Baloney." They'll vote for me.

But most of all, it will be the people who know that something must be done.[3]

The types of people who Goldwater thought would vote for him were stylists. They were not merely people who agreed with Goldwater on specific issues. Rather, they were people who harked back to basic principles, such as may be found in the nation's venerable documents, people who were suspicious of promises, who had courage, who were "sick to death of politicians," and who knew that something must be done.

Campaign Strategies

Fought between a political purist and a traditional politician, the 1964 election campaign was most peculiar by recent American standards. The parties appeared to slant their appeals somewhat differently from past emphases. The Democrats appealed much more to upper-income groups and the Republicans to lower-income groups than was usually the case. Despite (or perhaps because of) the larger differences in positions on issues, questions of personality and morality—was Goldwater irresponsible or Johnson a crook?—seemed to dominate the campaign. For the first time in many years, the Republicans made more appeals based on party identification than did the Democrats. And the candidate who put so much weight on consistency appeared to his opponents at least to be a most inconsistent man. Beginning with a brief discussion of the usual pattern of campaign strategies, we shall use our analysis of the Goldwater style and the specific context of the time in an effort to provide a coherent explanation of these apparent anomalies.

Holding the allegiance of approximately three out of every five voters, the Democratic party can expect to win any election which is determined on the basis of party preference. As a result, Democratic candidates typically stress their party identification, while Republican candidates play it down. In 1964, however, the fact that Senator Goldwater was so far to the right of most Republican voters gave President Johnson the opportunity to detach a significant portion of that party's traditional supporters. In search of this Republican vote, Johnson eschewed the usual partisan appeals. Instead, he went out of his way to praise the good old Republican party of yesteryear and to ask the electorate to reject the unnamed extremists who had temporarily taken control of it. While maintaining his party's historic position on welfare issues, Johnson carefully toned down his comments so as not to give moderate Republicans an excuse for voting against him. If he could not positively attract Republicans, he would do nothing to repel them. So the President adopted the stance of national unity, calling insistently on Americans to get together against certain demagogues and hotheads who might get the United States into a nuclear war or foment racial strife.

So far as domestic welfare policies were concerned, there was overwhelming evidence that the vast majority of voters were far closer to the liberal Democrats than they were to the most conservative Republicans. Hence Democratic candidates traditionally hit hard on "bread and butter" issues, while Republicans were caught in a dilemma: they could not please their conservative party activists and the voters at the same time. Since there are many more voters than activists, Republican candidates have normally chosen to go along with most welfare policies, claiming that they could carry out these measures better and cheaper. But Goldwater's conservatism and his unwillingness to change course to get votes made it difficult for him to make any appeal on welfare matters. As a result, Lyndon Johnson was placed in the unique position of being able to make gains on two issues—prosperity and poverty—even while playing down an aggressive pro-welfare stand in order not to alienate Republicans. And Goldwater spent a good deal of time plaintively arguing that he would not really take social security checks from the pockets of workers when they were not looking.

In the realm of foreign policy, the Democrats were subject to attack as "the party of war" because they happened to be in power during the three major wars of this century. Given Goldwater's proclivity for an adventurous foreign policy, however, a product in part of the style of "stand up and be counted," he could hardly expect to gain votes by appearing to advocate extension of military conflict in South Vietnam, Berlin, Cuba, and other places. After all, Eisenhower made political capital out of promising "to bring the boys back from Korea," not by promising to send more of them over there. Again, Goldwater was placed on the defensive. He had the extraordinary task of assuring voters that he would not launch a nuclear war immediately upon assuming office.

If voting behavior theory was correct, as the election returns would suggest, Goldwater could not pick up votes on either foreign policy or on the broad spectrum of domestic welfare policy. At the same time, he could not count on full support from normal Republican identifiers and thus had to make repeated calls for party unity. What kind of appeal, then, could he make and to whom?

The answer appeared to be that he could appeal to ordinarily Democratic working class as well as lower-middle-class voters on the racial issue. Hence the many references to safety in the streets and the scarcely veiled suggestions that women would know what he was talking about. Yet this approach also created problems for Goldwater. As a self-professed constitutional conservative, he could hardly call for a federal police force or for most forms of national action except, perhaps, for the appointment of tougher judges. His running mate, William Miller, could suggest that the jobs of workers would be taken by hordes of immigrants who would be let in by new immigration procedures proposed by the Johnson Administration. The trouble was that many of the workers who might have been influenced by this type of appeal came from ethnic groups sensitive to selective limitation of immigration.

A surface reading of the election returns suggests that outside the South the so-called "white backlash" could not have been very large. The workers whose "authoritarian tendencies" presumably left them responsive to a racial appeal, were among the most fervent supporters of the Democratic party. Racial feelings would have had to be highly salient and intense for them to vote against their traditional party and the social welfare legislation which is so important to them. If a group had felt its jobs threatened, or if it was desperately trying to ward off Negro encroachment on its residential areas, it might be sufficiently moved to change the direction of its vote. But there simply were not enough people in this kind of a position. Apparently, more Republicans were frightened by Goldwater than whites were frightened by Negroes.

On the basis of this analysis, derived from standard voting behavior theory, it was possible to predict long before the election that Goldwater would suffer a drastic defeat. Nor is there any reason to believe that the outcome will be different in 1968 or 1972 so long as the overwhelming purist component of the Goldwater conservatives prevents them from making more successful appeals to the voters. Indeed, immediately after the election Goldwater proposed that the parties be organized into pure conservative and liberal denominations. There cannot be much hope for the future when the first reaction of a leader who has suffered overwhelming defeat is to give away to the opposition a substantial percentage of his party's support—the Republican moderates and liberals.

Campaign Morality

The focus of the campaign upon problems of personal competence was directly connected with the existence of profound differences on public policy. No doubt it was naive to believe that the candidates could differ more and more over issues while saying better and better things about each other. Once Goldwater had moved rather far away from positions traditionally taken by Republican Presidential candidates, Johnson seized the opportunity to gain Republican votes by denouncing Goldwater as an extremist. The charge of extremism was built into a situation in which any party moved far from where it had been, especially if it also moved far from the voters. It would be easy to say that Goldwater responded to being called an extremist by raising the morality issue or that, lacking appeal on other issues, he used the Bobby Baker episode to undermine Johnson's claim to being defender of the traditional political faith. There may be some truth in this. But I believe that we have more significant answers at our disposal if we turn again to Goldwater and his followers as political purists.

If politics should be concerned with the private conscience of the political leader and his stock of basic principles, as many Goldwater supporters believe, then the morality of the candidates necessarily assumes prime importance. The politician is immediately condemned as immoral by virtue of his usual practices. He is immoral because he alters his role orientations to suit different constituencies. He is immoral because, at times, he alters his position to gain votes. Even when the politician hangs on to his fundamental position but gives a little to assure a wider consensus he is immoral because of his inconsistency and vacillation. Because Lyndon Johnson epitomizes the practicing politician, famed for his love of votes, compromise, bargaining, maneuver, and conciliation, his immorality was beyond all dispute for the political purists.

There is still another way in which concentration on political style made morality a central focus of election campaigns. The Goldwater purists were patently unwilling to believe that difficulties facing America, particularly in foreign affairs, might have been due to forces beyond the control of any leader. On the contrary, they thought that if the United States just had the right approach, if it stood up for what it believed and enunciated its principles with sufficient force, its problems would be solved. This was presumably what Goldwater meant when he said that he had a "rational solution" to the cold war, without specifying what it was, or when he insisted that our foreign policy difficulties were not complex but simple. If the world situation was not exactly rosy, therefore, the blame lay with immoral leaders who behaved as politicians instead of as purists. They sold out their country because they either did not have the right American principles or did not stand up for them or both. From the Goldwater point of view, it was necessary only to look at the state of the world to see that American political leaders were immoral. Reasoning from effect to cause, the purists would be bound to place the simple moral test—does the candidate have the right political style?—at the heart of a campaign taking place when decay had set in from the remotest Asian principality to the nearest city street.

Campaign Issues

Although the candidates in 1964 were not subject to the kind of abuse characteristic of the early days of the American republic, there apparently was more personal vilification than in the past decade or two. Of greater importance for our purposes, however, is the undoubted fact that in a campaign in which the parties were further apart on issues than they have been in our time, at least since 1936 and possibly in this century, there was relatively little discussion of issues. Certainly, the existence of wide and deep policy differences did not, as has sometimes been thought, lead directly to a campaign focusing on specific issues. Why not?

It might be the case that when candidates are virtually identical in their views, there is little else for them to talk about except their respective personalities. When they are moderately far apart, separated by marginal but real differences, however, the possibility for fruitful debate may be at its highest point. For the parties are then far enough apart to make debates meaningful and yet close enough together so that a real dialogue is possible. Both the candidates and attentive publics can understand what a marginal change from one proposal to another might mean. Yet when the parties and candidates are separated by a huge gulf there may literally be nothing to talk about. The differences may be so severe as to appear to be beyond discussion.

The experience of the 1964 Presidential campaign suggests that the old proposition, the greater the differences on issues, the greater the discussion of specific issues, might be replaced with a new hypothesis, discussion of issues varies directly with moderate, marginal disagreements on issues and inversely with the extremes of total agreement or total disagreement. Such has been the situation in France where election campaigns typically involved disagreements among the parties closest to each other and little or no direct confrontation among the parties which were furthest apart in ideology.

Campaign Consistency

In the light of Goldwater's professed devotion to consistency a major paradox of the campaign was his apparent inconsistency. The syndrome characteristically began with a Goldwater statement about atomic defoliation in South Vietnam, or giving military commanders control of "conventional" nuclear weapons, or about extremism not being a vice if it is in defense of liberty. In the ensuing furor, Goldwater complained that he had been misquoted or misconstrued; he issued clarifications which puzzled newsmen, and the cycle began again. In other instances, Goldwater maintained consistency; comments that the Tennessee Valley Authority ought to be sold to private interests are not usually made in the heart of the Tennessee Valley. How can we account for this ambivalence?

Goldwater's campaign managers did their best to keep him away from the press; not a single news conference was held during the campaign. One clue may be found in the disparity between the Goldwater supporters and the vast majority of voters. They simply could not believe they were so different from the vast majority of people. Statements unquestioningly accepted by the Senator's most enthusiastic supporters, therefore, occasioned an uproar in the world outside—to the Senator's genuine surprise.

In the final analysis, however, Goldwater's inconsistency may have arisen directly out of his political style. He and his supporters were impatient with the practical substance of policy decisions. They believed that if the government only approached politics in the right way then everything would be all right. They could hardly be bothered about verbal niceties when they knew in their hearts that their style was fundamentally correct. Traditional politicians may say inconsistent things to gather votes from an electorate which holds inconsistent policy preferences. Goldwater may take inconsistent positions because he is not seriously interested in specific policies.

What, then, have been the major consequences of having a purist candidate on the ballot? Compared to other recent campaigns, 1964 was (1) more bitter; (2) less moral; (3) more concerned with personalities; (4) less concerned with issues; (5) more involved with consistency; (6) less consistent, and (7) for the first time since the Civil War era introduced the explosive question of race relations as a major issue dividing the parties. But these distinctive accomplishments were at least confined to 1964. What will be the future of the party system if purists continue to represent one of the major parties?

The Future

It has often been said that parties in democratic countries like Great Britain are much more ideological, more strongly divided by serious cleavages over issues, than is the case in the United States. The evidence suggests that this view must be seriously modified. In Great Britain, for example, the political elites of the Labour, Conservative, and Liberal parties are extraordinarily united on domestic policy. They are almost all Keynesians in their economics, pragmatists in their policies on state intervention in the economy, supporters of the welfare state, and fundamentally at peace with the general development of governmental policy in the postwar world. The United States offers a striking contrast: a conservative political elite, disproportionately located in the Republican party, regards Keynesian economics as a dirty word, views governmental activity in the economy with ideological hostility, and is reconciled neither to the future growth of the welfare state nor to its steady development over the past 30 years. While not all political leaders in Great Britain are satisfied with its foreign policy, the impression is that most are agreed on essentials. There is no equivalent of the increasing frustration the Republican conservatives feel because the superior resources of the United States do not confer an automatic ability to control events beyond its borders. Of course, some Democrats share these feelings, but they cannot prevail within their national party.

This is not the place to argue about which views are correct or more nearly in tune with the realities of our time. But it is the place to say that the existence of a political elite, in a position to control a major national party, which holds views widely at variance both with the general voting population and its own followers, presents a major political problem in the United States. Goldwater's nomination and defeat are merely a sign of an old problem, but one hidden by the normal operation of the party system. What are some of the consequences for American political parties?

One possibility is that the Republican party will return to its previous course and seek out popular candidates whose moderate views will give it a chance to win Presidential elections. Once it is understood, however, that the Goldwater movement is not a temporary aberration, but represents a profound current within the Republican party, it becomes impossible for me to join the wishful thinkers who believe that the moderates and liberals in the party will automatically gain control after Goldwater's severe defeat in the election. A majority of party activists now support the political tendency Goldwater represented. (It might be well to recall that an Associated Press poll of Republican county chairmen, taken in April, 1964, showed that 722 chose Goldwater as their personal preference compared to 301 for Nixon.) If these conservatives are to be defeated they will have to be challenged by a rival, moderate elite, willing to engage in the daily tasks of political organization over the next four years. No one has been able to tell where these people will come from, especially after the Republican party has been swept out of office at all levels in a Johnson landslide.

The possibility cannot be ruled out that the Republican party will continue to nominate conservatives like Goldwater and will continue to lose badly. I believe that those who see in this development the likelihood of a realignment of the major parties along conservative and liberal lines will be grievously disappointed. What incentive would there be for conservative Democrats from the South to join a lost cause? On the contrary, they would more than ever be impelled to cling to the Democratic affiliation which at least promises them continued influence in Congress and some chance to modify the policies of Democratic Presidents. Republican moderates and liberals, however, might find association with the prevailing centers of power in the Democratic party more and more attractive.

In a study of state party systems, the late V. O. Key, Jr., has shown that as one party dominates the political scene by gaining continual electoral victories, nomination becomes tantamount to election; and there is a strong tendency for voters to move into the primaries of this party in order to gain some influence over its decisions. The minority party loses its moderates and becomes the preserve of the "diehards." Hence it becomes increasingly difficult for a candidate who might appeal to the electorate to win nomination in the minority party. Nor are the consequences for the majority party necessarily good. As it grows in relative size and importance it becomes more heterogeneous. At the same time the weakness of the opposition removes a powerful incentive to party cohesion.

Should this vision of the future materialize, we can expect an end to a competitive, two-party system. In its place we will have a modified one-party system with a dominant Democratic party. As its leaders find that their potential for controlling policy decisions has enormously increased they will also discover that greatly intensified factionalism within the party has strikingly diminished their capacity for united action. The immediate policy goals of an accelerated welfare state—medical care for the aged, aid to education, antipoverty programs—may be achieved ahead of schedule as a result of extraordinary Democratic party majorities in Congress. But these victories for liberal Democrats may be achieved at the price of inability to meet new problems. For the more overwhelming the dominance of their party, the less may be their importance within it. The success of liberal ideas will have been sacrificed to the triumph of their party. The Republican party, much diminished in size, will find that its greater potential for unity is accompanied by a drastically reduced capacity to get its preferences translated into government policy. It will have gained cohesion in exchange for impotence. The 1964 election may turn out to be a disaster for conservative Republicans and a Pyrrhic victory for liberal Democrats.

There has been a great deal of loose talk in the past about the desirability of having an avowed conservative run for the Presidency on the grounds that a severe defeat would put his backers "in their place" and demonstrate once and for all that they lack support in the country. The Goldwater candidacy, however, visibly increased the cost of losing the election to those who disagreed profoundly with him. As a result, there was a much more bitter campaign fraught with much greater anxiety than in the past. Will the comforts of a political system which is ordinarily kind to losers (because campaigns are fought between parties and candidates which differ somewhat but are not separated by too large a gulf) be more highly valued in the future? That depends on whether the rest of us learn the lessons which the Goldwater phenomenon has to teach us.

It is possible that the Goldwater phenomenon represents the beginnings of ideology in the United States. Although markedly different in their policy preferences, there are segments of the left as well as the right who are repelled by the usual patterns of democratic politics. There appears to be little difference in style between the Goldwater purists and the leftists who constantly complain about hypocrisy in public life and how the politicians sell out the people. Could it be that the United States is producing large numbers of half-educated people with college degrees who have learned that participation (passion and commitment) is good but who do not understand (or cannot stand) the normal practices of democratic politics? If this is true, we shall be hearing a great deal more from those who identify compromise with moral degeneracy. Political scientists might then wish to present their knowledge about the consequences of political purism. They might also wish to impart some wisdom on the relative desirability of flexible and inflexible political styles under varying conditions. For the Goldwater phenomenon, which once seemed so strange, may become a persistent feature of the American political scene, nonetheless disturbing because it reappears under different ideological guises.

NOTES

1. Since my conclusions may appear controversial, I shall indicate the major sources of the statements used here. Those concerning the normal operations of the party system are adapted from such standard works as Pendelton Herring, *The Politics of Democracy* (New York: Norton, 1966); Austin Ranney and Wilmoore Kendall, *Democracy and the American Party System;* V. O. Key, *Politics, Parties and Pressure Groups* (New York: Crowell, 1964); and Robert Dahl, *Preface to Democratic Theory* (Chicago: University of Chicago Press, 1963). The material on the goals of convention delegates comes from Nelson Polsby and Aaron Wildavsky, *Presidential Elections* (New York: Scribner's, 1964). Generalizations on voting behavior are drawn primarily from Campbell, Converse, Miller, and Stokes, *The American Voter* (New York: John Wiley, 1964). I have also relied heavily on the only systematic work comparing convention delegates and ordinary voters—Herbert McClosky et al., "Issue Conflict and Consensus Among Party Leaders and Followers," *American Po-*

litical Science Review 54 (June 1960): 406–427. (See also McClosky's "Consensus and Ideology in American Politics," *American Political Science Review* 53 (June 1964): 361–382).

After the 1956 conventions, McClosky distributed, and then analyzed, lengthy questionnaires filled out by large numbers of Republican and Democratic delegates and by samples of voters who identified with these parties. Using McClosky's work, one can make reliable statements about the characteristics and issue preferences of party leaders (represented at the conventions) and party followers (as they are found throughout the nation). Finally, I have made substantial use of some 150 interviews with Goldwater delegates held at the Hotel Fairmont in San Francisco, where the California, Illinois, and New Jersey delegates were housed. The interviews were conducted in the hotel lobby by myself, my sister, Judy Gordon, a friend, Maralyn Millman, and two graduate students—James Payne and Joseph Paff. Gerry Bass helped by monitoring the press for us. While these unstructured, probing interviews in no way represent a systematic sample of the delegates, they were undertaken because they have one great advantage over the usual mail questionnaire: the interviewer can try to insist on answers and pound away until some kind of response is forthcoming.

2. McClosky et al., "Issue Conflict and Consensus," p. 423.
3. *New York Times*, October 27, 1964.

14

THE MEANING OF "YOUTH" IN
THE STRUGGLE FOR CONTROL OF
THE DEMOCRATIC PARTY

The United States is witnessing a transformation of political styles. Traditional party politicians are being challenged not only on the substance of public policy but on their conduct of political activity. It is their behavior as political men as well as their position on issues that is under attack. Whatever their disagreements on specific policies, left and right-wing activists compete in excoriating the immorality of men in office. Everyone else has sold out, they say, and only we remain pure. These political purists consider the stock in trade of the politician—compromise and bargaining, conciliating the opposition, bending a little to capture public support —the epitome of hypocrisy. Their new style trades on declamation of principles and moral crusades. Since it is difficult to make public policy without compromising one's self in some way, there is an understandable tendency for these public men to stand outside of the main action and criticize.

The best place to seek changes in orientation toward politics was at the 1968 Democratic National Convention where delegates from hostile party factions could be observed and questioned under the heat of battle. My associates and I found the expected struggle for control of the party between the older elements and the newer McCarthy forces. Out of this conflict we discovered that a purist style evidencing distrust of politics was beginning to emerge on the left as it previously had with the Goldwaterites on the right. The symbol of the new style was "youth." New political styles might be expected to arise out of the moral fervor and demand for immediate satisfaction that characterize young people. What was unexpected, however, was the degree to which "youth" was imbedded in the central concerns of people over 30.

In hundreds of interviews my associates and I conducted at the 1968 Convention,[1] the idea of youth kept appearing in discussions of who would and should control the Democratic party. Important political conflicts have evidently been translated into the dominant symbol of the decade. If youth culture has not become a cult, as some claim, then it certainly has taken on a quasireligious quality that embodies a struggle between virtue and corruption. Insofar as the future belongs to youth, as the cliche has it, those who think they have a future want to be considered young. If youth means change in party controls, the defenders of the status quo and the purveyors of new creeds will put different values on age. The party regulars clearly saw their customary practices threatened by "youth" of all ages.

The Possessors: The Party of Adults

The theme of the party faithful at the Democratic National Convention was that the party was the domain of adults. To these regular Democratic party delegates with long years of service the McCarthy supporters were spoiled children. They were immature, unstable, and ungrateful. Like babies, the McCarthy delegates demanded immediate gratification. When their demands were rejected, they threw tantrums. It was up to the adults in the party, therefore, to play the parental role by showing the children proper limits and by socializing them into the grown-up world. Several times party regulars used the same analogy: "The McWhinnies [McCarthy supporters] are like little boys with marbles: you don't play by their rules —they want to break up the game."

In the adult world, party regulars insist, norms of apprenticeship are observed. One must work in the party for years before expecting to be in control. The regulars appear hurt and bewildered when faced with demands for immediate access to positions of party power. "The party structure is always open to people who are interested in working," said one party loyalist. "It's just that we have a sort of seniority system like Congress; those who make the most contribution get the largest say in what we do. That's only fair." Those who do most for the party are those who worked their way up from the bottom. "The problem," as one Humphrey delegate viewed it, "is that while the McCarthy kids want into the party they want in at the top. They aren't interested in the status which the beginner usually gets licking envelopes and things like that, which we did, all of us, when we were coming up." For "McCarthy kids" read "new pretenders to power," and the full import of the statement is clear. McCarthy supporters ought to accept a subordinate position until they prove themselves.

The norm of apprenticeship means more than just telling newcomers they have to wait their turn; it is based on a life of struggle and sacrifice for the party. "I worked for the coal company for 18 years," said a man who served his party for five decades. "But when I put my hat in the ring for Democratic councilman, I was thrown out of my job by the coal company who controlled everything in town." Another old timer recalls that it cost him a "fortune to fight the vested interests . . . to build a Democratic party. . . . I was running a trucking company, and they attacked me by revoking the license. They spread rumors against me. There were protests even within my family. You should tell the young people who are demonstrating that they are not the first people to try to change things." The feeling that youth gives no credit for their personal hardships rankles these party regulars. "My son, who is 17, takes all the advantages of the affluent society for granted. He does not realize what we went through to get them for him." The world has gone topsy-turvy in a lifetime. "In my day," an old timer said, "your father told you what to vote. Nowadays it's your son who tells you how to vote." The McCarthy forces, these men were saying, should act like the respectful sons of old.

Those new to party ways would be more respectful, the regulars believed, if they cast aside immediate gratification and adopted a longer time perspective. "You can't take over a political organization overnight or in one convention," a county chairman observed to an impatient youngster. "The time will come when you control the organization if you work hard."

Youth is, therefore, not only a matter of chronological age; delegates see it also as a question of whether one takes a short or a long-run perspective on party affairs. Consider the views of a 27-year-old committeeman. His understanding of party politics is that "this is just one inning of a long game. One goes into politics to increase one's influence over decisions, but that takes time. If one doesn't win one year, [he] can try again the next year. People that jump in and out don't understand this basic fact of political involvement." He was saying that McCarthy supporters should wait their turn and that he did not expect them to stay in politics. "They just came out of the woodwork this year," he observed, "and now they'll go back."

Because they were never really in the party, never served their apprenticeship, the McCarthy people were judged not important to it. The easiest way of disparaging them was just to say they were too young to participate. "Many of them are under 21 and can't vote anyway. A lot of whooping and hollering doesn't matter much."

The party regulars who supported Hubert Humphrey had, by contrast, a self-image as mature, experienced, and stable men. They identified with the Democratic party and had no difficulty in merging the party interest with their own. Whatever happened, they would be around to pick up the pieces. They would not desert the party in a fit of pique. They would take what they could get, even if it was not all they wanted, because they saw movement toward distant goals. They would not mistake the bawling of impatient juveniles for Joshua's trumpet of impending disaster.

Over and over again party regulars contended that McCarthy supporters would not retain their party strength because they were one-issue types. If the Vietnam war were over they would leave because they got what they wanted and if the war continued they would desert the party because their policy had been defeated.

The "one-issue" charge had broad ramifications. It was tied in with the belief that successful party activity required the adult ability to live with disappointment. "In politics you win and lose," a party regular commented, "sometimes mostly lose. But you can't give up, you must keep at it." The McCarthy "kids" did not have what it takes, the regular asserted, because they played the political game like little children who quit the "football team after losing one game."

The focus of the McCarthy forces on one issue was widely seen as preventing the normal give-and-take through which internal party differences should be resolved. When many issues are at stake, support for one can be traded for help on another. When issues are strung out over a period of time, early losses may be accepted as the price for later gains. According to exponents of party unity, McCarthy's men "pursue the single issue so hard that they become intolerant." A single issue of overriding importance at a moment in time breaks party solidarity.

It would be difficult to overemphasize the importance of loyalty to the party faithful. This is not, as their detractors would have it, a mere question of unthinking obedience. Nor is it, as the more sophisticated regulars would say, a matter of the requirements of effective party organization. The party loyalists identify themselves with the party and the party with the nation. "The Democratic party is the people," they say. "The Democratic party is the real majority party." How can the McCarthy people talk about fighting the "Establishment" when the Democratic party is the vehicle through which the people of the United States fight against the Establishment (or, as it used to be called, the "vested interests")?

Insofar as "youth" meant supporting "the people" against the privileged few, the Democratic party regulars believed themselves to be perpetually young. The traditional party system was dear to the hearts of the faithful because it pitted the good guys against the bad ones. It made them appear innovative and liberal (that is, young in their own eyes) by contrast. There are no heroes without villains. The Democrats need a Republican foil. So their loyalty extends to the two-party system itself. Insofar as McCarthyites talked about the two-party system at all, they saw it as excluding good men like themselves. But the Humphrey supporters, party regulars to a man, loved the system that had made a place for them. They were students in a great school of party life, and they did not want to change the curriculum.

The McCarthyite challenge, it must be understood, was quite different than the assault of the Kennedy forces on the bastions of party power. The Kennedy people (those who would have supported Robert Kennedy had he lived) were young in years but not in adherence to party norms. They impugned neither the party nor its activists. When the Kennedys challenged the party regulars in 1960, they told the party men to deal with them or be run over. However distasteful the prospect, the party loyalists understood the danger and could accommodate themselves to it. They made adjustments, and the party continued along familiar lines. The McCarthy forces, however, said that the party was no good and its regulars were even worse. Because the McCarthy supporters threatened to throw them out and reconstitute the party, the regulars felt they had to fight. When McCarthy delegates wondered why politicians who shared their views on Vietnam would not support their candidate, the explanation was all too simple: the party loyalists refused to commit political suicide.

When a person believes that the Democratic party is the best thing that ever happened to this country, that "without the Democratic party you would never get any good policies," it is difficult for him to understand how people who profess to belong to the party could hurt its electoral chances. If you came of age in the depression years of the 1930s when the Democratic party meant hope and progress and even life, the idea of abandoning its candidates is virtually incomprehensible. This wounded air of outrage is expressed by a Humphrey delegate from New York who asserts his unswerving loyalty: "I would never support a fourth party. I will work energetically for the ticket whatever it is. McCarthy people won't tell you that. [They] will only elect Republicans. Is that what they want? I just don't know about them; they say they are liberals, but they hurt the party. It just doesn't make any sense." Another delegate—"you can classify me as an old-line, hard-core party man"—said that "I could talk for two hours as to why I prefer Humphrey, but I'll tell you something that is a deciding factor: McCarthy's disloyal because he won't support the ticket."

The new pretenders to power were a mystery to the regulars because they would not abide by the rules of what the regulars regarded as proper party conduct. They would not serve an apprenticeship or wait for their chance to take over. Worst of all, they would not support the party's nominee for President. The underlying feeling among Humphrey delegates was that the McCarthy supporters were "politically immature," for if they had been older and been active in politics longer, they would have been aware of Humphrey's long-term accomplishments. The McCarthy people responded by saying Humphrey's men were living in the past. It would be more accurate to say that for these party regulars the future was an extension of the past. The future looks different to men for whom the past is a living memory rather than a dead weight whose load is to be lifted as soon as possible.

Men and women who have spent many years in the party are likely to interpret new events in the light of their past experience. They will try to assimilate current happenings into the understandable patterns of the past. Factional splits punctuated by loud withdrawals from the convention have occurred in the Democratic party. Yet the party goes on and most of its errant sons return to the fold. "I've seen many walkouts but they always come back." The McCarthy movement, therefore, was not seen as anything new by regular Democrats. Rather, they viewed it as a healthy phenomenon that gave everyone a chance to vent his feelings. "The rumors about a party split are old hat. It was said in '60 and in '48, when the Dixiecrats supported Dewey. In reality, every time we have a fight, it strengthens the party." The theory of perpetual renewal through open conflict was widespread among the delegates.

The evident fact of internal conflict may be turned around to refute charges that the party was controlled by an oligarchy. "If you have a truly representative party that isn't controlled by people at the top or by men with money, then you are sure to have fights between the different groups and factions . . ." A similar view conceives of internal party conflict as training for the coming election. "A boxer can't win the championship unless he's had practice trading blows in the ring." Intraparty conflict emerges again as a source of strength.

What looks to the young like a movement to change power relationships appears to the experienced party observer as part of the normal turn of party affairs. Challenges to party leadership appear to them to follow a cyclical pattern. "McCarthy kids are in revolt against the Establishment. I was like that in the 30's. Now I'm seen as part of the Establishment. Twenty years from now they'll be the Establishment, turn conservative and be rebelled against." There is glee in the thought of what the turn of events will do to the self-satisfied moralists of the moment. "Just as we came to terms with the Establishment of our day," a veteran party worker said, "so will the McCarthyites come to terms with us, but we'll have the last laugh because the kids of the future will want to throw them out."

The perception of whether important changes are taking place is influenced by the delegate's experience in his state party. Delegates from states in which there has been strong intraparty rivalry (between McCarthy neophytes and party regulars) are more willing to entertain the possibility of a nationwide defection of McCarthy supporters from the national candidate and from local and state candidates who support Humphrey. Delegates from such states appear more sensitive to changes in national political life over the last several years, and refer specifically to the increase in youth dissatisfaction and activism. Delegates from states in which there has been intense social conflict (racial disturbances, class conflict, etc.) appear more inclined to see the possibility of national political realignments, or the possibility of fourth-party formation.

Having seen it all, the party regulars waited for the tide of affairs to turn. They had the certainty of the possessors. The party was theirs by right. The idea that youth will prevail was replaced by the feeling that age will do its inevitable work. "McCarthy people are idealists; they will mellow as they get older." The McCarthy people were believed to be divided between the young, who might go for a fourth party "because they don't understand compromise," and the older McCarthy types, who "will realize they have had the effect they wanted and come back into the party." It takes a feeling that the universe is yours to believe that "as in the past, McCarthy supporters will support the party candidate and things will go on much as they have for the last 30 years."

A substantial minority of the party loyalists did sense that the nation was in strife and that change was inevitable. They felt that tokenism—letting 18-year-olds vote—would not do. But they were ambivalent about letting new people share power with them. The recognition of need combined with hesitation to follow through appears in statements like "The party has to make changes. Minority groups should get representation. But you can't get it all at once." It is not the inconsistency but the underlying feeling that makes the next comment so revealing: "The most crucial change [the Democratic party has to make] is to get in the young people. The young have to be in. Maybe youth caucuses or something. . . . We have to eliminate the back-room politicians, though they have to be in control, of course."

While the party faithful were reluctant to believe that their day had ended, those who supported Senator Robert Kennedy saw plenty of reason for change in political life: "The war, the cities, riots by our young people, dissatisfaction everywhere." But how and to what degree the Democratic party should respond to these changes was not as self-evident to them as to the McCarthy men. "You see the dissatisfaction reflected clearly enough, but I don't think you see it represented fairly. But I don't know; the whole thing confuses me a great deal. I just don't know what should be done. I had faith in Kennedy." It would be fair to say that the person of Robert Kennedy had helped resolve the doubts of his supporters by placing the nation's troubles in trustworthy hands. When Kennedy was assassinated, his supporters were faced with the necessity of analyzing the situation apart from their leader, and they could not quite make it. They lacked the essential complacency of the party regulars and the sense of being the elect that gave McCarthy people their air of confidence and optimism.

The Inheritors: The Party of Youth

McCarthy people see themselves as the wave of the future. They not only reflect the changes that are coming, they *are* these changes. History is on their side and it is only a matter of time before they sweep away the old party elements.

The McCarthyites claim they understand the changes that are taking place in America and their opponents do not. "We are in touch and they are out of it." "We know what's on the news programs. The Humphrey people don't." Their knowledge of emergent conditions provides McCarthy's supporters with an important link to youth. "The kids are part of what's happening. Like us, they see the changes that have to be made." Hence the claim that "the McCarthy worker is a new kind of worker." Like youth, his province is the future.

The supporters of Senator McCarthy accept with considerable pride the charge that they are new to the party. Youth and newness are, to them, indications that they will inherit control of the Democratic party. "To the extent that the party draws on youth," a delegate said, "it ensures its position as the party of the future."

The confidence of McCarthy forces in eventually gaining control of the Democratic party rested squarely on the idea of youth. They were the new men to whom the party would belong. They would make use of the energies of youth—new ideas and young bodies—to revitalize the party and bring it to victory. Whenever supporters of Senator McCarthy talked about giving youth its rightful voice or the danger of youth leaving the party, they meant that *they* must be given dominant voice and *they* must not be compelled to leave the party. "The big change in the country," McCarthy delegates insisted, "is the rising youth interest in government and their own destiny. The Democratic party better wake up to this or it will be in real trouble."

One of the most revealing outcomes of our interviews was the insight it gave into the extraordinarily high sense of political efficacy manifested by the McCarthy forces. Their work at the local level convinced them that the regular party was terribly weak and they were amazingly strong. They were young and energetic and the party regulars were old and tired. Probing the personal experience of McCarthy delegates generated many stories like this one: "Humphrey's organization is an empty shell. I found that out when I ran against these people for committeeman for my township. I won two-to-one with the help of the kids. I wish I were your age. What a political future there is for young people."

Secure in their vision of future triumph, the McCarthy delegates knew what would happen after Hubert Humphrey was nominated. "First off," a typical McCarthy delegate predicts, "a crashing and complete defeat this fall. And I'm glad of that. Get rid of a lot of deadwood. Then we can really take over."

The predicted temporary collapse of the Democratic party was viewed not only as inevitable but desirable. "The success of the Democratic candidate," a McCarthy delegate told us, "will just entrench the Democratic machines more firmly and will give impetus to shutting the average citizen out of participation in the political process." There are times, he believed, when you just have to "smash everything to bits" and start again. While it would be difficult to get control of a party whose leader occupied the presidency, it would be a great deal easier for McCarthy's supporters to pick up the pieces if Hubert Humphrey lost the election.

For the McCarthy people, the young are the hope of the future because they represent a counterweight to the elements traditionally strong in the Democratic party. Observe how delegates in California and Ohio make young people the engine for wresting party control.

In the last few years, with the waning of the power of the Young Democrats and the California Democratic Council, and even organized labor, which I think is overestimated, the real power has been the big money men. Savings and Loans, wealthy men, have become very powerful; some are liberal, others are not, but they are all powerful because they have a lot of money. The kids could have offset their influence—and they still can; I hope that Humphrey's nomination won't drive them out.

The party is controlled by people with money and the money-makers that operate through the party. The Republican Party in the late 19th century was too often a business venture for people who wanted to make a buck. The Democratic Party is too much like that right now. For instance, I could name you fifty people in Ohio politics who are there only to help their businesses. So the party is in bad shape this year, because there is a sudden swell of young people coming in who are interested in principles and in issues.

Many delegates spoke interchangeably about the influx of new McCarthy people and of youth into the party as vehicles for change in party control. The great question was whether they should seek to make the Democratic party "young" or try to build a fourth party made up of "youth" like them.

McCarthy's followers were certainly not tempted to remain in the Democratic party by their attraction to the candidacy of Hubert Humphrey. Only about one out of four of those we interviewed would even suggest that he might consider supporting Humphrey in the election. The Vice President's position on the Vietnam war was unacceptable. He reeked of party regularity. As a delegate put it, "I feel like a party hack just saying I might vote for him." These views were reinforced by the scars of internal party conflict that McCarthy delegates had picked up in the preconvention period. "I dislike the regular party types," a McCarthy activist reported. "They are immoral and fought in a petty fashion in Long Island. We had a hard time even getting registration lists."

Despite their evident unwillingness to support the party's nominee for President, however, the McCarthy people had no intention of leaving the Democratic party. Some delegates were tempted to leave but they could not stand the thought of indirectly helping Richard Nixon get elected as President of the United States. "This is a tough one. Yes, I would work for a fourth party. This answer troubles me because it means Nixon would get in. Change that—I'd say no, I wouldn't work for a fourth party." Other McCarthy supporters were kept in the party by their ability to work for a local candidate. Question: Would you support a fourth party? "I doubt it.

I am a Democrat. I will work for [Paul] O'Dwyer [running for the Senate from New York] this year." Senator McCarthy's refusal to endorse a fourth-party movement undoubtedly had great influence with his followers. "Gene says no." By far the most important reason McCarthy people had for rejecting a fourth party, however, was that they expected to take over the party themselves.

A heightened sense of future power explains much of the reluctance of the McCarthy delegates to walk out of a Democratic Convention where they were losing the fight for the nomination. At a caucus of McCarthy delegates a speaker put it this way: "I think we must remember that the vehicle for change in the United States is the Democratic party. We're part of it. If we walk out, we say we're not going to be part of that process at a time we are close to success. . . . The day is near when the party will return to its basic liberalism. [Loud applause]" At another McCarthy caucus a delegate cried, "We've shown our power. We've shown a majority of the country agrees with us. If we walk out, we lose our power." A similar theme was echoed by a delegate speaking at what was billed as a fourth-party convention on the day after Humphrey was nominated. His point was that 19 New Jersey delegates beat the machine in their areas and they did not want to sacrifice their gains by supporting any fourth party. McCarthy supporters were optimistic to the end. "I think we came off pretty well. We have a horrendous ticket, but I think these [McCarthy] guys—Peterson, Hoeh, and so on—are going to take over the party." Paul O'Dwyer put the matter with his customary ebullience: "It's not time for a fourth party. Stay within the Democratic Party because we've really won."

Events at the convention itself worked to reinforce the desire of the McCarthyites to go back into the Democratic party and gain control from the inside. The belief that police brutality was rampant enraged them. Their reaction was typified by one McCarthy delegate who said, "This has been a turning point in my life. I was going to leave politics, go home and play golf, but now I am going to stay in politics. We are going back and throw out the machine." The Hughes commission changes, such as the abolition of the unit rule, provided some hope for the future. Strong showings were made on the Texas and Georgia credentials challenges. The unity within dissident delegations (especially Oregon, Wisconsin, New York, and California) and the fact that those delegations were seated near one another on the convention floor (at the rear of the hall) produced an esprit de corps which helped lessen the feeling of powerlessness which might have been expected. The events which most increased solidarity among the dissidents were those associated with the management of the convention itself, as personified by Richard J. Daley, Mayor, as the signs everywhere advertised him. These events enabled the dissidents to feel that they were the spiritual leaders of the convention, the leaders of the future if not of the present (if only because Daley was so identified with the past). Instinctively they felt they were witnessing the last hurrah.

McCarthyites: The Power Orientation

While a sense of being the elect has been known to galvanize believers into action, predestination is not a substitute for effective political action. Important questions about the McCarthy movement remain to be answered. Will its members be able to accept organizational leadership and discipline? Will they be able to maintain unity? Will they retain their essential character once they have gained control of some segments of the Democratic party?

At first glance it would appear difficult for McCarthy supporters to accept central leadership. Their stress on individual conscience and personal participation might lead them to reject attempts at organization into a solid block. This is certainly the way they describe themselves. "McCarthy people represent a new type of worker and voter. They are different. They desire participation, dislike tight control. Every one must have his say."

Whatever their original predispositions, however, their experience at the convention led some McCarthy delegates to value leadership and solidarity. They learned how difficult it was for the ordinary delegate to exert influence on behalf of his candidate. The conclusion they arrived at was well put by a delegate who said, "Who am I, that I can persuade other delegates to vote with me? I just don't have enough clout. What we ought to do is to use some of our really big names." Participatory democracy was beginning to give way to centralized leadership.

As the convention wore on with its votes on contested delegations and the platform plank, McCarthy delegates began to see the value of central organization. They were dismayed by their inability to communicate with each other and with other delegates. They were delighted with the impact made by the large block of votes that a virtually unanimous California delegation delivered to the cause. Our report of the discussion at a caucus of the McCarthy delegates on the California delegation reveals a drastic change in the value these people put on the leadership provided by Speaker Jess Unruh. The change is the more remarkable because these political men had long been known as his opponents in state politics. As one important McCarthy delegate told his fellows, "We have to have Jess. The floor operation last night was murder. We might have won some votes if we had a decent operation, but we had nothing. You have to have someone with clout; Jess is the only one who could put together the kind of operation we need. Without him, nothing. It would be nice to have a lot of votes for McCarthy, but I think it's even more important to have Jess." These delegates had learned an important truth under fire. They would still prefer their kind of leadership to other people's in the future, but they were not likely to believe they would prevail without any kind of leadership at all.

There was, as the quotation above reveals, a substantial difference between delegates who cared about McCarthy as a person and those who saw him as a vehicle for making changes in the Democratic party. The followers who identified with McCarthy would contemplate no maneuver that would decrease his vote, while the delegates oriented to party affairs were at times willing to sacrifice McCarthy in order to help defeat Humphrey. They wanted power. The potential conflict between the two kinds of McCarthy supporters, temporarily muted by their common antagonism toward Humphrey, will emerge with greater force in the future.

If the power-oriented McCarthyites fail to win control of the Democratic party, their movement may disintegrate; its disappointed adherents might lapse into quiescence or, depending on the state of the nation, rejoin the Democratic party. They might move toward a more radical posture, but a national ticket in 1972 headed by Muskie or McGovern (the most likely nominees) would not give these McCarthyites much reason to desert their party. Nor can they unite in the next four years against a nonexistent Democratic President.

In some ways, however, these McCarthy forces have more to fear from victory than from defeat. They want victory and victory means that they will become the Democratic party in many localities. How will they retain their youth if they grow old in party service? Will not the desire to win office, to maintain unity, to assure internal discipline lead them to behave like the old party regulars they cast out? No doubt the presence of McCarthy people will move the Democratic party somewhat to the left (if that designation has any meaning at a time when liberals are questioning the dominant role of central government that used to be their chief stock in trade). There may be more party meetings concerned with debating issues. But there is no reason to believe that the power-oriented McCarthyites will prove any more successful than the people they displace in enacting and administering public policies. No more than their unhappy predecessors will they be able to achieve perfection—peace and security, equality and achievement, purity and power. Will they not, then, be subject to attack by the other McCarthyites who have found ways to remain active without compromising their morality?

McCarthyites: The Style Orientation

For many followers of Senator McCarthy there would be no point in taking over the Democratic party if it were to become just like it was in the past. There had to be a new politics to give life to a new party. But no one was successful in defining what that new politics might be. It had to do with enlisting greater citizen participation in public affairs. There was talk about democratizing party procedures. Aside from avoiding future Vietnams, however, there was little specific content to give substance to the future polity. Our interviews suggest that the meaning of the new politics lay not in substance but in style, not in policies but in people, not in what McCarthy did but in what his actions symbolized for his followers.

McCarthy's great attraction was his political style. From the comments of his supporters he emerges as the antithesis of the unscrupulous politician who changes his views on public policy in order to curry favor with the electorate. He opposed the Vietnam war before it was politically popular to do so. He is pictured as a man outside the ordinary political framework who holds the morally bankrupt politicians to account. When asked why they liked McCarthy, his supporters would say, "He's sincere and honest. He opposed the war in the primaries, and he's not a bullshitter."

Since McCarthy's integrity was his stock in trade, his supporters were concerned that he remain pure at all times. Many of his supporters eagerly assured us that "McCarthy wouldn't sell out. He wouldn't compromise. He won't accept the Vice Presidency with Humphrey." On hearing McCarthy say that he would support neither Humphrey or Nixon, a delegate leaped up and cried out, "What a man! What a man! What guts he has!" Telling established powers where to go was dear to the hearts of McCarthy men. This style went beyond McCarthy, as could be seen in a delegate's comment about the Democratic candidate for Senator from Ohio: "I like what Gilligan has done, more or less saying to organized labor, 'To hell with you'."

The idea that one should go into politics for personal gain was repellent to supporters of Senator McCarthy. McCarthy must not seek power. He must not seek personal gain. He must sacrifice himself but not his ideals. Yet the politics of selflessness posed problems for the McCarthyites. If they were not in it for themselves and their man was not in it for himself, how were they to justify their furious activity?

The first step was to say that McCarthy was upholding the ideals of his followers. "Gene is doing this for us. He'll never give away our policies and our ideals. He won't betray us." So McCarthy was not out for himself but for his supporters. The second step was to say that his followers were not out to get anything for themselves; they were out to help McCarthy. "We're for Gene, for what he stands for, because he isn't a politician. That's why we are doing all this." Putting the two kinds of statements together, you have the essential justification offered by McCarthy people: no one of them was after anything for himself; McCarthy was working for his followers and they were working for him.

McCarthy was the candidate of those who did not want and did not need to get material advantages from their participation in political affairs. By our observation as well as by common account, the McCarthy forces were largely middle and upper-middle class people. They had material things. What they lacked was psychic rewards—the desire to be counted important, to be active in behalf of a noble cause. No self-seeking for them. They could submerge a drive for power in their leader. He could use his power to strengthen them. McCarthy's conception of the Presidential office, which was so disturbing to the Kennedy supporters, pleased his followers no end. "The Federal government has too much power. McCarthy can do something about that. I like that quote of his: 'I see the office of President as setting free the energies of the people.' "

McCarthy could make his followers powerful but pure. His demeanor —slightly alienated, bemused, cynical, world-weary, detached, underplayed—fit in beautifully with the orientations of his followers. They could feel exalted without being corrupted. They could stress their own skills—argument, debate, and persuasion—in the pursuit of a better life for others. They saw McCarthy as they saw themselves, as an altruist for special interests.

McCarthy people regarded youth as a primary source of idealism; having youth with them signified that they had kept faith with themselves. The fear that Humphrey's nomination would alienate youth was for them a fear that the party would lose its connections with the purifying forces of idealism. "The kids, the young people are sometimes impractical," an older McCarthy delegate noted, "but they want us to live up to our ideals. If we lose them, we may be just like the others."

Youth is the conscience of the party. If you are just a little too comfortable, if you fear that you may one day be tempted to sell out or that adjustment to the status quo will somehow creep up on you unawares, the presence of the angel of youth might serve to prevent a fall from grace.

It should be clear by now that a central part of McCarthy's appeal to his style-oriented followers was that he did not act like a politician. He wrote poems, he was too reflective, he was too frank, he refused to bargain. He would not make the traditional gesture of supporting the party's nominee after he had lost. He attracted innocent children rather than worldly adults. His followers took all this as a sign that he was, like themselves, an outsider to the party who refused to become just another politician.

Yet the aspects of McCarthy's style that appeared attractive in a candidate led many delegates to wonder whether they were appropriate in a President. A Kennedy man insisted that "Presidents have to exercise power, not just pick flowers." There was no doubt about McCarthy's personal appeal, but as one respondent put it, he was "lacking in—I want to choose this word carefully—dynamics. He looks as if he were President somebody would steal the gavel away from him before he had a chance to use it."

McCarthy's supporters recognized that he might have difficulty in acting like the powerful Presidents of the past. Those whose affection for McCarthy was greatest wondered whether it was fair to send him out into the cruel political world. But in the end, the style-oriented McCarthyites consoled themselves with the thought that they did not want their candidate to be like other Presidents. He would raise their self-esteem instead of his own. If there were a new breed of party activists, why shouldn't McCarthy be a new kind of President? Why should he be a President at all unless he could come in on his own terms to put an end to traditional political practices?

Semipermanent Opposition

The McCarthy phenomenon is another harbinger of change in the style of political leadership in America. The reform Democrats described by James Q. Wilson brought an emphasis on open conflict over issues and ideology. The Goldwaterites added a purist stance in which the leader's attachment to private moral values took precedence over political agreement on feasible public policy. Compare, for example, the characterization of McCarthy with the adjectives the Goldwaterites used to describe their champion. When, in 1964, I asked Goldwater delegates to tell me what they most liked about their candidate only a few mentioned his position on the issues, and those who did were content with brief references to constitutional principles like states' rights. By far the most frequent characterizations of Goldwater referred to his consistency, honesty, integrity, and willingness to stick by principles. It was not so much his principles (though these were undoubtedly important) but the belief that he stuck to them that counted most with his supporters. "He is straightforward." "He does not compromise." "He doesn't pander to the public; he's against expediency." "He is frank." "He had courage." "He stands up for what he believes." As one of Goldwater's supporters perceptively observed, "He's different than most politicians."

Critical confirmation of the importance of style comes from a paper on "Amateurs and Professionals: A Study of Delegates to the 1968 Democratic Convention" by John W. Soule and James Clarke of Florida State University. They administered a questionnaire to a quota sample of delegates and found "that amateurs [purists], . . . and professionals [party regulars] are not distinguishable along ideological lines. . . . The differences . . . appear to be procedural and stylistic." Converting their language to our own, they find that purists are demonstrably younger, somewhat richer, enter party activity at a later age, and spend fewer years in the party than do the party regulars. Where party politicians value the party in and of itself because they have a deep attachment to it as an institution, I would add that the power-oriented McCarthyites take an instrumental view; they value the party only if they are in control. The style-oriented McCarthyites, however, value the Democratic party only if it also changes character to embody a purist conception of political life.

The contention that McCarthy's style is part of a trend in American political life is supported by an interesting finding: contrary to what we would expect, numerous polls reveal that approximately 20 percent of those who supported Senator McCarthy during the primaries ended up voting for Governor Wallace. In what ways might Wallace and McCarthy, despite their vast differences, appear to be similar? Perhaps voters who were disgusted with the major parties were attracted to leaders outside the system who stood up for what they believed and told off people in power. Wallace, who had no hopes in the regular political system, castigated the major parties for failing to represent citizens who were opposed to growing lawlessness and compulsory integration; McCarthy, who hoped to reconvert the Democratic party, blasted its leaders for failing to meet the aspirations of the young. Neither man has use for the people in control of party decisions. For much the same reasons the supporters of Barry Goldwater found his purist stance—no bargaining, compromise or pandering for votes—especially attractive as they attacked the eastern "Establishment" of the Republican party. No one is suggesting that McCarthy, Goldwater, and Wallace are at all equivalent in political life, but they do share a common characteristic that gives them appeal to people for whom the ordinary processes of political adjustment have become distasteful.

Where Goldwater sought to save a fundamentally sound political system by bearing witness to its potential purity, however, McCarthy takes the position of an outsider who is in semipermanent opposition to it. His position is correspondingly more difficult to understand. For he senses the disenchantment of his followers with normal politics and yet knows that he must at times bear an active relationship to existing political institutions. So he talks of basic changes in political processes but moves into action only when this consists of a form of opposition.

McCarthy's style may best be appraised through an understanding of his followers. He did not find them, they adopted him when he opposed the war in Vietnam in moral terms. McCarthy senses that his followers like him best when he attacks "the Establishment" or leads a moral crusade. They want him untainted. So he must be careful about the company he keeps and the commitments he makes.

The notion of a semipermanent opposition helps us understand Senator McCarthy's recent actions in voluntarily moving from the prestigious Foreign Relations Committee to the relatively obscure Government Operations Committee, and in supporting Russell Long over Edward Kennedy for the position of Democratic Whip in the Senate. Those who think of McCarthy as just a better man than the normal run of politician are puzzled and disheartened by his apparently perverse behavior. Yet McCarthy is being perfectly consistent with the role of semipermanent opposition he has set for himself. By removing himself from the Foreign Relations Committee, McCarthy relieves himself of association with the Senate "Establishment" and any remote implication in the foreign policies of the Nixon Administration. He is free to say what he will without violating any confidence. As a member of the Government Operations Committee, however, McCarthy, like his earlier namesake, can pursue the traditional work of that body: investigation and criticism of the bureaucracy. Just as he indicates that he has little hope for foreign policy under the existing political system, so does McCarthy symbolize his distaste for other political processes in refusing to vote for Edward Kennedy. By preferring an old Long from Louisiana rather than a new Kennedy from Massachusetts, McCarthy is saying that he has no hope for ordinary politics. There is no point, his action means, in refurbishing an unsatisfactory institution with a new cover. McCarthy opposes the ersatz youth that look young but act old. If we are going to have old politics, he suggests, you should not make the false promises that a Kennedy would suggest but face people with the reality that Russell Long epitomizes. In both cases, Senator McCarthy shows that he wants no part of government unless he is in control or in a position to criticize from the outside. Refusing to run for reelection to the Senate in 1970 is just his latest step in removing himself from responsibility for the acts of government.

As the legitimacy of the American political system has come increasingly under attack, the incentives for public activity have begun to change. If a politician fails in the difficult task of organizing disparate coalitions to support social legislation, he has little to show for his labors. If he succeeds, he is bound to be told that he has not accomplished anything worth doing. It is as if whatever the "Establishment" does is by definition small and inconsequential, so that the only way of knowing whether a policy is significant is that it does not gather support.

The greater the attack on the legitimacy of the political system, the less the willingness to accept responsibility for it. The greater the reduction of modest improvements in favor of wholesale changes, the less the ability of the political system to meet these requirements. Indeed, the more requirements are stated in stylistic terms, the less it is possible to know whether they have been met at all. As the demands for governmental performance become ever larger and more indefinite, the likelihood of any action receiving widespread approval decreases. Under these conditions, the temptation to engage in semipermanent opposition is bound to increase. No doubt there will still be a preponderance of governmental officials who will concentrate on the substance of public policy. But we can expect increasing numbers of them to seek what the French call "the cure of opposition."

More politicians may move into semipermanent opposition. They will learn how to generate opportunities that provide them with visible means of resolving moral dilemmas of government outside of a framework of responsibility. The French, for example, have long experience in combining the benefits of office with the advantages of opposition. It will take a while, however, before American politicians can rise to the sublime heights of General DeGaulle who, after witnessing prolonged rioting during his presidency, asked the citizenry to support his efforts in rescuing the nation from the misdeeds of the former regime.

NOTES

1. I am grateful to my colleagues at the University of California, Frank Levy and Andrew McFarland, to graduate students in the Political Science Department, Bill Cavala, Robert Nakamura, and Jeffrey Pressman, and to students at the University of Chicago, Philip Auerbach, Jo Freeman, Laura Martin, Wallet Rogers and Theodore Totman, for helping me carry out the interviews on which this paper is based. They also contributed many valuable suggestions. I also wish to thank Dean Sanford Elberg of the Graduate Division for providing the funds that made this research possible. There are approximately 500 interviews lasting from a few minutes to an hour. All the major delegations—California, New York, Illinois, Texas, Ohio, Pennsylvania—were covered, as were smaller delegations from every section of the nation. We placed ourselves in the hotels where the delegates stayed and were able to interview them easily from early in the morning until the late afternoon when the busses left for the convention hall. The violence that marked the convention week took place largely outside the hotels and did not inhibit our activities. We were never denied access to any hotel. The advantage of this type of interviewing is that it is possible to get answers on the spot and delve more deeply than is ordinarily possible in mail questionnaires or the usual sample surveys. We have no way of knowing how representative our responses are but the large number of interviews and the consistency of responses augurs well on that score.

15

COMPREHENSIVE VERSUS INCREMENTAL BUDGETING IN THE DEPARTMENT OF AGRICULTURE

WITH *Arthur Hammond*

In the Spring of 1962, the Department of Agriculture shunted aside traditional methods of budgeting and attempted a comprehensive and simultaneous evaluation of all departmental programs. The purpose of this essay is to describe this experiment and to evaluate its results, especially as they bear upon the controversy surrounding incremental versus comprehensive approaches to decision-making. After a brief description of the rival positions in this controversy, the procedures used by officials in the Department of Agriculture in comprehensive budgeting are described. Then we attempt to determine the extent to which the intended objectives of comprehensive budgeting were achieved, and to describe a number of unanticipated consequences of using this approach. We conclude with a series of recommendations.[1]

The Controversy

Whatever else they may be, budgets are manifestly political documents. They engage the intense concern of administrators, politicians, leaders of interest groups and citizens interested in the "who gets what and how much" of governmental allocations. Participants in budgeting use its political components as aids to calculation. They drastically simplify their task

From *Administrative Science Quarterly* 10 (December 1965), pp. 321–346. Reprinted by permission.

by concentrating on the relatively small portion of the budget that is politically feasible to change. The previous year's budget, the largest part of which is composed of continuing programs and prior commitments, is usually taken as a base needing little justification beyond that offered in the past. Attention is normally focused on a small number of incremental changes, increases and decreases, calling for significant departures from the established historical base of the agency concerned. Parts of the total budget are given to various administrative agencies, appropriations subcommittees, Budget Bureau divisions, and other interested parties for special attention. This fragmentation is increased because all budgetary items are not evaluated together, but are dealt with in sequence by the various participants, so that only a small number of items need be considered by any participant at any one time. Heavy reliance is placed on receiving feedback from interested parties, if a decision turns out to have adverse consequences for others. The existing budgetary process, therefore, may be described as incremental, fragmented, and sequential.[2]

A large part of the literature on budgeting in the United States has been devoted to a critique of the present process.[3] Aids to calculation like the incremental method have been attacked as arbitrary and inefficient. The fragmented and sequential budgetary operations have been severely criticized for leading to a lack of coordination and a neglect of important values.

Failure to consider the budget as a whole, each item competing for funds with the others, has been characterized as irrational. Although many statements could be cited to show how long and how consistently these views have been held, only a few illustrations are presented here. Writing in 1924, E. Hilton Young asserted:

It must be a temptation to one drawing up an estimate to save himself trouble by taking last year's estimate for granted, adding something to any item for which an increased expenditure is foreseen. Nothing could be easier, or more wasteful and extravagant. It is in that way obsolete expenditure is enabled to make its appearance year after year long after reason for it has ceased to be.[4]

This often-repeated theme was echoed in 1941 by Benton Biser: "Appropriations generally are built upon the basis of the preceding year's expenditure, plus or minus any known items of increase or decrease, without considering whether or not the past year's experience is the result of efficient and economical administration."[5] Arthur Smithies was more positive: "In general final expenditure decisions should not be made until *all* claims on the budget can be considered"[6] (italics supplied).

These norms are still held by participants in budgeting. Maurice Stans, who was budget director under President Eisenhower, stated: *"Every item in a budget ought to be on trial for its life each year* and matched against *all* the other claimants to our resources"[7] (italics supplied). The critics would prefer a budgetary process in which coordination would be made the explicit concern of a central hierarchy, which would consider a wide range of alternative expenditures and investigate rather fully the consequences of each and the probability of their occurring. No item would be automatically included, and each would be considered anew every year in the light of its relative priority compared to other items. Instead of proceeding from a historical base, there would be no base at all; therefore, this comprehensive budget is called a "zero-base" budget.

While it is evidently possible to talk about comprehensive, zero-based budgeting, the question arises as to whether it is possible to put it into practice.[8] This question cannot be shunted aside as unimportant, when one considers the constraints imposed by limited time and comprehension, by the lack of theory to predict consequences or means to calculate them fully, by the widespread political consensus on many programs and the statutory necessity of proceeding with others, and by inability to resolve the perennial question of the comparability of different preferences held with varying degrees of intensity. A direct test of the comprehensive approach has not previously been possible because (to the best of our knowledge) no major attempt has been made to try a zero-base budget. The effort of the Department of Agriculture to work with a zero-base budget in 1962 provides, therefore, a unique and valuable opportunity to undertake a direct test of this approach. The analysis of a "deviant case" (when compared with the usual mode of budgeting) has special advantages in highlighting features of the budgetary process that might otherwise escape notice. Despite the disadvantage of working with one case, one can obtain insights from a close view of problems of budgetary calculation.[9]

The study is based on an extended series of interviews, during the summer of 1963, with budget officers, directors or assistant directors, and staff people in nearly every agency in the Department of Agriculture, as well as department level officials. We attempted to interview every person at a high level who was intimately involved in the zero-base budget experiment, and succeeded in interviewing at least one person in all but two small agencies. Our 57 interviews constitute an overwhelmingly large sample of the important men available for discussion. All of the men interviewed were given an opportunity to comment upon a draft of this paper and to amplify their remarks to the senior author. Twelve reinterviews were undertaken in order to check on disputed points. Questions in the paper represent a transcription of notes taken during interviews or, when indicated, comments in letters written in response to the first draft.

Procedures

The origin of the experiment in zero-base budgeting may be traced to three circumstances: (1) The general climate of opinion favored comprehensive budgeting. (2) A letter from Director of the Budget, David Bell, to the Secretary of Agriculture, Orville Freeman, suggested that a more comprehensive approach to budgeting was in order. Dated August 16, 1961, the crucial sentence reads: "I think we should in a real sense reconsider the basic funding for each program—'justify from zero' in the budgetary phase." (3) Freeman had a strong interest in budgetary problems, which he had developed as governor of Minnesota.[10] Comments like "The Secretary pushed this" or "The Secretary's interest was the motivating force" clearly indicate where department officials found the immediate impulse behind the proposal.

When the decision was made to do a zero-base budget, staff members in the Department's Office of Budget and Finance made a quick survey of the literature and discovered that although much had been written criticizing the traditional methods of budgeting and advocating a comprehensive approach, there was little written about zero-base budgeting. After the staff members had consulted with leading department officials in order to get a clearer idea of the objectives, they began preparations.

In April, 1962, the Department Office of Budget and Finance sent out "Instructions for 1964 Agency Estimates," which called for radical changes.

A new concept has been adopted for the 1964 agency estimates; namely, that of zero-base budgeting. This means that all programs will be reviewed from the ground up and not merely in terms of changes proposed for the budget year. . . . The *total* work program of each agency must be subjected to an intensive review and evaluation. . . . Consideration must be given to the basic need for the work contemplated, the level at which the work should be carried out, the benefits to be received, and the costs to be incurred. . . .

The fact that certain activities have been carried out for a number of years will not, *per se,* adequately justify their continuation. Nor will the fact that programs are prescribed by statutory law necessarily be a controlling consideration. Program goals based on statutes enacted to meet problems or needs that are today of lesser priority must be reevaluated in terms of present conditions.

It is implicit in the zero-based budget approach that the need for programs and their recommended magnitude in the fiscal year 1964 be clearly and specifically demonstrated. . . . The justifications should be prepared on the assumption that *all* [italics supplied] information needed for making budget decisions should be included.[11]

The instructions for preparing a zero-base budget required the agencies to make three major types of calculations: (1) justification of the need for agency activities and programs without reference to congressional mandate or past practice, (2) justification of the requested level of expenditure (fund obligations) based on the needs, (3) justification of the costs of the needed programs from the ground up. How did agency officials react to the demands placed upon them by the zero-base budget? How did they go about putting together the huge amount of information they were required to submit?

APPLICATION OF ZERO-BASE CONCEPT

All the agencies had serious difficulty in conceptualizing circumstances in which there were no legislative mandates, no past commitments, no consideration of items to be included because other participants in the budgetary process would demand it, no programs for which support could not conceivably be expected; in a word, no history or learning based on that history. The words of one official, "Justifying the whole program is silly; it just equals rehashing the original legislation" were echoed by many others. So the agencies either assumed or quickly decided that their programs were needed. Many programs were justified at least in part by references to the language of their enabling legislation, despite the statement in the instructions that this would not be an overriding consideration. Besides pointing to statutory requirements, the agencies gave priority to showing how their program met objectives of the Kennedy-Freeman program: increasing recreation facilities, aiding low-income groups, and generally advancing rural development. This is, of course, what the agencies would usually have done in justifying their budgets, except that more detail and greater documentation were provided. Furthermore, time was precious and in short supply. "We didn't have time to analyze much" was a typical comment, reflecting the tendency for effort to be channeled into the large and pressing task of compiling supporting data.

One budget officer estimated that a "real examination" of the need for the programs carried out by his agency "would take at least a year." As a result, he explained, the continuation of major programs was not reexamined.

Agency people were far more concerned with the level of their programs than with whether there was a need for them at all. One stated, "We told our program people, 'These are the areas Congress has authorized us to participate in. Which need to be implemented in your state, and at what level?' "; and even here, "Mostly this was a justification of what we had." Program officials reported, apparently without realizing the implications for the theory behind the zero-base budget, that in preparing estimates, "We had to start from the previous year, then determine what increases we wanted for 1964." "Each staff officer reviewed his office. We all decided we needed what we had. Then we decided whether to ask for increases." The calculations involved in determining the precise figures were described by an agency head in terms generally applicable throughout the department: "In the matter of preparing budget estimates, the dollar emphases (priorities) are intended to represent a program which represents what the Secretary and Congress want to give emphasis to at that time. The dollar figures represent a compromise among the guidelines given by the need for the service (what the public has asked for), the wishes of the President and Secretary, and the indications given by Congress at 'Hill' hearings ('hold the line on this program next year!')." Other officials mentioned certain

limiting factors—the availability of trained personnel or physical resources, which set upper limits to what they could do. It is apparent that
agency people reduced their burden of calculation by actively seeking
guidelines or constraints—what Congress would approve, what the statutes
required, what could be done with available personnel and resources. The
major calculating device was to take the budget of the past year or two and
then consider increases or decreases.

Since the zero-base budget was designed to avoid this incremental procedure, we challenged the respondents to explain and defend their approach. Not all were aware at first that they were following an incremental
procedure. At times the respondents became agitated: "You've got to start
from where you are!" Two main grounds were advanced in support of this
proposition. First they knew most about their present status and could
make some reasonable estimate of the effect of more or less money for
particular programs. But they did not know what drastic changes, such as
eliminating their programs, or cutting them in half, or doubling them,
would mean: "Increases or decreases are about all we can swallow." Such
comments were reinforced by observing that at department budget hearings, agency representatives were typically confronted with the same kinds
of increase-decrease statements as in previous years: "How many people
do you have now? What did you spend for that last year? What do you
propose to do with the extra funds?"

The second argument was that the whole procedure was unreal. Why
such a great effort for a procedure which nobody with experience could
believe would lead to any significant results? Everybody knew that certain
programs were mandatory, others could not be modified, still others had to
be supported at approximately their current level, unless the President and
the secretary were prepared to make many more enemies than appeared to
be the case: "We knock our heads against the wall and then we know it
will all turn out the same." All this "waste of time and effort" when they
might have been working on programs they could really do something
about.

Considerations such as these were not entirely absent in the instructions
for the zero-base budget, where one statement was, "One of the Department's objectives will be to reduce overall net expenditures for the Department of Agriculture in 1964 and subsequent years below presently estimated levels for 1962 and 1963." If the agencies were expected to make a
fundamental analysis of the needs for their programs, regardless of budget
changes, such an admonition would seem superfluous.[12]

"My first reaction was to jump out the window," an agency budget officer revealed. As the agencies began work to justify the cost elements in
their estimates, however, the initial difficulties were forgotten in the attempt to meet the requirements set down for the zero-base budget. Those
agencies whose activities or experience lent themselves easily to work-load
analysis reacted differently from those whose activities made this proce-

dure impossible or inappropriate for them. An agency with a well-developed and widely accepted mode of work-load measures could meet the requirement that expenditures be justified from "the ground up" by attaching an explanation to tables of work-load statistics, supporting the expenditures. As one budget officer put it, "Work-load data is great for us. We're pioneers in this area. We'd been developing this data for years." A high-ranking official was explicit in stating that in his agency, "the zero-base approach made no difference, because to meet rapidly changing conditions, we're always preparing our budget zero-base style. Economic assumptions lead to size of expected program (required by statute), which leads to cost on basis of previous staffing and material needs. We don't know what the estimate will be until it pops out of the calculating machine."

For the agencies which did not or could not use work-load data, calculating the expected level of expenditures (budgetary obligations) in zero-base style was much more difficult, and the responsible officials tended to react much more negatively. "I don't know of any budget officer who liked zero-base budgeting," was a typical comment. "Work-load data is inappropriate for us," they explained. "It's not like building a bridge or something —you don't have 'units,' you have subject matter, and it is very difficult to know how many technical people are needed." Unable to talk in terms of so many applications processed, operations performed, or similar measures, the agencies with no work-load statistics had to find a substitute. In some cases an explanation of the problem was made, and the proposed levels of expenditure were justified by projecting the rate of growth of the previous few years into the future. A few agencies tried to develop new ways of dividing activities, although they did not think this realistic and expected no benefits from what they called "arbitrary categories." Developing supporting data meant breaking down costs differently and engaging in many hurried calculations without the feeling that something positive would result. As a result, these agencies were overburdened with work in which they had little confidence, although they did manage to submit estimates which were as much as ten or more times longer than previous ones. Six weeks after the instructions for the zero-base budget had been sent out, 25 sets of binders representing agency estimates, most taking up three feet of shelf space, appeared in the Office of Budget and Finance. "It nearly created a surplus storage problem," one official remarked in a pointed bit of humor.

COMPREHENSIVENESS OF ZERO-BASE APPROACH

"Theoretically," a department official said, "a zero-base budget is a way of evaluating needs and priorities more systematically and comprehensively than usual." How did the officials at the department level [13] analyze the voluminous material presented. Did they try to evaluate the relative merits of every item or program compared to every other? What procedures were actually used in making agency allowances?

The main problem was lack of time. "We knew we were getting into something horrendous," a respondent declared, "and it was obvious in advance that it would be impossible for all of us to analyze the material at all stages. The range of decision—the number of decisions to be made—increased almost infinitely. Although individual steps of the process at the department level were the same as always, this made such a quantitative difference as to amount to a qualitative one." Another official observed, "The stuff the agencies submitted was very complete, obviously too bulky for the Secretary himself to wade through." More direct confirmation came from an authoritative source, who said that the secretary "didn't read a great deal of material; he only has time for summary material." But he did spend more time than before on the budget. Of the eight members of the Budget Committee of the Department—the undersecretary (Chairman), six assistant secretaries, and the Director of Budget and Finance—it is doubtful that more than one or two actually had time to read all the material submitted. That the zero-base budget came up during the Billie Sol Estes episode and at a time when the appropriations bill was seriously behind schedule in Congress may have added to the time problem. The consensus, expressed by a high department official was "There was too much material in the zero-base budget for us to digest and use. I haven't read it all." What, then, did they do with the material they could read and digest?

The crucial question centers around the degree to which comparisons were made as to the relative desirability of programs spanning several different agencies. Nothing approaching a comparison of every program with every other (or of most programs with each other) was made. On the contrary, the majority of comparisons made by department officials concerned programs and activities within individual agencies. An official explained, "Questions at department hearings were in the same categories as usual—Why this program? Why this level? What would alternatives cost?—but in more detail. In analysis, we didn't consider why 65 rather than 64 or 66 man-years for project X, but why three times as much for project X as project Y." Only in a few cases involving closely related programs in different agencies, where this had been the practice, were comparisons made across agency lines. In fact, most of the analysis, as in previous years, dealt with the justification of an individual program at a particular level of expenditure. "Unavoidably," a department official revealed, "we ended up talking about how much more, about increases. Budget people seem to talk about a budget request of $5 million when actually that's just the increase."

When we faced him with these findings a department official declared that:

The ideal of a zero-base budget is actually impossible: It would require investigating why each research lab is where it is (which is tough to trace), giving an objective measure of how much can be justified for research in a given area, etc. If you have the type of program where you can identify units of work, budgeting on zero-base is relatively simple. But in a case like the Department of Agriculture, that often doesn't work. Our activities are so varied as to make quantitative comparisons between programs impossible. I don't agree that just because we put emphasis on increases, no one pays attention to the rest of it. We are always evaluating some programs in a basic sense and always trying to make improvements in management. If we do [place emphasis on increases] it's because that's the way appropriations committees like to operate.

This official and others appear to be saying (1) that they do not know how to make the calculations required for a zero-base budget; and (2) that a comprehensive approach is not necessary, because they do, from time to time, investigate various programs intensively, within the limitations of their time and knowledge. It is clear that those who would like a zero-base budget will have to show how it can be done if they wish to see it put into practice.

The Staff

Those engaged in analyzing the budget at the department level did make a serious effort to avoid increase-decrease analysis. "Naturally," a staff man explained, "we were interested in the fact that a program would be a new investment; that fact might raise or lower [its] priority. But increases and decreases as such were for the Bureau of the Budget [and later for submission to Congress]; they weren't even included in the detailed justifications." This procedure raises a question of some interest. If, as we have seen, top officials manifested a preponderant interest in increases and decreases for the purpose of making recommendations on the budget, what purpose was served by providing them with different kinds of data and analysis?

When this question was posed to department people, they began to alter the rationale they had originally offered for the zero-base budget. Two major lines of thought developed. The first professed to see in the zero-base budget a combination of psychological reassurance and strategic utility: "There has been a great hue and cry about the size of the agriculture budget. The purpose of it [the zero-base budget] is to reassure, if we can, the Secretary, the Director of the Budget, the members of the appropriations committees, that money is not being wasted and that it is being used to carry out only the most important projects in work that furthers the national interest." Although related to the first in its emphasis upon the psychological aspect, the second *post-hoc* rationale leans on the benefits to be derived from any radical change in habits of work and thought. "We were interested," the proponents of this view asserted, "in the zero-base budget as a therapeutic device for agency and budget people. It's easy to get into the habit of doing things the same way. Starting out with the idea that nothing is sacred is therapeutic in itself. Any device which will encourage people to give a deeper and broader consideration of operations will lead to better understanding of what is going on and of areas where improvements might be made." Note that the focus has shifted from external phenomena like comprehensive calculation from the ground up, from analyzing programs comparatively, to internal psychological states like breaking up people's habitual patterns of thinking and reassuring leaders. To what extent did "better understanding" lead to improvements? Consider the consequences of the zero-base budget for budgetary decisions within the department. What difference did it make in the kinds of decisions made?

Intended Objectives

The major purpose of the zero-base budget was to examine all programs at the same time and from the ground up to discover programs continuing through inertia or design that did not warrant being continued at all or at their present level of expenditure. Money released by the discovery of these "obsolete" programs could lead either to a decrease in the over-all size of the funds requested by the Department of Agriculture or to a more rapid expansion of the highest priority programs than was possible under the traditional incremental approach to budgeting. In brief, detailed information about all programs would for the first time be available in one place at one time for departmental review. As a result, relative priorities of total amounts for all programs could be considered, not merely amounts of increase and decrease for some programs.

We therefore asked each respondent to tell us whether any decision made by him or by others could in any way be attributed to the zero-base budget. Did the agency or department officials recommend different programs, different amounts for programs, or distribute funds among programs differently as a result of the zero-base approach? For the most part, the answer was negative.

Most statements were variants of "I don't think it made a damn bit of difference," or, "I don't think anyone would honestly tell you that they changed their budget." Agency personnel continually reiterated their doubts that the department was adequately staffed to digest the vast amounts of material. Asked for evidence, the respondents usually replied that, "The figures we put in have never been referred to as far as I know" or, "It [the zero-base budget data] was sent across the street [where the department offices are located] and we never heard of it again." In a few cases the respondent hedged: "I don't know that I personally learned anything new or different, but . . . I suspect it did make some difference, but I'd hate to have to prove it." A couple of times an exceedingly small change was reported though not without qualification. Although there was "no difference in the overall amounts requested or received from the department, analysis did lead to the transfer of $20,000 among programs. This analysis was, however, planned before the zero-base budget. . . ." An excess expenditure for files in one agency was also mentioned. In one instance a department official asserted, "I am confident that decisions were made which would not have been made or even considered in the absence of a zero-base budget." He could, however, give only one specific change—a reduction of $100,000 in an obsolete research program. The paucity of changes attributed to the zero-base budget is evident in the fact that this change was brought up repeatedly. (Many officials said they had heard of a change somewhere, but it always turned out to be this same change.) Another department official insisted that the zero-base budget procedure was not useful in "ferreting out all sorts of dark and sinister things that shouldn't be done, which would turn up quickly anyhow." Our general conclusion can be stated in the words of a person in a position to get a general view: "Some butterflies were caught, no elephants stopped."

There are a number of explanations for the paucity of changes. First, as an agency official put it, "Budgeting is continuous." Individual programs are constantly being evaluated. When authorizations run out, new studies are commonly undertaken and new justifications prepared. A change of party in the White House or the appearance of a new agency head often results in the reevaluation of some programs. Interest in Congress or the Bureau of the Budget, demands by clientele groups, and changes in the economy or in technology may lead to intensive analysis of specific programs. These take place in addition to periodic reviews scheduled within the agency in order to adjust to changing circumstances. Second, some of the department's programs have always been budgeted more or less in zero-base fashion because their operations lend themselves to quantification. These include the price support programs of the Commodity Credit Corporation, which make up the largest single item in the budget. For such programs, justifying a $600,000 program and justifying a $100,000 increase in a $500,000 program amount to much the same thing. Therefore the requests coming from the agencies—certainly a major determinant of what departmental officials will approve—were quite similar to those of previous years. Third, it is the responsibility of administrators to see that resources are expended for the programs they believe have the highest priorities. The head of one of the larger agencies indicated that when he goes to Congress with a request for an increase in his agency's budget, he must always be ready to admit that the increase will finance work of lower priority than is already being done; otherwise he will be criticized because he has not already transferred funds to the higher-priority activities. Nearly all agencies have many more programs than they can undertake or expand with the funds they have or are likely to get; they are not likely therefore, to allow an obsolete program to continue to drain resources from programs they deem more worth while.[14] Even those interested in expanding their organizations can seek expansion of those programs they believe most worth while.

The main reason that budgetary outcomes were not very different, however, is that the process by which budgets are calculated and justified is only one—and by no means the most important—determinant of program size, distribution, and content. Budget officials, particularly at the departmental level, continually qualified their remarks by saying that, after all, "The zero-base budget didn't affect the basic economic and political facts of life." There are mandatory programs like price supports for which expenditures must be made and which cannot be easily altered. The level of programs may depend a great deal on the state of the national economy (for service programs), on the existing state of knowledge and the availability of trained personnel (for research programs), and not on how programs are analyzed or written up. As many officials pointedly remarked, "Decisions are made on criteria other than the justification of the program itself. Frequently the figures are based on judgment factors of what the environment will permit taken in total." Whether political support exists for a program depends on party alignments in Congress and the executive branch, the preferences of the President, Director of the Budget, members of appropriations committees and other officials, and the activities of clientele groups. Budget people are well aware, for example, that the best possible justification may have little influence against a powerful budget-cutting drive. These factors find no place in the zero-base approach; therefore in a budgetary system in which there is necessarily much emphasis on "what will go," [15] a zero-base approach will not necessarily make much difference.

Although there was widespread agreement that the zero-base budget did not significantly affect outcomes, nearly half of those interviewed commented quite favorably on the experience after it was over. Was this merely a show of bureaucratic loyalty or were there other reasons for the favorable attitude? This unexpected finding led us to ask further questions, which produced perhaps the most interesting findings in the study.

Unanticipated Consequences

Activities may have outcomes which are unanticipated, even unperceived, by the participants in the activity.[16] The preparation of a zero-base budget resulted in a number of unanticipated consequences, which were probably more important (and certainly more interesting) than its expected results.

One of the difficulties faced by reflective people engaged in budgeting is that they hold implicit beliefs about desirable methods of calculations—comprehensive and simultaneous evaluation of means and ends being considered as synonymous with rationality—while they practice quite different—incremental and sequential—methods. For the large minority who expressed positive feelings about zero-base budgeting, the experience appears to have satisfied a longing to believe that they were proceeding according to the canons of rational methods of calculation. When asked why they liked zero-base budgeting, they would answer by describing the method and pronouncing it good: "Considering everything from the ground up at the same time is, well, good, the right way to do it, and not just letting things grow like Topsy." "The major benefit may well have been the much more intensive, thoroughgoing review, from the bottom up." But if the zero-base budget did not lead to changes, did they perhaps learn more?

Here there was a sharp split in the responses of the large minority that approved of the zero-base budget. Some respondents claimed that they learned nothing new; they had known about all their operations before. How, then, was the zero-base budget helpful? Agency personnel answered that the department people must have benefited; department-level personnel answered that agency personnel had benefited. "The zero-base budget," said an agency man, was "enlightening to Department officials who reviewed it. To us it was just an exercise." "We knew what was going on," department officials would say. "It was helpful in the agencies. I can't prove this, but I have no doubt that things turned up in the agencies that were never passed on." A variant of this argument was taken by an agency head: "I don't know that I personally learned anything new or different. But some of my staff who prepared material for me had clearer presentations than in other years." For these officials, the zero-base budget was good because it benefited other people.

The rest of the administrators who were favorably disposed toward zero-base budgeting did feel that they learned something new. Without exception these people had been in their positions less than three years and had not yet discovered how useful participation in budgeting and perusal of budgetary material could be in adding to their store of information. "I think everyone came out of this process with a great deal more information than they'd ever had before," a new appointee declared. "I went through all of the material, spent more time on budgeting than before [the previous two years], learned more about the scope of operations." Like others in his position, he knew what programs were being undertaken, but in some cases he had not realized the full extent of the operations until he read the budgetary data.

If this was the case, why did these officials not make use of the knowledge they had gained to alter their preferences or otherwise make somewhat different decisions? An important clue was furnished by one of these "learners" who remarked, "Some of these things I wouldn't have needed to know." Indeed, further questioning revealed that much of what was learned was simply not appropriate to the kinds of choices available to these men or, at least, was not perceived by them as being relevant in the context in which they operated.

Those who disliked the zero-base budget complained that they had done a lot of extra work, yet nothing had been changed as a result of their endeavors. Far from being unhappy at the absence of significant changes in their budgets, however, those who liked the zero-base budget seemed to find positive advantage in this circumstance. One official explained, the zero-base budget was good because "it tended to confirm what you had a notion of otherwise." It felt good "to satisfy yourself that you're doing a conscientious job," said another official, "instead of following the inevitable least resistance, less deep analysis, of the increases and decreases approach." The happy coincidence of doing a budget right all along was a morale booster. Before they had come to the department they had heard complaints that many of its programs were wasteful and unnecessary. Now that it had been demonstrated in detail just what the Department of Agriculture was doing and why, they were more certain of the necessity of the programs for which they were responsible.[17] The strength of this feeling may go a long way toward explaining their favorable reaction to the zero-base budget and all its extra work—even—indeed, *especially* when few changes were made as a result of it.

The zero-base budget experiment had focused attention on the budgetary process. For the first time in many years, a Secretary of Agriculture had attended department budget hearings and had made it known that he considered budgeting of primary importance. As a result, many officials informed us that, "There was a higher interest in budgeting than ever before." Much more time was spent on budgeting: "I worked ninety hours a week and still didn't have nearly enough time." "A tremendous number of man-hours were involved. I spent at least twice as much time on budgeting this year, lots of Saturdays and evenings." Budget people discovered that their function was rated more highly as program people became more involved in budgeting and were "forced . . . to sit down and justify their programs." And, as program personnel worked on budget justifications, they liked the feeling of being more involved in their activities regardless of whether they wanted to change them. They might well have learned as much (or more) in other years if they had spent as much time and energy on budgeting. The zero-base approach had value here not so much because it was necessarily a better way of planning a budget, but because it was a *different* one which prompted them to focus their attention on budgeting.

A large part of the felt benefits of engaging in zero-base budgeting may stem, therefore, from the well-known Hawthorne effect [18] in which the content of the experiment is less important than the fact that the sense of importance of those engaged in the experiment is enhanced. Greater interest and attention is devoted to the activity in question and the people who engage in it. Consequently, they feel that others are more interested in them and that, perhaps, their problems are in some sense better understood, regardless of whether this understanding is objectively real or leads to specific consequences for the pattern of decisions. Thus agency people felt good at being able to educate their departmental superiors. Top departmental officials believed that the zero-base approach helped agency people see their work in perspective. Through being compelled to justify the existence of their agency's programs, they would see how it fit into the total operations carried out by the Department of Agriculture. This line of reasoning may help explain why many officials were certain that the zero-base approach had helped people at other levels in the hierarchy, even if they were unable to suggest any way in which it had helped them.

POLITICAL USE OF BUDGET

Our analysis would not be complete without noting that the zero-base method of budgeting—whose advocates present it as a means of focusing on costs and benefits rather than on political maneuvering—was used for strategic purposes, thereby enhancing its appeal to some officials. They felt that the zero-base procedure was useful in dealing with the Bureau of the Budget and the appropriations committees. "We've examined these requests from the ground up," they would say in justifying their requests as "solid" and not subject to cuts. By stating that the desirability of changes had emerged from the zero-base analysis, several officials had the opportunity to call attention to changes they had wanted in previous years. In this way one agency was able to get approval for building funds denied the previous year. In general, the zero-base experiment helped those who had previously decided they wanted to review a program by providing them with an excellent reason for not delaying the review. Resistance to providing essential information was overcome to some extent because top agency officials "were armed with weapons which forced . . . the disgorging of the information they needed to get. . . . This is often like pulling teeth." And having proposed the change they had in mind, the responsible officials could use the belief that the zero-base approach was more rational to make their colleagues more amenable to the change.

ATTITUDE TOWARD ANNUAL ZERO-BASE BUDGET

No one suggested that the zero-base approach be followed every year. Among those who felt that the experiment should be repeated, the most common suggestions were: "not every year, periodically," "at intervals, every few years," or "every five years or so." Since new officials would stand to benefit the most, such officials reasoned, a zero-base budget would be useful only with changes in administration. Another view was that budgets changed little from year to year, so that an annual zero-base budget would result in "duplicating the same pages." The authors were cautioned to "remember that the budgetary process is not the only decision-making process for setting policy. Parts of operations are considered through other channels all the time." The general conclusion was that the zero-base method might be useful every five years "for a reference document," or "to find out where you are now," or so "we'll have a more recent base." It is apparent that even those who found some use for the zero-base approach began to assimilate it to the more familiar incremental method. They would use it from time to time to "take inventory" as one put it, and then take their bearings for the immediate future from that date.

Recommendations

No one, least of all the authors, would claim that an innovation like zero-base budgeting, which was confined to a single department for a single year, can be conclusively evaluated on the basis of this experience alone. Since this was the only experiment of its kind, however, it seems desirable to attempt at least a tentative appraisal. The first conclusion would be that comprehensive budgeting vastly overestimates man's limited ability to calculate and grossly underestimates the importance of political and technological constraints. The required calculations could not be made and would not have led to substantial changes. As a result, a great deal of effort went into zero-base budgeting with few specific changes attributable to this costly method.[19]

Had much more time been available, it might have been possible for the department to develop work-load measures for more programs. With more time and experience, the initial confusion might also have been overcome; but the basic problem of the zero-base budget still would not have been solved. In order to compare activities on the department-wide basis under a zero-base budget, the top officials would have had to develop categories cutting across agency programs, together with methods of relating their costs and benefits. Present methods of calculation are not equal to this task.

Failure to consider the contributions of the existing budgetary process toward calculation distorts the magnitude of the problem. New programs and substantial increases and decreases in old programs do receive close attention. The political system opens up subjects to special scrutiny as interest groups, politicians, or bureaucrats, demand an investigation. What escapes scrutiny is not the whole but only certain parts, which carry on much as before. The fact that certain activities do not receive intensive scrutiny is hardly reason for repeating everything every year. Indeed, we would argue that attempts to do everything are not only self-defeating, they are inefficient in diverting resources from tasks which can be managed and give promise of some results.

We advocate following an incremental approach, making use of the division of labor in government. Attention may be focused on those activities which do not change much from year to year, since these are the ones that may escape periodic review. Since they do not alter radically, a thorough review every four of five years ought to be sufficient. Nor need any one organization do it all. Department budget offices, the bureaus themselves, the Bureau of the Budget, and the House and Senate appropriations subcommittees and their investigating staffs, might use sampling techniques so that they review a few programs of this kind every year.[20] The results could then be used to see if more activity was warranted the next year. In this way a large part of the problem may be met while adding a little to the burden of calculation for any one participant.

Narrowing, fragmenting, and dispersing these budgetary reviews has considerable advantages from the viewpoint of encouraging experimentation and innovation. Because no participant is overburdened, the most thorough analysis is facilitated. More active participation by high-level officials is encouraged because the material to be considered at a given time is not overwhelming. As the knowledge and interest of top officials is fed back down the line, the significance of the activity and the importance of those who engage in it is likely to be enhanced. If these reviews can be freed from the peak periods of the formal budgetary cycle, the absence of immediate deadlines may encourage speculation and experimentation, while the increased probability of hierarchical superiors having time to listen would give promise that the efforts might lead to tangible results. The variety of organizations involved should also lead to consideration of a broad range of values and perspectives.

Although it may be useful at times to compel alterations in customary modes of analysis, there are other possibilities than comprehensive budgeting. One could as well move in the opposite direction and try a more radical version of incremental budgeting.[21] Instead of doing even a minimum amount of budgeting for programs that change little from year to year, these programs might be neglected for several years and efforts of the agency might be devoted to only a few major programs at a time. By shifting the emphasis every few years, it would be possible to direct the agency's efforts toward those programs that are undergoing the greatest amount of change and in which it is feasible to effect changes. Attention would thus be directed at those parts of the agency's budget which promise the greatest results from intensive analysis.

NOTES

1. We would like to thank the many officials in the Department of Agriculture whose generosity, time, and knowledge made this study possible. Thanks are also due to Rufus

Browning, Jesse Burkhead, Tom Blaisdell, Richard Fenno, Irving Fox, Frederick Mosher, Nelson Polsby, Allen Schick, and Larry Wade for criticizing various drafts of the manuscript, but we alone are responsible for the work presented here. The work was done while the senior author was a research fellow at Resources for the Future in Washington, D.C. The term "agency" refers to bureaus and other subunits in the Department of Agriculture.

2. See Aaron Wildavsky, *"Calculations" in The Politics of the Budgetary Process* (Boston: Little, Brown, 1964), Chapter 2, pp. 6–62.

3. See, for example, W. F. Willoughby, *The Problem of a National Budget* (New York: D. Appleton, 1918); A. E. Buck, *Public Budgeting* (New York: Harper, 1929); Commission on the Organization of the Executive Branch of the Government, *Budgeting and Accounting* (Washington, D.C.: U.S. Government Printing Office, 1949); Jesse Burkhead, *Government Budgeting* (New York: John Wiley, 1956); Arthur Smithies, *The Budgetary Process in the United States* (New York: McGraw-Hill, 1955); and Edward A. Kolodziej, Congressional Responsibility for the Common Defense: The Money Problem, *The Western Political Quarterly* 16 (March 1963): 149–160.

4. Quoted with evident approval by A. E. Buck in *The Budget in Governments of Today* (New York: Macmillan, 1934), p. 172.

5. "Some Shortcomings of Present Budgetary Practice," *Toward Better Budgeting* (Detroit: Governmental Research Association, 1941), p. 6.

6. Smithies, *op. cit.,* p. 16.

7. U.S. Senate Committee on Government Operations, Subcommittee on National Policy Machinery, *Hearings Organizing for National Security; The Budget and the Policy Process,* 87th Congress, 1st session, 1961, p. 1107.

8. David Braybrooke and Charles E. Lindblom, *A Strategy of Decision* (New York: The Free Press, 1963); also Lindblom's "Decision-Making in Taxation and Expenditure," in *Public Finances: Needs, Sources, Utilization* (Princeton: National Bureau of Economic Research, 1961), pp. 295–336.

9. See Patricia L. Kendall and Katherine M. Wolf, "The Two Purposes of Deviant Case Analyses," in P. F. Lazarsfeld and Morris Rosenberg, *The Language of Social Research* (Glencoe, Ill.: The Free Press, 1955), pp. 167–170. For excellent examples of the insight to be derived from an unusual case, see Herbert A. Simon, "Birth of an Organization: The Economic Cooperation Administration," *Public Administration Review* 13 (1953): 227–236, and S. M. Lipset, M. A. Trow, and J. S. Coleman, *Union Democracy* (Glencoe, Ill.: The Free Press, 1956).

10. Thomas Flinn, *Governor Freeman and the Minnesota Budget,* Inter-University Case Program, No. 60 (University of Alabama, 1961).

11. It should be clearly understood that this approach was being tried only at the Department of Agriculture and not in the Budget Bureau or Congress. As the "Instructions" pointed out, "Since it is anticipated that the Department Estimates for 1964 will be submitted to the Budget Bureau in accordance with existing . . . instructions, the justifications . . . will be primarily in terms of changes from 1963." Thus a list of "Increases and Decreases, 1964, Compared with Latest Estimate, 1963," was also requested of each agency.

12. An official at the Department level writes that this "sentence . . . appears to . . . contain an erroneous conclusion. As the author of the sentence referred to, I can clearly recall that at the time we very explicitly rejected the proposition that zero-base budgeting as such necessarily had to take place without regard to over-all limitations on financial resources. I felt then, and still feel, that the 'ceiling' technique and zero-base budget development and justification are logically compatible. As the article points out, the zero-base budget approach that was used involved not only the question of whether or not work should be done but also the amount of work proposed and the price tags. Each of these aspects is logically a variable but can be adjusted within a program or between programs in the light of over-all available resources. The reason the sentence was included in the instructions (and in a sense it was superfluous) was merely to make it very explicit to the agencies that we were not making the assumption that the budget decision making system would suddenly tolerate all 'justifiable' expenditures merely by virtue of a change in the technique of presenting the budget, and that the Secretary in fact had an over-all objective that he wished to attain with respect to the Department as a whole. The sentence, of course, was not intended to mean, and did not mean, that the objective applied to each individual program and activity separately."

13. The Secretary and his staff, the six Assistant Secretaries and their staff assistants, and the Director of Budget and Finance and his staff.

14. See the statement to this effect by the late William A. Jump, a noted budget officer in the Department of Agriculture, quoted in Wildavsky, *op. cit.,* pp. 23–24.

15. Wildavsky, "Deciding How Much to Ask For," in *op. cit.,* pp. 21–31. Despite our stress on the political aspects of budgeting, more than one official wrote: "Greater emphasis perhaps could also have been placed on the importance of the political imperative on the

budgetary process. At the point that budgeting begins, i.e., gathering of base information, there is often only meager guidance on economic and other assumptions on which to base estimates which are compatible with sound practices. This guidance consists of admonitions to be economy minded—guidance which may become meaningless if interest in program emphasis suddenly increases."

16. See Robert K. Merton, "Manifest and Latent Functions," in *Social Theory and Social Structure* (Glencoe, Ill.: The Free Press, 1957), pp. 19–84. We have avoided use of Merton's "manifest and latent function" because functional analysis has some inappropriate implications for this paper.

17. The reassurance function of the zero-base budget is clear from two quotations. A newcomer said:

> Coming into a big Department like this you need landmarks on which to justify your own opinions of the budget. This is difficult when the budget this year is based on last year which is based on the year before. You sometimes had the feeling that they were building it like a sort of poor skyscraper, piling on more and more steel, without knowing where the building was headed. [After the zero-base budget] you had the feeling that you understood the programs better . . . and had more confidence in the value of the services being performed.

An old timer in the Department confirmed this view and gave it a special twist in terms of the functions performed for the agencies.

> When new administrators come in, they see things they didn't know the Department of Agriculture was doing. They figure this is just the top of the iceberg and get worried. If you take the whole iceberg out of the water and drop it on their desks, and they're too overwhelmed to look at it, they don't have an excuse to nag you anymore. This is the major benefit from the agency point of view: to the extent that their superiors looked at the stuff they were reassured; to the extent they didn't, they no longer have an excuse to nag them [the agencies].

18. Elton Mayo, *The Social Problems of an Industrial Civilization* (Cambridge: Graduate School of Business Administration, Harvard University, 1945); Fritz Roethlisberger, *Management and Morale* (Cambridge: Harvard University Press, 1941).

19. If one makes the conservative estimate that at least 1,000 administrators above the level of clerk-typist and messenger were involved in bringing together parts of the zero-base budget throughout the Department of Agriculture and its many field offices, and that they spent an average of 30 hours a week for six weeks preparing the data, above and beyond their usual budgetary work, then at least 180,000 man-hours may be charged directly to this activity. With the generous estimate that $200,000 worth of changes (without going into their desirability) can be attributed to the zero-base budget, it appears that the government achieved a return of something more than one dollar per hour (leaving out the cost of facilities, paper, clerical help, and depreciation of human talent). Nor do we know what these officials missed in terms of opportunities foregone during the time they worked on the zero-base budget. The point is not that the reader should place too much credence in these estimates (respondents differ as to whether we are too high or too low) but that under any reasonable estimate, the return to the government would be very small. Had anything like the same amount of effort been devoted to studies of filing, the flow of paper, or similar operations, much greater returns might have been achieved. Since half of these men were not usually involved in budgeting, however, there might well have been important intangible benefits that we have not taken into account.

One respondent went further and wrote that "The author might find it advisable or worth while to really set about analyzing the present cost of budget preparation and justification throughout its entire process. While this is an important activity, there is little written evidence as [to] the resources going into the preparation and justification of agency budgets within the Department, the Bureau of the Budget, and the Congress of the United States. A careful analysis might reveal that possible shorter steps or involvement by fewer people would be in order."

20. "It has been my experience during 27 years of government employment," an official writes, "that what you propose is frequently and regularly taking place in Department budget offices and in the bureaus . . . whether or not [it is] recognized and with little publicity."

21. See Wildavsky, "Toward a Radical Incrementalism: A Proposal to Aid Congress in Reform of the Budgetary Process" (from *Congress: The First Branch of Government* [Washington, American Enterprise Institute for Public Research, 1966], pp. 115–165), Chapter 23 of this volume.

16

BILL LONG:
PORTRAIT OF AN ACTIVIST

In this chapter we turn to the fascinating question of how the remarkable individual gets involved in community affairs, how he makes his will felt, how he operates, and what satisfactions he gets from his activities.

James F. "Bill" Long was born on January 7, 1913, in Baltimore, Maryland, the second oldest of six children in the family of a produce and seafood distributor. After attending high school in Baltimore, Long joined his father's business for a period of four years. During that time he came under the influence of clergymen from the Evangelical and Reformed Church who preached the social gospel with much fervor. Long became interested in the typical ideological concerns of the reform movements of the 1930s, bringing about greater economic justice, reducing racial prejudice, ending war. From this period we can date his passion for conversion, for getting other people to see the light, not only on religious but on social matters. With the intention of studying for the ministry, he enrolled at Heidelberg College, Tiffin, Ohio, and studied history and English until his graduation in 1940. By that time, however, he had lost his theological bent (though not his reformist ardor) and gave up a fellowship to the Yale Divinity School in order to take a position with the Ohio Farm Bureau and Cooperative Association, thus transferring his "missionary" activities to the cooperative movement. Six months later, he moved to Wooster, Ohio, as organizational and education director for that area. He was married in 1942 and has four children.

The coming of World War II found Long faced with a crisis because of his pacifist convictions. He initially registered as a conscientious objector but in the light of Nazi activities, his loss of religious conviction, and his own active temperament, he decided that he could not maintain this

From Aaron Wildavsky, *Leadership in a Small Town* (Totawa, N.J.: Bedminster Press, 1964), pp. 236–252. Copyright © 1964 by The Bedminster Press, Inc. Reprinted by permission.

position and went into the Army. He was in the Medical Corps from 1942–1946, went to Officers Candidate School and served as an administrator and a detachment commander at a hospital. He found that he had administrative talent and liked the work. He could never stand to watch mismanagement and, indeed, has never found an organization run by others which was handled as well as it could be.

After the war Long rejoined the Farm Bureau in Bucyrus, Ohio. In 1948 he attempted to pioneer a cooperative store in Lorain, and when CIO officials sponsoring it became less than enthusiastic, he moved to Oberlin to take charge of the Co-op stores.

Most people receive their primary satisfactions through their jobs, friends, families, hobbies, and not through participation in the seemingly esoteric and threatening realms of public affairs. Like them, Bill Long was so busy during the years from 1949 to 1952 trying to put the Co-op bookstore and foodstore on their feet that he had little time and inclination to do much else. But his work as manager of the Co-op bookstore brought him into contact with many people in the community, especially with college professors with whom he had to deal many times in the procurement of text books. Samuel Goldberg, a Professor of Mathematics, became a close confidant of Long's. Professor Kenneth Roose, who was to become his most intimate associate in the Oberlin Improvement and Development Company, and Professor William Hellmuth, who was to serve two terms with him on City Council, were both presidents of the Co-op. Interested in discussing national affairs, debating religious questions, and exploring such exotic areas as game theory, Long soon found that he had more in common with faculty members and their friends among the "out-of-town" executives, than he did with the downtown merchants.

At the same time his business activities brought him into conflict with leading members of the local business community. Upon discovering that the head of the People's Bank, Ira Porter, was hostile to the Co-op, Long transferred the organization's funds to the other bank in town. On one occasion he had difficulties in arranging essential loans and was able to survive only by going out of town for some Co-op funds and raising additional amounts through internal subscriptions. When he wanted to move the Co-op stores to advantageous locations, he was temporarily blocked, he believed, by the actions of John Cochrane who controlled the necessary leases. The stage was set for conflict but it took time to mature.

One day, as a result of prodding from the wife of an Oberlin College math professor, he decided to attend a meeting of citizens for the purpose of organizing a recreation committee in Oberlin. He soon found that there was a lot of talk, most of it terribly confused, in his opinion, and beside the point. Being irrepressible, Long then asked a series of questions to try and clarify what the participants were trying to do. When an unofficial recreation committee was set up pending the results of the campaign for the new charter in 1955, Long was asked to serve. After the charter was approved, and an official commission of five was appointed by council, Long was chosen again. A year later it transpired that no one else sought the job of chairman of the Recreation Commission, and that Long's activity seemed to make him the logical choice. As he put it, "I'd just as soon run it if I'm going to be on it." The incident illustrates a typical process of self-selection: an individual manifests interest in and shows some capacity for a particular chore; he is immediately drawn in by others who are looking for people willing to work. The incident also shows certain of Long's most prominent characteristics, his impatience with what he considers sloppy thought and procedure, and his desire to run things more effectively as he views effectiveness.

When it became known that Long was willing to do things, he became drawn into other activities. A committee to promote fluoridation had been established and someone told its chairman that Long was good at writing advertisements (he had done some snappy ones for the Co-op). Ken Roose brought Long in as a member of the Board of the American Civil Liberties Union.

During this period Long was a member of the NAACP as well, reflecting his life-time interest in eliminating racial prejudice. He hired Negroes in the Co-op, gave them positions of responsibility, and sought to set an example for the community. He was thwarted by the unwillingness of the NAACP to take positive action, such as threats of picketing, to improve employment opportunities, and he constituted himself a one-man committee to prod and goad them into doing things. He would, on occasion, taunt his own employees about the Negro community's lack of action and its inability to use the ballot to reward friends and punish enemies. Looking back on these events, Long perceives a considerable change in the Negroes' willingness to vote and, to a lesser extent, to act in a manner to benefit members of their race. But he takes no credit for this, ascribing it, instead, to the determination of about a dozen Negro families in Oberlin.

In 1951, Long was still only mildly interested in town politics. A friend suggested that Long run for City Council and he agreed in a lukewarm manner provided that the friend got the required signatures on the nominating petition. The "campaign" consisted of one speech at a meeting. Long was soundly defeated.

By 1957, Long was much more interested and active in city affairs. He had a network of acquaintances, knew his way around, and had had some dealings with the City Council, serving as chairman of the Recreation Commission. When Dan Kinsey came up with the notion that the existing waterworks would eventually be abandoned and that the reservoir, together with a large arboretum owned by the college, would make a splendid city recreation area, Long did the organization work and pushed the idea, getting Councilman Andrew Stofan interested. Meeting opposition from other councilmen, Long arrived at the conclusion that this negative attitude reflected fear that a municipal swimming pool would involve interracial activity. (He was not aware then of the discussions within the Public Utility Commission related to the water problem.) During 1957 Long had begun to venture in the realm of real estate. Together with Ken Roose he had acquired some land near the new Co-op bookstore and the two men had made preliminary planning efforts to redevelop this area as a community shopping center. This led to reflection on problems concerning the community as a whole especially with regard to economic factors related to growth. It was the combination of these two interests: recreation and community planning which led to Long's decision to run for council.

Although Long came in third out of the first seven, he was named chairman of the council. This came about because neither Stofan nor Comings, the two vote leaders, wanted the job whereas Long was more than willing. Among other things, he stressed the need for an early selection of a chairman to take the lead in choosing a new city manager, the old one having resigned on election day.

During the pre-election period and in his first few months in office, Long had an opportunity to attend many council and commission meetings, experiences which changed his views about the difficulties which the city was facing. He had previously thought that there were a number of irreconcilable reactionaries, "old buzzards," running the town to suit themselves, determined to protect their own interests. In the election campaign he had complained about decisions being made by small groups at coffee time, all of them businessmen or their allies. But as Long came to observe their behavior he decided that while such groups existed, they were ineffective, did not know how to get things done. He found their procedures "hit and miss" rather than systematic. Their meetings rambled on without sharp questions being posed or determined efforts made to get all the relevant information. Most important of all, Long decided that there was no real attempt to plan, to anticipate problems, and as a result council reeled from one to another half-hearted attempt to meet immediate crises. He determined to change all this.

Since serving on council, Long has wandered far afield in gathering basic information about the problems a city faces. He reads extensively on city planning, drawing his basic philosophy from architect Victor Gruen, architect Eliel Saarinen's book entitled *The City,* and Lewis Mumford's recent book *The City in History.* For month to month stimulation in this area he is a regular reader of *Architectural Forum* and *House and Home,* two of the trade journals for builders.

Long sees his role as an initiator, builder of support, gainer of consent, and decider of wide-ranging policies. His task as a councilman and citizen, as he views it, is to be continually active on a broad front and to see that decisions are made (after public discussion) which he believes are wise. Naturally, he identifies his own views with the common interest. A passive role as registrar of other people's sentiments or keeper of the city's consensus is not for him. He feels his job is aggressively to promote policies (such as a new water system) desirable for the city and to veto others which threaten these goals. When other people propose policies he prefers, as in the housing code, he may be content to do his part in gaining consent and leave it at that. When serious opposition appears, he is ready and willing to take his side to the public and to present the case with full force. He not only recognizes the right of others to dissent, but he prizes discussion and takes pride in arranging the fullest possible opportunity for debate. Indeed, he has an almost mystical view of truth emerging from what others would call the market place of ideas, a feeling not unconnected, perhaps, with his zest and talent for debate.

Long does see certain limits in his role. Although clear in definition, they are rather fuzzy in practice. He does not deem it proper to interfere in administrative matters within the province of the city manager. But he tends to view the area of policy, belonging to council, as wide enough to do what he wants. Whenever possible, he will back up the City Manager and refer matters dealing with working conditions, traffic tickets, and that kind of thing to him. Long's close relationship with Dunn no doubt helps in this regard. Indeed, Long has insisted upon and largely secured an open, critical relationship with Dunn, in which both feel free to criticize the other and disagreements take place. It is mutually profitable, however, for both men to minimize their disagreements and their zealousness in defining their spheres of action helps prevent encroachments.

Dunn, and, especially, Long are pragmatists. They have held many discussions over what constitutes "administration" in a city like Oberlin, and have come to the conclusion that it is a combination of city manager and staff, council and its chairman, and boards and commissions. The way to get things done, they agreed, was to use this machinery in any possible combination in order to achieve the desired results.

The degree to which self-interest creeps into human affairs is difficult to describe with precision. The notion that what is good for General Motors is good for the country is well nigh universal. And if we need a reminder, Reinhold Niebuhr has insistently pointed out the degree to which self-love can contaminate the highest human aspirations. So far as he is conscious of his own interests, Long tries rigorously to exclude them from his official acts. He is not averse to taking actions which apparently run counter to his immediate interests, such as bringing in a chainstore to compete with the Co-op or opposing parking on a street near the bookstore. And when the downtown shopping center developed, requiring council action for parking space, he announced that he would not vote and would not run for reelection in order to avoid possible conflict of interests. It remains to be seen whether he is correct in his assumption that his moves for industrial development and his complementary council actions are both in the general interest.

For Long the explanation of his leadership is rather simple. He puts in a lot of time and energy, he is persuasive, and he knows how to do things in business and local affairs. This is not a bad short explanation. For our analytic purposes, however, it is desirable to essay a more detailed and systematic discussion of his resources (his bases of influence), the attributes and positions he uses to make an impact on community decisions.

There is no doubt that Long devotes more time to community affairs than anyone else in Oberlin except for the city manager who works at it full time. He is constantly thinking about city problems, working out policy alternatives, talking to people, taking action. As one resource can be converted into another, the nature of his job permits him to spend more time, and make more effective use of it, than would otherwise be the case. Although he spends much time working, he is free to attend to city affairs when the occasion demands. He is not tied to a particular schedule, and he uses various economizing devices to make the most of the available time. Working at the produce counter in the foodstore, he can talk to people about town problems. Going to and from the two Co-op stores, he can see people and have brief discussions. He keeps a list of things that need doing in his pocket, attends to them in spare moments, thinks about them whenever he can, catches people on the run.

Where other people have hobbies like golfing and fishing, Long is pretty much of a "cause" man and has been for most of his life except for the time spent in the Army. Prior to his college days the cause was working for what he calls the old-fashioned concept of the Brotherhood of Man under the Fatherhood of God. After college and war service the cause was the cooperative movement. In Oberlin, up until his election to council, it was the Oberlin Co-op. But after election it became the city with its many problems and complex relationships.

The pattern of Long's social life differs from that of other citizens. He does not like chit-chat or discussions about the weather. He does not socialize for the sake of going out or just to meet people. One result is that his evenings are largely "free" for community business. Another is that what social life he does have, and it is not inconsiderable, tends to revolve about his interests in the city. A good example is the origins of a study group in which he now participates. One night at a social gathering at Dunn's house attended by the Don Peases and the Longs, the three couples began speculating on the possibility of establishing a group where they might engage in discussion of philosophical subjects not necessarily connected with city problems, topics like religion, the purpose of life, and so on. Later they expanded the initial group to twelve. During the 1960 national convention period, four meetings were devoted to presentations about the rival candidates. City questions did come up sporadically and the individuals present had a chance to communicate about these before or after the discussions. One night some group member raised the question of quality in the schools and Long suggested getting Superintendent Duncan down. The offer was accepted, and a lengthy discussion ensued. One result was [a] new brochure advertising the school system. . . . Another was that school board member, George Hoover, who visited the group one night, made a very favorable impression and probably generated support in a circle which previously had suspected him of being a poor board member.

The time which Long spends is not a sacrifice for him; this is what he enjoys doing. He will think nothing of writing six drafts of a speech or report, revising continually in odd moments, to satisfy his desire to excel and to make the best possible impression for the policy he is proposing. He is a political man.

Time and interest are not enough; one also must have the energy to pursue one's objectives. It is an understatement to say that Long is phenomenal in this respect. Apparently tireless, he continually spews forth ideas and works at them. Of middle height, in good health and rather chunky, he manifests remarkable resiliency. Inevitably he comes in for his share of rebuffs, as in the early days of the industrial development campaign, but he can take a lot of punishment and come back for more. He enjoys the give and take, the rough and tumble of public affairs. What all this energy signifies for his personal psychology is beside the point for present purposes; the fact is that it exists and must be taken into account like any other imposing natural phenomenon.

Information is a prerequisite of influence. Ordinarily one must know that events are taking place and know something about them in order to affect the outcome. Bill Long is probably the best informed person in town (over the widest range of issues) other than the city manager. There are some who know more than he does about specific issues, such as Homer Blanchard on the light plant, but none who can rival him over the general field and over those issues, like industrial development, of which he makes a particular specialization. As regards information in the sense of knowing what is happening, Long tries to learn as much as possible. He sees or phones the city manager constantly, talks to other councilmen, city employees, and commission members, converses with customers in his stores, and seeks out others who are in a position to inform him. Though subject to much heckling, he occasionally goes down to the restaurant where the downtown businessmen hang out for coffee, and frequently manages to discover what they are doing, a technique that is handy at times when strategic moves depend upon knowing who is on what side, who is wavering, and who can be persuaded.

Referring now to information in the sense of knowledge about issues, Long is uniformly better prepared than his opponents. No doubt this must in part be a subjective judgment. But it is one which is supported by the evidence in this book and by many of his opponents who recognize a deficiency on their own parts in that respect. Typical of Long's emphasis upon being informed are the research he did on John Cochrane's record as councilman for use in the 1959 election campaign, and his familiarity with the various water plans useful in rebutting Ira Porter. Long's intelligence is high and he has a quick mind. But he is also willing to spend time and energy building up a storehouse of information. His answers are always based on some kind of evidence, and even if his opponents are correct in saying that his conclusions are highly fallacious, it is difficult for them to meet something with nothing.

Bill Long's position as Co-op manager provides him with many resources—control over jobs, access to money, a friendly clientele, a "dispensable" occupation, status as a businessman—which he has exploited with considerable success. (Unlike most retail merchants, Long's clientele is a "committed" group, held to him in part by the Co-op ideology.) It must not be thought that Long can use jobs in the traditional sense of patronage; he cannot and does not. But he can employ Negroes and, whether intended or not, this may be useful to him at election time and in raising his prestige among those interested in providing equal opportunities in employment.

By serving people at the Co-op stores and working with Co-op Board members, Long becomes identified with them and he gains a popularity which may be translated into votes, letters to the editor, or even more active support on various issues. We already have spoken of the value of his job as a listening post, information center, conversion hall, and general focus of activity which he can leave when he has to attend to other matters. Yet it is perhaps in a negative sense that being manager of the Co-op has been most helpful. Long has a reasonably safe job utterly outside the control of bankers, businessmen, college officials, or any others who might conceivably threaten him. He cannot be controlled through his job. Had the Co-op been unable to raise capital, the refusal of the local banks to lend might have proven fatal as Long was faced with the choice of losing his position, of knuckling under or leaving town. But this did not happen. His success in building the Co-op from a $30,000 a year business in 1949 when he came to a $750,000 a year business in 1960 has raised his prestige. It is only fair to add that this further infuriates his opponents among the downtown businessmen who cannot abide the thought that a "radical" with so "difficult" a personality has made a success of even a subsidized business like the Co-op.

Legitimacy, the acknowledged right to hold public office and exercise its functions, has obviously been a valuable resource for Long. It has given him access to information, a forum for publicity, a means of persuasion, and public acknowledgment of support (whatever that might mean) from voters. Most important, his position as councilman gave him one vote out of seven and the widespread expectation that it was proper for him to try to convince other members to support his views. While the position of chairman is chiefly an honorary one, it had extra advantages for Long during the two years that he held it. It enabled him to establish a special relationship with the city manager by making it customary for them to discuss all matters appearing on the agenda, a practice which Mayor Nord continues, though to a lesser extent. The position of chairman also legitimatized the notion that leadership should come from that direction. And in chairing the meetings Long was able to expedite matters on the agenda and see to it that the debate was carried on according to his conception of proper procedure.

Popularity is a difficult resource with which to deal. All we need say here, however, is that so long as he won victories at the polls, Bill Long's opponents could not do much to stop him. His popularity among Negro and high-income college people as well as out-of-town executives was an indispensable base for his influence.

That resource called skill is an important part of what makes Long an effective leader. Being intangible, it is often neglected, to the detriment of the study of politics. Properly used it may seem effortless and appear to require no explanation. Nor is it possible to show on every occasion that a less skillful person might have failed and a more skillful one might have succeeded. For the sake of convenience we shall speak here of technical skill, skill in persuasion, skill in coalition-building, and skill in devising strategies.

The ability to manage two stores, to run a development corporation, to juggle mortgages, to understand financial operations, has enabled Long to do things which other men could not. His skill as a business technician has served him well.

He has, moreover, proved himself to be an exceedingly persuasive person, capable of altering the views of others. He presents his case fluently, with a wide array of factual material, emphasizing the public interest involved, stressing the real coincidence in goals between himself and the other person. He is adept at feeling out the kind of arguments which will have attraction to specific individuals. He appeals to a sense of reasonableness by denying that his statements are perfect but asking whether the other person has anything better to suggest, because if so, he would certainly like to hear about it and give it serious consideration. The policy alternatives (or some selected set) at his fingers, Long marshals them in verbal columns so that one or two emerge as clearly desirable if not the only possible solutions. Whatever else happens, he is certain to present a barrage of arguments, sometimes assuming volcano-like proportions. Although some doubt has been expressed as to whether Long really convinces others or merely wears them out, these techniques are effective. And for those who are disposed to agree with him, Long's proclivity for explicit statement provides them with ready-made rationales, prepared for use when challenged, to justify their position. In a community where leaders exercise virtually no coercive authority over followers, a talent for persuasion is no mean asset.

Skill in building coalitions is perhaps the supreme art of the politician. It requires finding agreement among previously disparate and possibly conflicting individuals and groups. It demands finesse in convincing the participants that their varying desires will be served. Long demonstrated this skill (though only in part) by bringing conservatives into government to ward off criticism and expand support, by encouraging Negroes to participate and by being flexible about the form of various policies, such as accepting the housing formula which would win the most widespread support and the vote according to investment on the OID.

A sense of strategy is helpful to anyone who participates in collective life. It can be used to create opportunities and to seize upon the favorable moment. Opponents may be maneuvered into untenable positions. The kinds of strategies which Long pursues are rather simple and direct. His study of game theory has not, of course, resulted in any direct applications to the real world. But it has further sensitized him to thinking in terms of alternative approaches and different kinds of pay-offs. When a policy arises he asks himself which person or body has the formal right of decision. (. . . he may try to alter the locus of decision if the outcome seems destined to go against him.) From his store of past information he will concentrate on those necessary to make a majority. Knowing he cannot coerce, he will seek to persuade. If that fails, or he has reason to believe that it will, he will try to find someone on his side who has a better chance of approaching the key individuals. . . . He is not averse to rumors suggesting that he has inordinate power because this leads to a sense of fatalism on the part of his opponents—he cannot be beaten—and makes him seem more powerful than he really is. He maintains that certain issues will always be fought tooth and nail by a handful of conservative people, that the job is always to force these people to give reasons for their positions, and that if this is done their arguments will fall apart and they will then be defeated. Long is concerned not only with the immediate present but with future decisions and seeks to recruit a corps of personnel who share his general orientation. He is tireless in suggesting that this or that person serve on a committee or commission and rarely misses an opportunity to draw a person into more active participation. Sometimes, as with Blanchard and Nord, people who were already on city commissions when he was elected, and who were also well known as conservative Republicans, he urges them to move from the commissions and run for the council seat. To be better prepared than his opponents, to move first and fast, at the right place and time, to come early and stay late, represents his mode of operation.

The multiple activities of Bill Long provide an example *par excellence* of the pyramiding of resources. Long first used his energy to build up the Co-op. His solid position there was used to gain contacts, information and popularity. These resources were then parlayed into a council victory which was used to gain further popularity and respect. Legitimacy and respect were used to further the cause of industrial development; some success here increased his ability to raise funds to promote a shopping center which, in turn, increased his chances of fostering the type of community development which he preferred. While it is conceivable that Long might have done even more than he has, there can be little doubt that he has exploited the resources available to him at a higher rate and with greater efficiency than anyone in town with the possible exception of the city manager. Since there are inevitably vast reservoirs of resources which may be tapped when their possessors feel sufficiently concerned to make this worthwhile, Long's pyramiding was eventually answered by increased and more intensive opposition.

What kind of a person is Bill Long? In attempting to answer this question, we do not intend, even if it were possible, to provide a psychological case study. Knowledge of political psychology is not sufficiently advanced to permit us to say that under "X" conditions certain characteristics will probably lead an individual to "Y" political activity and under "A" conditions to "B" activity. Instead of relying on this fascinating but inconclusive procedure, let us seek out politically relevant aspects of Bill Long's personality based on depth interviews lasting several hours, observation over an extensive period of time, and a questionnaire he filled out and made available.

Bill Long is an activist. He cares deeply about local and national politics, though not state politics. He votes in all elections, talks incessantly about public affairs, writes to public officials, expresses opinions frequently, is a Democratic precinct committeeman, contributes to campaigns, asks others for political support, and is approached to give his in turn. He has joined five organizations and is active in all to which he belongs. On anyone's index of political participation, he would score 100 percent.

Long evidences a high degree of civic obligation which is probably deeply internalized. He believes that what governments do is very important and that every citizen has an obligation to participate even if (though he is inclined to hedge a bit here) he really does not like it. He disagrees strongly with the notion that it is best to stay out of community affairs, and thinks it is probably true that participation in Oberlin politics raises one's prestige in the community.

Far from being a pessimist, or exhibiting feelings of impotence in the public arena, Long has an extremely high sense of political efficacy. Governmental decisions are by no means too complicated for the citizen to understand. Politicians do care about what he thinks. They do not really manipulate people very much. The community arena is open and subject to change by the citizenry.

Long may be described as a person who is sociable, aggressive, and confident. He likes to meet people, to argue with them and to convince them, and he is rarely at a loss for words or possessed by feelings of awkwardness. He utterly rejects the notion that he should not take sides in arguments between people he knows even though he recognizes that a person might lose friends by such actions. He believes that one must be aggressive to succeed in politics, that this is a risk which must be taken. Ultimately, he is confident that things will turn out well.

Everything that Long does demonstrates a tremendous need for achievement. The objective of man, he believes, is to strive and achieve. But he does not believe that he seeks achievement for the accumulation of power, prestige or wealth, but rather for an idealistic end which he would clearly define as being to obtain the best interests of the community. Long relates how, in discussion with Leonard Barr, one of the most successful of the out-of-town businessmen who eventually gave him support, he was prodded as to what he was really up to and responded with a now favorite saying of his: "There is a bit of the creator in every man, an urge to put something where nothing was, a desire to be able to say 'this happened because of me.'" Long says all this without embarrassment.

Linked with this drive toward achievement is a characteristic which could be described as a need for control over events. He insists that planning ahead is indispensable. He vigorously objects to the idea that an individual's success or failure is dependent on the operation of uncontrollable outside forces. On the contrary, he believes that the individual is responsible for his success or failure. He would stand with Cassius in proclaiming that the fault lies not in our stars but in ourselves.

Like most people in our society, Long is ambivalent about exercising power over others. He agrees somewhat with the notion that people should not exercise control over others but he is convinced that politicians have to exercise control over others in order to do their jobs. Thus he uses the legitimacy of public office to resolve this dilemma.

On the basis of some roughly comparative findings by others, it appears likely that the portrait of Bill Long we have presented is quite similar to that of other activists. They also tend to feel that they are effective, to internalize civic obligation, to enjoy socializing, to have a high need for achievement, to believe the individual is responsible for his own fate.

Why is Long so active? He would say that he thinks people *ought* to be active and that he is an active type of person. He would also stress the importance to the community of the goals which he has set out to achieve. The question arises as to whether his temperament is such that he would be active regardless of the content of the goals. Perhaps. But the goals are really inseparable from the activity. He might find it difficult to live with himself without the sustaining belief that his activity was useful for others besides himself. A desire to be of service may well be fused with a need to achieve.

It has occurred to Long that Oberlin may be too small an arena for his talents. Yet he feels that in a small town an individual can do concrete things and see the results in an immediate way that might not be possible, say, in Washington. There are many matters on which others are more proficient than he is, as he readily acknowledges. But in the realms of community development and the solving of civic problems he has yet to find anyone whose talent matches his. He would like to find such a person, to compare notes, to pit himself against him. Once, when his wife asked what he would most like to do for a vacation, he suggested attending one of those seminars for business leaders which he had read about in *Fortune* so that he could see if these leaders really were superior to him in solving problems; Long's few contacts with big businessmen have not convinced him that this is so.

There is in Long a joy in civic combat which few others share. He does not get involved in every possible combat—he has refused to become involved in controversies at the golf club and over welfare policies. He likes opposition, likes to overcome it, to outmaneuver it, to defeat it. Exercising his skills, picking the crucial element in a problem, solving it, brings him considerable satisfaction. If he can be accused of being insensitive on occasion to the feelings of particular individuals, he is acutely aware of group sentiments and has a feeling for dealing with them. Not given to introspection, Long is happiest when engaged in many activities. Where other men would wilt under the strain, he appears to thrive.

In conclusion, it is well to point out that the purpose of these comments has been to focus attention on a single individual whose leadership qualities mark him off from the mass. A sympathetic view has been taken in the belief that his qualities could be best appreciated in that way. Yet the writer is aware, and the reader can hardly have failed to notice, that many of the characteristics which make Long a leader also produce antagonism. His brash manner, informal attire, and generally aggressive behavior result in opposition and negative criticisms. An elderly lady once commented, "I could forgive him a lot if he would just button his shirt collar." The wide scope of his interests and activity make him an obvious target for hostility which he might not suffer if he were more specialized. The advantages he accrues from being manager of the Co-op are partially offset by the suspicion engendered by that organization and its label as a center of radicalism. His insistence on moving forward sometimes overpowers his awareness of the importance of timing, as when he brought up zoning ordinance difficulties about apartments over local stores just before the 1959 election, thus intensifying the opposition to him. His ability to pyramid resources has led to charges of conflict of interest and some uneasiness even among those who normally consider themselves supporters. It has led to his withdrawal from the council and enforced circumspection in some areas where the city is involved in industrial development. To say all this, however, is to signify that he has the defects of his virtues. For if he did not have these disabilities it is unlikely that he would be the kind of person he is, an outstanding leader in the community.

PART IV

Political Analysis

17

THE TWO PRESIDENCIES

The United States has one President, but it has two presidencies; one presidency is for domestic affairs, and the other is concerned with defense and foreign policy. Since World War II, Presidents have had much greater success in controlling the nation's defense and foreign policies than in dominating its domestic policies. Even Lyndon Johnson has seen his early record of victories in domestic legislation diminish as his concern with foreign affairs grows.

What powers does the President have to control defense and foreign policies and so completely overwhelm those who might wish to thwart him?

The President's normal problem with domestic policy is to get congressional support for the programs he prefers. In foreign affairs, in contrast, he can almost always get support for policies that he believes will protect the nation—but his problem is to find a viable policy.

Whoever they are, whether they begin by caring about foreign policy like Eisenhower and Kennedy or about domestic policies like Truman and Johnson, Presidents soon discover they have more policy preferences in domestic matters than in foreign policy. The Republican and Democratic parties possess a traditional roster of policies, which can easily be adopted by a new President—for example, he can be either for or against Medicare and aid to education. Since existing domestic policy usually changes in only small steps, Presidents find it relatively simple to make minor adjustments. However, although any President knows he supports foreign aid and NATO, the world outside changes much more rapidly than the nation inside—Presidents and their parties have no prior policies on Argentina and the Congo. The world has become a highly intractable place with a whirl of forces we cannot or do not know how to alter.

From *Trans-action*, December 1966, pp. 7–14. Reprinted by permission.

The Record of Presidential Control

It takes great crises, such as Roosevelt's hundred days in the midst of the depression, or the extraordinary majorities that Barry Goldwater's candidacy willed to Lyndon Johnson, for Presidents to succeed in controlling domestic policy. From the end of the 1930s to the present (what may roughly be called the modern era), Presidents have often been frustrated in their domestic programs. From 1938, when conservatives regrouped their forces, to the time of his death, Franklin Roosevelt did not get a single piece of significant domestic legislation passed. Truman lost out on most of his intense domestic preferences, except perhaps for housing. Since Eisenhower did not ask for much domestic legislation, he did not meet consistent defeat, yet he failed in his general policy of curtailing governmental commitments. Kennedy, of course, faced great difficulties with domestic legislation.

In the realm of foreign policy there has not been a single major issue on which Presidents, when they were serious and determined, have failed. The list of their victories is impressive: entry into the United Nations, the Marshall Plan, NATO, the Truman Doctrine, the decisions to stay out of Indochina in 1954 and to intervene in Vietnam in the 1960s, aid to Poland and Yugoslavia, the test-ban treaty, and many more. Serious setbacks to the President in controlling foreign policy are extraordinary and unusual.

Table 17–1 compiled from the Congressional Quarterly Service tabulation of Presidential initiative and congressional response from 1948 through 1964, shows that Presidents have significantly better records in foreign and defense matters than in domestic policies. When refugees and immigration—which Congress considers primarily a domestic concern—are removed from the general foreign policy area, it is clear that Presidents prevail about 70 percent of the time in defense and foreign policy, compared with 40 percent in the domestic sphere.

World Events and Presidential Resources

Power in politics is control over governmental decisions. How does the President manage his control of foreign and defense policy? The answer does not reside in the greater constitutional power in foreign affairs that Presidents have possessed since the founding of the Republic. The answer lies in the changes that have taken place since 1945.

The number of nations with which the United States has diplomatic relations has increased from 53 in 1939 to 113 in 1966. But sheer numbers do not tell enough; the world has also become a much more dangerous place. However remote it may seem at times, our government must always be aware of the possibility of nuclear war.

Yet the mere existence of great powers with effective thermonuclear weapons would not, in and of itself, vastly increase our rate of interaction with most other nations. We see events in Assam or Burundi as important because they are also part of a larger worldwide contest, called the cold war, in which great powers are rivals for the control or support of other nations. Moreover, the reaction against the blatant isolationism of the 1930s had led to a concern with foreign policy that is worldwide in scope. We are interested in what happens everywhere because we see these events as connected with larger interests involving, at the worst, the possibility of ultimate destruction.

TABLE 17–1

Congressional Action on Presidential Proposals from 1948–1964.

POLICY AREA	CONGRESSIONAL ACTION		NUMBER OF PROPOSALS
	PERCENT PASS	PERCENT FAIL	
Domestic policy (natural resources, labor, agriculture, taxes, etc.)	40.2	59.8	2499
Defense policy (defense, disarmament, manpower, misc.)	73.3	26.7	90
Foreign policy	58.5	41.5	655
Immigration, refugees	13.2	86.0	129
Treaties, general foreign relations, State Department, foreign aid	70.8	29.2	445

SOURCE: Congressional Quarterly Service, *Congress and the Nation, 1945–1964* (Washington, 1965)

Given the overriding fact that the world is dangerous and that small causes are perceived to have potentially great effects in an unstable world, it follows that Presidents must be interested in relatively "small" matters. So they give Azerbaijan or Lebanon or Vietnam huge amounts of their time. Arthur Schlesinger, Jr., wrote of Kennedy that "in the first two months of his administration he probably spent more time on Laos than on anything else." Few failures in domestic policy, Presidents soon realize, could have as disastrous consequences as any one of dozens of mistakes in the international arena.

The result is that foreign policy concerns tend to drive out domestic policy. Except for occasional questions of domestic prosperity and for civil rights, foreign affairs have consistently higher priority for Presidents. Once, when trying to talk to President Kennedy about natural resources, Secretary of the Interior Stewart Udall remarked, "He's imprisoned by Berlin."

The importance of foreign affairs to Presidents is intensified by the in-

creasing speed of events in the international arena. The event and its consequences follow closely on top of one another. The blunder at the Bay of
Pigs is swiftly followed by the near catastrophe of the Cuban missile crisis.
Presidents can no longer count on passing along their most difficult problems to their successors. They must expect to face the consequences of
their actions—or failure to act—while still in office.

Domestic policy-making is usually based on experimental adjustments to
an existing situation. Only a few decisions, such as those involving large
dams, irretrievably commit future generations. Decisions in foreign affairs,
however, are often perceived to be irreversible. This is expressed, for example, in the fear of escalation or the various "spiral" or "domino" theories of international conflict.

If decisions are perceived to be both important and irreversible, there is
every reason for Presidents to devote a great deal of resources to them.
Presidents have to be oriented toward the future in the use of their resources. They serve a fixed term in office, and they cannot automatically
count on support from the populace, Congress, or the administrative apparatus. They have to be careful, therefore, to husband their resources for
pressing future needs. But because the consequences of events in foreign
affairs are potentially more grave, faster to manifest themselves, and less
easily reversible than in domestic affairs, Presidents are more willing to
use up their resources.

The Power to Act

Their formal powers to commit resources in foreign affairs and defense
are vast. Particularly important is their power as Commander-in-Chief to
move troops. Faced with situations like the invasion of South Korea or the
emplacement of missiles in Cuba, fast action is required. Presidents possess both the formal power to act and the knowledge that elites and the
general public expect them to act. Once they have committed American
forces, it is difficult for Congress or anyone else to alter the course of
events. The Dominican venture is a recent case in point.

Presidential discretion in foreign affairs also makes it difficult (though
not impossible) for Congress to restrict their actions. Presidents can use
executive agreements instead of treaties, enter into tacit agreements instead
of written ones, and otherwise help create *de facto* situations not easily reversed. Presidents also have far greater ability than anyone else to obtain
information on developments abroad through the Departments of State and
Defense. The need for secrecy in some aspects of foreign and defense policy further restricts the ability of others to compete with Presidents. These
things are all well known. What is not so generally appreciated is the
growing Presidential ability to *use* information to achieve goals.

In the past Presidents were amateurs in military strategy. They could not even get much useful advice outside of the military. As late as the 1930s the number of people outside the military establishment who were professionally engaged in the study of defense policy could be numbered on the fingers. Today there are hundreds of such men. The rise of the defense intellectuals has given the President of the United States enhanced ability to control defense policy. He is no longer dependent on the military for advice. He can choose among defense intellectuals from the research corporations and the academies for alternative sources of advice. He can install these men in his own office. He can play them off against each other or use them to extend spheres of coordination.

Even with these advisers, however, Presidents and Secretaries of Defense might still be too bewildered by the complexity of nuclear situations to take action—unless they had an understanding of the doctrine and concepts of deterrence. But knowledge of doctrine about deterrence has been widely diffused; it can be picked up by any intelligent person who will read books or listen to enough hours of conversation. Whether or not the doctrine is good is a separate question; the point is that civilians can feel they understand what is going on in defense policy. Perhaps the most extraordinary feature of Presidential action during the Cuban missile crisis was the degree to which the Commander-in-Chief of the Armed Forces insisted on controlling even the smallest moves. From the positioning of ships to the methods of boarding, to the precise words and actions to be taken by individual soldiers and sailors, the President and his civilian advisers were in control.

Although Presidents have rivals for power in foreign affairs, the rivals do not usually succeed. Presidents prevail not only because they may have superior resources but because their potential opponents are weak, divided, or believed that they should not control foreign policy. Let us consider the potential rivals—the general citizenry, special interest groups, the Congress, the military, the so-called military-industrial complex, and the State Department.

Competitors for Control of Policy

THE PUBLIC

The general public is much more dependent on Presidents in foreign affairs than in domestic matters. While many people know about the impact of social security and Medicare, few know about politics in Malawi. So it is not surprising that people expect the President to act in foreign affairs and reward him with their confidence. Gallup Polls consistently show that Presidential popularity rises after he takes action in a crisis—whether the action is disastrous as in the Bay of Pigs or successful as in the Cuban missile crisis. Decisive action, such as the bombing of oil fields near Haiphong, resulted in a sharp (though temporary) increase in Johnson's popularity.

The Vietnam situation illustrates another problem of public opinion in foreign affairs: it is extremely difficult to get operational policy directions from the general public. It took a long time before any sizable public interest in the subject developed. Nothing short of the large scale involvement of American troops under fire probably could have brought about the current high level of concern. Yet this relatively well developed popular opinion is difficult to interpret. While a majority appear to support President Johnson's policy, it appears that they could easily be persuaded to withdraw from Vietnam if the administration changed its line. Although a sizable majority would support various initiatives to end the war, they would seemingly be appalled if this action led to Communist encroachments elsewhere in Southeast Asia.[1]

Although Presidents lead opinion in foreign affairs, they know they will be held accountable for the consequences of their actions. President Johnson has maintained a large commitment in Vietnam. His popularity shoots up now and again in the midst of some imposing action. But the fact that a body of citizens do not like the war comes back to damage his overall popularity. We will support your initiatives, the people seem to say, but we will reserve the right to punish you (or your party) if we do not like the results.

SPECIAL INTEREST GROUPS

Opinions are easier to gauge in domestic affairs because, for one thing, there is a stable structure of interest groups that covers virtually all matters of concern. The farm, labor, business, conservation, veteran, civil rights, and other interest groups provide cues when a proposed policy affects them. Thus people who identify with these groups may adopt their views. But in foreign policy matters the interest group structure is weak, unstable, and thin rather than dense. In many matters affecting Africa and Asia, for example, it is hard to think of well-known interest groups. While ephemeral groups arise from time to time to support or protest particular policies, they usually disappear when the immediate problem is resolved. In contrast, longer-lasting elite groups like the Foreign Policy Association and Council on Foreign Relations are composed of people of diverse views; refusal to take strong positions on controversial matters is a condition of their continued viability.

The strongest interest groups are probably the ethnic associations whose members have strong ties with a homeland, as in Poland or Cuba, so they are rarely activated simultaneously on any specific issue. They are most effective when most narrowly and intensely focused—as in the fierce pressure from Jews to recognize the state of Israel. But their relatively small numbers limits their significance to Presidents in the vastly more important general foreign policy picture—as continued aid to the Arab countries shows. Moreover, some ethnic groups may conflict on significant issues such as American acceptance of the Oder-Neisse line separating Poland from what is now East Germany.

THE CONGRESS

Congressmen also exercise power in foreign affairs. Yet they are ordinarily not serious competitors with the President because they follow a self-denying ordinance. They do not think it is their job to determine the nation's defense policies. Lewis A. Dexter's extensive interviews with members of the Senate Armed Services Committee, who might be expected to want a voice in defense policy, reveal that they do not desire for men like themselves to run the nation's defense establishment. Aside from a few specific conflicts among the armed services which allow both the possibility and desirability of direct intervention, the Armed Services Committee constitutes a sort of real estate committee dealing with the regional economic consequences of the location of military facilities.

The congressional appropriations power is potentially a significant resource, but circumstances since the end of World War II have tended to reduce its effectiveness. The appropriations committees and Congress itself might make their will felt by refusing to allot funds unless basic policies were altered. But this has not happened. While Congress makes its traditional small cuts in the military budget, Presidents have mostly found themselves warding off congressional attempts to increase specific items still further.

Most of the time, the administration's refusal to spend has not been seriously challenged. However, there have been occasions when individual legislators or committees have been influential. Senator Henry Jackson in his campaign (with the aid of colleagues on the Joint Committee on Atomic Energy) was able to gain acceptance for the Polaris weapons system and Senator Arthur H. Vandenberg played a part in determining the shape of the Marshall Plan and so on. The few congressmen who are expert in defense policy act, as Samuel P. Huntington says, largely as lobbyists with the executive branch. It is apparently more fruitful for these congressional experts to use their resources in order to get a hearing from the executive than to work on other congressmen.

When an issue involves the actual use or threat of violence, it takes a great deal to convince congressmen not to follow the President's lead. James Robinson's tabulation of foreign and defense policy issues from the late 1930s to 1961 (Table 17–2) shows dominant influence by Congress in only one case out of seven—the 1954 decision not to intervene with armed force in Indochina. In that instance President Eisenhower deliberately sounded out congressional opinion and, finding it negative, decided not to intervene—against the advice of Admiral Radford, chairman of the Joint Chiefs of Staff. This attempt to abandon responsibility did not succeed, as the years of American involvement demonstrate.

THE MILITARY

The outstanding feature of the military's participation in making defense policy is their amazing weakness. Whether the policy decisions involve the size of the armed forces, the choice of weapons systems, the total defense budget, or its division into components, the military have not prevailed. Let us take budgetary decisions as representative of the key choices to be made in defense policy. Since the end of World War II the military has not been able to achieve significant (billion dollar) increases in appropriations by their own efforts. Under Truman and Eisenhower defense budgets were determined by what Huntington calls the remainder method: the two Presidents estimated revenues, decided what they could spend on domestic matters, and the remainder was assigned to defense. The usual controversy was between some military and congressional groups supporting much larger expenditures while the President and his executive allies refused. A typical case, involving the desire of the Air Force to increase the number of groups of planes, is described by Huntington in *The Common Defense:*

The FY [fiscal year] 1949 budget provided 48 groups. After the Czech coup, the Administration yielded and backed an Air Force of 55 groups in its spring rearmament program. Congress added additional funds to aid Air Force expansion to 70 groups. The Administration refused to utilize them, however, and in the gathering economy wave of the summer and fall of 1948, the Air Force goal was cut back again to 48 groups. In 1949 the House of Representatives picked up the challenge and appropriated funds for 58 groups. The President impounded the money. In June, 1950, the Air Force had 48 groups.

The great increases in the defense budget were due far more to Stalin and modern technology than to the military. The Korean War resulted in an increase from 12 to 44 billions and much of the rest followed Sputnik and the huge costs of missile programs. Thus modern technology and international conflict put an end to the one major effort to subordinate foreign affairs to domestic policies through the budget.

It could be argued that the President merely ratifies the decisions made by the military and their allies. If the military and/or Congress were united and insistent on defense policy, it would certainly be difficult for Presidents to resist these forces. But it is precisely the disunity of the military that has characterized the entire postwar period. Indeed, the military have not been united on any major matter of defense policy. The apparent unity of the Joint Chiefs of Staff turns out to be illusory. The vast majority of their recommendations appear to be unanimous and are accepted by the Secretary of Defense and the President. But this facade of unity can only

TABLE 17–2

Congressional Involvement in Foreign and Defense Policy Decisions

ISSUE	CONGRESSIONAL INVOLVEMENT (HIGH, LOW, NONE)	INITIATOR (CONGRESS OR EXECUTIVE)	PREDOMINANT INFLUENCE (CONGRESS OR EXECUTIVE)	LEGISLATION OR RESOLUTION (YES OR NO)	VIOLENCE AT STAKE (YES OR NO)	DECISION TIME (LONG OR SHORT)
Neutrality Legislation, the 1930's	High	Exec	Cong	Yes	No	Long
Lend-Lease, 1941	High	Exec	Exec	Yes	Yes	Long
Aid to Russia, 1941	Low	Exec	Exec	No	No	Long
Repeal of Chinese Exclusion, 1943	High	Cong	Cong	Yes	No	Long
Fulbright Resolution, 1943	High	Cong	Cong	Yes	Yes	Long
Building the Atomic Bomb, 1944	Low	Exec	Exec	Yes	Yes	Long
Foreign Services Act of 1946	High	Exec	Exec	Yes	No	Long
Truman Doctrine, 1947	High	Exec	Exec	Yes	No	Long
The Marshall Plan, 1947–1948	High	Exec	Exec	Yes	No	Long
Berlin Airlift, 1948	None	Exec	Exec	No	Yes	Long
Vandenberg Resolution, 1948	High	Exec	Cong	Yes	No	Long
North Atlantic Treaty, 1947–1949	High	Exec	Exec	Yes	No	Long
Korean Decision, 1950	None	Exec	Exec	No	Yes	Short
Japanese Peace Treaty, 1952	High	Exec	Exec	Yes	No	Long
Bohlen Nomination, 1953	High	Exec	Exec	Yes	No	Long
Indo-China, 1954	High	Exec	Cong	No	Yes	Short
Formosan Resolution, 1955	High	Exec	Exec	Yes	Yes	Long
International Finance Corporation, 1956	Low	Exec	Exec	Yes	No	Long
Foreign Aid, 1957	High	Exec	Exec	Yes	No	Long
Reciprocal Trade Agreements, 1958	High	Exec	Exec	Yes	No	Long
Monroney Resolution, 1958	High	Cong	Cong	Yes	No	Long
Cuban Decision, 1961	Low	Exec	Exec	No	Yes	Long

SOURCE: James A. Robinson, *Congress and Foreign Policy-Making* (Homewood, Ill.: Dorsey Press, 1962)

be achieved by methods that vitiate the impact of the recommendations. Genuine disagreements are hidden by vague language that commits no one to anything. Mutually contradictory plans are strung together so everyone appears to get something, but nothing is decided. Since it is impossible to agree on really important matters, all sorts of trivia are brought in to make a record of agreement. While it may be true, as Admiral Denfield, a former Chief of Naval Operations, said, that "On nine-tenths of the matters that come before them the Joint Chiefs of Staff reach agreement themselves," the vastly more important truth is that "normally the *only* disputes are on strategic concepts, the size and composition of forces, and budget matters."

MILITARY INDUSTRIAL

But what about the fabled military-industrial complex? If the military alone is divided and weak, perhaps the giant industrial firms that are so dependent on defense contracts play a large part in making policy.

First, there is an important distinction between the questions "Who will get a given contract?" and "What will our defense policy be?" It is apparent that different answers may be given to these quite different questions. There are literally tens of thousands of defense contractors. They may compete vigorously for business. In the course of this competition, they may wine and dine military officers, use retired generals, seek intervention by their congressmen, place ads in trade journals, and even contribute to political campaigns. The famous TFX controversy—should General Dynamics or Boeing get the expensive contract?—is a larger than life example of the pressures brought to bear in search of lucrative contracts.

But neither the TFX case nor the usual vigorous competition for contracts is involved with the making of substantive defense policy. Vital questions like the size of the defense budget, the choice of strategic programs, massive retaliation vs. a countercity strategy, and the like were far beyond the policy aims of any company. Industrial firms, then, do not control such decisions, nor is there much evidence that they actually try. No doubt a precipitous and drastic rush to disarmament would meet with opposition from industrial firms among other interests. However, there has never been a time when any significant element in the government considered a disarmament policy to be feasible.

It may appear that industrial firms had no special reason to concern themselves with the government's stance on defense because they agree with the national consensus on resisting communism, maintaining a large defense establishment, and rejecting isolationism. However, this hypothesis about the climate of opinion explains everything and nothing. For every policy that is adopted or rejected can be explained away on the grounds that the cold war climate of opinion dictated what happened. Did the United States fail to intervene with armed force in Vietnam in 1954? That must be because the climate of opinion was against it. Did the United States send troops to Vietnam in the 1960s? That must be because the cold war climate demanded it. If the United States builds more missiles, negotiates a test-ban treaty, intervenes in the Dominican Republic, fails to intervene in a dozen other situations, all these actions fit the hypothesis by definition. The argument is reminiscent of those who defined the Soviet Union as permanently hostile and therefore interpreted increases of Soviet troops as menacing and decreases of troop strength as equally sinister.

If the growth of the military establishment is not directly equated with increasing military control of defense policy, the extraordinary weakness of the professional soldier still requires explanation. Huntington has written about how major military leaders were seduced in the Truman and Eisenhower years into believing that they should bow to the judgment of civilians that the economy could not stand much larger military expenditures. Once the size of the military pie was accepted as a fixed constraint, the military services were compelled to put their major energies into quarreling with one another over who should get the larger share. Given the natural rivalries of the military and their traditional acceptance of civilian rule, the President and his advisers—who could claim responsibility for the broader picture of reconciling defense and domestic policies—had the upper hand. There are, however, additional explanations to be considered.

The dominant role of the congressional appropriations committee is to be guardian of the treasury. This is manifested in the pride of its members in cutting the President's budget. Thus it was difficult to get this crucial committee to recommend even a few hundred million increase in defense; it was practically impossible to get them to consider the several billion jump that might really have made a difference. A related budgetary matter concerned the planning, programming, and budgeting system introduced by Secretary of Defense McNamara. For if the defense budget contained major categories that crisscrossed the services, only the Secretary of Defense could put it together. Whatever the other debatable consequences of program budgeting, its major consequence was to grant power to the secretary and his civilian advisers.

The subordination of the military through program budgeting is just one symptom of a more general weakness of the military. In the past decade the military has suffered a lack of intellectual skills appropriate to the nuclear age. For no one has (and no one wants) direct experience with nuclear war. So the usual military talk about being the only people to have combat experience is not very impressive. Instead, the imaginative creation of possible future wars—in order to avoid them—requires people with a high capacity for abstract thought combined with the ability to manipulate symbols using quantitative methods. West Point has not produced many such men.

THE STATE DEPARTMENT

Modern Presidents expect the State Department to carry out their policies. John F. Kennedy felt that State was "in some particular sense 'his' department." If a Secretary of State forgets this, as was apparently the case with James Byrnes under Truman, a President may find another man. But the State Department, especially the Foreign Service, is also a highly professional organization with a life and momentum of its own. If a President does not push hard, he may find his preferences somehow dissipated in time. Arthur Schlesinger fills his book on Kennedy with laments about the bureaucratic inertia and recalcitrance of the State Department.

Yet Schlesinger's own account suggests that State could not ordinarily resist the President. At one point, he writes of "the President, himself, increasingly the day-to-day director of American foreign policy." On the next page, we learn that "Kennedy dealt personally with almost every aspect of policy around the globe. He knew more about certain areas than the senior officials at State and probably called as many issues to their attention as they did to his." The President insisted on his way in Laos. He pushed through his policy on the Congo against strong opposition with the State Department. Had Kennedy wanted to get a great deal more initiative out of the State Department, as Schlesinger insists, he could have replaced the Secretary of State, a man who did not command special support in the Democratic party or in Congress. It may be that Kennedy wanted too strongly to run his own foreign policy. Dean Rusk may have known far better than Schlesinger that the one thing Kennedy did not want was a man who might rival him in the field of foreign affairs.

Schlesinger comes closest to the truth when he writes that "the White House could always win any battle it chose over the [Foreign] Service; but the prestige and proficiency of the Service limited the number of battles any White House would find it profitable to fight." When the President knew what he wanted, he got it. When he was doubtful and perplexed, he sought good advice and frequently did not get that. But there is no evidence that the people on his staff came up with better ideas. The real problem may have been a lack of good ideas anywhere. Kennedy undoubtedly encouraged his staff to prod the State Department. But the President was sufficiently cautious not to push so hard that he got his way when he was not certain what that way should be. In this context Kennedy appears to have played his staff off against elements in the State Department.

The growth of a special White House staff to help Presidents in foreign affairs expresses their need for assistance, their refusal to rely completely on the regular executive agencies, and their ability to find competent men. The deployment of this staff must remain a presidential prerogative, however, if its members are to serve Presidents and not their opponents. Whenever critics do not like existing foreign and defense policies, they are likely to complain that the White House staff is screening out divergent views from the President's attention. Naturally, the critics recommend introducing many more different viewpoints. If the critics could maneuver the President into counting hands all day ("on the one hand and on the other"), they would make it impossible for him to act. Such a viewpoint is also congenial to those who believe that action rather than inaction is the greatest present danger in foreign policy. But Presidents resolutely refuse to become prisoners of their advisers by using them as other people would like. Presidents remain in control of their staff as well as of major foreign policy decisions.

How Complete is the Control?

Some analysts say that the success of Presidents in controlling foreign policy decisions is largely illusory. It is achieved, they say, by anticipating the reactions of others, and eliminating proposals that would run into severe opposition. There is some truth in this objection. In politics, where transactions are based on a high degree of mutual interdependence, what others may do has to be taken into account. But basing Presidential success in foreign and defense policy on anticipated reactions suggests a static situation which does not exist. For if Presidents propose only those policies that would get support in Congress, and Congress opposes them only when it knows that it can muster overwhelming strength, there would never be any conflict. Indeed, there might never be any action.

How can "anticipated reaction" explain the conflict over policies like the Marshall Plan and the test-ban treaty in which severe opposition was overcome only by strenuous efforts? Furthermore, why doesn't "anticipated reaction" work in domestic affairs? One would have to argue that for some reason Presidential perception of what would be successful is consistently confused on domestic issues and most always accurate on major foreign policy issues. But the role of "anticipated reactions" should be greater in the more familiar domestic situations, which provide a backlog of experience for forecasting, than in foreign policy with many novel situations such as the Suez crisis or the Rhodesian affair.

Are there significant historical examples which might refute the thesis of Presidential control of foreign policy? Foreign aid may be a case in point. For many years, Presidents have struggled to get foreign aid appropriations because of hostility from public and congressional opinion. Yet several billion dollars a year are appropriated regularly despite the evident unpopularity of the program. In the aid programs to Communist countries like Poland and Yugoslavia, the Congress attaches all sorts of restrictions to the aid, but Presidents find ways of getting around them.

What about the example of recognition of Communist China? The sentiment of the country always has been against recognizing Red China or admitting it to the United Nations. But have Presidents wanted to recognize Red China and been hamstrung by opposition? The answer, I suggest, is a qualified "no." By the time recognition of Red China might have become a serious issue for the Truman administration, the war in Korea effectively precluded its consideration. There is no evidence that President Eisenhower or Secretary Dulles ever thought it wise to recognize Red China or help admit her to the United Nations. The Kennedy administration viewed the matter as not of major importance and, considering the opposition, moved cautiously in suggesting change. Then came the war in Vietnam. If the advantages for foreign policy had been perceived to be much higher, then Kennedy or Johnson might have proposed changing American policy toward recognition of Red China.

One possible exception, in the case of Red China, however, does not seem sufficient to invalidate the general thesis that Presidents do considerably better in getting their way in foreign and defense policy than in domestic policies.

The World Influence

The forces impelling Presidents to be concerned with the widest range of foreign and defense policies also affect the ways in which they calculate their power stakes. As Kennedy used to say, "Domestic policy . . . can only defeat us; foreign policy can kill us."

It no longer makes sense for Presidents to "play politics" with foreign and defense policies. In the past, Presidents might have thought that they could gain by prolonged delay or by not acting at all. The problem might disappear or be passed on to their successors. Presidents must now expect to pay the high costs themselves if the world situation deteriorates. The advantages of pursuing a policy that is viable in the world, that will not blow up on Presidents or their fellow citizens, far outweigh any temporary political disadvantages accrued in supporting an initially unpopular policy. Compared with domestic affairs, Presidents engaged in world politics are immensely more concerned with meeting problems on their own terms. Who supports and opposes a policy, though a matter of considerable interest, does not assume the crucial importance that it does in domestic affairs. The best policy Presidents can find is also the best politics.

The fact that there are numerous foreign and defense policy situations competing for a President's attention means that it is worthwhile to organize political activity in order to affect his agenda. For if a President pays more attention to certain problems he may develop different preferences; he may seek and receive different advice; his new calculations may lead him to devote greater resources to seeking a solution. Interested Congressmen may exert influence not by directly determining a Presidential decision, but indirectly by making it costly for a President to avoid reconsidering the basis for his action. For example, citizen groups, such as those concerned with a change in China policy, may have an impact simply by keeping their proposals on the public agenda. A President may be compelled to reconsider a problem even though he could not overtly be forced to alter the prevailing policy.

In foreign affairs we may be approaching the stage where knowledge is power. There is a tremendous receptivity to good ideas in Washington. Most anyone who can present a convincing rationale for dealing with a hard world finds a ready audience. The best way to convince Presidents to follow a desired policy is to show that it might work. A man like McNamara thrives because he performs; he comes up with answers he can defend. It is, to be sure, extremely difficult to devise good policies or to predict their consequences accurately. Nor is it easy to convince others that a given policy is superior to other alternatives. But it is the way to influence with Presidents. For if they are convinced that the current policy is best, the likelihood of gaining sufficient force to compel a change is quite small. The man who can build better foreign policies will find Presidents beating a path to his door.

NOTE

1. See Seymour Martin Lipset, "The President, the Polls, and Vietnam," *Trans-action,* September–October 1966.

18

BUDGETING AS A
POLITICAL PROCESS

Budgets are predictions. They attempt to specify connections between words and numbers on the budget documents and future human behavior. Whether or not the behavior intended by the authors of the budget actually takes place is a question of empirical observation rather than one of definition. The budget of the Brazilian government, for example, has long been known as "a great lie" (Alionar Baleeiro, reported by Frank Sherwood), with little if any connection between what is spent for various purposes and what is contained in the formal document. Nor is there any necessary connection between the budgets of Soviet and American industrial firms and the expenditures they make or the actions they take.[1]

Budgeting is concerned with the translation of financial resources into human purposes. Since funds are limited, a budget may become a mechanism for allocating resources. If emphasis is placed on receiving the largest returns for a given sum of money, or on obtaining the desired objectives at the lowest cost, a budget may become an instrument for pursuing efficiency.[2] A proposed budget may represent an organization's expectations; it may contain the amounts which the organization expects to spend. A budget may also reflect organizational aspirations; it may contain figures the organization hopes to receive under favorable conditions. Since the amounts requested often have an effect on the amounts received, budget proposals are often strategies. The total sum of money and its distribution among various activities may be designed to have a favorable impact in support of an organization's goals. As each participant acts on the budget he receives information on the preferences of others and communicates his own desires through the choices he makes. Here a budget emerges as a

From David L. Sills, ed., *The International Encyclopedia of the Social Sciences* (New York: Crowell Collier and Macmillan, 1968), 2: 192–199. Copyright © 1968 by Crowell Collier and Macmillan, Inc. Reprinted by permission of the publisher.

network of communications in which information is being continuously generated and fed back to the participants. Once enacted a budget becomes a precedent; the fact that something has been done before vastly increases the chances that it will be done again.[3]

For our purposes we shall conceive of budgets as attempts to allocate financial resources through political processes. If politics is regarded as conflict over whose preferences are to prevail in the determination of policy, then the budget records the outcomes of this struggle. If one asks who gets what the (public or private) organization has to give, then the answers for a moment in time are recorded in the budget. If organizations are viewed as political coalitions,[4] budgets are mechanisms through which subunits bargain over conflicting goals, make side-payments, and try to motivate one another to accomplish their objectives.

Viewed in this light, the study of budgeting offers a useful perspective from which to analyze the making of policy. The opportunities for comparison are ample, the outcomes are specific and quantifiable, and the troublesome problem of a unit of analysis with which to test hypotheses—there is no real agreement on what a decision consists of—is solved by the very nature of the transactions in budgeting. Although a major effort has been made to collect budgetary material from many different countries, levels of government, and private firms, the results have only been fragmentary at best. Very little is available in any language on how budgeting is actually carried on. From Stourm's classic work on the budget [5] to the present day, virtually the entire literature on budgeting has been normative in tone and content.[6] Yet the glimpses we do get of budgetary behavior in different systems suggest that there may be profound uniformities underlying the seeming diversities of form and structure.

Budgetary Calculations

Decisions depend upon calculation of which alternatives to consider and to choose. Calculation involves determination of how problems are identified, get broken down into manageable dimensions, and are related to one another, and how choices are made as to what is relevant and who shall be taken into account. A major clue toward understanding budgeting is the extraordinary complexity of the calculations involved. In any large organization there are a huge number of items to be considered, many of which are of considerable technical difficulty. Yet there is little or no theory in most areas of policy which would enable practitioners to predict the consequences of alternative moves and the probability of their occurring.[7] Man's ability to calculate is severely limited; time is always in short supply; and the number of matters which can be encompassed in one mind at the same time is quite small.[8] Nor has anyone solved the imposing problem of the interpersonal comparison of utilities. Outside of the political process, there is no agreed upon way of comparing and evaluating the merits of different programs for different people whose preferences vary in kind and in intensity.

SIMPLIFICATION

Participants in budgeting deal with their overwhelming burdens by adopting aids to calculation. They simplify in order to get by. They make small moves, let experience accumulate, and use the feedback from their decisions to gauge the consequences. They use actions on simpler matters they understand as indices to complex concerns. They attempt to judge the capacity of the men in charge of programs even if they cannot appraise the policies directly. They may institute across-the-board ("meat axe") cuts to reduce expenditures, relying on outcries from affected agencies and interest groups to let them know if they have gone too far.[9] Hospital boards in Great Britain, unable to determine what costs should be in an absolute sense, rely on comparisons with comparable institutions. County councils keep close track of expenditures in only a few major areas to cut down on the bulk of overspending. The timing of new starts on projects is used as a simplifying device for regulating total expenditures. Another way local authorities keep spending within limits is through the practice of "rate rationing," or allowing committees so many pence or shillings of each pound of income.[10] Industrial firms use the percentage of total industry sales or some percentage of earnings on assets employed before taxes in setting budgetary goals. Many organizations use the number of personnel as strategic control points in limiting expenditures.[11] Constraints are actively sought as in the common practice of isolating "prunable" items when looking for places to cut the budget.[12]

INCREMENTAL METHOD

By far the most important aid to calculation is the incremental method. Budgets are almost never actively reviewed as a whole in the sense of considering at once the value of all existing programs as compared with all possible alternatives. Instead, this year's budget is based on last year's budget, with special attention given to a narrow range of increases or decreases. The greatest part of any budget is a product of previous decisions. Long-range commitments have been made. There are mandatory programs whose expenses must be met. Powerful political support makes the inclusion of other activities inevitable. Consequently, officials concerned with budgeting restrict their attention to items and programs they can do something about—a few new programs and possible cuts in old ones.

When a British Treasury official warns in 1911 against "the habit of regarding each year's estimate as the starting-point for the next . . . ,"[13] one can be sure that the practice has become well established. Both the practice and the complaints continue unabated in Great Britain.[14] Incremental budgetary calculations can be found in such different places as Canadian provinces [15] and Michigan cities (where a sample budgetary guideline to department heads reads, "Budgets should be for the same level of service as the current year unless a variation is previously approved . . ." [16]

EXPECTATIONS OF PARTICIPANTS

Incremental calculations proceed from an existing base. By "base" we refer to commonly held expectations among participants in budgeting that programs will be carried out at close to the going level of expenditures. The base of a budget, therefore, refers to accepted parts of programs that will not normally be subjected to intensive scrutiny. Since many organizational units compete for funds, there is a tendency for the central authority to include all of them in the benefits or deprivations to be distributed. Participants in budgeting often refer to expectations regarding their fair share of increases and decreases.[17] Argyris [18] quotes a supervisor as observing that employees had a well-developed notion of a fair output. In talking about the Philadelphia capital budget, Brown and Gilbert [19] observe that every department got a share because projects were considered partly as contributions toward keeping the departments going. The widespread sharing of deeply held expectations concerning the organization's base and its fair share of funds provides a powerful (though informal) means of coordination and stability in budgetary systems which appear to lack comprehensive calculations proceeding from a hierarchical center.

COORDINATION AND SUPERVISION

The most powerful coordinating mechanisms in budgeting undoubtedly stem from the role orientations adopted by the major participants. Roles (the expectations of behavior attached to institutional positions) are parts of the division of labor. They are calculating mechanisms. In American national government, the administrative agencies act as advocates of increased expenditure, the Bureau of the Budget acts as Presidential servant with a cutting bias, the House Appropriations Committee functions as a guardian of the Treasury, and the Senate Appropriations Committee serves as an appeals court to which agencies carry their disagreement with House action. The roles fit in with one another and set up a stable pattern of mutual expectations, which markedly reduces the burden of calculation for the participants. The agencies need not consider in great detail how their requests will affect the President's overall program; they know that such criteria will be introduced by the Budget Bureau. Since the agencies can be depended upon to advance all the programs for which there is prospect of support, the Budget Bureau and the appropriations committees can concentrate respectively on fitting them into the President's program or paring them down. If the agencies suddenly reversed roles and sold themselves short, the entire pattern of mutual expectations would be upset, leaving the participants without a firm anchor in a sea of complexity. For if agencies refuse to be advocates, Congressmen would not only have to choose among the margins of the best programs placed before them, they would also have to discover what these good programs might be. Indeed, the Senate Appropriations Committee depends upon agency advocacy to cut its burden of calculation; if the agencies refused to carry appeals from House cuts, the senators would have to do much more work than their busy schedules permit.[20]

A writer on Canadian budgeting [21] refers to the tendency for an administrator to become "an enthusiastic advocate" of increased funds for his policies. When disagreements over departmental budgets arise, as they frequently do in private firms, the controller and the departmental representatives come to a meeting armed to the teeth to defend their respective positions.[22] The same interministerial battles go on in Great Britain, the Netherlands, and the Soviet Union, where "serious clashes" arise when ministries and republics ask for greater funds to fulfill their plans.[23]

In a discussion which deserves to be better known, W. Drees [24] points out that agency heads can defend the interests of their sectors because it is so difficult for them to relate their modest part in total expenditures to the overall budgetary situation. Anything they could save through a spirit of forbearance would be too small a portion of the total to make the sacrifice worthwhile. From their point of view, total expenditures are irrelevant.

The role of guardian or defender of the treasury apparently did not come naturally. In the early days of public finance in France, "Financiers appropriated to themselves without restraint the spoils of the nation, and used for their own profit the funds intended for the Treasury; the only restraint lay in the fact that when their plundering exceeded the measure of tolerance they were hanged. It was a summary procedure of control *a posteriori* . . ." [25] It took centuries to develop a finance minister like Louis Thiers, whose definition of his role included that "ferocity . . . needed to defend the Treasury." [26] The members of the U.S. House Appropriations Committee consider themselves guardians of the Treasury who take pride in the high degree of frequency with which they reduce estimates.[27] They reconcile this role with the defense of constituency interests by cutting estimates to satisfy one role and generally increasing amounts over the previous year to satisfy the other.

Among the legislatures of the world, however, guardianship appears to be quite rare. Drees [28] reports that in the Netherlands the legislative specialists concerned with finance, by advocating higher appropriations, defend the interests of the policy areas over which they have jurisdiction to a degree overriding party lines. Much the same thing happened in France during the Fourth Republic.[29] It may be that guardianship depends, first, on appropriations committees that have continuing power to affect outcomes—a rare occurrence in the modern world—and, second, on the development of cultural values and legislative mores that support an insistent financial check on the bureaucracy. Legislative committees in nations like Mexico, where virtually complete budgetary power is in the hands of the President, who heads the single great party,[30] or Great Britain, where party responsibility overwhelms parliamentary initiative,[31] are hardly in a position to develop a role of guardianship.

BUDGETARY GOALS

Possessing the greatest expertise and the largest numbers, working in the closest proximity to their policy problems and clientele groups, desirous of expanding their horizons, administrative agencies generate action through advocacy. But how much shall they ask for? Life would be simple if they could just estimate the costs of their ever-expanding needs and submit the total as their request. But if they ask for amounts much larger than the appropriating bodies believe are reasonable, the credibility of the agencies will suffer a drastic decline. In such circumstances, the reviewing organs are likely to apply a "measure of unrealism," [32] with the result that the agency gets much less than it might have with a more moderate request. So the first decision rule is: Do not come in too high. Yet the agencies must also not come in too low, for the assumption is that if agency advocates do not ask for funds they do not need them. Since the budgetary situation is always tight, terribly tight, or impossibly tight, reviewing bodies are likely to accept a low request with thanks and not inquire too closely into the rationale. Given the distribution of roles, cuts must be expected and allowances made.

The agency decision rule might therefore read: Come in a little high (padding), but not too high (loss of confidence). But how high is too high? What agency heads do is to evaluate signals from the environment—last year's experience, legislative votes, executive policy statements, actions of clientele groups, reports from the field—and come up with an asking price somewhat higher than they expect to get.[33] In Michigan cities, for example, city managers sound out councilmen to determine what will go or get by in their budgets.[34] Departments and local authorities in Great Britain commonly make assessments "of how much spending is likely to be acceptable to the governing body." [35] After first determining what the mayor, finance director, councilmen, and other key participants will "die for," together with other projects which "cannot be moved," the men in charge of Philadelphia's capital budget let other projects by if they seem sound and if the request is not too far out of line.[36]

The Bureau of the Budget in the United States takes on the assigned role of helping the President realize his goals when it can discover what they are supposed to be. This role is performed with a cutting bias, however, simply because the agencies normally push so hard in asking for funds. The bureau helps the President by making his preferences more widely known throughout the executive branch so that those who would like to go along have a chance to find out what is required of them. Since Congress usually cuts the President's budget, bureau figures tend to be the most the agencies can get, especially when the items are not of such paramount importance as to justify intensive scrutiny by Congress. Yet the power of the purse remains actively with Congress. If the Budget Bureau continually recommended figures which were blatantly disregarded by Congress, the agencies would soon learn to pay less and less attention to the President's budget. As a result, the bureau follows consistent congressional action; [37] it can be shown empirically that bureau recommendations tend to follow congressional actions over a large number of cases.

In deciding how much money to recommend for specific purposes, the House Appropriations Committee breaks down into largely autonomous subcommittees in which the norm of reciprocity is carefully followed.[38] Specialization is carried further as subcommittee members develop limited areas of competence and jurisdiction. Budgeting is both incremental and fragmented as the committees deal with adjustments to the historical base of each agency. Sequential decision-making is the rule as problems are first attacked in the jurisdiction in which they appear and then followed step-by-step as they manifest themselves elsewhere.[39] The subcommittee members treat budgeting as a process of making marginal monetary adjustments to existing programs, rather than as a mechanism for reconsidering basic policy choices every year.[40] Fragmentation and specialization are further increased through the appeals functions of the Senate Appropriations Committee, which deals with what has become (through House action) a fragment of a fragment. When the actions of subcommittees conflict, coordination may be achieved by repeated attacks on the problem or through reference to the House and Senate as a whole when the appropriations committees go beyond the informal zone of indifference set up by the more intense preferences of the membership. When one thinks of all the participants who are continually engaged in taking others into account, it is clear that a great many adjustments are made in the light of what others are likely to do.

BUDGETARY STRATEGIES

Having decided how much to ask for, agencies engage in strategic planning to secure their budgetary goals. Strategies are the links between the goals of the agencies and their perceptions of the kinds of actions which their political environment will make efficacious. Budget officers in the U.S. national government uniformly believe that being a good politician —cultivating an active clientele, developing the confidence of other officials (particularly of the appropriations subcommittees), and using skill in following strategies that exploit opportunities—is more important in obtaining funds than demonstration of efficiency. Agencies seek to cultivate a clientele that will help them to expand and that will express satisfaction to other public officials. Top agency officials soon come to learn that the appropriations committees are very powerful; their recommendations are accepted approximately 90 percent of the time.[41] Since budgetary calculations are so complex, the legislators must take a good deal on faith. Hence their demand that agency budget officers demonstrate a high degree of integrity. If the appropriations committees believe that they have been misled, they can do grave damage to the career of the offending budgeting officer and to the prospects of the agency he represents. While doing a decent job may be a necessary condition for success, the importance of clientele and confidence are so great that all agencies employ these strategies.[42]

In addition to these ubiquitous strategies there are contingent strategies which depend upon time, circumstance, and place. In defending the base, for example, cuts may be made in the most popular programs so that a public outcry results in restoration of the funds. The base may be increased within existing programs by shifting funds between categories.[43] Substantial additions to the base may come about through proposing new programs to meet crises and through campaigns involving large doses of advertising and salesmanship.[44] The dependence of these strategies on the incremental, increase—decrease type of budgetary calculation is evident. By helping determine the ways in which programs are perceived and evaluated, the forms of budgetary presentation may assume considerable importance.

One major strategy deserves separate attention—the division of expenditures into capital and expense budgets. In practice, as Mosher says, "The Capital budget is a catalogue of prospective budgets for which money may be borrowed . . ." [45] The attempted distinction between capital assets with future returns and ordinary expenditures soon breaks down under the pressure of avoiding tax increases or the appearance of deficits by borrowing for items designated in the capital budget.[46] The ideological emphasis on the size and growth of the deficit in the United States makes it likely that the introduction of a capital budget would permit substantially greater expenditures as apparent deficits become converted into formal surpluses.

Organizations wish to maintain themselves in their environment. For governmental agencies this can be taken to mean maintenance of political support from clientele groups and other governmental participants. We expect that policies are chosen not only because of any intrinsic merit but also because they add to, or at least do not seriously detract from, the necessary political support. The heads of agencies can expect to lose internal control, to be fired, to see their policies overturned, or even to find their organization dismembered if their recommendations are continually disapproved. They therefore seek to maintain a reasonable record of success (to guard their professional reputation, as Richard Neustadt puts it) in order to maintain the confidence of the key people in and out of their agency. Thus, they are compelled to consider the probable actions of others differently situated who have a say in determining their income. These notions may be tested by observing how agency requests vary with the treatment they receive from the Budget Bureau and Congress.

Suppose that we wish to explain the level of appropriations which agencies request of Congress through the Bureau of the Budget and the amounts which Congress provides through appropriations laws. The goals of the participants may be conceived of as constraints which are represented by the role orientations adopted by members of the appropriations committees and by top agency officials. Moreover, we know that budgetary calculations are incremental. Thus, it becomes possible to create in symbolic form, as linear, stochastic differences equations, a series of simple decision rules embodying the relationships we expect to find. Given the availability of appropriations laws and of Budget Bureau requests for individual agencies, the decision rules can be tested for their fit in accommodating the times series comprising 15 or 20 years' figures.

In the simplest form, for example, a decision rule might be that the funds requested by an agency in a particular year are a direct function of its appropriation in the previous year up to a normally distributed random error. A second decision rule might make allowance for the difference between what the agency asked for and actually received from Congress in the previous year. Should an agency decide to pad its request to make up for a cut, should it decide to insist on the worth of its programs despite congressional action—strategies such as these can be represented as separate decision rules. Davis, Dempster, and Wildavsky [47] are now able to show that basic parts of the federal budgetary process can be precisely described by a small number of relatively simple decision rules.

BUDGETS OF FIRMS

Treatment of budgets as political instruments is justified not only in governmental activities but also in industrial enterprises. A more political phenomenon than budgeting in Soviet industrial firms has not been invented. Rewards to managers depend on meeting production quotas assigned in economic plans. But the supplies, skilled labor, and financial resources are often lacking. The first consequence is that the quota is not set from above but becomes the subject of bargaining as the managers seek to convince the ministries that quotas should be as low as possible. The managers find it prudent not to exceed their quota hugely, for in that case next year's quota will be raised beyond attainment. The second consequence is that production is not rationalized to yield the greatest output at the lowest cost but is geared instead to meeting specific incentives. Heavy nails, for example, are overproduced because quotas are figured by weight. Maintenance may be slighted in favor of huge effort for a short period in order to meet the quota. Funds are hidden in order to provide slack that can be used to pay "pushers" to expedite the arrival of supplies. The list of essentially deceitful practices to give the appearance of fulfilling the quota is seemingly endless: producing the wrong assortment of products, transferring current costs to capital accounts, shuffling accounts to pay for one item with funds designated for another, declaring unfinished goods finished, lowering the quality of goods, and so on.[48] The point is that the budgetary system arranges incentives so that managers cannot succeed with lawful practices. Communist China reveals the same pattern.[49] When similar incentives are set up in American industrial firms similar practices result, from running machines into the ground, to "bleeding the line," to meeting a monthly quota by doctoring the accounts.[50]

As in the Soviet Union, American firms often use budgets not to reflect or project reality but to drive managers and workers toward increased production. Indeed, some firms base their budgets on historical experience plus an added factor for increased performance.[51] Budgets are conceived of as forms of pressure on inherently lazy people so that (to paraphrase Mao Tse-tung) the more the pressure, the better the budget. Inevitably, managers and workers begin to perceive budgets as "perpetual needlers." In some cases this type of budget leads to discouragement because it is apparent that whatever the effort, the budget quota will be increased. Since accounting takes place by subunits in the firm, it is not surprising that fierce negotiations occur to assign costs among them. As a result, top officials find it necessary to engage in campaigns to sell budgets to the units. Otherwise, sabotage is likely.[52] While some attention has been given to human relations in budgeting,[53] only Stedry [54] has attempted to explore the essential motivational problems of budgeting within a political, institutional framework. Yet without an understanding of the impact of different goals and incentive systems on human activity, reliable statements about the likely consequences of budget documents can hardly be made.

Intensive study of budgetary behavior has just begun. Despite the relative paucity of comparative data, patterns of behavior appear to be remarkably consistent across private and public organizations [55] and national and state boundaries. After the appearance of monographs on different budgetary systems in various environments, it should be possible to create a small number of budgetary models specifying the elements of the organization coalition, the distribution of roles among the principal actors, the most prevalent aids to calculation, the strategies which appear as responses to types of incentives, and the outcomes to be expected in terms of amounts requested and received. Computer simulation may be used to test the effect of shocks to the budgetary systems. The study of budgeting as a political phenomenon in an organizational context may then become a major aid in the comparative analysis of governmental policy.

NOTES

1. Joseph Berliner, *Factory and Manager in the U.S.S.R.* (Cambridge, Mass: Harvard University Press, 1957); Chris Argyris, *The Impact of Budgets on People* (New York: Controllership Foundation, 1952); Bernard H. Sord and Glenn A. Welsch, *Business Budgeting: A Survey of Management Planning and Control Practice* (New York: Control Foundation, 1958).

2. Arthur Smithies, *The Budgetary Process in the United States* (New York: McGraw-Hill, 1955).

3. Aaron B. Wildavsky, *Politics of the Budgetary Process* (Boston: Little, Brown, 1964).

4. Richard M. Cyert and James C. March, *A Behavioral Theory of the Firm* (Englewood Cliffs, N.J.: Prentice-Hall, 1963).

5. René Stourm, *The Budget* (New York: Appleton, 1917).

6. Smithies, *op. cit.*, Jesse Burkhead, *Government Budgeting* (New York: John Wiley, 1956); A. E. Buck, *Public Budgeting: A Discussion of Budgetary Process in the National, State, and Local Government of the United States* (New York: Harper, 1929) and *The Budget in Governments of Today* (New York: Macmillan, 1934); William F. Willoughby, *The Movement for Budgetary Reform in the States* (New York: Appleton, 1918) and *The National Budget System* (Baltimore: Johns Hopkins Press, 1927).

7. David Braybrooke and Charles E. Lindblom, *A Strategy of Decision: Policy Evaluation as a Social Process* (New York: Free Press, 1963).

8. Herbert A. Simon, *Models of Man: Social and Rational: Mathematical Essays on Rational Human Behavior in a Social Setting* (New York: John Wiley, 1947–1956).

9. Wildavsky, *op. cit.*, pp. 1–13.

10. Royal Institute of Public Administration, *Budgeting in Public Authorities* (New York: Macmillan, 1959).

11. Sord and Welsch, *op. cit.*

12. Royal Institute, *op. cit.*, pp. 115–116.

13. Henry Higgs, *The Financial System of the United Kingdom* (London: Macmillan, 1914), pp. 135–136.

14. Ronald J. Mitchell, *State Finance: The Theory and Practice of Public Finance in the United Kingdom* (London: Pitman, 1935); Royal Institute, *op. cit.*

15. T. H. McLeod, "Budgeting Provincial Expenditure," in *Proceedings of Fifth Annual Conference,* Institute of Public Administration of Canada (Toronto: The Institute, 1953), pp. 11–19.

16. Thomas W. Kressbach, *The Michigan City Manager in Budgetary Proceedings* (Ann Arbor: Michigan Municipal League, 1962), p. 41.

17. Wildavsky, *op. cit.*, pp. 16–18.

18. Argyris, *op. cit.*

19. William H. Brown, Jr. and C. E. Gilbert, *Planning Municipal Investment: A Case Study of Philadelphia* (Philadelphia: University of Pennsylvania Press, 1961).

20. Wildavsky, *op. cit.*

21. Norman Ward, *The Public Purse* (Toronto: University of Toronto Press, 1962), p. 162.

22. Argyris, *op. cit.*, p. 9.

23. Herbert Brittain, *The British Budgetary System* (New York: Macmillan, 1959), p. 216–217; William Drees, *On the Level of Government Expenditure after the War* (Leiden, Netherlands: Stenfert Kroese, 1955), pp. 61–71; Robert W. Davies, *The Development of the Soviet Budgetary System* (Cambridge: Cambridge University Press, 1958), p. 184.

24. Drees, *op. cit.*

25. Stourm, *op. cit.*, p. 536.

26. *Ibid.*, p. 69.

27. Richard F. Fenno, "The House Appropriations Committee as a Political System: The Problem of Integration," *American Political Science Review* 56 (1962): 310–324.

28. Drees, *op. cit.*

29. Philips M. Williams, *Crisis and Compromise: Politics in the Fourth Republic,* 3rd ed. (Hamden, Conn: Shoe String Press, 1964).

30. Robert E. Scott, "Budget Making in Mexico," *Inter-American Economic Affairs* 9 (1955): 3–20.

31. Brittain, *op. cit.*
32. Royal Institute, *op. cit.*, p. 245.
33. Wildavsky, *op. cit.*, pp. 21–32.
34. Kressbach, *op. cit.*, p. 5.
35. Royal Institute, *op. cit.*, p. 57.
36. Brown and Gilbert, *op. cit.*, pp. 71–88.
37. Wildavsky, *op. cit.*, pp. 4–42.
38. Fenno, *op. cit.*
39. Wildavsky, *op. cit.*, pp. 56–64.
40. Fenno, *op. cit.*
41. *Ibid.*
42. Wildavsky, *op. cit.*, pp. 65–98.
43. Kressbach, *op. cit.*, p. 51; Stourm, *op. cit.*, p. 348.
44. Wildavsky, *op. cit.*, pp. 101–123.
45. Frederick C. Mosher, *A Report to the Governor of the State of New York and the Mayor of the City of New York,* New York State–New York City Fiscal Relations Committee, 1956, pp. 65–84.
46. Burkhead, *op. cit.*, p. 182; Mosher, *op. cit.*, p. 70; Jacob W. Sundelson, *Budgetary Methods in National and State Governments* (Albany, New York: Lyon, 1938), pp. 146–148.
47. Otto Davis, M. A. H. Dempster, and Aaron Wildavsky, *A Theory of Budgetary Process, American Political Science Review,* 60 (September 1966), pp. 529–547. Chapter 19 of this volume.
48. Berliner, *op. cit.*
49. Ronald Hsia, *Economic Planning in Communist China* (New York: Institute of Pacific Relations, International Secretariat, 1953); Cho-min Li, *Economic Development of Communist China: An Appraisal of the First Five Years of Industrialization* (Berkeley: University of California Press, 1959).
50. Frank Jasinsky, "Use and Misuse of Efficiency Controls," *Harvard Business Review* 34 (1956): 105–112.
51. Charles F. Axelson, "What Makes Budgeting So Obvious?" *Business Budgeting* 11 (1963): 22–27.
52. Sord and Welsch, *op. cit.*, pp. 140–150.
53. Arnold A. Bebling, "A Look at Budgets and People," *Business Budgeting* 10 (1961): 15–18.
54. Andrew C. Stedry, *Budget Control and Cost Behavior* (Englewood Cliffs, N.J.: Prentice-Hall, 1960).
55. Aaron Wildavsky, "Private Markets and Public Arenas," *American Behavioral Scientist,* 9 (1965): 33–37, Chapter 29 of this volume.

19

A THEORY OF THE
BUDGETARY PROCESS

WITH *Otto A. Davis* AND *M. A. H. Dempster*

There are striking regularities in the budgetary process. The evidence from over half of the nondefense agencies indicates that the behavior of the budgetary process of the United States government results in aggregate decisions similar to those produced by a set of simple decision rules that are linear and temporally stable. For the agencies considered, certain equations are specified and compared with data composed of agency requests (through the Bureau of the Budget) and congressional appropriations from 1947 through 1963. The comparison indicates that these equations summarize accurately aggregate outcomes of the budgetary process for each agency.

In the first section of the essay we present an analytic summary of the federal budgetary process, and we explain why basic features of the process lead us to believe that it can be represented by simple models which are stable over periods of time, linear, and stochastic.[1] In the second section we propose and discuss the alternative specifications for the agency-Budget Bureau and congressional decision equations. The empirical results are presented in section three. In section four we provide evidence on deviant cases, discuss predictions, and future work to explore some of the problems indicated by this kind of analysis. An appendix contains informal definitions and a discussion of the statistical terminology used in the essay.

From *American Political Science Review* 60 (September 1966), pp. 529–547. Reprinted by permission.

I. The Budgetary Process

Decisions depend upon calculation of which alternatives to consider and to choose.[2] A major clue toward understanding budgeting is the extraordinary complexity of the calculations involved. There are a huge number of items to be considered, many of which are of considerable technical difficulty. There is, however, little or no theory in most areas of policy which would enable practitioners to predict the consequences of alternative moves and the probability of their occurring. Nor has anyone solved the imposing problem of the interpersonal comparison of utilities. Outside of the political process, there is no agreed upon way of comparing and evaluating the merits of different programs for different people whose preferences vary in kind and in intensity.

Participants in budgeting deal with their overwhelming burdens by adopting aids to calculation. By far the most important aid to calculation is the incremental method. Budgets are almost never actively reviewed as a whole in the sense of considering at once the value of all existing programs as compared to all possible alternatives. Instead, this year's budget is based on last year's budget, with special attention given to a narrow range of increases or decreases.

Incremental calculations proceed from an existing base. (By "base" we refer to commonly held expectations among participants in budgeting that programs will be carried out at close to the going level of expenditures.) The widespread sharing of deeply held expectations concerning the organization's base provides a powerful (although informal) means of securing stability.

The most effective coordinating mechanisms in budgeting undoubtedly stem from the roles adopted by the major participants. Roles (the expectations of behavior attached to institutional positions) are parts of the division of labor. They are calculating mechanisms. In American national government, the administrative agencies act as advocates of increased expenditure, the Bureau of the Budget acts as Presidential servant with a cutting bias, the House Appropriations Committee functions as a guardian of the Treasury, and the Senate Appropriations Committee as an appeals court to which agencies carry their disagreements with House action. The roles fit in with one another and set up patterns of mutual expectations which markedly reduce the burden of calculation for the participants. Since the agencies can be depended upon to advance all the programs for which there is prospect of support, the Budget Bureau and the Appropriations Committees respectively can concentrate on fitting them into the President's program or paring them down.

Possessing the greatest expertise and the largest numbers, working in the closest proximity to their policy problems and clientele groups, and desiring to expand their horizons, administrative agencies generate action through advocacy. But if they ask for amounts much larger than the appropriating bodies believe reasonable, the agencies' credibility will suffer a drastic decline. In such circumstances, the reviewing organs are likely to cut deeply, with the result that the agency gets much less than it might have with a more moderate request. So the first guide for decision is: do not come in *too* high. Yet the agencies must also not come in too low, for the reviewing bodies assume that if agency advocates do not ask for funds they do not need them. Thus, the agency decision rule might read: come in a little too high (padding), but not too high (loss of confidence).

Agencies engage in strategic planning to secure these budgetary goals. Strategies are the links between the goals of the agencies and their perceptions of the kinds of actions which will be effective in their political environment. Budget officers in American national government uniformly believe that being a good politician—cultivation of an active clientele, development of confidence by other officials (particularly the appropriations subcommittees), and skill in following strategies which exploit opportunities—is more important in obtaining funds than demonstration of agency efficiency.

In deciding how much money to recommend for specific purposes, the House Appropriations Committee breaks down into largely autonomous subcommittees in which the norm of reciprocity is carefully followed. Specialization is carried further as subcommittee members develop limited areas of competence and jurisdiction. Budgeting is both incremental and fragmented as the subcommittees deal with adjustments to the historical base of each agency. Fragmentation and specialization are increased through the appeals functions of the Senate Appropriations Committee, which deals with what has become (through House action) a fragment of a fragment. With so many participants continually engaged in taking others into account, a great many adjustments are made in the light of what others are likely to do.

This qualitative account of the budgetary process contains clear indications of the kind of quantitative models we wish to develop. It is evident, for example, that decision-makers in the budgetary process think in terms of percentages. Agencies talk of expanding their base by a certain percentage. The Bureau of the Budget is concerned about the growth rates for certain agencies and programs. The House Appropriations Committee deals with percentage cuts, and the Senate Appropriations Committee with the question of whether or not to restore percentage cuts. These considerations suggest that the quantitative relationships among the decisions of the participants in the budget process are linear in form.

The attitudes and calculations of participants in budgeting seem stable over time. The prominence of the agency's "base" is a sign of stability. The roles of the major participants are powerful, persistent, and strongly grounded in the expectations of others as well as in the internal requirements of the positions. Stability is also suggested by the specialization that occurs among the participants, the long service of committee members, the adoption of incremental practices such as comparisons with the previous year, the fragmentation of appropriations by program and item, the treatments of appropriations as continuously variable sums of money rather than as perpetual reconsiderations of the worth of programs, and the practice of allowing past decisions to stand while coordinating decision-making only if difficulties arise. Since the budgetary process appears to be stable over periods of time, it is reasonable to estimate the relationships in budgeting on the basis of time series data.

Special events that upset the apparent stability of the budgetary process can and do occur. Occasionally, world events take an unexpected turn, a new President occupies the White House, some agencies act with exceptional zeal, others suffer drastic losses of confidence on the part of the appropriations subcommittees, and so on. It seems plausible to represent such transient events as random shocks to an otherwise deterministic system. Therefore, our model is stochastic rather than deterministic.

The Politics of the Budgetary Process contains a description of strategies which various participants in budgeting use to further their aims. Some of these strategies are quite complicated. However, a large part of the process can be explained by some of the simpler strategies which are based on the relationship between agency requests for funds (through the Budget Bureau) and congressional appropriations. Because these figures are made public and are known to all participants, because they are directly perceived and communicated without fear of information loss or bias, and because the participants react to these figures, they are ideal for feedback purposes. It is true that there are other indicators—special events, crises, technological developments, actions of clientele groups— which are attended to by participants in the budgetary process. But if these indicators have impact, they must quickly be reflected in the formal feedback mechanisms—the actions of departments, the Bureau of the Budget, and Congress—to which they are directed. Some of these indicators (see section iv) are represented by the stochastic disturbances. Furthermore, the formal indicators are more precise, more simple, more available, more easily interpreted than the others. They are, therefore, likely to be used by participants in the budgetary process year in and year out. Present decisions are based largely on past experience, and this lore is encapsulated in the amounts which the agencies receive as they go through the steps in the budgetary cycle.

For all the reasons discussed in this section, our models of the budgetary process are linear, stable over periods of time, stochastic, and strategic in character. They are "as if" models: an excellent fit for a given model means only that the actual behavior of the participants has an effect equivalent to the equations of the model. The models, taken as a whole, represent a set of decision rules for Congress and the agencies.

II. The Models

In our models we aggregate elements of the decision-making structure. The Budget Bureau submissions for the agency are used instead of separate figures for the two kinds of organizations. Similarly, at this stage in our analysis, we use final congressional appropriations instead of separating out committee action, floor action, conference committee recommendations, and so on. We wish to emphasize that although there may be some aggregation bias in the estimation of the postulated structure of decision, this does not affect the linearity of the aggregate relationships. If the decisions of an agency and the Bureau of the Budget with regard to that agency depend linearly upon the same variable (as we hypothesize), then the aggregated decision rule of the two, treated as a single entity, will depend linearly upon that variable. By a similar argument, the various congressional participants can be grouped together so that Congress can be regarded as a single decision-making entity. While the aggregating procedure may result in grouping positive and negative influences together, this manifestly does not affect the legitimacy of the procedure; linearity is maintained.[3]

Our models concern only the requests presented in the President's budget for an individual agency and the behavior of Congress as a whole with regard to the agency's appropriation. The models do not attempt to estimate the complete decision-making structure for each agency from bureau requests to departments to submission through the Budget Bureau to possible final action in the Senate and House. There are several reasons for remaining content with the aggregated figures we use. First, the number of possible decision rules which must be considered grows rapidly as each new participant is added. We would soon be overwhelmed by the sheer number of rules invoked. Second, there are genuine restrictions placed on the number of structural parameters we can estimate because (a) some data, such as bureau requests to departments, are unavailable, and (b) only short time series are meaningful for most agencies. It would make no sense, for example, to go back in time beyond the end of World War II when most domestic activity was disrupted.[4]

Since the agencies use various strategies and Congress may respond to them in various ways, we propose several alternative systems of equations. These equations represent alternative decision rules which may be followed by Congressional and agency-Budget Bureau participants in the budgetary process. One important piece of data for agency-Budget Bureau personnel who are formulating appropriations requests is the most recent congressional appropriation. Thus, we make considerable use of the concept "base," operationally defined as the previous congressional appropriation for an agency, in formulating our decision rules. Since the immediate past exercises such a heavy influence on budgetary outcomes, Markov (simultaneous, difference) equations are particularly useful. In these Markov processes, the value of certain variables at one point in time is dependent on their value at one or more immediately previous periods as well as on the particular circumstances of the time.

We postulate several decision rules for both the agency-Budget Bureau requests and for congressional action on these requests. For each series of requests or appropriations, we select from the postulated decision rules that rule which most closely represents the behavior of the aggregated entities. We use the variables

y_t the appropriation passed by Congress for any given agency in the year t. Supplemental appropriations are not included in the y_t.

x_t the appropriation requested by the Bureau of the Budget for any given agency for the year t. The x_t constitutes the President's budget request for an agency.

We will also introduce certain symbols representing random disturbances of each of the postulated relationships. These symbols are explained as they are introduced.

A. EQUATIONS FOR AGENCY-BUDGET BUREAU DECISION RULES

The possibility that different agencies use different strategies makes it necessary to construct alternative equations representing these various strategies. Then, for each agency in our sample, we use time series data to select that equation which seems to describe best the budgetary decisions of that agency. In this section we present three simple models of agency requests. The first states agency requests as a function of the previous year's appropriation. The second states requests as a function of the previous appropriation as well as a function of the differences between the agency request and appropriation in the previous year. The third states requests as a function of the previous year's request. In all three linear models provision is made for a random variable to take into account the special circumstances of the time.

An agency, while convinced of the worth of its programs, tends to be aware that extraordinarily large or small requests are likely to be viewed with suspicion by Congress; an agency does not consider it desirable to make extraordinary requests, which might precipitate unfavorable congressional reaction. Therefore, the agency usually requests a percentage (generally greater than one hundred percent) of its previous year's appropriation. This percentage is not fixed: in the event of favorable circumstances, the request is a larger percentage of the previous year's appropriation than would otherwise be the case; similarly, the percentage might be reduced in the event of unfavorable circumstances.

Decisions made in the manner described above may be represented by a simple equation. If we take the average of the percentages that are implicitly or explicitly used by budget officers, then any request can be represented by the sum of this average percentage of the previous year's appropriation plus the increment or decrement due to the favorable or unfavorable circumstances. Thus

(1) $x_t = \beta_0 y_{t-1} + \xi_t$

The agency request (through the Budget Bureau) for a certain year is a fixed mean percentage of the congressional appropriation for that agency in the previous year plus a random variable (normally distributed with mean zero and unknown but finite variance) for that year.

is an equation representing this type of behavior. The average or mean percentage is represented by β_0. The increment or decrement due to circumstances is represented by ξ_t, a variable which requires some special explanation. It is difficult to predict what circumstances will occur at what time to put an agency in a favorable or unfavorable position. Numerous events could influence Congress's (and the public's) perception of an agency and its programs—the occurrence of a destructive hurricane in the case of the Weather Bureau, the death by cancer of a friend of an influential congressman, in the case of the National Institutes of Health, the hiring (or losing) of an especially effective lobbyist by some interest group, the President's becoming especially interested in a program of some agency as Kennedy was in mental health, and so on. (Of course, some of them may be more or less "predictable" at certain times to an experienced observer, but this fact causes no difficulty here.) Following common statistical practice we may represent the sum of the effects of all such events by a random variable that is an increment or decrement to the usual percentage of the previous year's appropriation. In equation (1), then, ξ_t represents the value which this random variable assumes in year t.

We have chosen to view the special events of each year for each agency as random phenomena that are capable of being described by a probability density or distribution. We assume here that the random variable is normally distributed with mean zero and an unknown but finite variance. Given this specification of the random variable, the agency makes its budgeting decisions as if it were operating by the postulated decision rule given by equation (1).

An agency, although operating somewhat like the organizations described by equation (1), may wish to take into account an additional strategic consideration: while this agency makes a request which is roughly a fixed percentage of the previous year's appropriation, it also desires to smooth out its stream of appropriations by taking into account the difference between its request and appropriation for the previous year. If there were an unusually large cut in the previous year's request, the agency submits a "padded" estimate to make up for the loss in expected funds; an unusual increase is followed by a reduced estimate to avoid unspent appropriations. This behavior may be represented by equation or decision rule where

(2) $$x_t = \beta_1 y_{t-1} + \beta_2 (y_{t-1} - x_{t-1}) + \chi_t$$

The agency request (through the Budget Bureau) for a certain year is a fixed mean percentage of the congressional appropriation for that agency in the previous year plus a fixed mean percentage of the difference between the congressional appropriation and the agency request for the previous year plus a stochastic disturbance.

χ_t is a stochastic disturbance, which plays the role described for the random variable in equation (1), the β's are variables reflecting the aspects of the previous year's request and appropriation that an agency takes into account: β_1 represents the mean percentage of the previous year's request which is taken into account, and β_2 represents the mean percentage of the difference between the previous year's appropriation and request $(y_{t-1} - x_{t-1})$ which is taken into account. Note that $\beta_2 < 0$ is anticipated so that a large cut will (in the absence of the events represented by the stochastic disturbance) be followed by a padded estimate and vice-versa.[5]

Finally, an agency (or the President through the Bureau of the Budget), convinced of the worth of its programs, may decide to make requests without regard to previous congressional action. This strategy appeals especially when Congress has so much confidence in the agency that it tends to give an appropriation which is almost identical to the request. Aside from special circumstances represented by stochastic disturbances, the agency's request in any given year tends to be approximately a fixed percentage of its request for the previous year. This behavior may be represented by

(3) $$x_t = \beta_2 x_{t-1} + \rho_t$$

The agency request (through the Budget Bureau) for a certain year is a fixed mean percentage of the agency's request for the previous year plus a random variable (stochastic disturbance).

where ρ_t is a stochastic disturbance and β_2 is the average percentage. Note that if the agency believes its programs to be worthy, $\beta_3 > 1$ is expected.[6]

These three equations are not the only ones which may be capable of representing the actual behavior of the combined budgeting decisions of the agencies and the Bureau of the Budget. However, they represent the agency-Budget Bureau budgeting behavior better than all other decision rules we tried.[7]

B. EQUATIONS FOR CONGRESSIONAL DECISION RULES

In considering congressional behavior, we again postulate three decision equations from which a selection must be made that best represents the behavior of Congress in regard to an agency's appropriations. Since Congress may use various strategies in determining appropriations for different agencies, different congressional decision equations may be selected as best representing congressional appropriations for each agency in our sample. Our first model states congressional appropriations as a function of the agency's request (through the Budget Bureau) to Congress. The second states appropriations as a function of the agency's request as well as a function of the deviation from the usual relationship between Congress and the agency in the previous year. The third model states appropriations as a function of that segment of the agency's request that is not part of its appropriation or request for the previous year. Random variables are included to take account of special circumstances.

If Congress believes that an agency's request, after passing through the hands of the Budget Bureau, is a relatively stable index of the funds needed by the agency to carry out its programs, Congress responds by appropriating a relatively fixed percentage of the agency's request. The term "relatively fixed" is used because Congress is likely to alter this percentage somewhat from year to year because of special events and circumstances relevant to particular years. As in the case of agency requests, these special circumstances may be viewed as random phenomena. One can view this behavior as if it were the result of Congress' appropriating a fixed mean percentage of the agency requests; adding to the amount so derived a sum represented by a random variable. One may represent this behavior as if Congress were following the decision rule

$$(4) \qquad\qquad y_t = a_0 x_t + n_t$$

The congressional appropriation for an agency in a certain year is a fixed mean percentage of the agency's request in that year plus a stochastic disturbance.

where a_0 represents the fixed average percentage and n_t represents the stochastic disturbance.

Although Congress usually grants an agency a fixed percentage of its request, this request sometimes represents an extension of the agency's programs above (or below) the size desired by Congress. This can occur when the agency and the Bureau of the Budget follow Presidential aims differing from those of Congress, or when Congress suspects that the agency is padding the current year's request. In such a situation Congress usually appropriates a sum different from the usual percentage. If a_0 represents the mean of the usual percentages, this behavior can be represented by equation or decision rule

$$(5) \qquad\qquad y_t = a_1 x_t + v_t$$

where v_t is a stochastic disturbance representing that part of the appropriations attributable to the special circumstances that cause Congress to deviate from a relatively fixed percentage. Therefore, when agency aims and congressional desires markedly differ from usual (so that Congress may be said to depart from its usual rule) the stochastic disturbance takes on an unusually large positive or negative value. In order to distinguish this case from the previous one, more must be specified about the stochastic disturbance v_t. In a year following one in which agency aims and congressional desires markedly differed, the agency makes a request closer to congressional desires, and/or Congress shifts its desires closer to those of the agency (or the President). In the year after a deviation, then, assume that Congress will tend to make allowances to normalize the situation. Such behavior can be represented by having the stochastic disturbance v_t generated in accordance with a first order Markov scheme. The stochastic component in v_t is itself determined by a relation

$$(6) \qquad\qquad v_t = a_2 v_{t-1} + \epsilon_t$$

where ϵ_t is a random variable. The symbol v_t therefore stands for the stochastic disturbance in the previous year (v_{t-1}) as well as the new stochastic disturbance for the year involved (ϵ_t). Substituting (6) into (5) gives

$$(7) \qquad\qquad y_t = a_1 x_t + a_2 v_{t-1} + \epsilon_t$$

The congressional appropriation for an agency is a fixed mean percentage of the agency's request for that year plus a stochastic disturbance representing a deviation from the usual relationship between Congress and the agency in the previous year plus a random variable for the current year.

as a complete description of a second congressional decision rule. If Congress never makes complete allowance for an initial "deviation," then $-1 < a_2 < 1$ is to be expected.

To complete the description of this second congressional decision rule, we will suppose $0 < a_2 < 1$. Then, granted a deviation from its usual percentage, Congress tends to decrease subsequent deviations by moving steadily back toward its usual percentage (except for the unforeseeable events or special circumstances whose effects are represented by the random variable ϵ_t). For example, if in a particular year $v_{t-1} > 0$, and if in the following year there are no special circumstances so that $\xi_t = 0$, then $v_t = a_2 v_{t-1} < v_{t-1}$. The deviation in year t is smaller than the deviation in year $t-1$. However, if $-1 < a_2 < 0$ after an initial deviation, Congress tends to move back to its usual rule (apart from the disturbances represented by the random variable ϵ_t) by making successively smaller deviations which differ in sign. For example, if $v_{t-1} > 0$, then apart from the disturbance ϵ_t it is clear that $v_t = a_2 v_{t-1} < 0$, since $a_2 < 0$. Finally, if $a_2 = 0$, decision rule (7) is the same as the previous rule (4).

The specialization inherent in the appropriations process allows some members of Congress to have an intimate knowledge of the budgetary processes of the agencies and the Budget Bureau. Thus, Congress might consider that part of the agency's request (x_t) which is not based on the previous year's appropriation or request. This occurs when Congress believes that this positive or negative remainder represents padding or when it desires to smooth out the agency's rate of growth. If Congress knows the decision rule that an agency uses to formulate its budgetary request, we can let λ_t represent a dummy variable defined as $\lambda_t = \xi_t$ if the agency uses decision rule (1); $\lambda_t = \beta_2(y_{t-1} - x_{t-1}) + \chi_t$ if the agency uses decision rule (2); and, $\lambda_t = \rho_t$ if the agency uses decision rule (3). Suppose that Congress appropriates, on the average, an amount which is a relatively fixed percentage of the agency's request plus a percentage of this (positive or negative) remainder λ_t. This behavior can be represented by the "as if" decision rule

$$(8) \qquad\qquad y_t = a_3 x_t + a_4 \lambda_t + v_t$$

The congressional appropriation for an agency is a fixed mean percentage of the agency's request for a certain year plus a fixed mean percentage of a dummy variable which represents that part of the agency's request for the year at issue which is not part of the appropriation or request of the previous year plus a random variable representing the part of the appropriation attributable to the special circumstances of the year.

where v_t is a stochastic disturbance whose value in any particular year represents the part of the appropriation attributable to the agency's special circumstances of the year. One might expect that Congress takes only "partial" account of the remainder represented by λ_t, so $0 < a_4 < 1$.

III. Empirical Results

Times series data for the period 1947–1963 were studied for fifty-six nondefense agencies of the United States Government. The requests (x_t) of these agencies were taken to be the amounts presented to Congress in the President's budget. For eight subagencies from the National Institutes of Health, data for a shorter period of time were considered, and the requests (x_t) of these eight subagencies were taken to be their proposals to the Bureau of the Budget.[8] In all instances the congressional decision variable (y_t) was taken to be the final appropriation before any supplemental additions. The total appropriations (without supplements) of the agencies studied amounted to approximately 27 percent of the nondefense budget in 1963. Over one-half of all nondefense agencies were investigated; the major omissions being the Post Office and many independent agencies. A minimum of three agencies was examined from each of the Treasury, Justice, Interior, Agriculture, Commerce, Labor, and Health, Education and Welfare Departments.[9]

If the agency-Budget Bureau disturbance is independent of congressional disturbance,[10] the use of ordinary least squares (OLS) to estimate most of the possible combinations of the proposed decision equations is justified. OLS is identical to the simultaneous full information maximum likelihood (FIML) technique for most of the present systems. This is not so, however, for some systems of equations because of the presence of an autocorrelated disturbance in one equation of the two and the consequent nonlinearity of the estimating equations. In equation (6) the stochastic disturbance for year t is a function of the value of the disturbance in the previous year. In a system of equations in which autocorrelation occurs in the first equation, an appropriate procedure is to use OLS to estimate the alternative proposals for the other equation, decide by the selection criteria which best specifies the data, use the knowledge of this structure to estimate the first equation, and then decide, through use of appropriate criteria, which version of the first equation best specifies the data.

The principal selection criterion we used is that of maximum (adjusted) correlation coefficient (R). For a given dependent variable this criterion leads one to select from alternative specifications of the explanatory variables, that specification which leads to the highest sample correlation coefficient. The estimations of the alternative specifications must, of course, be made from the same data.[11] The second criterion involves the use of the d-statistic test for serial correlation of the estimated residuals of a single equation.[12] This statistic tests the null hypothesis of residual independence against the alternative of serial correlation. We used the significance points for the d-statistic of Theil and Nagar.[13] When the d-statistic was found to be significant in fitting the congressional decision equation (4) to an agency's data, it was always found that equation (7) best specified congressional behavior with respect to the appropriations of that agency in the sense of yielding the maximum correlation coefficient. A third criterion is based on a test of the significance of the sample correlation between the residuals of (4) and the estimated λ_t of the equation selected previously for a given agency. David's significance points for this statistic were used to make a two-tailed test at the five percent level of the null hypothesis that the residuals are uncorrelated.[14] When significant correlation occurred, it was always found that congressional decision equation (8), in which a function of the deviation from the usual relationship between request and the previous year's appropriation enters explicitly, best specified appropriation behavior with respect to the agency in question.

The statistical procedures were programmed for the Carnegie Institute of Technology's Control Data G-21 electronic computer in the 20-Gate algebraic compiling language. The selection among alternate specifications according to the criteria established was not done automatically; otherwise all computations were performed by machine. Since the results for each agency are described in detail elsewhere,[15] and a full rendition would double the length of the paper, we must restrict ourselves to summary statements.

TABLE 19–1

Best Specifications for Each Agency Are High

| | FREQUENCIES OF CORRELATION COEFFICIENTS | | | | | | | | | | |
	1 – .995	– .99	– .98	– .97	– .96	– .95	– .94	– .93	– .90	– .85	–
Congressional	21	8	15	4	5	2	2	1	5	2	2
Agency-Bureau	9	2	2	8	5	2	4	3	5	11	10

The empirical results support the hypothesis that, up to a random error of reasonable magnitude, the budgetary process of the United States government is equivalent to a set of temporally stable linear decision rules. Estimated correlation coefficients for the best specifications of each agency are generally high. Although the calculated values of the multiple correlation coefficients (R's) tend to run higher in time series than in cross-sectional analysis, the results are good. We leave little of the variance statistically unexplained. Moreover the estimated standard deviations of the coefficients are usually, much smaller than one-half of the size of the estimated coefficients, a related indication of good results. Table 19–1 presents the frequencies of the correlation coefficients.

The fits between the decision rules and the time series data for the congressional decision equations are, in general, better than those for the agency-Bureau of the Budget equations. Of the 64 agencies and subagencies studied, there are only 14 instances in which the correlation coefficient for the agency (or subagency) equation was higher than the one for the corresponding congressional equation. We speculate that the estimated variances of the disturbances of the agency-Budget Bureau decision rules are usually larger because the agencies are closer than Congress to the actual sources that seek to add new programs or expand old ones.

Table 19–2 presents a summary of the combinations of the Agency-Bu-

TABLE 19–2

Budgetary Behavior is Simple

SUMMARY OF DECISION EQUATIONS			
Agency-Budget Bureau	1	2	3
	4 44[a]	1	8
Congress	7 1	0	0
	8 12	0	0

[a] Including eight subagencies from the National Institutes of Health

reau of the Budget and congressional decision equations. For those agencies studied, the most popular combinations of behavior are the simple ones represented by equations (4) and (1) respectively. When Congress uses a sophisticated "gaming" strategy such as (7) or (8), the corresponding agency-Bureau of the Budget decision equation is the relatively simple (1). And, when Congress grants exactly or almost exactly the amount requested by an agency, the agency tends to use decision equation (3).

Our discussion thus far has assumed fixed values for the coefficients (parameters) of the equations we are using to explain the behavior underlying the budgetary process. In the light of the many important events occurring in the period from 1946 to 1963, however, it seems reasonable to suppose that the appropriations structure of many government agencies was altered. If this is correct, the coefficients of the equations—literally, in this context, the values represented by the on-the-average percentages requested by the agencies and granted by Congress—should change from one period of time to the next. The equations would then be temporally stable for a period, but not forever. The year when the coefficient of an equation changes from one value to another is termed the "shift point." The time series we are using are so short that it is possible to find only one meaningful shift point in each of the two equations that describe the budget request and appropriation best fitting an agency. We, therefore, broke each time series into two parts and used Chow's F-statistic [16] to determine temporal stability by testing the null hypothesis that the underlying coefficients did not shift (against all alternatives) for the individual equations. We used four categories for the coefficients of a decision equation defined as follows:

Temporally very stable: The F-statistic is small and the coefficients estimated from the first and last parts of the series are virtually the same.
Temporally stable: The F-statistic is small, but the coefficients estimated from the first and last parts of the series appear to be different.
Not temporally stable: The F-statistic is large but not significant at the ten percent level and the coefficients estimated from the first and last parts of series appear to be different.
Temporally unstable: The F-statistic is significant at the ten percent level.

Of the congressional decision equations, six were temporally very stable, 12 were temporally stable, 12 were not temporally stable, and 28 were temporally unstable. Of the agency-Bureau of the Budget decision equations, four were temporally very stable, 18 were temporally stable, 18 were not temporally stable, and 18 were temporally unstable.[17] Since a substantial majority of cases fall into the not temporally stable and temporally unstable categories, it is evident that while the process is temporally stable for short periods, it may not be stable for the whole period.

Table 19–3 presents a summary of the combinations of the agency-Bureau of the Budget and Congressional decision equations when each series is broken into two parts. These specifications are referred to as "first period" and "second period" for all agencies even though the years at which the time series were broken vary. While the most frequent combinations of behavior are the simple ones represented by equations (4) and (1) respectively, there is a marked tendency for congressional behavior to become more sophisticated: the incidence of the gaming behavior represented by equation (8) increases over time.[18]

TABLE 19–3

*Congressional Behavior Tends to
Become More Sophisticated*

FIRST-PERIOD DECISION EQUATIONS

	1	2	3
4	45	0	10
7	1	0	0
8	2	0	0

SECOND-PERIOD DECISION EQUATIONS

	1	2	3
4	35	1	9
7	1	0	0
8	12	0	0

The budgetary process seems to become more linear over time in the sense that the importance of the "special circumstances" appears to diminish. Table 19–4 presents frequencies of the correlation coefficients for the first and second periods. Although there is a different number of correlation coefficients in each period (111 in the first period and 114 in the second)[19] Table 19–4 shows clearly that fits are better for the second period, which is sufficient evidence of increasing linear tendencies. To us it seems reasonable to expect an increasing use of simplifying rules of thumb as the budget grows in size and the pressure of time on key decision makers increases. Yet this is only one of a number of possible explanations. For example, the data are not deflated for changes in the price level during the early years. Since there were larger increases in the price level during the early years, this might help explain why the fits are better during the second period.

When only one shift point is presumed, most shifts are discovered during the first two budgets of the Eisenhower Administration (1954–1955). Table 19–5 presents, for both congressional and Agency-Budget Bureau decision equations, frequencies of the shift points for (a) those equations whose coefficients are in the not temporally stable or temporally un-stable categories and (b) those agencies for which the decision rules of the partic-

TABLE 19–4

The Budgetary Process Is Becoming More Linear

| | FREQUENCIES OF CORRELATION COEFFICIENTS | | | | | | | | | | |
	1 – .995	– .99	– .98	– .97	– .96	– .94	– .92	– .90	– .80	– .60	– 0
First period	9	5	8	5	3	6	8	4	18	24	21
Second period	27	5	13	8	8	15	7	5	12	8	6

TABLE 19–5

Likely Shift Points Are Concentrated in the First Years
of the Eisenhower Administration

| | FREQUENCIES OF SHIFT POINTS | | | | | | | | | | | | | | | |
YEAR	48	49	50	51	52	53	54	55	56	57	58	59	60	61	62	T
Congressional	0	2	3	1	0	1	17	16	1	1	3	0	0	1	0	46 (40)
Agency-Bureau	0	2	4	0	2	3	15	13	3	0	2	1	0	2	1	37 (36)

ipants appeared to change. While it is certainly possible that shift points do not occur as dramatically and as sharply as shown here, and that it may take several years for actual behavior to change noticeably, Table 19–5 nevertheless makes it clear that likely shifts are concentrated in the first period of the Eisenhower administration.

We said, in the second section, that we expected β_0, β_1, and β_3, to be greater than one, and β_2 to be negative. In 56 instances this expectation is satisfied, but eight exceptions were noted. In the two cases where the estimated $\beta_3 < 1$, explanations are immediately available. First, the fit for the Bureau of Employment Security is not good. Second, the Office of Territories evidences most un-Parkinsonian behavior: its activities decline with a decrease in the number of territories. In the six other exceptions, the estimated coefficient is $\beta_0 < 1$. For three of these, Congress tends to appropriate an amount greater than the request, and two of the three represent an interesting phenomenon. When those parts of requests and appropriations directly related to loans are omitted from the data for both the Rural Electrification Administration and the Federal Housing Administration, the estimated coefficients are of the magnitudes expected with $\beta_0 > 1$ and $a_0 < 1$. However, when the data relating to loans are included, then $\beta_0 < 1$ and $a_0 > 1$. Apparently, Congress favors the loan programs more than do the agencies or the Budget Bureau.

As a rule, the d-statistics resulting from fitting the best specifications were not significant. It would thus appear that all major underlying trended variables (with the possible exception of variables with the same trend) have been accounted for by these specifications. When an exception to this rule did exist, the authors made a careful examination of the residuals in an effort to determine the reason for such a situation. It appeared that in most of these instances the cause was either (a) that the coefficients shifted slowly over several years and not abruptly at one point in time, or (b) that restricting the search to only one shift point left undetected an additional shift either very early or very late in the series.

In an attempt to unmask the trended variable most likely (in our opinion) to have been ignored, and to cast some light upon the notion of "fair share," final appropriations y_t for each agency were regressed on total non-defense appropriations z_t. This time series was taken from the *Statistical Abstract of the United States*. The results were poor. Indeed, the sample correlations between y_t and z_t are usually worse than those between y_t and x_t. Moreover, the d-statistics are usually highly significant and the residual patterns for the regression show the agency's proportion of the nondefense budget to be either increasing or decreasing over time. However, it should be noted that even those exceptional cases where the agency trend is close to that of the total nondefense appropriation do not invalidate the explicit decision structure fitted here. A similar study, with similar results, was conducted at the departmental level by regressing y_t for the eight National Institutes of Health on y_t for the Public Health Service, the agency of which they are a part. Finally, the y_t for selected pairs of agencies with "similar" interests were regressed on each other with uniformly poor results.

Although empirical evidence indicates that our models describe the budgetary process of the United States government, we are well aware of certain deficiencies in our work. One deficiency, omission of certain agencies from the study, is not serious because over one-half of all nondefense agencies were investigated. Nevertheless, the omission of certain agencies may have left undiscovered examples of additional decision rules. We will shortly study all agencies whose organizational structure can be traced. We will also include supplemental appropriations.

A more serious deficiency may lie in the fact that the sample sizes, of necessity, are small. The selection criterion of maximum sample correlation, therefore, lacks proper justification, and is only acceptable because of the lack of a better criterion. Further, full-information maximum likelihood estimators, and especially biased ones, even when they are known to be consistent, are not fully satisfactory in such a situation, although they may be the best available. However, the remedy for these deficiencies must await the results of future theoretical research on explosive or evolutionary processes.

The Deviant Cases and Prediction: Interpretation of the Stochastic Disturbances

The intent of this section is to clarify further the interpretation of the stochastic disturbances as special or unusual circumstances represented by random variables. While those influences present at a constant level during the period serve only to affect the magnitude of the coefficients, the special circumstances have an important, if subsidiary, place in these models. We have indicated that although outside observers can view the effects of special circumstances as a random variable, anyone familiar with all the facts available to the decision-makers at the time would be able to explain the special circumstances. It seems reasonable therefore to examine instances where, in estimating the coefficients, we find that the estimated values of the stochastic disturbances assume a large positive or negative value. Such instances appear as deviant cases in the sense that Congress or the agency-Budget Bureau actors affected by special circumstances (large positive or negative values of the random variable) do not appear to be closely following their usual decision rule at that time but base their decisions mostly on these circumstances. The use of case studies for the analyses of deviant phenomena, of course, presupposes our ability to explain most budgeting decisions by our original formulations. Deviant cases, then, are those instances in which particular decisions do not follow our equations. It is possible to determine these deviant instances simply by examining the residuals of the fitted equations: one observes a plot of the residuals, selects those which appear as extreme positive or negative values, determines the year to which these extreme residuals refer, and then examines evidence in the form of testimony at the Appropriations Committees, newspaper accounts and other sources. In this way it is possible to determine at least some of the circumstances of a budgetary decision and to investigate whether or not the use of the random variables is appropriate.[20]

Finally, it should be pointed out that in our model the occurrence of extreme disturbances represents deviant cases, or the temporary setting aside of their usual decision rules by the decision-makers in the process, while coefficient shifts represent a change (not necessarily in form) of these rules.

From the residuals of one-half of the estimated congressional decision equations, a selection of 55 instances (approximately 14 percent of the 395 congressional decisions under consideration) were identified as deviant.[21] Table 19–6 shows the yearly frequency of the occurrence of deviant cases. It is apparent that deviancy grows in years of political change: in 1948 the Republican 80th Congress made a determined effort to reduce appropriations submitted by the Democratic President; the years 1953 through 1955 mark the beginning of Eisenhower's presidency; the large number of deviant cases in 1962 and 1963 are related to the accession to

TABLE 19–6
Deviant Cases Cluster in Years of Political Change

YEAR	1948	1949	1950	1951	1952	1953	1954	1955
Number of cases	8	2	1	1	1	4	6	4

YEAR	1956	1957	1958	1959	1960	1961	1962	1963
Number of cases	1	1	2	3	4	2	8	7

office of Kennedy and Johnson. The latter category of deviant cases, we will explain later, may be misclassifications in the sense that the passage of time and the corresponding accumulation of additional evidence may reveal shift points, i.e., changes in the "average percentages" of the decision processes, rather than "exceptional circumstances." Nevertheless, this fact causes no particular problem in light of our purposes here, and the cases may be viewed as if they are appropriately classified.

TABLE 19–7
*Deviant Cases May be Viewed
as Random Events*

CATEGORIES OF DEVIANCE	NUMBER OF CASES
Significant policy change	20
Fiscal policy change	8
Felt need of congressional supervision	6
Amended estimate due to a time factor	6
Single event	5
Large new legislative program	4
Reorganization of agency	1
Non-identifiable	5
TOTAL N =	55

Table 19–7 categorizes the cases according to estimates ot why deviance occurred. It should be noted that the largest category, significant policy change, involves the lack of a budgetary base for the agency in question. In order to highlight the meaning we give to random phenomena, an illustration of each category follows. This analysis explains why, although the deviant cases are understandable to an experienced observer or participant, an outsider would have to regard them as essentially random disturbances to an otherwise deterministic system. Indeed, no two events in the categories of Table 19–7 are likely, *a priori,* either to be the same or to occur in any particular year.

SIGNIFICANT POLICY CHANGE

The Southwestern Power Administration is typical of agencies whose appropriations fluctuate unduly because basic policy is being negotiated. Deviance was evident in 1948, 1949, 1954, and 1955. The SPA continually requested funds for the building of transmission lines, and Congress repeatedly eliminated the request from their appropriations, insisting that private enterprise would supply the necessary facilities. In 1948 the Bureau of the Budget recommended $7,600,000 of which only $125,000 was appropriated, with stringent and explicit instructions that printing and mailing of materials calculated to increase clientele among rural and municipal electrical cooperatives cease.

The Korean War increased demands for electric power. Deviance occurred in 1955 not because of appropriations cuts but because of House floor amendments and Senate Appropriations Committee increases. Public policy then became stabilized as Congress established a budgetary base. The following years fit our equations.

FISCAL POLICY CHANGES

The Foreign Agricultural Service's 1963 appropriation is deviant in appropriation figures, but, because $3,117,000 was provided by transferring funds from Sec. 32, the total budget for FAS is close to the Budget Bureau's initial request.

FELT NEED OF CONGRESSIONAL SUPERVISION

The House Committee reports on Office of Territories for 1953 show a lack of confidence in the agency. The tenor can be judged by House Report 1622: "The Department was advised last year that the Committee did not intend to provide appropriations for an endless chain of capital investment in the Alaska Railroads. Army testimony was conflicting as to the need for a road and railways. There is need for a coordinated plan before the Committee can act intelligently with regard to the railroad."

AMENDED ESTIMATE DUE TO TIME FACTOR

Typical of this type of deviance is the Commodity Stabilization Service's appropriation for 1958. On the basis of figures from County Agricultural Agents, Secretary Ezra Taft Benson scaled down his request from $465 million to $298 million. A more accurate estimate was made possible because of added time.

LARGE NEW LEGISLATIVE PROGRAM

This is especially apt to affect an agency if it is required to implement several new programs simultaneously. The Commissioner of Education said in reference to the student loan program, "We have no way of knowing because we never had such a program, and many of the institutions never had them." The NDEA Act alone had ten new entitlements.

REORGANIZATION OF AN AGENCY

The only example is the Agricultural Marketing Service's appropriation for 1962. Funds were reduced because of a consolidation of diverse activities by the Secretary of Agriculture and not through reorganization as a result of congressional demands.

NONIDENTIFIABLE

This applies, for example, to the Public Health Service where a combination of lesser factors converge to make the agency extremely deviant for 1959, 1960, 1961, and 1962. Among the apparent causes of deviance are publicity factors, the roles of committee chairmen in both House and Senate, a high percentage of professionals in the agency, and the excellent press coverage of health research programs. No one factor appears primarily responsible for the deviance.

Our models are not predictive but explanatory. The alternate decision equations can be tried and the most appropriate one used when data on requests and appropriations are available. The appropriate equation explains the data in that, given a good fit, the process behaves "as if" the data were generated according to the equation. Thus, our explanatory models are backward looking: given a history of requests and appropriations, the data appears as if they were produced by the proposed and appropriately selected scheme.

The models are not predictive because the budget process is only temporally stable for short periods. We have found cases in which the coefficients of the equations change, i.e., cases in which there are alterations in the realized behavior of the processes. We have no *a priori* theory to predict the occurrence of these changes, but merely our *ad hoc* observation that most occurred during Eisenhower's first term. Predictions are necessarily based upon the estimated values of the coefficients and on the statistical properties of the stochastic disturbance (sometimes called the error term). Without a scientific method of predicting the shift points in our model, we cannot scientifically say that a request or an appropriation for some future year will fall within a prescribed range with a given level of confidence. We can predict only when the process remains stable in time.

If the decision rules of the participants have changed, our predictions may be worthless: in our models, either the coefficients have shifted or, more seriously, the scheme has changed. Moreover, it is extremely difficult to determine whether or not the observation latest in time represents a shift point. A sudden change may be the result either of a change in the underlying process or a temporary setting aside of the usual decision rules in light of special circumstances. The data for several subsequent years are necessary to determine with any accuracy whether a change in decision rules indeed occurred.

It is possible, or course, to make conditional predictions by taking the estimated coefficients from the last shift point and assuming that no shift will occur. Limited predictions as to the next year's requests and appropriations could be made and might turn out to be reasonably accurate. However, scholarly efforts would be better directed toward knowledge of why, where and when changes in the process occur so that accurate predictions might be made.

The usual interpretation of stochastic (in lieu of deterministic) models may, of course, be made for the models of this paper, i.e., not all factors influencing the budgetary process have been included in the equations. Indeed, many factors often deemed most important such as pressure from interest groups, are ignored. Part of the reason for this lies in the nature of the models: they describe the decision process in skeleton form. Further, since the estimations are made, of necessity, on the basis of time series data, it is apparent that any influences that were present at a constant level during the period are not susceptible to discovery by these methods. However, these influences do affect the budgetary process by determining the size of the estimated coefficients. Thus, this paper, in making a comparative study of the estimated coefficients for the various agencies, suggests a new way of approaching constant influences.

No theory can take every possible unexpected circumstance into account, but our theory can be enlarged to include several classes of events. The concentration of shift points in the first years of the Eisenhower administration implies that an empirical theory should take account of changes in the political party controlling the White House and Congress.

We also intend to determine indices of clientele and confidence so that their effects, when stable over time, can be gauged.[22] Presidents sometimes attempt to gear their budgetary requests to fit their desired notion of the rate of expenditures appropriate for the economic level they wish the country to achieve. By checking the Budget Message, contemporary accounts, and memoirs, we hope to include a term (as a dummy variable) which would enable us to predict high and low appropriations rates depending on the President's intentions.

Significance of The Findings

We wish to consider the significance of (a) the fact that it is possible to find equations which explain major facets of the federal budgetary process and (b) the particular equations fitted to the time series. We will take up each point in order.

A. It is possible to find equations for the budgetary process. There has been controversy for some time over whether it is possible to find laws, even of a probabilistic character, which explain important aspects of the political process. The greatest skepticism is reserved for laws which would explain how policy is made or account for the outcomes of the political process. Without engaging in further abstract speculation, it is apparent that the best kind of proof would be a demonstration of the existence of some such laws. This, we believe, we have done.

Everyone agrees that the federal budget is terribly complex. Yet, as we have shown, the budgetary process can be described by very simple decision rules. Work done by Simon, Newell, Reitman, Clarkson, Cyert and March, and others, on simulating the solution of complex problems, has demonstrated that in complicated situations human beings are likely to use heuristic rules of thumb to enable them to find satisfactory solutions.[23] Braybrooke and Lindblom have provided convincing arguments on this score for the political process.[24] Wildavsky's interviews with budget officers indicate that they, too, rely extensively on aids to calculation.[25] It is not surprising, therefore, as our work clearly shows, that a set of simple decision rules can explain or represent the behavior of participants in the federal budgetary process in their efforts to reach decisions in complex situations.

The most striking fact about the equations is their simplicity. This is perhaps partly because of the possibility that more complicated decision procedures are reserved for special circumstances represented by extreme values of the random variable. However, the fact that the decision rules generally fit the data very well is an indication that these simple equations have considerable explanatory power. Little of the variance is left unexplained.

What is the significance of the fact that the budgetary process follows rather simple laws for the general study of public policy? Perhaps the significance is limited; perhaps other policy processes are far more complex and cannot be reduced to simple laws. However, there is no reason to believe that this is the case. On the contrary, when one considers the central importance of budgeting in the political process—few activities can be carried on without funds—and the extraordinary problems of calculation which budgeting presents, a case might better be made for its comparative complexity than for its simplicity. At present it is undoubtedly easier to demonstrate that laws, whether simple or complex, do underlie the budgetary process than to account for other classes of policy outcomes, because budgeting provides units of analysis (appropriations requests and grants) that are readily amenable to formulating and testing propositions statistically. The dollar figures are uniform, precise, numerous, comparable with others, and, most important, represent an important class of policy outcomes. Outside of matters involving voting or attitudes, however, it is difficult to think of general statements about public policy that can be said to have been verified. The problem is not that political science lacks propositions which might be tested. Works of genuine distinction like Herring's *The Politics of Democracy,* Truman's *The Governmental Process,* Hyneman's *Bureaucracy in a Democracy,* Neustadt's *Presidential Power,* Buchanan and Tullock's *The Calculus of Consent,* contain implicit or explicit propositions which appear to be at least as interesting as (and potentially more interesting than) the ones tested in this paper. The real difficulty is that political scientists have been unable to develop a unit of analysis (there is little agreement on what constitutes a decision) that would permit them to test the many propositions they have at their command. By taking one step toward demonstrating what can be done when a useful unit of analysis has been developed, we hope to highlight the tremendous importance that the development of units of analysis would have for the study of public policy.

B. *The significance of the particular equations.* Let us examine the concepts that have been built into the particular equations. First, the importance of the previous year's appropriation is an indication that the notion of the base is a very significant explanatory concept for the behavior of the agencies and the Budget Bureau. Similarly, the agency-Budget Bureau requests are important variables in the decisions of Congress. Second, some of the equations, notably (7) and (8) for Congress, and (2) for the agency-Budget Bureau, incorporate strategic concepts. On some occasions, then, budgeting on the federal level does involve an element of gaming. Neither the Congress nor the agencies can be depended upon to "take it lying down." Both attempt to achieve their own aims and goals. Finally, the budgetary process is only temporally stable. The occurrence of most changes of decision rules at a change in administration indicates that alterations in political party and personnel occupying high offices can exert some (but not total) influence upon the budgetary process.

Our decision rules may serve to cast some light on the problem of "power" in political analysis. The political scientist's dilemma is that it is hardly possible to think about politics without some concept of power, but that it is extremely difficult to create and then to use an operational definition in empirical work. Hence, James March makes the pessimistic conclusion that "The Power of Power" as a political variable may be rather low.[26] The problem is particularly acute when dealing with processes in which there is a high degree of mutual dependence among the participants.

In budgeting, for example, the agency-Budget Bureau and congressional relationships hardly permit a strict differentiation of the relative influence of the participants. Indeed, our equations are built on the observation of mutual dependence; and the empirical results show that how the agency-Budget Bureau participants behave depends on what Congress does (or has done) and that how Congress behaves depends on what the agency-Budget Bureau side is doing (or has done). Yet the concept of power does enter the analysis in calculations of the importance that each participant has for the other; it appears in the relative magnitude of the estimated co-efficients. "Power" is saved because it is not required to carry too great a burden. It may be that theories which take power into account as part of the participants' calculations will prove of more use to social science research than attempts to measure the direct exercise of influence. At least we can say that theories of calculation, which animate the analysis of *The Politics of the Budgetary Process* and of this paper, do permit us to state and test propositions about the outcomes of a political process. Theories of power do not yet appear to have gone this far.

In the field of economics, work has long been done on organizational units called industrial firms. In political science, however, despite the flurry of excitement over organization theory, there has been no empirical demonstration of the value of dealing with various public organizations as comparable entities. By viewing governmental bodies not as distinctly different agencies but as having certain common properties (here, in budgetary calculations and strategies), we hope to have shown the utility to empirical theory of treating organizations *qua* organizations. Despite the differences among the organizations studied—some follow different decision rules and are affected by different random disturbances—it is analytically significant to explain their behavior by virtue of features they share as organizations.

It should be clear that we are dealing with general models of organizations and not with individual policies. One cannot say anything directly about water, land, health, or other transportation policies, from inspection of our models of a given agency. But this limit is not inherent in our approach. It is possible, for example, to calculate from our data present and future estimated rates of growth for virtually all domestic agencies since World War II. Agencies with similar growth rates may be segregated and examined for common features. The growth rates of agencies in similar areas of policy, such as public health and natural resources, may be compared, and the fortunes of policies in those areas deduced. Individual agencies may be broken down into subunits or the courses of certain policy programs charted to explain the differential treatment they receive. While pursuing this type of analysis, we hope to have one advantage. We shall be working from a general model of the budgetary process. It will, therefore, be possible for us to locate our efforts within this larger scheme. To know whether one is dealing with a normal or deviant case, to know one's position in this larger universe, is to be able to give more general meaning to the individual and particular circumstances with which one must be involved in handling small parts of the total process.

The general mode of analysis we have developed here may be pursued in many different contexts. Similar studies could be undertaken in state and local governments as well as foreign countries.[27] Private firms and public agencies may be conceptualized in parallel terms through their budgetary mechanisms.[28] By comparing the processes underlying budgeting in a variety of political and economic systems, it may be possible to state more elegantly and precisely the conditions under which different forms of behavior would prevail.

Appendix

ON THE DEFINITION OF TERMS

Certain of the technical terms required in the paper are here given informal definitions.

Coefficient. A coefficient of an equation is a parameter or number that is said to have some given but usually unknown value. The α's and β's used in the models are the coefficients of the equations in which they appear. Since the values of the coefficients are usually unknown, they must be estimated statistically from available data. In this paper, the coefficients (α's and β's) are average representations of the real percentages of requests made by agencies and appropriations granted by Congress.

Linear. An equation is linear if it has no square or higher order terms. Thus $y = \alpha x$ is linear whereas $y = \alpha x^2$ is not linear. (Remember that for two variables linear means "in a straight line.")

Stochastic. A variable is stochastic, a term meaning random, if the particular value that it assumes is a matter of chance and the set of values that it can assume is capable of being described by a probability distribution or density. The distribution gives the probability of the random variable assuming the various allowable values.

Variance. The variance is defined as $E(x - \mu)^2$ where x is a random variable, μ is its mean, and E stands for "the expected value of." One can think of variance as a measure of the dispersion or spread of the probability distribution governing the random variable.

Linear Regression Equation. A linear regression equation is a particular model of the relationship between two or more variables. The model has the form

$$y_i = \beta_0 + \beta_1 x_{1i} + \beta_2 x_{2i} + \cdots + \beta_k x_{ki} + \epsilon_i$$

where β_0 is the unknown constant term, the other β's are unknown coefficients, and ϵ_i is a random variable. In this notation, y_i represents the value of the dependent variable on the ith observation and x_{1i}, x_{2i}, $\cdots$, x_{ki} represents in a similar manner the values of the independent variables for the same observation. From a set of n observations, each of which consists of particular values for the dependent and independent variables, the regression operation estimates values for the unknown coefficients and the constant term; the regression operation also estimates n values of the random variable, which are called residuals. When the sets of observations on the dependent and independent variables refer to successive periods, the observations are called time series and we say that the values of y_i are generated by a stochastic process.

Stochastic Disturbance. This is a name for the random variable in a regression equation. It is also called the error term. Thus, in the equation $y = ax + \epsilon$, the term ϵ_i represents a stochastic disturbance (or random variable), which is usually assumed to be normally distributed with mean zero and finite but unknown variance.

Difference Equation. An equation which describes the value of a variable in one period in terms of the value of either that variable or another variable in some previous period is a difference equation. For example, $x_t = \beta y_{t-1}$ is a difference equation. If a random variable is present, the equation is called a stochastic difference equation. Thus, if ϵ is a random variable, $x_t = \beta y_{t-1} + \epsilon_t$ is a stochastic difference equation and the successive values of x may be thought of as a stochastic process.

Unstable, Evolutionary or Explosive Process. A process is said to be unstable, evolutionary, or explosive if the expected values of the successive values taken by the process are increasing. For example, the stochastic difference equation $y_t = \gamma y_{t-1} + \epsilon_t$, where $\gamma > 1$, generates an evolutionary process.

Serially Independent. If successive realizations of a random variable are serially independent, the value it assumes in one period is independent of the value it assumed in a previous period. This can be described mathematically as $E(x_i x_{t-1}) = E(x_t)$, meaning that the expected value of random variable x at period t does not depend upon the value that the random variable x assumed at period t-1. It follows that the expected simple correlation between x_t and x_{t-1} will be zero, if the random variable x is serially independent. For example, in our models, the assumption of serial independence of the disturbances reflects the belief that special circumstances in one year either do not affect special circumstances in succeeding years or that their influence enters explicitly into our model (as in equation (8) and the equations of footnote 4).

THE MEANING OF A MARKOV PROCESS

For our purposes, a Markov process generating some random variable x, is a process for which the value of x at time t depends upon the values assumed by that random variable at one or more earlier periods plus the value assumed by some stochastic disturbance at time t. A Markov process is "first order" if the variable x_t takes on a value that depends only upon the value of the variable x_{t-1} in the previous period plus the value of a stochastic disturbance at time t. Thus

$$x_t = \alpha x_{t-1} + \epsilon_t$$

is a first order Markov process where ϵ_t is a random variable with a given distribution and α is a nonzero constant. A second order Markov process can be described by

$$x_t = \alpha_1 x_{t-1} + \alpha_2 x_{t-2} + \epsilon_t$$

where both α_1 and α_2 are nonzero constants. The value of the variable x_t now depends upon its values in two previous periods.

ON THE MEANING OF GOODNESS OF FIT

An intuitive notion of good fit for a linear regression equation is that in a scatter diagram the observations should cluster about the fitted line. Probably the most popular measure of good fit is the square of the multiple correlation coefficient (R^2), which may often be interpreted as the percentage of the variance of the dependent variable that is explained by the postulated linear relationship (regression). For our models however, this interpretation is not valid, although the adjusted R gives a rough measure of the goodness of fit. The closer to 1 that the adjusted R is, the better the fit.

ON STANDARD DEVIATIONS OF COEFFICIENT ESTIMATES

Speaking roughly, these standard deviations measure the reliability of the estimates of the coefficients. The smaller the estimated standard deviation, the more accurate the estimated coefficient is likely to be. If we had another series of data generated from the same process, the smaller the standard deviation of the coefficient (estimated from the first data) in relation to the size of this coefficient, the more likely it is that a new estimate made on the basis of the hypothetical new series of data would be close to the estimate made from the original data. Generally, one hopes the estimated standard deviation of the coefficient is at least as small as one-half the size of the estimated coefficient.

ON BIASED AND UNBIASED ESTIMATORS

Think of the problem of trying to determine the average IQ of students at a large university. Suppose the administration would not allow access to

records and one did not wish to give IQ tests to all students. One might select a certain number of students at random (a sample) and give them the
tests. The test scores of these students are sample observations. One might
compute the average of these test scores and claim that he has an estimate
of the mean IQ of all students at the university. The estimator is the formula for the average of the sample observations. If he repeated the process, taking a new sample, it is possible that the estimator would produce a
slightly different estimate of the mean. However, the estimator would still
have a certain expected value. If the expected value of the estimator can
be proven to equal the population parameter (the mean IQ of all the students example) then the estimator is said to be unbiased. Otherwise, it is
said to be biased.

ON CONSISTENT ESTIMATORS

An estimator is consistent if it approaches nearer and nearer to the true
value of a parameter (in our case, a coefficient) as the size of the sample is
increased. A consistent estimator may be biased (it may approach closer to
but never actually equal the parameter), but if the sample from which it is
estimated is large enough this bias will be small.

ON LEAST-SQUARES ESTIMATORS AND THE MEANING OF
TEMPORALLY STABLE PROCESSES

This discussion specifically refers to process (4) although it is equally
applicable to all processes. Consider

$$y_t = \alpha_0 x_t + \eta_t$$

where α represents the coefficient of the equation or the "on the average"
percentage of the request that is granted by Congress and η_t is a stochastic
disturbance (random variable) that represents the variation in the request
over time that may be assigned to special circumstances. We assume that η_t
is normally distributed with mean zero and finite but unknown variance.
The coefficient is unknown and must be estimated on the basis of available
data. The data are the requests x_t and the corresponding appropriations y_t.
We do not know the values assumed by the stochastic disturbance. Our estimates of the values assumed by the stochastic disturbance are the residuals of the fitted regression equation. If, for a given agency, we observe the
requests and appropriations over a specified period of time, we could plot
the data in a scatter diagram (Figure 19–1). The line drawn in Figure
19–1 would be our estimated line (the line resulting from our estimate of
α).

The vertical positive and negative distances of the points from the fitted
line are the values of the residuals, our estimates of the values assumed by

the stochastic disturbance. The least-squares estimates of the coefficients are those values of the coefficients which make the sum of the squares of these distances a minimum. In Figure 19–1, there is no discernible pattern of departure of the points from the line.

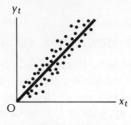

FIGURE 19–1

Thus, we can say that the process is temporally stable (i.e., fixed over time) and presume that the true value of the coefficient (we know only its estimated value) remained constant during the period under consideration. A temporally stable process is one in which the value of the true coefficient does not change during the period under consideration. This should not be confused with a stable or nonevolutionary process, i.e., one whose values do not tend to grow, but fluctuate about some level.

If we again plotted the requests and appropriations data for an agency and found the results to be as in Figure 19–2, the longest line would rep-

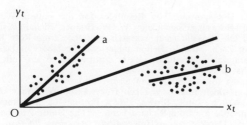

FIGURE 19–2

resent our first fitted equation (or the equation resulting from our first estimate of the value of the coefficient). The points (alternately the residuals) form a pattern of departure from the fitted line. In the early years (a) they fall mostly above the line and in the later years (b) they fall mostly below the line. The process must have been temporally unstable for the period as a whole, i.e., the coefficient had one true value during the first years of the period and a different true value during the last years.

A temporally unstable process is one in which the true coefficient assumes two or more values during the period under consideration. Since we only know the estimated coefficient, we must examine the residuals to determine whether such a pattern is present. Then, we select what appears to be the probable year of change, and fit two lines such as those drawn in above. We then compute the F-Statistic to make our statistical test to determine, at a given level of significance, whether or not the true value of the coefficient shifted. If it was found to shift, the process was temporally stable for some period of time but not necessarily for the entire series of time periods examined.

THE MEANING OF A SHIFT POINT AND A BREAK POINT

The two second lines fitted to Figure 19–2 represent the true process. The year during which the coefficient changes (the year when the pattern shifts from clustering about line (a) to clustering about line (b) is referred to as a shift point. If what appears at first to be a shift in the true value of the coefficient is actually an alteration in behavior so that one equation fits the first subperiod and another equation must be used for the second subperiod, we still refer to the year of the change in realized behavior as a shift point. Break point is the term used to describe a suspected shift point but for which the F-test indicates that the true coefficient value did not shift.

N O T E S

NOTE: The research was sponsored by Resources for the Future. We received valuable criticism from Rufus Browning, Sam Cohn, W. W. Cooper, Richard Cyert, Nelson Polsby, Herbert Simon, and Oliver Williamson, research assistance from Rose Kelly, and editorial assistance from Jean Zorn. Mrs. E. Belton undertook the laborious task of compiling the raw data. We are grateful to Resources for the Future and to our colleagues, but the sole responsibility for what is said here is our own.

1. See the Appendix for explanations of terms and concepts.

2. The description which follows is taken from Aaron Wildavsky. *The Politics of the Budgetary Process* (Boston: Little, Brown, 1964). Portions of the comments on the House Appropriations Committee are from Richard Fenno, "The House Appropriations Committee as a Political System: The Problem of Integration," *American Political Science Review* 56 (1962): 310–324.

3. See H. Thiel, *Linear Aggregation of Economic Relations* (Amsterdam, 1954).

4. Our subsequent discussion of "shift" or "break" points should also make clear that it is not realistic to expect meaningful time series of great length to be accumulated for most agencies in the United States government.

5. Since some readers may not be familiar with the notation we are using, a brief explanation may be in order. As a coefficient of the equation, β_2 is an unknown number that must be estimated from the data, and this coefficient multiplies another number ($y_{t-1} - x_{t-1}$) that may be computed by subtracting last year's request from last year's appropriation. We want the equation to say that the agency will try to counteract large changes in their appropriations by changing their normal requests in the next year. If the agency asks for much more than it thinks it will get and its request is cut, for example, the expression ($y_{t-1} - x_{t-1}$) will be a negative number written in symbolic form as ($y_{t-1} - x_{t-1}$) < 0. A rule of multiplication says that a negative number multiplied by another negative number gives a positive number. If an agency pads its request, however, it presumably follows a cut with a new request which incorporates an additional amount to make allowance for future cuts. In order to represent this behavior, that is to come out with a positive result incorporating the concept of padding, the unknown coefficient β_2 must be negative ($\beta_2 < 0$).

6. The agency that favors its own programs should increase its requests over time. In the absence of the stochastic disturbance (when the random variable is 0), the request

in a given year should be larger than the request in the previous year so that $x_t > x_{t-1}$. Therefore, the unknown coefficient β_2 must be larger than one ($\beta_2 > 1$) since it multiplies last year's request.

7. Other gaming strategies are easily proposed. Suppose, for example, that a given agency believes that it knows the decision rule that Congress uses in dealing with it, and that this decision rule can be represented by one of (4), (7), or (8), above. Presume, for reasons analogous to those outlined for (8), that this agency desires to take into account that positive or negative portion of the previous year's appropriation y_{t-1} that was not based on the previous year's request x_{t-1}. This consideration suggests

$$x_t = \beta_4 y_{t-1} + \beta_5 \Delta_{t-1} + \delta_t$$

as an agency decision rule where Δ_{t-1} is a dummy variable representing in year $t-1$ the term not involving x_{t-1} in one of (4), (7) or (8) above. If one believes that agency and Bureau of the Budget personnel are sufficiently well acquainted with the Senators and Congressmen to be able to predict the value of the current stochastic disturbance, then it becomes reasonable to examine a decision rule of the form

$$x_t = \beta_6 y_{t-1} + \beta_7 \Delta_t + \delta_t$$

where Δ_t is defined as above. No evidence of either form of behavior was found, however, among the agencies that were investigated. We also estimated the parameters of the third order autoregressive scheme for the requests of an individual agency in

$$x_t = \beta_8 x_{t-1} + \beta_9 x_{t-2} + \beta_{10} x_{t-3} + \tau_t$$

an attempt to discover if naive models would fit as well as those above. In no case did this occur and generally the fits for this model were very poor. A similar scheme was estimated for the appropriations y_t of an individual agency with similar results with respect to equations (4), (7) and (8) above. Since the "d" statistic suggests that no higher order Markov process would be successful, no other rules for agency behavior were tried.

8. Agency proposals to the Bureau of the Budget are not reported to the public and could be obtained only for these eight subagencies.

9. Three interrelated difficulties arise in the analysis of the time series data x_t, y_t for an agency. The first problem is the choice of a technique for estimating the parameters of the alternate schemes in some optimal fashion. Given these estimates and their associated statistics, the second problem is the choice of criteria for selecting the model best specifying the system underlying the data. Finally, one is faced with the problem of examining the variability of the underlying parameters of the best specification. We believe that our solution to these problems, while far from optimal, is satisfactory given the present state of econometric knowledge. See our presentation in "On the Process of Budgeting: An Empirical Study of Congressional Appropriations," by Otto Davis, M. A. H. Dempster, and Aaron Wildavsky, in Gordon Tullock, ed., *Papers on Non-Market Decision Making* (Charlottesville, Va.: Thomas Jefferson Center, University of Virginia, 1966). See especially section 4 and the appendix by Dempster, which contains discussions and derivations of estimation procedures, selection criteria and test statistics for the processes in Section II of this paper.

10. We make the assumption that these two disturbances are independent throughout the paper. Notice, however, that dependence between the disturbances explicitly enters decision equation (8) of section II and those of footnote 7. For these equations, the assumption refers to the disturbance of the current year. That is, we allow the possibility that special circumstances may affect a single participant (Bureau of the Budget or Congress) as well as both. When the latter case occurred, our selection criteria resulted in the choice of equation (8) as best specifying congressional behavior.

11. We are estimating the unknown values of the coefficients (or parameters) of regression equations for each agency. All of our estimators are biased. We use biased estimators for the simple reason that no unbiased estimators are known. The property of consistency is at least a small comfort. All of our estimators are consistent. It might be noted that all unbiased estimators are consistent, but not all consistent estimators are unbiased.

12. This statistic is known as the Durbin-Watson ratio. A description of the test may be found in J. Johnston, *Econometric Methods* (New York: McGraw-Hill, 1963), p. 92.

13. H. Theil and A. L. Nagar, "Testing the Independence of Regressional Disturbances," *Journal of the American Statistical Association* 56 (1961): 793–806. These significance points were used to construct further significance points when necessary. See Davis, Dempster, and Wildavsky, *op. cit.*

14. The test is described in T. W. Anderson, *An Introduction to Multivariate Analysis* (New York: John Wiley, 1958), pp. 69–71. See Dempster's appendix to Davis, Dempster, and Wildavsky, *op. cit.*, for some justification of the use of the test.

15. See Davis, Dempster, and Wildavsky, *op. cit.*

16. G. C. Chow, "Tests of Equality between Sets of Coefficients in Two Linear Regressions," *Econometrica* 28 (1960): 591–605, and the appendix to Davis, Dempster, and Wildavsky, *op. cit.*

17. In a few instances an inspection of the residuals indicated that a shift point occurred so early or so late in the series that it was not possible to compute a meaningful stationarity F-Statistic. In these few cases the deviant observations were dropped and the usual analysis performed on the shortened time series. Thus we "forced" a break in every case in order to perform subsequent operations.

18. The apparent discrepancy between the latter part of Table 19–3 and Table 19–1 is caused by the fact that for two agencies, the Bureau of Census and the Office of Education, although the Agency-Bureau of the Budget decision equations are temporally stable and best specified as (1), when a shift point is forced, the criteria indicate (3) for the latter period.

19. Some of the shift points appeared to occur so early in the series that it was not possible to calculate a correlation coefficient.

20. The importance of analyzing deviant cases is suggested in: Milton M. Gordon "Sociological Law and the Deviant Case," *Sociometry* 10 (1947); Patricia Kendall and Katharine Wolf, "The Two Purposes of Deviant Case Analysis," in Paul F. Lazarsfeld and Morris Rosenberg, eds., *The Language of Social Research* (Glencoe, Ill.: The Free Press, 1962), pp. 103–137; Paul Horst, *The Prediction of Personal Adjustments: A Survey of the Logical Problems and Research Techniques* (New York, 1941); and Seymour Lipset, Martin Trow, and James Coleman, *Union Democracy* (New York: Doubleday, 1960).

21. We are indebted to Rose M. Kelly, a graduate student in the Department of Political Science, University of California, Berkeley, who did the research on the deviant cases and provided the data for Tables 19–6 and 19–7.

22. See Wildavsky, *op. cit.*, pp. 64–68, for a discussion of clientele and confidence. In his forthcoming book, *The Power of the Purse* (Boston: Little, Brown, 1966), Richard Fenno provides further evidence of the usefulness of these categories.

23. Geoffrey P. E. Clarkson, *Portfolio Selection: A Simulation of Trust Investment* (Englewood Cliffs, N.J.: Prentice-Hall, 1962); G. P. E. Clarkson and H. A. Simon, "Simulation of Individual and Group Behavior," *American Economic Review* 50 (1960): 920–932; Richard Cyert and James March, eds., *A Behavioral Theory of the Firm* (Englewood Cliffs, N.J.: Prentice-Hall, 1963); Allen Newell, "The Chess Machine: An Example of Dealing with a Complex Task by Adaptation," *Proceedings of the Western Joint Computer Conference* (1955), pp. 101–108; Allen Newell, J. C. Shaw, and H. A. Simon, "Elements of a Theory of Human Problem Solving," *Psychological Review* 65 (1958): 151–166; Allen Newell and H. A. Simon, "The Logic Theory Machine: A Complex Information Processing System," *Transactions on Information Theory* (1956), 61–79; W. R. Reitman, "Programming Intelligent Problem Solvers," *Transactions on Human Factors in Electronics*, HFE-2 (1961), pp. 26–33; H. A. Simon, "A Behavioral Model of Rational Choice," *Quarterly Journal of Economics* 60 (1955): 99–118; and H. A. Simon, "Theories of Decision Making in Economics and Behavioral Science," *American Economic Review* 49 (1959): 253–283.

24. David Braybrooke and Charles Lindblom, *A Strategy of Decision* (New York: Free Press, 1964).

25. Wildavsky, *op. cit.*, pp. 8–63.

26. James March, "The Power of Power," in David Easton, ed., *Varieties of Political Theory* (Englewood Cliffs, N.J., Prentice-Hall, 1966), pp. 39–70.

27. See the forthcoming studies by John P. Crecine on budgeting in Pittsburgh, Detroit, and Cleveland, and by Donald Gerwin on the Pittsburgh School District. Aaron Wildavsky will attempt to apply variations of the models in this paper to Oakland, California.

28. Aaron Wildavsky, "Private Markets and Public Arenas," *The American Behavioral Scientist* 9 (September 1965): 33–39.

PART V

What Difference Does Reform Make?

20

WHAT DIFFERENCE DOES IT MAKE?

When at gatherings of political scientists the inevitable questions are raised—What is political science (public administration)? How should one approach it?—the best response is undoubtedly to leave the room. Why? Because it is a matter of empirical observation that such discussions degenerate into a futile search for essences. The result may be to leave the discussant angry, annoyed, dissatisfied, or even bemused, but never, it seems, enlightened. Far better to take an eclectic attitude—let us all go and do something and then we will see whether it is any good. "By their works shall ye know them" appears to be a much more useful guide than "by their definitions of political science" shall their worth be known.

Discussions of this or that approach to the study of politics typically become bogged down in fruitless (and seemingly endless) quarrels about whether the approach is or is not "behavioral." What on earth can this mean? Does anybody study nonbehavior? Are courses given and books written on things rarely contemplated but never done? Broadly conceived, "behavior" appears to be just a synonym for politics, for what men think and for how they act in the political sphere. Since most investigators are concerned with what political actors do or might do, the question comes down to asking which methods are most appropriate for studying a particular kind of behavior. This kind of question is amenable to answer by standards traditional to scholarly inquiry. Is the method appropriate to the purpose? Are the conclusions interesting and are they supported by reasonable evidence? Which method tells us the most about the subject in the least space and with greatest relevance to other work? And, by far most important, what has actually been done to demonstrate the usefulness of an approach as opposed to making claims or telling other people what to do or issuing proclamations. That superbly revealing distinction between work which is good, bad, or indifferent, is more than adequate for the purpose of distinguishing political scientists from one another.

A large part of the literature on public administration in the United States consists of uncritically held normative statements. Whether the subject is the organization of the Executive Branch,[1] civil service,[2] budgetary reform,[3] the creation of metropolitan governments,[4] the role of the expert,[5] or the forms of urban administrative activity,[6] unexamined normative assumptions are more important in determining the results of inquiries than is observation of what happens. No matter how much the famous politics-administration dichotomy is formally rejected, for example, it continues to color a great deal of the writing on administration. While the claim that administrators do not exercise discretion is abandoned explicitly, it is reintroduced, among other ways, in pleas for central planning and for decision-making by experts. As a result, the literature is full of proposals for reform whose radical implications for the outcomes of politics are not appreciated, and it is noticeably lacking in analysis of existing practices whose profound effect upon outcomes is not noticed. In view of the existing state of the discipline, this paper suggests that much greater stress on what actually happens, on the development of descriptive (positive) theory is in order.

This is not to say that I am guilty or innocent or advocating something terrible called by the awkward title of "a value-free social science." One of the most obnoxious trends of the times is the strident demand that we all choose up sides when many of us do not want to play this particular game at all. It seems reprehensible to me that a scholar has to apologize for trying to be descriptive (or normative) when that is the aspect which interests him at a particular time, or else face critics who contend that he has prostituted himself if he has not bowed to their special deity on every occasion. Why can we not try to be as value-free as possible when we feel like it and as full of value statements as possible when we feel like it without having to pass this arbitrary social science litmus test every time we venture forth.

The problem for the scholar is not so much whether to be normative or descriptive or usually both, but to be clear as to what he is about and to make his intentions clear to others. To be above-board, to put one's cards on the table is an essential requirement of scholarship. Now in politics it is often good tactics to be rather muddy about what is involved for various interests in a given situation. The participants may never be able to agree if everyone is all too clear about what is precisely at stake. But I doubt if we would commend this procedure to the scholar ostensibly trying to communicate with his fellows. It is one thing, to cite another example, for military officers to use the artificial distinctions between command and staff officers for purposes of bureaucratic infighting, and quite another for scholars to perpetuate this distinction on ostensibly scientific grounds.[7] It would be far better if academics were to face up to the normative pose in which many feel most comfortable and openly consider how to best realize their values, than to pretend to be describing while actually prescribing. A thoroughgoing normative bent would also offer the special advantage of highlighting the lack of descriptive propositions on which to base reforms.

One of the many things which students of politics are interested in is outcomes. Why this decision rather than that, why this distribution of losses and gain rather than another, why one kind of outcome in a particular political system and a different kind of another one? We study Congress as an institution partly because of the belief that its operations help determine the kinds of outcomes which take place, that is, because the way Congress works makes a difference to our politics. If the kinds of decisions which the American national legislature made remained the same regardless of whether there was a congressional system, a parliamentary system, or any other system, then there would be little point in studying Congress. Only an antiquarian or an addict of the German footnote school would feel obliged to study an institution whose distinguishing characteristics made no difference to the kind of legislation enacted in the United States and hence had no impact on its inhabitants. Students of Soviet politics do not study what passes for the national legislature in trying to discover how legislation is made; they turn to the party or the bureaucracy or the secret police or some center where there is some reason to believe that what happens makes some difference. Whether one is primarily normative or descriptive, one's inquiry is in some sense guided by a belief that the institution or practice one is explaining or is interested in changing makes some difference in the outcomes of a political system.

In studying a practice or an institution or a proposed change in accustomed ways of doing things, I have found it useful to ask, what difference it makes to the outcomes of the political system. Would we, for example, get different kinds of Presidents who would prefer different kinds of policies if we counted votes in other ways than through an Electoral College mechanism? Would we get different kinds of Representatives who preferred different kinds of policies and acted on these preferences if the rules governing apportionment were different? Since the answers seem to be emphatically, "yes," it appears worthwhile to try to specify the consequences for the outcomes of our politics of the rules concerning representation. If the answer were "no," as might have been the case if we had asked whether the basic maladies of Fourth Republic France could have been overcome by changing the election laws, we would have searched elsewhere for the factors that would have made a difference.

Rather than leave the reader with some general advice—go and inquire about the differences that variations in administrative practices make to the outcomes of the political process—it would be more useful to present examples hopefully demonstrating both the need for and the utility of this approach. This volume contains several essays which are useful for the purpose. The article on "Salvation by Staff" surveys some of the unrecognized consequences of proposals to help the President which are anything but helpful to him. "The Political Implications of Budgetary Reform", "The Political Economy of Efficiency," and "Rescuing Policy Analysis from PPBS" are concerned with the different impact of program versus line item budgeting. Here it may be helpful to deal with a subject that is often discussed but almost never analyzed, namely, the proliferation of committees. Instead of concentrating on the kinds of committee arrangements that facilitate or hinder action, or that move decisions in one direction or another, the usual approach is to complain that there are too many of them. Proposals to eliminate interdepartmental committees, for example, founder because they either involve changes that make no difference or that presuppose too great a difference in outcomes. Let us look into the matter a little further.

Whenever anything goes wrong in the federal government, especially when some interests and their supporters in academic life do not get the action they want, someone is sure to say that the difficulty lies with all those interdepartmental committees. In fact, when a scapegoat is needed for almost any purpose the proliferation of committees is a handy target. All the noise to the contrary not withstanding, however, the problem of committees, when posed in this fashion, is strictly illusory.

Consider two of the most elementary propositions about national political administration: (1) most important issues involve several agencies; (2) departments and bureaus represent somewhat independent areas of influence to the extent that the President frequently cannot command their obedience but must work through persuasion, bargaining, and conflict. It follows that "government by committee" is inevitable, for only if the expertise and support of various agencies is not necessary can they be bypassed. No doubt a person with a pathological fear of committees may avoid them by going around serially to all the agencies represented and securing the essential clearances. This process contains the essence of the committee principle—clearance; it just takes longer and requires a more athletic person.

Putting the blame on the committee system may serve to hide the fact that the Chief Executive does not want to act. It is an error to assume that the only purpose of committees is to make decisions, and that something must be wrong with them if this purpose is not served. Committees may and do serve many other purposes as the following brief enumeration should demonstrate. Committees may

1. Delay decisions until the President and other participants are ready to act.

2. Postpone interdepartmental conflicts by insisting on further discussion before the conflict spills over into the public arena.

3. Kill a proposed action by keeping the matter under consideration

endlessly with no intent to do anything about it. This is the administrative version of the filibuster.

4. Divorce the President from an issue when he is unwilling to use up his influence but is willing to accept whatever agreement may be bargained out by the interested agencies. In the absence of widespread agreement among the participants, the result may be inaction or a vastly watered down policy. Sometimes the conferees may decide that some agreement is better than none and will come up with something. Whatever happens or fails to happen the President has succeeded in avoiding unwanted involvement.

5. Spread the responsibility where no one participant feels able to assume the risk. In bureaucratic jargon a request to "initial" a document is often interpreted as meaning, "let's spread the risk." Rather than necessarily inhibiting action, a committee mode of operation may facilitate it by permitting the sharing of risks and obligations and, if necessary, of the sanctions which may follow.

6. Add legitimacy to an outcome, thus increasing the commitment to abide by it.

7. Increase the bargaining power of the President through a version of what T. C. Schelling has called the commitment tactic. By claiming that a committee has limited his freedom, or that he has given it a solemn pledge, a President may be able to induce others to accept his position since he has limited his ability to accept theirs.

To spell out in detail the differences in outcomes attributable to varieties of interdepartmental committees would be a worthy undertaking. To ask that they be eliminated, however, is to suggest a radical change in the national political system in which the pluralism of interests in the federal bureaucracy which gives them life would be undermined. What difference would it make if interdepartmental committees were abolished? A great deal, almost too much, since this would have been accompanied by a change to another political system in order to be effective. Very little, if things remain as they are because some equivalent of the committees would be certain to appear so long as agencies represent interests which cannot be coerced.

NOTES

1. See Norton Long, "Power and Administration," *Public Administration Review* (1949), pp. 257–264; Simon, Smithburgh and Thompson, *Public Administration*, 1950; and Karl A. Bosworth, "The Politics of Management Improvement in the States," *American Political Science Review* (1953), pp. 84–99.

2. See Herbert Kaufman, "Emerging Conflicts in the Doctrines of Public Administration," *American Political Science Review* (1956), pp. 1057–1073; Herman M. Somers, "Some Reservations about the Senior Civil Service," *Personnel Administration* 19: 10 ff; and mimeographed paper by Wallace Sayre delivered at the Conference on the Political Executive, Princeton, 1956.

3. See Aaron Wildavsky, "Political Implications of Budgetary Reform," *Public Administration Review* 21 (1961): 183–190, Chapter 9 of this volume.

4. See Edward Banfield, "The Politics of Metropolitan Area Organizations," *Midwest Journal of Political Science* (1957), pp. 62–75.

5. See York Wilburn, "Professionalization in the Public Service," *Public Administration Review* (1954), pp. 13–21.

6. See Lawrence Herson, "The Lost World of Municipal Government," *American Political Science Review* (1957), pp. 330–345.

7. See Paul Hammond, *Organizing for Defense* (Princeton: Princeton University Press, 1961), especially pp. 118–122.

21

SALVATION BY STAFF: REFORM OF THE PRESIDENTIAL OFFICE

By all accounts, the presidency is the most important political institution in American life. To many people, Presidents symbolize the nation. It is not surprising, therefore, that citizens have large expectations concerning the man who fills the presidency. Presidents are expected to lead the nation. They must maintain prosperity. They must strive constantly to preserve a just and honorable peace. They must secure social justice. They must manage a vast governmental apparatus. They must exercise power without being overbearing. They must act for all the people while building and furthering the fortunes of their own political party. Several years ago, when a national game was made out of defining national goals, it became apparent that even if the citizenry was unable to define its own goals, the President was expected to perform this function. It is clear that the expectations are so great that no man or institution can fulfill them. It is also clear that the expectations are often mutually inconsistent if not contradictory.

The overwhelming expectations surrounding the presidency have naturally led many people to suggest that the President needs help and to devise means for ostensibly helping him. This is one case, however, where Presidents need to be more wary of their friends than their enemies. There are proposals for helping the President by taking his job away. There are proposals for helping him by making him take advice from people he has not chosen and he may not like.

Suggestions for lightening the burden of the presidency are many and often contradictory. Should help consist largely in simplifying the govern-

From Aaron Wildavsky, ed., *The Presidency* (Boston: Little, Brown, 1969), pp. 694–700. Reprinted by permission.

mental structure so that, supposedly, it will be easier to manage? Or should it take quite the opposite course, calling on more people, more agencies, and more devices?

Before 1939, the President officially had only three assistants assigned to him. Today the Executive Office has some 5,000 functionaries and employees. It includes the Budget Bureau and the Council of Economic Advisers. There are numerous special Presidential assistants. There is the regular White House office personnel. There are the National Security Council, the Office of Defense Mobilization, and the President's Advisory Council on Government Organization. But despite the phenomenal growth in the number of people who are supposed to help the President, his job remains as difficult as ever.

In view of the confusion as to what causes the trouble, let's first make a brief analysis of the problems which the President faces. We can then turn to the question of what changes in the Executive Office might result in a real contribution toward easing the tremendously difficult job of being President.

The President of the United States needs—perhaps more than anything else—these three things to help him in his task. He needs knowledge—an immense supply of knowledge—to enable him to make his plans and decisions wisely. He needs time to do his thinking and to perform the work essential to meeting the responsibilities of the presidency with greatest effect and success. And he needs support—from his Cabinet, from the Congress, from the people—if he is successfully to carry out his program.

But these are the very things often denied him, at least in part. No man, no matter how wise, can possess within himself the knowledge which a President requires to deal with the countless number of problems and questions that confront him. He must rely to a very considerable extent on the knowledge and information of others to help brief him. The President's time tends to be gobbled up not only by essentials but by seeming nonessentials. Some of the demands on his time can perhaps be lightened by improvements in the organization of the government and of the Office of the Presidency itself.

But it would be a grave error to suggest that he give up all acts of symbolic importance, such as lighting the national Christmas tree and putting medals on the chests of those who have performed heroic acts. For Presidents soon discover that many things they do lead to criticism; it is in the very nature of the job that everyone cannot be satisfied. It is all the more important, then, that Presidents appear occasionally in symbolic roles that enable them to act for all the people in a noncontroversial way. Presidents need all the support they can get.

No President can carry out a program simply by issuing orders. The carrying out of his program depends on the degree of support which he can muster for it. Nor can a President count on an assured basis of support for everything he wants to accomplish just because he has won the general support of the citizenry in the Presidential election. Individuals and interest groups which support him on one policy may oppose him on another. Indeed, he has to be careful not permanently to antagonize important interests on any one thing because he may need their support when it comes to other issues.

Given the fragmentation of power in the national political system, today's opponents are often tomorrow's indispensable allies. Presidents try to enact their policies through creation of a series of *ad hoc* coalitions varying from issue to issue and from time to time. They are well advised not to prematurely close off sources of support. The fact that we have a vital federal system in which groups with special interests are concentrated in various geographical areas means that they demand and often receive special representation in Congress.

Congress holds the vital power of the purse and the general legislative authority which the President needs and without which he can accomplish little. Yet the President is unable to control the actions of most legislators because he cannot either help or harm them by affecting their chances for nomination or election. Presidential intervention would be resented on grounds of local autonomy and is likely to prove ineffectual because the interests that the Presidents represent are unlikely to be mirrored exactly in many congressional districts around the country. The most influential men in Congress are the committee chairmen whose power is based on the seniority which comes with continuous service. These men tend to come from safe districts which reelect them year after year. The result is that the President is dependent on Congressmen whose tenure in office is relatively invulnerable to anything he can do and whose constituencies are much narrower than his.

Even in making Cabinet appointments, the President is not entirely free to follow his own preferences. He may have to "give away" appointments to placate an opposing wing of his own party, to secure the support of a powerful interest group, or to mitigate the antagonism of an influential Congressman. Moreover, department heads are expected to champion the cause of the labor, commerce, veteran, and other clientele groups which they serve and represent. Indeed, Cabinet members must serve these interests to some extent if they are to serve the President. For if a large number of important interests become hostile to the President at the same time, he would not find this advantageous even if the excuse was that his Cabinet members were putting his preferences before those of their clientele. It is, therefore, a profound error in American politics to say that merely because the President has formal power of appointment he necessarily controls a particular agency.

His task is to get support wherever he can in order to build up coalitions of interests on each particular policy. And to do this he must do a great deal more bargaining and persuading than ordering.

How can the President's degree of support be strengthened—and should it be strengthened? He already has the veto power, and extensive powers over the military forces and over foreign affairs. He can avail himself of some patronage in making appointments. He has unparalleled publicity facilities for letting the citizenry know his views. He wields great moral force as the symbol of the nation.

One way to increase the influence he now holds would be to give him powers to compel the allegiance of a majority of Congress. Another way would be to enable him to discipline members of his party who disagreed with his policies. It soon becomes apparent that the measures necessary to give the President significantly greater assured support would involve radical changes in the American system of government.

"Salvation By Staff"

The fact that the President's time and knowledge are limited means that he can deal only with a small number of the thousands of issues that come up within the administrative apparatus.

So here is where the President can truly be helped by getting aid from other people. He can hire observers to tell him what is going on in the government and country. He can hire experts to supply information. He can use advisers to suggest courses of action. He can use negotiators to deal with others on his behalf. He can delegate areas of decision to others. Yet the President's use of other people to overcome some of his limitations creates serious problems.

The first problem that the President encounters in using the help of other people is related to the question of support of his policies. Although a Cabinet officer presumably handles decisions for the President, he may be beholden to others and fail fully to represent the President's policy preferences.

Furthermore, how can the President be certain that an adviser will perform or recommend actions in accord with the President's own preferences? If the President lays down detailed instructions, the problem is minimized. But the greater the detail which the President gets into, the greater the amount of time and effort he must expend. And the President is still dependent on his staff for initial advice as to what his preferences ought to be in cases where his knowledge is limited, his time is short, or he has not yet formed opinions.

A further problem is that in seeking "salvation by staff" the President runs into serious managerial difficulties. There is a limit to the amount of information or advice it is useful for the President to have or on which he has time to act. After a while, the addition of new staff just multiplies his managerial problems without giving him valuable service in return.

The multiplication of staff members creates another problem. When these men discover that the President is receiving all the information and advice he can assimilate, they are apt to be left without enough to do. In this circumstance there is a tendency to make work by taking over the operational responsibilities of the regular agencies. But this tendency destroys the one quality above all others which the staff must have if it is directly and dispassionately to serve the Chief Executive: the ability to view problems from the broad perspective of the presidency rather than from the necessarily narrower perspectives of the operating agencies.

Still another problem stems from the protectiveness which staff members may come to feel for the President. They may try to shield him from unpleasant information or contacts. They may try to cheer him up by telling him what they think he wants to hear. Jealous of their access to him, they may screen out people whom they do not want him to see. It is up to the President to make certain that he has alternative channels of information and that the lines of access to him are not blocked. For if the President lets a staff man act as his Prime Minister, he will find himself relegated to the status of a constitutional monarch with only symbolic powers.

The President is not only served by his staff; he must also constantly guard against becoming its victim. There is no more certain way of controlling a President than controlling the people available to help him. President Truman recognized this in his relationship to the Council of Economic Advisers. The council was established in 1946 to advise the President on general economic problems relating to the maintenance of a high degree of employment. The original structure provided for a three-man body appointed by the President subject to senatorial confirmation. The expectation was that men of differing points of view would be chosen, that they would be impartial, and that they would also serve as congressional advisers. But this scheme proved unworkable.

Difficulties arose when members of the council who did not share the preferences of the President sought to give him their advice. There were also council members who would give advice but would not tackle the critical task of seeking political support for their recommendations.

As for the council's dual function of serving also in advisory capacity to Congress, experience proved that no cohesive group of legislators in Congress could make effective use of the council to put through a unified program. The reason is that there is no group of men in Congress sufficiently small to be able to act, sufficiently cohesive to be able to agree, and sufficiently powerful to guarantee that their program will be adopted in Congress. There is a name for a governing body that does all of these things —it is called a Cabinet under the British model. As a result the council's organization was changed so that the President appointed the chairman as its chief officer solely responsible to him.

Judging from what has been discussed, what are the conditions under which appointees or additions to the presidential staff are most useful to the President?

These criteria might serve as a rule of thumb:

First, staff members must represent the President's personal choice and not that of any other person or group. Second, they must accept political responsibility for mustering support behind his programs. Third, he must be able to use them as he sees fit and not as others dictate. Fourth, their value to him must be greater than the additional burden of management caused by their presence. Fifth, they must not relieve his burdens by also relieving him of the most important prerogatives of his office.

Reform by Organization Chart

A perennial type of reform (advanced by the President's Commission on Administrative Management in 1937 and by the two Hoover Commissions in 1949 and 1955) calls for reducing the number of government agencies reporting to the President by putting them under a few great departments.

The rationale behind these proposals is that the President would exercise greater control over government agencies by placing them directly under his line of command through faithful Cabinet Officers. The difficulty with plans of this kind is that they confuse clarity and simplicity on an organization chart with an actual increase of presidential control. All the President might get would be a paper integration, because his need for support would still necessitate giving away appointments to high positions and would still prevent him from controlling agencies with powerful congressional and interest-group support. After all, if the President were able to be sure that Cabinet members would follow and enforce his preferences, he would not need the large Executive Office staff he has now.

One can imagine that all federal agencies were put within the Executive Office of the President. The result of this extreme move would be to create additional employment for sign painters, but not much else. For underneath the title on every office would have to be painted in "of the Executive Office of the President." But it is easy to see that nothing else would happen because people would still remain in the same buildings and their relationships to the President would not have been changed at all.

Critics of American foreign and defense policies in the past have complained that the National Security Council subordinated our military position to budgetary requirements. They suggested reorganizing the NSC to give higher priority to national defense. Presumably, these critics believed that changing the NSC's structure would also change the President's policy preferences. Yet it is difficult to see how any organizational change will prevent the President from getting advice he wants to take from the Budget Director or the Secretary of the Treasury unless he is forbidden to see these people. As is so often the case, what we have here are differences in policy masquerading in the more palatable guise of organizational reform. Making the President adopt other people's policies is an odd form of aid.

Another type of reform is contained in the proposal that the President should be served by a new management staff with its personnel drawn largely from the civil service. But what would happen then to the role of the President as a political leader with an overwhelming need for responsiveness and support? How could the President afford to take advice from people who, because of their civil service status, could not become fully identified with his program and openly develop support for it? The result would be to compel the President to take advice from people whose preferences may differ from his, whom he has not had a completely free hand in choosing, but who are in a position to exercise great influence over the information he receives and the alternatives he considers.

Other Reorganizational Suggestions

In recent years there has been a rash of proposals for the appointment of an Assistant President to take over some of the Chief Executive's responsibilities. For example, it has been suggested that a sort of Super-Secretary be created to handle the development and coordination of military and foreign policies. But this is precisely the President's greatest task at the present time. To delegate this task to someone else would virtually mean abdicating his office. If this person were a man of independent influence he would use his resources to thwart the President in cases of disagreement. Furthermore, if he had no considerable political support to bring to the job in order to get the program accepted, there is no reason to believe that he would be more successful at it than the President.

Some people propose giving the Vice President extraordinary responsibilities. They forget that he often represents a different party faction than the President. He may very possibly not agree with the President on key policies.

A more drastic proposal calls for the establishment of a plural executive —that is, three presidents instead of one. They might each have more time to work (and perhaps to disagree) but the scheme would sacrifice what is probably the major asset of the President today—his ability to speak with a single voice and propose a single line of policy.

At bottom, these proposals represent an abiding distrust of the President and a desire to protect the country against him if he should prove weak. But does guarding against weak Presidents by thwarting strong ones seem like a valid answer to the problem?

Saving the President's Time

Another set of suggestions for helping the President involves proposals for saving the President's time so that he can have some moments for reflection. Giving him more staff, however, may actually insulate him from currents of thought he should be aware of in the agencies which have operating responsibility for meeting the nation's problems. The President might have more time to think at the expense of not having much to think about.

No doubt there are ceremonial duties which he might give up to save time. But can he avoid them all, since he has a role to perform as symbol of the nation and this role helps him gain support for his other activities? Without at all minimizing the problem of time, it does appear that this has been overemphasized in relation to the President's overriding problem of gaining support for his policies. Even as things now are, the number of policies which our Presidents find time to propose always exceeds the number for which they can find support.

Coordination or Coercion?

Virtually all proposals insist that the President needs help in coordinating the activities of the Executive Branch.

There is considerable truth in this assertion. The Chief Executive does need people to report on glaring inconsistencies in policy or to point out activities which are carried on at cross-purposes. And he already has many (perhaps too many) coordinators assigned to this task.

As long as the lack of coordination is a result of ignorance of other people's activities or the complexity of organization, there is a good chance of overcoming it by dedicated staff work. But in many cases lack of coordination is a result of conflicting views about policy which are held by men and agencies which have independent bases of influence in society and Congress. The only way to secure coordination in these cases is for one side to convince or coerce or bargain with the other. When it is understood that "coordination" is often just another word for "coercion," the full scope of the President's difficulties becomes even more apparent. For he is frequently unable to coerce others and the use of staff personnel for this purpose cannot be expected to be any more effective than the President's personal intervention.

Maybe the Job Has To Be as Tough as It Is

It has become fashionable to speak of helping the President as if everyone were agreed that this was a good idea. This is not necessarily so. Of course we all want the President to be able to do his very best both at home and abroad. But in a democracy like ours people have many conflicting interests and there exist legitimate differences of opinion over what the government should do. If the President is made more effective this means that the interests which he represents will have an advantage over competing interests which may find their views more fully represented in Congress. Strengthening the President is not a neutral goal; it has vital implications for the kinds of decisions the government makes. Those who stand to gain and those who stand to lose necessarily take different positions. Consequently, powerful opposition to any move to alter existing relationships in order to make the going smoother for the President is certain to develop.

Conclusion

Is there nothing, then, that we can do to help the President?

One course of action is obvious yet rarely mentioned: we can give him our active political support if we believe he is right—not just be passive bystanders.

In regard to staffing the presidency, the best rule to follow would seem to be letting the President help himself by allowing him the utmost flexibility in the choice, number, characteristics and deployment of his staff. Every President has different personal needs and priorities. Compelling him to use staff as we should like him to is a means of forcing our preferences on him. We ought not be surprised if he resists this kind of "help."

Ultimately, the American people have to decide whether a strong President has now become so indispensable to national survival that, whether he represents our individual preference or not, fundamental changes in the political system must be made to permit him to act more effectively. We deceive ourselves if we think that organizational reforms or piling on multitudes of staff will help the President overcome his biggest problem of all, the problem of obtaining support for his program.

22

RESCUING POLICY
ANALYSIS FROM PPBS

Everyone knows that the nation needs better policy analysis. Each area one investigates shows how little is known compared to what is necessary in order to devise adequate policies. In some organizations there are no ways at all of determining the effectiveness of existing programs; organizational survival must be the sole criterion of merit. It is often not possible to determine whether the simplest objectives have been met. If there is a demand for information the cry goes out that what the organization does cannot be measured. Should anyone attempt to tie the organization down to any measure of productivity, the claim is made that there is no truth in numbers. Oftentimes this is another way of saying, "Mind your own business." Sometimes the line taken is that the work is so subtle that it resists any tests. On other occasions the point is made that only those learned in esoteric arts can properly understand what the organization does, and they can barely communicate to the uninitiated. There are men so convinced of the ultimate righteousness of their cause that they cannot imagine why anyone would wish to know how well they are doing in handling our common difficulties. Their activities are literally priceless; vulgar notions of cost and benefit do not apply to them.

Anyone who has weathered this routine comes to value policy analysis. The very idea that there should be some identifiable objectives and that attention should be paid to whether these are achieved seems a great step forward. Devising alternative ways of handling problems and considering the future costs of each solution appear creative in comparison to more haphazard approaches. Yet policy analysis with its emphasis upon originality, imagination, and foresight, cannot be simply described. It is equivalent to what Robert N. Anthony has called strategic planning: ". . . the

From *Public Administration Review* 29 (March–April 1969), pp. 189–202. Reprinted by permission.

process of deciding on objectives of the organization, on changes in these objectives, on the resources used to attain these objectives. . . . It connotes big plans, important plans, plans with major consequences." [1] While policy analysis is similar to a broadly conceived version of systems analysis,[2] Yehezkel Dror has pointed up the boundaries that separate a narrow study from one with larger policy concerns. In policy analysis,

1. Much attention would be paid to the political aspects of public decision-making and public policy-making (instead of ignoring or condescendingly regarding political aspects). . . .
2. A broad conception of decision-making and policy-making would be involved (instead of viewing all decision-making as mainly a resources allocation). . . .
3. A main emphasis would be on creativity and search for new policy alternatives, with explicit attention to encouragement of innovative thinking. . . .
4. There would be extensive reliance on . . . qualitative methods. . . .
5. There would be much more emphasis on futuristic thinking. . . .
6. The approach would be looser and less rigid, but nevertheless systematic, one which would recognize the complexity of means-ends interdependence, the multiplicity of relevant criteria of decision, and the partial and tentative nature of every analysis. . . .[3]

Policy analysis aims at providing information that contributes to making an agency politically and socially relevant. Policies are goals, objectives, and missions that guide the agency. Analysis evaluates and sifts alternative means and ends in the elusive pursuit of policy recommendations. By getting out of the fire-house environment of day-to-day administration, policy analysis seeks knowledge and opportunities for coping with an uncertain future. Because policy analysis is not concerned with projecting the *status quo,* but with tracing out the consequences of innovative ideas, it is a variant of planning. Complementing the agency's decision process, policy analysis is a tool of social change.

In view of its concern with creativity, it is not surprising that policy analysis is still largely an art form; there are no precise rules about how to do it. The policy analyst seeks to reduce obscurantism by being explicit about problems and solutions, resources and results. The purpose of policy analysis is not to eliminate advocacy but to raise the level of argument among contending interests. If poor people want greater benefits from the government, the answer to their problems may not lie initially in policy analysis but in political organization. Once they have organized themselves, they may want to undertake policy analysis in order to crystallize their own objectives or merely to compete with the analyses put forth by others. The end result, hopefully, would be a higher quality debate and perhaps eventually public choice among better known alternatives.

A belief in the desirability of policy analysis—the sustained application of intelligence and knowledge to social problems—is not enough to insure its success, no more than to want to do good is sufficient to accomplish noble purposes. If grandiose claims are made, if heavy burdens are placed on officials without adequate compensation, if the needs of agency heads are given scant consideration, they will not desire policy analysis. It is clear that those who introduced the PPB system into the federal government in one fell swoop did not undertake a policy analysis on how to introduce policy analysis into the federal government.

In a paper called "The Political Economy of Efficiency," [4] written just as PPBS was begun in national government, I argued that it would run up against serious difficulties. There is still no reason to change a single word of what I said then. Indeed, its difficulties have been so overwhelming that there is grave danger that policy analysis will be rejected along with its particular manifestation in PPBS. In this essay I shall assess the damage that the planning-programming-budgeting system has done to the prospects of encouraging policy analysis in American national government. Then I would like to suggest some ways of enabling policy analysis to thrive and prosper.

Why Defense Was a Bad Model

A quick way of seeing what went wrong with PPBS is to examine the preconditions for the use of this approach in the Defense Department, from which it was exported throughout the federal government. The immediate origins of PPBS are to be found in The RAND Corporation,[5] where, after World War II, a talented group of analysts devoted years of effort to understanding problems of defense policy. It took five years to come up with the first useful ideas. Thus the first requisite of program budgeting in defense was a small group of talented people who had spent years developing insights into the special problems of defense strategy and logistics. The second requisite was a common terminology, an ad hoc collection of analytical approaches, and the beginnings of theoretical statements to guide policy analysis. When Secretary of Defense Robert McNamara came into office, he did not have to search for men of talent nor did he have to wait for a body of knowledge to be created. These requisites already existed in some degree. What was further necessary was his ability to understand and to use analytical studies. Thus the third requisite of program budgeting is top leadership that understands policy analysis and is determined to get it and make use of it.

The fourth requisite was the existence of planning and planners. Planning was well accepted at the various levels of the Defense Department with the variety of joint service plans, long-range requirement plans, logistical plans, and more. Military and civilians believed in planning, in coping with uncertainty and in specifying some consequences of policy decisions. The problem as the originators of PPBS saw it was to introduce cost considerations into planning; they wanted to stop blue-sky planning and to integrate planning and budgeting. They wanted to use the program budget to bridge the gap between military planners, who cared about requirements but not about resources, and budget people, who were narrowly concerned with financial costs but not necessarily with effective policies.

Policy analysis is expensive in terms of time, talent, and money. It requires a high degree of creativity in order to imagine new policies and to test them out without requiring actual experience. Policy analysis calls for the creation of systems in which elements are linked to one another and to operational indicators so that costs and effectiveness of alternatives may be systematically compared. There is no way of knowing in advance whether the analysis will prove intellectually satisfying and politically feasible. Policy analysis is facilitated when: (1) goals are easily specified, (2) a large margin of error is allowable, and (3) the cost of the contemplated policy makes large expenditures on analysis worthwhile. That part of defense policy dealing with choices among alternative weapons systems was ideally suited for policy analysis. Since the cost of intercontinental missiles or other weapons systems ran into the billions of dollars, it was easy to justify spending millions on analysis.[6] The potential effectiveness of weapons like intercontinental missiles could be contemplated so long as one was willing to accept large margins of error. It is not unusual for analysts to assume extreme cases of damage and vulnerability in a context in which the desire for reducing risk is very great. Hence a goal like assuring sufficient destructive power such that no enemy strike could prevent devastation of one's country may be fuzzy without being unusable. If one accepts a procedure of imagining that possible enemies were to throw three times as much megatonage as intelligence estimates suggest they have, he need not be overly troubled by doubts about the underlying theory. If one is willing to pay the cost of compensating against the worst, lack of knowledge will not matter so much. The point is not that this is an undesirable analytic procedure, quite the contrary, but the extreme cases were allowed to determine the outcomes.

INERTIA

The introduction of new procedures that result in new policies is not easy. Inertia is always a problem. Members of the organization and its clientele groups have vested interests in the policies of the past. Efforts at persuasion must be huge and persistent. But there are conditions that facilitate change. One of these is a rising level of appropriations. If change means that things must be taken away from people in the organization without giving them anything in return, greater resistance may be ex-

pected. The ability to replace old rewards with larger new ones helps reduce resistance to change. The fact that defense appropriations were increasing at a fast rate made life much easier for Mr. McNamara. The
expected objections of clientele groups, for example, were muted by the
fact that defense contractors had lots of work, even if it was not exactly
what they expected. Rapid organizational growth may also improve the
possibilities for change. The sheer increase in organizational size means
that many new people can be hired who are not tied to the old ways. And
speedy promotion may help convince members that the recommended
changes are desirable.

The deeper change goes into the bowels of the organization, the more
difficult it is to achieve. The more change can be limited to central management, the greater the possibility for carrying it out. The changes introduced in the Defense Department did not, for the most part, require acceptance at the lower levels. Consider a proposed change in the organization
of fighting units that would drastically reduce the traditional heavy support
facilities for ground forces. Such a change is not easily manipulated from
Washington. But the choice of one weapons system over another is much
more amenable to central control. The kinds of problems for which program budgeting was most useful also turned out to be problems that could
be dealt with largely at the top of the organization. The program budget
group that McNamara established had to fight with generals in Washington
but not with master sergeants in supply. Anyone who knows the Army
knows what battle they would rather be engaged in fighting.

The ability of an organization to secure rapid change depends, of
course, on the degree of its autonomy from the environment. I have argued
elsewhere [7] that the President of the United States has much more control
over America's foreign policy than over its domestic policy. In almost any
area of domestic policy there is a well-entrenched structure of interests. In
foreign and defense policy, excluding such essentially internal concerns as
the National Guard, the territory within the American political system is
not nearly so well defended; there are far fewer political fortifications,
mines, and boobytraps.

PERSONNEL

Experienced personnel may be a barrier to change. They know something about the consequences of what they are doing. They may have tried
a variety of alternatives and can point to reasons why each one will not
work. If I may recall my low-level Army experience (I entered as a private first class and was never once demoted), the usual reply to a question
about the efficacy of present practice was, "Have you ever been in combat,
son?" But the most dramatic changes introduced in the Pentagon had to do
with questions of avoiding or limiting nuclear war, in which no one had a
claim to experience and in which the basic purpose of analysis is to make

certain that we do not have to learn from experience. If the system fails, the game is over. And since McNamara's men possessed a body of doctrines on defense policy, they had an enormous advantage over regular military who were for a long time unable to defend themselves properly in the new field.[8]

The new policy analysts did not accept the currency of military experience. In their view, naked judgment was not a satisfactory answer to why a policy should be adopted. The Army might know the fire-power of an infantry division, but fire-power was not "effectiveness." Competition among the services for appropriations, however, was favorable to PPBS. There was a defense budget that covered virtually all of the department's subject matter. There were defense missions in which trade-offs could be made between the services. Resources could actually be diverted if the analysis "proved" a particular service was right. Programs could easily be developed because of the facile identification of program with weapons systems and force units. Once the military learned the jargon, they were willing to play the game for an extra division or carrier. So long as dollar losses in one program were more than made up by gains in another, the pain of policy analysis was considerably eased.

The favorable conditions for the limited use of program budgeting in the Department of Defense do not exist in most domestic agencies. There are no large groups of talented policy analysts expert in agency problems outside of the federal government. These nonexistent men cannot, therefore, be made available to the agencies. (The time has passed when eighth-rate systems engineers in aerospace industries are expected to solve basic social problems overnight.) Most agencies had few planners and even less experience in planning. There is no body of knowledge waiting to be applied to policy areas such as welfare and crime. A basic reason for wanting more policy analysis is to help create knowledge where little now exists. There are only a few agencies in which top managers want systematic policy analysis and are able to understand quantitative studies. Goals are not easily specified for most domestic agencies. Nor do they usually have handy equivalents for programs like expensive weapons systems. What Thomas Schelling has so pungently observed about the Department of State—it does not control a large part of the budget devoted to foreign policy—is true for the domestic departments and their lack of coverage as well.[9]

Except for a few individual programs like the proposals for income supplements or assessing the desirability of a supersonic transport, the cost of most domestic policies does not rise into the billions of dollars. Congress and interested publics are not disposed to allow large margins of error. Instead of increasing, the availability of federal funds began declining soon after the introduction of program budgeting. A higher level of conflict was inevitable, especially since the acceptance of proposed changes required the acquiescence of all sorts of people and institutions in the far-flung reaches of the agencies. Social workers, city officials, police chiefs, welfare mothers, field officers, and numerous others were involved in the policies. Program budgeting on the domestic side takes place in a context in which there is both less autonomy from the environment and a great deal more first-hand experience by subordinates. On these grounds alone no one should have been surprised that program budgeting in the domestic agencies did not proceed as rapidly or with as much ostensible success as in the Defense Department.[10]

No One Can Do PPBS

In past writings I argued that program budgeting would run up against severe political difficulties. While most of these arguments have been conceded, I have been told that in a better world, without the vulgar intrusion of political factors (such as the consent of the governed), PPBS would perform its wonders as advertised. Now it is clear that for the narrow purpose of predicting why program budgeting would not work there was no need to mention political problems at all. It would have been sufficient to say that the wholesale introduction of PPBS presented insuperable difficulties of calculation. All the obstacles previously mentioned, such as lack of talent, theory, and data, may be summed up in a single statement: *no one knows how to do program budgeting*. Another way of putting it would be to say that many know what program budgeting should be like in general, but no one knows what it should be in any particular case. Program budgeting cannot be stated in operational terms. There is no agreement on what the words mean, let alone an ability to show another person what should be done. The reason for the difficulty is that telling an agency to adopt program budgeting means telling it to find better policies and there is no formula for doing that. One can (and should) talk about measuring effectiveness, estimating costs, and comparing alternatives, but that is a far cry from being able to take the creative leap of formulating a better policy.

PATTERN OF EVENTS

On the basis of numerous discussions with would-be practitioners of program budgeting at the federal level, I think I can describe the usual pattern of events. The instructions come down from the Bureau of the Budget. You must have a program budget. Agency personnel hit the panic button. They just do not know how to do what they have been asked to do. They turn, if they can, to the pitifully small band of refugees from the Pentagon who have come to light the way. But these defense intellectuals do not know much about the policy area in which they are working. That takes time. Yet something must quickly come out of all this. So they produce a

vast amount of inchoate information characterized by premature quantification of irrelevant items. Neither the agency head nor the examiners in
the Bureau of the Budget can comprehend the material submitted to them.
Its very bulk inhibits understanding. It is useless to the Director of the
Budget in making his decisions. In an effort to be helpful, the program
analysis unit at the Budget Bureau says something like, "Nice try, fellows;
we appreciate all that effort. But you have not quite got the idea of program budgeting yet. Remember, you must clarify goals, define objectives,
relate these to quantitative indicators, project costs into the future. Please
send a new submission based on this understanding."

Another furious effort takes place. They do it in defense, so it must be
possible. Incredible amounts of overtime are put in. Ultimately, under severe time pressure, even more data is accumulated. No one will be able to
say that agency personnel did not try hard. The new presentation makes a
little more sense to some people and a little less to others. It just does not
hang together as a presentation of agency policies. There are more encouraging words from the Budget Bureau and another sermon about specifying
alternative ways of meeting agency objectives, though not, of course, taking the old objectives for granted. By this time agency personnel are desperate. "We would love to do it," they say, "but we cannot figure out the
right way. You experts in the Budget Bureau should show us how to do
it." Silence. The word from on high is that the Bureau of the Budget does
not interfere with agency operations; it is the agency's task to set up its own
budget. After a while, cynicism reigns supreme.

PPBS must be tremendously inefficient. It resembles nothing so much as
a Rube Goldberg apparatus in which the operations performed bear little
relation to the output achieved. The data inputs into PPBS are huge and its
policy output is tiny. All over the federal government the story is the
same: if you ask what good has PPBS done, those who have something favorable to say invariably cite the same one or two policy analyses. At one
time I began to wonder if the oil shale study [11] in the Interior Department
and the maternal and child health care program [12] in Health, Education,
and Welfare were all that had ever come out of the programming effort.

The orders to expand PPBS did not say, "Let us do more policy analysis
than we have in the past." What it said was, "Let us make believe we can
do policy analysis on everything." Instead of focusing attention on areas of
policy amenable to study, the PPBS apparatus requires information on *all*
agency policies.

PROGRAM STRUCTURE

The fixation on program structure is the most pernicious aspect of PPBS.
Once PPBS is adopted, it becomes necessary to have a program structure
that provides a complete list of organization objectives and supplies information on the attainment of each one. In the absence of analytic studies

for all or even a large part of an agency's operations, the structure turns
out to be a sham that piles up meaningless data under vague categories.[13]
It hides rather than clarifies. It suggests comparisons among categories for
which there is no factual or analytical basis. Examination of a department's program structure convinces everyone acquainted with it that policy
analysis is just another bad way of masquerading behind old confusions. A
mere recitation of some program categories from the Department of
Agriculture—Communities of Tomorrow, Science in the Service of Man,
Expanding Dimensions for Living—makes the point better than any comment.

Even if the agency head does understand a data-reduction-summariza-
tion of the program budget, he still cannot use the structure to make decisions, because it is too hard to adjust the elaborate apparatus. Although
the system dredges up information under numerous headings, it says next
to nothing about the impact of one program on another. There is data but
no causal analysis. Hence the agency head is at once oversupplied with
masses of numbers and undersupplied with propositions about the impact
of any action he might undertake. He cannot tell, because no one knows,
what the marginal change he is considering would mean for the rest of his
operation. Incremental changes at the Bureau of the Budget at the agency
level are made in terms of the old budget categories. Since the program
structure is meant to be part of the budget, however, it must be taken as a
statement of current policy and it necessarily emerges as a product of organizational compromise. The program structure, therefore, does not embody a focus on central policy concerns. More likely, it is a haphazard arrangement that reflects the desire to manipulate external support and to
pursue internal power aspirations. Being neither program nor budget, program structure is useless. It is the Potemkin Village of modern administration. The fact that generating bits of random data for the program structure takes valuable time away from more constructive concerns also harms
policy analysis. The whole point of policy analysis is to show that what
had been done intuitively in the past may be done better through sustained
application of intelligence. The adoption of meaningless program structures, and their perversion into slogans for supporting existing policies,
does not—to say the least—advance the cause of policy analysis.

GORHAM TESTIMONY

I do not mean to suggest that the introduction of PPBS has not led to
some accomplishments. Before we consider the significance of these accomplishments, however, it is essential that we understand what PPBS has
manifestly *not* done. One could hardly have a better witness on this subject
than William Gorham, formerly Assistant Secretary (Program Coordination), Department of Health, Education, and Welfare, and now head of the

Urban Institute, who is widely acknowledged to be an outstanding practitioner of program budgeting.

At the highest level of generality, it is clear that PPBS does not help in making choices between vast national goals such as health and defense, nor is PPBS useful in making tradeoffs between more closely related areas of policy such as health, education, and welfare. In his testimony before the Joint Economic Committee, Gorham put the matter bluntly:

> Let me hasten to point out that we have not attempted any grandiose cost-benefit analysis designed to reveal whether the total benefits from an additional million dollars spent on health programs would be higher or lower than that from an additional million spent on education or welfare. If I was ever naïve enough to think this sort of analysis possible, I no longer am. The benefits of health, education, and welfare programs are diverse and often intangible. They affect different age groups and different regions of the population over different periods of time. No amount of analysis is going to tell us whether the Nation benefits more from sending a slum child to pre-school, providing medical care to an old man or enabling a disabled housewife to resume her normal activities. The "grand decisions"—how much health, how much education, how much welfare, and which groups in the population shall benefit—are questions of value judgments and politics. The analyst cannot make much contribution to their resolution.[14]

It turns out that it is extremely difficult to get consensus on goals within a single area of policy. As a result, the policy analysts attempt to find objectives that are more clearly operational and more widely acceptable. Gorham speaks with the voice of experience when he says:

> Let me give you an example. Education. What we want our kids to be as a result of going to school is the level of objective which is the proper and the broadest one. But we want our children to be different sorts of people. We want them to be capable of different sorts of things. We have, in other words, a plurality of opinions about what we want our schools to turn out. So you drop down a level and you talk about objectives in terms of educational attainment—years of school completed and certain objective measures of quality. Here you move in education from sort of fuzzy objectives, but very important, about what it is that you want the schools to be doing, to the more concrete, less controversial, more easily to get agreed upon objectives having to do with such things as educational attainment, percentage of children going to college, etc.
>
> I think the same thing is true in health and in social services, that at the very highest level objective, where in theory you would really like to say something, the difficulty of getting and finding a national consensus is so great that you drop down to something which is more easily and readily accepted as objectives.[15]

What can actually be done, according to Gorham, are analytic studies of narrowly defined areas of policy. "The less grand decisions," Gorham testified, "those among alternative programs with the same or similar objectives within health—can be substantially illuminated by good analysis. It is this type of analysis which we have undertaken at the Department of Health, Education, and Welfare." [16] Gorham gives as examples disease control programs and improvements in the health of children. If this type of project analysis is what can be done under PPBS, a serious question is raised: Why go through all the rigamarole in order to accomplish a few discrete studies of important problems?

A five-year budget conceived in the hodge-podge terms of the program structure serves no purpose.[17] Since actual budget decisions are made in terms of the old categories and policy analysis may take place outside of the program structure, there is no need to institutionalize empty labels. If a policy analysis has been completed, there is no reason why it cannot be submitted as part of the justification of estimates to the Bureau of the Budget and to Congress. For the few program memoranda that an agency might submit, changes could be detailed in terms of traditional budget categories. Problems of program structure would be turned over to the agency's policy analysts who would experiment with different ways of lending intellectual coherence to the agency's programs. There would be no need to foist the latest failure on a skeptical world. Nor would there be battles over the costs of altering a program structure that has achieved, if not a common framework, at least the virtue of familiarity. The difference is that stability of categories in the traditional budget has real value for control [18] while the embodiment of contradictions in the program structure violates its essential purpose.

Incentives for Policy Analysis

PPBS discredits policy analysis. To collect vast amounts of random data is hardly a serious analysis of public policy. The conclusion is obvious. The shotgun marriage between policy analysis and budgeting should be annulled. Attempts to describe the total agency program in program memoranda should be abandoned. It is hard enough to do a good job of policy analysis, as most agency people now realize, without having to meet arbitrary and fixed deadlines imposed by the budget process.[19] There is no way of telling whether an analysis will be successful. There is, therefore, no point in insisting that half-baked analyses be submitted every year because of a misguided desire to cover the entire agency program. The Budget Bureau itself has recently recognized the difficulty by requiring agencies to present extensive memoranda only when major policy issues have been identified. It is easier and more honest just to take the program structure out of the budget.

The thrust of the argument thus far, however, forces us to confront a major difficulty. Policy analysis and budgeting were presumably connected in order to see that high quality analysis did not languish in limbo but was translated into action through the critical budget process. Removing policy analysis from the annual budget cycle might increase its intellectual con-

tent at the expense of its practical impact. While formal program structures should go—PPBS actually inhibits the prospects for obtaining good
analysis that is worth translating into public policy—they should be replaced with a strong incentive to make policy analysis count in yearly
budgetary decisions. I am therefore proposing a substitute for PPBS that
maintains whatever incentive it provided for introducing the results of policy analysis into the real world without encouraging the debilitating effects.

The submission of program memoranda supported by policy analysis
should be made a requirement for major dollar changes in an agency's
budget. The Bureau of the Budget should insist that this requirement be
met by every agency. Agency heads, therefore, would have to require it of
subunits. The sequence could operate as follows:

1. Secretary of agency and top policy analysts review major issues and
legislation and set up a study menu for several years. Additions and dele-
tions are made periodically.
2. Policy analysts set up studies which take anywhere from six to twenty-
four months.
3. As a study is completed for a major issue area, it is submitted to the
secretary of the agency for review and approval.
4. If approved, the implications of the study's recommendations are
translated into budgetary terms for submission as a program memorandum
in support of the agency's fiscal year budget.

No one imagines that a mechanical requirement would in and of itself
compel serious consideration of policy matters. No procedure should be
reified as if it had a life of its own apart from the people who must implement it. This conclusion is as true for my suggestion as for PPBS. We must
therefore consider ways and means of increasing the demand for and supply of policy analysis.

INCREASING DEMAND AND SUPPLY

The first requirement of effective policy analysis is that top management
want it. No matter how trite this criterion sounds, it has often been violated, as Frederick C. Mosher's splendid study of program budgeting in
foreign affairs reveals.[20] The inevitable difficulties of shaking loose information and breaking up old habits will prove to be insuperable obstacles
without steady support from high agency officials. If they do not want it,
the best thing to do is concentrate efforts in another agency. Placing the
best people in a few agencies also makes it more likely that a critical mass
of talent will be able to achieve a creative response to emerging policy
problems.

Policy analysis should be geared to the direct requirements of top management. This means that analysis should be limited to a few major issues. Since there will only be a few studies every year, the secretary should have time to consider and understand each one. The analytical staff should be flexible enough to work on his priority interests. Consequently, one of the arguments by which program budgeting has been oversold has to be abandoned. Policy analysis will not normally identify programs of low priority. Top management is not interested in them. They would receive no benefit from getting supporters of these programs angry at them. Instead, agency heads want to know how to deal with emergent problems. Practitioners of policy analysis understand these considerations quite well. Harry Shooshan, Deputy Undersecretary for Programs, Department of the Interior, presents a perceptive analysis:

. . . We have tried to more heavily relate our PPB work and our analytical work to the new program thrusts, and major issues, not because it is easier to talk about new programs, but rather, there is a good question of judgment, on how much time one should spend on ongoing programs that are pretty well set. So you restate its mission and you put it in PPB wrapping and what have you really accomplished?

There are going to be new program proposals, new thrusts of doing something in certain areas. Let's relate our analyses to that and get the alternatives documented as well as we can for the decision-makers. So it is a combination of on the one hand it being difficult to identify low priorities in a manner that really means something and on the other hand, it is the fact of what have we really accomplished by simply putting old programs in new wrappings when new programs really should get the emphasis right now in terms of what are the decisions now before, in my case, the Secretary of the Interior, in terms of what should he know before he makes decisions relative to where he is attempting to go. If I can relate PPB to the decision on his desk today and the near future, I can sell him and in turn, our own Department on the contribution that we can make.[21]

The implications of Shooshan's point go beyond making policy analysis more desirable by having it meet the needs of top management. The subjects for policy analysis ought to be chosen precisely for their critical-fluid-emergent character. These are the places where society is hurting. These are the areas in which there are opportunities for marginal gains. Indeed, a major role for top management is scanning the political horizon for targets of opportunity. Yet the characteristics of these new problems run counter to the criteria for selection that PPBS currently enforces, since they are identified by ambiguity concerning goals, lack of data upon which to project accurate estimates of costs and consequences, and pervasive uncertainty concerning the range of possible changes in program.

There would be a much larger demand for policy analysis if it were supplied in ways that would meet the needs of high level officials. Let us consider the example of the President of the United States. He can certainly use policy analysis to help make better decisions. Substantial policy studies would give him and his staff leverage against the bureaucracy.

Knowledge is power. Indeed, command of a particular field would enable Presidents to exert greater control over the agenda for public decision and would give them advantages in competition with all sorts of rivals. Presidents could use perhaps a dozen major policy studies per year of their most immediate concerns. If even a few of these turn out well, the President may be motivated to make use of them. Contrast this with the present inundation of the Executive Office by endless streams of program "books," summaries, and memoranda that nobody ever looks at.

What is true of the President is also true for important executives in the agencies. Policy-oriented executives will want to get better analysis. Executives wishing to increase their resource base will be interested in independent sources of information and advice. Those who would exert power need objectives to fight for. It is neither fashionable nor efficient to appear to seek power for its own sake. In polite society the drive is masked and given a noble face when it can be attached to grand policy concerns that bring benefits to others as well as to power seekers. The way to gain the attention of leaders is not to flood them with trivia but to provide examples of the best kind of work that can be done. The last years of the Johnson Administration witnessed a proliferation of secret commissions to recommend new policies. The department secretary often became just another special pleader. If they have any interest in curbing this development, secretaries may find that producing their own policy analyses allow them to say that outside intervention is not the only or the best way to generate new policies.

CONGRESSIONAL DEMAND

If strategically located Congressmen demanded more policy analysis, there is little doubt that we would get it. What can be done to make them want more of it? The answer does not lie in surrounding them with large staffs so that they lose their manifestly political functions and become more like bureaucrats. Nor does the answer lie in telling Congressmen to keep away from small administrative questions in favor of larger policy concerns. For many Congressmen get into the larger questions only by feeling their way through the smaller details.[22] A threat to deprive Congressmen of the traditional line-item appropriations data through which they exert their control of agency affairs also does not appear to be a good way of making Congressmen desire policy analysis.

Policy analysis must be made relevant to what Congressmen want. Some legislators desire to sponsor new policies and they are one clientele for analysis. For other Congressmen, however, policy is a bargainable product that emerges from their interactions with their fellows. These members must be appealed to in a different way. They often have a sense of institutional loyalty and pride. They know that Congress is a rare institution in this world—a legislative body that actually has some control over public policy. They are aware that the development of new knowledge and new techniques may freeze them out of many of the more serious decisions. Policy analysis should be proposed to these men as an enhancement of the power of Congress as an institution. The purpose of analysis would be, in its simplest form, to enable Congressmen to ask good questions and to evaluate answers. Oftentimes it is hardest for a layman to recognize the significant questions implicit in an area of policy. Are there other and better questions to be asked, other and better policies to be pursued?

A Congress that takes seriously its policy role should be encouraged to contract for policy analysis that would stress different views of what the critical questions are in a particular area of policy. Each major committee or subcommittee should be encouraged to hire a man trained in policy analysis for a limited period, perhaps two years. His task would be to solicit policy studies, evaluate presentations made by government agencies, and keep Congressmen informed about what are considered the important questions. In the past, chairmen have not always paid attention to the quality of committee staffs. Following the lead of the Joint Economic Committee, seminars might be held for a couple of weeks before each session. At these seminars discussions would take place between agency personnel, committee staff, and the academics or other experts who have produced the latest policy analysis. If all went well, Congressmen would emerge with a better idea of the range of issues and of somewhat different ways of tackling the problems, and the policy analysts would emerge with a better grasp of the priorities of these legislators.

SUPPLIERS OF POLICY ANALYSIS

Thus far we have dealt solely with the incentive structure of the consumers who ought to want policy analysis—agency heads, Presidents, Congressmen. Little has been said about the incentive structure of the suppliers who ought to provide it—analysts, consultants, academics. Our premise has been that the supply of policy analysis would be a function of the demand. Now, the relationships between supply and demand have long been troublesome in economics because it is so difficult to sort out the mutual interactions. Upon being asked whether demand created supply or supply created demand, the great economist Marshall was reported to have said that it was like asking which blade of the scissors cuts the paper. There is no doubt, however, that changes in the conditions and quality of supply would have important effects on the demand for policy analysis.

Disengaging policy analysis from PPBS would help build the supply of policy analysis by:

1. Decreasing the rewards for mindless quantification for its own sake. There would be no requests from the Bureau of the Budget for such information and no premium for supplying it.

2. Increasing the rewards for analysts who might try the risky business of tackling a major policy problem that was obviously not going to be considered because everyone was too busy playing with the program structure. Gresham's Law operates here: programmed work drives out unprogrammed activity, make-work drives out analysis.

One way of increasing the supply of policy analysis would be to improve the training of people who work directly in the various areas of policy. Instead of taking people trained in policy analysis and having them learn about a particular policy area, the people in that area would be capable of doing policy analysis. Three-day or three-month courses will not do for that purpose. A year, and possibly two years, would be required. Since it is unlikely that the best people can be made available for so long a period, it is necessary to think in terms of education at an earlier period in their lives. There is a great need for schools of public policy in which technical training is combined with broader views of the social context of public policy. Although no one knows how to teach "creativity," it is possible to expose students to the range of subjects out of which a creative approach to public policy could come.

Another way of increasing the supply of policy analysis would be to locate it in an organizational context in which it has prestige and its practitioners are given time to do good work. Having the policy analysis unit report directly to the secretary or agency head would show that it is meant to be taken seriously.[23] But then it is bound to get involved in day-to-day concerns of the agency head, thus creating a classic dilemma.

TACTICS

The effective use of a policy analysis unit cannot be specified in advance for all agencies. There are certain tensions in its functions that may be mitigated on a case-by-case basis but cannot be resolved once and for all. Serious policy analysis requires months, if not years, of effort. A unit that spends its time solely on substantial policy analysis would soon find itself isolated from the operational concerns of the agency. There would be inordinate temptations on the part of its members to go where the action is. Before long, the policy unit might become more immediately relevant at the expense of its long-term impact. The frantic nature of day-to-day emergencies drives out the necessary time and quiet for serious study and reflection. What can be done? One tactic is for the policy unit to consider itself an educational as well as an action group. Its task should be to encourage analysis on the part of other elements of the organization. It should undertake nothing it can get subunits to do. The role of the policy unit would then be one of advising subunits and evaluating their output.

A second tactic would be to contract out for studies that are expected to take the longest period of time. The third tactic is the most difficult, because it calls for a balancing act. Immediate usefulness to top management may be secured by working on problems with short lead times while attempting to retain perhaps half of the available time for genuine policy analysis. To the degree that serious policy analysis enters into the life of the organization and proves its worth, it will be easier to justify its requirements in terms of release from everyday concerns. Yet the demand for services of the analysts is certain to increase. Failures in policy analysis, on the other hand, are likely to give the personnel involved more time for reflection than they would prefer. Like headquarters-field relationships, line and staff responsibilities, and functional versus hierarchical command, the problems of the policy unit are inherent in its situation and can only be temporarily resolved.

These comments on incentives for increasing the supply and demand for policy analysis are plainly inadequate. They are meant merely to suggest that there is a problem and to indicate how one might go about resolving it. We do not really know how to make policy analysis fit in with the career requirements of Congressmen, nor can we contribute much beside proverbial wisdom to the structure and operation of policy-analysis units. There are, however, opportunities for learning that have not yet been used. One of the benefits flowing from the experience with PPBS is that it has thrown up a small number of policy analyses that practitioners consider to be good. We need to know what makes some live in the world and others remain unused. Aside from an impressive manuscript by Clay Thomas Whitehead,[24] however, in which two recent policy analyses in defense are studied, there has been no effort to determine what this experience has to teach us. Despite the confident talk about policy analysis (here and elsewhere), a great deal of work remains to be done on what is considered "good" and why. The pioneering work by Charles E. Lindblom should not be wrongly interpreted as being antianalysis, but as a seminal effort to understand what we do when we try to grapple with social problems.

REEXAMINATION

Critical aspects of policy analysis need to be reexamined. The field cries out for a study of "coordination" as profound and subtle as Martin Landau's forthcoming essay on "Redundancy." [25] That most elemental problem of political theory—the proper role of the government versus that of the individual—should be subject to a radical critique.[26] The fact that cost-benefit analysis began with water resource projects in which the contribution to national income was the key question has guided thought away from other areas of policy for which this criterion would be inappropriate. There are policies for which the willingness of citizens to support the activity should help determine the outcome. There are other policies in which presently unquantifiable benefits, like pleasure in seeing others better off or reduction of anxiety following a visible decrease in social hostility, should be controlling. Although social invention is incredibly difficult, the way is open for new concepts of the role of government to liberate our thoughts and guide our actions.

In many ways the times are propitious for policy analysis. The New Deal era of legislation has ended and has not yet been replaced by a stable structure of issues. People do not know where they stand today in the same way they knew how they felt about Medicare or private versus public electric power. The old welfare state policies have disenchanted former supporters as well as further enraged their opponents. Men have worked for 20 years to get massive education bills through Congress only to discover that the results have not lived up to their expectations; it takes a lot more to improve education for the deprived than anyone had thought. There is now a receptivity to new ideas that did not exist a decade ago. There is a willingness to consider new policies and try new ways. Whether or not there is sufficient creativity in us to devise better policies remains to be seen. If we are serious about improving public policy, we will go beyond the fashionable pretense of PPBS to show others what the best policy analysis can achieve.

NOTES

NOTE: I wish to thank Arnold Meltsner, a graduate student in the Department of Political Science, for his critical comments and for giving me the benefit of his experience with defense budgets. I also wish to thank Robert Biller, Yehezkel Dror, Todd LaPorte, Frederick C. Mosher, and Nelson Polsby for helpful comments. Peter Dahl made useful stylistic suggestions. No one who reads this paper will doubt that I mean to take all the blame.

1. Robert N. Anthony, *Planning and Control Systems: A Framework for Analysis,* (Boston: Harvard University Press, 1965), p. 16.

2. Aaron Wildavsky, "The Political Economy of Efficiency," *Public Administration Review* 26 (December 1966): 298–302.

3. Yehezkel Dror, "Policy Analysts: A New Professional Role In Government Service," *Public Administration Review* 27 (September 1967): 200–201. See also Dror's major work, *Public Policy-Making Reexamined* (San Francisco: Chandler, 1968).

4. Wildavsky, *op. cit.*

5. See David Novick, "Origin and History of Program Budgeting" (Santa Monica, Calif.: The RAND Corporation, October 1966, p. 3427).

6. I once tried to interest a graduate student who had experience with defense problems in doing research in the City of Oakland. He asked the size of Oakland's budget. "Fifty million dollars," I said. "Why, in the Air Force we used to round to that figure," was his reply.

7. Aaron Wildavsky, "The Two Presidencies," *Trans-action* 4 (December 1966): 7–14 (chapter 17 of this book).

8. For further argument along these lines see my article, "The Practical Consequences of the Theoretical Study of Defense Policy," *Public Administration Review* 25 (March 1965): 90–103.

9. Thomas C. Schelling, "PPBS and Foreign Affairs," memorandum prepared at the request of the Subcommittee on National Security and International Operations of the Committee on Government Operations, U.S. Senate, 90th Congress, 1st session, 1968.

10. Dr. Alain Enthoven, who played a leading role in introducing systems analysis to the Defense Department, has observed that: "The major changes in strategy, the step-up in production of Minutemen and Polaris and the build-up in our non-nuclear forces including

the increase in the army, the tactical air forces, and the air lift . . . were being phased in at the same time that PPBS was being phased in. . . . We speeded up the Polaris and Minuteman programs because we believe that it was terribly important to have an invulnerable retaliatory force. We built up the Army Land Forces because we believed it was necessary to have more land forces for limited non-nuclear wars. We speeded up the development of anti-guerrilla forces or special forces because we believed that was necessary for counter-insurgency. "Those things would have happened with or without PPBS. PPBS does not make the strategy." Subcommittee on National Security and International Operations of the Committee on Government Operations, U.S. Senate, *Hearings, Planning-Programming-Budgeting*, 90th Congress, 1st session, Part 2, September 27 and October 18, 1967, p. 141.

11. *Prospects For Oil Shale Development* (Washington, D.C.: Department of the Interior, May 1968).

12. The study is presented in *ibid.*, pp. 10–45.

13. Similar difficulties under similar conditions evidently occur in the business world. It is worth citing Anthony's comments: "Strategic planning [that is, policy analysis] is essentially *irregular*. Problems, opportunities, and 'bright ideas' do not arise according to some set timetable; they have to be dealt with whenever they happen to be perceived. . . . Failure to appreciate the distinction between regular and irregular processes can result in trouble of the following type. A company with a well-developed budgeting process decides to formalize its strategic planning. It prepares a set of forms and accompanying procedures, and has the operating units submit their long-range plans on these forms on one certain date each year. The plans are then supposed to be reviewed and approved in a meeting similar to a budget review meeting. Such a procedure does not work. . . . There simply is not time enough in an annual review meeting for a careful consideration of a whole batch of strategic proposals. . . . It is important that next year's operating budget be examined and approved as an entity so as to ensure that the several pieces are consonant with one another. . . . Except for very general checklists of essential considerations, the strategic planning process follows no prescribed format or timetable. Each problem is sufficiently different from other problems so that each must be approached differently." Anthony, *op. cit.*, pp. 38–39.

14. Joint Economic Committee, Congress of the United States, *Hearings, The Planning, Programming-Budgeting System: Progress and Potentials,* 90th Congress, 1st session, September 1967, p. 5.

15. *Ibid.*, pp. 80–81. One might think that a way out of the dilemma could be had by adopting a number of goals for an area of policy. When Committee Chairman William Proxmire suggested that more goals should be specified, Gorham replied, "I would like to be the one to give the first goal. The first one in is always in the best shape. The more goals you have, essentially the less useful any one is, because the conflict among them becomes so sharp" (p. 83).

16. *Ibid.*, p. 6.

17. Anthony again supplies a useful comparison from private firms that makes a similar point: "An increasing number of businesses make profit and balance sheet projections for several years ahead, a process which has come to be known by the name 'long-range planning.' . . . A five-year plan usually is a projection of the costs and revenues that are anticipated under policies and programs *already approved,* rather than a device for consideration of, and decision on, new policies and programs. The five-year plan reflects strategic decisions already taken; it is not the essence of the process of making new decisions. . . . In some companies, the so-called five-year plan is nothing more than a mechanical extrapolation of current data, with no reflection of management decisions and judgment; such an exercise is virtually worthless." Anthony, *op. cit.,* pp. 57–58.

18. An excellent discussion of different purposes of budgeting and stages of budgetary development is found in Allen Schick, "The Road to PPB: The Stages of Budget Reform," *Public Administration Review* 26 (December 1966): 243–258.

19. In another paper ("Toward A Radical Incrementalism"), I have proposed that policy analysis would be facilitated by abolishing the annual budget cycle. One of the great weaknesses of governmental policy making is that policies are formulated a good two years before funds become available. Given the difficulties of devising policies in the first place, the time lag wreaks havoc with the best analysis. Since no one seems disposed to consider this alternative seriously, I mention it merely in passing as a change that would fit in with what has been suggested.

20. Frederick C. Mosher, "Program Budgeting in Foreign Affairs: Some Reflections," memorandum prepared at the request of the Subcommittee on National Security and International Operations of the Committee on Government Operations, U.S. Senate, 90th Congress, 2nd session, 1968.

21. *Hearings, The Planning-Programming-Budgeting System: Progress and Potentials,* pp. 77–78.

22. "Toward A Radical Incrementalism," pp. 27–29.

23. When Charles Hitch was Controller of the Defense Department, the policy-analysis unit reported directly to him, as did the budget unit. One reported result is that the policy unit was able to do its work without being drawn into the daily concerns of the budget men. When policy analysis (called systems analysis) was given separate status, with its own assistant secretary, there was apparently a much greater tendency for its members to insist upon control of immediate budgetary decisions. Hence the distinction between longer-run policy analysis and shorter-run budgeting tended to be obscured. It would be interesting to know whether the participants saw it in this way. Optimal placement of a policy-analysis unit is bound to be a source of difficulty and a subject of controversy.

24. Clay Thomas Whitehead, "Uses and Abuses of Systems Analysis" (Santa Monica, Calif.: The RAND Corporation, September 1967).

25. See Martin Landau, "Redundancy," *Public Administration Review* (July/August 1969), pp. 346–358.

26. For a fine example of original thought on this question, see Paul Feldman, "Benefits and the Role of Government in a Market Economy," Institute For Defense Analysis, Research Paper, February 1968, p. 477.

23

TOWARD A RADICAL INCREMENTALISM:
A PROPOSAL TO AID CONGRESS
IN REFORM OF THE
BUDGETARY PROCESS

I have said—if it were possible for man to be so constituted, as to feel what affects others more strongly than what affects himself, or even as strongly—because, it may be well doubted, whether the stronger feeling or affection of individuals for themselves, combined with a feebler and subordinate feeling or affection for others, is not, in beings of limited reason and faculties, a constitution necessary to their preservation and existence. If reversed—if their feelings and affections were stronger for others than for themselves, or even as strong, the necessary result would seem to be, that all individuality would be lost; and boundless and remediless disorder and confusion would ensue. For each, at the same moment, intensely participating in all the conflicting emotions of those around him, would, of course, forget himself and all that concerned him immediately, in his officious intermeddling with the affairs of all others; which, from his limited reason and faculties, he could neither properly understand nor manage. Such a state of things would, as far as we can see, lead to endless disorder and confusion, not less destructive to our race than a state of anarchy. It would, besides, be remediless—for government would be impossible; or, if it could by possibility exist, its object would be reversed. Selfishness would have to be encouraged and benevolence discouraged. Individuals would have to be encouraged, by rewards, to become more selfish, and deterred, by punishments, from being too benevolent; and this, too, by a government, administered by those who, on the supposition, would have the greatest aversion for selfishness and the highest admiration for benevolence.

To the Infinite Being, the Creator of all, belongs exclusively the care and superintendence of the whole.

—JOHN CALHOUN, *A Disquisition on Government*
(New York: Political Science Classics, 1947),
pp. 5–6. (Brought to my attention by H. D. Price.)

From *Congress: The First Branch of Government* (Washington: American Enterprise Institute for Public Research, 1966), pp. 115–165. Reprinted by permission.

My purpose in writing this essay is to aid Congress in reforming the budgetary process from the viewpoint of legislators in a representative assembly. The usual proposals for helping Congress by taking its job away or by shifting its responsibilities to the executive or by recommending that it confine itself to those actions of which it is least capable will not be found here. I shall propose a radical incremental approach designed to improve the calculating capability of all governmental participants in the budgetary process. I shall also propose mechanisms for improving the essential political information on budgeting available to Congress, somewhat at the expense of the Chief Executive, though not without some compensations for him as well. Finally, I shall suggest that Congress sponsor research which, for the first time, would be directly geared to improving its ability to act on appropriations in terms best suited to its limitations and opportunities.

My approach is based on considerations (as old as political theory itself) which do not seek vainly to condemn natural political behavior, but rather to so arrange the interaction of political forces as to secure desirable results. At one point in the *Politics*,[1] Aristotle devised a solution to a vexing political problem. It seems that the poor were so busy trying to make a living that they could not afford to attend the assembly, while the rich found so much profit in their private activities that it did not appear worthwhile for them to participate. This violated the balance of political forces whereby justice emerges from a clash of interests. Aristotle's solution was characteristically ingenious: the poor were to be paid to attend and the rich fined if they failed to attend. We might also recall how the Greeks saw to it that men of wealth paid their subscriptions to the state. If one man claimed he could not pay, any man willing to do so could substitute his property for the property of the man who alleged he could not pay. Children recognize the considerations involved when they divide a valued object by having one of them cut it in half and the other select the piece for himself. Spinoza's *Tractatus Politicus*[2] is full of suggestions for mechanisms by which the passions of men may, by their strength and predictability, be usefully employed. He suggests, for example, that military leaders be paid from the receipts of import and export duties so that they will be motivated to defend the state but not to engage in continual wars, since this would interrupt commerce and with it their source of income. The Constitution of the United States, with its separation and sharing of powers, its federalism, its staggered elections, and overlapping constituencies, is based on this kind of consideration, as the words of the framers so clearly reveal. I would take my stand with the authors of the *Federalist* (especially in their 51st number) who argue that political practices should be so arranged "that the private interest of every individual may be a sentinel over the public rights."

In order to provide necessary background, the first section of the paper is devoted to an analysis of the nature of reform proposals. Following this is a brief description of the budgetary process in the United States. After

an analysis of the major criticisms of the budgetary process, the paper
ends with an exposition and defense of radical incrementalism as a desirable approach to budgeting in the United States.

The Political Meaning of Budgetary Reform

A large part of the literature on budgeting in the United States is concerned with reform.[3] The goals of the proposed reforms are couched in
similar language—economy, efficiency, improvement, or just better budgeting. The President, the Congress and its committees, administrative
agencies, even the interested citizenry are all to gain by some change in
the way the budget is formulated, presented, or evaluated. There is little or
no realization among the reformers, however, that any effective change in
budgetary relationships must necessarily alter the outcomes of the budgetary
process. Far from being a neutral matter of "better budgeting," proposed
reforms inevitably contain important implications for the political system.

A crucial aspect of budgeting is whose preferences are to prevail in disputes about which activities are to be carried on and to what degree, in the
light of limited resources. The problem is not only generally "how shall
budgetary benefits be maximized," as if it made no difference who received them, but also specifically "who shall receive budgetary benefits and
how much." One of the central problems of social conduct consists of
somehow aggregating different preferences so that a decision may emerge.
How can we compare the worth of expenditures for irrigation to certain
farmers with the worth to motorists of widening a highway, or the desirability of aiding old people to pay medical bills with the degree of safety
provided by an expanded defense program? All this is further complicated
by the necessity of taking into account the relative intensity of preference
with which policies are sought by different people. The process developed
for dealing with interpersonal comparisons in government is not economic
but political. Conflicts are resolved (under agreed upon rules) by translating different preferences through the political system into units called
votes or into types of authority like a veto power. Therefore, if the present
budgetary process is rightly or wrongly deemed unsatisfactory, one must
alter in some respect the political system of which the budget is an expression. It is impossible to make drastic changes in budgeting without
also altering the political system and the distribution of influence within
it.[4]

By far the most significant way of influencing the budget would be to introduce basic political changes (or to wait for secular changes like the
growing industrialization of the South). Imagine that the Electoral College
were changed to favor conservatives or that the seniority system were altered to favor more liberal committee chairmen; give the President an item

veto or provide him with more powers enabling him to control the votes of his party in Congress; enable a small group of congressmen to command a majority of votes on all occasions so that they can push their program through. Then you will have exerted a profound influence on the content of the budget.

Since the budget represents conflicts over whose preferences shall prevail, one cannot speak of "better budgeting" without considering who benefits and who loses or demonstrating that no one loses. Just as the supposedly objective criterion of "efficiency" has been shown to have normative implications,[5] so a "better budget" may well be a cloak for hidden policy preferences. To propose that the President be given an item veto, for example, represents an attempt to increase the influence of the particular interests which gain superior access to the Chief Executive rather than, say, to the Congress. Only if one could eliminate the element of conflict over expenditures could it be assumed that a reform is "good enough" if it enables an official to do a better job from his point of view; since conflict over expenditures cannot be eliminated, the policy implications for others must be taken into account.[6]

Perhaps there are reforms which promise benefits for all and deprivations for none, or benefits for some and deprivations for none. But this cannot be assumed; it must be demonstrated especially to groups which anticipate deprivations for themselves. I am proposing that we be explicit about our intentions and demonstrate some awareness of the likely consequences of our proposals. (This advice is meant for the scholars whose task presumably includes being open with their colleagues, and not for the political participants for whom it might not always be wise to reveal what they are about.) It is clear, then, that before reforms are suggested, we need some idea of how the federal budgetary process operates in its political context. Then we may get a better idea of the consequences of reform proposals in comparison with the consequences of the present budgetary process.

The Budgetary Process

For our purposes, we shall conceive of budgets as attempts to allocate financial resources through political processes. If politics is regarded as conflict over whose preferences are to prevail in the determination of policy, then the budget records the outcomes of this struggle. If one asks "who gets what the (public or private) organization has to give?" then the answers for a moment in time are recorded in the budget. If organizations are viewed as political coalitions,[7] budgets are mechanisms through which subunits bargain over conflicting goals, make side-payments, and try to motivate one another to accomplish their objectives. In a study such as this, which stresses the appropriations process in Congress, the political context of budgeting can hardly be overemphasized.

The making of decisions depends upon calculation of which alternatives to consider and to choose. Calculation involves determination of how problems are identified, get broken down into manageable dimensions, are related to one another, and how choices are made as to what is relevant and who shall be taken into account. A major clue toward understanding budgeting is the extraordinary complexity of the calculations involved. In any large organization, there are a huge number of items to be considered, many of which are of considerable technical difficulty. Yet there is little or no theory in most areas of policy which would enable practitioners to predict the consequences of alternative moves and the probability of their occurring.[8] Man's ability to calculate is severely limited; time is always in short supply; and the number of matters which can be encompassed in one mind at the same time is quite small.[9] Nor has anyone solved the imposing problem of the inter-personal comparison of utilities. Outside of the political process, there is no agreed upon way of comparing and evaluating the merits of different programs for different people whose preferences vary in kind and in intensity.

Participants in budgeting deal with their overwhelming burdens by adopting heuristic aids to calculation. They simplify in order to get by. They make small moves, let experience accumulate, and use the feedback from their decisions to gauge consequences. They use actions on simpler matters that they understand as indices to complex concerns. They attempt to judge the capacity of the men in charge of programs even if they cannot appraise the policies directly. They may institute across-the-board ("meat axe") cuts to reduce expenditures, relying on outcries from affected agencies and interest groups to let them know if they have gone too far.[10]

By far the most important aid to calculation is the incremental approach. Budgets are almost never actively reviewed as a whole in the sense of considering at one time the value of all existing programs compared to all possible alternatives. Instead, this year's budget is based on last year's budget, with special attention given to a narrow range of increases or decreases. The greatest part of any budget is a product of previous decisions. Long-range commitments have been made. There are mandatory programs whose expenses must be met. Powerful political support makes the inclusion of other activities inevitable. Consequently, officials concerned with budgeting restrict their attention to items and programs they can do something about—a few new programs and possible cuts in old ones.

Incremental calculations, then, proceed from an existing base. By "base" we refer to commonly held expectations among participants in budgeting that programs will be carried out at close to the going level of expenditures. The base of a budget, therefore, refers to accepted parts of programs that will not normally be subjected to intensive scrutiny. Since many organizational units compete for funds, there is a tendency for the central authority to include all of them in the benefits or deprivations to be distributed. Participants in budgeting often refer to expectations regarding their fair share of increases and decreases. The widespread sharing of deeply held expectations concerning the organization's base and its fair share of funds provide a powerful (although informal) means of coordination and stability in budgetary systems that appear to lack comprehensive calculations proceeding from a hierarchical center.[11]

Roles (the expectations of behavior attached to institutional positions) are parts of the division of labor. They are calculating mechanisms. In American national government, the administrative agencies act as advocates of increased expenditure, the Bureau of the Budget acts as Presidential servant with a cutting bias, the House Appropriations Committee functions as a guardian of the Treasury, and the Senate Appropriations Committee as an appeals court to which agencies carry their disagreement with House action.

Possessing great expertise and large numbers, working in close proximity to their policy problems and clientele groups, and desirous of expanding their horizons, administrative agencies generate action through advocacy. But how much shall they ask for? Life would be simple if they could just estimate the costs of their ever-expanding needs and submit the total as their request. But if they ask for amounts much larger than the appropriating bodies believe is reasonable, their credibility will suffer a drastic decline. In such circumstances, the reviewing organs are likely to apply a "measure of unrealism" [12] with the result that the agency gets much less than it might have with a more moderate request. So the first decision rule for agencies is: do not come in too high. Yet the agencies must also not come in too low, for the assumption is that if the agency advocates do not ask for funds they do not need them. Since the budgetary situation is always tight, terribly tight, or impossibly tight, reviewing bodies are likely to just accept a low request with thanks and not inquire too closely into its rationale. Given the distribution of roles, cuts must be expected and taken into account. Thus, the agency decision rule might read: come in a little high (padding), but not too high (loss of confidence). But how high is too high? What agency heads usually do is to evaluate signals from the environment—last year's experience, legislative votes, executive policy statements, actions of clientele groups, reports from the field—and come up with an asking price somewhat higher than they expect to get.[13]

Having decided how much to ask for, agencies engage in strategic planning to secure their budgetary goals. (Strategies are the links between the goals of the agencies and their perceptions of the kinds of actions which their political environment will make efficacious.) Budget officers in American national government uniformly act on the belief that being a good politician—cultivation of an active clientele, development of confidence by other officials (particularly the appropriations subcommittees), and skill in following strategies which exploit opportunities—is more important in obtaining funds than demonstration of efficiency. Top agency officials soon learn that the appropriations committees are very powerful; committee recommendations are accepted by Congress approximately 90 percent of the time.[14] Since budgetary calculations are so complex, the legislators must take a good deal on faith; thus, they require agency budget officers to demonstrate a high degree of integrity. If the appropriations committees believe that an agency officer has misled them, they can do grave damage to his career and to the prospects of the agency he represents. While doing a decent job may be a necessary condition for the agency's success in securing funds, the importance of having clientele and the confidence of legislators is so great that all agencies employ these strategies.[15]

In addition to these ubiquitous strategies, there are contingent strategies which depend upon time, circumstance, and place. In defending the base, for example, cuts may be made in the most popular programs so that a public outcry will result in restoration of the funds. The base may be increased within existing programs by shifting funds between categories. Substantial additions to the base may come about through proposing new programs to meet crises and through campaigns involving large doses of advertising and salesmanship.[16] The dependence of these strategies on the incremental, increase-decrease type of budgetary is evident.

The Bureau of the Budget in the United States has the assigned role of helping the President realize his goals (when it can discover what they are supposed to be). This role is performed with a cutting bias, however, simply because the agencies normally push so hard in making requests for funds. The bureau helps the President by making his preferences more widely known throughout the executive branch so that those who would like to go along have a chance to find out what is required of them. Since Congress usually cuts the President's budget, bureau figures tend to be the most that agencies can get, especially when the items are not of such paramount importance as to justify intensive scrutiny by Congress. Yet the power of the purse remains actively with Congress. If the Budget Bureau continually recommended figures which were blatantly disregarded by Congress, the agencies would soon learn to pay less and less attention to the President's budget. As a result, the bureau follows consistent congressional action.[17] It can be shown empirically that bureau recommendations tend to follow congressional actions over a large number of cases.[18]

In deciding how much money to recommend for specific purposes, the House Appropriations Committee breaks down into largely autonomous subcommittees in which the norm of reciprocity is carefully followed.[19] Specialization is carried further as subcommittee members develop limited areas of competence and jurisdiction. Budgeting is both incremental and fragmented as the committees deal with adjustments to the historical base of each agency. Sequential decision-making is the rule as problems are first attacked in the subcommittee jurisdiction in which they appear and then followed step-by-step as they manifest themselves elsewhere.[20] The subcommittee members treat budgeting as a process of making marginal monetary adjustments to existing programs rather than as a mechanism for reconsidering basic policy choices every year.[21] Fragmentation and specialization are further increased through the appeals functions of the Senate Appropriations Committee which deals with what has become (through House action) a fragment of a fragment. When the actions of subcommittees conflict, the difficulties are met by repeated attacks on the problem or through reference to the House and Senate as a whole.[22]

The members of the United States House Appropriations Committee consider themselves guardians of the Treasury who take pride in the frequency with which they reduce estimates.[23] They reconcile this role with their role as representatives of constituency interests by cutting estimates to satisfy one role and generally increasing amounts over the previous year to satisfy the other. As guardians of the public purse, committee members are expected to cast a skeptical eye on the blandishments of a bureaucracy ever anxious to increase its dominion by raising its appropriations. In order to provide an objective check on the effectiveness of the committee's orientation, Fenno [24] examined the appropriations histories of 37 bureaus concerned with domestic policies from 1947–1959 and discovered that the committee reduced the estimates it received 77.2 percent of the time.

Tough as they may be in cutting the budgets of their agencies, appropriations committee members, once having made their decision, generally defend the agencies against further cuts on the floor. This kind of action is in part self-interest. The power of the appropriations subcommittees would be diminished if their recommendations were successfully challenged very often. Members believe that the House would "run wild" if "orderly procedure"—that is, acceptance of committee recommendations—were not followed. The role of defender also has its roots in the respect for expertise and specialization in Congress, and the concomitant belief that members who have not studied the subject should not exercise a deciding voice without the presence of overriding consideration. An appeal to this norm usually is sufficient to block an attempt to reduce appropriations.[25]

A member of the Senate Appropriations Committee is likely to conceive of his proper role as the responsible legislator who sees to it that the irrepressible lower House does not do too much damage either to constituency or to national interests. The Senators are rather painfully aware of the House committee's preeminence in the field of appropriations and they know that they cannot hope to match the time and thoroughness that the House body devotes to screening requests. For this reason, the Senate committee puts a high value on having agencies carry appeals to it. The Senators value their right to disagree on disputed items as a means of maintaining their influence in crucial areas while putting the least possible strain on their time and energy. The Senate role of responsible appeals court is dependent, of course, upon agency advocacy and House committee guardianship.

The Budgetary Process Reconsidered

In describing the budgetary process, we have identified a number of basic characteristics that have called forth a great deal of criticism from many sources. For example, the aids to calculation have been described as arbitrary and irrational. It has been said that, instead of concentrating on grand policy alternatives, the appropriations committees interfere mischievously with the administrative process through excessive concern with small details. Some critics go so far as to state that this petty intervention takes place without adequate information so that administrators are harassed for all the wrong reasons by men who lack knowledge. The specialized, incremental, fragmented, and sequential budgetary procedures have been faulted as leading to a lack of coordination and a neglect of consequences of the actions that are taken. At the same time, Congress is said to be losing its control of appropriations because its meager efforts cannot keep pace with the superior information resources of the federal bureaucracy. Nor, the critics add, are the appropriations committees willing to make the vast increase in staff which would enable them to make their will felt through intelligent decisions on broad policies. Instead, they combine dependence on the executive for information with "irrational" practices such as across-the-board cuts. The participants in budgeting have been taken to task for serving local interests rather than the national public interest. Their roles are considered to be excessively narrow, and the strategies they follow are condemned as opportunistic if not immoral. Finally, the appropriations process is deemed much too slow and too late: actions are taken on material which is out of date, and administrators are left uncertain how much money they will have until long after the previous fiscal year has ended.

It is immediately evident that many of these criticisms are contradictory. Increasing the staff of the appropriations committees hardly seems like a good way to cut down on detailed oversight of administration. Concern with local interests is one way of dealing with the differential consequences of national policy. Congress can hardly interfere less with administrators by making all the basic policy decisions for the executive agencies. That the critics of Congress are confused is an old story; let us make the best sense we can out of the criticisms and deal with the serious concerns which they raise.

The alternative budgetary process envisioned by the critics is quite different from the one we now have. Instead of aids to calculation such as the incremental method, they prefer comprehensive and simultaneous evaluation of means and ends. In their view, coordination should be made the explicit concern of a central hierarchy that should consider a wide range of alternative expenditures and investigate rather fully the consequences of each and the probability of their occurring. Each participant should seek to protect the general interest rather than the particular interests directly within his jurisdiction. Strategies should be eschewed or, at least, based on the merits of the program rather than on making the best possible case. Congressmen should avoid interferences in the administrative process and concentrate on developing superior knowledge and greatly enlarged staff assistance in order to make the most general determinations of governmental policy. The following pages deal in detail with various critical approaches.

COMPREHENSIVENESS

One prescription offered by the critics for "rationally" solving problems of calculation is to engage in comprehensive and simultaneous means-ends analysis. But budget officials soon discover that ends are rarely agreed upon, that they keep changing, that possible consequences of a single policy are too numerous to describe, and that knowledge of the chain of consequences for other policies is but dimly perceived for most conceivable alternatives. The result, as Charles Lindblom has demonstrated, is that although this comprehensive approach can be described, it cannot be practiced because it puts too great a strain by far on man's limited ability to calculate.[26] What budget officials need are not injunctions to be rational but operational guides that will enable them to manage the requisite calculations. Commands like "decide according to the intrinsic merits," "consider everything relevant," "base your decision on complete understanding," are simply not helpful. They do not exclude anything; unlike the aids to calculation, they do not point to operations that can be performed to arrive at a decision.

All that is accomplished by injunctions to follow a comprehensive approach is the inculcation of guilt among good men who find that they can never come close to fulfilling this unreasonable expectation. Worse still, acceptance of an unreasonable goal inhibits discussion of the methods actually used. Thus, responsible officials may feel compelled to maintain the acceptable fiction that they review (almost) everything; and yet when they describe their actual behavior, it soon becomes apparent that they do not. The vast gulf between the theories espoused by some budget officials and their practice stems, I believe, from their adherence to a norm deeply imbedded in our culture, which holds that the very definition of rational decision is comprehensive and simultaneous examination of ends and means. In this case, however, the rational turns out to be the unreasonable. Sad experience warns me that even those who agree with the analysis thus far are prone to insist that governmental officials must "take a look at the budget as a whole," even though neither they nor anyone else has any idea of what that might mean or how it might be accomplished. Surely, considering "the budget as a whole" does not mean merely putting it between the covers of one volume, or letting one's eyes run over the pages, or merely pondering the relationship between income and expenditures. Yet, if (to take current examples) evaluating the most important relationships between the space program, the war on poverty, and aid to education appears to be extraordinarily difficult, what is the point of talking about reviewing "the budget as a whole" in the real sense of analyzing the interrelationships among all the important programs. The perpetuation of myth is an old story. What is unfortunate is that insistence on an impossible standard takes our attention away from real possibilities for change.

Failure to consider the contributions toward calculation of the existing budgetary process distorts the magnitude of the problem. New programs and substantial increases and decreases in old programs do not receive close attention when interest groups, politicians, or bureaucrats, anxious to make an issue, demand an investigation. What escapes intensive scrutiny is not the whole but only certain parts, which carry on as before. The fact that some activities do not receive intensive scrutiny is hardly sufficient reason to do everything over every year. In my recommendations, I shall deal with the problem that remains.

COORDINATION

The fact that the budgetary process is not comprehensive has given rise to charges that it is uncoordinated. Indeed, the very terms that we have used to describe budgetary practices—specialized, incremental, fragmented, sequential, nonprogrammatic—imply that at any one time the budget is not effectively considered as a whole so as to systematically relate its component parts to one another. As long as the lack of coordination is the result of ignorance of other people's activities or the complexity of organization, there is a good chance of overcoming it by dedicated staff work or some formal coordinating mechanism. But, in many cases, lack of coordination is a result of conflicting views about policy that are held by men and agencies that have independent bases of influence in society and in Congress. The only way to secure coordination in these cases is for one side to convince or coerce or bargain with the other. When it is understood that "coordination" is often just another word for "coercion," the full magnitude of the problem becomes apparent. For there is no one, the President and congressional leaders included, who is charged with the task of dealing with the "budget as a whole" and who is capable of enforcing his preferences. Vesting of formal power to coordinate the budget effectively would be tantamount to a radical change in the national political system, requiring the abolition of the separation of powers and a federally controlled party system, among other things.

What may be said about coordination, then, if we take the existing political system as not subject to drastic change? By taking as our standard of coordination the existence of a formal structure charged with the task and capable of executing it, we come up with an obvious answer: there is very little coordination excepting what the President can manage through the Budget Bureau. By accepting the possibility of informal coordination, of participants who take into account what others are doing, we can say there is a great deal of coordination that has escaped the notice of observers.

Let us pose the following question: how does an appropriations subcommittee know when things are not working out in other areas affected by its actions? Are its budgetary decisions coordinated with those decisions made by other subcommittees? Part of the answer is found in a comment by a committee member to the effect that "People can't be too badly off if they don't complain." The subcommittees do not consider themselves to be the only participants in budgeting. They expect, in accordance with sequential decision making, that committees and organizations in the affected areas will take corrective action. When an agency shouts more loudly than usual, when an interest group mounts a campaign, when other Congressmen begin to complain, subcommittee members have a pretty good idea that something is wrong. If their perceptions of the array of political forces lead them astray, the appropriations subcommittees can be brought back into line by a rebellion within the full committee or by an adverse vote on the floor. For, as we noted earlier, unless members have an exceedingly intense preference, they will try to come up with appropriations that will not be reversed on the floor; to do otherwise would be to risk losing the great prestige the committee enjoys. The subcommittee may be thought of as exercising discretion over a zone of indifference, within which others are not aware enough or not concerned enough to challenge them, but beyond which others will begin to mobilize against them. In this way, a semblance of coordination is maintained. And as time passes, the participants come to develop a tacit understanding as to the general level of most appropriations, a phenomenon we have previously designated by the notion of fair shares. No one has to check up on everyone; it is sufficient that occasional marked departures from commonly held notions of fair shares would generate opposition.

Widespread acceptance of this concept of fair shares may go a long way toward accounting for the degree of coordination (the extent to which participants take into account what others do) that does exist in calculating expenditures totals. The total budget was rarely drastically out of line with expenditures before it was formalized in 1921, and even without control by a central authority today we do not usually get extraordinary increases or decreases except during national emergencies. There has been much more subtle and informal coordination by tacit agreements and accepted limits than there has previously been thought to be.

To some critics the procedure by which the agencies (as well as the Appropriations Committee and the Budget Bureau to a lesser extent) try to gauge "what will go" may seem unfortunate. They feel that there must be a better justification for programs than the subjective interpretation of signals from the environment. Yet we live in a democracy in which a good part of the justification for programs is precisely that they are deemed desirable by others. What is overlooked is that these informal procedures are also powerful coordinating mechanisms: when one thinks of all the participants who are continuously engaged in interpreting the wishes of others, who try to feel the pulse of Congress, the President, interest groups, and special publics, it is clear that a great many adjustments are made in anticipation of what other participants are likely to do. This, it seems to me, is just another term for coordination, unless one insists that coordination be redefined to require conscious control by a single individual or group.

The interaction between appropriations committees and administrative agencies include at least seven modes of coordination:

1. Laws commanding specific actions;

2. Committee reports demanding specific action on (implicit) pain of future penalties;

3. Exchange of indulgences;

4. Taking each other's preferences into account with direct contact;

5. Accommodations to prior actions of the other without consultation;

6. Argument in which one side convinces the other;

7. Granting of side payments by one participant in return for action by the other.

NEGLECT OF CONSEQUENCES

The budgetary process is sometimes attacked for its apparent neglect of consequences, and there can be no doubt that lack of comprehensiveness in budgeting means that a participant making a specific decision will often neglect important values affected by that decision. However, Lindblom has proposed that consequences neglected by one participant may be considered by another, or by the same participant working on another problem.[27] To the extent, therefore, that all significant interests tend to be represented in a fragmented political system, decision-makers may reduce their information costs, by neglecting many alternatives, in the confidence that they will be picked up by others or by themselves at another time. Thus, the budgetary process as a whole may be considered rational even though the actions of individual participants may not seem to be because they omit from their calculations consequences important for others.

The political process in a democracy has a built-in feature that assures that some presently neglected values will be considered. This mechanism exists because politicians and interest-group leaders are motivated, by their hope of retaining or winning office, to find needs that have not been met and proposing to fulfill them in return for votes.

No doubt the neglect of some values (say those dear to Negroes) could be better avoided by increasing the weight of the appropriate interests in the political process. There is no point, it seems to me, in faulting the budgetary process for the lamentable failure of some groups to be properly represented in the political life of the nation. Political mobilization of Negroes will obviously do much more to protect their neglected interests than any change in the mechanism for considering budgets.

The most powerful coordinating mechanisms in budgeting undoubtedly are the various roles adopted by major participants in the budgetary process. Because the roles fit in with one another and set up a stable pattern of mutual expectations, they do a great deal to reduce the burden of calculations for the individual participants. The agencies need not consider in great detail how their requests will affect the President's overall program; they know that such criteria will be introduced in the Budget Bureau. The Appropriations committees and the Budget Bureau know that the agencies are likely to put forth all the programs for which there is prospect of support and can concentrate on fitting them into the President's program or on paring them down. The Senate committee operates on the assumption that if important items are left out through House action the agency will carry an appeal. If the agencies suddenly reversed roles and sold themselves short, the entire pattern of mutual expectations might be upset, leaving the participants without a firm anchor in a sea of complexity. If the agency were to refuse the role of advocate, it would increase the burden on the Congressmen; they would not only have to choose among desirable items placed before them with some fervor, but they would also have to discover what these items might be. This is a task ordinarily far beyond the limited time, energy, information, and competence of most Congressmen.

The roles appear to be "natural" to the occupants of these institutional positions. A man who has spent many years working in, say, the natural resources area can be expected to believe that his programs are immensely worthy of support. (He may try to eliminate programs he deems unworthy, but there are always others to take their place.) Indeed, he would hardly be worth having as a governmental employee if he did not feel this way in his position. By serving as advocate in the real world, he sees to it that important values in his area are not neglected if he can help it.

The House Appropriations Committee's role of guarding the Treasury, with its emphasis on reducing requests, makes sense in the context of agency advocacy. If the Congressmen can be reasonably certain that the agency has put its best foot forward, then their decisions may be viewed as choices along the margins of the top percentage of expenditures advocated by the agencies. The role of guardianship provides the Congressmen with a stance that supplies reasonably clear instructions—cut the estimates—while keeping the area within which they must focus their attention (the largest increases) manageable in terms of their limited time and ability to calculate.

Some critics suggest that appropriations committee members should adopt a different role. In this "mixed" role, the Congressman would be oriented toward neither cutting nor increasing but to doing both in about equal proportions. Each case would have to be considered on its own merits. To some extent, of course, this balance occurs under the present system. The difference is one of degree, but not less important for being so. For where they are in doubt or do not care to inquire in detail, the Congressmen may now follow their prevailing orientation—usually to cut at the margin—expecting to receive feedback if something drastic happens. Under a "mixed" role, however, an exhaustive inquiry into all or most items would be called for. The resulting increase in amounts of calculation required would be immense. And to the extent that other participants adopted a mixed role, the pattern of role expectations upon which participants are now dependent as a calculating device would no longer prove stable. The calculation of preferences, essential in a democratic system, would become far more burdensome since inquiries would have to be instituted to find out what the various groups wanted in specific cases.

Furthermore, the adoption of a mixed role would be likely to lead to a greater neglect of values affected by decisions. Unless the ability of each participant to calculate the consequences of his actions is much more impressive than the evidence suggests, he is bound to neglect more if he attempts to do more. Yet this is precisely what a mixed role would force him to do. Instead of concentrating on a limited range of values within his jurisdiction, as his present role requires, he would have to consider the widest possible range of values in order to make a mixed role work. In place of the reasonable certainty that each participant does a good job of looking after the relatively narrow range of values entrusted to his care, there would be little certainty that any particular value would be protected because no one had been especially directed to look after it. Let us explore this question further as a fundamental problem in normative political theory.

INTERESTS

Why, it may be asked, should the various participants take a partial view? Why should they not simply decide in accordance with what the public interest requires? Actually, this is the principle that participants think they are following now; they all believe that their version of the public interest is correct. It is their differing institutional positions, professional training, and group values that lead to perspectives producing somewhat different interpretations of the public interest. Let us, then, rephrase the question and ask whether it is better for each participant to put first the achievement of his own goals (including the goals entrusted to him by virtue of his position) when he considers what is meant by "public interest," or whether he should view the goals of others as of prime or at least equal importance to this consideration?

I am prepared to argue that the partial-view-of-the-public-interest approach is preferable to the total-view-of-the-public-interest approach, which is so often urged as being superior. First, it is much simpler for each participant to calculate his own preferences than for each to try to calculate the preferences of all. It is difficult enough for a participant to calculate how the interests he is protecting might best be served without requiring that he perform the same calculation for many others who might also be affected. The "partial" approach has the virtue of enabling others to accept as an input in their calculations the determination of each participant as to his preferences, which is not possible under the total approach. The danger of omitting important values is much greater when participants neglect the values in their immediate care in favor of what seem to them a broader view. How can anyone know what is being neglected if everyone speaks for someone else and no one for himself?

The partial approach is more efficient for resolving conflicts, a process that lies at the heart of democratic politics. Because the approach is partial, it does not require its practitioners to discover all or most possible conflicts and to work out answers to problems that may never materialize. It permits each participant to go his own way until he discovers that the activities of others interfere. Effort can then be devoted to overcoming the conflicts that arise. The formation of alliances in a political system requiring them is facilitated by the expression and pursuit of demands by those in closest touch with the social reality from which they issue. It is not, then, *noblesse oblige* but self-interest that assures that all demands insist on being heard and find the political resources to compel a hearing. A partial adversary system in which the various interests compete for control of policy (under agreed-upon rules) seems more likely to result in reasonable decisions—that is, decisions that take account of the multiplicity of values involved—than one in which the best policy is assumed to be discoverable by a well-intentioned search for the public interest for all by everyone.

STRATEGIES

If it is granted that budgetary practices based on a partial view of the public interest are desirable, then it would appear necessary to accept the use of strategies designed to secure appropriation goals. It is not surprising, however, that critics find something basically underhanded, even undemocratic, in the maneuvering of "special interests" for strategic advantage. Would not a straightforward approach based on the "merits" of each program be preferable?

Requiring that an individual commit suicide for the public good may at times have an acceptable rationale; suggesting that it become a common practice can hardly claim as much. I shall take it as understood, then, that asking participants in budgeting consistently to follow practices extremely disadvantageous to themselves and their associates is not reasonable. The participants must be able to maintain themselves in the environment.

The notion that administrators go around telling each other (or believing in secret) that the purposes for which they request funds are not valid but that they want the money anyway in order to advance themselves and build empires is not worthy of consideration. It would be exceedingly difficult to keep people in an organization if they could not justify its purposes to themselves. Such an attitude would be bound to come to the attention of other participants, who would take appropriate action. It would be bad strategically as well as morally. Attempts to reduce a complex distributive process like budgeting to the terms of a western melodrama—the good men ride white horses and advance on their merits; the bad men wear black masks and rely on strategies—do away with the great problem of deciding upon expenditures advocated by officials who are sincere believers in their proposals, and who know that all demands can be satisfied.

Budgetary strategies may generally be characterized as attempts to make the best case for the agency at the best time and thus to get as large an appropriation as possible. This behavior follows from the role of the agency as advocate. As a practical matter, we would expect any agency head worth his keep to respond to opportunities for increasing appropriations and warding off cuts. The contrary position—making the worst case at the worst time—is not likely to be greeted with enthusiasm by either Congressmen or agency staff.

Seizing on the opportune moment for advancing the agency's budgetary goals has much to commend it. The nation is served by initiative in meeting the needs of the time. An element of flexibility is generated that helps ensure that opportunities for action will be taken. "Crisis" strategies belong in this category. What is the difference, we may ask, between using a crisis to increase appropriations and acting to meet the nation's requirements in an hour of need? The desire to present the agency's requests in the best light can be used in a positive sense to improve the thinking of the operating units. The budget office can play an important mediating role because it must explain and justify agency actions to the outside world. By playing devil's advocate to agency personnel, by pointing out that justifications are not clear or persuasive, by saying that the program heads have to do better to convince the Budget Bureau or the Appropriations Committee, the budget office may compel or encourage thinking from diverse perspectives. In this way, a wider range of interests and values receive consideration.

Clientele and confidence strategies are desirable as well as inevitable in a democratic society. The feedback that clientele give to the participants is essential political information about who wants what programs, at what level, and with what degree of intensity. The establishment of confidence in an agency and its officers provides the trust necessary for Congressmen who must live with complexity; the sanctions upon that agency that follow from lack of congressional confidence represent a great safeguard against duplicity. That morality is to some extent the handmaiden of necessity does not make it any less real or valuable.

A naked recital of strategies is bound to suggest that a certain amount of trickery is involved. Some strategies that appear to be deceitful represent amoral adjustments to an environment that does not give the participants much choice. Consider the kind of duplicity that appears to be involved in the game wherein agency people make believe that they are supporting the President's budget while actually encouraging Congressmen to ask questions that will permit them to talk about what they would really like to have. Is this behavior immoral or does the immorality belong to the Executive Office directive that tries to compel agency personnel to say things that they do not believe in order to support the President? Congress has the power of the purse and it is difficult to argue that it should not have the kind of information about what the people in charge of the program think they ought to get that might help it to arrive at decisions. If one wants to get rid of Congress, then the problem solves itself. But if one accepts the separation of powers, then it may well be that it would be destructive to deny Congress information it would like to have, especially when for Congress to have it is manifestly in the interests of administrators. The Biblical injunction against excessive temptation is appropriate here.

MERITS

Despite all that has been said, the very idea that strategies are employed may still appear disturbing. Why cannot programs be presented on their merits and their merits alone? The most obvious answer is that the question presupposes popular, general agreement on what constitutes merit when the real problem is that people do not agree. That is why we have politics. To lay down and enforce criteria of merit in budgeting would be, in effect, to dispense with politics in favor of deciding what the government shall do in advance.

Much of what is meant by merit turns out to be "meets my preferences" or "serves my interests" or "the interests of those with whom I identify." It would be most peculiar for a nation calling itself a democracy to announce that only the most meritorious policies were carried out despite the fact that they were not preferred by any significant group in the population. The degree to which widespread preferences are met not only *is* but *ought* to be *part* of why policies are deemed meritorious.

We all know that people do not always realize what is good for them.

They are occupied with many things and may not recognize the benefits flowing from certain policies. They may find it difficult to support policies that are meritorious but not directly related to their own immediate needs. Here is where strategies come in. Where support is lacking, it may be mobilized; where attention is unfocused, it may be directed by advertising; where merits are not obvious, they may be presented in striking form. Ability to devise strategies to advance the recognition of merit is immensely more helpful than cries of indignation that political artistry should be necessary.

Merit consists, in part, of the effectiveness with which programs are formulated and carried out. No one should doubt that this criterion is recognized in the budgetary process; estimates, justifications, and presentations are directed to this end. Though effectiveness is indispensable—confidence would be lacking without it, for one thing; clientele would be dissatisfied, for another—agencies find that it does not take them far enough. An agency may be wonderfully effective in formulating and carrying out its programs and yet see its fortunes suffer because of the need for Congress to cut that year or to shift funds to some other vital area. Defense appropriations are often a function of domestic concerns; stabilization policy may be constrained by military needs; the complexity of a project or the difficulty of demonstrating immediate results may militate against it. Consequently, the agency invariably finds that in some areas its good works and best efforts are not being rewarded. Prizes are simply not distributed for good deeds alone. The agency's mode of adapting to this circumstance is to use demonstration of good works as one among a number of strategies. Forbidding agencies to use strategies designed to give its good requests a better chance, because bad requests can also be dressed up, seems inadvisable as well as unlikely to succeed.

Motivation

Instead of bewailing the use of strategies, it would be immensely more fruitful to arrange incentives within the system so as to insure that good strategies and good programs will go together as often as possible. Budgeting would be conceived of in this sense as constituting a problem in human motivation. When motivation is disregarded, it is no wonder that unsatisfactory results ensue. In order to demonstrate that this problem is by no means peculiar to the national budgetary process let us take a brief look at budgeting in Soviet and American industrial firms.

Rewards to managers in Soviet industrial firms depend on their meeting production quotas assigned in economic plans. But necessary supplies—skilled labor and financial resources—are often lacking. The first consequence of this is that the quota is not set from above but becomes the subject of bargaining as the managers seek to convince the ministries that quotas should be as low as possible. Yet the managers find it prudent not to hugely exceed their quota, for in that case next year's quota will be raised beyond attainment. The second consequence is that production is not rationalized to produce the greatest output at the lowest cost, but is geared instead to meeting specific incentives. Heavy nails are overproduced, for example, because quotas are figured by weight. Maintenance may be slighted in favor of huge effort for a short period in order to meet the quota. Funds are hidden in order to provide slack that can be used to pay "pushers" to expedite the arrival of supplies. The list of essentially deceitful practices to give the appearance of fulfilling the quota is seemingly endless: producing the wrong assortment of products, transferring current costs to capital accounts, shuffling accounts to pay for one item with funds designated for another, declaring unfinished goods finished, lowering the quality of goods, and so on.[28] The point is that the budgetary system arranges incentives in such a way that managers cannot succeed with lawful practices. When similar incentives are applied in American industrial firms, similar practices result, from running machines into the ground, to "bleeding the line," to meeting a monthly quota by doctoring the accounts.[29]

As in the Soviet Union, American firms often use budgets not to reflect or project reality but to drive managers and workers toward increased production. Budgets are conceived of as forms of pressure on inherently lazy people [30] so that (to paraphrase Mao Tse-tung) the greater the pressure the better the budget. Inevitably, managers and workers begin to receive budgets as "perpetual needlers" or as "the hammer that's waiting to hit you on the head." [31] In some cases, this leads to discouragement because it is apparent that whatever the effort, the budget quota will be increased. Since accounting is separate for subunits in the firm, it is not surprising that fierce negotiations take place to assign costs among them. As a result, top officials find it necessary to engage in campaigns to sell budgets to the units. Otherwise, sabotage is likely.[32] While some attention has been given to human relations in budgeting,[33] only Stedry [34] has attempted to explore the essential motivational problems of budgeting within an organizational framework. Yet, without an understanding of the impact of different goals and incentive systems on human activity, reliable statements about the likely consequences of different budgetary incentives can hardly be made. I shall attempt to deal with this problem in my recommendations.

POWER

The strategy which critics of the budgetary process find most objectionable is Congress' use of the appropriations power to alter policies of executive agencies. To say that Congressmen interfere too much in the details of administration, however, is to consign them to impotence. Grand policy

decisions come few and far between. Most policy is made through interpretation of statutes by administrators or through a succession of marginal
adjustments in the form of legislative amendments. If by "administrative
detail" one means "trivial," then it would seem that the administrators
who are presumably being defended would have little to worry about. A
basic analytic problem, preventing meaningful thought, is that "policy" is
identified with "Congress" and "administration" with the executive branch.
By definition, Congress should not tell administrators what to do, because
administrators administrate and Congress is supposed only to make policy.
I agree so completely with the position taken by Richard Fenno that I
would like to quote his comments at some length:

> To relegate Congress to the making of broad policy decisions and to oversight
> in terms of broad program management is to prescribe precisely those tasks
> which Congress is least capable of performing. To criticize Congress for inter-
> vening in a specific and detailed fashion is to attack it for doing the only thing
> it can do to effectively assert its influence. Specifics and details are the indis-
> pensable handles which Congressmen use to work inductively toward broader
> kinds of oversight judgments. Specifics and details are what concern the con-
> stituents on whose behalf Congressmen must intervene with the bureaucracy.
> Specific and detailed requests from an interested Congressman to a bureau head
> or division chief do more to "galvanize the internal disciplines of administra-
> tion" (Arthur Macmahon's phrase) than any broad statement of policy. The
> profusion of committees and subcommittees make possible a degree of speciali-
> zation which gives to Congressmen the detailed and specific information they
> find most useful in influencing executive behavior.
>   Specific and detailed controls by individuals and small committees give Con-
> gressmen their maximum influence because these controls are best adapted to
> the realities of executive decision-making. If executive decision-making is basi-
> cally piecemeal, incremental and marginal, then congressional control, if it is
> to be effective, must be basically piecemeal, incremental and marginal. What is
> or is not "appropriate" congressional control cannot be prescribed *a priori*.
> . . . Congressional control is or is not appropriate in the context of the reali-
> ties of legislative and executive decision-making. The legislator ought not to
> be criticized for using those controls which are available to him and which
> his experience tells him bring the greatest influence over executive activity.
> If we do not recognize this, we will continue to prescribe impossible control
> tasks. . . .[35]

The power of Congress to control budgetary decisions depends on the
power of its appropriation committees. For no large assembly of men can
develop the expertise, self-direction, cohesiveness, and dispatch which are
necessary to do the large volume of budgetary business. A good index of
the power of any legislature is whether it develops and follows committees
of experts in specific areas of decisions. Where such committees are absent, as in Great Britain, the power of Parliament becomes a fiction. (A
common definition of a Cabinet is a committee which permits no rivals.)
The appropriation committees measure up exceedingly well when we consider that their recommendations are adopted by the houses of Congress
approximately 90 percent of the time. Although one might contemplate

with equanimity some reduction in this record of success, a drop below, say, 75 percent would seriously compromise the appropriations committees with the President and the agencies. For a great deal of the ability to have agencies follow congressional will is dependent on the knowledge that the appropriations committees are watching and that their actions will be upheld with a high degree of certainty. Once the power gets transferred to Congress as a whole, its exercise becomes so uncertain and diffuse that no one can count on it. Congressmen simply do not have the time and the knowledge to debate a very large number of appropriations with sense and then follow through. The general body of congressmen do well to keep the appropriations committees in line with an occasional defeat on the floor to remind them whom they are ultimately beholden to.

The great power of the appropriations committees consists in the extent to which agencies and the Bureau of the Budget systematically take account of their preferences. Anyone who has seen budget offices in operation knows that the unseen hand of Congress is never far from the surface. The agency practice of holding mock hearings in which some officials are assigned the role of appropriations committee members is a vivid illustration of how Congress makes its will felt indirectly.

The power of the appropriations committees depends on their ability to command regular support in Congress, support which in turn is dependent on the cohesiveness of the committees. Fenno [36] has shown that support for the House Appropriations Committee drops markedly when its subcommittees issue split recommendations. The internal norms and calculating mechanisms whereby the committee achieves a high degree of integration are therefore of extreme importance in the maintenance of congressional power. The incremental, fragmented, nonprogrammatic, and sequential procedures of the present budgetary process aid in securing agreement. It is much easier to agree on an addition or reduction of a few thousand or a million dollars than to agree on whether a program is good in the abstract. It is much easier to agree on a small addition or decrease than to compare the worth of one program to that of all others. Conflict is reduced by an incremental approach because the area open to dispute is reduced. Agreement comes much more readily when the items in dispute can be treated as differences in dollars instead of as basic differences in policy; calculating budgets in monetary increments facilitates bargaining and logrolling. It becomes possible to swap an increase here for a decrease there or for an increase elsewhere without always having to consider the ultimate desirability of programs blatantly in competition. Procedures that deemphasize overt conflicts among competing programs also encourage secret deliberations, nonpartisanship, and the recruitment of personnel who feel comfortable in sidestepping policy decisions most of the time. The prospects for agreement within the House Appropriations Committee are enhanced by closed hearings and mark-up sessions, and by a tradition against publicity. Were deliberations to take place in public—"open covenants openly arrived at"—committee members might find themselves accused of "selling out" if they made concessions. Willingness to compromise, to be flexible, is a quality sought in choosing members to serve on the appropriations committees. Party ties might be disruptive of agreement if they focused attention on the policy differences between the two political persuasions. Instead, party differences are submerged during committee deliberations, and the usual process of taking something from a program here, adding to a program there, swapping this for that, can go on.

However, the committee's practices are subject to attack precisely because of their deemphasis on large policy considerations. Manifestly, the House Appropriations Committee does not normally consider its task to lie in rehashing every year the arguments over the fundamental desirability of the legislation already considered by the substantive committees and passed by Congress. Fortunately, Richard Fenno [37] has provided us with a splendid analysis of a committee whose members took fierce partisan and ideological positions on virtually all the issues that came before them. The norm of reciprocity—accepting the recommendations of other subcommittees if they accept yours—was unknown on the House Education Committee in the years after World War II. The members went after each other with abandon. They appeared to glory in differences and to stress the ultimate values which divided them. As a result, the committee was supremely ineffective in getting its recommendations accepted in the House. Internal committee warfare contributed to the long delay in producing any important legislation on education. Were these norms to prevail on the appropriations committees it is doubtful that a congressional budget could be produced at all. In the presence of delay and confusion and in the absence of party majorities to resolve these matters consistently on a strict partisan basis, Congress would be faced with the choice of abandoning its budgetary prerogatives or of indulging in the grossest forms of action leading to wild and unpredictable swings in the levels of appropriations.

REFORM PROPOSALS

The literature on reform is replete with suggestions for improving the rationality of the budgetary process, which turn out to have vast implications for the distribution of power. Identifying rationality with a comprehensive overview of the budget by a single person or group, Arthur Smithies despairs of the fragmented approach taken by Congress and proposes a remedy. He suggests that a Joint (congressional) Budget Policy committee be formed and empowered to consider all proposals for revenue and expenditure in a single package and that its decisions be made binding by a concurrent resolution. He presents this reform suggestion as a moderate proposal to improve the rationality of the budget process.[38] If the proposed Joint Committee were unable to secure the passage of its recommendations, as would surely be the case, it would have gone to enormous trouble without accomplishing anything but a public revelation of futility. The impotence of the Joint Committee on the Economic Report,[39] the breakdown of the single congressional attempt to develop a comprehensive legislative budget,[40] and the failure of congressional attempts to control the Council of Economic Advisers [41] and the Budget Bureau,[42] all stem from the same cause. There is no cohesive group in Congress capable of using these devices to affect decision making by imposing its preferences on a majority of Congressmen. Smithies' budgetary reform presupposes a completely different political system from the one which exists in the United States. In the guise of a procedural change in the preparation of the budget by Congress, Smithies is actually proposing a revolutionary move which would mean, if it were successful, the virtual introduction of the British Parliamentary system.

In a sophisticated advocacy of budgetary reform, John Saloma suggests a Joint (congressional) Committee of Fiscal Policy, which he believes can operate within the existing political system. The Joint Fiscal Committee would have a small membership drawn from leading members of the two appropriations and the two finance committees of Congress. The Joint Committee would be well staffed. According to Saloma:

The Joint Committee should not be required to submit a formal legislative budget for congressional enactment. At most it should develop budgetary guidelines to assist the fiscal committees (guidelines that probably would be kept confidential). Primarily it should provide a forum for continuing Congressional consideration of the budget, changing economic and political assumptions on which the budget is based, and the status of authorization and appropriation measures.[43]

Saloma [44] believes that the Joint Fiscal Committee would improve communications between the houses of Congress, enable Congress "to express its sentiments on broad fiscal policy," provide a continuing picture of the budget which Congress does not have, and provide guidelines to a coordinating committee of appropriations subcommittee chairmen on levels of appropriations. Smithies' proposal has been made more realistic at the cost of emasculating it. What is the point of the Joint Fiscal Committee if, unlike the Joint Committee on Atomic Energy, it cannot make recommendations for action on the floor of Congress? Why should any other committee pay attention to its recommendations? Experience with the Joint Economic Committee suggests that advisory committees of this character have hardly any influence at all on governmental policy.[45] If the budgetary guidelines of the Joint Fiscal Committee were adopted, which is doubtful, we would have in effect a steering committee of Congress, which Saloma recognizes is unrealistic. If they were rejected, as is likely, disillusionment would be inevitable, despite Saloma's warning that expectations should not be too high. Whatever information is desired on the outstanding authorizations and appropriations can be had through the existing committees of Congress or through some simple information service. It seems to me that Saloma's proposal, a variation of the McClellan Committee bill, is simply a bow to the gods of comprehensiveness. As usual, no demonstration is made of the feasibility of a comprehensive approach; instead, the gods are appeased by providing an umbrella committee, much as if incantation of the Joint Fiscal Committee's name would reveal the divine presence of a rational view of the budget as a whole.

SUMMARY

In appraising the budgetary process, we must deal with real men who know that, in this real world, the best they can get is to be preferred to the perfection they cannot achieve. Unwilling or unable to alter the basic features of the political system, they seek to make it work for them rather than against them in budgeting. Participants in budgeting not only work within the specified constitutional rules, they also make active use of them. Problems of calculation are mitigated by the division of labor in the separation of powers; morality is enforced by substantial external checks as well as by inner motives; a wider range of preferences is taken into account by making the institutional participants responsible for somewhat different ones. A great deal of informal coordination takes place as participants adjust to their expectation of others' behavior. An incremental approach guards against radical departures most of the time, whereas agency advocacy and strategies designed to take advantage of emergent needs help ensure flexibility. A basic conclusion of this appraisal is that the existing budgetary process works much better than is commonly supposed.

There is, however, no special magic in the status quo. Inertia and ignorance as well as experience and wisdom may be responsible for whatever problems exist in the present state of affairs. Improvements of many kinds are undoubtedly possible and desirable. The heart of the problem of budgetary reform lies in the inevitable tension between the practice of incrementalism and the ideology of comprehensiveness. The assumption of all previous proposals for reform has been that incrementalism must be sacrificed to comprehensiveness. But as this section has suggested formal coordination and comprehensive calculation of budgets are unfeasible, undesirable, or both. If comprehensiveness is rejected, however, there turn out to be other significant directions for reform that have not yet been tried. My view is that the present budgetary process should be taken as far as it will go and then corrected for its worst deficiencies. Proposals for reform should advocate a more thoroughgoing incremental approach, not its opposite—a more comprehensive one. There should be greater use of aids to calculation rather than less. Agencies should not be told to give up advocacy, but should be motivated to make their best case even more persuasive. There should be even less formal unity and more conflict in budgeting than there is today.

Radical Incrementalism

The President, the agencies, and Congress are now compelled to give at least *pro forma* consideration to all the activities in the whole budget in a limited period of time. This results in a brief period characterized by frantic activity and the rote presentation of masses of information, most of which is not subject to change and of no special interest to anyone at that time. Why? Because of unthinking acceptance of the idea that there must be a budget containing all expenditures presented and considered at one time. As the federal budget grows, and life and budgeting become more complex, the demand for central direction increases. Yet the overload of information is already staggering; aids to calculation are used in a desperate attempt to simplify consideration of small parts of the budget. The time has come to cast aside the myth of comprehensiveness. Theory should be brought in line with experience so that there will be a chance of improving the experience. The budget needs to be further fragmented. Attention needs to be directed to matters of political interest which can be changed. Evaluation of budgetary requests must be spread out so that greater time and attention may be devoted to each of them. The development and refinement of further aids to calculation should assume a high research priority. The delays in the budgetary process should be markedly reduced by permitting the most immediate response to budgetary requests.

My proposal is that we abandon the annual budgetary process, as it is now known, and substitute a continuous consideration of incremental changes to the existing base. Each agency will assume that the funds for its programs will automatically be continued. All appropriations will be continuous, except for a small number designed for a limited time period. When an agency wishes to increase or decrease its funds for a program or to eliminate an old program or begin a new one, it will submit a request to Congress through the Bureau of the Budget. The President may submit requests for change to Congress, and have them considered right away. The appropriations committees may call for testimony at any time on any budgetary matter and change appropriations irrespective of the fiscal year. By altering authorizations to spend, the substantive committees may also bring reconsideration of budgetary matters. I call this proposal radical incrementalism because it is based on pushing the evident incremental tendencies in budgeting to encompass the entire process.

A basic purpose of radical incrementalism is to facilitate speedy and continuous adaptation to emergent problems. While some programs may remain in a steady state, others can be reviewed as often as any participant deems it necessary. Supplemental appropriations would become a thing of the past. Demands could be dealt with as they arise. If the latest incremental move suggests a new step requiring changes in appropriations, a decision

could be made right then and there. The tyranny of the annual budget—
requiring formal review of programs of little immediate interest and inhibiting action on programs which need attention at the moment—would be
ended.

Suppose that a subcommittee wished to look at trends in personnel or
building costs. It could simply ask for these figures and act on them as it
saw fit. Should a subcommittee want to view any budgetary item in relation to an agency's total appropriations, it could request both sets of figures. In order to facilitate this procedure, the appropriations committee
should require agencies to develop quick and inexpensive methods of estimating expenditures. The agencies as well as the appropriations committees need to develop better aids to calculation. It may well be the case that
much agency budgetary work is far too expensive and cumbersome for the
results achieved. The development of rough and ready cost estimates
should make it possible for agencies to provide serviceable breakdowns of
their activities from a variety of conceptual viewpoints. Instead of being
stuck with a rigid set of program categories, terribly expensive to maintain
under proper accounting, the agencies and the subcommittees would have
the advantage of being able to look at activities from diverse perspectives.

An objection that might be raised to radical incrementalism is that certain programs could escape scrutiny over a period of years. This potential
problem may be solved by appointing people to review periodically those
programs or activities that do not change very much from year to year,
and would, therefore, tend to escape frequent scrutiny. Since they do not
alter radically, a thorough going over every five years or so would be sufficient. Nor need any one organization do it all; the incremental approach
can make use of the division of labor that is a part of the national system.
Departmental budget offices, the bureaus themselves, the Bureau of the
Budget, and the House and Senate appropriations subcommittees and their
investigating staffs, might use sampling techniques so that each would review a few programs of this kind every year. The results could then be
used to see if congressional scrutiny were warranted the next year. In this
way, a large part of the problem may be met while adding only a little to
the burden of the participants. Should the appropriations committee decide
that they wish to review every activity as often as every five to eight years,
they could make it a rule that each appropriation lapses five to eight years
after the last congressional act.

Narrowing, fragmenting, and dispersing these budgetary reviews has
considerable advantage from the viewpoint of encouraging experimentation
and innovation: because no one organization is overburdened, the most
thorough analysis is facilitated; more active participation by high level officials is encouraged because the material to be considered at any one time
is not overwhelming; as the knowledge and interest of top officials is fed
back down the line, the significance of the activity and the importance of

those who engage in it is likely to be enhanced. If budgetary reviews can be liberated to some extent from the peak periods of the formal budgetary cycle, imagination and creativity can be given freer play. The absence of immediate deadlines may encourage speculation and experimentation, while the increased probability that hierarchical superiors have time to listen gives greater promise that the efforts may lead to tangible results. The variety of organizations involved should also lead to consideration of a broad range of values and perspectives.

At first glance, it might appear that problems of coordination would be made more difficult than they are today. I think not; unless, of course, one is prepared to define coordination as placing all appropriations within the cover of one huge book at one time. Nor does it make much sense to define coordination as a central review, since this begs the question of whether policies have actually been related to one another in a reasonable way. It is a lot easier to mesmerize oneself with talk about central coordination than it is to practice it. Radical incrementalism, however, can be practiced. Each increment of the budget can be considered as it comes up. Attempts can be made to adapt the new policy, through successive approximation, to major features of the environment as revealed by experience. Thus, a series of rapid adjustments can be made in a budgetary system which encourages (indeed, compels) decision-makers to take into account the preferences of others and to mitigate the adverse consequences that policies may have for them. Under radical incrementalism, adaptation can be undertaken with greater intelligence because (1) the action is close in time to awareness of the problem; (2) changes are smaller, quicker, alterable, and, therefore, more easily made; (3) the decision-makers are enabled to have a better grasp of where they are in relation to where they want to be; (4) each change can be separately evaluated against a general picture of the most relevant programs then in operation instead of, an immensely more complicated task, multitudes of suggested changes being pitted against each other simultaneously; (5) every change is always important in the sense that a major participant in the system wants it.

Nothing in radical incrementalism prevents any participant in the budgetary process from using any and all analytic techniques at his disposal. Everyone is permitted to be as wise as he knows how to be. If the day should come when a simultaneous comparison of all governmental programs appeared desirable, the President or Congress could consider the budget in just that way. If it appears desirable to consider all programs dealing with water or land or any other area of policy, the President or the appropriations committees can call for action. Indeed, a radical incrementalism might foster such an approach by permitting scheduling when other great matters were not up for immediate decision. The endless search for "needless duplication," "sheer waste," and "irrational decisions" could go on with as much, or as little, sense as before.

CONSEQUENCES OF RADICAL INCREMENTALISM FOR MAJOR PARTICIPANTS

What would happen to the President's budget? It would represent the President's preferences on any and all budgetary items on which he cared to express an opinion. It could be as complete a document as he (through the Budget Bureau) knows how to make, or it could contain positions only on selected matters. It would go to Congress as a source of information, but it would not be the action document that it is now. Instead, action on Presidential requests would take place when he sent specific demands for specific items to the appropriations committees. The President's budget would be much like his State of the Union message where he presents his legislative priorities and shopping list, but where he does not necessarily comment on policies he does not wish changed. When he wants action, he follows up his address by submitting a series of concrete proposals for action. Then, as his pending requests are acted upon, the President takes these decisions into account in submitting his next wave of requests. The President would gain flexibility he does not have now because he would not have to commit himself in advance on all appropriations requests as is the case under the annual budget approach. Nor would he and his chief advisors have to engage in the chaotic activity of the fall, when tired and overburdened men work furiously to put together all appropriations. Outgoing Presidents would not have to go through the charade of developing a budget with which to stick their successor, and incoming Presidents would not have to face the immediate task of putting together another full-scale budget to counteract the one that is then operative. The new President could deal with the most vital matters first, and then take up the rest in a more leisurely way.

The President's ability to pursue economic policies would be enhanced rather than diminished by radical incrementalism. There would be no decrease in his ability to plan for a desired relationship between revenue and expenditures. He could set out the relationship he believes desirable in his budget message or in his economic report or in any other way he deems appropriate. And he could propose action to meet his preferences through regular legislation, appropriations, or executive action. But he would not be compelled to do this at any specific time as is now the case. He could wait until he thought a change was necessary, receive the most current predictions of current revenue and expenditure, and act at once. When emergencies require increased expenditure, as in the Vietnam situation, or when long-range estimates proved to be faulty, as frequently happens, he could modify his plans. Since the possibility of substantial change in expenditures is confined to a few areas of policy, these could be re-studied when necessary. While automatic stabilizers, such as unemployment compensation, work well in guarding against depressions, voluntary action by the federal government has not proved effective.[46] Perhaps the flexibility provided by radical incrementalism will permit speedier and more appropriate adaptation to contemporary needs.

A possible objection to radical incrementalism might be that Congress would suffer because agencies would not have to come before the appropriations committees every year for all the appropriations that (aside from trust funds and the like) are usually included in the annual budget. However, instead of concentrating their attention on appropriations requests only in the once-a-year period when all requests are made, agencies would be continually thinking of the prospect of making their next request. On vital matters, the agencies might be called for repeated appearances. To the extent that Congress is more often on their mind its influence should grow rather than decrease.

Opinion on radical incrementalism will probably be divided in Congress. Some members who identify with a Presidential constituency might object on the grounds that welfare policies would be hurt by enhancing the power of the appropriations committees to cut in crucial places. However, this would not happen, because, while conservatives now gain somewhat by the special positions they hold on committees, this advantage is rapidly disappearing.[47] There is good reason to believe that the seniority system will increasingly benefit proponents of welfare legislation. Both Presidents and the formal congressional leadership have ample means at their disposal to place members who represent preferences of the party majority on the appropriations committees, and they have already used this to good effect in the House. Deviance from the party majority is largely a southern, Democratic phenomenon and will diminish in size and importance with the growth of Negro voting, population shifts out of the deep South, and increased Democratic party representation elsewhere. Moreover, the best analysis we have of the appropriations committees in Congress (see forthcoming book by Professor Richard F. Fenno, Jr. of the University of Rochester, Rochester, New York) suggests that they do not markedly transgress on the preferences of the mass of other legislators. While it is true that service on the appropriations committees does tend to make members suspicious of executive advocacy, it is also true that the substantive committees are generally packed with legislators whose constituency interests suggest a more expensive view of governmental programs. A creative tension between the somewhat differing orientations of the two levels of committees does not appear to be a bad thing.

Fiscal conservatives might also oppose radical incrementalism for fear that it would result, in general, in higher governmental expenditures. Such critics might argue that, in considering programs one at a time, Congress would lose track of the implications for the total rate of expenditure. However, there would be little difficulty in arranging for a reporting service in Congress that would issue frequent statements on total approved expenditures. The solution to the problem of securing decreases, or holding down increases, in expenditure lies in the elimination of programs and not in budgetary procedures. If fiscal conservatives wish to make a drastic impact on expenditures, they will have to elect many more legislators who support their views than is now the case. Barring this unlikely development, there is no point in making the appropriations process the whipping post for developments that represent secular trends in the political system as a whole. Where appropriations subcommittees appear to stand in the way of expenditures desired by a significant majority of their colleagues, they may be outvoted on the floor, or congressional majorities may resort to backdoor spending or to other devices that take control of appropriations out of the offending subcommittees' hands. When fiscal conservatives, or liberals for that matter, are able to assert themselves in Congress, radical incrementalism should provide somewhat better opportunities for selective intervention than now exist.

In my opinion, the most serious obstacle to the acceptance of radical incrementalism is an ideological one. The proposals may not receive serious consideration because they run counter to the reigning ideologies of comprehensiveness and annual budgeting. But I still think them useful to have at hand if and when Congress gets serious about improving its capabilities as an institution.

STRATEGIC POLITICAL KNOWLEDGE

By reducing the information requirements of budgetary decisions, radical incrementalism increases the possibility of reasonable action. Whatever knowledge exists can be brought to bear on the problem by some participant in the system. Knowledge may be increased in the sense that the data are more recent and the feedback from one action can be immediately used in the next appraisal. But knowledge about how to deal with problems is only one kind of knowledge. There is a prior knowledge which often assumes greater political importance: namely, what problems should be considered? A radical incrementalism provides an important aid to calculation in that it focuses attention on those changes from the status quo which are important to some participant. But there are other ways of being alerted to matters of importance which would be especially useful to congressmen.

The Budgeting and Accounting Act of 1921 provides for Presidential submission of agency budgets to Congress through the Bureau of the Budget. The appropriations committees do not formally receive original agency requests but only those requests as amended or deleted by the Chief Executive. We all know, to be sure, that when ties between agencies and appropriations committee chairmen are close the original agency demands may be brought out in private or in committee hearings. But, agency officials are under restrictions in how far they can go in open advocacy. In any event, junior members of the appropriations committees may never discover this information, and the same will most certainly be true of most other members of Congress.

As political men in a representative assembly, legislators are, above all, dealers in preferences. Since they are makers, shapers, molders, brokers, and bargainers of preferences, the most important information for them to have is information about what people want. Related to this as an aid to calculation is information on where preferences of key participants differ and why, for it alerts legislators to a conflict of preferences in which they may wish to intervene. Congress could well use Franklin D. Roosevelt's well-known practice of programming for conflict, which was designed to assure him that he would be called in on important matters, that is, matters on which preferences and policies differed. This kind of strategic political knowledge is of special importance to congressmen because they appear to be more skilled in reconciling conflicting preferences than in evaluating complicated sets of budgetary figures.

Therefore, I propose that, along with radical incrementalism, there should be a legal requirement that the original requests of agencies be made public, together with a statement by the Budget Bureau giving its reasons for making changes. Congressmen would be immediately alerted to a conflict of preferences and would have the rationales of both the agency and the Budget Bureau presenting rival arguments. Both the agencies and the Budget Bureau would be highly motivated to make the best possible case for their demands. If they were also motivated to reach an agreement through bargaining, the very fact of their success would be one indicator that the matter was not of the highest priority for congressional attention. While some agencies might try to raise their demands inordinately for bargaining purposes, a series of attempts would soon reveal that consistently coming in too high would not serve their interests and would be abandoned.

Thus far I have deliberately used the general word "agency" to avoid complicating the argument with distinctions between bureaus and departments. My initial recommendation is that each department retain its present power to make secret recommendations to the President on behalf of the bureaus within its jurisdiction. In this way, general Presidential influence on initial bureau requests could be maintained through his power to hire and fire cabinet members and other heads of organizations. Since department heads must maintain themselves in an environment which necessarily differs from that of the President, their recommendations may sometimes be expected to differ from his on crucial matters. (If this were not the case, the President would have much less need for a Budget Bureau and an Executive Office.) The congressional purpose of unearthing significant political matters through the airing of conflicts would be served. Should this proposal prove insufficient, Congress could go further and require department heads to present in writing their reasons for disagreements with the Budget Bureau request.

Under a system of congressional programming for conflict, the President would lose his ability to maintain the fiction that agencies uniformly support his budget. If this means that Congressmen would learn more about where to intervene, there might be a corresponding decrease of the Presidential influence now gained by keeping Congress in the dark. Undoubtedly, the proposal will be fought for that reason. But, in fact, the President's support would still be terribly important to the agencies. Congress would still rely on the President's figures as a starting point for their consideration and as a bench mark for making cuts or (less frequently) increases. Agencies would almost always be better off with the President's support than without it; since Congress tends to cut the President's budget, an agency would have to mount a special campaign, with no certain prospect of success, in order to have a chance for victory. It would hardly be advisable, therefore, for agencies to flaunt the Chief Executive. The President might gain in another direction through his ability, under radical incrementalism, to intervene continuously in the appropriations process rather than to confine his energy largely to consideration of the annual budget.

I have no intention of proposing a system that would interfere with the confidential relationship between the President and the Bureau of the Budget. All communications from the Budget Bureau to the President would be as privileged as they are today. Nothing would prevent the Budget Bureau from presenting one kind of argument to the President and another to Congress. The only requirement would be that the President (through the Bureau of the Budget) comment on the differences between his recommendations and those of the agency involved.

A painful adjustment on the part of the Bureau of the Budget would undoubtedly be required. It has grown up in an environment which nurtures secrecy. Its confidential relationship with the President has been used to prevent public scrutiny of its action. Rationalizations of its positions on issues, which have become partly implicit in the subculture of the Executive Office, would have to be raised to the surface at some point. The bureau's claim to a more rational mode of decision making in the public interest (as opposed to irrational procedures in agencies surrounded by special interests) would become open to public examination. The Bureau of the Budget could no longer operate entirely as if it were guided by an informal version of the Official Secrets Act, which so effectively shields executive personnel in Great Britain from outside intervention. While bureau personnel would gain by being liberated from the physically and mentally exhausting task of putting together an entire governmental budget in a few frantic weeks, they might not be happy with a radical incremental approach to budgeting.

By raising conflict to a more public and hence more visible level, interest groups may be stimulated to greater activity. In a democracy, where public knowledge is generally deemed good, this hardly appears to provide an objection to radical incrementalism. Recent scholarship has suggested that in many cases the power of interest groups in relation to public officials has been exaggerated. Where interest groups are already very powerful, as in the case of the Rivers and Harbors Congress, the chances are that they are privy to the additional information that would be made public under the new system. Thus, the proposals for increasing the availability of strategic information might work to strengthen groups presently weak while adding little or no additional power to the strong.

KNOWLEDGE ABOUT POLICIES

Although it might be agreed that strategic political information is of the highest importance to a political body like Congress, knowledge about the fields of policy themselves is also significant. Since the specialization of subcommittee members, together with long service in particular areas of policy, undoubtedly does more to augment the substantive information of the legislators than anything which might be suggested, it follows that proposals that drastically increase the turnover of legislators or prevent them from specializing should be resisted. One minor suggestion, however, might be useful. The appropriations committees might hire one or two staff members whose purpose would be to recruit *ad hoc* teams of scholars and practitioners to give a special kind of advice. These men would produce very brief reports telling the subcommittees two things: the questions deemed to be of greatest importance in the relevant field of policy, and the best known ways of looking at the problems involved. Then, if the members of a subcommittee were interested, they could spend a few days at the beginning of the session discussing general policy considerations with their consultants. The best that could be said for this approach would be that it might sensitize Congressmen to different kinds of questions and approaches divorced from the immediate need to make a decision. The worst would be that nothing useful would happen. The approach seems worth a try on a low priority basis.

Under a radical incremental approach, with programming for conflict, each organizational unit in the executive branch would be highly motivated to bring forth its best programs and to back them up with the best knowledge at its command. Congress could then use the resources in the executive branch to improve the quality of information that goes into its own decisions. It could still be possible, however, for situations to exist in which all the participants lack useful knowledge. No amount of competition or conflict or reconciliation of divergent preferences would produce reasonable decisions where everyone is poverty-stricken in regard to knowledge. One can say that in the midst of universal lack of knowledge a centrally directed and enforced policy would be by far the worst kind since its impact would be more far-reaching and its reversal would be far more difficult. Such a problem is not peculiar to Congress; universal ignorance is a defect of the society, not merely of a single institution. Yet Congress does have an obligation to increase the sum total of knowledge relevant to carrying out its policy-making functions. The best way for individual Congressmen to become aware of gaps in information is to carry on intimate association with program personnel in the agencies and with experts from industry and academic life who might be most sensitive to what we do not know. Beyond this, the task force of experts described above might make suggestions for research in areas where crucial knowledge is lacking. The aid given governmental bodies by organizations such as RAND, also suggests that Congress should look kindly upon the establishment of research corporations in all major areas of policy. Although these corporations would have ties to executive agencies, the increase in information which they would generate would also be useful to Congress. By increasing the number of men trained in various policy areas, research corporations like RAND also increase the possibilities for Congress to gather information from knowledgeable men during and (especially) after their term of employment has ended.

The usual solution suggested for the problem of lack of knowledge in Congress is simply to add to staff resources. In this undifferentiated form, however, the proposal is not terribly helpful. How great an increase in staff, for whom, and for what purpose? The appropriations committees now are entitled to as many staff assistants as they want. In addition, they have virtually unlimited call on the General Accounting Office and other agencies for as much help as they ask for. However, while the staff members are by and large immensely knowledgeable—they may well know more about programs than the highest executive officials—they tend to serve the subcommittee chairmen and ranking minority members rather more than the junior members. But not all junior members would want an additional staff person, responsible only to themselves, who would help out on appropriations. Some members might be tempted to engage in subterfuge by using their appropriations staff for other purposes they deem more valuable. To encourage open behavior it would be advisable to give all legislators a couple of extra staff people at high pay. Then those appropriations committee members who wanted extra assistance could use a staff man for that purpose or not as they saw fit. In this way, a few members might be helped without encouraging a direct conflict with subcommittee chairmen and regular committee staff who might view the earmarking of additional staff for appropriations work as a threat to them. Of course, some conflict over new staff is probably inevitable. A very large increase in personnel or committee staff would seem undesirable on the ground that Congressmen are valuable as representatives and not as office managers.

But this discussion still begs the question of what kind of knowledge Congressmen need. As a self-respecting body. Congress ought to have research carried on which is expressly designed to help its members in the context in which they work. There is no point in preparing vast volumes of general data to be added to the tomes Congressmen already have no time to read. Nor is there much point in preparing comprehensive decision procedures which Congress could not and would not use. It would be most desirable, however, for researchers to study ways and means of developing and introducing scanning mechanisms which would tell Congressmen what matters were worth their attention. Forcing conflicts to the surface is one such mechanism. So is increase-decrease analysis. Congressmen need more devices which gear the budgetary process toward producing signals which direct attention to important problems or to strategic opportunities for intervention at low cost in time and high payoff in control. A research group on "aids to calculation" might prove exceedingly useful in this respect.

To the best of my knowledge no one has ever undertaken a study designed to tell Congressmen how they might best get compliance with their directives. The lack of knowledge of budgetary motivation has previously been mentioned. What relationship should there be between agency and Budget Bureau requests and grants of funds to secure the highest degree of sensitivity to congressional preferences? What kind of division of functions between and within agencies would maximize opportunities for congressional knowledge and intervention? What simple budgetary forms could be devised to remind executives of congressional interest? The President has found a new Machiavelli in Richard Neustadt; Congress finds no one to give it advice about its special power stake.

INCREASE IN CONFLICT

A predictable consequence of the adoption of the reforms proposed here would be a moderate increase in conflict within Congress over specific appropriations. By highlighting the matters that do receive consideration by the appropriations committees, a radical incremental approach should moderately increase the awareness of interested Congressmen. By increasing staff possibilities for junior members of the committees, their ability to disagree with the more senior members should be enhanced somewhat. Emphasizing differences between the President and the agencies should increase political knowledge for all interested members of Congress. Since committee recommendations now receive such a high level of support in Congress, a modest increase in conflict would enable ordinary Congressmen to have a little more influence without disrupting the budgetary process. The ability of the system to withstand conflict would also be enhanced by a radical incremental approach because it decreases the need to reach formal agreement on the entire budget. If conflict within Congress leads to lack of agreement and some delay, the agencies can continue to spend at the same level while waiting for a decision on proposed changes. Moreover, only incremental parts of the budget would be delayed while the rest would continue as before. By relaxing the inhibitions created by the overwhelming need to agree on a whole budget every year, the creative aspects of conflict would be given greater scope in budgetary matters as they are in other legislation.

Conclusion

The change to radical incrementalism would not require as great a change in budgetary practices as it would in perceptions of these practices. Incremental practices are a part of the present budgetary process; but, because participants believe that the ideal budgetary process is comprehensive and coordinated hierarchically, they view incrementalism, with an attitude somewhere between desperation and contempt, as a necessary evil that was adopted only because they did not know any better. At present, incremental practices take place within the framework of annual considerations of the entire budget; this arbitrary time schedule, which is designed to give the appearance of comprehensiveness, actually serves neither the theory of comprehensiveness nor the practice of incrementalism. While comprehensiveness, which cannot be practiced, is touted as a lofty ideal, incrementalism, which could be practiced, is hidden in the scullery like an unloved but necessary Cinderella.

If Congress were willing or able to delegate its powers to an executive committee of compatible legislators, it could, of course, achieve central direction in the same limited sense as the President has: the final word on budgetary decisions would come from a single source whose unity would be visible. But, if Congress is unwilling and unable to do this, as is surely the case, then it should seek to manifest its influence in ways appropriate to a body of legislators capable of unity on an *ad hoc* basis but not consistently over a wide range of measures. Its ability to continually form and reform *ad hoc* coalitions addressed to emergent political problems should be enhanced through a radical incrementalism. Congress is in the business of correcting mistakes—consequences of decisions with adverse impact on people—and should improve its ability to do so with dispatch. The weaknesses of Congress as a highly fragmented institution are self-evident. I am suggesting that Congress could gain strength by making use of its essential nature rather than by running away from it.

NOTES

1. Richard McKeon, ed., *Basic Works of Aristotle* (New York: Random House, 1941), pp. 1185–1187, 1212–1224.

2. A. G. Wernham, *Benedict de Spinoza, The Political Works* (Oxford: The Clarendon Press, 1958), *inter alia.*

3. Arthur E. Buck, *Public Budgeting* (New York: Harper and Brothers, 1929); Jesse Burkhead, *Government Budgeting* (New York: John Wiley, 1956); Hoover Commission on the Organization of the Executive Branch of the Government, *Budget and Accounting* (Washington, D.C., 1949); Edward A. Kolodziej, "Congressional Responsibility for the Common Defense: The Money Problem," *The Western Political Quarterly,* 16 (1963): 149–160; Arthur Smithies, *The Budgetary Process in the United States* (New York: McGraw-Hill, 1955); Robert Ash Wallace, "Congressional Control of the Budget," *Midwest Journal of Political Science* 3 (1959): 151–167; and William Franklin Willoughby, *The National Budget System* (Baltimore: Johns Hopkins Press, 1927).

4. Aaron Wildavsky, *Politics of the Budgetary Process* (Boston: Little, Brown, 1964), pp. 127–144.

5. Dwight Waldo, *The Administrative State* (New York: the Ronald Press, 1948), *inter alia;* Herbert A. Simon, *Administrative Behavior,* 2d ed. (New York: Macmillan, 1957), pp. 172–197.

6. Wildavsky, *op. cit.,* pp. 127–144.

7. Richard Cyert and James March, eds., *A Behavioral Theory of the Firm* (Englewood Cliffs, N.J.: Prentice-Hall, 1963).

8. David Braybrooke and Charles Lindblom, *A Strategy of Decision* (New York: Free Press, 1963).

9. Simon, *op. cit.*

10. Wildavsky, *op. cit.,* pp. 1–13.

11. *Ibid.,* pp. 16–18.

12. J. S. Hines (Research Officer) and R. W. Edwards (Chairman), *Budgeting in Public Authorities* (New York: A Study Group of the Royal Institute of Public Administration, 1959), p. 245.

13. Wildavsky, *op. cit.,* pp. 21–32.

14. Richard F. Fenno, Jr., "The House Appropriations Committee as a Political System: The Problem of Integration," *American Political Science Review* 56 (1962): 310–324.

15. Wildavsky, *op. cit.,* pp. 65–98.

16. *Ibid.,* pp. 101–123.

17. *Ibid.,* pp. 4–42.

18. Otto Davis and Aaron Wildavsky, "An Empirical Theory of Congressional Appropriations." (Mimeograph, 1965.)

19. Fenno, *op. cit.*

20. Wildavsky, *op. cit.,* pp. 56–64.

21. Fenno, *op. cit.*

22. Wildavsky, *op. cit.*

23. Fenno, *op. cit.*

24. *Ibid.,* p. 312.

25. *Ibid.;* Wildavsky, *op. cit.*

26. Charles Lindblom, "The Science of 'Muddling Through,'" *Public Administration Review* 19 (1959): 79–88.

27. See his *Decision-Making In Taxation and Expenditures, Public Finances, Needs, Sources and Utilization* (Princeton: National Bureau of Economic Research, 1961), pp. 295–336.

28. Joseph S. Berliner, *Factory and Manager in the USSR* (Cambridge: Harvard University Press, 1957).

29. Frank Jasinsky, "Use and Misuse of Efficiency Controls," *Harvard Business Review* 34 (1956): 107; Chris Argyris, *The Impact of Budgets on People* (New York: Controllership Foundation, Inc., 1952), pp. 12 ff.

30. Argyris, *op. cit.,* pp. 6 ff.

31. *Ibid.,* pp. 12–13.

32. *Ibid., inter alia;* Burnard H. Sord and Glenn A. Welsch, *Business Budgeting: A Survey of Management Planning and Control Practices* (New York: Controllership Foundation, Inc., 1958), pp. 140–50.

33. Arnold A. Bebling, "A Look at Budgets and People," *Business Budgeting* 10 (1961): 16.

34. Andrew C. Stedry, *Budget Control and Cost Behavior* (Englewood Cliffs, N.J.: Prentice-Hall, 1960).

35. Richard F. Fenno, Jr., review of Joseph P. Harris, *Congressional Control of Administration,* in *American Political Science Review* 58 (1964): 674.

36. Fenno, "The House Appropriations Committee as a Political System: The Problem of Integration."

37. Frank Munger and Richard Fenno, Jr., *National Politics and Federal Aid to Education* (Syracuse, N.Y.: Syracuse University Press, 1962), pp. 106–136.

38. Smithies, *op. cit.,* pp. 192 ff.

39. Avery Leiserson, "Coordination of the Federal Budgetary and Appropriations Procedures Under the Legislative Reorganization Act of 1946," *National Tax Journal* 1 (1948): 118–126.

40. Wallace, *op. cit.;* Dalmas H. Nelson, "The Omnibus Appropriations Act of 1950," *Journal of Politics* 15 (1953): 274–288; John Phillips, "The Hadacol of the Budget Makers," *National Tax Journal* 4 (1951): 255–268.

41. Roy Blough, "The Role of the Economist in Federal Policy-Making," *University of Illinois Bulletin* (1953), p. 51; Lester Seligman, "Presidential Leadership: The Inner Circle and Institutionalization," *Journal of Politics,* 1956, 410–426; Edwin G. Nourse, *Economics in the Public Service: Administrative Aspects of the Employment Act* (New York: Harcourt Brace, 1953); Ronald C. Hood, "Reorganizing the Council of Economic Advisors," *Political Science Quarterly,* 59 (1954): 413–437.

42. Fritz Morstein Marx, "The Bureau of the Budget: Its Evolution and Present Role, II," *American Political Science Review* 39 (1945): 869–898; Richard Neustadt, "Presidency and Legislation: The Growth of Central Clearance." *American Political Science Review* 48 (1954): 641–671; Seligman, *op. cit.*

43. John S. Saloma, "The Responsible Use of Power," in Saloma and Murray L. Weidenbaum, *Congress and the Federal Budget* (Washington, D.C.: The American Enterprise Institute for Public Policy Research, 1965), p. 182.

44. *Ibid.,* pp. 175–193.

45. Ralph K. Huitt, "Congressional Organization and Operations in the Field of Money and Credit," in William Fellner et al., *Fiscal and Debt Management Policies: A Series of Research Studies prepared for the Commission on Money and Credit* (Englewood Cliffs, N.J.: Prentice-Hall, 1963), pp. 399–495.

46. Wilfred Lewis, Jr., *Federal Fiscal Policy in the Postwar Recessions* (Washington, D.C.: The Brookings Institution, 1962).

47. Raymond E. Wolfinger and Joan Heifetz, "Safe Seats, Seniority and Power in Congress," *American Political Science Review* 49 (1965): 337–349.

BIBLIOGRAPHY

Argyris, Chris. *The Impact of Budgets on People.* New York: Controllership Foundation, Inc., 1952.

Axelson, Charles F. "What Makes Budgeting So Obnoxious?" *Business Budgeting* 11 (1963): 22–27.

Bebling, Arnold A. "A Look at Budgets and People." *Business Budgeting* 10 (1961): 16 ff.

Berliner, Joseph S. *Factory and Manager in the USSR.* Cambridge: Harvard University Press, 1957.

Blough, Roy. "The Role of the Economist in Federal Policy-Making." *University of Illinois Bulletin* 51 (1953).

Braybrooke, David and Charles Lindblom. *A Strategy of Decision.* New York: Free Press of Glencoe, 1963.

Buck, Arthur E. *Public Budgeting.* New York: Harper and Brothers, 1929.

Burkhead, Jesse. *Government Budgeting.* New York: John Wiley, 1956.

Cyert, Richard and James March, eds. *A Behavioral Theory of the Firm.* Englewood Cliffs, N.J.: Prentice-Hall, 1963.

Davis, Otto and Aaron Wildavsky. "An Empirical Theory of Congressional Appropriations." Mimeo, 1965.

Fenno, Richard F., Jr. "The House Appropriations Committee as a Political System: The Problem of Integration." *American Political Science Review* 56 (1962): 310–324.

———. Review of Joseph P. Harris, *Congressional Control of Administration,* in *American Political Science Review* 53 (1964): 673–675.

Hines, J. S. (Research Officer), R. W. Edwards (Chairman). *Budgeting in Public Authorities.* New York: A Study Group of the Royal Institute of Public Administration, 1959.

Hood, Ronald C. "Reorganizing the Council of Economic Advisors," *Political Science Quarterly* 69 (1954): 413–437.

(Hoover) Commission on the Organization of the Executive Branch of the Government. *Budget and Accounting.* Washington, D.C., 1949.

Huitt, Ralph K. "Congressional Organization and Operations in the Field of Money and Credit," in William Fellner et al., *Fiscal and Debt Management Policies: A Series of Research Studies prepared for the Commission on Money and Credit.* Englewood Cliffs, N.J.: Prentice-Hall, 1963, pp. 399–495.

Jasinsky, Frank. "Use and Misuse of Efficiency Controls," *Harvard Business Review* 39 (1952): 105–112.

Kolodziej, Edward. "Congressional Responsibility for the Common Defense: The Money Problem," *The Western Political Quarterly* 16 (1963): 149–160.

Leiserson, Avery. "Coordination of the Federal Budgetary and Appropriations Procedures Under the Legislative Reorganization Act of 1946." *National Tax Journal* 1 (1948): 118–126.

Lewis, Wilfred, Jr. *Federal Fiscal Policy in the Postwar Recessions.* Washington, D.C.: The Brookings Institution, 1962.

Lindblom, Charles. *Decision-Making in Taxation and Expenditures, Public Finances, Needs, Sources and Utilization.* Princeton: National Bureau of Economic Research, 1964, pp. 295–336.

——. "The Science of 'Muddling Through.'" *Public Administration Review* 19 (1959): 79–88.

Marx, Fritz Morstein. "The Bureau of the Budget: Its Evolution and Present Role, II." *The American Political Science Review* 39 (1945): 869–898.

McKeon, Richard, ed. *Basic Works of Aristotle.* New York: Random House, 1941.

Munger, Frank and Richard F. Fenno, Jr. *National Politics and Federal Aid to Education.* Syracuse, New York: Syracuse University Press, 1962.

Nelson, Dalmas H. "The Omnibus Appropriations Act of 1950." *Journal of Politics* 15 (1953): 274–288.

Neustadt, Richard. "Presidency and Legislation: The Growth of Central Clearance." *The American Political Science Review* 48 (1954): 641–671.

Nourse, Edwin G. *Economics in the Public Service: Administrative Aspects of the Employment Act.* New York: Harcourt Brace, 1953.

Phillips, John. "The Hadacol of the Budget Makers." *National Tax Journal* 4 (1954): 255–268.

Saloma, John S. "The Responsible Use of Power," in Saloma and Murray L. Weidenbaum, *Congress and the Federal Budget.* Washington, D.C.: The American Enterprise Institute for Public Policy Research, 1965, pp. 103–205.

Seligman, Lester. "Presidential Leadership: The Inner Circle and Institutionalization." *Journal of Politics* 18 (1956): 410–426.

Simon, Herbert A. *Administrative Behavior,* 2nd edition. New York: Macmillan, 1957.

Smithies, Arthur. *The Budgetary Process in the United States.* New York: McGraw-Hill, 1955.

Sord, Burnard H. and Glenn A. Welsch. *Business Budgeting: A Survey of Management Planning and Control Practices.* New York: Controllership Foundation, Inc., 1958.

Stedry, Andrew C. *Budget Control and Cost Behavior.* Englewood Cliffs, N.J.: Prentice-Hall, 1960.

Sundelson, J. Wilner. *Budgetary Methods in National and State Governments.* Albany, New York: J. B. Lyon Co., 1938.

Waldo, Dwight. *The Administrative State.* New York: The Ronald Press, 1948.

Wallace, Robert Ash. "Congressional Control of the Budget." *Midwest Journal of Political Science* 3 (1959): 151–167.

Wernham, A. G. *Benedict de Spinoza, The Political Works.* Oxford: The Clarendon Press, 1958.

Wildavsky, Aaron. *Politics of the Budgetary Process.* Boston: Little Brown and Company, 1964.

——. "Private Markets and Public Arenas." *The American Behavioral Scientist* 9 (September 1965): 33–37.

Willoughby, William Franklin. *The National Budget System.* Baltimore: Johns Hopkins Press, 1927.

Wolfinger, Raymond E. and Joan Heifetz. "Safe Seats, Seniority and Power in Congress." *American Political Science Review* 59 (1965): 337–349.

24

THE THEORY OF
PREEMPTIVE REVOLUTION

Criticizing American foreign policy has replaced baseball and Monopoly as the national pastime. And winning the game depends on making profound statements like: "The United States is always reacting to events instead of enacting them," or "America should be molding the New World, instead of vainly trying to stem the forces of change," and "Born in revolution, the American government finds itself in the anomalous position of supporting conservative regimes." How much better it would be, the various critics seem to suggest, if the United States found itself part of the revolutionary vanguard. Then, the American people would be loved abroad, instead of hated, and an American could raise his head in a foreign land with some small feeling of pride. It gives me great pride to announce that a new discovery in political science (or, rather, the adaptation of an old one) now permits the United States government to accomplish all of these goals—and many other desirable ends as well.

The new discovery is, of course, the *Theory of Preemptive Revolution.* As one would immediately suspect, this theory is merely a subtheory of Gresham's Law: "bad revolutions drive out good ones." In its opening phases, the Theory calls for the United States to single out the three most hopeless countries in Latin America, in Africa, and in Asia. These should be nations whose extraordinary dearth of natural resources is matched only by the virtually total incapacity of their populations. These countries must be such sinkholes that billions of dollars would disappear into their vast slums and vaster wastelands without producing a molecule of visible improvement. Unless, of course, it was to be found in the unremitting hostility of the populations of these countries to the nation that had supplied the funds.[1]

Once having chosen three unpromising countries in each area, the United States will immediately set about to cause Communist revolutions in them. If there is no nascent Communist movement, the United States will start one. Unlimited funds and weaponry will be supplied to all those who give promise of pulling off a Communist revolution at the earliest possible moment. No delays will be tolerated. All socialist, democratic, or conservative forces will be rigorously suppressed. The rallying cry will be: "All power to the Communist party—At Once."

Once the Communist revolutions have succeeded, the party leaders will be encouraged to ally themselves, as openly and loudly as possible, with the Soviet Union. Dedicated party members in each country, having introduced governments modeled on that of the Soviet Union, will make it unmistakably clear that their struggling but aspiring nations are truly and genuinely Communist, loyal parts of the socialist camp, and dedicated to following the Soviet lead—and to accepting Soviet aid—in all matters.

What alternatives will confront the Soviet Union? If she accepts these nine countries as part of her sphere of influence, she will be required to support them. At an enormously high expenditure. It is estimated that Cuba, one of the three wealthiest countries in Latin America before its revolution, currently costs the Soviet Union around a million dollars a day. How much more will these nine other countries cost? And for how long will they require support? Note that the Soviet Union will be supporting them, and the United States, once the revolution has succeeded, will not be spending a penny. If the Soviet Union refuses to recognize the claims of these countries to her protection and support, her hollow pretensions to world leadership will be exposed. The Soviets will have to choose between solvency and saving face. (Nor can the Chinese Communists take up the slack; they can afford it even less. At the moment, the Chinese are specializing in places like Zanzibar, where much revolution can be accomplished at minimal expenditure.) A third possibility for the Soviet Union would be to attempt to stem the revolution in these Asian, African, and Latin American countries. In this case, United States foreign policy will have put the Soviet Union in the position of a status quo power, which keeps insisting that various countries hurry, but very slowly, along the road to Communism.

What about the so-called developing countries? The great problem at the moment is that the United States keeps pursuing them, shouting at the top of its lungs that they are in danger of being taken over by Communism. Naturally, these countries do not quite believe this, and wonder if Uncle Sam does not have either some ulterior motive or paranoia. Their best bet is to play both ends against the middle and to try to get the most they can out of the Soviet Union and the United States. But, consider the startling change that will overcome their policies the moment the United States seriously undertakes to put into practice the Theory of Preemptive Revolution. Instead of being able to take the status quo policies of the United States for granted, the developing countries will suddenly find themselves having to worry a great deal about the United States. If they look too hopeless, they may find the United States not only leaving them to the mercies of the local Communists, but perhaps even actively helping the revolutionary process along. The developing countries will have to demonstrate to the United States that they are worth saving from Communism. Countries who see their neighbors under Communist rule may decide that the Communist menace is a possibility for them, too, and ask for American assistance. The United States will then be in the much more enviable position of being able to play hard to get. As a result, the Soviet Union will end up supporting only the utterly hopeless countries—and using the money it would have liked to spend on more prosperous countries to do so.

The image of the United States as a conservative status quo power will be gone forever. No longer fear-ridden, no longer forever worrying about which little piece of African, Asian, or Latin American real estate might go Communist, it will be a proud and confident nation, which is continually in the enviable position of being asked to help others and must choose carefully those lucky places to which it will lend its support. Instead of being a wall flower, or, what is worse, actively forcing partners to dance with it, the United States will be much sought after—and on its own terms. Its foreign policy will be both active and judicious. No longer will it be the passive reactor-to-events that it is now. On the contrary, it will always be actively contemplating the possibility of fomenting revolutions in the hopeless countries that need them most. The Communists will have little time, no incentive, and no funds to aid revolutions in countries that could really cause harm to American interests. Developing countries will have much greater incentive to defend themselves, and to call upon American assistance in doing so. By adopting the Theory of Preemptive Revolution, the United States will break out of the vicious cycle in which it now finds itself. . . .

NOTE

1. Names of possible target countries have been omitted in order not to cause unnecessary offense at this stage and, also, not to alert our enemies to new policies.

25

A THIRD-WORLD
AVERAGING STRATEGY

WITH *Max Singer*

WASHINGTON (AP)—U.S. policymakers privately voiced unhappiness Thursday over the coup in Peru, but they expect the new military leadership to be pro-West and anti-Communist. And eventual recognition of the new regime seems likely. [Later dispatches reveal that the United States has suspended diplomatic relations and is reconsidering its foreign aid program in Peru.]

On the record, the State Department held to a strict no comment on judging the pre-dawn Army overthrow of President Fernando Belaunde Terry.

Press officer Robert J. McCloskey indicated the United States would consult with its hemisphere allies on what posture to adopt toward the new regime—but would like Latin Americans to make the first move.

Off the record, U.S. authorities acknowledged the military takeover came as a setback to the goal of U.S. policy and of the U.S.-supported Alliance for Progress hemisphere development program.

Covey T. Oliver, assistant secretary of state for inter-American affairs, had been citing the absence of a coup in Latin America since the June 1966 Argentine military takeover as a sign of growing democratic stability in the area.

Just what Washington will do next depends on developments.

After the latest previous coup in Peru, in 1962, the Kennedy administration tried to show U.S. disapproval by breaking off U.S. relations and aid. [*Berkeley Daily Gazette,* Friday, October 4, 1968.]

This routine press dispatch epitomizes everything that is wrong with American foreign policy toward developing nations. Why should American foreign policy makers be unhappy about a coup in Peru? Why should a normal, regular, and all too predictable event be interpreted by American officials as a setback in foreign policy? Why should the success of American policy be predicated upon stability in areas characterized by turmoil? Why should the United States consult with anyone on what pos-

From Paul Seabury and Aaron Wildavsky, eds., *U.S. Foreign Policy: Perspectives and Proposals for the 1970s* (New York: McGraw-Hill, 1969). Reprinted by permission of McGraw-Hill Book Company. Copyright © 1969 by McGraw-Hill, Inc.

ture to take when there is no apparent reason for being anything other
than correct in its behavior toward Peru? Why should the United States
government be going through the old routine of considering whether or not
to maintain diplomatic relations and foreign-aid programs in a nation that
has done nothing to it? Why should the democratic character of a weak
and strife-torn country be of greater concern to State Department officials
than apparently it is to many of its citizens?

Our purpose is to suggest new ways of thinking about and implementing
American foreign policy toward developing nations. These nations can do
little either to help or to hinder the United States; yet for several decades
the United States has been involved in frantic efforts to obtain their support and blunt their hostility. The resulting policies have been both unsuccessful and unnecessary, and still no one knows how to devise adequate
policies toward these chaotic countries. We recommend abandoning the attempt to devise specific policies for each developing nation; instead the
United States should adopt an averaging strategy by which the same policy
of friendly benevolence and minimum political involvement is applied to
all of them. We begin with consideration of how the international system
has been perceived by those who make and debate American foreign policy. This discussion is essential because we believe that the supporters and
the opponents of American foreign policy base their positions on images
of international instability that are inappropriate for developing countries.
Bad policies are the result of bad models. The frantic reflex action of intervention adopted toward nations like Peru is understandable only if one
holds an image of a world perched on the brink of disaster unless America
acts.

The International System

At a low level of analysis the nature of the controversies over American
foreign policy seems to be reasonably clear. The "hawks" and the "doves,"
the unilateral disarmers and the proponents of preventive war, appear to
be urging diametrically opposed policies. And so they are, up to a point.

At a middle level of analysis it is possible to discern two opposing models of international conflict. On the one hand, those who espouse the spiral
model of nuclear war believe that nations get caught up in a cycle of
events in which their responses become involuntary and extreme as they
mistakenly believe they have enemies who are out to get them. Each side
expects the other to do the worst and, by its very precautions, justifies its
initial predictions. The conflict escalates as each party responds to the presumed provocations of the other until the spiral of events gets completely
out of hand. The adherents of the rival appeasement model, on the other
hand, see a world bully as the ultimate danger. As the great aggressor is

appeased, its appetite grows until it becomes so inordinate as to threaten the complete destruction of others. The result is the same as with the spiral model—a final confrontation in a nuclear holocaust. Whether the disputants conceive of armaments and aggressive postures (spiral model) or lack of sufficient armaments and weak postures (appeasement model) as the major cause of world destruction, they agree that if their remedies are not followed cataclysmic events will take place. Although there are more subtle and complex versions of these positions, public debate and official action have been guided essentially by the more blatant models.

At a higher level of abstraction, beliefs about the nature of the international system are powerful determinants of a nation's foreign policy. In a "stable" system, small causes have small effects that generate countervailing influences which return the system to its former equilibrium. In an unstable system, small causes have large effects that throw the system into ever greater disequilibrium as (appropriately) in a nuclear chain reaction. It is evident that since the end of World War II most American decision-makers have considered the international system to be unstable. Hence the United States has been concerned to halt the advance of Communism everywhere lest a small cause such as a Communist victory in the Dominican Republic, Guatemala, or the Congo build up such large effects as to threaten American security. In a world it believed to be stable, the United States could view the apparent rise of some Communist regimes as small events whose consequences would soon be counteracted.

Perceptions about the stability of the international system are not the only perceptions about the system that influence foreign policy. In a "tightly coupled" system the component elements are so closely related that a disturbance of one link can transmit effects to many and distant links. In a "loosely coupled" system, however, most effects are localized in a particular subsystem and do not shake the entire edifice. If the international system is thought to be loosely coupled, then the occasional rise of Communist regimes can be seen as having essentially local impact. The ascendancy of Communists in Ghana or Guinea would be of primary interest and concern to the immediately surrounding countries (or at most to the entire subcontinent) but not to the United States.

Perceptions of the polarization of nations also affect America's foreign policy. Government officials in the United States feel they are operating in a primarily bipolar (or if China is included, a tripolar) world. Events, therefore, are interpreted not only for their intrinsic significance but also for their impact on the contest between America and the great Communist powers. The world is not only unstable and tightly coupled, it is also divided into two or three great camps. The importance of local events is magnified if they are viewed as part of a larger contest that the United States cannot afford to lose. A retreat here or a failure there is amplified because of its purported significance for whichever camp is ahead or behind in the cold war. In a multipolar world, however, there may be many contests only distantly related to one another: The Dominican Republic might be part of a Caribbean power struggle but it would not automatically be considered a part of the cold war.

Now the time has come to question the assumptions about the international system—instability, tight coupling, and bipolarity—that have guided the debate about American foreign policy. As a rough operational guide we can say that the international system has gone beyond the bounds of stability if there is a major cost to the United States (like World War II) or a comparable defeat to the Soviet Union. The international system appears in the past two decades to have operated within the limits of stability. Although violence between nations has occurred, it has been contained without spreading very far or involving a direct confrontation of the superpowers. While potential sources of instability exist, they have not yet manifested themselves. Unfortunately, the world may appear stable only to those who lack the wit to sense the disruptive forces building up behind the facade of seemingly insignificant events.

The trouble is that it is either too easy or too hard to confirm the existence of systemic instability. If a moderate level of violence is the major measure of instability, almost any continent where there is some open conflict appears unstable. The absence of revolutionary violence then becomes the only sign of stability. On the other hand, when the analyst must identify the faintly emerging causes of instability its presence is too difficult to verify. (For example, can it be said that the United States is unstable because of its race riots?)

Fortunately, we do not have to confront this dilemma directly. For if the world system is loosely coupled, causes in the developing areas are unlikely to have effects around the globe. Whether or not parts of the world are unstable, Communist victories or other ominous events in Latin America or Africa are unlikely to have continuously amplifying bad effects elsewhere. Instead, evident forces such as nationalism and disorganization are likely to interfere with trends in directions bad for America as well as with efforts in directions good for it.

The question of whether the world is bipolar or multipolar is one of power: who controls international decisions? Or, differently expressed, it is a question of causal relations: What nations cause events to happen in the international arena? If only two or three nations control international decisions, then the world system may be described as bipolar or tripolar. If many nations exercise power, then the world is multipolar. Stated in this way, however, the test assumes that those who have power have all of it and those who lack it are totally devoid of it. Here it is crucial to specify the areas of policy over which power is being exercised. Actors may be powerful in some areas and lack influence in others. While the Soviet Union and the United States come close to monopolizing control of intercontinental delivery systems for atomic weapons, their ability to control the future of NATO or the international Communist movement is in grave doubt. It seems likely, therefore, that the international system is unipolar or bipolar in some respects, tripolar in others, and multipolar so far as different areas of policy are concerned.

In the unstable, tightly coupled, and polarized international system perceived by many Americans every change is continuously amplified—thereby causing ever greater instability. Forces restoring the system to a more stable position are absent. The United States must provide countervailing power in every instance, therefore, in order to prevent disaster. Those who wish to change American foreign policy must argue, as we do, that a policy of permanent intervention is not necessary, because events in the developing areas are unlikely to blow up the rest of the world.

We believe that developing nations exist in a state of dynamic stability in which there is much action but little overall result. The combination of large populations and high volatility produces internal turbulence but not external force. The image of dynamic stability suggests that the great danger the developing nations pose for the United States lies not in their intrinsic importance but in the temptation to intervene in their affairs. Permanent chaos for them is mistaken for overwhelming danger for us. It would make better sense for the United States to loosen the connections between its national interests and events in developing countries. Instead of rushing to intervene, the United States should be reluctant to get involved. Outside of nonpartisan grants of foreign aid allocated on an objective basis, the American posture should be one of friendly concern but not of direct intervention. We shall attempt to justify these policy recommendations by showing, first, that developing nations cannot affect America's national interests and, second, that America cannot, in any event, devise effective policies toward these nations.

Are Developing Nations A Threat to Anyone Outside Their Area of the World?

The question of national survival today is dominated by high-yield nuclear weapons, superpowers, and the possibility of central war. Since the concept of central war, in turn, is dominated by intercontinental missiles, submarines, satellites, and aircraft capable of delivering nuclear weapons over long distances, strategic points on the earth's surface are becoming much less significant than they have been. The developing areas lack the capability to engage in or interfere with central war. They are, therefore, increasingly less important in regard to ultimate problems of American survival.

It is not beyond human ingenuity, of course, to perceive overwhelming importance in these developing nations. By insisting that the world is unstable, tightly coupled, and bipolar the United States can interpret the most minor event as crucial to its well-being. A central war that vastly reduced the strength of the superpowers would obviously enhance the importance of those nations left relatively intact. By then, of course, few Americans would be left to care who was taking their place in the pantheon of nations.

It is still worth considering, however, whether there are less catastrophic but still real dangers emanating from developing nations. Access to their markets, we are told, is essential to the prosperity of the United States. Perhaps America will suffer if these nations ally themselves with hostile superpowers. In the background there is the vision of continents on fire—and the implication that the United States must put out these fires or eventually be consumed in the conflagration. Each of these arguments is worth examination.

Before a nation can be a threat to anyone it must be able to organize itself. Because the developing nations cannot solve the problem of providing adequate government, we believe they threaten no one but themselves.

Adequate government is a supreme human triumph and it has only rarely been achieved. By adequate government we mean one able to assure internal peace and order, to provide for orderly succession of power, to defend itself against outside forces, and to reasonably satisfy most of its citizens. It seems unlikely that many of the underdeveloped countries will move rapidly toward adequate government. We can learn about the prospects for adequate government from the South American countries; they have not generally achieved it, although their task probably was not as difficult as that which now faces the African countries. We are not, therefore, in a position where with effort, skill, and luck we could bring about a fairly smooth and happy transitional period for the underdeveloped areas. Although we may have the resources to moderate the fate of these countries, many of them are destined for turbulence and misfortune regardless of what we do.

Most of us take government for granted. For us the words "country" or "nation" represent a group of people occupying a fairly well-defined area and having institutions reasonably capable of performing the usual functions of the state. Similarly we assume that power to control the state passes from one group to another in accordance with accepted practices. At least, we feel, control can pass; that is, the country can be taken over, and one can say who is in control. But even this is not always true. There may be no "control" which can make effective use of the resources of a country—which can be taken over, combined, or otherwise figured in the political calculus in the same way as the more familiar integers.

The factors that look so formidable to us as we consider the possibilities for peace, order, and growth in the underdeveloped countries also limit the danger to us from these countries, even if they "go Communist." The developing nations have highly volatile national systems and few national institutions or regularized patterns of action. Their expectations from the past have been disrupted without being replaced by new ones to regularize their social and political behavior. Internal groups exhibit hostility toward one another and do not evidence a strong sense of national identity. Desperate efforts are made to find instruments of nationhood through the army, party, bureaucracy, or some form of secularized religion; communications are poor; talent is woefully scarce. Though terribly small elites can cause large degrees of disruption and coups and countercoups take place with some regularity, nothing much really changes.

Unable to order their national life, developing nations are tempted to look for solutions outside of their territory. But, as they can hardly secure a minimum level of agreement at home, they are quite unable to maintain effective supranational arrangements abroad. Hostile to former colonial rulers, they are no more favorably disposed to neighboring countries in view of traditional enmities or tribal differences. Should a foreign nation (or its ideology) establish a visible presence in or near these developing countries, a counterreaction is likely. "What are these (white, red, yellow) foreigners doing? No doubt they want to enslave us again." It may not be possible to know exactly what the new nations want, but it is obvious that what they do not want is outside interference.

It is difficult for the developing nations to follow any consistent course: They have trouble allying with other nations; their rulers are practically unable to predict the directions in which they are likely to move. It is most unlikely, therefore, that any force will move whole regions and continents in a single direction. These nations are too upset, too conflicted, too inconsistent, too suspicious, and too weak to be a large cause of anything much beyond their borders.

Conditions of Instability Applied to Developing Nations

Our argument has been that the chronic weakness of developing nations means that they are unlikely to threaten American interests. Other observers have argued that it is precisely the pervasive disorder of these nations that compels the United States to take defensive measures before the chaos spreads to its shores. This brings us back to the tricky concept of international instability. Perhaps we can move the discussion forward by briefly examining the conditions of instability in the most important case since 1945—Soviet expansion into Europe.

After the end of World War II, Soviet armies had extended their dominion in Eastern Europe, Czechoslovakia had been toppled by a combination of external threat and internal subversion, and attempts were underway to repeat the process in France and Italy. These attempts were large causes, threatening to have large effects, and the United States responded appropriately in a massive way. The Soviet thrust was contained through active intervention in Greece, threats of force elsewhere, and large injections of economic aid in Western Europe. Had the Communist advance continued, Soviet control of the productive capacity and manpower of Western Europe might have directly threatened the security of the United States. This instability occurred under the following conditions: (1) the presence of a superpower with large ground forces and (2) economic capacity that (3) had already subjugated a series of contiguous nations. (4) These nations were near other threatened nations (5) which possessed trained manpower and great industrial capacity and (6) which had strong local organizations tied to the superpower. Under these conditions, processes with the potential for radically changing the system were clearly at work. These processes were checked by another superpower, which possessed equal or greater resources and was willing to use or threaten limited force, cooperating with local talented economic and political groups opposed to the aggressive superpower.

This set of conditions does not obtain, however, in those areas of the world in which most of the developing nations are located. None of the six potential destabilizing conditions of the European case exist in Africa. There is no superpower in physical possession of territory on the African land mass. No nation has "gone Communist" in the usual sense, though a few countries seem to lean toward one or another superpower. No African nation can be described as a great source of trained manpower with great industrial capacity, like France, Germany, or Italy. Nor are there substantial local Communist parties to invite speculations about whether they are closely allied with Moscow or Peking. Indeed there is doubt whether some of these peoples have the capacity to support "real" Communist parties. Moreover, such immediate success as the Soviets and Chinese appeared to have achieved has been rapidly reversed. Having been kicked in the teeth numerous times the superpowers have temporarily retreated from major participation in the area's internal disputes.

If there is any superpower dominating Latin America it is the United States rather than the Soviet Union. However, an American thrust through Mexico down the isthmus into Central America seems unlikely, to say the least. If the United States does have the equivalent of satellites, it does not seem to be running them very well. The Soviets do not appear to have made anything like a satellite out of Cuba and the Castroites have been remarkably unsuccessful in spreading their brand of revolution. There are Soviet, Chinese, and Castroite groups here and there but these do not seem to be strong. Competition between them, as in Bolivia, limits the chances that any of them will succeed. There is certainly no immediate prospect that numbers of Latin American countries will choose some version of the Communist path. Except for Argentina, Brazil, and Venezuela (in different ways), Latin America possesses only limited economic resources and does not have the trained manpower and organization to exploit fully the resources it does have. From the partial viewpoint of defense of American interests, none of the conditions of international instability in Western Europe in the late 1940s exist in Latin America today.[1]

The Economic Importance of the Developing Areas to the United States

If events in developing nations do not seriously threaten America's political interests, what about the long-standing belief that America's economic welfare depends on cheap supplies of raw materials and privileged trading relationships? We can largely discard the assumption that the United States needs the developing areas as a market (or as an outlet for investments) in order to maintain roughly the standard of living it now has. Only a very small part of the goods and services produced by Western nations are sold in the developing areas. Trade with industrial Japan will soon be worth more to America than the rest of Asia combined. Although a good portion of the raw material used by the West is obtained from the underdeveloped areas, technological developments have reduced the importance of this raw material contribution. The increasing substitutability of resources (resulting in part from the ability to synthesize new materials and in part from the generally increased sophistication of modern technology) reduces the monopoly power of any single raw material. Raw materials, moreover, are becoming a less important part of total goods and services. Therefore, the West can afford to pay a substantially higher price for raw materials—or their alternatives—without a major effect on its total economy. For these reasons, hostile control of the underdeveloped areas cannot produce a critical, long-term effect on the American economy.

This analysis is greatly strengthened if it is looked at from the other side. The goods and services which the underdeveloped areas receive from the West are a decisive part of their economies, particularly if they are to raise their standard of living. These countries are far more dependent on selling than America is on buying, as the abortive Arab oil boycott recently demonstrated. We cannot imagine that anyone can organize and control the underdeveloped areas in the next generation to such a degree that they can all be cut off from the West.

Calculating Good Policies

A decision to act should be based not only on a determination that one's interests are involved but also upon a corresponding judgment that one is capable of taking effective action. Having argued that American interests need not be seriously involved in the lives of developing countries, we should like to complete our case with the claim that the United States (like other nations) lacks the knowledge to make wise decisions about individual policies toward developing countries.

In order to exercise political influence in the developing countries we must be able to make the hardest kinds of judgment about their affairs—predictions of the political effects of proposed actions and possible counteractions. Politics in America are stable and familiar compared to the politics of developing countries. Change takes place in small steps so that the political environment possesses a fundamental continuity. Yet it is exceedingly difficult to predict the outcomes of major elections or to discover long-term trends. If picking a winner or judging the extent of racial animosities is a dubious exercise in America, how can we expect to pick winners and judge the extent of racial animosities in West Africa? We can surely fall into evil ways, but we have little reason to believe we can do good except by accident. Merely trying to do good is not enough. We are sophisticated enough to understand that "good can come from evil and evil from good." If we want to play chess with history, we have to be able to think at least one or two moves ahead. Yet we can hardly figure out what went wrong with our past moves, let alone estimate the consequences of future actions.

The formulation of foreign policy is a complicated process. The difficulties for an individual to try to understand the political situation in any one of the developing countries are magnified when all those in our country who participate in determining foreign policy come to grips with the intricate problems of all 75 or so developing countries.

Let us suppose that a shift in the situation in Tanzania requires a change in American policy. The first problem would be for those dealing with Tanzania to recognize that the situation is changing, to determine the direction of change, and to predict the impact upon U.S. goals and policies. (It is not easy to make these judgments: though there were plenty of reports from Germany during the 1930s about the profound changes taking place and the powerful forces at work, no generally accepted understanding of even the basic elements of the situation was arrived at in England or America until very late.) Reports from officials concerned with Tanzania will then have to be considered by the State Department people responsible for making policy in wider areas. It is unlikely that all of the diagnoses will agree.

Since the hypothetical change in the Tanzanian situation requires a shift in American policy, the ideas of Assistant Secretaries of State, policy planners, and numerous other officials will have to be changed. Since there probably was some controversy when the existing policy was adopted, and there is certainly controversy about related situations in other countries, the decision-makers will be reluctant to throw out an agreed-upon attitude and will be suspicious of the advice that it is necessary to do so, because of the relation of this advice to other controversies.

The efforts to change the ideas of the policy-makers about Tanzania must compete with their concern for 75 other underdeveloped countries and the other half of the world. They must also compete for their attention against efforts to carry out the old policy.

If a policy change is to be made and supported, it probably will have to face—sooner or later—opposition in Congress, the press, and small interested publics. Those people who have not learned about the changing facts in Tanzania, or who do not believe them, will oppose the new policy because it is in conflict with their understanding of the facts. In some cases it will not be possible for the State Department to reveal the new facts or the theory which produced the new policy. Thus special interests built up around the old policy will resist change. The change in Tanzanian policy may become involved in irrelevant disputes in Congress or elsewhere.

If two groups in the administration, the Congress, and the public have different approaches to problems of the underdeveloped areas or foreign policy in general, they are likely to differ on many specific policy questions. These differences will be mediated by our political process, and neither side will win all the time. Therefore, people from all schools of thought must expect that they will consider some of the decisions to be wrong. There is an inherent tendency toward inconsistency in this process of give and take. For the country to "understand" what is happening in the underdeveloped countries necessarily involves a great deal more than the intellectual difficulties confronting any individual.

To some it may appear that the United States is uniquely ill suited to carry out large numbers of discriminating policies for developing nations. The fragmentation of power in the political system militates against fast action and consistent policies. The taking of incremental steps and the use of feedback to judge the next small move—procedures that work reasonably well in a stable, democratic country—may be irrelevant to problems of developing nations. The impatience of the population and the desire for clear-cut outcomes may prevent the careful handling of intractable problems. Yet there is no need to carry analysis further. While the American system has defects, so do the Soviet and Chinese systems, and these nations handle such problems as badly as the United States, if not worse. Indeed, it does not appear that any great power is able to handle these problems. If, as we suggest, the difficulties reside both in the characteristics of the developing nations and the inherent weaknesses of complex organizations like the United States government, the proper course is to devise a policy orientation that takes these sources of difficulty into account.

Averaging Strategies

The United States government can adopt three general decision-making postures toward the developing nations. The first is to call for the adoption of policies appropriate to the special circumstances of each country under varying conditions. American policy before, during, and after bloody racial warfare in the Sudan would fit in this category. The second posture is to recommend devising individual policies only for a few nations chosen for their special interest or critical position. Whenever a crisis occurred in or near these nations, new policies would be devised; the rest of the developing nations would be covered by general policy guidelines. The preferential treatment once afforded Nigeria, when it was regarded as the hope of the African heartland, belongs in this category. The third posture of decision-making specifically rejects creating special policies for each developing country. Nor does it single out a few nations for unusual attention. Instead, this alternative maintains the same policy for all such nations. The rationale for adopting the same policy for an entire class of nations is that the results would, on the average, be better than trying to work out specific policies for all or a few of them.

Averaging strategies originate as a response to conditions that make it prohibitively expensive to calculate new policies for each new situation. As an example, consider the problem that every corporation faces of making sure executives retire before they are too old. We can assume that when people exhibit a certain degree of senility, they should be required to retire; however, people reach this degree of incompetence at different ages. (There is, after all, the "young fogy" problem.) The organization loses out if people are forced to retire either too early or too late. In order to do justice to each employee and to retain the best people, new organizations often begin by considering each case on its merits. Determining "the merits," however, turns out to be much more difficult than it had originally appeared. Not everyone agrees on criteria of excellence in work—on the trade-off, for instance, between experience and vigor. A great deal of time must now be spent working out detailed criteria. The alternative is to act intuitively toward each individual—this one looks good and that one should go—but the absence of formal criteria leads to charges of favoritism. If the man forced into retirement merely feels aggrieved, the cost is only personal unhappiness. But if he happens to be highly placed, or if the decision regarding him is taken as symbolic of a factional conflict, the costs are likely to be much higher. A relatively small matter has now been invested with much larger significance. A campaign for support is initiated; a *cause célèbre* is in the making. Feelings run high almost in inverse proportion, it seems, to the intrinsic importance of the case.

After a number of traumatic episodes, an organization will usually adopt an averaging strategy called an automatic retirement rule. Top executives know that it may be possible to specify the age at which any individual should be retired with more accuracy than the automatic rule provides, but rather than saying to those involuntarily retired, "You are senile," most organizations would rather take the small losses due to early and delayed retirements by making the much less invidious statement, "You are 65." The averaging strategy results in small losses due to people being retired when they might be productive for another few years. On the other hand, considering each retirement on its merits leads to substantial costs of search (investigating each case), decision (time, energy, negotiation), and organizational strain (because fighting over the outcome is regarded as a loss or gain for various factions). An averaging strategy is desirable when the inherent significance of the problem is minor, because the possible gains from correct individual decisions are much smaller than the likely losses from wrong ones. Conversely the high cost of individual bad decisions may be avoided by accepting the low cost of having an automatic policy.

The case for adopting averaging strategies toward developing countries is much stronger than suggested by the problem of executive retirement. No one could doubt the ability of intelligent men to make basically sound decisions about who should retire early and who should be kept on a job. There is no reason to believe, however, that capable men know enough to devise good policies for developing nations. The risk of disaster is always there. And the costs incurred by making these many individual choices must also be measured by opportunities lost to devise better policies in more critical areas.

Suppose that the United States faced a choice of active intervention in 100 developing nations. Direct action might be justified in fifteen cases. But there is no theory or observation to decide which of the hundred deserve the investment. In order not to overlook most nations deserving of intervention, at least double that number must be tried. Yet some nations requiring direct action must be left out and others in no great need are included. Multiple interventions increase foreign policy difficulties enormously. Instead of seeming active and in control, the United States paradoxically appears insecure and on the defensive, because it is always trying to extricate itself from an unfortunate involvement. It is difficult to know when success has come because it was never clear whether the theatened danger was real or whether it would have been mitigated by local conditions. What is clear is that the stakes of intervention in some cases have dramatically increased because of the importance the United States has ascribed to the case. Yet American ability to control events does not escalate along with its deeper involvement. We need an averaging strategy to bring investments and risks in line with potential gains and losses.

A Special Proposal

Consider the following major components of the proposed averaging policy:

1. A policy of abstaining from the internal politics of the underdeveloped countries, dealing with each on the basis of tolerance and generous correctness. What is proposed here is *not* a withdrawal of the United States from these areas, but a change in its mode of participation in their affairs.

2. A large-scale economic aid program in which a regular part of our national income (or national growth) is committed to helping any of the underdeveloped countries that wish such aid.

3. An ability and willingness to fight overt military aggression. The United States should be prepared to nullify the effect of Russian or Chinese military power by its readiness to come to the aid of victims of that power. But America should be cautious about committing itself to providing immediate assistance to nations that do not really need the help and use American participation as a weapon against their neighbors.

Each case would be decided on its own merits: the ability of the United States to successfully defend the threatened nation, its willingness to help defend itself, its importance to vital American interests, the presence or absence of democratic processes, all these should play a part in the American decision.

Abstaining from the politics of the underdeveloped countries would mean:

1. Not trying to maintain particular governments in power.

2. Not making alliances, or encouraging countries to commit themselves between the East and the West.

3. Not having particular "friends" or "enemies" among the countries of the underdeveloped areas. The United States should treat all of these nations with equal respect and propriety regardless of their policies and personnel. (This does not mean that the government should allow countries to abuse it by provocative acts, e.g., requiring the United States to reduce its diplomatic staff to 14 people on 48 hours notice.)

4. Finally, abstention would mean not trying directly, except by advice and persuasion, to end any internal political policy such as feudalism or repression. The United States would not, for example, use its aid in order

to keep a "good relationship" with anti-Communist governments. The United States would not associate itself in special relationships with particular governments or countries to try to prevent them from "going Communist." The United States would not allocate aid among underdeveloped countries on the basis of which are in the greatest danger of "going Communist."

If the United States approves of some governments and disapproves of others it will be hard for it to avoid having to pass judgment on all governments, and people will read approval or disapproval into everything it says or does. If the United States becomes tied to the success of particular governments by making them, in effect, its protégés, at the same time, if it builds policies that depend on the success of particular governments, it takes on possibilities of defeat in situations which it cannot control, without gaining in return a reasonable likelihood of benefit. This way America loses its freedom of action. It is forced to adjust policies out of loyalty to these governments or for fear of weakening them, regardless of principles or long-run interest. The United States cannot always force reform on governments it depends on, but often, if they do not reform, they fall and the United States suffers. Furthermore, when it becomes associated with a particular government, the United States is tempted to use short-term efforts to save it. When these actions fail the government never knows whether more intervention will save the day or whether the situation is hopeless.

Of course it would be foolish to treat these prescriptions as absolute rules; rather they should be treated as general rules which the government should be extremely reluctant to violate. In the nature of things there will always be temptations to intervene. There will be a constant series of situations where political action by the United States seems necessary to prevent some terrible thing from happening (or to seize some lovely but fleeting opportunity). But these situations will be misleading. If the value of abstention could be seen in such immediate situations there would be no need for a general rule. The general rule of abstention is proposed precisely because it would be unwise on the whole to do what seems wise in each particular case. The way to stay thin is to abstain from eating too much. Even though each piece of cake tastes good and has no immediately visible bad effect, most pieces of cake must be rejected. The fact that temptation is tempting makes it hard to resist and that is why one must make a resolution to resist.

America's proper attitude towards the underdeveloped countries should be friendly politeness or correctness to all. It should have a large economic aid program whose explicit motivation is benevolence or altruism. The President should decide whether benevolence is a sufficient justification for a large nonmilitary development assistance program (say 0.5 percent of gross national product per year). If he does, he should present the case for a decision to recognize this obligation of benevolence.

The position should be that the program is justified even if it involves no advantage to the national interest; that the American people can hope in the long run a policy of generosity and benevolence will turn out to be of some value in ways that cannot be predicted. This should be more a matter of faith than of explicit reasoning (like "honesty is the best policy"). Furthermore, there is only a modest chance that more explicit calculations of the national interest would lead to a more effective program, and there are advantages to not trying to make such a calculation.

Selling the program to Congress and the public should stress the argument of benevolence and duty. The case is very simple: they are very poor and we are very rich; therefore we should help them.

It would be consistent with the American character to undertake regular foreign aid as an obligation of generosity. Even today many people think of it in these terms. The altruistic case for foreign aid is a good case. We believe that the American people can be convinced of the merits of a regular foreign-aid program on this basis, although a decision of this scope takes a long time to make. There must be widespread public discussion, articles in magazines, resolutions by national organizations and their local chapters. There must be long congressional struggle, hearings, bills, amendments, compromises, debate, delay. But when a decision is evolved out of this kind of struggle and debate, it survives; it is not challenged every year. Social security and medical care for the aged are good examples of accepted policies. Although it would be the target of regular peripheral sniping, such a major decision on foreign aid probably would become an automatic part of everybody's platform like past reforms enacted amid much controversy.

Once the decision is made that simple humanity requires our giving a small part of our income to the underdeveloped nations each year, there will be no good basis for the annual argument about the need for and value of foreign aid, because every year the situation will be the same: they will be poor and we will be rich. If foreign aid is not considered a way to stop the spread of Communism, to induce countries to become our allies, or to assure peace and democracy in the underdeveloped areas, then there cannot be annual debates about whether it is working or not. If there are no short-term objectives there can be no short-term failures. If the aid is to be allocated on the basis of standards which, compared with a crusade against the Reds, seem prosaic, objective, and technical, then Congress will not be so concerned about having a major share in the decision-making; the allocation of foreign aid will become a settled policy.

If over a number of years we do not use our aid as a political device, if we give without bias or favor, the nature of our program will come to be understood, and people will learn that our aid is not support for particular governments. All factions in recipient countries will know that if they gain power the aid will continue to come on the same basis as before. To this end, our aid should be allocated and administered on principles designed to minimize as much as possible the relationship of the aid to the particular governments in power in the recipient countries.

A vast bureaucracy is now employed to see that foreign aid is spent for the purposes the United States regards as most desirable. The result is that America courts hostility from the recipient nation in order to achieve an indifferent level of success in securing worthwhile expenditures. The bureaucratic and decision-making costs of foreign aid may be virtually eliminated by simply providing grants to whatever government exists on an objective basis.[2] No doubt a fair amount of money might be squandered, but that is the case today. And the United States might avoid the difficulties of trying to maintain control through large foreign-aid establishments abroad. Each recipient nation would have to justify to its own population the use of these funds. Despite evident difficulties, this policy would center responsibility where it belongs—on the nation receiving the funds. If our foreign-aid proposal is regarded as too radical, its essence might be assured by channeling all funds through international organizations, regional associations, and multination consortiums whose major personnel are not American. The amount of aid would still be geared to objective criteria and the amount determined by the United States; how and for what the aid was spent would be determined by others.

The existence of India, with a huge population, and nations like Pakistan, Indonesia, and Brazil, with large populations, raises the question of whether they should be treated as special political cases. Under our proposal they would be treated differently in one crucial respect: since the amount of aid would be determined by such criteria as population size, these countries would naturally get more than others. We could not go beyond this point without endangering the policy of nonintervention. After a while, the cutoff point for special consideration would be difficult to determine. Population is not the only factor that might serve as a basis for special treatment. Interest in oil or uranium might bring in other countries. The United States would then be in the same situation from which it was trying to extricate itself. The past American enthusiasm for India is a case in point. The Chinese Communists disrupted the Pakistani-American alliance simply by invading India. Immediate American overreaction led to large arms shipments to India. The result was that Pakistan was alienated even though we did not have strong reason to believe that India was really in danger of conquest. The maintenance of special relationships is similarly fraught with danger throughout the world.

Can the United States Move Toward an Averaging Strategy for Southeast Asia?

While an averaging strategy might have made sense before the United States became deeply involved in the developing nations, it may appear that its time has passed. Too many commitments have been made. Too many acts of intervention have taken place to permit a policy of self-imposed restraint. Has the original sin become the everlasting flaw? Having once eaten the fatal fruit, must the United States forever choose a steady diet of intervention? The toughest test of our averaging strategy is Southeast Asia.

In the 1950s the United States could have afforded the absorption of South Vietnam by North Vietnam. South Vietnam was not intrinsically important, but the huge American intervention made that nation a symbol of American ability to protect small nations. This action made the possibility of victory for North Vietnam much more costly to the United States than it would have been had we not intervened. One of the benefits that is sought by a policy of very limited intervention is a reduction of the risk of such artificially created costs.

The question before us now, however, is not whether the United States should enter Vietnam but whether it can extricate itself. A policy of helpful and respectful distance will not be applicable to South Vietnam for a long time. But the United States could, over a four- or five-year period, gradually withdraw its troops. This policy requires no coalition government or agreement with the Vietcong or the North Vietnamese. Should the South Vietnamese government collapse, that would end the immediate problem. Should that government survive, the United States would continue to provide military and economic assistance for a decade. The objective of American policy would be to disengage from South Vietnam sufficiently to permit an averaging strategy to be applied in the surrounding area.

There are ample opportunities to move toward an averaging strategy elsewhere in Southeast Asia. If Japan, for example, were in danger of overthrow through internal subversion or external aggression, the United States would have to consider armed intervention. Japan is a potential superpower, and its dependence is of critical importance to the United States. But the Japanese refuse to believe that they are in serious danger. And so long as South Korea remains independent, it will be difficult to convince the Japanese to do more for their own defense. America should not be more interested in the defense of a country than its own people are. Running after a reluctant ally creates a false position, which is bad for American self-respect and Japanese capacity to assess its own interests.

Americans may ask whether they really gain anything from a maintenance of military bases in Japan. In order to keep these bases, America now makes disadvantageous economic agreements. (For example, the Japanese sell us their excellent cameras, but we may not sell our superior color film in Japan.) A new policy should be adopted. Having arranged for commercial ship repair facilities and transit rights for airplanes, the United States could move its military bases to Okinawa. Legal sovereignty over Okinawa would be returned to Japan as the United States withdrew its obsolete atomic weapons from the island. Even this limited arrangement should not be made without public acknowledgment by the Japanese government of its own interest in keeping the American bases.

Indonesia is the kind of troubled developing nation with whom the United States should avoid special relationships: the "low posture" policy currently being followed by the American embassy is excellent, except that it is threatened by the large number of administrators required to do the paper work on foreign aid. Malaysia, which has never received American aid because it manages its affairs too well, should at least get some economic assistance. Nascent nationalism and economic piracy in the Philippines should be met by a marked reduction in America's military and civilian personnel. The historic relationship between the United States and the Philippines might justify continued subsidies in the form of a special sugar quota, but history does not justify vast military bases and a swollen civilian bureaucracy. As rising nationalism leads the Philippines to look for scapegoats for its poverty and injustices, the United States should be making itself scarce. American troops should remain in Korea, however, where a strong and vigorous government is determined to defend its people against the real threat of armed attack. Should the unexpected occur—a full-scale North Korean invasion of South Korea backed by Communist China—the United States might again find itself at war, but one far better adapted to its moral and military strength than Vietnam. The provocation would be obvious, as would the capacity of the Koreans to assist in their own defense. There would then be no need to urge the Japanese to rearm; they would figure out where their safety lay without our help. Over a period of time, therefore, the United States (while still capable of direct action under special conditions) could move toward limited engagement in Southeast Asia.

Conclusion

The United States is a great world power and, as such, cannot escape being a prime actor in world affairs. Thus it must inevitably appear to some to be "throwing its weight around." Though history has decreed against escapism, playing a major, often unpopular role in world affairs need not mean total involvement everywhere all the time. A sense of proportion should be introduced into American foreign policy: distinctions need to be made between major events and minor annoyances. The present overload on foreign policy-making machinery, introduced by constant concern about developments in dozens of developing nations, should be reduced. A sense of calm and restraint should replace the frenetic atmosphere that induces intervention as a reflex action. We hope that it will prove helpful to replace the old view of the international system as highly unstable, tightly coupled, and bipolar with a fresh view of it as stable, loosely coupled, and multipolar particularly as regards the developing nations.

We believe that an averaging policy toward developing nations, based on genuine friendship, aid, and respectful distance, will enhance the quality of American foreign policy. Such a stance will facilitate greater attention to more important matters. Armed intervention, if and when it occurs, will take place under more clearcut circumstances—more likely to enhance support from the threatened nation and from the American people. The self-image of Americans as decent, responsible, and effective citizens will be improved, and fateful days of decision will not be clouded by endless petty squabbles about trivial issues in unimportant places. No doubt developments that might have been headed off by direct action when they were small will grow larger. But such action is as likely to fail as to succeed and to it must be added numerous difficulties resulting from unwanted or unskillful intervention. There will still be failures. But on the average the United States should do better and feel better about what it is doing.

NOTES

1. We are saving Vietnam and Southeast Asia for later in order to test the relevance of our policy recommendations in the toughest case.

2. Our objective is to set up a foreign aid system that will (1) commit the United States to substantial yearly expenditure, (2) remove the political costs of supervising aid, and (3) provide incentives to encourage recipient nations to oversee each other. Our immediate purpose is to show how a new foreign-aid program would fit in with our averaging strategy. Considerations of specific criteria—population, birth rates, spending by other growing nations, stability of currency, and measures of effort for development—must wait for a separate paper.

26

A STRATEGY FOR
POLITICAL PARTICIPATION

That the opportunities for expression and protection provided by a democratic political system exist does not mean that they will be used. Those who cannot see the connection between what governments do and their own welfare are not likely to inform themselves or to act. Those who lack a sense of efficacy are unlikely to translate any concern they may have into action. In the absence of training in the skills of participation—speaking, communicating, organizing, understanding—these people are dependent upon leaders who will represent them. Rival parties, factions, personalities have an incentive to provide this leadership in order to obtain office in a competitive political system. But no one can be certain that leaders will arise who can articulate and pursue the interests of those ordinarily unwilling or unable to protect themselves. While the political system places limits beyond which citizens cannot be deprived, it by no means guarantees them against deprivations. We all take our chances and it is no secret that the less well endowed in the requirements of our political culture can expect to suffer more than most.

What of those citizens, however, who do possess the necessary skills, who do wish to participate, but who find the prospect overwhelming? Participation may seem to them to require so much effort that the very thought is fatiguing as well as defeating. I propose to discuss the situation and to suggest a strategy through which the individual can make himself effective.

What would life be like, we may ask, if the citizen fulfilled even a small part of the endless injunctions given him to be interested, knowledgeable, and active? Where would he find time for family activities, for social life and friendships, for hobbies and reading, and for just plain relaxation?

From Aaron Wildavsky, *Leadership in a Small Town* (Totawa, N.J.: Bedminster Press, 1964), pp. 352–360. Copyright © 1964 by The Bedminster Press, Inc. Reprinted by permission.

Imagine the family life of Mr. and Mrs. Model Citizen who obey all the commands about participation. On Monday and Tuesday nights they attend meetings of the local sewer service board because it is clear that without adequate sanitation the community cannot exist. Wednesday and Thursday evenings are spent dealing with police problems because public safety is essential for the good life. Fridays are reserved for pollution, which is so threatening to our way of life. Saturdays go to mental health, because if people don't think straight they can't do anything else. Caucuses on Vietnam naturally take up Sundays. The week has left Mr. and Mrs. Model Citizen deeply unsatisfied, of course, because they have had to stand by while the Middle East situation deteriorates, national forests are cut down, and the United Nations withers away without their help.

The next week promises to be just as hectic as mother, leaving TV dinners in the oven, rushes off to a meeting of the Council on Juvenile Delinquency. She has failed to notice that daughter has not been home for two days and has just been caught in a raid where abusive drugs were found. Father was late to work again, because no moral man should miss the meeting at which the Welfare Council decides how to deal with indigent families. The Geratsco Fertilizer Company, however, is callously indifferent to Mr. Model Citizen's public service and insists that he pay more attention to his job or consider joining the relief rolls himself. Father was going to take his son on a hike, but there was too much to be done to preserve the ecological balance of his region, so the boy starts running around with a juvenile gang and gets picked up for burglary. With both their children in jail, Mother and Father Model Citizen console themselves with the thought that they will now have more time to spend on the problems of our penal institutions.

To sacrifice life on the altar of citizen participation seems excessive. Helping society by contributing to its social problems seems odd. No wonder there are few truly political men.

These comments may seem like sacrilege coming from a political scientist who devotes his life to the study of public affairs and who would be thought to desire the widest possible citizen participation. Although there is much to be said for emphasizing the quality rather than the quantity of participation, there being citizens whom one might wish to remain apathetic, I hasten to assure the reader that I do teach and advocate citizen participation. The point of the remarks thus far has been that the usual exhortations to do everything are quite impossible to fulfill. All they really succeed in doing is to inculcate guilt at having failed or a sense of utter futility in view of the magnitude of the task. They may actually harm the cause they set out to advance by setting sights so high that more manageable goals are not even attempted. If we are interested not merely in the amount of participation but in its effectiveness and its reasonable relationship to the whole life of the individual, then we must suggest a goal and appropriate strategies which take into account both genuine interest and competition from other essential activities.

The goal is to become a specialist and the strategy is to specialize. It is vain to think that any one of us can become generalists. We don't have the time and even if we did we probably wouldn't be willing to devote it solely to this purpose. Even an extraordinarily active person like Bill Long [1] is a generalist only for local affairs and not on the state or national level. But it is possible for any reasonably intelligent person, with a high school education or its equivalent in experience or ability to read, to become an effective issue specialist. This goes for issues as far apart as disarmament and whether to sell the local electric plant. The first question is how to decide the issue in which to specialize.

We can all find the time to read a decent newspaper and perhaps a good supplementary weekly for local affairs. If such a paper is not available in a particular region, it is easy enough to get a subscription to something like the *Christian Science Monitor* or the news magazines. By making a quick survey of the news day-by-day, aided now and then by news broadcasts, the citizen can decide what it is that interests him most. Soon he builds up a small fund of information on a variety of issues which should better enable him to choose his specialty. If there is no paper which contains even the barest account of local events, it may be necessary to attend a few meetings and find out who is well-informed so that these people can be approached from time to time for a résumé of happenings. Having chosen a specialty, the next question is how to become sufficiently informed to develop one's own preferences about what needs to be done.

Where to begin? This is not easy because the citizen does not yet have the background which enables him to pinpoint the literature which best meets his needs. There are, however, a number of ways to proceed which may help to cut information costs. If the citizen is fortunate and knows someone whom he respects and regards as informed, he can ask that person for recommendations as to what to read. Once having begun with something worthwhile, there are almost always additional references to other highly regarded works. Occasionally, the citizen may develop a liking for a columnist or news commentator who suggests appropriate reading. If these resources are not available, a foraging expedition to the local library is indicated. He can leaf through several books and articles on the subject of interest and see which has the most immediate appeal. The point is to begin somewhere and keep at it. For there are few issues (and none of central importance, in my opinion) that cannot be mastered once the citizen has discovered the relevant literature.

In the realm of local affairs there may not be literature which appears immediately relevant to the problem at hand. But the chances are that this is not so and that at least some comparative experience on housing, planning, education, and the like is readily available. To be informed on local differences, however, may require reading special reports and attending meetings devoted to the issue. Take heart! There may be many meetings on many issues; there are rarely an inordinate number on any single one.

There is always the danger that the unwary citizen may be submerged by a flood of material on a well-known issue without being aware of how to extricate himself. He will soon discover, if he is careful, that after two or three books and a half dozen articles, the amount of repetition rises rapidly and he can get by more than adequately with his newspaper, a book, and a few articles every year. It is necessary to know when to stop as well as when to begin.

While it is difficult to imagine the citizen doing this kind of research constantly, it is not utopian to believe that he can do it from time to time if he specializes. Suppose there is an emergency or the issue comes up for a decision immediately? The obvious way to handle this is to plunge right in. But a few plunges will prove tiring if not tiresome. The optimum strategy is to specialize not only in specific problems—shall we teach Russian in the high school or shall we put a sewer in on X street—but in a broader area such as education or utilities or public safety. Then one will always have a store of information by which to judge events when they turn up.

Specialization increases the fund of information in many ways. The citizen may find that he gets acquainted with people who share his interests, who attend the same meetings and join the same organizations, and who welcome discussion in the area of their mutual concern. Each participant may pick up pointers from the others. When some new development takes place, the specialist is more likely to be informed because his interest has become known. After a while, his right to know is likely to become established through usage and public and private officials inform him as a matter of course. The better acquainted he is with the material, the more agile his mind is likely to become in making the required associations, thus increasing the efficiency of his efforts to acquire information.

The need for participants is so great in most public organizations that anyone who manifests interest is likely to be coopted. By attending meetings, speaking up on occasion, volunteering his services, or just letting it be known that he cares, the citizen can vastly increase the probability of being asked to take part. The more time and energy he has to devote to this issue area, which is partly a function of his specialization, the greater the likelihood that he will be asked to do more. And the more he does the more likely he is to do still more. Patience is required, however, for it must not be thought that the moment the citizen shows that he is interested, people will flock around demanding his services. A period of time must elapse to demonstrate his genuine interest and for others to judge that he has taken the trouble to become informed.

Yet specialization may not be a useful strategy for the citizen who is repelled by the general tenor of governmental policies. He may find the style of life in his community at variance with his own values. He may discover that other citizens simply do not share his preferences. In that case he has two choices. He can attempt to become a general activist in order to mount an across-the-board attack on the policies and personnel he does not like. The costs of doing this are enormously high, as we have seen, in terms of alternatives forgone. If he is disaffected with local policies, the citizen is far more likely to "vote with his feet" by moving to a community that contains a mix of policies closer to his liking. How much easier it is to move his place of residence than to fight continuously on a dozen fronts with no assurance he will prove victorious. Specialization is most useful, therefore, only if the citizen is at least willing to tolerate most policies and to rest content with attempting to alter the ones in which he is most interested.

There can be no guarantee, of course, that the preferences of the citizen who actively specializes will actually be met. There may be others who are equally active and who possess superior resources which he cannot match. Unless the citizen finds himself isolated to the point where few other interested persons share his preferences, however, he does have a good chance to become influential. The probability of his exercising an impact upon decisions will certainly be much greater.

In pluralist political systems where the prizes go to the interested and the active, and where so few others bring their resources to bear, the specialist has great advantages. Most other people do not possess his information, knowledge, and skills in this area and they certainly do not match his rate of participation. Routine decisions are likely to be made by specialists because no one else is concerned. Even when a controversy arises which tends to broaden participation, the specialist has a much better chance of knowing the disposition of forces, the intentions and capabilities of leaders, the degree of solidarity or agreement among them, the kinds of other people who might be mobilized, and similar political data. He will be looked to for leadership by others who are novices in this area compared to him.

The value of specialization comes through in a remarkable book, *The Great Impostor,* which tells the story of a series of impersonations enabling Ferdinand DeMara to assume positions of leadership in several organizations and communities. He draws from his experiences the lesson that there is leadership sort of lying around the streets to be had for the asking. But he enters a persuasive caveat: always be certain that you are not stepping on someone's shoes; avoid this elemental conflict and you can expand your resources considerably before anyone else finds it worthwhile to try and stop you. By implication, DeMara suggests that ours is a society in which there are many unused and inefficiently exploited resources. These, however, are available to many people. For this reason he recommends following a strategy in which your moves do not immediately conflict with those of others, since there is in any event plenty of room to expand your operations in a narrow sphere without running into opposition. It would not be out of place to suggest that those who would be community leaders might find the same rationale convincing.

Granted that specialization is a useful strategy for increasing the influence of the citizen, doubts may arise as to whether it is socially desirable. Is it desirable for citizens to limit themselves to a narrow segment of community affairs? An immediate retort might be that they can hardly do anything else, since considerably increased participation is wholly unrealistic. But this smacks of a debater's trick and I will offer additional arguments. Specialization need not imply total neglect of other areas and I have already advised attention to the general picture through newspapers, broadcasts, and other media of information. It does require the use of various techniques to cut the cost of making one's preferences as effective as possible without large scale participation. The party system, for example, serves as a mechanism for registering an important general preference and does not require knowledge on all issues. The citizen can simply choose the party which on past knowledge he believes best reflects his views. He can see how well the parties operate in the area of his specialization and make deductions from that. He can try to get in touch with specialists in other areas whose opinion he respects and trade information. There are well-known commentators in the public media who express their views for all to see. If things go badly in his opinion, the citizen can always decide that it is worthwhile to switch his specialization or temporarily take on a new one until he is satisfied.

To say that the specialist need not suffer overly in other areas because of his particular strategy is not to demonstrate that his mode of operation results in a political system which meets preferences widely held in society. I shall argue that it does, providing that one gives up the belief that it is realistic to expect or essential to achieve a political system in which most decisions are made in accordance with the active will of a majority of citizens.

For most citizens most of the time most community affairs are not of active concern. They may have reason to know that things are going well from their point of view and see no reason to participate. It is more likely that the negative is true; they have no reason to believe that things are not going well and it is not worth the cost in time and energy to establish beyond any doubt that this is so. From time to time events do occur which lead them to take an interest and perhaps participate sporadically on a few matters of great concern. If citizens are able for the most part to bring the leaders in these areas into a responsive position on these few matters, so that their preferences are taken into account, then in large measure the community may be said to be ruled in accordance with their wishes or, more accurately, the wishes which are important to them. If the specialists who predominate in each issue area are representative of and can be made responsive to those who care the most about it, then we have a situation in which different minorities rule in different areas and the same result ensues. Given the reservoir of resources which most citizens possess, their willingness to use them at a higher rate in the few areas of their concern, and the interest rival leaders have in taking their case if they are dissatisfied, the rule of minority satisfaction should apply. This is not majority rule in the sense that all or most community decisions accord with the preferences of a majority of citizens; it is majority rule in the special sense that the minority who feel intensely about an issue make up a majority of those who receive consideration and some satisfaction from the outcome. In this way specialization serves the public interest in contributing to a political system which comes closer than others to meeting the widest range of preferences.

NOTE

1. See "Bill Long: Portrait of an Activist," Chapter 16 of this volume.

INDEX